אם הבנים שמחה

EM HABANIM SEMEHA

RESTORATION OF ZION AS A RESPONSE DURING THE HOLOCAUST

Yissakhar Shlomo Teichthal

אם הבנים שמחה

EM HABANIM SEMEHA

RESTORATION OF ZION AS A RESPONSE DURING THE HOLOCAUST

Editor, Translation and Notes by

Pesach Schindler

KTAV PUBLISHING HOUSE, INC.
HOBOKEN, NEW JERSEY

Library of Congress Cataloging-in-Publication Data

Taikhtel, Yisakhar Shelomoh, b. 1884 or 5.
  [Em ha-banim semehah. English]
  Em habanim semeha : restoration of Zion as a response during the Holocaust /
Yissakhar Shlomo Teichthal ; editor, translation, and notes by Pesach Schindler.
    p. cm.
  Includes bibliographical references and index.
  ISBN 0-88125-441-X
  1. Jews--Restoration. 2. Zionism. I. Title: Restoration of Zion as a response during the
Holocaust. II. Schindler, Pesach. III. Title.

BS649.J5 T3513 2000
296.3'1174--dc21   99-088873

Distributed by
KTAV Publishing House, Inc.
900 Jefferson Street
Hoboken, NJ 07030

Dedicated to the memory of our dear daughter

Geeta Schindler Schwartz, z"l

אם הבנים ואשת חיל

CONTENTS

Introduction by Rabbi Dr. Walter Wurzburger ix

Acknowledgements xi

Editor's Introduction xiii

First Preface 3

Second Preface 17

Foreword 37

First Chapter 61

Second Chapter 87

Third Chapter 133

Fourth Chapter 335

Appendix 393

Index 401

INTRODUCTION

by Rabbi Dr. Walter Wurzburger

Pesach Schindler, the author of a pioneering study of *Hasidic Responses to the Holocaust*, has made another significant contribution to the understanding of this tragic era with his most readable translation of Rabbi Shlomo Teichthal's classic, *A Happy Mother of Children.*

Especially valuable is the Editor's Introduction to the work; it enables even readers unfamiliar with the historic background to appreciate the momentous nature of Rabbi Teichthal's "conversion" from radical anti-Zionism to passionate advocacy of Religious Zionism. Dr. Schindler succeeds in pointing out how, in the wake of the new realities created by the Holocaust, Rabbi Teichthal felt constrained to recant his previous position, which had reflected the prevailing ethos of Hungarian Orthodoxy. At the risk of jeopardizing his reputation among his co-religionists, he pleaded with them to abandon their rejectionist ideology and join even non-Orthodox Jews in the sacred task of settling Eretz Yisrael and returning to Mother Zion.

Rabbi Teichthal's tract suffers from having been hastily composed under most trying conditions during his brief stay in Budapest as a refugee from Slovakia. That is why even individuals who can read the Hebrew original will derive much benefit from Dr. Schindler's excellent notes and commentary. With the tools of scholarship at his disposal, he is able to illumine what would otherwise have remained obscure to those who cannot match his extensive knowledge of talmudic and Hasidic literature.

By making Rabbi Teichthal's fascinating tract accessible to a larger circle, Dr. Schindler will also help lay to rest the canard that tradition-oriented Jews are so overwhelmed by the past that they cannot respond to newly emergent situations. Rabbi Teichthal provided convincing evidence that truly great minds and spirits are capable of transcending deeply ingrained ways of thinking and, while employing traditional categories of thought, can successfully respond to the challenge of momentous upheavals.

ACKNOWLEDGEMENTS

It was Professor Emil Fackenheim who urged me to translate *Em Habanim Semeha*, and to provide a commentary and notes for the English reader. I also express my appreciation to Professor Netanel Katzburg, former director of the Center of Holocaust Research at Bar Ilan University.

My thanks to the staff at the Schocken Library in Jerusalem, and the National Library at the Hebrew University in Jerusalem, to whom I owe my courtesies without which the research could not possibly have been carried out.

To Vivienne Mintz, my devoted secretary, who worked with this manuscript from its inception, and who shared a keen interest with me in the significance of this project. To Julie Paritsky, who typed final proofs, my thanks. I am grateful to the editors at KTAV who were most helpful in advising me on delicate tasks of style and editing, and to Mrs. Denah Stilerman for a meticulous job of proofreading, and Mr. Bernard Scharfstein for his patience and fortitude.

EDITOR'S INTRODUCTION

On January 24, 1945 (10 *Sh'vat,* 5705, according to the Jewish calendar), Rabbi (R.) Yissakhar Shlomo Teichthal, scion of generations of Eastern Jewish scholarship and piety, was murdered in a German cattle car transporting the remnants of Auschwitz ahead of the pursuing Russian armies.[1] Unlike millions of fellow Jews who took with them to their death their personal feelings, R. Teichthal recorded a remarkable work in Budapest between January 4, 1943 and December 23, 1943. It is not the usual war narrative of an historian or an eye-witness. Nor is it a diary, although it contains elements of Holocaust history and personal testimony. *Em Habanim Semeha*[2] (*EHS*) is a prodigiously documented polemic written in rabbinic Hebrew and addressed to the *Haredi* (ultra-Orthodox) leadership and learned layman. Against the background of the unfolding horror of the *hurban* (destruction) of European Jewry, the author formulated a merciless confession of what

---

1 Variant versions appear as unnamed eye-witness reports in S. Roseman, *Rashei Golat Ariel* ("Exiled Leaders of Ariel" [Poetic reference to Jerusalem as per Isa. 29:1–8] Brooklyn, N.Y., Zikhron Kedoshim, 1979), p. 193; H.M. Teichthal [Biographic introduction by the son of the author], in *Responsa Mishneh Sakhir* (Jerusalem, HaVa'ad Lehotza'at Kitve HaMehaber, 1973) [preliminary unpaginated p. 10]; Yitzhak Levin (ed.) *Eileh Ezkerah* ["These Will Be Remembered"] (New York, Research Institute for Religious Jewry, 1972), vol. 7, pp. 122–123.

2 "A Happy Mother of Children," based on Ps. 113:9. The choice of the title is explained at the close of the Second Preface. See also *EHS,* 148 and *EHS,* 206–207. The three major editions in their order of appearance are: *Em HaBanim Semeha* (Budapest, Salomon Katzburg, 1943) (New York, H.S. Teichthal, 1969). [Photostat of first edition] Foreword by R. Teichthal's son Shimon, the publisher (Jerusalem, Machon Pri Ha'Aretz, 1983), with foreword by publishers and the author's son, H.M. Teichthal, with selected textual references in footnotes. This English edition utilized *EHS* Budapest, 1943.

might have, and should have been. The Holocaust is also the tragic stage upon which is presented the plan for the national-religious reconstruction of the Jewish people in the postwar era. The text is replete with the documentation of the fallacies of religious leaders in the past. They are the results of the prolonged and enervating struggle in exile, which twisted Jewish theology, as it was perceived or misperceived. The author exposes the prevalent fatalistic streams of dependence on miraculous Divine intervention which inhibited the progress of Jewish history and paralyzed human initiative in search of national redemption. Thus, the destruction of European Jewry was the calamitous combination of missed opportunities and prompted by theological considerations.

The Balfour Declaration of 1917 which "looked with favour" on a Jewish national homeland in Palestine, had been such an opportunity, according to *EHS*. Among the dramatic passages in the volume are the author's plea for *tikkun* (restoration, reconstruction) of the Jewish people, and the concomitant parallel Unity of the Divine. This restoration could only come about through the return of the people to its homeland in Eretz Yisrael, based on the spiritual foundations of Torah, while employing the modern instruments of a modern nation-state.

Most remarkable are the writer's defense of *sinners* and *heretics*. In Teichthal's view, the non-observant Zionists settlers of the Land who were objects of the scorn and hostility on the part of *Haredi* leaders, are in fact the true catalysts of *tikkun*. Their love for the Land—expressed in dedication, toil, and self-sacrifice, without any claims to piety—contributed more to the realization of *tikkun* than all the prayers of pious Jews, who have bewailed the long exile while passively, and often comfortably, remaining ensconced in exile.

Hence, Teichthal breaks with the prevailing theological position of his ultra-Orthodox contemporaries. Yet, it was only three and a half years prior to the outbreak of World War II that Rabbi Teichthal's own vehement public opposition to settlement in Palestine was included in the ultra-Orthodox *Tikkun Olam*,[3] which was published at the behest

---

3 *Tikkun Olam* was published in Munkatch in 1936, authored and edited by

of R. Hayyim Elazar Shapira, the Rebbe of Munkatch (Munkacs).[4]

Although the author clearly attributed his recantation to the cataclysmic events of the Holocaust,[5] the documentation for his activist redemptive ideology was drawn from a massive cross-section of sources in classic Judaica. Hence the author may have begun struggling with his counter-ideology even prior to the Shoah. It is clear that R. Teichthal was familiar with the writings of one of the forerunners of modern Zionism—especially the form which synthesizes piety and religious observance with the duty to settle the Holy Land—R. Zvi Hirsch Kalischer (1795–1874). The rabbinic endorsements (*haskamot*) for Kalischer's important Zionist work *Derishat Zion* ("Seeking Zion"), published in 1862, were utilized by Teichthal as posthumous, albeit controversial, support by acknowledged rabbinic authorities for his own statement on religious Zionism.[6]

This introduction will examine the four introductory sections and

Moshe Goldstein. The work is a massive polemic supported by letters and statements of major rabbinic and community leaders, vehemently opposing Zionist settlement efforts in Eretz Yisrael. The Orthodox *Agudat Yisrael* and *Mizrahi* movements especially came under harsh criticism. Among the 150 rabbinic leaders who lent their name to this volume, by way of signatures or supporting documents, was R. Yissaskhar Shlomo Teichthal. His letter of February 9, 1936 to the editors of the *Yidishe Tsaytung* in Munkatch (reprinted pp. 104–107) attacks the Zionist settlement efforts and the *Agudat Yisrael* party for premature political involvement in Eretz Yisrael at the expense of Torah study.

4   *EHS* 314. Rabbi of Munkatch, descendant of the Bnei Yessaskhar, R. Zvi Elimelekh of Dinov, and leader of the Munkatch-Shapira dynasty from 1904 to his death in 1937. Though a zealous opponent of all forms of political Zionism, he also opposed the emerging ultra-Orthodox *Agudat Yisrael*. This movement was founded in Katowitz (Katowice) in May 1912, and may have competed politically with Munkatcher community interests. See A. Fuchs, *Yeshivot Hungaria Begadlutan Uvehurbanan* ("Hungarian *Yeshivot*: From Grandeur to Holocaust") (Jerusalem, A. Fuchs, 1978), pp. 497–505.

5   *EHS*, 314.

6   It is not clear if R. Teichthal had access to the writings of his elder contemporary R. Abraham Isaac Kook (1865–1935), who as the first chief rabbi of Palestine during the British mandate, opposed by the ultra-Orthodox camp, supported every builder of Eretz Yisrael, including non-believers. See R. Abraham Isaac Kook, *Orot* ("Lights") (Jerusalem, Mosad HaRav Kook, 1961), pp. 70–72, 80, 148–151. Also A. Hertzberg, *The Zionist Idea* (New York, Atheneum, 1977), pp. 422, 430. Attempts at charting any channels of influence are, therefore, difficult, though the Kook-Teichthal texts contain many similarities. The endorsements appear in *EHS*, 2–12.

four chapters of this important contribution to the primary literature of the Holocaust. As a guide to the reader it may be helpful to focus on the following issues raised by the author of this remarkable work:

> 1. *Why?* Is there a Divine purpose to the Shoah? "Who among all these does not know that the hand of the Lord has done this?" (Job 12:9). Does the Jobian certainty apply to Rabbi Teichthal's view of human and national disaster?

> 2. *What?* Are there lessons to be learned by the Jewish people, its leadership, especially the religious leaders?

> 3. *How?* Can these lessons be applied? Are there resources for reconstruction (*tikkun*)? Where shall one find redeeming sources for consolation?

In preparing the reader to confront this prodigiously documented work, texts will be selected in order to shed light on several significant aspects of this work: the theological-sociological climate in which R. Teichthal functioned prior to and during the Holocaust; the readership for whom the volume was intended; possible causes of his radical change of views; sources which may explain the continued post-Holocaust ambivalence and hostility of ultra-Orthodoxy to the Jewish State; and, clues as to the attitude the author might have assumed towards the modern State of Israel had he lived to witness its emergence.[7]

THE AUTHOR[8]

Rabbi Teichthal was born in Hungary in 1885. He received the traditional, intensive Jewish education of a young boy within ultra-Orthodox

---

7 With the exception of the translation and notes of the Second Preface in *Tradition*, 21 (Fall 1984), 63–79, text selections appear in English for the first time.

8 The source for biographic material is from the introduction by his son, R. Hayyim Menahem, to the Jerusalem edition (1974) of R. Teichthal's *Responsa Mishneh Sakhir* (Bardiow, Slovakia, 1924). The author's place of birth, Nadihalas, cited in S. Roseman, *op. cit.*, p. 181, is probably Nagyhalász, a town in northeastern Hungary, in the province of Szabalcs.

circles in Eastern Europe, leading to scholarly achievements, rabbinic ordination, and the growing responsibilities of a religious communal leader. The intense communal responsibilities expected of a young rabbi in the resort town of Piestany in Slovakia did not prevent him from devoting his scholarship to rabbinic legal writings, as well as serving as head of the Yeshivah (talmudic academy) Moriah in Piestany. The first volume of his Responsa collection, *Mishneh Sakhir*, was published in Slovakia in 1924. The second volume was in the process of publication when the war intervened. Some manuscripts were hastily deposited with a non-Jewish acquaintance and subsequently recovered by one of the author's daughters. His son, Hayyim Menahem Teichthal of Jerusalem, has issued the second volume of *Mishneh Sakhir*.[9] A diary is planned for publication. These documents may shed light on the intimate thought processes of the author, and offer evidence for the radical changes in his thinking, evident in *Em HaBanim Semeha*.

THE CONTINUING AGENDA OF THE VOLUME

This writer first encountered Teichthal's work when researching Hasidic responses to the Holocaust for a doctoral dissertation at New York University.[10] The issues raised by R. Teichthal in 1943 continue to challenge the Jewish people today. The reality of an independent Jewish state represents the physical realization of the pioneers who settled Palestine and received the belated praise and support of the martyred author. But Teichthal's sharp critique of his ultra-Orthodox colleagues is still relevant. The responses to the Jewish State by *Haredi* Judaism range from ambivalence to hostility. The author's description of the Jew who prefers the stepmother (diaspora) over his natural mother (Eretz Yisrael)[11] goes to the heart of the theological debate on the question of religious Zionism. The encounter between the

---

9 Jerusalem, HaVa'ad Lehotza'at Kitve HaMehaber, 1987.

10 Subsequently published as *Hasidic Responses to the Holocaust in the Light of Hasidic Thought* (Hoboken, New Jersey, Ktav, 1990).

11 JT Ber. 2:8. *EHS*, 148.

world of passive belief in supernatural intervention as opposed to the activist school of national redemption continues unabated.

THE INDICTMENT

> Now who is actually responsible for this innocent blood which has been spilled in our time, due to our many iniquities? It seems to me that these very leaders who prevented Jews from joining and participating with the builders[12] cannot atone (for their wrongs) by exclaiming: Our hands did not shed blood.[13]

With this accusation, made even before preparing the reader with three introductory prefaces, the author presents his thesis: the ultra-Orthodox leadership in Europe is responsible for much of the innocent Jewish blood which has been shed. The guilt is collective; so are the implications for the restoration of the Jewish people, since "all Jews are held responsible for one another."[14] Throughout the generations leaders should have

> travelled among the Jewish communities, a day in each . . . teaching Jews the proper path, over a period of a year, two or three, until Israel will have settled in its land and thereby glorify and sanctify the name of the Holy One, blessed be He. . . . They did not do so. Rather, each entered into his own field, his own vineyard [enjoying] his own wine exclaiming: "All is well with me"[15] so as not to burden themselves [with responsibilities].[16] This is true in our present day as well. They [the

---

12 *HaBonim* (the builders); referring to the *halutzim*, the Jewish pioneers of the late 19th and early 20th century in Eretz Yisrael who were opposed by the ultra-Orthodox on ideological and theological grounds. The supporting and opposing arguments are among the major themes which run through the *EHS* volume.

13 Cf. Deut. 21:7. The biblical passage describes the absolution of the town elders from guilt in the event that one is found slain (by an unknown assailant) in a neighboring field. *EHS*, 14–15. All references are from the 1943 Budapest edition.

14 Shav. 39a; Sanh. 27b. *EHS*, 15.

15 See Ta'an. 11a, "When the community is in trouble let not a person exclaim: 'I will enter my home, eat, drink, and all will be well with me.'"

16 *EHS* partial citation of *Tanna DeBei Eliyahu* (Lemberg, 1864), Ch. 11.

leaders] should have been involved in this matter, teaching Jews to return to the Holy Land in the spirit of the Torah. Where might we have been today had all of the *tzadikim* (righteous) and *haredim* (pious) in former generations given their support. Many thousands of Jewish souls would have been saved![17] (*EHS*, 15)

The biblical spies [Numbers 13–14] are the prototypes of self-seeking leaders who sacrifice the interest of the people, the Land and, hence, redemption.

Was there anyone more fit for a mission than the spies [sent by Moses]?[18] But since their drive for authority was firmly rooted within them, as elaborated in the *Zohar*,[19] and the *Shelah*,[20] they were afraid that should they come to Eretz Yisrael they will lose their positions of authority. They turned against this lovely Land and deceived others as well, thereby causing this exile, as elaborated by our sages. . . .[21] The current situation is similar even among rabbis, *rebbes* and their hasidim. This one has a good rabbinic post; another is endowed with a lucrative *rebistve*.[22] This one owns a profitable business or factory, or is appointed to a good and prestigious position offering great satisfaction. They are frightened that should they move to Eretz Yisrael their status will be shaken. (*EHS*, 31)

---

17   This condemnation is repeated in *EHS*, 17, 161 and 216–217.

18   Num. 13:1–16. Rashi on the term *all the men* (13:3) notes: "Whenever *anashim* (men) are referred to in Scripture, this signifies prominence. Indeed, they were at that moment worthy men."

19   Zohar III, 158b. "All men being leaders." (*Kulam anashim*, etc.). They were all virtuous, but they were misled by false reasoning. They said: "If Israel enters the Land we will be replaced, since it is only in the wilderness that we were considered worthy to be leaders. This was the cause of their death and the death of all who followed them."

20   *Sefer Luhot HaBrit* (The Tablets of the Covenant) of R. Isaiah b. Abraham HaLevi Horowitz (1565–1630) (the *She'lah HaKadosh*), *Parashat Shelah*, part II (Furth, 1764), p. 68a.

21   NumR. 16:20; Ta'an. 29a; Sot. 35a; Zohar II, 161a.

22   Leadership and control of a particular hasidic community or dynasty. Rebbe (pl. Rebbes, Rebbeim) denotes the hasidic rabbinic leader or master.

THE VOW

Religious traditions offer at least two spiritual sanctuaries for the
devoted adherent in crisis. In one, the person of faith seeks stability;
in the other, one searches for hope. One is situated in the past, and
the second lies expectant in the future.

In the *First Preface* R. Teichthal develops a two-faceted system in
which he seeks both support and hope. For the first he chooses the
Patriach Jacob, the prototype of one who faced mortal danger, wrestled
with both the human and Divine, persevered and, albeit wounded,
prevailed.[23] Though the assuring expression "have no fear" is a familiar
biblical landmark,[24] it is the phrase *al tira avdi Ya'akov* ("Have no fear,
My servant Jacob")[25] which has become a motif in Jewish tradition.[26]

Teichthal, however, does not retreat into a passive protective sanctuary. He selects an active Jacobian model. From amidst adversity is
forged a vow which becoms a vital life-sustaining force protecting the
integrity of the person of faith.

> Our holy Torah has already noted the act of Jacob our Patriarch, may
> he rest in peace. When he was in distress he made an important vow to
> the Lord as it is written: "Jacob then made a vow, saying, 'If God
> remains with me and gives me bread to eat and clothing to wear and if
> He protects me on this journey that I am making and if I return safe to
> my father's house, etc.'"[27] Our sages of blessed memory noted:[28] "What

---

23 Gen. 32:25–33.

24 From Abraham, in confrontation with those hostile to him (Gen. 15:1) to the
comforting of Zion by the prophet Zephaniah (Zeph. 3:16).

25 Jer. 30:10; 46:27–28.

26 The twenty-two line acrostic of unknown authorship employing *al tira avdi
Ya'akov* as the repetitive refrain has been incorporated into the liturgy at the conclusion
of the Sabbath.

27 A rearrangement of Gen. 28:20–21. The subsequent vow made by Jacob when
fleeing from Esau pledged the future building of a House of God and a permanent
tithe contribution from his income.

28 GenR. 70:1. The full text reads: "It is written (Ps. 66:14): '[I enter Your house
... with vows] that my lips pronounced, that my mouth uttered in my distress.' Rabbi
Yitzhak the Babylonian said, 'That my mouth uttered when I was in distress.' He
vowed to perform a mitzvah (religious precept) when in distress. For what purpose?

is its significance?[29] We learn from here that one must make a vow when in distress." Therefore, I shall also make a significant vow to the God of Israel. I will pray for all of Israel in the spirit of our ancient Patriarch of blessed memory described previously. If God will be with me during these difficult persecutions; will watch over me against those who wish to harm me; will provide me with bread to eat and clothing to wear; will permit the merits of Eretz Yisrael to protect me and my family; that harm, hurt or confrontation shall not befall me or my household until imminent redemption will come to all of Israel; that suffering shall be commanded: Enough![30]; that the following verse will be speedily realized in our day: "A righteous man falls seven times and rises again, but the wicked stumble at once,"[31] that our Holy Land will arouse its merit on our behalf so that we may be speedily remembered for redemption and in compassion since we have no power left to hold out; and that the suffering of these past years which have befallen us will be the pangs preceding the Messiah,[32] that our righteous Messiah

---

In order to teach future generations to utter a vow when they will be in distress.'"

29 Of the verses Gen. 28:20–21.

30 A commonly employed anthropomorphism, based on *Tanh. Miketz.* "He, therefore prayed to the God, *Shaddai* declaring: 'He who restricted heaven and earth *Dai* (enough), shall also instruct my suffering: enough!'" *Shaddai* would therefore be read "that it may be enough (*She'dai'*)."

31 Prov. 24:16. Actual reading: "For a righteous man falls seven times and rises again, but the wicked stumble under adversity." See also Prov. 28:18.

32 *Hevlei Mashiah* (the pangs preceding the Messiah). A major concept in the apocalyptic themes of the Talmud. Pes. 118a, Ket. 111a, Meg. 17b, and especially Sanh. 97–98); Kabbalah, G. Scholem, *Major Trends in Jewish Mysticism* (New York, Schocken Books, 1954), pp. 245–247, and Hasidic literature; see P. Schindler, *Hasidic Responses, op. cit.*, pp. 37–39, 49–50. The pre-messianic suffering is a central theme in Teichthal's thesis. "However, our prophets as well as our sages of blessed memory have predicted in the literature of the Talmud, the Midrash, and Kabbalah, the period of great suffering, persecutions and slaughter which will befall the Jewish people in the end of days prior to the advent of the Messiah. From these [demonstrations of suffering], one may already recognize the period in which the light of the Messiah glows, as it is related in our sacred texts; the hardships of exile will be felt only after the era of redemption has commenced." See *Avodat Avodah* (Zolkiew, 1865), 20b, by R. Solomon Kluger of Brody, on the tractate Avodah Zarah (AZ) 9a, commencing on "two thousand years will be the duration of the epoch of the Messiah." As Rashi interprets the verse (Isa. 26:17): "Like a woman with child approaching childbirth writhing and screaming in her pangs, so are we become because of You, O Lord."

will come and redeem us from their clutches, though we may not be
privy to God's will with respect to the coming of the Messiah since He
did not reveal His thoughts on the subject[33] (*EHS*, 23).

SUFFERING IN EXILE

The purpose of the volume is to explain the suffering of the Jewish
people during the course of history and especially the tragedy in
progress. If such has any meaning, according to the author, it must
lead to *tikkun*. The people and, specifically, its religious leadership
are responsible for sowing the seeds of *galut* (exile) which are harvested
at the expense of *ge'ulah* (redemption).

> The suffering which befalls Israel is due to bad leaders. I dared to
> survey and research [the literature] devoted to the continued persistence
> of the exile. I proceed to compose this work, with the help of God, in
> which I publicly express my views to advise my people as to what
> should be done to advance redemption, speedily in our day. . . . After
> some respite following my arrival here in the capital,[34] fulfilling my
> vow, I began work on the volume devoted to the rebuilding of our
> Holy Land; to raise it from the mounds of dust[35] to simulate love and
> affection in the hearts of our Jewish brethren, old and young, so that
> they would endeavor to return to our Land, the Land of our forefathers,
> and not remain here in the lands of exile. As expounded in the Midrash
> Rabba:[36] "It is preferable to live in the deserts of Eretz Yisrael and not
> in palaces outside the Land."
>
> Furthermore, the purpose of all of the plagues with which we were

---

Rashi: "We are witness to renewed suffering and believe these to be indications of
redemption and salvation, since we are surely to be redeemed amidst sorrow and
distress, like a woman in childbirth, due to Your decrees." [An extended paraphrase
of Rashi, Isa. 26:17] *EHS*, 22–23, 60–61.

33   The author employs the Rabbinic Aramaic *liba lefuma la galya*. EcclR. 12:10;
MPs. 9:2.

34   The author arrived in Budapest from Nitra, following the High Holy Days
5703, likely between October 25 and 28, 1942. See preface to *EHS* to Jerusalem
(1974) edition, p. 8 of the nonpaginated biography.

35   Cf. Neh. 3:34.

assailed during our periods of exile was to arouse us to return to our Holy Land (*EHS*, 28).

Among the central motifs to which the author returns repeatedly are:

> 1. The shortcircuiting of communication between the Divine and the Jewish people, while the latter linger in exile, and its inversion.

> 2. The active and necessary initiative of a people rebuilding its land, which represents not only a sign of faithfulness, but *tikkun*, the requisite step towards redemption.

The *Tosefta* in Avodah Zarah (chapter 5) remarks upon the verse:

"And I will faithfully plant them in this Land"[37] [Whenever they shall be on the Land they will be as if I had planted them before Me, faithfully, with all My heart and soul],[38] [but if they] are not settled upon her, they will not be planted before Me faithfully, neither with My whole heart nor soul.[39]

It is indeed startling for the Holy One, blessed be He, to declare that when Israel is not in its Land they are not at one with Him in heart nor soul. What has befallen us in our time and the limited degree of evident [Divine] providence should not astonish us, since He is not faithfully linked to us with His entire heart and soul. We are after all in the land of other nations. When we shall attempt to return to her, then we will immediately cleave to Him with all heart and soul. As it is explained in the *Kuzari* (2:14), the Shekhinah [Divine Presence] descended upon Ezekiel despite the statement of our sages of blessed memory that the Shekhinah does not rest outside the Land of Israel.[40] Since he prophesied in the interest of Eretz Yisrael, the Shekhinah rested [upon him] outside

---

36 GenR. 39:10.

37 Jer. 32:41, "I will rejoice in treating them graciously and I will faithfully plant them in this Land, with My whole heart and soul."

38 This section of the *Tosefta* is omitted in *EHS*.

39 *Tosefta*, Zuckermandel, ed. (Jerusalem, Wahrman Books, 1970), p. 466.

the Land of Israel [as well].

Primarily, God expects us to assume the initiative and yearn to return to our Land. We should not wait until He Himself brings us there. Therefore, we are told, "I will faithfully plant them in this Land."[41] That is to say, we are consciously to strive and yearn for this purpose, faithfully, and with all our abilities. Then He will successfully complete the task for us (*EHS*, 28–29).

ERETZ YISRAEL:
THE SCRIPTURAL INHERITANCE THAT COMMITS

Among the primary poles upon which the volume turns is the central role of Eretz Yisrael in the contract which binds the Divine to the Jewish people. First, Eretz Yisrael is the natural habitat within which both the Divine and the people reach their ultimate fulfillment. Jewish religious and economic activities, outside the Land, no matter how positive, are unnatural and delay the process of redemption. Perhaps the statement which most marks Teichthal's departure from classic *Haredi* theology, is his rejection of reliance on supernatural miracles.

I chanced upon the holy volume *Bet Elohim* of our teacher HaMabit.[42] He notes that Joshua was compelled to conquer the Land by conventional means of war. The Ramban in his commentary on the Pentateuch in Shelah, Numbers (13) has emphasized that the Torah does not rely on miracles.[43] Rabbi Bahya[44] also makes this point.[45] It is also noted in

---

40 J. Halevi, *The Kuzari* (New York, Schocken Books, 1964), pp. 89–92.

41 Jer. 32:41.

42 R. Moshe ben Yosef Trani (1505–1585) descendent of the distinguished Trani family, originating in the 12th century in Italy, contemporary of R. Joseph Karo; author of Responsa bearing an acronym of his name (Mabit), a commentary on the Bible and Talmud (*Kiryat Sefer*, Venice, 1551), and *Bet Elohim* (Venice, 1576), a volume devoted to ethics and belief.

43 *Perush HaTorah LeRabbenu Moshe ben Nahman* (The Torah Commentary of Nahmanides), vol. 2, H.D. Chavel, ed. (Jerusalem, Mosad HaRav Kook, 1960) pp. 199, 241. "Since the Torah does not rely on a miracle whereby one [warrior] pursues a thousand . . . because Scripture will not always depend upon miracles but will in fact command the warriors to seek refuge, to beware, and to lie in ambush."

Rashi, Shabbat 23 b.[46] The Jerusalem Talmud, Yoma 1:4, teaches us not to rely on miracles in order that you "do not test the Lord your God."[47] It is further taught in the chapter Tamid Nishhat 64,[48] that we do not rely on miracles.[49]

Rabbi Teichthal compares the tragic misconception of the *golus Yid* (the Jew with the *galut* mentality), who is trapped in the vicious cycle of reliance on miracles, and dependence on the good will of others, rather than initiating acts of self redemption, to Peretz *gabbai* in the following story.

With regard to the excerpt from the Talmud: "What must a person do that he may have male children?"[50] I am reminded of a story told to me by an aged hasid of R. Eliezer of Komarno.[51] The holy Rebbe was attended by an elderly bachelor. Though he was of limited intelligence,

---

44 R. Bahya ben Asher, 13th century commentator and kabbalist, student of R. Solomon ibn Abraham Adret. Noted for his commentary (and encyclopedic compilation of commentaries) on the Pentateuch (Naples, 1492).

45 *Rabbenu Bahya: Be'ur al HaTorah*, vol. 3, H.D., Chavel, ed. (Jerusalem, Mosad HaRav Kook, 1968) p. 79. "for if someone does not prepare and relies upon a miracle he will surely fall into enemy hands."

46 No reference to miracles is noted in Rashi, Shab. 23b. Likely reference is to Rashi, Shab. 53b regarding R. Nahman's statement: "Miracles do occur, but food is not so readily created by miracles." Supernatural or revealed miracles appear when the people are fully worthy. Since this is not the reality, redemption must be pursued "in the natural course of events by a natural process." *EHS*, 86. Further, this form of redemption is to be gradual since one long in the dark exile "could not enjoy the sudden exposure to brilliant light." *EHS*, 89.

47 Deut. 6:16. The JT Yoma text reads: "Are these not among the miracles performed in the Temple? Said Rabbi Avin: Therefore, do not test [the Lord your God]."

48 Pes. 64b.

49 This is the view of Raba. The doors of the Temple court were manually closed by those assigned this task on the Passover holiday when throngs of pilgrims would enter the courtyard in three regulated shifts (see *Mishnah* Pes. 64a). Unlike Abaye's opinion that the doors were locked miraculously, Raba insists "that we do not rely on a miracle."

50 Nid. 70b–71a.

51 D. 1898, son of R. Yitzhak Isaac Safrin, founder of the Komarno hasidic dynasty.

he was a God fearing person. He was called Peretz "gabbai."[52] They
asked this Peretz: "Why do you not marry a woman?" He replied:
"Why do I need a woman? Do I lack anything being with the Rebbe?"
They replied: "But a man is in need of children!" He retorted: "Children?
I will submit a *kvittel*[53] to the Rebbe and I will have children!" When
they related Peretz's words to the Rebbe he laughed, exclaiming: "That
is the kind of image one acquires—like that of a Peretz—when one
relies completely on the Rebbe."[54] We learn from this that one without
the other is insufficient. Prayer [in this instance] not accompanied by
the marrying of a woman, is inadequate. One cannot emulate a Peretz
gabbai who relied on the prayers of the Rebbe and would not marry a
woman![55]

On the other hand, the natural relationship which would permit
the people to inherit the Land as part of the covenant, would require
the observance of Torah without which Eretz Yisrael would be in-
complete. The Land however, provides the inspirational environment
by which Torah observance can reach its ultimate realization.

Now in accepting the *morashah* [legacy] of Torah we will also be worthy
of the *morashah* of Eretz Yisrael. Should we depart from her [Torah]
either right or left,[56] so that it no longer be our *morashah*, then Eretz
Yisrael can no longer be our *morashah*. This occurred to our forefathers
and to ourselves because of our sins. Furthermore, we cannot grasp the
true profound mysteries [of Torah] except in Eretz Yisrael. As [our

---

52   The attendant of a hasidic rebbe. In this instance, the term may have been
applied in jest.

53   Yiddish for a written petition of the *hasid* to his rebbe. For the origin of the
kvittel in the hasidic tradition see A. Wertheim, *Halakhot VeHalikhot BaHasidut*
(Jerusalem, Mosad HaRav Kook, 1960), pp. 161–164 and n. 39; see *Law and Custom
in Hasidism* (Hoboken, Ktav, 1992), pp. 241–248, n. 39 on p. 245.

54   In the original text the latter portion of the story appears in Yiddish.

55   As additional material is introduced emphasizing the futility of prayer which
is not accompanied by personal effort (*EHS*, 103–104), the author describes his
difficulty in accurately citing sources away from his study and library. וכעת אי אפשר לי
לציין על הספר והמקום שאני כותב כעת בלי ספרים מחמת גלותי שברחתי מחדר הורתי מחמת המציק)

56   Jos. 1:7.

sages] said:"The atmosphere of Eretz Yisrael makes one wise."[57] They also related the advantage of studying Torah in Eretz Yisrael.[58] Upon this background it will be understood why I, at the very outset presented [the premise] that Torah and Eretz Yisrael were commanded simultaneously and that they function as two inseparable companions. (*EHS*, 52)

The tripartite relationship between God, People and Land is biblically transferred by inheritance through the ages and commits all concerned for all time, irrespective of subsequent political or military events.

Now the strongest case for [our ties to] Eretz Yisrael is based on inheritance, as it is written in the verse: ". . . to give you this Land as a possession."[59] Neither the argument of acquisition [by purchase] nor the argument of military conquest are valid. With regard to the latter; one conquest may cancel a previous one. The holy Torah is our contract and proof; it remains eternal and is evident to all nations. (*EHS*, 45–46)

The paradox is now complete. This classic fundamentalist position of scriptural absolutes is challenged, by Teichthal's radical defense of secular sinners.

THE REDEMPTIVE *TIKKUN* OF THE SINNERS — THE BLUNDER OF THE PIOUS

Whereas much of ultra-Orthodoxy vehemently rejected political Zionism,[60] attacking those "who meddled in hastening the End of Days," the young Zionist settlers, many of whom either rejected their traditional roots or were educated in the secularism of post-emancipation,

---

57 BB 158 b. "The atmosphere of Eretz Yisrael inspires wisdom."

58 See GenR. 16:7; "There is no wisdom like the wisdom of Eretz Yisrael, and there is no Torah like the Torah of Eretz Yisrael." *Bet Elohim, op. cit.*, 96b.

59 Gen. 15:7.

60 See M. Selzer (ed.), *Zionism Reconsidered: The Rejection of Normalcy* (New York, Macmillan, 1970), pp. 1–47.

were elevated by Teichthal, to the highest level of religious fulfillment. It is likely that he was attacked for embracing the "heretical" *halutzim* as much as he was villified for his ideological "backsliding."

> I shall presently address myself to the builders of our Holy Land in our own generation. By these things [the Divine promise and fulfillment] men live.[61] And through them the Lord's purpose may prosper.[62] It is as clear as day that your endeavors and labors are pleasing to God. You have built cities. From waste land you have created flourishing fields. This was achieved by means of difficult and dedicated efforts. You succeeded in cleansing bodies of water which had been infected with many diseases. You then directed these to choice and fruitful fields. I shall demonstrate that your works are indeed pleasing to the Lord.[63] (*EHS*, 53)

Of major moment in Teichthal's defense of the *halutzim* is his reinforcing the Jewish legal principle of the intrinsic worth of every mitzvah (commandment) performed, irrespective of the motive or the quality of observance of other mitzvot.

> The Hatam Sofer states in his novellae [*hiddushim*] on the tractate Sukkah 35[64] that the acts of plowing and sowing in Eretz Yisrael are as if one performs the commandments of tefillin [phylacteries], sukkah [the booth], or lulav [the palm], one of the four vegetative species required for the Sukkot festival.[65] (*EHS*, 54)

---

61   Isa. 38:16. A contextual homiletical reading may have been intended for this complex verse: "May the Divine spirit dwell upon them."

62   Variation of Isa. 53–10.

63   The expression מעשים רצויים לפני הבורא or רצויה לפני הקב"ה is identified in Hasidism with the desired experience of *deveikut* (clinging) to the Divine. This experience may take place irrespective of any conscious efforts. See R. Dov Ber, *Maggid Devarav LeYa'akov*, ed. R. Schatz (Jerusalem, Magnes Press, 1976), p. 76 and note to paragraph 53.

64   Actually *Suk.* 36a.

65   Biblical commandments based on Ex. 13:9; Ex. 13:16; Deut. 6:8; Deut. 11:18; Lev. 23:42–43; Deut. 16:13; Lev. 23:40.

THE INFINITE WORTH OF THE FINITE

Beyond this censure of fundamentalism, which insists on examining total patterns of "religious behaviorism,"[66] emerges a remarkable theory of *tikkun*, scaled down to finite segments of human realities. Each segment at any given time represents an independent redeeming element for which a particular individual or group may have been specifically created.

It seems to me, that this simple individual who builds the Land, without any religious pretenses, but merely for his own advantage, fulfills a greater act of *tikkun* in the upper spheres than even the most righteous of *tzadikim* with his Tikkun Hatzot[67] and his wailing and bewailing the Shekhinah and exile. . . .[68] The text in Sanhedrin 102b reiterates this teaching as does our master[69] in his introduction to the volume *Reshit Hokhma*. *Tikkun* (restoration) is achieved by the actual performance of

---

66   Heschel's terminology for "an attitude toward the law as well as a philosophy of Judaism as a whole," characterized by an exaggerated emphasis on "orthopraxis" which "reduces Judaism to a sort of sacred physics, with no sense for the imponderable, the introspective, the metaphysical." See A.J. Heschel, *God in Search of Man* (New York, Harper and Row, 1966), pp. 320–335.

67   *Lit.* "the institution of midnight" or the "midnight vigil." The practice of rising at midnight to recite prayers in memory of the destruction of the Temple and to plead for the restoration (*tikkun*) of Eretz Yisrael. The talmudic basis is found in related passages Ber. 3a–4a. The mystic R. Isaac Luria formalized the practice. For the broader ramifications of *tikkun* in Kabbalah, see G. Scholem, *Kabbalah* (Jerusalem, Keter, 1974), pp. 140–144, specifically, p. 143, dealing with the influence of human activity on *tikkun* in the lower and upper worlds.

68   The concept of the Shekhinah in exile appears in the Talmud and Zohar as reflecting Divine empathy with the suffering of His people and His special love for them. "Wherever they were exiled, the Shekhinah accompanied them." (Meg. 29a; JT *Ta'an.* 1:1; Zohar I, 120b, 211b.) In Kabbalah and Hasidism, the burden of releasing the Shekhinah from exile is transfered to the individual. The performance of the mitzvah, the pious act "below," releases the holy sparks from their imprisonment among the *kelipot* (impure shells). On the other hand "acts of Edom," sinful acts, compel the Shekhinah to "accompany" the alien action in exile in Edom. See R. Shneur Zalman of Liadi, *Tanya, Likutei Amarim* (Kfar Habad, Israel, *Otzar HaHasidim*, 1959), p. 23. The Baal Shem Tov expressed the exile of the Shekhinah and the redeeming act of man in terms of *koved ha-rosh*, sharing the "burden of the Source."

69   R. Elijah ben Moses de Vidas.

the mitzvah. . . .[70] I found similar support in the volume *Yismah Moshe*,[71] [that is to say,] the active aspect of the mitzvah, though not based on any specific intent, is more effective than a mitzvah which lacks activity, although it is accompanied by great intentions. . . .[72] According to the halakhic authorities as well, it is clear that a mitzvah which involves action does not require intent. The mitzvah is fulfilled without intent.[73] Note also the Rashba[74] on Yevamot 103: The act which results in a mitzvah cannot be retracted even should such action have come about by way of a transgression, Heaven forbid. Furthermore, the mitzvah is not negated in any manner.[75] This major principle is valid here as well. The Yishuv [Jewish settlement] in Palestine has expanded due to their deeds. These are irreversible and cannot be denied. After all, we are the benefactors of the fruits of their labor. Even if this may have come about by means of transgression, Heaven forbid, the mitzvah has been convincingly fulfilled, in all its revealed as well as esoteric aspects. . . . Therefore, every Jew who is truly faithful to God, and whose love for

---

70 *Reshit Hokhmah, op. cit.*, 2b. "It is true that the main objective of Torah is to bring the act towards realization." The world to come is achieved by performing deeds (4a). "Further, the Shekhinah is restored by action, more so than by words" (4b). The author of *Reshit Hokhmah* cites the Zohar I, prologue, 8a for support.

71 Classic volume for homiletical commentary on the Bible (Siget, 1898) by R. Moshe ben Zvi Teitelbaum (1759–1841), founder of the Teitelbaum dynasty of Hasidic leaders in Galicia, Poland and Hungary; pupil of the master R. Yaakov Yitzhak, "The Seer" of Lubin.

72 *Yismah Moshe, op. cit.*, 30a. "It becomes evident that one who actually acts upon this mitzvah easily achieves the particular act of restoration intended for that mitzvah although it was simply performed. His Will is done although not accompanied by mystical and esoteric thoughts, and though [the mitzvah was] not [performed] with appropriate purity, utmost sanctity, awe and love."

73 Probably reference to the Rabbenu Yonah (ben Abraham Gerondi c. 1200–1263) commentary on *Alfasi*, Ber. 3a and 8b and *Pahad Yitzhak* (R. Isaac Hezekiah ben Shmuel Lampronti, 1679–1756) (Livorno, 1839), vol. 5, p. 187. "Even according to the [legal] position that *mitzvot* do not require concentration, this is so only in the event that it [the mitzvah] is characterized by action. Action replaces intent."

74 R. Shlomo ben Abraham Adret (1235–1310), among the most notable of Spanish rabbinic authorities and prolific author of responsa.

75 *Hiddushei Yebamot LeHaRashba* (Constantinople, 1720), p. 129a concerning the questionable motives of the levir when enacting the ceremony of *halitzah*, as per Deut. 25:5–10.

God and His people takes precedence over self-conceit, will be grateful and appreciate your acts of building our Holy Land. (*EHS*, 54–55)

In sanctifying the acts of the secular pioneers, the author did not negate the preferred option for a Jewish state founded and operating on the basis of Torah. Yet, the *Haredi* detractors rejected Teichthal's positive synthesis of secular activism and divine purpose. Possibly, aspects of this synthesis became apparent to the author in the midst of the *hurban* which bound the secular and the pious together within a common crucible of fate and faith.

DESTRUCTION AND DOUBT

It is clear from the text that Teichthal's redemptive, activist theology did not evoke enthusiastic response from his suffering community, reminiscent of Moses' rejection by the Israelites in slavery. Nevertheless, the author pleads for fortitude by accepting the pre-messianic pangs with love. Worthiness of redemption will be enhanced by suffering which is endured with faith, or weakened by enervating doubt.

We must endure with love these misfortunes, difficult decrees and pogroms which have befallen us at this time. We must brave them with all our strength, since they are as important to us as if they were a whole burnt offering.[76] However, the last of the prophets, Malachi, warned us what will occur to us in the end of days when we shall be entangled in suffering during the period of the pangs of the Messiah. There will be those who will exclaim: "It is useless to serve God. What have we gained by keeping His Torah? Those who have done evil have found favor in the eyes of God. It is indeed they whom the Lord prefers."[77] Where is the God of Justice? Yet these are precisely the words heard during these bitter times! But those who revere the Lord and cling to Him talk to one another. They do not adhere to their

---

76 *Kekorban kalil ve'olah* implies sacrificial components. Lev. 1:3–17. Lev. 6:16.
77 A liberal paraphrasing of Mal. 3:14.

wicked deeds but encourage and strengthen one another.[78] As it is written in Isaiah 8:[17] "So I will wait for the Lord Who is hiding His face from the house of Jacob, and I will trust in Him." Though He hides His face from the house of Jacob, nevertheless he [Isaiah] will be patient and trust in Him. The Holy One, blessed be He, notes these words spoken by those who revere the Lord on the day of suffering. He records their words in a scroll of remembrance. Then with the coming of the day of retribution and redemption the Lord will distinguish between those who clung to Him and those who abandoned Him.[79] It seems to me that it is in reference to these righteous who are inscribed in the scroll of remembrance that Daniel states: "And at that time your people shall be delivered, every one that shall be found written in the book."[80] (I believe this interpretation is to be found in one of the commentaries on Daniel. As I prepare this manuscript for publication I do not have any texts available to me and therefore cannot cite the exact source.)[81] Therefore, during these trying times every Jew must surely brace himself, that his feet not slip.[82] It is worthwhile to bear the full brunt of the yoke of exile since this will reflect the magnitude of the reward which shall be granted to us by the Almighty when everyone shall be compensated in accordance with one's dealing with the Holy One blessed be He. (*EHS*, 61)

THE DECEPTIVE EXILE

Though the *hurban* represents the consequences of opportunities wasted in exile, the author assumes a position neither of self-pity nor despair. Rather, he identifies with the victims of the tragedy and seeks the redemption of the remnant. The faith of the remnant in its

---

78 Paraphrase of Mal. 3:16.

79 Conclusion of the paraphrase of Mal. 3:14–18.

80 Dan. 12:1.

81 The R. Saadia Gaon (889–942), R. Abraham Ibn Ezra (1089–1164) and R. David Altschuler (*Metzudat David*, 18th century) in their commentaries on Dan. 12:1, relate this verse to Mal. 3:16.

82 II Sam. 22:37, Ps. 18:37 ולא מעדו קרסלי.

will to rebuild the Jewish people will be the reward of redemption. *EHS* is a theology of hope. The suffering, albeit a problem of human failure, is also the mysterious existential "void prior to existence" associated with redemption.[83] The byways of suffering experienced by the Jewish people characterized by the mysterious need of "void prior to existence" is supplemented, however, by Rabbi Teichthal with a rational, behavioral approach to suffering and redemption.

Now, should redemption take place in a setting of goodness, tranquility and calm among the nations, many of our Jewish brethren would never consider leaving. What would they lack here in exile? They are well-to-do, prominent and fill important posts among the nations, such as the Rothschilds and Jewish barons who have achieved fame and have been elevated to positions of officialdom and aristocracy. What is their link to the Messiah and Eretz Yisrael? They have their own Messiah, Jerusalem is right here. They need not seek a better Messiah than the one they already have here [in exile]. . . .[84] The mystery of Exile and the hardships of the decrees which have constantly been our lot are designed to arouse us from our slumber in exile. This is the voice of our Beloved. This refers to the Holy One, blessed be He, who pounds[85] at the portal of our hearts, to stimulate within us a desire and longing to return to our Holy Land, neglected for almost two thousand years. We have instead compromised for a nominal and tenuous life of calm among the nations, thereby, rejecting the glory of God and the splendor of our nation and Holy Land. We have sold the birthright of Israel for a portion of lentil stew of the nations.[86]

---

83 Redemption need not necessarily be linked to suffering if Israel is worthy. Since Israel is not worthy, perhaps for having spurned opportunities for self redemption, it must accept the path of adversity in good faith. *EHS*, 62, citing *San.* 98 a, and the *Or HaHayyim* commentary in Num. 24:17. This view is also supported by R. Judah Loew ben Bezalel of Prague in *Netzah Yisrael* (Warsaw, 1886), 44 a and R. Yaakov Emden (17 th century), *Siddur Tefillah* (Altoona, 1745) 219 b–220 a.

84 The author refers to the legendary rejection of the Worms Jewish community of Ezra the Scribe's call to return to Jerusalem. ("You live in the Greater Jerusalem. We shall remain here in the smaller Jerusalem.") *EHS*, 33.

85 Song 5:2. Also CantR. 1:12. ‏"יבא דודי: זו השכינה‎.

86 A caustic reference to Gen. 25:29–34. Whereas Esau had exchanged his precious

THE *HAREDI* ANACHRONISTIC THEOLOGY

The negation of exile takes on a tragically renewed connotation during the disaster to which the author is witness. Eretz Yisrael is not only a sacred dwelling of a people in the historic-theological reality, but now has become an emergency life-raft for the sacred remnant.

> Israel is a dispersed flock of sheep,[87] lost among the nations with nothing which would unite one Jew with another. They are like dismembered organs dangling from their various places of residence, neither linked to the individual and certainly not with the [Jewish] totality. We are all as abandoned fish in the sea. As we have witnessed during recent years, even the lowest and most common scoundrel has felt free to do with us as he wishes; commit against us depravities and murder without having to account to anyone. Such [anarchy] could not be possible if we were to found, with the help of God, a center in Eretz Yisrael which would raise our glory with honor before all nations of the earth. We too would be considered a distinguished nation. Thus the individual who remains in exile would not be irresponsibly abandoned. Anyone considering acts of violence against us must understand that he will be accountable to someone for his acts. He will be held responsible and therefore would refrain from acting towards us with hostility. [The ingathering] would also cause the hearts of Jews to be reunited, even those in exile. Peace will reign among us. Thereby we shall attain, with good hope, the final redemption, speedily in our time, Amen. (*EHS*, 92)

The *haredi* theologies represent an illusory luxury of the past, a cruel anachronism during the current catastrophic realities.

> [Even] as I clearly respond throughout to all the arguments of our master and rabbi, the author of *Minhat Elazar*, of Munkatch (I too was among his circle), I am also aware that his premises were based upon a form of miraculous and wondrous redemption. Those who took matters

---

birthright for momentary physical satisfaction, it was now the descendants of Jacob who rejected their heritage for the delusion of tranquility among the nations.

87   Cf. Jer. 50:17.

into their own hands were considered to be meddlers. These arguments
are maintained in all of his works.

Without detracting from his revered status, I must respectfully indicate
that he viewed all things from a meritorious perspective based on his
[lofty] standards. Yet, in truth, this last generation, due to our many
transgressions is "not worthy." Redemption must, therefore, be disguised
as a natural process.

It is worth adding that had our rabbi, the author of *Minhat Elazar*,
been with us to witness all these terrible decrees and acts of murder
which have befallen us, Heaven help us, he too would acknowledge that
we must abandon the lands of exile, return to Eretz Yisrael which had
provided us [in the past] with royalty, and not wait for the call to the
Messiah. (*EHS*, 94)

Haredi leaders, who continued to oppose redemptive initiatives as
if nothing has changed, come under scathing attack throughout the
volume. Applying the teaching in the *Kuzari* of R. Yehudah HaLevi,[88]
R. Teichthal notes:

Thus we have a clear option from this divine personage. Even if, Heaven
forbid, Eretz Yisrael becomes inhabited with forces of obscenity, it is
still preferable to live there than anywhere else. This should serve as an
example for those in our own day who drape themselves in piety, and
slander the Land, claiming that it does not meet their religious standards.
(*EHS*, 96)

THE CLOAK OF PIETY AND FOLLY

In the latter sections of the volume the author exposes the costly
factionalism among Jews, especially among the pious and their relations
with others, "their manner of separation and isolation from the total
nation, the Jewish people" (*EHS*, 251). Their orbit is "the house of
worship, morning and evening," and "the Talmud study circle". . . .
They have no attachment and affinity with the masses since their

---

88   Halevi, *op. cit.*, pp. 99–100.

outlook is limited to the narrow circle within which they revolve"
(*EHS*, 251). These "cloaked" Jews are referred to as "*sheine Yidden*"[89]
who have left the masses vulnerable to the mortal danger from without.
The folly of unbridled piety reached such proportions that some
Haredi elements were convinced that "the reason our fellow Jews in
Hungary have been saved is due to their not being involved in the
movement to build the Land."[90] The author, appalled at such conclu-
sions, responds with the dismissal of disdain:

> Our heart truly pains us as we have to listen to so many fools who
> speak, saying that the Holy One, blessed be He, is compassionate with
> our fellow Jews who dwell in Hungary because they rejected the move-
> ment to build the Land and did not cooperate on its behalf. May the
> Almighty spare us from such opinions! Go see the extent of their obsti-
> nacy. With such people one should not argue at all. Solomon referred
> to them when he remarked: "Do not answer a fool in accord with his
> folly [else you will become like him]" (*EHS*, 357). . . .[91] May the good
> Lord forgive them for this deed. (*EHS*, 423)

---

89   *Lit.* "beautiful Jews," a caustic Yiddish expression for Jews who flaunt their
piety. ובציצית העטופים בטליתות is the phrase of the *Mahari Kohen* commentary, cited by
EHS, 328. The expression is found in the commentary on MPs. 18:44 (Warsaw,
1875), 54. R. Yitzhak ben Shimshon Katz HaKohen (d. 1624), son-in-law of R. Judah
Loew b. Bezalel of Prague, commentator on the Midrash to Samuel, Psalms and
Proverbs.

90   The Germans invaded Hungary in mid March 1944, more than seven months
after this episode occurred. Further, from March 9, 1942 to March 17, 1944, Hungary
was led by Prime Minister Miklos Kallay who pragmatically began to draw nearer to
the Allied cause in 1943 and provided some protection to the Jewish population.
This was interpreted by the *Haredi* anti-Zionist factions as reward for their efforts.
For a less favorable evaluation of Kallay see Bela Vago, "Germany and the Jewish
Policy of the Kallay Government," in R. L. Braham (ed.), *Hungarian Jewish Studies*
(vol. 2) (New York, World Federation of Hungarian Jews, 1969), pp. 183–210.

91   Prov. 26:4. See also *EHS*, 235.

TIKKUN WITHIN THE HOLOCAUST

Em HaBanim Semeha looks beyond the complex strata of massive grief. The work relentlessly forges elements of *tikkun* from which the Jewish people will be reconstructed.

A. The *Tikkun* of Exile (*Galut*)

The Jewish relationship with exile is to be forthwith and interminably severed. This is an example of where the vessel is to be completely shattered before it can be reconstituted. The stepmother is to be cast aside for the mother who has been eagerly awaiting the return of her children; hence, the title of the volume.

> Hundreds and thousands of years were lost to us in exile, all of our energy and blood we gave to our stepmother. Now we have received from her in appreciation for all of our care on her behalf a stick with which she has proceeded to beat us cruelly without mercy and compassion. She has wounded our entire body from head to toe without a spot that remained unblemished.[92] She has proceeded to expel us with vehemence. She has taken our wealth from us, compelled us to leave her home naked and bereft. So many of our fellow Jews, in the thousands and tens of thousands, died horrible deaths at the hands of our stepmother. Shall we now express our trust in her by returning to her once again? What guarantee do we have that after a few decades she will not again act towards us in this manner? In fact, our history has demonstrated that these acts recur in cycles throughout the years. Thus far, we have not learned from our past. We can no longer trust the lands of exile, because of all this which has happened—never, never! Never shall we return to our stepmother. Rather we will rise and ascend to our genuine mother. We will dedicate to her all of our energies, from now and forever. We will rebuild her walls and reconstruct her ruins. (*EHS*, 207–208)

---

92 Cf. Isa. 1:6.

B. The *Tikkun* of Tragedy

The martyrs of the Holocaust are to be redeemed only if the Jewish people redirect energies towards the resurrection of their homeland.

> It is acknowledged, therefore, that in abandoning these countries of exile and returning to Eretz Yisrael, not only do we redeem the souls of our Jewish brethren who were murdered and fell here in exile, because they compelled us to return to the domain of our forefathers, but we hasten their resurrection. Hence, their martyrdom was actually not in vain. (*EHS*, 213)

C. The *Tikkun* of Attitude

Redemptive efforts would have to include the adoption of a tolerant and balanced posture towards other Jews, and the rejection of polarizing positions in the name of "religious integrity and piety."

> Now it is said in the name of our holy Rabbi, R. Naftali of Ropshitz,[93] who was known for his clever remarks, that a proper Jew must be at once "good, pious and wise."[94] One without the other is not sufficient. One who is exclusively good is an adulterer.[95] To be pious only, is to be a fool. To be clever alone, is to be a sceptic. To be good, and pious, and clever is the proper course of a Jew. These were his words. (*EHS*, 274)

D. The *Tikkun* of Discord

The seeds of destruction are sown from within. Disunity proclaims to the potential perpetrator that the potential victim is prepared to participate in one's own undoing. Consistent with Teichthal's mystical

---

93   Hasidic master (1760–1827), pupil of the Hozeh of Lubin, the Maggid of Koznitz and R. Elimelekh of Lizhensk.

94   In Yiddish.

95   Deriving personal pleasure from being good without the broader moral religious motive. The mere act of good performance can be self-indulgent.

views, discord in the world below prevents unity in the cosmos, hence delaying redemption.

> In the [commentary of the] portion of *Kedoshim*,[96] the *Pardes Yosef*[97] cites a text from the Haggadah [of Passover]: "Not just one [tyrant][98] rose up against us to destroy us. . . ." The intent of *lo ehad bilvad* [not only one] refers to the fact that we are not one [united] among ourselves. This alone is cause to destroy us, God forbid.[99] Then the Lord, blessed be He, will bring our hearts closer, one to another, and unity shall reign in Israel. Amen, may this be His will. (*EHS*, 228)

The unity motifs increase in vehemence with the close of the volume. The catastrophe is linked to the tragedy of discord, to the futility of uniting the God in exile with His people in exile, to the *tikkun* which is necessary and possible.

> Our entire redemption and destiny is tied to the one condition that we remain united and consolidated as one complete entity; that we unite within ourselves people representing every sector found among us, from the person on the extreme right to the one on the extreme left. [This is to be done] until all of Israel becomes a unified perfect whole. Then we will conquer the Divine attribute of strict Justice. We will silence the adversary [Satan] so that he cannot scheme against us,[100] as indicated earlier.
>
> Yet, how is it possible to remedy all this? Who is capable of bringing them all together? How can one include and gather all of Israel from the four corners of the earth and forge them into one flock with such different points of view and features? Indeed, this difficulty was raised

---

96 Lev. 19:1–20:27.

97 An anthology of commentaries related to Rashi and Nahmanides of R. Yosef Pachanovsky (d. 1930).

98 I.e., Pharaoh.

99 *Pardes Yosef,* (Lodz, 1930), part 3, p. 236b. ובהגדה ישלא אחד בלבד עמד עלינו לכלותינו ילא א ח ד׳ בלבד מה שלא יש אחדות ביניינו זה גורם לכלותינו.

100 Cf. ותגער בשטן לבל ישטיננו from the *hineni* personal prayer of the *hazzan* prior to the Musaf service on the High Holy Days.

by our rabbi [the author of] *Hafla'ah*[101] [commenting] at the close of
Ketubot [112 b] on the eventual unification of all of Israel in our time,
which was forestalled due to the differences in views among them.[102]

Our sages of blessed memory have instructed us saying: Do not
underrate the importance of anything.[103] Even the ordeal of the abnormal
periods which we have endured teach us that events which people had
believed to be unrealistic, proved to be very real. And things which no
man even believed were possible in this world were eventually realized.
Similarly, incorporating all of Israel into a unified whole is a likely
possibility and is not contrary to its natural inherent tendency, as I shall
proceed to relate with the help of the Almighty.[104] (*EHS*, 255–6)

E. The *Tikkun* of Love (*Ahavah*)

The concluding fourth chapter is devoted entirely to the theme of
Ahavat Yisrael (love for a fellow Jew). Paradoxically, it is this motif
which emerges most dramatically from the hostile context of the
hurban.

The numerical value of *Ohev Yisrael*[105] is identical to the numerical
value of *takkanah*,[106] in order to teach that only it can be the solution
for Israel, none other.[107] (*EHS*, 317)

---

101   The extensive commentary on the tractate of *Ketubot* by R. Pinhas HaLevi Ish
Horowitz (1730–1805), whose Hebrew initials form the Hebrew title.

102   *Hafla'ah* (Jerusalem, Hafla'ah Publishers, 1961) on Ket. 112 b, pp. 49 b–50a.

103   Avot 4:3.

104   To those for whom piety is of greater value than unity, the author cites the
admonition of R. Eleazer ben David Fleckeles of Prague (1754–1862) in his volume
of responsa *Teshuvah Me'ahavah* (Prague, n.p., 1809) no. 61, p. 33b. "If building the
Holy Temple can only be achieved by means of discord, it is best that it not be built."
The Jerusalem *EHS* edition (1983) copies the inaccurate citation (part 1, 205) noted
in the original (*EHS*, 327).

105   One who genuinely cares for an Israelite.

106   "Reconstruction," "remedy." אוהב ישראל and תקנה both equal 555 in *gematria*.

107   ". . . so will [*Ahavat Yisrael*] be the remedy for every Jew who approaches the
Lord, each in his own fashion," Introduction to *Ohev Yisrael* (Zitomer, *Siftei Tzadikim*,
1863), p. 2, by R. Meshulam Zusya of Zinkow, grandson of the author, R. Abraham
Yeshoshua Heshel of Apt (1755–1825), disciple of R. Elimelekh of Lizhensk.

R. Teichthal's plea for the *tikkun* of love was not a pious platitude but grounded in the harsh internecine fractionalism which often characterized the competitive and complex *Haredi* world in which the author functioned. Epithets such as *rasha* (wicked), *poshe'a Yisrael* (a Jewish villain), and *kofer* (heretic) were commonly employed against the non-conformist. This destructive orbit of random hostility is noted.

> I also looked at the text *Malbushei Yom Tov* of the holy Zidachover[108] who cites R. Menaham Mendel of Rimanov.[109] Accordingly, the second son in the Haggadah [of Passover] will also benefit from the *tikkun* [restoration] of the final redemption. Due to his love for Israel this holy person refused to refer to him as a villain [*rasha*], but rather "the second son." Note to what extent one should love a fellow Jew. Not even a relentless villain, such as the second son in the Haggadah, was to be referred to as a villain." (This should be an example for all those who tend to evalute others with the expression *rasha*.)[110] (*EHS*, 67)

F. The *Tikkun* of Error

The potential to be retransformed from the *Golus Yid* mentality to redemptive-oriented people, assumes recognizing and acknowledging errors of the past. *Tikkun* of error is the most difficult of tasks for people of faith, inclined to fatalistic thought and behavior. Yet his own agonizing experience within the Holocaust, fortified by classic Jewish sources, demonstrates that the *tikkun* of error is possible.

---

108 R. Yissakhar Dov of Zhidachov (d. 1923) grandson and disciple of R. Isaac, founder of the Zhidachov dynasty (d. 1872). *Malbush Shabbat VeYom Tov* (Munkatch, Bernart Meisels, 1927), p. 51b, is a collection of Hasidic commentary on the weekly portion of scripture.

109 Major Hasidic leader (d. 1814), disciple of R. Shmelke of Nikolsburg and R. Elimelekh of Lizhensk.

110 The author is pained as to why Jews would question and evaluate anyone's Jewish identity when for the foe there is no such problem. Citing the responsa of Rabbi Moshe Sofer, the Hatam Sofer, *Yoreh De'ah*, no. 333 (New York, Hod Publishers, 1972) p. 143, regarding a non-observant Jew who was killed by gentiles in 1811: "A Jew who is killed by a gentile, is a *kadosh* [sacred martyr], though he may have been a transgressor and *rasha*" *EHS*, 109.

I proceeded to preach on this subject with considerable passion. Many
were upset with me.[111] This reached the attention of this *gaon*[112] who
reacted as follows: in reality, it has turned out we were in error in
withdrawing from the movement to build the Land. [Yiddish.] These
were the very words of this great *gaon*, a leader of his generation. And
he said further: A great many of our Jewish brethren would have been
saved had we all been involved in the rebuilding of our Land and not
feuded among ourselves. He then burst forth weeping, for some of his
children, as well, who were trapped in Slovakia. (*EHS*, 161)

The author proceeds to underscore a major principle in his dynamic
philosophy of the halakhah process, relevant to the debate at hand.
Only those involved in the contemporary life struggle are in a position
to participate in rabbinic legal discourse. Those no longer active in
the affairs of this world "be it even Moses or the angels," are not to
rule on legal matters which concern the present generation. Consequently, rabbinic attitudes and rulings on the Zionist question which
may have been appropriate in previous generations are not necessarily
valid in the present. Dynamics of change are assumed by those who
are directly affected by such change. Anachronistic considerations
compound the error, which in the case of the *hurban* proved to be
fatal.[113]

R. Teichthal recants openly:

Now that the situation has changed so have the demands. I have already
indicated at the outset of this volume,[114] that I had never been able to
grasp the profound meaning of this obligation.[115] Now that I have
become engrossed in this duty[116] and become convinced of my error I
will proceed to do what many of our sages in the Talmud did. They

---

111   For approving of the Zionist enterprise.

112   R. David Meisels, rabbi, scholar in the community of Ohel in northeast Hungary,
and a contemporary of the author.

113   *EHS*, 162–164.

114   *EHS*, 17–18.

115   The obligation to settle the Land of Israel.

116   *Lit*, "After I lodged in the valley of the Law [*halakhah*]." See Meg. 3b.

admitted: "My statements to you were in error."[117] Also among legal authorities we find that they changed their rulings from previously expressed opinions. Note this well! (*EHS*, 314)

THE CONTEMPORARY SIGNIFICANCE
OF *EM HABANIM SEMEHA*

Em HaBanim Semeha has assumed its place among the masterpieces of *hurban* literature. R. Teichthal is an authentic voice of witness and prophecy, the lament of the witness, the plea and hope of the prophet. As such, the work stands on its own as a major work of religious response, as well as an expression of spiritual resistance during the Holocaust.

Its position in the post-Holocaust period as one might expect, varies in extremes. The Jewish nationalist right—especially the orthodox wing of that camp, represented by Yeshivat Mercaz HaRav in Jerusalem, and many of the settlements in the territories—revere the author. *EHS* is a textbook studied in their upper schools. The anti-Zionist (in the political sense of the term) *Haredi* world, to the degree that it is aware of the work, holds Rabbi Teichthal in contempt or pity. They see him as an unfortunate aberration, and a victim, a survivor who has lost his mind. Needless to say, his work is banned in a world which has changed little since the *hurban*. The heresies of pre-Auschwitz remain heresies—perhaps more so, since some of the basic assumptions of the author have been realized.

Yet, despite the reality of the State of Israel—and one can only hazard a guess as to what might have been the relationship of R. Teichthal to that reality—most of the issues targeted for the *tikkun* of the Jewish people in the wake of the Shoah have not been addressed or resolved. Jews continue to embrace their various stepmothers. They continue to adopt their habits and thoughts of their exilic existence. In this regard *EHS* is uncannily prophetic.

---

117   Er. 16b, 104a; Shab. 63b and others דברים שאמרתי לפניכם טעות הן בידי.

The decree is likely to cease.[118] Surely there will come a period of rest
and respite for Israel. They will readjust to their original state and will
remain here in exile. Furthermore, should they come upon a good
enterprise or lucrative income, they will console themselves with various
pretexts in order to tie themselves once again to their stepmother.
They will continue to betray their genuine mother, Eretz Yisrael. They
will make a mockery of themselves, believing that their stepmother will
now continue to be kind to them. They will regress to their former way
and forget about Eretz Yisrael. (*EHS*, 211)

Irrespective of the partisan feelings which it evokes, this volume,
conceived and written by a man of deep faith, raises searing theological
questions. The author links the current catastrophic events and "the
diminution of Divine Concern for us" (*EHS*, 29) to Israel's lack of
concern for its homeland, and, hence, its God. It is the "Cause of all
Causes" Who incites the nations against a people who have forgotten
their identity and rejected their portion.[119] Is this to be taken literally?
Are these mere conventional phrases of rabbinic language? Would
even such standard parlance have been expunged by the author had
he known in 1943 the true extent and final consequences of the
Shoah? Surely, a treatise which places *Ahavat Yisrael* in the center of
its concern would not simultaneously allow the architects of the Final
Solution to appear even remotely as agents of the Divine, Who seeks
to return the people to His fold. Though Pharaoh and Nebuchadnezzar
were depicted as God's agents in rabbinic literature, no serious scholar
would go so far with Hitler. Any explanation other than the dichotomy
between the style of language addressed to a particular audience and
the substance of its radical context, would remove from the perpetrators
any moral responsibility to humanity and to God for their crimes.

A literal reading of the author's references to Divine Will with
regard to the Shoah would not only make absurd the principle of
absolute moral responsibility of the individual, but would empty of
any significance Teichthal's own thesis of *Hevlei Mashiah*, and his

---

118 ועבדא גזירה דבטלא *vs.* גזירה עבידא דבטלא, Ket. 3b.

119 *EHS*, 33. See also *EHS*, 20, 64–65, 78–79, 219.

rejection of reliance upon supernatural events in human history.[120] The author himself responds to this paradox.

> Perhaps, my brethren, you will claim that this is all a decree from Heaven, part and parcel of the exile which has been fated for us until the Messiah will come, speedily in our day and [therefore] we need not do anything about it. Let it be known, my brothers, that I do not agree with you. . . . On the contrary, from the teaching of Nahmanides,[121] we learn that we are to blame ourselves for all this. (*EHS*, 221)

Exile and redemption, consequences as well as merits, are ultimately determined by man's own will and action. Evil is, therefore, defined as the exploitation of free will by the perpetrator in response to the passivity of the victim who has surrendered fields of initiatives to others. For Teichthal, exile is the vacuum of powerlessness. Eretz Yisrael represents the redemptive realm of sovereign initiatives.

How precisely such a sovereign Jewish state, inspired and guided by the principles of Torah Judaism, would function in a world of secularism, modern technology and finance, and international *realpolitik*, is not addressed. All pales when considering the immediate and only priority of Eretz Yisrael as a sanctuary for the remnants of a repentant people returning to their homeland, to reunite with their God Who shared His people's fate throughout their long exile.[122]

References to "Divine causes" during the Shoah are in fact the descriptions of a man of faith but one who is cognizant of human failings, who acknowledges people as free agents, created in the Divine image, who can blunder and create hazardous consequences to their own undoing. These, according to Rabbi Teichthal, are the realities which operate in the Divine-human nature of things.

The author anticipated the rejection of his views. These were anathema to *Haredi* elements who defended their particular theology of

---

120 The mystical meaning of suffering prior to redemption as well as the imperative of continued human struggle on behalf of that redemption is pushed beyond any form of reductionism with the possibility of a mass criminal serving Divine ends.

121 *Commentary on Leviticus* 26:44.

122 *EHS*, 75–77, 170.

Divine dominance in the affairs of people and nations.[123]

The debate which was joined in the heat of the Holocaust continues. R. Yissakhar Shlomo Teichthal, who was murdered in a cattle car at the age of sixty, understood that the messages sent from Budapest in 1943 would continue to challenge the post-Auschwitz Jewish agenda.

> My contemporaries, I will yet come back to you in writing and by means of discourse, with the help of God. (*EHS*, 349)

Em HaBanim Semeha remains the focus of such discourse even as it echoes the author's last prayer for his people:

> May the Lord bind up His people's wounds and heal the injuries it has suffered,[124] speedily in our day. (*EHS*, 349)

---

123 *EHS*, 347–348. On one occasion, likely in the latter part of 1943, Rabbi Teichthal was refused the privilege of leading Shabbat morning services in a hasidic synagogue, after his views became known in Budapest. *EHS*, 228–231.

124 Cf. Isa. 30:26.

THE ENGLISH EDITION

When I first encountered *Em HaBanim Semehah*, one of numerous primary sources examined in the course of preparing my doctoral dissertation, it was clear that an English edition of this monumental work was essential.

Em HaBanim Semeha is a *cri de coeur*, and appears as unrelenting waves of argument piled on argument, without clear patterns of priority development or persuasiveness. It is clear that the author had neither the means, the time or moments of repose conducive to reorganizing the manuscript and assuming the tedious and rigorous tasks of editing. To ease the path for the English reader, editing and some condensation was essential.

The learned Hebrew reader is directed to the original source. I had the difficult task of deleting passages which seemed to repeat or supplement points of argumentation already presented. I assume responsibility in the choice of deletions, designated by ellipses, which were done with obvious regret, since the cumulative and various layers of documentation reflect an astounding grasp of the classic sources of Judaica. Wherever possible and necessary, in order to sustain continuity, a summary of the omissions is provided in the notes.

Text inserted between square brackets is either stylistic clarification not clearly evident in the original, or the completion of a source referred to in the original. The notes represent my efforts to trace and elaborate on sources, persons, or historical points not always identified in the text or referred to only in passing.

As editor and translator, I can only hope that the spirit in which *Em HaBanim Semeha* was written has been captured and retained, and that the accompanying notes will contribute to a fuller appreciation and understanding of this exceptional work. May it serve as a memorial to the victims of the Holocaust, and as a vibrant message to future generations.

Pesach Schindler
Jerusalem, 5757/1997

EM HABANIM SEMEHA

A·HAPPY
MOTHER·OF
CHILDREN

FIRST PREFACE

I read the following in a letter sent in the year 5562[1] by our Master, the author of the *Tanya*,[2] to our Rabbi of Berdichev,[3] may their merits protect us, when he was informed of his release from prison in St. Petersburg.[4]

I shall often repeat how the Lord worked great wonders[5] on this earth. Who am I, a lowly being, that the Lord was made great and sanctified because of me? . . . It was the Lord's will that the virtue of the Holy Land and its inhabitants protected us. This (merit) will help us against every enemy and rescue us from distress.

---

1 1802 would be mistaken. The letter as recorded in Rabbi Hayyim Meir Hellman's *Bet Rebbi* (vol. I, 69–70), lists the year 5559 (1799), more accurately parallel to the date of Rabbi Shneur Zalman's release from prison. See n. 4, below.

2 Rabbi Shneur Zalman of Liadi (1745–1813), a disciple of Rabbi Dov Ber of Mezeritch (1719–1772). The latter assumed the leadership of the Hasidic fellowship from its founder Rabbi Yisrael Baal Shem Tov (1700–1760). R. Shneur shaped the philosophic, reflective Habad approach of Hasidism. For a narrative history of the period, the reader will still benefit from the classic, *History of the Jews in Russia and Poland* (Vols. 1 & 2) by Simon Dubnow. (Philadelphia, Jewish Publication Society, 1946). The *Encyclopedia Judaica* articles in vol. 7 and the Dynasty Chart (vol. 1, 160–167) are helpful.

3 The legendary Rabbi Levi Yitzhak of Berdichev (1740–1809), among Rabbi Dov's disciples, and close colleague of Rabbi Shneur Zalman in the battle against Hasidism's opponents.

4 The bitter struggle between the Hasidim and their opponents, the Mitnagdim, led to the formal charges by the latter to the Russian authorities. The documents accused Rabbi Shneur Zalman and his followers of acts inimical to the empire. R. Zalman was arrested and tried in October 1798. On the 19th of Kislev 5559 (November 28, 1798) he was acquitted and released for lack of proof. This day continues to be celebrated by Habad Hasidim as the "Holiday of Deliverance."

5 Joel 2:21.

3

. . . I discovered from these holy and relevant words something heretofore unknown to me, which I had not noted in any literature: When a Jew is in trouble, Heaven forbid, he can be saved due to the merits of Eretz Yisrael and its inhabitants. . . . The teacher of the author of *Tanya*, of blessed memory, our Holy Master Rabbi Ber of Medziboz[6] of blessed memory, may his merit protect us, noted in his will written to his son[7] of blessed memory, that the wisdom (of the author of *Tanya*), his understanding, and knowledge[8] have no bounds.

Indeed, his intuitive reasoning reflects prophecy in miniature. . . . I elaborate upon the well-known exceptional qualities of our teacher, the author of *Tanya* only to underscore the holy teaching which was heretofore new to me, which I had not noted in the holy rabbinic literature. Because his words are imbued with the Holy Spirit, his point concerning the protective merits of Eretz Yisrael is completely reliable. I then reviewed the literature and the Almighty enlightened me. I discovered an authentic source in the very teaching of Moses which supported the words of our rabbi.[9] In the portion of *Behukotai*[10] it is written:

> Then will I remember My covenant with Jacob; I will remember also My covenant with Isaac, and also My covenant with Abraham; and I will remember the Land.[11,12]

Our teachers in *Midrash Rabba* have already drawn our attention to the reference of Land (in the covenant passage). Check the original source.[13]

---

6 Should read "Mezeritch," the community of Rav Dov Ber, and teacher of Rabbi Shneur Zalman.

7 R. Abraham (1741–1776), friend and student of Rabbi Shneur.

8 Utilizing the very terms by which the Hasidic trend developed by Rabbi Shneur Zalman is known: *Hokhmah* (wisdom), *Binah* (understanding), *Da'at* (knowledge)—*HaBaD.*

9 R. Shneur Zalman of Liadi.

10 The weekly portion of Scripture: Lev. 26:3–27:34.

11 Lev. 26:42.

12 LevR. 36:4.

13 The Midrash reads: "Why does He note both the merit of our Patriarchs and

However, our Rabbi's point is further validated when one examines Rashi's commentary:[14]

Why were they[15] listed in reverse order? As if to say: For Jacob, the youngest—for his sake alone.[16] If he will not deserve it, then Isaac shall join him. And if they on their own shall not be deserving, then Abraham too will join them.[17]

Now according to this explanation one can add: If none of these shall be considered worthy, and—God forbid—the merits of the patriarchs shall have been exhausted, nevertheless, "I will remember the Land."[18] The merit of Eretz Yisrael will rescue them from their distress. Thus, we have a pure source in the Torah of our master Moses which clearly supports our Rabbi's assertion that the merits of Eretz Yisrael stands above all our other merits. Indeed, it is greater than the merit of our Patriarchs. Should these not suffice, it will rescue us during times of misfortune, may the Lord help us.

And here I discovered another source in the *Mekhilta* in the chapter of *Beshalah*[19] commenting on the verse "Why do you cry out to Me? Tell the Israelites to go forward!"[20]

---

the merit of the Land? Resh Lakish said: 'This may be compared to a king who had three children and a maidservant who raised them. Whenever the king would inquire about the welfare of his children he would at the same time send greetings to the nursemaid. Thus, whenever the Holy One, blessed be He, mentions the Patriarchs, He includes the Land with them, for it is written: "Then will I remember My convenant with Jacob etc. . . . and I will remember the Land." This teaching may be linked to GenR. 84:13: "A person must inquire about the welfare of the subject from which he benefits."

14 To Lev. 24:42. Reference to the great scholar, teacher and commentator Rabbi Solomon ben Isaac (Rashi), 1040–1105.

15 The Patriarchs.

16 Would the Lord invoke the convenant.

17 The original Rashi text adds: "For he (Abraham) is deserving." The commentator actually paraphrases GenR. 36:5: "Why were the Patriarchs mentioned in reverse order? To say: If Jacob's deeds will not suffice, those of Isaac will be worthy. Were those of Isaac not sufficient, those of Abraham would be worthy."

18 Lev. 26:42.

19 *Mekhilta* (Ed. I. H. Weiss, Vienna, 1865), *Beshalah*, 35.

20 Ex. 14:15.

Rabbi Ishmael says: "For the sake of Jerusalem, I will divide the sea for them, for it is written, etc."[21]

Indeed they were in distress and the merit of Jerusalem sustained them. One wonders: What is the relationship to Jerusalem [of the miracles] of the exodus from Egypt? . . .

However, our sages of blessed memory have at times noted in the teachings of the Midrash[22] that "Eretz Yisrael" is synonymous with "Jerusalem," since it is the center of Eretz Yisrael. Also the *Vayera* portion of the *Midrash HaNe'elam* of the Zohar[23] notes: "All of Eretz Yisrael is incorporated within Jerusalem."

Thus the words of the author of the *Tanya* are specially reflected in Scripture and in the *Midrash* of our rabbis. His teaching is as valid as that of Moses, who received these from the Almighty. Since we the Children of Israel are presently in great distress, may the Merciful One speedily save us!

Misfortunes have entangled themselves about our necks. They recur daily, in fact, every hour. Sufficient paper to describe them all does not exist. I shall leave that to future historians. But most important, in my opinion, is that we remember the degree of our great distress, may the All-Merciful save us! There is not a day which does not bring curses exceeding those of the previous day. We are now certainly in need of the merits of our Holy Land to protect us and bring relief from our enemy and deliver us from our distress.

Our holy Torah has already noted the act of Jacob our Patriarch, may he rest in peace. When he was in distress he made a vow to the

---

21 "Awake, awake, O Zion! Clothe yourself in splendor! Put on your robes of majesty, Jerusalem, holy city! For the uncircumcized and the unclean shall never enter you again" (Isa. 52:1). R. Yishmael links Jerusalem with the crossing of the Red Sea motif in Isa. 51:9–10 via the identical עורי עורי "Awake, Awake!" call.

22 Likely reference to *Tanh. Kedoshim,* 10. ארץ ישראל יושבת באמצעיתו של עולם, וירושלים באמצעיתה של ארץ ישראל "Eretz Yisrael is located in the center of the universe, and Jerusalem is located in the center of Eretz Yisrael." See also, EstR. 1:9 where "city" is defined as "country," employing Jerusalem as the model *via* Ezek. 9:4.

23 Zohar I, 114a, מלמד דכל ארץ ישראל בכלל ירושלים היא The *Midrash HaNe'elam* is probably the earliest of three strata of the mystical Zohar literature according to Gershom Scholem, *Zohar: The Book of Splendor* (New York, Schocken Books, 1949), 14–15.

Lord as it is written: "Jacob then made a vow, saying, 'If God remains with me and gives me bread to eat and clothing to wear and if He protects me on this journey that I am making and if I return safe to my father's house, etc. . . .[24]

Our sages of blessed memory noted:[25] "What is its significance? . . .[26] We learn from here that one must make a vow when in distress". . . Therefore, . . . I shall also make a significant vow to the God of Israel, I will pray in the name of all of Israel in the spirit of our ancient Patriarch of blessed memory described previously. If God will be with me during these difficult persecutions; will watch over me against those who wish to harm me; will provide me with bread to eat and clothing to wear; will permit the merits of Eretz Yisrael to protect me and my family; that harm, hurt or confrontation shall not befall me or my household until the imminent redemption will come to all of Israel; that suffering shall be commanded: Enough!;[27] that the following verse will be speedily realized in our day: "A righteous man falls seven times and rises again, but the wicked fall but once;"[28] that our Holy Land will arouse its merit on our behalf so that we shall be speedily remembered for redemption and compassion since we have no power left to hold out; and that the suffering of these past years which have befallen us will be the pangs preceding the Messiah;[29]

---

24 A rearranged version of Gen. 28:20–21. The subsequent vow made by Jacob when fleeing from Esau pledged the future building of a House of God and a permanent tithe contribution from his income.

25 GenR. 70:1. The full text reads: כתיב: יאשר פצו שפתי ודבר פי בצר לי. (תהלים ס"ו:יד)
א"ר יצחק הבבלי יזדבר פי ודבר פי בצר לי' שנדר מצוה בעת צרתו. מהו לאמר? לאמר לדורות כדי שיהיו נודרין בעת צרתן. "It is written (Ps. 66:14): '[I enter your house . . . with vows] that my lips pronounced, that my mouth uttered when I was in distress.' He vowed to perform a mitzvah (religious precept) when in distress. For what purpose? In order to teach future generations to utter a vow when they will be in distress."

26 Of the verses Gen. 28:20–21.

27 An anthropomorphism commonly used based on *Tanh. Miketz* (Jacob's plea), and the play on *Shadai* לפיכך היה מתפלל באל שדי ואומר: מי שאמר לשמים וארץ די, יאמר ליסורי די "He, therefore, prayed to the God, *Shadai*, declaring: 'He who restricted heaven and earth, (*dai*) "enough!" shall also restrict my suffering, declaring, 'enough!'"

28 Prov. 24:16. Actual reading: "For a righteous man falls seven times and rises again, but the wicked succumb to adversity." See also Prov. 28:18.

29 חבלי משיח "The pangs preceding the Messiah." A major concept in the apocalyptic

that our Righteous Messiah will come and redeem us from their
clutches, though we may not be privy to God's will with respect to
the coming of the Messiah since He did not reveal His thoughts on
the subject.[30]

How the Messiah shall appear remains a mystery to all. This has
been indicated in the *Derashot* of the Ran:[31] Just as we shall not know
the timing of his coming so we shall not know the manner of his
coming (as will be explained further); whether it shall be by means of
a revealed miracle or by a miraculous act disguised within natural
means. Following the cessation of our suffering and God's granting
us relief, should the coming of the Messiah nevertheless be delayed,
Heaven forbid, (until such time when the Divine will decree his
coming,) then[32] will I take upon myself a vow, similar to the vow of
Jacob our Patriarch. [I promise] to write a book as soon as God will
bring us relief from our enemies. This volume will be devoted to the
glory of Eretz Yisrael. It will attempt to seek its merits and raise its
prestige. Above all, [the book will] demonstrate how much we are
obligated to rebuild and to improve her, to reestablish her on High
and to raise her from the dust.[33] Every Jew must attempt to participate
in the rebuilding of our Holy Land, for our entire redemption hinges
upon it. Eretz Yisrael is the mother of the Jewish nation, as described
in the Jerusalem Talmud (towards the end of the second chapter.)...[34]

---

themes of the Talmud (Pes. 118a, Ket. 111a, Meg. 17b, and especially Sanh. 97–98);
Kabbalah (Gershom Scholem, *Major Trends in Jewish Mysticism* [New York, Schocken
Books, 1954], 245–247) and hasidic literature (Pesach Schindler, *Hasidic Responses*,
37–39,49–50). A central theme in Rabbi Teichthal's thesis in confronting the Holocaust
events.

30   The author employs a rabbinic Aramaic expression: ליבא לפומא לא גליא "The
heart does not reveal [thoughts] to the mouth." Cf. EcclR. 12:10; MPs. 9:2. The
author's vow follows.

31   A collection of essays by Rabbi Nissim Reuben Gerondi, one of the leading
fourteenth-century talmudists in Spain. The exposition appears the end of Essay 11.

32   The resolution of the author's lengthy series of hypotheses which leads to the
declaration of his vow.

33   ולהרימה מעפרה. Allusion to Isa. 52:2.

34   JT Ber. 2:8. The author's major theme is presently introduced. Eretz Yisrael
as the mother of the Jewish people appears in the dialogue between Rabbi Kahana
and Rabbi Yohanan. בר נש דאימיה מבסרא ליה, ואיתתיה דאבוהי מוקרא ליה, להן ייזול ליה?

May we, therefore, benefit from the Almighty's protection of all of Israel who are in peril, including myself. I pray hopefully to God, Guardian of Israel, that He may shield me against destructive forces. May I be strengthened with vigorous health. May they [the oppressors] not have any power over me, my family and all of Israel . . . May the merits of Eretz Yisrael, which I revere, deliver me from the enemy and enable me to fulfill my vow with satisfaction and sincerity, speedily in our day. Amen, so be it the will of God.

It seems to me that this was the very essence of Jacob's vow during his ordeal. . . to return to Eretz Yisrael, to revere it greatly and to invest one's entire resources in its settlement. In this fashion, he intended to stimulate the merit of Eretz Yisrael on his behalf . . . Thus he declared in making his vow: ". . . and if I return safely to my father's house the Lord shall be my God."[35]

Now "and if I return safely to my father's house" was in fact the vow he made![36] This resolves the difficulty of the commentators with regard to Jacob's statement "(if I return safely . . .) the Lord shall be my God." For is it indeed possible that Jacob would premise his vow on this condition?[37] The well-known maxim of our sages, however, appearing at the close of the tractate of Ketubot [will also confirm

---

The context is ironic. "A man's mother degrades him while his father's wife honors him—to whom shall he go?" While Rabbi Kahana was mistreated in Eretz Yisrael, he was greatly respected in Babylonia. See below, 33–36, 199–203, 206, 236.

35 Gen. 28:21.

36 While the focus of the vow appears in Gen. 28:22, the author prefers to place the emphasis on verse 21 as the core of Jacob's declaration; not the condition, but the vow itself.

37 Is it conceivable that Jacob's belief in God was conditional? The commentators *Or HaHayyim* (Venice 1742) Moses Ibn Hayyim Attar (1696–1743); *Kli Yakar* (Lublin 1602) Ephraim Solomon ben Aaron of Luntshiz (1550–1619); Ramban (Moses ben Nahman of Gerona known as Nahmanides, 1194–1268); the *Tosafist* School (12th century France) respond to the author's difficulty and anticipate his reply. Conditions made it difficult for Rabbi Teichthal to consult all of the primary literature. The author frequently alludes to his writing without texts or sources. Rabbi Teichthal's daughter described her father's constant movements among cellar hideouts during the period in which this volume was written. (Communicated orally on April 5, 1983 to the editor by Rabbi Hayyim Menahem Teichthal, the son of the author, and a resident of Jerusalem.)

this point].

> . . . for whoever lives in the Land of Israel may be considered to have a
> God, but whoever lives outside the Land may be regarded as one who
> has no God.[38]

Thus Jacob's statement, "If I return safely to my father's house, the
Lord shall be my God" signified that when he would return to Eretz
Yisrael, then, indeed, the Lord would be his God. This was the vow!
He would return to Eretz Yisrael.

I also encountered a source in the *Midrash Tanhuma, Parshat Re'eh*
which describes Jacob's longing for her (that is to say, Eretz Yisrael)
based on the verse "If I return safely to my father's house."[39] Similarly,
I found the following in the Zohar, *Parshat Vayetze*:

> Another interpretation: "If I return safely to my father's house": The
> Holy Land is there. It is there so that I may achieve perfection. And the
> Lord shall be my God.[40]

These are indeed my exact thoughts with regard to Jacob's vow. I
was happily privileged to concur with the opinion of the pious teacher
Rabbi Shimon bar Yohai. . . .[41] When I shared this interpretation
with my dear friend, the distinguished scholar and teacher Rabbi
Yisrael Weltz, may he live long and happily, *dayan* (rabbinic judge)
and righteous teacher,[42] here in the Jewish community, he brought to
my attention a passage which appeared in the *Tosefta, Avodah Zarah,*[43]

---

38   Ket. 110b. כמו (*kemo*) vs. כמי (*kemi*) "as one" in the original.

39   *Tanh. Re'eh*, 8 (based on Deut. 12:29). 'יעקב נתאוה לה וגו "Jacob longed for her,
etc."

40   Zohar I, 150b דתמן הוא ארעא קדישא "The Holy Land is there" (based on Gen.
28:21).

41   The Zohar literature is attributed by tradition to Rabbi Shimon bar Yohai,
the mid-second century master of the mishnaic period.

42   Rabbinic scholar in Budapest (1887–1973) and author of *Hok LeYisrael* (Budapest,
1927) devoted to the laws of *Erev Pesah* (the day of Passover eve) which coincides
with the Sabbath. Assumed editorship of the rabbinic journal *Tel Talpiot* in 1937. See
below, 127 and 243.

43   Based on Lev. 25:38.

similar to the Zohar selection, as follows:

> When you will be in the Land of Canaan, I shall be your Lord. When
> you will not be in the Land of Canaan, He will not be your Lord.[44]

Hence, the *Tosefta* also substantiates that Jacob's vow was intended
to compel him to return to Eretz Yisrael. . . . In this light we shall
also understand the Midrash in the portion of *Vayishlah*,[45] interpreting
the verse, "and Jacob was greatly frightened."[46] He said: "During all
of these years, he (Esau) lived in Eretz Yisrael. Perhaps he will confront
me with the force of Eretz Yisrael."[47]

This seems surprising.[48] Yet as implied previously, Jacob's fear is
well founded. Since Jacob's own prayer[49] was entirely premised on
the hoped-for protection of the merits of Eretz Yisrael (provided that
he return to live there), our patriarch's fear was justified. Jacob's
present ties with Eretz Yisrael were theoretical, while the evil man
Esau *actually* resided there. Perhaps this evil man's merits will exceed
his own! He was therefore in a state of fear. Therefore, Jacob our
Patriarch vowed in his moment of travail to return to Eretz Yisrael,
to improve and establish [the Land], so that its merits would protect
him.

Obviously, we should at this critical time examine and emulate
Jacob's act. We must vow to return to our Holy Land. We must try
to reestablish its glory. Then too its merits will release us from our
distress, quickly in our day, Amen.

This then is the meaning of the Midrash:

---

44 *Tosefta*, AZ 5:2.

45 Gen. 32:4–36:43.

46 וירא יעקב מאד (Gen. 32:8).

47 GenR. 76:2. While Jacob flees from Esau's wrath to his uncle Laban in (Haran),
his brother continues to reside in Eretz Yisrael. The merits of uninterrupted residence
in Eretz Yisrael, Jacob fears, may give his brother the advantage in the anticipated
confrontation.

48 In the light of God's repeated promises of protection (Gen. 31:3, 28:13–15)
and Isaac's second blessing (Gen. 28:1–4), Jacob's fear is unexpected.

49 Gen. 28:21.

The Almighty transformed the conversations of our Patriarchs into models of redemption for their children.[50]

And here I discovered in the holy book *Divrei Emet* (Words of Truth),[51] of our teacher, the Godly personality from Lublin, of blessed memory,[52] from the portion of *Vayetze*:[53]

Jacob's vow was entirely intended for us to this day who walk in the footpaths of the Messiah[54] in order that we return safely to the Holy Land, the Land of our Fathers. This is the intent of the phrase Jacob

---

50　GenR. 70:6. נטל הקב״ה שיחתן של אבות ועשאן מפתח לגאולתן של בנים The positive commitment of והיה ד׳ לי לאלהים (Then shall the Lord be my God) reechoes via the והיה (Then shall . . .) in the redemptive passages of Zech. 14:8. והיה ביום ההוא יצאו מים חיים מירושלים "Then shall it come to pass in that day, that living waters shall emerge from Jerusalem." Isa. 11:11. והיה ביום ההוא יוסיף אדני שנית ידו לקנות את שאר עמו "Then shall it come to pass in that day, that the Lord will set His hand again the second time, to recover the remnant of His people." Joel 4:18. והיה ביום ההוא יטפו ההרים עסיס. "Then shall it come to pass in that day, that the mountains shall drop down sweet wine." Isa. 27:13. והיה ביום ההוא יתקע בשופר גדול "Then shall it come to pass in that day, that the great shofar shall be blown."

51　Yaakov Yitzhak HaLevi Horowitz, *Sefer Divrei Emet al HaTorah* (Words of Truth [of commentaries] on the Torah). (Lemberg, 1859), 9b.

52　Reference to Rabbi Yaakov Yitzhak, the Seer (*Hozeh*) of Lublin; among the early great masters of Hasidism (d. 1815), disciple of Rabbi Dov Ber, the Maggid of Mezeritch who inherited the mantle of leadership of the movement from its founder Rabbi Yisrael Baal Shem Tov.

53　Gen. 28:10–32:3.

54　בעקבתא דמשיחא. Term indicating the imminence of the Messiah (Sot. 49b). The full text in *Sefer Divrei Emet* (see above, n. 51) is cited herewith bearing on this point as well the following reference to the Zohar is cited herewith וישא יעקב רגליו׳ דהנה איתא שנדר יעקב אבינו הנדר על בניו בגלות לשוב לשלום: וקאמר שפעל בנדרו ובקשתו דהנה כמה פעמים נזכר עקבות משיחא ובזוהר עד דמטו רגלין ברגלין שיעלו ניצוצות מאדם בליעל להקדושה גם מהרגלין וזה בסוף וזה לשון עקבות, וזה וישא יעקב רגליו. "'Jacob lifted his feet' [Jacob resumed his journey]. This refers to the vow made by Jacob our Father on behalf of his children in exile, so that they would return in peace. It states that his vow and his wish were effective. A number of times is [the term] *ikvot Meshiha* (in the footsteps of the Messiah) noted in the Zohar, [A play on the name יעקב (Jacob) which is related to the root עקב, hence, עקבות (*ikvot*), to the extent that from [the interaction of] the lifting of the feet, sparks will ascend from a worthless person towards sanctity. They [the sparks] [will ascend] even from the feet, that is to say, from the lowest point. This is the meaning of *ikvot* ["related to the heel," hence, the lowest portion of the body]. And this is the interpretation of [the verse] 'And Jacob lifted up his feet.'"

"lifted up his feet."[55]

This denotes "in the footsteps of the Messiah,"[56] which the Zohar defines as *raglin*.[57]

The holy scholar, the Mabit of blessed memory,[58] noted in his work *Bet Elokim* that according to our Rabbis the entire vow of Jacob was directed to us so that we may know how to hasten the redemption in the end of days. . . .[59] Now note the Rashi commentary on the

---

55 Gen. 29:1. The symbolism of רגל "foot" as employed by mystical tradition requires here the literal translation rather than the idiomatic "[Jacob] resumed his journey," of JPS, *The Torah* (1962).

56 See above, n. 54.

57 The author relies on the *Divrei Emet* text quoted in full in n. 54 for the Zohar references. The Zohar in Gen. 29:1 does not enter into the mystical exegesis, but the redemptive allusions associated with the רגלין term are amply evidenced in the literature. The *Bet Aharon* commentary (Rabbi Aaron of Karlin, 1736–1792, disciple of Rabbi Dov Ber of Mezeritch) on the verse וישא יעקב רגליו "And Jacob lifted his feet" associated it with the messianic prophecy of Zech. 14:4 ועמדו רגליו ביום ההוא על הר הזיתים "And his feet shall stand in that day upon the Mount of Olives." Rabbi Nahman of Bratzlav (1772–1810) takes the Lurianic teaching of רגלין to its ultimate redemptive resolution. The "sifting out of the sparks," בירור הניצוצות) is linked to both the רגלין motif, to the Zech. 14:4 verse and to the resolution of "raising" from the seeming lowest point (symbolized by רגלין) to the pinnacle of restoration referred to as תיקון הניצוצות, the restoration of the sparks. The Luria and Bratzlaver texts are herewith cited. רגלין ברגלין, כשיתברר גם הניצוצין שברגלין אז יבוא המשיח "Feet intermingled with feet. When these will be sifted so that the sparks among them will be evident, then shall the Messiah come." (*Etz Hayyim*, Section 39:1) ובחי זאת של בירור הניצוצות נעשה בכל יום עד ביאת המשיח, עד שיתקיים יעמדו רגליו ביום ההוא על הר הזיתים" (זכריה יד:ד) כי עקר תיקון הנצצות הוא בבחי רגלין (ליקוטי מוהרי"ן, חי"א, עה) "This aspect of sifting the spark occurs daily until the coming of the Messiah, until the realization of [the verse in Zech. 14:4]: 'And his feet shall stand on that day upon the Mount of Olives,' since רגלין [the feet] are an aspect of rehabilitating the [holy] sparks." (*Likute Moharan*, Part I, 75.) Thus Jacob's "lifting the feet" coincides with the metaphysical, cosmological redemptive dynamics.

58 Rabbi Moshe ben Yosef Trani (1505–1585) descendent of the distinguished Trani family, originating in the 12th century in Italy, contemporary of Rabbi Joseph Karo, author of responsa literature, bearing his name (Mabit), a commentary on the Bible and Talmud (*Kiryat Sefer*, Venice 1551), and *Bet Elohim* (Venice, 1576), a volume devoted to ethics and belief.

59 וענין תפילת יעקב אבינו בזה המקום הוא תפילה על גלותנו זה האחרון, כי גלות מצרים וגאולתן היא מצד אברהם אבינו, וגלות בבל וגאולתן מיצחק, וגלות זה וגאולתן מצד יעקב . . . וכמו שהם התפללו על בנין ירושלים ובית המקדש ונתקבלה תפילתם בבית ראשון ובבית שני, רצה הוא להתפלל על בנין ירושלים ובית המקדש ונתקבלה תפילתם בבית זאת קרובה לביאת השמש שהוא רמז לגלות הארוך הזה. "שער התפילה") (פרק יח) ספר בית אלהים, ווארשא: תרלב (1872) כה "The implication of the prayer [and vow] of Jacob our Father at this specific place [Bet El, Gen. 28:19–22] is

verse in I Chronicles, chapter 29.[60] At a time when a person is in difficulty and makes a vow to God, he must recall Jacob our Patriarch, who was our mentor in this respect. This is the intent of the *Midrash*,[61] namely, to emulate Jacob our Father, and in my own vow I have indeed emulated Jacob our Father in utilizing the merits of settling in Eretz Yisrael. Hence, the merits of Eretz Yisrael will surely protect us, as was the case with Jacob our Father. I shall fulfill my vow *in toto*. God willing, my book shall stimulate the hearts of our brethren in exile so that they will presently reject the lands of other people and will arouse the desire to return to the Land of Delight which we inherited from our fathers. We shall therefore be privileged to experience complete redemption quickly in our own day.

I wrote this introduction on the seventh day of *Av* in the year "do not turn away Your annointed,"[62] when I and my family were in grave danger and we miraculously escaped. There was no doubt in my mind that only the merit of Eretz Yisrael saved us because of my great vow to the Lord. . . .

And note the introduction in the volume of *Derashot*[63] of the

---

that it represents a prayer concerning this, our final exile. In fact the exile to Egypt and redemption is linked to Abraham our Father. The Babylonian exile and redemption is tied to Isaac. This [current] exile and [eventual] redemption is related to Jacob. . . Just as they [Abraham and Isaac] prayed for the rebuilding of Jerusalem and the Holy Temple, and their prayers were answered with regard to the first and second Temples, so he [Jacob] desired to pray for the future reestablishment of Jerusalem and the Holy Temple. Therefore, his prayer was recited in close proximity to sunset [Gen. 28:11] [See GenR. 68:12 and the reference to the setting of the sun and exile in Jer. 15:9] which alludes to this lengthy exile." (*Sefer Bet Elohim, Sha'ar HaTefillah* [The Gate of Prayer], ch. 18. Warsaw, 1872, 25a.)

60   Reference is to verse 10. King David in his vow singles out "The Lord of Israel our Father." The author mistakenly refers to the *Rashi* commentary (R. Shlomo ben Isaac, 1040–1105, the leading medieval commentator of the Bible and Talmud), rather than Radak (R. David Kimchi, Bible commentator and grammarian 1160–1235) who actually cites the relevant Midrash (GenR. 70:1). For the text see above, n. 25.

61   See closing citation in previous note.

62   Corresponding to Tuesday, July 21, 1942. The verse in Ps. 132:10 and II Chron. 6:42 תשב פני משיחך, contains both the year תש״ב (702) as well as the redemptive theme. The term לפ״ק following the verse signifies לפרט קטן, namely, the Jewish year as cited in abbreviated form without the prefix ה the equivalent of 5000 years; thus התשי״ב—5702, which corresponds to 1942.

63   Homilies, homiletical interpretations.

Hatam Sofer[64] concerning the exposition of the verse: "Do it Israel, willingly and faithfully . . . a land flowing with milk and honey, as the Lord the God of your fathers spoke to you."[65] This text is difficult to grasp. [He proceeded to explain.] In all of these chastising [Biblical] themes, Eretz Yisrael is repeatedly cited. It is a marvellous remedy, since the very mention of the Holy Land generates sanctity in the heart of the listener. The same holds true for [the realm of] abomination which "should not be heard out of your mouth."[66] Thus, "he who exclaims Rahab!" (*Megillah* 15a)[67] or the contrary, in reference to holiness, [such as] the mention of the Holy Land and holy people[68] [indicating that verbal activity, whether negative or positive, influences corresponding action].

Hence, declared the Holy One, blessed be He: "To such a degree will everyone in Israel be sanctified that when the name 'Israel' will be heard, one will surely preserve and fulfill God's commandments." This is the intent of "Hear, O Israel."[69] If the name of Israel is heard, then you will respond to His voice, by the mere mention of the name of Israel.[70] As an example the verse then concludes in every instance with "as [the Lord, the God of your fathers] spoke to you, a land,"[71]

---

64 *Homilies of the Hatam Sofer* (Sarat, 1929). See also Rabbi Moshe Sofer, "The Legal Aspects Concerning One Who Makes a Vow in Distress," *Sefer Zicharon* (Memorial Volume). Jerusalem: 1957, 73–74.) Rabbi Moshe Sofer (1762–1839), known by the title of his responsa volumes, *Hatam Sofer*, was among the foremost scholars of his time and the indefatigable leader of the Orthodox communities in Europe in the struggle against the Reform movement and liberal tendencies.

65 Deut. 6:3. ושמעת (*Veshamata*) will be literally interpreted in relation to "hearing" vs. acting as suggested in the JPS Torah translation.

66 Ex. 23:13.

67 Reference to the passage Meg. 15 a: תנו רבנן: רחב בשמה . . . אמר ר׳ יצחק כל האומר רחב! רחב! מיד ניקרי "Our Rabbis taught: Rahab inspired lust by her name . . . R. Isaac said: Whoever but mentions 'Rahab! Rahab!' has a seminal emission at once."

68 Allusion to Ex. 22:30. ואנשי קודש תהיון לי "You shall be holy unto Me."

69 Deut. 6:3. See n. 65.

70 Additional support for verbal activity affecting action.

71 Deut. 6:3.

so that this avowal will reinforce the state of sanctity. Similarly, in our case. . . .[72] It [Eretz Yisrael] generates such power that it will surely multiply in force in order to rescue us whenever there is trouble. Whenever we will place its name upon our lips, and will long to return to her, to dwell in her as in former days, [we will be rescued]. Amen, so be it the word of God, speedily in our day, Amen.

---

72 The author concludes with a restatement of the Hatam Sofer selection. See n. 64.

SECOND PREFACE

Dejected, I perceive the ruin of my people [1] overwhelmed in these times in their exile. We are as captives in prison. *There* is the reality of all suffering. As it is written: "Those destined for death shall die; those by the sword, shall be put to the sword; those by famine, shall starve; and those meant for captivity shall be made captive." [2] Each is more extreme than the next (as elaborated in tractate Baba Batra 8). All forms of suffering are included [within the punishment of] captivity (see Rashi). [3] The glory of all Israel has been cut down. Never in all of Israel's history has there been such misfortune. True, there have been difficult periods in the past. But these were spaced during different periods and places which permitted our forefathers alternate sites for refuge. The massive and comprehensive form of the current destruction of this European continent, (which had heretofore been a center of Jewish life from which emerged many of the great personalities and sages during recent centuries) is now characterized by complete imprisonment with no opportunity for escape. Everything is being destroyed. Every nation has shut its gates before us.

"Strip her, strip her, to its very foundation!" [4] "And they were entirely

---

1 Cf. שבר בת עמי "Over the ruin of my poor people" Lam. 2:11, 3:48, 4:10.

2 Jer. 15:2.

3 ואמר ר׳ יוחנן: כל המאוחר בפסוק זה קשה מחברו . . . שבי קשה מכולם דכולהו איתנהו ביה שהוא ביד העכומ״ז לעשות בו כל חפצו אם למות אם לחרב אם לרעב (רש״י, ב״ב ח). "R. Yohanan said: Each punishment mentioned in this verse is more severe than the one before. . . . Captivity is harder than all, because it includes the sufferings of all." (BB 8b). "Since the worshippers of idols and the stars can determine his fate, whether to die by the sword or famine" (Rashi, BB 8b).

4 Interlacing of Ps. 137:7. האומרים ערו ערו עד היסוד בה "How they cried, 'Strip

17

enclosed. No one could leave or enter."[5] This has not occurred since the time of Haman the evil one. He too decreed the destruction of the entire Holy people. He also shut before them the gates of the nations, as the Midrash explains.[6] And now that so much daily life is without pleasure[7] and my mind is preoccupied with the suffering of this generation I am unable to concentrate on regular study as is my habit. The study of halakhah requires concentration.[8] To make matters worse, due to the storms of exile which have assaulted us, the yeshivot and houses of study have been eliminated. On that bitter day[9] when the pogroms of the people broke out in all their fury and trampled under them all that was holy, yeshivah students were evicted from their schools. I remained alone, absorbed in my thoughts of the destruction of the people and communities of Israel. . . . Why did the Lord do such a thing?[10] Why the extraordinary anger?[11]

---

her, strip her, to her very foundation.'"

5 Variant of Jos. 6:1. ויריחו סגרת ומסגרת מפני בני ישראל אין יוצא ואין בא. "Now Jericho was shut up tight because of the Israelites; no one could leave or enter."

6 Possible allusion to EstR. 7:23.

7 Cf. Eccl. 12:1. אין לי בהם חפץ. "I have no interest in them."

8 צלותא (zaluta) should read צילותא (ziluta) "clarity" as in Meg. 28b: משום דשמעתא בעא צילותא כיומא דאסתנא. "Because the discussion of a legal point requires clarity, like a clear day" and Rashi: צילותא: דעת צלולה ומיושבת שאינו טרוד בכלום מחשבה. "Clarity: A clear and settled mind which is not distracted with other concerns."

9 Since the author's second preface was dated in Budapest, January 7, 1943 ר"ח שבט תש"ג (The New Moon of Shevat, 5703) the event described could not refer to the subsequent reign of terror of October 1944 by the Arrow-Cross Fascist party. The reference may be to a number of anti-Jewish measures by the Hungarian regime, under strong pressure from Nazi Germany, beginning in October 1942 through early 1943. Forced conscription of male Jews aged 18–48 into labor brigades was operative in Hungary throughout the pre-occupation period of 1940–1944. This may have accounted for some of the depletion of the Yeshivah student population. When such periodic measures failed to move the relatively moderate regime of Miklos Kallay to enact more drastic anti-Jewish measures, including mass evacuation of the Jewish population (among numerous other German dissatisfactions with their half-hearted ally), the formal occupation of Hungary took place on March 19, 1944 (code name: Operation Margaret). It is also unlikely that the reference is to the atrocities of Autumn 1941 and January 1942 which did not affect Budapest Jewry. Livia Rotkirchen, "Korot Tekufat HaShoah: Toldot Yehudei Hungaria," in Pinkas HaKehilot (Jerusalem, 1976), 106–18.

10 Deut. 29:23; I Kings 9:8; Jer. 22:8.

Hence, I decided to examine the 2,000 year chronicles of our people during their exile and persecutions among the nations. True, I never before dealt with questions of this sort. After all I was always trained in the House of God and resided in the world of halakhah and responsa literature. I was privileged to learn and to teach. I published works in the field which were well received and praised by the scholars, thank the Almighty. (See the endorsements of the great masters in my *Mishneh Sakhir*, part one, published in the year 5684.[12] See also the letter to me from the holy person of Ostrowtza[13] published in my volume *Tov Yigael* in the year 5686).[14] I never took the time to be concerned with matters affecting the welfare of our holy nation, since this mitzvah[15] could be left to others with the claim that "all of your goods cannot equal her."[16] I did not believe that the study of Torah should be neglected on its account (as elaborated in Moed Katan[17] and the legal ruling in *Yoreh Deah*).[18]

During the present upheaval, however, it is impossible to limit oneself to the teachings of Abaye and Raba[19] and other complex legal matters. My students have been forcibly removed from me. No one remains with whom I can engage in halakhic study. Thus I have been stimulated to question as in the Book of Daniel: "How long until the end of these awful things?"[20] Are we not as yet close to the eve of the

---

11   Deut. 29:3.

12   1923–24.

13   Rabbi Meir Yehiel HaLevi Halstuk (1851–1928) was among the great hasidic masters of pre-Holocaust Poland.

14   1925–26.

15   Religious obligation, commandment of biblical origin or rabbinic derivation.

16   Prov. 3:15. Wisdom, more specifically Torah, was to take precedence over all other pursuits.

17   MK 9b. במצוה שאפשר לעשותה ע״י אחרים, וגו׳ "Where the obligation can be discharged through another person."

18   *Shulhan Arukh, Yoreh De'ah, Hilkhot Talmud Torah*, 246:18.

19   3rd–4th century CE, 4th generation Amoraim, leading talmudic masters in Babylonia. The "teachings of Abaye and Raba," became the standard expression for talmudic-rabbinic study.

20   Dan. 12:6. עד מתי קץ הפלאות! "How long until the end of these awful things?"

Sixth Day? As it is written "at evening time there shall be light."[21] Note Rashi's commentary: "Prior to the completion of the millenium the shining light shall appear."[22]

See the *piyyut* for the second day of Rosh HaShanah, which gives a similar time, "when the sun tends to the west, two-thirds of an hour from darkness. Light for the upright will shine before evening." It would seem that we have already reached this time. (I also found this in the commentary on [*Midrash*] *Tanna d'Bei Eliyahu, Tosafot Ben Yehiel,* at the beginning of Chapter 2.)

Nevertheless the son of Yishai[23] has not come. There must surely be some restraint upon us which delays our redemption. We are, therefore, compelled to identify and understand this obstacle so that it is removed from our midst. Clear "the highway"[24] for our Righteous Messiah, who will surely and speedily rescue us from distress in our own day and raise the Shekhinah from this dust. With the help of He Who favors man with knowledge,[25] I decided to investigate this area as much as my limited abilities would allow me. Further, I recalled the statement of our sages of blessed memory cited in "The Chapter on Judges," *Reshit Hokhmah,*[26] as follows: "One who is decent and fears sin should be involved in the needs, burdens and sufferings of Israel." Indeed such a person sustains the entire world, as it is written: "By justice a king sustains the land, etc."[27] But one who refrains from sharing their burden, from mending their broken fences and acts as if

---

21   Zech. 14:7. והיה לעת ערב יהיה אור. Allusion to the light on the eve of redemption. See *Yalkut Shimoni* II, 585. See below, 105.

22   Rashi, Zech. 14:7 probably based on Sanh. 97a. See also GenR. 2:2. Additional support for the redemption at hand is offered from the High Holyday and *Midrash* literature.

23   The Messiah, descended from David the son of Yishai.

24   Cf. Isa. 62:10.

25   Cf. the fourth of the Eighteen Benedictions in the daily liturgy אתה חונן לאדם דעת.

26   Reference to R. Elijah ben Moses de Vidas' major work on morals first published in Venice in 1579. R. Elijah, a 16th century mystic in Safed, was a pupil of R. Moses Cordovero, the great kabbalist of the Safed school. The citation (based on *Tanh. Mishpatim* 2) appears on p. 391 of the first edition.

27   Prov. 29:4. מלך במשפט יעמיד ארץ.

he were a priestly offering set aside from the dough,[28] it is as if he tramples upon the world and destroys it, as it is written: "But a fraudulent man tears it down. . . ."[29]

This is the extent to which our sages insisted that we be concerned with the plight of the Jew even during times of normalcy and tranquility in the world. Certainly this is incumbent on every Jew when the Jewish people is disgraced,[30] when they writhe in their own blood and are utterly abandoned as fish in the sea. Then he must, to the best of his God-given knowledge . . . seek a way in which they may be extricated from their distress. Our master Rabbi Moses Cordovero in his work *Tomer Devorah*[31] (seventh chapter), observes that one must entertain positive thoughts on behalf of all of Israel, for their benefit. Note the comment of *Ya'arot Devash*[32] (part two) discussing the blessing, "O Lord return our judges."[33] There, as well, the responsibility for directing constructive thoughts towards Israel is placed upon the leadership.

According to the author, the suffering which befalls Israel is due to bad leaders. . . . I dared to survey and research [the literature] devoted to the continued persistence of the exile. I proceeded to compose this work, with the help of God, in which I publicly express my views in

---

28 A "privileged" individual who believes himself exempt from communal responsibilities. Reference to the ritual gift offering in Num. 15:18–21.

29 Prov. 29:4. Homiletic on the term איש תרומות, which is made to refer to a selfish, ambitious leader who prefers gifts without assuming reciprocal responsibilities for his people's plight.

30 *Lit.* "to cut down the horns of Israel." Cf. Lam. 2:3.

31 The chapter in this volume by the great master and innovator of Kabbalah of Safed (1522–1570), is devoted to the responsibilities of the scholar who is cautioned against assuming a stance of arrogance towards others. אלא יתנהג עמהם בנחת על פי דרכם "Rather let him behave towards them with gentle ways in accordance to their needs." *Tomer Devorah* (Koenigsberg, 1858), 18a.

32 Volume of moral homiletics by the 18th century controversial scholar of Talmud and Kabbalah, Jonathan Eybeschutz. *Sefer Ya'arot Dvash*, 1926, 7a. Likely reference to the first homily, part I (p. 17), though there are numerous references which highlight the laudable aspects and traits of the people of Israel. See ibid., part 2, 32b, 52b, 54b, 58a, 66b.

33 From the daily liturgy of the Eighteen Benedictions השיבה שפטינו.

order to advise my people as to what should be done to advance
redemption speedily in our day. . . . After some respite following my
arrival here in the capital,[34] fulfilling my vow, I began work on the
volume devoted to the rebuilding of our Holy Land; to raise it from
the mounds of dust;[35] to stimulate love and affection in the hearts of
our Jewish brethren, old and young, so that they would endeavor to
return to our Land, the Land of our forefathers and not remain here
in the lands of exile. As expounded in the *Midrash Rabba*:[36] "It is
preferred that one lives in the deserts of Eretz Yisrael and not live in
palaces outside the Land."

Furthermore, the purpose of all of the plagues with which we were
assailed during our periods of exile were mainly intended to stimulate
us to return to our Holy Land. As it is explained in *Midrash Shoher
Tov* (section 17)[37] concerning King David during the time of the
pestilence, the Holy One, blessed be He, sent to him Gad the prophet,
as it is written: "Gad came to David and said to him 'Go and set up
an altar to the Lord.'"[38] This may be compared to one who strikes his
son and the son doesn't know why he is being struck. After the
beating he [the father] addresses him as follows: Go and discharge
that which I have ordered you to do today, and in days past, but
which you have neglected to act upon. Thus was it with the thousands
who were slain in David's day[39] merely because they did not demand
the building of the Temple. From this we can argue the following: If
these,[40] who neither witnessed the building of the Temple nor its
destruction were destined to be punished in this fashion because they

---

34   The author arrived in Budapest from Nitra, following the High Holy Days
5703, likely between 25–28 October, 1942. See "Preface" to Jerusalem 1974 edition,
p. 8 of nonpaginated biography of the author by his son R. Hayyim Teichthal. See
below, 288, n. 1059.

35   Cf. Neh. 3:34.

36   GenR. 39:10.

37   MPs. 17:4. See below, 204.

38   II Sam. 24:18.

39   Specific reference to the seventy thousand victims of the pestilence. Ibid.
24:1–15.

40   The Jews in the era of King David, who lived before the Temple was constructed.

did not insist on building the Temple, we who witnessed its destruction and nevertheless do not mourn, nor receive compassion,[41] how much more so [are we deserving of punishment]. Rashi in Hosea 3[42] quotes the following: "Rabbi Shimon b. Menassiah said: 'The Jewish people will not be shown a good omen until they repent and seek the Kingdom of Heaven, the Kingdom of the House of David and the building of the Temple as it is written: "Afterwards the children of Israel shall return and seek the Lord their God and David their King, etc. . . ."[43]

Now included in our plea to return to Eretz Yisrael are these very three conditions. "Whoever resides in Eretz Yisrael may be considered to have a God."[44] The building of the Temple will also be realized with our return, and with the help of God, as explained in Talmud *Megillah* [19].[45] Thereafter the Messiah will come. This is the [fulfillment] of the House of David. . . First and foremost, however, we must endeavor to return to Eretz Yisrael and then with the help of God all three conditions will be fulfilled.

The *Tosefta* in *Avodah Zarah* (chapter 5) remarks upon the verse: "And I will faithfully plant them in this Land,"[46] "[Whenever] they shall be on the Land they will be as if I had planted them before me, faithfully, with all my heart and soul,[47] [but if they] not be settled upon her, they will not be planted before me faithfully, neither with my whole heart nor soul."[48] It is indeed startling for the Holy One, blessed be He, to declare that when Israel is not in its Land they are

---

41 Following the *Midrash* text: ולא מקבלים רחמים.

42 Hos. 3:5. See below, 102.

43 Ibid. See below, 102, n. 85.

44 Ket. 110b. הדר בארץ ישראל כאלו יש לו אלוה. The condition for the Kingdom of Heaven is thereby fulfilled.

45 More likely Meg. 17b–18, describing the various stages of redemption. The Meg. 19a reference is to the erroneous calculations of Ahasuerus which prompted him to use the vessels of the Temple. By his account the seventy years referred to in Dan. 9:2 had lapsed. See also Meg. 11b. These passages thus allude to the simultaneous return of the people to their Land and the use of the Temple facilities.

46 Jer. 32:41 "I will rejoice in treating them graciously and I will faithfully plant them in this Land, with my whole heart and soul."

47 This section of the *Tosefta* text is omitted.

48 *Tosefta* (Zuckermandel ed., Jerusalem, 1937), 466.

not at one with Him in heart or soul. What has befallen us in our time and the limited degree of evident [divine] providence should not astonish us, since He is not faithfully linked to us with His entire heart and soul. We are after all in the land of other nations. When we shall attempt to return to her, then we will immediately cleave to Him with all our heart and soul. As it is explained in the *Kuzari* (2:14)[49] . . . the Shekhinah descended upon Ezekiel despite the qualification of our sages of blessed memory that the Shekhinah does not rest outside the Land of Israel.[50] Since, however, he prophesised in in regard to Eretz Yisrael the Shekhinah rested [upon him] outside the Land of Israel. . . .

Primarily, God expects us to assume the initiative and yearn to return to our Land. We should not wait until He Himself brings us there. Therefore, we are told "I will faithfully plant them in this Land."[51] That is to say, we are consciously to strive and yearn for this purpose, faithfully, and with all our abilities. Then He will successfully complete the task for us.

In this spirit, the Zohar (*Noah*) writes concerning Solomon's Temple. Although it was prefabricated,[52] nevertheless the Holy One, blessed be He, waited in expectation for our handiwork.[53] Then did God complete the building. So must it be with us in the settling of Eretz Yisrael . . . I came upon a similar lesson with regard to David in I Chronicles 13:2, where he first consulted with [the people of] Israel.[54]

---

49   The *Kuzari* (Jerusalem, Schocken 1968), 75–76. Brought to the author's attention via the gloss of R. Zvi Hirsh Hayot (1805–1855) on MK 25a (Vilna ed.). כיון שנתנבא בשביל ארץ ישראל שורה השכינה אף בחוץ לארץ. See the discussion on MK 25a and Rashi there. Also LamR, *Petihta*, 24.

50   The text in the *Mekhilta, Bo*, 2: תדע שאין השכינה נגלית בחוצה לארץ, therefore, should read: "The Shekhinah is not revealed outside of Israel." Cf. Rashi on Deut. 2:17.

51   Jer. 32:41.

52   The Zohar reading of והבית בהבנתו "When the House was built" (I Kings 6:7) suggests that the artisans merely had to initiate the building process which was preconceived completely by the Almighty. Zohar (*Noah*), Sperling-Simon transl. (London, 1931), 251.

53   Solomon's artisans.

54   In anticipation of returning the Holy Ark to Jerusalem.

It is stated: "If you approve, and if the Lord our God agrees, let us send far and wide to our remaining kinsmen throughout the territories of Israel. . . ." One should take note of David's partiality towards Israel, prefacing "If you approve and if the Lord our God agrees."

This [reversal of order] is prohibited as noted towards the close of *Yadayim.*[55] Rashi's commentary,[56] is revealing: "David said to them: You have now achieved [placing a king at your helm[57]] for your benefit [so that he may help you]. Now you should devote yourself to paying homage to God." David's plan to return the Ark to Jerusalem involved some act in honor of God. This is why he did not refer to God first, but to Israel, so that he would motivate them.

That which related to the reverence for Heaven, should rightfully emanate first from them and not from above . . . We learn from this that all which is of divine concern requires first the human act. Thereafter, the individual is assisted by Heaven. . . .[58]

I emphasize that my writings are intended for the Jew who is interested in learning the sober truth emanating from the discussions of halakhah. Redemption[59] is also a subject for halakhah as taught by our sages in *Shabbat* 138[60] and *Tanna DeBei Eliyahu.*[61] "The word of the Lord this is halakhah. The word of the Lord, this is *haketz.*"[62]

---

55   Mishnah Yadayim 4:8. The Sadducees are reprimanded for placing the name of the ruler above the Name of God upon divine documents.

56   On I Chron. 13:1.

57   Deleted in the author's text.

58   Human initiative as the precondition to redemption is central to our author, and is amply documented in this work. See variation of this theme in R. Kalonymos Kalmish Shapira *Sefer Esh Kodesh*, a major source of the religious literature of the Holocaust, written in the Warsaw Ghetto (Tel Aviv, 1966, p. 9). See also Pesach Schindler, "*Zidduk HaDin Mitokh HaShoa*," *Petahim* 55–56 (Sept. 1981), p. 44 and n. 13 for supporting evidence from the Zohar, R. Levi Yitzhak of Berdichev and R. Aaron of Karlin.

59   *Haketz, lit.* "the end."

60   Shab. 138b.

61   *Pirke Derekh Eretz* (l). *Eliyahu Zutra* 16. See also *Tosefta, Eduyot* 1:1.

62   The exegesis in Shab. 138b of the terms דברי ד׳ "the words of the Lord" and דבר ד׳ "the word of the Lord" in Amos 8:11–12 leads to an exposition of the interrelationship between halakhah and the process by which redemption is to be realized. The author documents the legal significance of all aspects related to rebuilding

Thus they taught that all which concerns redemption lies within the realm of halakhah and requires legal discussion of scholars. . . .

However, one who is thoroughly predisposed to a particular view will never be objective and admit to our viewpoint. No amount of evidence will suffice. They are blinded by their partiality. They go as far as denying the obvious. Was there anyone more fit for a mission than the spies [sent by Moses]?[63] But since their ambition for authority was firmly rooted within them, as elaborated in the Zohar,[64] and the *Shelah*,[65] they were afraid that should they come to Eretz Yisrael they will lose their positions of authority. They turned against this lovely land and deceived others as well, thereby causing this exile, as elaborated by our sages.[66] Joshua and Caleb challenged [their fellow leaders] in order to demonstrate the trustworthiness of Moses and his Torah, saying "Let us go up at once and occupy it! . . ."[67]

They elaborated upon their arguments [in defense of Moses and the Land] insisting that they could succeed [despite the threatening inhabitants] as Rashi indicates.[68] Nevertheless, their efforts at persuasion did not succeed since the spies suffered from a deeply rooted bias because of selfish motives. The current situation is similar even among rabbis, *rebbes* and their *hasidim*. This one has a good

---

Eretz Yisrael as imperatives of halakhah (ובנין ארץ ישראל). *EHS*, 30–31.

63   Num. 13: 1–16. Rashi on the term (כלם אנשים) "All of them were men" (13:3) notes: כל "אנשים" שבמקרא לשון חשיבות ואותה שעה כשרים היו. "All references to 'men' in Scripture imply importance. At the time [of their selection as scouts] they were fit [to assume their trustworthy roles.]"

64   Zohar III, 158b. "Everyone a leader" (כלם אנשים). They were all virtuous, but they were misled by false reasoning. They said: If Israel enter the Land we will be replaced, since it is only in the wilderness that we were considered worthy to be leaders. This was the cause of their death and the death of all who followed them." See below, 287, n. 1056.

65   *Shenei Luhot HaBrit* of R. Isaiah b. Abraham HaLevi Horowitz (1565–1630) (the *Shelah HaKadosh*), *Parshat Shelah* part II, 68a. *Shelah* is the acronym of this major work on ethics, philosophy and law by this distinguished scholar, kabbalist and communal leader in Poland, Frankfurt, Prague, Jerusalem and Safed/Tiberias.

66   NumR. 16:20; Ta'an. 29a; Sot. 35a; Zohar II, 161a.

67   Num. 13:30.

68   Rashi, Num. 13:30.

rabbinic post; another is endowed with a lucrative *Rebistve*.[69] This one owns a profitable business or factory, or is appointed to a good and prestigious position offering great satisfaction. They are frightened that should they move to Eretz Yisrael their status will be shaken. . . . Note the comments of the *Divrei Hayyim* on Hanukkah.[70] A person perceives what he wishes to perceive. . . .[71]

Also, that man of God, the *Hatam Sofer,* in the sixth volume of his Responsa (responsum 59)[72] writes in a similar vein.

> . . . but not merely the ignorant and the multitude. The learned as well, even rabbis who do not utter the truth that is in their heart or embody decency and righteousness, or keep a distance from them and do not walk in their paths.[73]

If they wrote thus in their generation which was yet, truly, a learned generation, what shall we say in our generation? . . . Truly, the movement of *aliyah* [settlement in the Land of Israel], to ascend and return to Eretz Yisrael, is not new. Great and saintly sages responded in the past as I indicated above. Since, however, that period was one of emancipation for Jews and they resided in the lands of exile in peace and tranquility, no one paid attention to what was said with divine inspiration.

Note Rashi's observation (Kiddushin 69b) concerning the return of Ezra [to Eretz Yisrael] with only the poor and the hardpressed, while

---

69 Leadership and control of a particular hasidic community and/or dynasty.

70 R. Hayyim Halberstam of Zans (Nowy Sacz) (1793–1876), founder of the Zans hasidic dynasty in western Galicia in the mid-19th century. Reference to the second of three volumes titled *Divrei Hayyim* devoted to the weekly portion and the festivals.

71 The likely excerpt: כי נפשם מזוהמים מתאוות והגאות והבלי עולם הזה ולכן אין דבר שבקדושה נרשם בשכלם כי המה מדמים בשקר. . . כי ידוע אשר מי שנוטה נגד צד אחד אינו יכול להכריע ולבא בעיונו על האמת כי שכלו מכריעו לצד נטיה שלו. "Their souls were polluted with appetites, pride and vanities of this world. Therefore, sacred matters do not register in their minds because of the false imaginings. . . . As is well-known when someone is biased he cannot freely confront the truth since his mind is inclined towards his bias." Krakau [Cracow] 1892, Hanukkah, [Hebrew pagination] 13.

72 *Sefer Hatam Sofer*, vol. 6 (Bratislava, 1864).

73 Ibid. 20a.

those who had lived in comfort in exile did not join him.[74] See *Seder HaDorot*,[75] which cites our master the *S'M'A'*,[76] who in turn makes reference to the following which he read in the *Sefer Ma'aseh Nissim*, of our Rabbi Eleazer of Worms, the author of the *Rokeah*.[77] Ezra sent letters to all the communities of the exile requesting them to ascend with him to Eretz Yisrael. One such communication was received in the city of Worms in Germany where Jews resided at the time.[78]

They replied: "You may live in Great Jerusalem. We shall dwell here in Little Jerusalem. (Since at that time they were considered to be distinguished among the lords and gentiles.) [Besides] they were very wealthy. They dwelt there at ease and in peace . . . Because of this, major and difficult decrees befell the Jews of Germany, and Worms particularly. During the destruction of the first Temple they had settled there. After the completion of the seventy years [of exile] Ezra wrote and beseeched them to join him. They did not ascend.

Indeed, as we know from our people's history, all the suffering and punitive decrees emanated from the Germanic countries, as presently

---

74   Rashi explains "I reviewed the people" ואבינה בעם (Ezra 8:15). Ezra was compelled to scrutinize the returnees. Those who returned of their own accord were not only of low descent genealogically, but socio-economically depressed as well. הכשרים לא מצא לפני שהיו יושבים בבבל בשלוה והעולים בירושלים היו בעוני ובטורח המלאכה ובאימת כל סביבותיה. "He [Ezra] did not encounter any who were fit since these were peacefully ensconced in Babylonia. Those who ascended to Jerusalem were poor, harrassed with work and frightened by their [hostile] surroundings."

75   The classic chronology-history by R. Yehiel Heilpern (1660–1746), (Warsaw, 1897), 251. The year under scrutiny is 1620.

76   Acronym for *Sefer Me'irat Einayim*, a commentary on the *Hoshen Mishpat* by R. Joshua Falk (1555–1614), who is referred to by the name of his famous work.

77   Reference to R. Eleazar of Worms (c. 1165–c. 1230) among the last masters of Hasidei Ashkenaz in medieval Germany and noted for his halakhic work *Sefer HaRokeah* (hence his title) and his volume on theology *Sodei Razaya*. The legend appears in the 1696 edition of *Sefer Ma'aseh Nissim* (Amsterdam) describing events in Worms during their tragic periods. There is no evidence that the *Baal HaRokeah* edited and authored the volume. The introduction is written by Eliezer Lieberman, the son of R. Yiftach Yosef Shamash who narrates the stories.

78   The first documented evidence of Jews in Worms approximates the year 1000 C.E. though a legend related them to the descendants of the tribe of Benjamin and refers to the existence of a congregation during the Roman period. (*Jewish Encyclopedia*, vol. 12, 560.)

in our day. . . . So it has always been throughout Israel's tranquil periods in exile. They refused to respond to *aliyah*. . . .

Now, however, the prime Advisor, Planner and Mover of all that is formidable and awe-inspiring, has seen fit to cause all of our gentile neighbors to persecute us with oppressive decrees.[79] It is no longer possible to remain here among them. Every Jew would now consider himself fortunate if he could return to our Holy Land. He would surely respond to the summons for *aliyah* with love and affection.

This may have been the sense of the interpretation of the Midrash of the Song of Songs verse "Draw me to you, we will run after you. . . ."[80] "Because you have incited my evil neighbors against me."[81] That is to say, for some time now we have lived with our gentile neighbors on good and amicable terms. Suddenly, they have been transformed into enemies and evil neighbors who hound us. But this is only because they have been incited against us by a particular Source. This impulse emanates from the profound purpose of God, in order that "we will run," to ascend to Eretz Yisrael, since Eretz Yisrael instantaneously follows God [in rank][82] (as explained in the holy book *Tzeror HaMor*[83] in the reading of *Mas'ei*)[84] . . . .

The *Midrash Tanhuma, Tetzaveh* writes as follows:[85]

---

79 Invoking the classic theological principle that God is the First Cause [*The Cause*]. This implies that freedom of action (or its limits) for either the perpetrator or victim in the Holocaust context lies with Him. This theme is subsequently developed by the author, especially in his treatment of the redemption themes.

80 Song 1:4 משכני אחריך נרוצה.

81 CantR. 1:4 דבר אחר ימשכני אחריך נרוצה׳ ממה שגרית בי שכני הרעים. The root to draw משך (draw, pull) is transposed to שכן (neighbor) in משכני "Draw me."

82 Thus completing the interpretation of אחריך נרוצה "We will run after you."

83 A commentary on the Pentateuch (Venice, 1522, Constantinople, 1514; Cracow, 1595) by the Spanish scholar and mystic R. Abraham ben Jacob Saba (c. 1508).

84 The commentary on Num. 33–37, pp. 126b–128a in the Cracow 1595 edition. R. Abraham Saba describes the difficult journeys of the people of Israel in the wilderness as a prelude to the redemptive entry into the Land. A similar pattern will characterize the Jewish people's final exile and their eventual "fourth redemption." In his text, R. Teichthal confuses R. Abraham Saba (סבע) with R. Joseph Karo's father-in-law, R. Isaac Saba (סבא).

85 *Tetzaveh*, 13.

When [the people of Israel] were exiled to Babylon what did Ezra say
to them? "Ascend to Eretz Yisrael." They did not respond. So it was
Ezra who replied:[86] "You have sowed much and brought in little, you
eat without being satisfied;[87] you clothe yourselves but no one gets
warm[88] and he who earns anything earns it for a 'leaky purse. . . . '"[89]
Similarly it is written in Zephania: "And I will punish the men who rest
untroubled as would wine on its sediment, who say to themselves 'The
Lord will do nothing, good or bad'. Their wealth shall be plundered
and their homes laid waste. They shall build houses, but will not dwell
in them. They shall plant vineyards, but not drink their wine. . . ."[90]

This is precisely what has occurred in our time in nearly all of the
European nations. This has come about due to their being remiss and
not ascending to Eretz Yisrael (as explained previously in the *Midrash
Tanhuma*).

Indeed the great *Yavetz*[91] in the preface to the *Siddur Sulam Bet
El*[92] grieves over our neglect to return to and dwell in Eretz Yisrael.
We continue to live calmly outside the Land as if we have discovered
another Eretz Yisrael and Jerusalem. That is the reason for the tragedies
which have befallen the Jews when they dwelled in comfort in Spain
and other countries. Once again they were expelled.

Not a Jew remains in that country. Righteous indeed is God,[93]
since their exile has made them lose their mind entirely as they

---

86   The *Tanhuma* text interpolates the Haggai text with the Ezra statement.

87   אוכל ולא לשבעה in our text vs. אוכל ואין לשבעה in Haggai. שתו ואין לשכרה "You
drink without being intoxicated" of the original text is deleted.

88   לבוש ואין לחום vs. לבוש ואין לחום לו of the original.

89   Hag. 1:6. צרור נקוב vs. צרור הנקוב. The interpretation of Haggai suggests that
Israel's toil in exile will be frustrated and not bear fruit.

90   Zeph. 1:2–13.

91   R. Yaakov ben Zvi Emden (1697–1776) rabbinic scholar in Germany, leading
opponent of the adherents of Shabbetai Zvi and critic or R. Jonathan Eybeschutz.
See below, 287, 302.

92   The first of three parts of his commentary, grammatical and ritual annotations
to the *Siddur Tefillah* published in Altona 1745–48. The relevant passage in the
original follows, n. 95 below.

93   To have caused their expulsion. Cf. Lam. 1:18.

assimilated among the nations. All this has befallen us because "we abandoned the glorious Land. . . ."[94,95]

This explains what is happening to our people in these countries. "My Beloved is calling"[96] in order to awaken in us the desire to return to our Land. Surely, after all that is occurring to us during these difficult days there is no doubt that our words will fall upon fertile ground. . . . They will surely ponder on the [merit of their] conduct here in exile. All their pursuits are in vain. The fruits of their toil benefit Esau. Not alone does he plunder their assets and property, but, as is evident in Europe presently, he robs their bodies, their very life. During such times they will surely listen to me.

I further discovered in the volume *Hon Ashir* (by the author of *Mishnat Hasidim*[97]) expounding upon the *Mishnah* at the close of the

---

94 ארץ צבי שכחנו Cf. Dan. 11:16; 11:41; Jer. 3:19. Also see Ket. 112 a for a homiletical exposition of the term.

95 The full text of R. Emden reads: ולא תועיל הכוונה במקום שאין טענת אונס גמור ובשעת רווח. ולזה צריך כל אדם מישראל לעשות בלבו הסכמה קבועה ותקועה לעלות בא"י . . . אין איש שם על לב מבקש אהבתה, דורש שלומה וטובתה, ולא מצפה לראותה, כמדומה לנו בהיותנו בשלוה בחו"ל שכבר מצאנו א"י וירושלים אחרת דוגמתה, ע"כ באו עלינו כל הרעות בשבת ישראל בארץ שפניא וארצות אחרות בשלוה בכבוד גדול מימי החורבן זמן רב קרוב לאלפים שנה. ושוב נתגרשו ממנה עד שלא נשאר שם שארית לישראל בארץ ההיא. צדיק הוא ד' כי יצא מדעתם לגמרי ענין גלותם והתערבו בגוים וילמדו מעשיהם ויעשו נאצות . . . כל זאת באתנו. כי כארז נמשלנו ארץ צבי שכחנו, לשוב אל ארץ מולדתנו לא זכרנו. (ר' יעקב עמדן, סידור תפילה בית אל, הקדמה, ל: סימן ו See below, 316).

"Intent is of little value when we cannot claim that [we are] forced [to remain in exile] by compulsion, at a time of calm. That is precisely when every Jew ought to firmly resolve to ascend to Eretz Yisrael . . . [yet] no one seeks its love, and is concerned for its welfare. No one wishes to see her. It seems that when we live in tranquility outside the Land, we have already discovered the like of Eretz Yisrael and Jerusalem. Therefore, has all this evil befallen us in the land of Spain and other countries where we lived peacefully for so long, almost two thousand years after the destruction [of the Temple]. Once again we were expelled [from exile] until hardly a Jew remains in that land. The Lord is righteous (Ps. 145:17). They have completely lost the sense of their exile. They have become assimilated among the nations, acquired their ways and committed impieties (Neh. 9:18) . . . All this has befallen us although we have been compared to [the strength of] a cedar (Num. 24:6) we have abandoned the glorious Land. We have forgotten to return to the Land of our birth."

96 Song 5:2 קול דודי דופק.

97 R. Immanuel Hai ben Abraham Ricchi (1688–1743) rabbinic scholar and kabbalist in Italy. *Hon Ashir* (Amsterdam, 1731) is his commentary on the Mishnah; *Mishnat Hasidim* (Amsterdam, 1727), his principal work, a treatise on Lurianic Kabbalah.

tractate *Sota*, "The Galilee will be destroyed,"[98] in which he writes as
follows: "The homes shall be laid waste as it is written 'And your
cities shall be made waste.'[99] When I was privileged by the Almighty
to ascend to Eretz Yisrael, here in Safed, (may it be speedily rebuilt
and established in our days, Amen[100]), in the year 5478,[101] this being
Galilee. [The city was] filled with homes in ruins, the result of our
many sins. 'My eyes beheld this, and no one else.'[102] Thank Heaven, I
was happy to be present during these past two years and witness their
daily rebuilding. I claim this to be an indication of the coming of the
redeemer (speedily in our day), since should he come while all is in a
state of desolation, there would be no space to accommodate the
ingathering of the exiles. So it was with the 'First Coming'"[103] Our
rabbis commented:

> The Holy One, blessed be He, purposefully delayed Israel in the
> wilderness for forty years in order to allow the Land to be restored
> following the destruction of its trees and houses which were uprooted
> by the Amorites[104] during the exodus from Egypt. They had thought
> that Israel would enter the Land immediately and find it in a state of
> destruction. It was only when the Land was eventually restored that He
> brought them in. So it will be with God's help with the coming of our
> Messiah, speedily in our day, and be revealed first in this land, as is
> mentioned in the Zohar.

---

98   Sot. 9:15.

99   Lev. 26:33.

100   ותבנה ותכונן במהרה בימינו אמן] תובב״א. The traditional petition following the
mention of any of the four holy cities in Eretz Yisrael: Jerusalem, Hebron, Safed,
Tiberias.

101   1718. During two years in Safed, R. Immanuel devoted his studies to the
teachings of R. Isaac Luria and R. Hayyim Vital. The 1720 epidemic compelled him
to return to Europe in preparation for entry into the Holy Land.

102   Job 19:27.

103   The forty years in the wilderness in preparation for entry into the Holy Land.

104   The *Mekhilta* (*Beshalah*) reads "Canaanites." The midrashic text indicating
that it was the Canaanites themselves who were compelled to restore the Land to its
original state, is not reflected in the *Hon Ashir* summary. See also ExR. 20:15.

I was astounded with this discovery. I interpreted this to be a response from Heaven to the question which I posed earlier—how much longer [must we wait] for the wonderous end of days? It is God, blessed be He, who sustains the exiles until the time when Eretz Yisrael is rebuilt, as indicated by these holy words written by one imbued with the Holy Spirit and who received the revelation of the prophet Elijah, as is known. . . . Who, after all, are we in this day and age to dispute his views? Presently, and especially in recent years, when a significant portion of the Land is being rebuilt and transformed into a productive land, the words of the holy kabbalist[105] should indeed direct us to recognize [this process] as an indication of redemption....

One is astonished, therefore, as to why some of these who fear God's word should oppose this. The subject [of returning to Eretz Yisrael] is practically one of abhorrence and loathing for them. This can only be explained by what we quoted previously from the holy teachings of R. Elijah of Greiditz.[106] It is the force of the *kelipah* which compels them to delay [redemption]. It [the *kelipah*] knows that with the building of the Land her existence comes to an end. It may also be their own self-interest which accounts for their remaining here as it was with the spies. . .[107]

I have consequently proven to all my Jewish brethren in exile that the present time is the most opportune moment to do all within our means to leave the *Eretz Ha'amim*,[108] to return to our Holy Land and to attend to its restoration. By means we shall bring closer the coming of the Messiah, speedily in our own day.

I entitled this volume *Em HaBanim Semeha*,[109] based on the Jerusalem tractate of Berakhot, (towards the close of the second chapter) which portrays Eretz Yisrael as the mother of Israel and the lands of

---

105 R. Immanuel Hai Ricchi.

106 Outstanding 19th century scholar and kabbalist, a student of R. Akiva Eiger.

107 The impure corrupting forces of the *kelipah* are sustained by *Galut*. It is therefore in the interest of the *kelipah* to resist the redemptive process. See below, 205, 229.

108 *Lit.* "Land of Nations," but cf. Mishnah Oholot 2:3; Shab. 15a; Nazir 54b–55a.

109 Ps. 113:9. "To be a joyful mother of children."

exile as the stepmother.[110] Our sages describe our mother of Zion who weeps and laments when we are in exile.[111] She awaits our return to her bosom. "In my own flesh I behold God,"[112] when in the year 5702 before Passover[113] a terrible decree was issued in Slovakia by the cursed villains. Young Jewish women from the age of sixteen were forcibly transported to a distant place and to an unknown destination.[114] To this very day we do not know what occurred to the thousands of innocent Jewish souls who were deported. May God avenge them on our behalf.

The Jewish community was in a state of great panic. I knew a person who sought to rescue his young daughters from this evil trap. He tried to cross the border[115] with them. This happened during the intermediate days of Passover.[116] He promised to send his wife a telegraphed confirmation that he had arrived safely together with his daughters at the predesignated point. The mother waited at home with great anticipation for the good news. As it happened they seized the father together with his daughters before they crossed the border. They were arrested and interned in a prison near the border. The

---

110 JT Ber. 2:8. See above, 9 and below, 199-203, 195, 229.

111 Likely reference to the Midrashim and Zohar related to Jer. 31:15. קול ברמה נשמע נהי בכי תמרורים רחל מבכה על בניה מאנה להנחם על בניה כי איננו. LamR., *Petihta* 24 (Zion identified with Rachel); LamR. 1:27 (Zion identified with Sarah and Hannah). Zohar III, 20.

112 Job 19:26. The author utilizes the verse in accordance with Rashi who accepts אלוה in the sense of infliction and suffering, i.e. I have personally experienced suffering.

113 Passover in 1942 began on the eve of April 14.

114 Clear reference to the first mass deportation of unmarried Jews aged 16–35 in March and April, 1942. They were sent under the guise of forced labor for the German war effort but were actually dispatched to the Auschwitz and Lublin (Maidanek) concentration camps. The first transport, consisting of 999 young women left Poprad, Slovakia, on March 26 for Auschwitz, 19 days prior to Passover. For documentary evidence including railroad timetables and related correspondence of the Ministry of the Interior and railroad officials, see, Livia Rotkirchen, *The Destruction of Slovak Jewry* (Jerusalem, Yad Vashem, 1961), 21–24; 57–77; 96–129.

115 Hungary to the south was the most frequently sought border at the time since it was not as yet directly involved in the war, nor occupied by Nazi German forces. This episode is partly autobiographical. See *Mishneh Sakhir* (Jerusalem, 1974 edition), p. 8 of nonpaginated biography of our author by his son R. Hayyim Teichthal.

116 Corresponding to April 17–20, 1942.

rest of the Passover festival was spent in jail. They were now in great danger of being immediately deported to an unknown destination of doom. This was the anticipated penalty for violating the laws of illegal departure. Those caught for this offence were given a harsher sentence than the other prisoners.

We can imagine the bitter disappointment of the mother when she realized what had actually transpired. The initial joy turned into grief. The holiday [of Passover] was transformed into an occasion of mourning[117] for her husband and daughters. . . . She understood the fate which awaited them. We must now recall with praise the dedicated and valiant efforts. . . . of the *gaon*, *tzadik* and hasid our master R. Shmuel David Ungar, may he be blessed with a long and good life, the senior *dayan* of the holy community of Nitra.[118] He did not rest or relent until he had ransomed the three captives with a considerable sum. They were set free and returned safely to their home. One can well imagine the reaction of the unfortunate woman when she was informed by telephone that her husband and daughters were free, safe from the clutches of the enemy. From that moment on she waited with yearning for their return. The following day she could no longer be contained. She sat near the entrance of the courtyard with great anticipation waiting for the moment of their return.

Immediately upon seeing them she burst into tears and poured out all the emotions of her heart. Her excitement was so intense that she was unable even to express words of thanks to the Holy One,

---

117 Poignant allusion to the thanksgiving to God of the Passover Haggadah "for having transformed mourning into celebration (מאבל ליום טוב)."

118 R. Ungar was among the prominent rabbinic personalities in prewar Eastern Europe. Originally head of the Tranava Yeshivah, he was appointed to lead the Nitra Yeshivah in 1932, developing it into a major talmudical academy. He served on the *Moetzet Gedolei HaTorah* (Council of Torah Sages) within the prewar *Agudath Israel* movement. His son-in-law, Michael Ber Weissmandel was in the forefront of Holocaust rescue efforts and is the author of the classic *Min HaMetzar* (Jerusalem, 3rd edition; 1960). The Nitra Yeshivah continued to function under the most hazardous conditions until it closed on the 17th of Elul, 5704, Sept. 5, 1944 (*Min HaMetzar*, 34) among the last yeshivot still functioning during Holocaust conditions. R. Ungar was smuggled into the forest under partisan control, but the difficult conditions took their toll. He died in the forest on the 9th of *Adar*, 5405/February 22, 1945. (Avraham Fuchs, *Yeshivot Hungaria Begidulotan Uvehurbanan* (Jerusalem, 1979), pp. 127–141.

blessed be He, for the great miracle which transpired for her and for her family. . . . Those who did not witness this reunion, the tears, and emotions of happiness of a joyous mother [reunited] with her children, never were privileged to have witnessed genuine joy. . . .[119]

I imagine that such would be the experience of joy of our Mother Eretz Yisrael at the time when we shall return to her after a terrible captivity such as in our present time. I have, therefore, called my volume *Em HaBanim Semeha* ("A Happy Mother of Children"). May the Lord grant me the privilege of utilizing my book for the purpose of returning the children to their Land[120] and thereby fulfilling speedily in our own day [the hope of] a Joyous Mother of Children.[121] May we ascend to Zion in gladness,[122] speedily in our day, Amen.

The second preface is now completed in the fifth millenium of the weekly portion "I have also heard the cries of the children of Israel,"[123] on the New Month of *Shevat*. . . . the year 703[124] in the city of Budapest.

---

119   The incident is autobiographic as indicated in *EHS*, p. 3 of the introduction in the original source.

120   Cf. Jer. 31:16 ושבו בנים לגבולם "The children shall return to their borders."

121   Ps. 113:9.

122   Cf. Isa. 35:10, 51:11 ובאו ציון ברינה "They come to Zion with joy."

123   Ex. 6:5, referring to the scripture reading of the week, *Va'erah* (Ex. 6:2–9:35). It is customary to identify the date of publication of a volume or parts thereof by referring to an apt verse or phrase culled from the scripture reading of that particular week.

124   Totaling 5703. The second preface was completed on January 7, 1943. The numerical value 703 is symbolically structured אל הקודש (703) גשת (*lit.* "approaching holiness"). Cf. Num. 8:19.

FOREWORD

Torah and Eretz Yisrael were uttered in one divine breath.[1] They represent two inseparable companions. With regard to Torah, it is written: "Moses commanded us a Torah, the inheritance [of the community of Jacob]."[2] Concerning Eretz Yisrael it is written: "I will give it to you as a heritage."[3] Indeed they were both conceived and united into one expression—*morashah*. The *morashah* formulation in both instances sums up for us their essence.

I shall first explain, with the help of God, the theme of *morashah* as it relates to Torah. What is its meaning? Following this, I propose with the help of God to expand upon *morashah* as it relates to Eretz Yisrael. We shall see clearly how these two concepts are inextricably connected. It is not possible to separate them.

Isaiah the prophet declared: "No weapon formed against you shall succeed, and every accusation that challenges you at law you shall defeat. Such is the lot of the servants of the Lord; they shall be justified through Me (Is. 22:17). . . ."[4,5] "You may therefore be assured that the Torah in our Land is the true Torah of God given to us by

---

1 Cf. שמור וזכור בדבור אחד "'Keep' and 'Remember' were [used in one word]," from the *Lekha Dodi*, Friday eve liturgy.

2 Deut. 33:4 [קהילת יעקב] תורה צוה לנו משה מורשה.

3 Ex. 6:8 ונתתי אותה לכם מורשה.

4 Misprint or misquote in the text reads: מאתם "through them" *vs.* מאתי "through me."

5 Actually Isa. 54:17. Our author proceeds to quote and summarize extensively from *Iggeret Teiman* of Maimonides addressed to the Jewish community in Yemen (c. 1172), in response to their call of despair when threatened with conversion to Islam or death.

37

the Master of all prophets.[6] It is this very Torah which differentiates us from citizens of the world. The truth of our Torah is not based on wondrous signs or miracles. It is, however, verified by a sustained experience of seeing and hearing our King and our Creator on Mount Sinai. With our own ears we heard how he spoke with Moses declaring: "I the Lord am your God,"[7] and the balance of the Commandments.[8]

Behold, the verse explicitly affirms: "I will come to you in a thick cloud, in order that the people may hear when I speak with you and so trust you thereafter."[9] So it was that we also witnessed the Lord on Mount Sinai, as did Moses. We too heard God's word, as did he. Consequently we conferred upon him [Moses] our complete and unceasing confidence, as it is written: "and so trust you thereafter." Together with Moses we may be compared to two witnesses who gave evidence, each being confident that the other's testimony is identical to his own.[10] "So it is with us. We the congregation in Israel always were convinced of the authenticity of Moses our teacher since we saw him at the time of the Divine revelation at Sinai. It was not because of miracles [that we trusted him]."[11] Miracles are sought [as confirmation] only in the event of doubt. One cannot rely upon them as evidence. It is said: Seeing is superior to hearing.[12] Therefore the greatness of this [Sinai] event. "It is befitting that you should educate your children in the light of this majestic experience. Recount its greatness [glory][13] and splendor among the community and congregation since it is the very pillar around which our faith revolves

---

6 *Iggeret Teiman* in *Iggarot HaRambam*, ed. M.D. Rabinowitz (Jerusalem, Mosad HaRav Kook, 1960), 114

7 Ex. 20:2.

8 Ibid. 3–14.

9 Ibid. 19:9. Quoted in *Iggeret Teiman, op. cit.,* 130.

10 *Iggeret Teiman, op. cit.,* 148.

11 Ibid.

12 As opposed to miracles which may operate in the realm of illusion. Israel's presence together with Moses at Sinai represent actual proof of the historic experience which transcends the supernatural. For the preference of direct vision to indirect auditory messages, see RH 25b. לא תהא שמיעה גדולה מראייה "Hearing should not exceed seeing."

13 Not in the *Iggeret* text.

and it is *the* evidence which leads to [the discovery] of truth."[14] It was none other than we alone, "an entire nation listening to the word of God, seeing glory face to face. This event took place only in order that faith might be strengthened within our hearts, never to be changed by anyone who wishes to make changes [in religion]. . . ."[15]

"Should the hand of the coercer[16] prevail"[17] and legislate edicts of forced conversion and suffering, or should they compel us to exchange our holy religion, we shall declare to them: "Duplicate for us the Sinai experience, when the respective camps of the Lord and Israel stood facing one another. Then we will respond to your advice."[18] He [Maimonides] then proceeded to explain the verse: "for God has come only in order to test you and that the fear of Him may be ever with you so that you do not go astray."[19] That is to say, that Revelation at Sinai was so apparent, assuring that they [the Jewish people] would stand up to all the tests of time. Their hearts would persevere. They would not go astray. . . .[20]

. . . Now, my brothers and friends, you may see for yourself that our rabbis' teachings [concerning heritage] are embodied in the words of Rashi on the verse: "This is my God and I will glorify Him; the God of my father and I will exalt Him."[21] I am not the first to experience Divine holiness. It had already been acquired and bequested to me since the days of my forefathers. . . ." I have now demonstrated that the

---

14   *Iggeret Teiman, op. cit.,* 131.

15   Ibid. 132.

16   Maimonides' reference to the forced conversion practices of Christianity and Islam of his day.

17   Ibid.

18   Ibid. 133. Our author's text reads אז אשוב לעדתכם "Then shall I return to your community" *vs.* אז אשוב לעצתכם "Then shall I respond to your advice."

19   Ex. 20:16.

20   *EHS* proceeds to elaborate (pp. 39–43) upon the significance of the Revelation and the special nature of the heritage of Torah to the Jewish people, the actual meaning of which is beyond the grasp of the ordinary person.

21   Ex. 15:2. זה אלי ואנוהו, אלהי אבי וארוממנהו. Rashi paraphrases, interpreting the variant אלהי אבי "The God of my father" and זה אלי "This is my God."

very presence of the Torah in our possession is linked to its inheritance from our forefathers. We can now better understand the term *morashah* as it appears in the verse "Moses commanded us with the Torah, as the heritage of the community of Jacob. . . ."[22] This represents the validity of the Torah in our possession. This is the significance of the term *morashah* in our Torah, pointing to its firm foundations and its eternal character. . . . No one shall be able to destroy it. It shall remain firm forever . . . Those who attempt to tamper with it, will in due course be destroyed, as was the case with all those who attempted to so do in the past. We shall not eliminate even an iota [of Jacob]. [Torah] shall never, ever be surrendered. . . .

Now, I wish to explain with the help of God, the term *morashah* as it pertains to Eretz Yisrael. Indeed, when Man was fashioned in the universe by the Creator, may His Name be blessed and elevated, he was separated [by the Almighty] into the nations of the world, seventy in all. God then assigned them to guardian angels. Each nation was positioned below its respective angel and its sphere of influence. The respective rank of the angel in heaven would determine the place of the nation on earth. Ascendency of the patron angel above would bring about the ascendency of its people below. With the fall of the angel above would follow the fall of its people below, as it is written: "[On that day] the Lord will punish the host of heaven in heaven and the kings of the earth on earth. . . ."[23]

---

22 Deut. 33:4, Jacob representing the eternal ancestral heritage of Torah.

23 Isa. 24:21. והיה ביום ההוא יפקד ד' על צבא המרום במרום, ועל מלכי האדמה על האדמה. See the commentators Radak and Abrabanel who follow Abraham Ibn Ezra in identifying the צבא מרום (The host of heaven) with the מלאכי שרי האומות (patron angels of the princes of nations). "Many interpret this prophecy as a reference to an eclipse of the sun and moon; but more correctly it is referred to the angels, that are ready to assist or to attack a nation. Comp. Dan. 10:13, 20. These words are therefore followed by: the kings of the earth on the earth, for the reign of the kings is in connection with the reign of the angels." (Translation in *The Commentary of Ibn Ezra on Isaiah*, vol. 1 by M. Friedlander, London, 1873, p. 112 and n. 30).

The author grafts onto the depiction of the patron angel the mirror imagery of Kabbalah in which impulses from "above" trigger parallel responses "below." See *Tanh. Re'eh* 8: אתה מוצא כשברא העולם חלק הארצות לשרי האומות ובחר בארץ ישראל.

"One discovers that when He created the world He apportioned the countries among the princes of the nations, but He [alone] chose Eretz Yisrael." Ibid. *Mishpatim*,

One Land, however, God preferred to keep under His own jurisdiction. He did not assign it to any patron angel, declaring: "This Land I shall set aside for Myself and My dominion. When I will meet a compatible person upon this earth I will bring him close to me,[24] and settle him in this Land. He will be under my direct guidance[25] and influence without any intermediary patron angels from above. . . . This person was Abraham our Patriarch. He was completely at one with the Creator of the entire world, in heart and mind, in the full meaning of the word. Scripture amply confirms this: "You are . . . the Lord, God, Who chose *Abram* and brought him out of Ur of the Chaldeans, and named him *Abraham*. You regarded him as being faithful to you."[26] God considered him worthy to be settled in the Land to be selected and chosen for his apportionment. This is reflected in the *Midrash Tanhuma* (the weekly portion of *Re'eh*):[27]

> Beloved is Eretz Yisrael, since it was chosen by the Holy One, blessed be He. You will find that when He created the universe He apportioned the lands among the patron angels of the nations. He selected Eretz Yisrael. How is this known? Moses declared: "When the Most High gave nations their homes, etc."[28] and chose Israel for Himself, as it is written: "But the Lord's portion is His people, Jacob His own allotment,"[29] said the Holy One, blessed be He: "Let the people Israel who have been apportioned to Me, settle the Land which is being allotted to Me."

What prepared Abraham for the privilege of partaking in this Divine scheme? This was due to his total devotion to God and to the extent

---

אמר הקב"ה: אומות העולם בגדו בי ונתתי להם שרים שיהו משמשין אותן, וגו' 17.
"Said the Holy One, blessed be He: The nations of the world acted unfaithfully towards me, so I assigned princes who would serve them, etc." See below, 262.

24 ושמתיך כחותם כי בך בחרתי Cf. Hag. 2:23 אשימנו כחותם על לבי. "I will bring you close to me for I have chosen you." See also Jer. 22:24.

25 Probably השגחתי "my guidance" *vs.* השגתי "my understanding."

26 Neh. 9:7–8.

27 *Tanh. Re'eh* 8, treating the verse Deut. 12:29.

28 Deut. 32:8.

29 Ibid. 32:9.

that he sanctified His blessed Name beyond what was ever achieved by any other person on this earth. He was originally selected because he sanctified God's name among the people in Ur of the Chaldees. . . .

This was to be the first of ten trials in which Abraham stood the test as explained by Rabbi Ovadia Bartenoro in the fifth chapter of *Avot*. . . .[30] I also noted that the holy volume *Bet Elohim* (of the rabbi and master the Mabit, colleague of the *Bet Yosef* [31] and a member of his court), in the Gate of Foundations, chapter 32, elaborates on Abraham's act of kiddush HaShem in Ur-Kasdim, thereby gaining for him the privilege of settling in Eretz Yisrael. "It was then that God vowed to give the Land to his offspring. As the Lord said: 'I am the Lord who brought you out of Ur-Kasdim in order to give you this land, to inherit it.'"[32] This declaration was also spoken on the occasion of [the Covenant] of the Pieces. . . .[33] This [repeated declaration] was to inform him that the intention to give him the Land goes back to the time of his being brought out from Ur-Kasdim. . . .[34]

---

30 Avot 5:3. Ovadia Bartenoro, 15th century commentator on the Mishnah, lists the celebrated trial of Abraham of *Ur-Kasdim* when King Nimrod compelled him to enter into the fiery furnace. GenR. 34:9, 38:13, 39:3, 39:8, 44:13.

31 Joseph Karo. See above, 13, n. 58.

32 Gen. 15:7.

33 Gen. 15:8–21.

34 *Bet Elohim, op. cit.*, 96. The full text is significant: ותדע ותשכיל ממוצא דבר ירושת
הארץ מפי האל' יתב' עד ירושתה תפ״ח שנים כמו שיש מהתחלת קבלת התורה עד תשלומה תפ״ח שנים .
. . שכשהיה אברהם בן ב״ן שנה שנשלמו שני אלפים ליצירה נחשב כהתחלת קבלת התורה שאז השלים
אברהם אבינו הכרת הבורא ית' ונפלאותיו אשר עשה עמו שהצילו אז מאור כשדים בהיותו בן נ״ב שנה.
ואז נדר לתת לזרעו את הארץ הזאת לרשתה. כי גם שדבור זה נאמר לו במעמד/ברית/בין הבתרים שהיה
בן שבעים שנה הרי הודה והודיע לו כי מאז שהוציא מאור כשדים היתה הכוונה לתת לו את הארץ, וגו'
והרי הוא כאלו מאז נדר לו בזכות מה שמסר עצמו על קדוש שמו ית', אם כן הרי שני אלפים תהו, כי כל
זמן שלא ניתנה התורה ולא ישבו ישראל על אדמתם היה העולם כאלו לא נברא והיה תהו. ומשהתחיל
אברהם אבינו לקבל ולקיים התורה כשנשלמו ב' אלפים והיה בן ב״ן וזכה אז ג״כ לירושת הארץ נחשב
העולם כאלו הוא בנוי ומשוכלל בתורה ובא״י" "You should know that from the time of the origins of the legacy of the Land as promised by the Divine, until the actual settlement [of the Land] 488 years elapsed. These 488 years also constitute the period from the time when the Torah was first acknowledged until its full realization [the Revelation] . . . [the time that] Abraham was 52 years old, corresponding to 2000 years since Creation, is considered the beginning of the acceptance of the Torah at Sinai. It was

Now note, my brethren, that at the very outset, when the Lord, blessed be He, vowed to give the Land to Abraham, He also declared that His intention was to give the Land not only to him, but also to his offspring in every generation. And thus, we who are the offspring of Abraham, Isaac and Jacob, were privileged to receive the Land of Israel, which is God's own portion. . . . And since God chose Abraham to take part in His portion, we too were privileged to take part in the portion of the Holy One, blessed be He.

Our sages of blessed memory commented appropriately:

> Said the Holy One to the people of Israel: "Eretz Yisrael is my portion" as it is written—"It is a land on which the Lord always keeps His eye and looks after,"[35] "and you are my portion," as it is written—"But the Lord's portion is His people."[36] It will be proper for My portion [the people of Israel] to live in "My portion'"[Eretz Yisrael].'"[37]

Now the strongest case for [our relationship to] Eretz Yisrael is based on inheritance, as it is written in the verse: "to give you this

---

then that Abraham our father recognized the blessed Creator, and all of God's wonders from which he benefited when, being 52 years old, he was saved from Ur-Kasdim. He then vowed to give to his (Abraham's) seed this Land as an inheritance. Although this promise was also made on the occasion [of the Covenant] Between the Pieces, when he was 70 years old, God informed him that from the very time he had left Ur-Kasdim it was His intention to give him the Land, etc. It was, therefore, as if the vow was operative from that point [in Abraham's history] because he had dedicated himself to sanctifying His Name. Hence, the [first] two millenia may be considered to have been in a state of void. After all, if the Torah had not yet been given and Israel had not yet been settled on its Land, it is as if the world had not yet been created and was in a state of void. But when Abraham our father accepted and fulfilled the Torah upon the completion of two thousand years [of creation], at the age of 52 years, and concurrently merited the inheritance of the Land, then the world was considered as [fully] built and perfected by means of Torah and Eretz Yisrael."

35 Conflation of Deut. 11:12. ‏ארץ אשר ד' אלהיך דרש אותה תמיד עיני ד' אלהיך בה.‏ "It is a Land which the Lord your God looks after, on which the Lord your God always keeps His eye."

36 Ibid. 32:9.

37 A variant of *Tanh. Re'eh* 8. The Midrash employs Deut. 32:8 ‏בהנחל עליון גוים‏ "He fixed the boundaries of peoples," *vs.* our author's Deut. 11:12 (see n. 35). Consequently: ‏אמר הקב"ה: יבואו ישראל שבאו לחלקי וינחלו את הארץ שבאה לחלקי.‏ See also *NumR.* 23:7.

Land as a possession."[38] Neither the argument of acquisition [by purchase] nor the argument of military conquest are as valid. . . . With regard to the latter; one conquest may cancel a previous one. . . . The holy Torah is our contract and proof; . . . it remains eternal and is evident to all the nations.

Observe what is written in the holy book *Netzah Yisrael* of the divine scholar, our Rabbi, the Maharal of Prague.[39]

> Nature is the strongest of the forces [as opposed to human trial and error]. It is independent, and does not permit any obstacle to obstruct its natural process. If an obstruction does occur, it is of a temporary nature. Eventually it is overcome. Nature then returns to its essential process . . . as originally determined by God. . . . So it is with our kinship to Eretz Yisrael. We may be certain that Eretz Yisrael will return to us with the help of the Creator. . . . The Creator of the universe implanted it [the partnership between Eretz Yisrael and the Jewish people] into the natural process of things. Being dispersed and divided among the other nations, in exile from our Land, is an unnatural state of affairs. Exile is an obstruction to the Divine process. . . . Therefore, God who governs the universe will intervene in various ways until our Holy Land will return to us, as was originally intended . . . (these are the words of the Maharal.)

It is important to note that just as the gift of Eretz Yisrael represented God's vow to Abraham because he sanctified the Holy Name, so too this inheritance requires that we also follow the ways of our Fathers. Then we as their offspring will be worthy of this inheritance. If, God forbid, we stray from their ways then we shall not have a share in this inheritance. This is explicitly stated in Scripture. "Sarah saw the son whom Hagar the Egyptian had [borne to Abraham] playing."[40] Our

---

38   Gen. 14:7.

39   R. Judah Loew ben Bezalel (c. 1525–1609), a rabbinic scholar, philosopher, moralist, and mathematician. His work *Netzah Yisrael* (Prague, 1599) is devoted to the process of exile and redemption. The author proceeds to summarize one of the major premises in the Maharal work in chapter one. See below, 161, n. 185, 260.

40   Gen. 21:9. אשר ילדה לאברהם "Whom [Hagar the Egyptian] had borne to Abraham" deleted in our text.

sages of blessed memory commented (as well as Rashi on this text):[41]

"He had heard that he [Ishmael] had become corrupt."[42] "She said to Abraham: 'Cast out that slave woman and her son, for the son of that slave shall not share in the inheritance with my son Isaac.'"[43] It is precisely because Ishmael became corrupt that he received no portion in his father's inheritance. Further, God agrees with Sarah, as the verses indicate: "The matter distressed Abraham greatly, for it concerned a son of his. But God said to Abraham: "Do not be distressed over the boy [or your slave]; whatever Sarah tells you, do as she says, for it is through Isaac that your offspring shall come forth. . . .'"[44] And Abraham our father did as commanded by God, as it is written: "Early next morning, Abraham took some bread and a skin vessel of water and gave them to Hagar. He placed them over her shoulder, together with the child, and sent her away. . . ."[45] Now it is clear why the story of Sarah [and Hagar] appears [in Scripture] next to the binding [of Isaac].[46] When she declared "for the son [of that slave] shall not share in the inheritance with my son Isaac," she also confirmed that Isaac was worthy of the inheritance. Just as Abraham sanctified the blessed Name of God, so did he. He was indeed a son worthy of the inheritance. . . .

We now find[47] that the Holy One, blessed be He, at the very outset of the conquest of the Land, made the following stipulation with Joshua, as it is written: "After the death of Moses . . . the Lord said to Joshua. . . . Prepare to cross the Jordan, together with all this people, into the Land which I give to the Israelites. . . ."[48] Be strong

---

41 Ibid. 11 על אודות בנו "For it concerned a son of his."

42 Expanded in GenR. 53:15 and Ex. 1:1.

43 Gen. 21:10.

44 Ibid. 11–12 כי כל אשר תאמר "Because whatever [Sarah] tells you," vs. כל אשר תאמר "Whatever [Sarah] tells you," in Scripture. Inheritence of ethnic, national and religious claims as dependent upon walking in the religious path of God and Torah is reinforced in the midrash [GenR. 53:16] and Maimonides [*Iggeret Teiman*] EHS, 47.

45 Ibid. 14.

46 Ibid. 22:1–19.

47 The author proceeds to demonstrate that Isaac's inheritance could also not be taken for granted. The lesson of Ishmael also has implications for Israel.

48 Jos. 1:1–2.

and resolute for you shall apportion to this people the Land that I
swore to their fathers to give them. But you must be very strong and
resolute to observe faithfully the entire Torah that My servant Moses
enjoined upon you. Do not deviate from it to the right or to the left,
that you may be successful wherever you go. Let not this Book of
Torah cease from your lips, but recite it day and night . . . and only
then will you be successful. I charge you: Be strong and resolute, do
not be terrified or dismayed, for the Lord your God is with you
wherever you go. Joshua thereupon gave orders to the officials of the
people. . . .[49] But everyone of your fighting men shall cross [the
Jordan] armed and in front of your brethren. You shall assist them."[50]
Now the Lord instructed Joshua to observe two commands:

1. To be strong and resolute regarding matters of war and
to encourage and arm fighting men who will engage the
nations which inhabit the Land in order to conquer it...[1]

2. To observe all that Moses enjoined [upon the people of
Israel] in the holy Torah.[52]

I found in the holy volume *Bet Elohim* of our teacher HaMabit,[53]
That Joshua was compelled to conquer the Land by conventional
means of war. The Ramban in his commentary on the Pentateuch in
Numbers, *Shelah* has emphasized that the Torah does not rely on
miracles.[54]

---

49 Ibid. 10.

50 Ibid. 14. Reference to the tribes of Reuben, Gad and the half tribe of Menashe
who were now to fulfill their pledge as described in Num. 32.

51 Ibid. 2–6; 10–15.

52 Ibid. 7–8.

53 *Op. cit.*, 96 See above, 13, 44, and below 104.

54 *Ramban al HaTorah* Vol. 2, ed. Hayyim Dov Chavel (Jerusalem, 1960), 199. כי
אלף אחד שירדוף הנס על תסמוך לא התורה. ibid. 241. "The Torah will not rely upon a
miracle where one will pursue a thousand." יצוה אבל הנס על מעשיו בכל יסמוך לא הכתוב כי
ולארוב ולהשמר להחלץ בנלחמים. "The verse will not relate to acts which rely upon a
miracle. It will, however, urge the warriors to prepare, to be on guard and to wait in
ambush." See also ibid., 137. הנס על באזהרותיה התורה תסמוך לא כי. "The Torah in its
exhortations will not depend upon the miracle."

Rabbi Bahya [55] also makes this point. [56]

It is also noted in Rashi, Shabbat 23 b. [57] The Jerusalem Talmud, Yoma 1:4 teaches us not to rely on miracles in order that you "do not try the Lord your God. . . ." [58] It is further taught in the chapter *Tamid Nishhat* 64, [59] that we do not rely on miracles. . . . [60]

Now in accepting the *morashah* [legacy] of Torah we will also be worthy of the *morashah* of Eretz Yisrael. Should we depart from her [Torah] either right or left, [61] so that it no longer is our *morashah*, then Eretz Yisrael can no longer be our *morashah*. This occurred to our forefathers and to ourselves because of our sins.

Furthermore, we cannot grasp the true profound mysteries [of Torah] except in Eretz Yisrael. As [our sages] said: "The atmosphere of Eretz Yisrael makes one wise." [62] They also related on the advantage of studying Torah in Eretz Yisrael. [63,64] Upon this background it will

---

55 R. Bahya ben Asher, 13th century commentator and kabbalist and student of R. Solomon ibn Abraham Adret. Noted for his commentary (and encyclopedic compilation of commentaries) on the Pentateuch (Naples, 1492).

56 *Rabbenu Bahya al HaTorah, Shelah* (ed. Hayyim Dov Chavel) (Jerusalem, 1968), 80.

57 No reference to miracles noted in Rashi Shab. 23 b. Likely reference is to Rashi Shab. 53b on R. Nahman's statement: "The proof is that miracles do occur but food is not so readily created by miracles."

58 Deut. 6:16. The JT Yoma text reads ולא מן הניסים שהיו נעשין בבית המקדש הן? א"ר אבין: על שם לא תנוסון. "Were these not among the miracles which occurred in the Temple? R. Abin said: Due to [the caution] 'Do not try [the Lord your God.']"

59 Pes. 64 b.

60 This the view of Raba. The doors of the Temple court were manually closed by those assigned this task on the Passover holiday when throngs of pilgrims would enter the courtyard in three regulated shifts (see *Mishnah*, ibid. 64a). Unlike Abaye's opinion that the doors were locked miraculously, Raba insists "that we do not rely on a miracle." The author proceeds to develop the theme of "the miracle within nature," the efficacy of which is contingent on the degree of study and observance of Torah. Employing the commentaries on Jos. 1:7 with regard to the emphatic terms רק (*rak*) "but"—and מאד (*me'od*) "very"—the Torah as a prerequisite to the physical and "natural" means by which the Land would be conquered, is clearly established.

61 Jos. 1:7.

62 BB.158 b. אוירא דא"י מחכים.

63 See GenR. 16:7 אין חכמה כחכמת א"י, ואין תורה כתורת א"י. "There is no wisdom as the wisdom of Eretz Yisrael, and there is no Torah comparable to the Torah of Eretz Yisrael."

be understood why I, at the very outset presented [the premise] that
Torah and Eretz Yisrael were commanded simultaneously and that
they function as two inseparable companions. Note, therefore, the
statement of R. Moshe Cordovero, our teacher, the divine personage,
in the volume *Or Ne'erav*[65] the fifth chapter: [66]

> It is known that the relationship of Eretz Yisrael to the Torah is that of
> the heart to the totality of existence. The lifeline to the universe is
> Torah, as it is written: ". . . and has planted within us life eternal."[67]
> The habitat of life's forces and the soul lies in the heart. Its vital
> functions are situated there and extend to the rest of the body. So it is
> with Torah. Its primary functions are situated in Eretz Yisrael.

After having noted the above [*morashah* themes] I discovered a
further reference in the Jerusalem Talmud of Baba Batra, Chapter 8,
at the close of the second halakhah.[68] There, too, the comparison is
made between the concept of inheritance as it applies to the Land
and as it applies to Torah, as well . . . As in the case of Torah, when
one begins to study he encounters difficulties and doubts. As one
continues to delve further into study it becomes the object of greater
desire and, eventually, pleasure. So it is with Eretz Yisrael. The
expression *dey-he* [69] signifies feebleness and doubt.[70] We shall indeed

---

64   *Bet Elohim, op. cit.*, 96b.

65   (Furth, 1701, 18b). An introductory treatise on the Kabbalah.

66   Chapter six in the Furth edition (no. 12283) in the Schocken Library, Jerusalem.

67   From the blessings recited at the Torah reading אשר נתן לנו תורת אמת וחיי עולם
נטע בתוכנו. "Who has given us the Torah of truth, planting within us life eternal." And
the allusion to Prov. 3:18. See *Siddur Bet Ya'akov* (R. Yaakov Emden), *op. cit.*, 84. עי
חיים היא למחזיקים בה. "It is a tree of life for those who grasp it."

68   א״ר הושעיה: כל מקום שנאמר מורשה לשון דיהא התיבון והכתיב ׳מורשה קהילת יעקב׳ אמר
לית דיהא סוגין מיניה. מן דו לעי היא משכח כולה. "R. Hoshaya said: Wherever the term
morashah is used it is a faint [vague] expression, as when it is written '. . . the heritage
of the congregation of Jacob' (Deut. 33:4). He indicates that there is none vaguer
than this [expression], yet whoever exerts effort obtains the whole of it."

69   As it appears in the Yerushalmi text לשון דיהא, Ibid.

70   The *Torah Temimah* commentary of R. Baruch HaLevi Epstein (1860–1942)
points to the verse in Ex. 6:8 ונתתי אותה לכם מורשה "And I will give it to you for a
possession" and the discussion in BB 119b comparing the unqualified term ירושה

experience a number of uncertainties and obstacles at the outset. We will find it very difficult. But in the course of applying ourselves diligently to the task, we shall eventually overcome. All of our objectives will be realized, as is the way with Torah. . . .

I shall presently address myself to the builders of our Holy Land in our own generation. "By these things [the Divine promise and fulfillment] men live."[71] And through them the Lord's purpose may prosper.[72] It is as clear as day that your endeavors and labors are pleasing to God. You have built cities. From waste land you have created flourishing fields. This was achieved by means of difficult and dedicated efforts. You succeeded in cleansing bodies of water which had been infected with many diseases. You then directed these to choice and fruitful fields.

That your works are indeed pleasing to the Lord,[73] I will eventually demonstrate. I shall presently cite only one notable source from the tractate of Sanhedrin 102b[74] which surely cannot be challanged.[75] "Rabbi Yohanan said: Why was Omri worthy of royalty?[76] Because he added a city in Eretz Yisrael. . . ."[77]

(inheritance) to the more ambiguous מורשה (legacy, possession).

71 Isa. 38:16. A contextual homiletical reading may have been intended for this complex verse: "May the Divine spirit dwell upon them" אדני עליהם יחיו.

72 Variation of Isa. 53:10.

73 The expression רצויה לפני הקב״ה "Pleasing to the Holy One blessed be He" or מעשיהם רצויים לפני הבורא "Their deeds are pleasing to the Creator" is identified in Hasidism with the desired experience of דבקות (cleaving) to the Divine. This experience may take place irrespective of any conscious human efforts. (See *Maggid Devarav LeYa'akov*, ed. Rivka Schatz, Jerusalem, 1976, 76, n. in paragraph 53.)

74 Erroneously printed in the text as 108.

75 Obvious reference to the rabbinic leadership in Eastern Europe which zealously opposed modern Zionist efforts of reclaiming Eretz Yisrael politically, economically, and demographically. One of their arguments among others claimed that the *halutzim*, who denied the Torah and its Divine origins, are tampering with the Divine redemption process and do so with impudent unholy means. They were considered *"posh'ei Yisrael"* (sinners of Israel) and unworthy of their self proclaimed task. Our author vehemently opposed these assumptions.

76 His iniquities are described in I Kings 16:25.

77 א״ר יוחנן: מפני מה זכה עמרי למלכות? מפני שהוסיף כרך אחד בא״י.

In the volume of Kabbalah, *Otzrot Yosef*, [78] by the outstanding intellect Rabbi Yosef Engel,[79] the question is posed as to why, in fact, did the Holy One, blessed be He, reward him [Omri] with *malkhut* [royalty] for this act, as opposed to another reward. It is known that the kabbalists considered Eretz Yisrael to be identified with the sphere of Divine *malkhut*.[80] Since he restored an aspect of *malkhut* by the addition of one city in Eretz Yisrael he became worthy of a kingdom,[81] although Omri was one of the wicked kings.

An entire verse in Scripture testifies (I Kings 16):[82] [And Omri ascended[83]] "then he bought the hill of Samaria from Shemer for two talents of silver; he built upon the hill and named the city which he built Samaria [after Shemer the owner of the hill], Omri did what was displeasing to the Lord; he was worse than all who preceded him. He followed all the ways of Jeroboam son of Nebat and the sins which he committed and caused Israel to commit." And even this city which he established was established for selfish reasons and not for the sake of Heaven, [for he exclaimed]: "What Jerusalem signifies for Judah, Samaria will be for the kings of Israel."[84] Though his building efforts involved such grave transgressions, he nevertheless fulfilled thereby the positive commandment of the settling of Eretz Yisrael. Were it not so, he would not have been rewarded measure for measure. . . .[85]

---

78   Yosef Engel, *Sefer Otzrot Yosef* (Vienna, 1928), 4.

79   R. Yosef Engel (1859–1920), among the leading Polish rabbinic authorities of the period; was noted for his creative studies in halakhah, aggadah, and kabbalah, and his attempt to integrate these disciplines. Many of his works were destroyed during the Holocaust.

80   The tenth in the sequence of ten spheres (*sefirot*) of Divine manifestations central to kabbalah and prominent in the Zohar. (Gershom Scholem, *Major Trends in Jewish Mysticism*, New York: 1954, 212–217.) See below, 239.

81   Consistent with the kabbalistic doctrine that human initiative in the world below stimulates reciprocal action above in a related heavenly sphere.

82   Verses 24–26.

83   Addition of the author.

84   *Yalkut Shimoni* II, 756. The author previously referred to this source in a deleted passage.

85   מדה כנגד מדה. The Divine reward or punishment befits the human deed. Sanh. 90a שכל מדותיו של הקב״ה מדה כנגד מדה. "Since all of God's ways reflect measure for

This is, therefore, irrefutable evidence that even the most heinous transgressor, one such as Omri, who would reject the entire Torah, Heaven forbid, nevertheless was worthy [of a reward] when he devoted himself to the building of a city in Eretz Yisrael. . . . Similarly, those who assume the task of building the Land in our own day, though they have unfortunately abandoned the Torah, surely they are not worse than Omri. . . . Their works [as well] are desirable before the Lord. . . .[86] The *tikkunim* and *yihudim*[87] were achieved by these builders who have expanded the Land and made it fruitful (which is the main purpose of settling the Land, as indicated by the Maharsha[88] in Berakhot 58, that the essential mitzvah of building the Land is by means of fields and vineyards. . . .[89] Similarly, our master the Hatam Sofer in his volume of *derashot*, in the *derashah* for *Shabbat HaGadol* 5558[90] explains that the lands of Sihon and Og were never designated as "inhabited," though they were in fact inhabited. This was so since their lands were never cultivated, either by gentiles or Jews. . . .[91] It seems to me that we have clear support for our rabbi [the Hatam Sofer] for the verse in *Vayishlah*: "These were the sons of Seir the

---

measure."

86 Though their acts are not religiously motivated. See n. 73, above.

87 The union of human endeavors in thought and action with the Divine will (*yihud*) for the purpose of achieving a form of *ruah hakodesh* (the Holy Spirit) and *tikkun* (the state of reconstruction or restoration of the imperfect), thus hastening redemption, is central to both Kabbalah and Hasidism.

88 R. Samuel Eliezer ben Judah HaLevi (1555–1631) a major commentator on the Talmud in Poland known for his classic commentaries *Hiddushei Halakhot* and *Aggadot Maharsha*

89 R. Jeremiah, the son of Elazar, said: "When Samaria was cursed, its neighbors were blessed, as it is written (Micah 1:6), 'Therefore, I will make Samaria a heap in the open country, a place for planting vineyards.' It is thus a curse for Israel, the inhabitants of Israel. (Maharsha's commentary on Ber. 58a.) This suggests that Israel's displacement (the curse) is equated with the planting of vineyards which will benefit enemy neighbors. However, note the Maharsha further: ועוד יישוב א"י עדיף משדות וכרמים. "Further, the settlement of Eretz Yisrael is preferred over the [planting of] fields and vineyards," which would contradict our author's argument based on this text.

90 Delivered on the Sabbath prior to Passover 5558 (1798).

91 Hatam Sofer: *Derashot*, vol. 2 (Jerusalem, 1974), 466.

Horite, who were settled in the Land."[92] They expounded upon this
verse in *Shabbat* 85[93] and Rashi notes that they [the sons of Seir] were
experts at cultivating the land. [They used to say] "this complete acre
[of land is fit] for olives, this complete acre is fit for vines. . . . They
tasted the earth and knew for which crop it was suited."[94] This then
was the primary function of settling the Land. Note also the responsa
of the Rashbash, sections 1, 2 and 3.[95] Similarly, the Hatam Sofer
states in his novellae *[hiddushim]* on the tractate *Sukkah* 35[96] that the
acts of plowing and sowing in Eretz Yisrael are as if one performs the
commandments of *tefillin* [phylacteries], *sukkah* [the booth] or *lulav*
[palms, one of the four vegetative species required for the *Sukkot*
festival].[97]

But there is more. It seems to me, that this ordinary person who
builds the Land, without any religious pretenses, but merely for his
own advantage, fulfills a greater act of *tikkun* in the upper spheres[98]
than even the most righteous of *tzadikim* with his *tikkun hatzot*[99] and
his wailing and bewailing the Shekhinah and exile which certainly

---

92   Gen. 36:20. The phrase יושבי הארץ "who were settled in the land. . ." stimulates
the discussion in the Talmud.

93   Shab. 85a *vs.* 88 in the text.

94   The author intersperses partial text from the Talmud and the Rashi commentary.

95   Leghorn, 1742. R. Shlomo ben Shimon Duran, prominent 15th century North
African rabbinic authority, son of the Tashbaz (R. Shimon ben Zemah) major author
of responsa. The first three responsa are devoted to the legal parameters of fulfilling
the commandment of settling the Land (וישב ארץ ישראל) especially his summary of the
discussions in the Talmud ישראל דארעה ישובא משום דברים כמה אמרו וכן: "And they also
taught a number of lessons with regard to [the mitzvah of] settling the Land."

96   Actually *Suk.* 36a פסול לכושי דומה "Similar to a black *etrog* which is invalid, etc."

97   Biblical commandments based on Ex. 13:9; Ex. 13:16; Deut. 6:8; Deut. 11:18;
Lev. 23:42–43; Deut. 16:13; Lev. 23:40.

98   Based on the symmetrical symbiosis defined in the system of the .Zohar,. See
n. 100, below.

99   *Lit.* "the institution of midnight" or the "midnight vigil." The practice of
rising at midnight to recite prayers in memory of the destruction of the Temple and
to plead for the restoration (*tikkun*) of Eretz Yisrael. The talmudic basis is found in
related passages Ber. 3a–4a. The mystic R. Isaac Luria formalized the practice. For
the broader ramifications of *tikkun* in Kabbalah, see Gershom Scholem, *Kabbalah*
(Jerusalem, 1974), 140–144, specifically 143, dealing with the influence of human
activity on *tikkun* in the lower and upper worlds.

accomplishes a great *tikkun*. . . .[100] The text in Sanhedrin[101] reiterates this teaching as does our master[102] in his introduction to the volume *Reshit Hokhma*, namely, *tikkun* (restoration) is achieved by the actual performance of the mitzvah.[103] I found similar support in the volume *Yismah Moshe*,[104] [that is to say] the active aspect of the mitzvah, though not based on any specific intent, is more effective than a mitzvah which lacks activity, although it is accompanied by great

---

100   The concept of the Shekhinah in exile appears in the Talmud and reflecting Divine empathy with the suffering of His people and His special love for them שבכל מקום שגלו שכינה עמהם. "Wherever they were exiled the Shekhinah was with them." (Meg. 29a; JT Ta'an. 1:1; Zohar I, 120b and, 211b. In Kabbalah and Hasidism, the burden of releasing the Shekhinah from exile is transferred to the individual. The performance of the mitzvah, the pious act "below," releases the holy sparks from their imprisonment among the *kelipot* (impure "shells"). On the other hand "acts of Edom," sinful acts, compel the Shekhinah to "accompany" the alien action in exile in Edom. (*Tanya, Likutei Amarim*, Kfar Habad, 1959, Chapter 17, 23.) The *Baal Shem Tov* expressed the exile of the Shekhinah and the redeeming act of man in terms of אין מתפללים אלא מתוך כובד ראש (ברכות ה:א) sharing the "burden of the Source." אין עומדין להתפלל אלא מתוך כובד ראש: פרוש אל תתפלל בשביל דבר שחסר לך כי יקובל תפלתך, אלא כשתרצה להתפלל התפלל על כבידות שיש בראש, כי הדבר שחסר לך החסרון יש בשכינה, כי אדם חלק אלקי ממעל והחסרון שיש בחלק יש בכלל. "'One does not pray without a sense of sobriety (*koved rosh*)' (Ber. 5:1); One should not rise to pray without a sense of sobriety. That is to say—do not pray for something which you lack and hope that your prayer will be accepted. But, when you do pray, pray for the burden (*koved*) carried by the Source (*Rosh*). After all, that which you lack is also missing within the Shekhinah, since man is a divine segment of that which is Above and that which is lacking within the segment must necessarily also be lacking within the totality. (*Tzva'at HaRibash [The Testament of Rabbi Yisrael Baal Shem Tov]* Tel Aviv, 1961, 224).

101   102b cited above, relating to the act of Omri, King of Israel.

102   R. Elijah ben Moses de Vidas.

103   *Reshit Hokhmah, op. cit.*, 2b אמת שעקר עסק התורה הוא להביא לקיום המעשה. "It is a fact that the main concern of Torah study is to direct action," מצינו שקניית חיי העולם הבא הוא על ידי מעשה. "We find that the aquisition of a place in the world to come is brought about by the performance of an act." וכן שכינה מתתקנת במעשה יותר מדיבור "The Shekhinah is restored by acts more so than by words." The Shekhinah is more effectively restored by means of action than by study or talk. The author of *Reshit Hokhmah* cites the Zohar I, Prologue, 8a for support.

104   Classic volume of homiletical commentary on the Bible (Lemberg, 1848–61; Siget, 1898) by R. Moshe ben Zvi Teitelbaum (1759–1841), founder of the Teitelbaum dynasty of hasidic leaders in Galicia, Poland and Hungary; pupil of the master R. Yaakov Yitzhak, "The Seer" of Lublin.

intentions. . . .[105]

According to the halakhic authorities as well, it is clear that a mitzvah which involves action does not require intent. The mitzvah is fulfilled without intent.[106] Note also the Rashba[107] on Yevamot 103: The act which results in a mitzvah cannot be retracted even should such action have come about by way of a transgression, Heaven forbid. Furthermore, the mitzvah is not negated in any manner. . . .[108] This major principle is valid here as well. [Jewish] settlement in the Land has expanded due to their deeds. These are irreversible and cannot be denied. After all, we are the benefactors of the fruits of their labor. Even if this may have come about by means of transgression, Heaven forbid, the mitzvah has been convincingly fulfilled, in all its revealed as well as esoteric aspects. . . . Therefore, every Jew who is truly faithful to God, and, whose love for God and His People takes precedence over self-conceit, will be grateful and appreciate your acts of building our Holy Land.

However, you must be aware, my brethren and friends, and recall the supplication of Moses our teacher, who prayed before the Holy One, blessed be He: "In [Your going with us] we are distinct, I and

---

105 *Yismah Moshe* (Siget, 1898), 30a. ונמצא העושה המצוה בפועל הוא בנקל שיעשה התיקון והיחוד שראוים להיות ע"י מצוה זו, אף בעשיה כפשוטו אמר ונעשה רצונו אף בלי כונת סודות נסתרים ואף אם אין הטהרה והקדושה, הגדולה והיראה והאהבה הראויה. "Thus, one who actually performs the mitzvah, easily will achieve the proper *tikkun* and motivation for this particular mitzvah even though the manner of performing it is simply executed, without any esoteric intentions, and though it lacks the proper purity, sanctity, awe and love."

106 Probable reference to the Rabbenu Yonah (ben Abraham Gerondi c. 1200–1263) commentary on Alfasi, Ber. 3a and 8b and the *Pahad Yitzhak* (R. Isaac Hezekiah ben Shmuel Lampronti, 1679–1756) summary (Livorno, 1839) vol. 5, 187. דאפילו מי שסובר שמצות אינם צריכות כוונה, ה"מ בדבר שיש בו מעשה, שהמעשה במקום כוונה, כגון נטילת לולב, וכיוצא. "Even the authority who would not require proper intent in the performance of *mitzvot*, would claim so only with regard to a mitzvah which involves performance. In such an instance the actions takes the place of intent, as in the case of taking the lulav [on the Festival of Sukkot] and the like."

107 R. Shlomo ben Abraham Adret (1235–1310) among the most notable of Spanish Rabbinic authorities and prolific author of responsa.

108 *Hiddushei Yebamot LeHaRashba* (Constantinople, 1720) 129a (Concerning the questionable motives of the levir when enacting the ceremony of *halitzah*). As in Deut. 25:5–10.

Your people, from all the people that are upon this earth."[109] The
essence of our people is not founded on the exclusive concept of
"nationality" alone, as is the case with other people upon this earth.
We are a "holy people."[110] This state of holiness rests upon the sacred
Torah commanded to us by God. Only by means of Torah do we
become a people, as it is written: "This day you have become the
people [of the Lord your God]."[111] The Arab sage referred to us as the
"people of the Book."[112] Sages of other nations describe us as the
"people of the Spirit." Mistaken are those who believe that the concept
of nationality alone is sufficient for us. . . .

In the *Midrash Lamentations* it is written: "Should a person tell you
there is wisdom among the nations, believe it. [But if he tells you]
there is Torah among the nations, do not believe it."[113] Note the
Tiferet Yisrael[114] of our master the Maharal: The Torah has the capacity
to remove us from the natural world and elevate us to a status beyond
nature. If we consider ourselves to be the people of Torah and set our
ways in accordance with the spirit of Torah then we are elevated by
Torah beyond nature.[115] What is unattainable by natural means we
may achieve by the merit of Torah.

Without Torah, life does not exist for us, as in the parable of the
fish related by R. Akiva in Berakhot. . . .[116]

In the event, Heaven forbid, that we deviate from the path of
Torah, our claim [to Eretz Yisrael] will be forfeited. We will no
longer deserve it. When one who helps, falls, the helped one shall fall

---

109 Ex. 33:16.

110 Ex. 19:6.

111 Deut. 27:9.

112 *Ahl al-Kitaab.* Quran 3:64, etc.

113 LamR. 2:17.

114 (Prague 1598, Slawuta [Ukraine], 1793.) Philosophic treatise on the uniqueness
of Torah by R. Judah Loew ben Bezalel of Prague.

115 Paraphrase of *Tiferet Yisrael, op. cit.,* 4b–5b. ‏והאומה היחידה הוא על הטבע לכך ראוי‏
‏לישראל התורה שהיא על הטבע‏ "Because it is the only nation which exists beyond nature,
is Israel thereby privileged to receive the Torah which is beyond nature."

116 61b. As the fish cannot survive without being immersed in water, so the
people Israel cannot function without Torah.

as well.[117] We have witnessed the many obstacles[118] which you and all
of Israel have encountered in recent years since you have begun to
build the Land. How many innocent Jews have been killed in the
Holy Land at the hands of Arab extremists![119]

All this occurred because our claim of inheritance was not in complete
accord with the spirit of our holy Torah. This is not to suggest,
Heaven forbid, that your actions are in vain. However, together with
your *aliyah* to the Land you brought with you the influence of the
nations in which you dwelled while in exile, as it is written: "They
were mingled among the nations and learned their words."[120] It is
actually the spirit of an alien people which ferments among you,
causing you to stumble and falter.[121] Were it only "that My people
would listen to Me. . . .[122] I would soon subdue their enemies."[123]
Abandon the disposition of the peoples which you have brought with
you. Seek to follow the advice of the great sages of the Torah. Our
holy Torah is rich in knowledge. It is best able to resolve questions of
daily life and those in the political sphere. . . . As it is related in the
midrash to the Song of Songs, "The daughters of Jerusalem,"[124] "Do
not read this as 'the daughters of Jerusalem,'[125] rather, 'the builders of
Jerusalem,'[126] these are the Great Sanhedrin[127] who sit in session and
provide an interpretation[128] for every difficulty and case. . . ."[129] My

---

117 Variant of Isa. 31:3 ונפל עוזר, וכשל עוזר. I.e., without the support of Torah,
Israel cannot stand alone.

118 עקולא ופשורי "twisting bays and shallow waters" (AZ 34b).

119 Probable reference to the Arab hostilities of 1929 in Hebron, the Jewish
Quarter in Jerusalem, Beer Tuvia, Hulda, and the 1936–39 riots in many of the
Jewish settlements in Palestine.

120 Ps. 106:35 ויתערבו בגוים ולימדו מעשיהם.

121 Cf. I Sam. 25:31 לפוקה ולמכשול לב.

122 Ps. 81:14, 15.

123 Ibid. 15.

124 Song 1:5.

125 בנות ירושלים (*benot Yerushalayim*).

126 בונות ירושלים (*bonot Yerushalayim*).

127 The High Court in Jerusalem.

128 מבינים referring to בינה (*bina*). Thus בנות (*benot*) assumes the multiple meaning

brethren, my people are your people. I am as one with you. We are of one soul. [130] We both wish to see the success of our Holy Land and to exalt it. Therefore, listen to me. If you wish to succeed in your endeavors, submit to the sages, the great ones of the generation, who bear aloft the flag of Torah, do not be stubborn. You do not require them. . . . [131] Since "'not by might nor by power, but by My spirit' said the Lord of Hosts." [132] [However,] we do require you. As in the days of Solomon who selected among experts the craftsmen for each task, [133] so in our time, it is obvious that without skilled people we will be unable to build the Land. Yet you must understand that you will require the Torah sages, so that all is accomplished within the spirit of Torah. Then surely, your work will be sustained. A similar situation is recorded in Sanhedrin 49a. [134] If it were not for David who studied Torah, Joab the son of Zeruiah [135] would not have succeeded in war. But were it not for Joab who waged war, David could not have devoted himself to the study of Torah. [136]

May the merits of our holy Father encourage the Divine will to help you fulfill your tasks. May no enemy or evil force confront you. "No man shall stand up to you." [137] "May those engaged in iniquity be scattered." [138] Wherever we turn, may the purpose of the Lord prosper [139]

---

of building together with understanding and wisdom.

129   CantR. 1:37. Cf. ExR. 23:10.

130   Cf. II Kings 3:7.

131   Probable reference to the secular and specifically, the socialist ideologies of the *halutzim* settlers.

132   Zech. 4:6.

133   Reflecting the wealth and variety of craftsmanship depicted in I Kings 6, 7.

134   Cited as Sanh. 45 in the text. See below, 187.

135   King David's military commander. I Sam. 8:16.

136   דאמר רבי אבא בר כהנא: אלמלא דוד לא עשה יואב מלחמה, ואלמלא יואב לא עסק דוד בתורה. "Said R. Abba the son of R. Kahana: 'Were it not for David, Joab could not have engaged in war. And were it not for Joab, David could not have studied Torah.'"

137   Deut. 11:25.

138   Ps. 92:10. יתפרדו כל פועלי און.

139   Cf. Isa. 53:10.

in our hands. As a great blessing, the Land will bring forth its fruit.[140]
Likewise, we shall benefit much and receive great abundance from
Above. Thus the explanation of Rashi on the verse, "May your
abundance last you all your years:"[141] "The days in which you fulfill
the will of God, shall surely be plentiful. Silver and gold from all the
lands will flow[142] to Eretz Yisrael. [This is since] you will be blessed
abundantly with produce and thus sustain all the lands. In exchange
they will pour out to you all of their silver and gold."[143] We shall
deserve this only if the Land is rebuilt in the spirit of Torah, in
accordance with the advice of the great Torah sages. . . . Then the
former glory of Eretz Yisrael shall be restored, reflecting her "beautiful
landscape, the joy of the entire earth."[144] The Name of Heaven will
be glorified and sanctified by our acts leading up to the complete
redemption, the coming of the son of David, our righteous Messiah,
speedily in our own time, Amen. May God echo [this prayer]. Amen,
Amen.

We have now completed the Foreword of the volume. Praised be
the Lord, Creator of the universe.

---

140   Cf. Lev. 25:19.
141   Deut. 33:25. וכימיך דבאך.
142   The root דבא designates flowing and abundance.
143   Rashi on Deut. 33:25. See below, 297.
144   Ps. 48:3. יפה נוף משוש כל הארץ.

My volume is arranged into four chapters.

The First Chapter: The Chapter of Suffering and Messianic Pangs

The Second Chapter: The Chapter of Redemption and Deliverance

The Third Chapter: The Chapter of Settlement and Building

The Fourth Chapter: The Chapter of Unity and Peace

THE FIRST CHAPTER:
OF SUFFERING AND MESSIANIC
PANGS—ALSO ENTITLED:
THE TREATISE "MY BELOVED IS
CALLING"[1]

As is well-known, the belief in the advent of the righteous Messiah is basic to the offspring of Abraham, Isaac, and Jacob, the disciples of Moses our teacher; the servants of our master, King David. This belief is deeply imbedded in our hearts, among our adults and our children. Not all the storms, revolutions, and convulsions in the universe are able to move it, even slightly, from our hearts. "Though he lingers, we nevertheless wait for him"[2] every day that he may come, speedily in our time. Amen. "We do not fix a time nor seek evidence from Scripture for his coming."[3] This [phenomenon of the Messiah] belongs to the mysterious realm of events hidden from and closed to every living person. As Rabbi Shimon bar Yohai stated in *Midrash Kohelet Rabba*[4] "Should someone tell you when the time for redemption is coming,[5] do not believe him, for the heart has not even revealed it

---

1 Song 5:2.

2 The twelfth of thirteen Articles of Faith, *Commentary of Maimonides* on Mishnah Sanhedrin, 10th Chapter: אם יתמהמה, חכה לו "If he lingers, wait for him." See also Hab. 2:3.

3 Ibid. ולא ישים לו זמן, ולא יעשה לו סברות במקראות להוציא זמן ביאתו.

4 12:10. The text cites *Midrash Song of Songs*. See also MPs. 9:2.

5 The text: "When the Son of David is coming."

61

to the mouth." Maimonides elaborates upon this subject in his commentary on the Mishnah Sanhedrin, tenth chapter, [6] and, again in his magnificent sacred *Iggeret Teiman*.[7]

However, our prophets, as well as our sages of blessed memory, have predicted in the literature of the Talmud, the Midrash and Kabbalah,[8] the period of great suffering, persecutions and slaughter which will befall the Jewish people in the end of days prior to the advent of the Messiah. From these [demonstrations of suffering], one may already recognize the period in which the light of the Messiah glows, as it is related in our sacred texts: the hardships of exile will be felt only after the era of redemption has commenced. (See *Avodat Avodah* of R. Solomon Kluger of Brody on Avodah Zarah 9a, commenting with "Two thousand years will be the duration of the epoch of the Messiah.")[9] As Rashi interprets the verse (Isaiah 26:17): "Like a woman with child approaching childbirth writhing and screaming in her pangs, so are we become because of You, O Lord."[10] Rashi: We are witness to renewed suffering and believe these to be indications of redemption and salvation, since we are surely to be redeemed amidst sorrow and distress, like a woman in childbirth, due to Your decrees.[11]

We must endure these misfortunes with love, these difficult decrees and pogroms which have befallen us at this time. We must brave

---

6 Maimonides cites a variant of "Blasted be the bones of those who calculate the end" (Sanh. 97b) תיפח רוחן של מחשבי קיצין. *vs.* תיפח עצמן של מחשבי קיצין.

7 Iggeret Teiman, op. cit., 151. הרי ראשית מה שאתה צריך לדעת כי הקץ בדיוק לא יוכל שום אדם לדעת אותו בעולם, וגו׳ "First you should be aware that the exact time [of the advent of the Messiah] no one in the entire world can ever know, etc."

8 See *EHS* (Jerusalem, Pri Ha'Aretz, 1983), p. 63, nn. 4–7, for suggested citation.

9 *Avodat Avodah* (Zolkiew, 1865), 20b. R. Solomon Kluger (1795–1869), among the great scholars of his generation in Poland, renowned for his erudition in responsa literature ולפי״ז הנה ידוע דקישיי הגלות אין מתחיל רק אחר זמן צמיחת הגאולה וכמ״ש במצרים שהתחיל עיקר השעבוד משנולדה מרים ושנמנה להם לגואל. "Accordingly, as is known, the hardships of exile begin only after the era of redemption has commenced. So it was in Egypt. The actual bondage began with the birth of Miriam, who was reckoned by them [the people] as a redeemer."

10 כמו הרה תקריב ללדת תחיל תזעק בחבליה, כן היינו מפניך ד׳.

11 An extended paraphrase of Rashi, Isa. 26:17.

them with all of our strength, since they are as important to us as if they were a whole burnt offering. . . .[12] However, Malachi, the last of the prophets, forewarned what will occur to us in the end of days when we shall be entangled in suffering during the period of the pangs of the Messiah. There will be those who will exclaim: "It is useless to serve God. What have we gained by keeping His Torah? Those who have done evil have found favor in the eyes of God. It is indeed they whom the Lord prefers."[13] Where is the God of Justice? Yet these are precisely the words heard during these bitter times! But "those who revere the Lord and cling to Him talked to one another," not to adhere to their wicked deeds but to encourage and strengthen one another.[14] As it is written in Isaiah 8: "So I will wait for the Lord Who is hiding His face from the house of Jacob, and I will trust in Him."[15] Namely, though He hides His face from the house of Jacob, nevertheless he (Isaiah) will be patient and trust in Him. The Holy One, blessed be He, notes these words spoken by those who revere the Lord on the day of suffering. He records their words in a "scroll of remembrance." Then, with the coming of the day of retribution and redemption, the Lord will distinguish between those who clung to Him and those who abandoned Him.[16] It seems to me that it is in reference to these righteous who are inscribed in the scroll of remembrance that Daniel states: "And at that time your people shall be delivered, everyone that shall be found written in the book."[17] (I believe this interpretation is to be found in one of the commentaries on Daniel. As I prepare this manuscript for publication, I do not have any texts available to me and therefore cannot cite the exact source.[18])

---

12 כקרבן כליל ועולה "as a complete whole burnt offering" combines sacrificial components in Lev. 1:3–17 and Lev. 6:16.

13 A liberal paraphrasing of Mal. 3:14.

14 Paraphrase of Mal. 3:16.

15 Verse 17.

16 Conclusion of the Mal. 3:14–18 summary.

17 Dan. 12:1.

18 The author will make repeated references to his working from memory, reflecting the conditions under which he wrote. R. Saadia Gaon (882–942), R. Abraham Ibn Ezra (1089–1164) and R. David Altschuler (*Metzudat David*—18th century) in

Therefore, during these trying times every Jew must surely brace himself, that his feet not slip. . . . [19] It is worthwhile to bear the full brunt of the yoke of exile since this will reflect the magnitude of the reward which shall be granted to us by the Almighty when everyone shall be compensated in accordance with one's dealing with the Holy One, blessed be He.

However, it is indeed most extraordinary that the Lord should bring the Messiah by means of great suffering. Is it conceivable, Heaven forbid, that God is unable to redeem us without suffering? Surely the Messiah could come in the wake of good fortune from which we would benefit! [20]

The text *Netzah Yisrael* of our master the Maharal of Prague suggests a rationale for the suffering during the pangs of the Messiah: They represent the void prior to actuality. [21] According to the degree of void one may recognize the degree of actuality which will be provided for us by God, may He be blessed, during redemption. [22] I noted as well the yearning of the Gaon Yavetz in his Siddur: [23] "Greatness and success in most instances develop after a period of despair. The awesome fall must come first. One of the four principles of actuality and reality

---

their commentaries on Dan. 12:1 relate this verse to Mal. 3:16.

19   Cf. II Sam. 22:37 and Ps. 18:37 ולא מעדו קרסלי "And my feet have not slipped."

20   The author anticipates the second chapter devoted to themes of redemption, citing texts from the *Or HaHayyim* commentary, on Num. 24:17, Talmud Sanhedrin and Rashi (subsequently to be cited in chapter two) in which the *form* of redemption (adversity *vs.* prosperity) depends upon the worthiness of Israel. The text of Sanh. 98a: זכו עם ענני שמיא; לא זכו עני רוכב על חמור "If they are meritorious [he, the Messiah will come] with the clouds of heaven; if not, lowly and riding upon an ass."

21   Following the traditional definition of "negative" being the absence of "positive" in order to deny an independent reality to "evil." Genuine actuality according to this view must incorporate elements of redemption, since these flow directly from the Divine.

22   *Netzah Yisrael*, 44a כי כל הוי יוקדם לה העדר. . . כמו שיוקדם הלילה לפני היום יוקדם עוה"ז לפני עוה"ב, ולכך ראוי שיוקדם לפני זה העדר וחסרון, הוא הגלות. "Every actuality is preceded by void . . . as the night precedes the day, and as this world precedes the world to come, so it follows that this void and emptiness shall also come first. This is exile."

23   R. Yaakov Emden, *Siddur Tefillah* (Altona, 1745) 219b–220a. Great 18th-century scholar who led the anti-Sabbatian forces and opposed other deviant groups within the Jewish community.

is the prerequisite of the void." As our sages taught: [But in the case of a young bird] it develops [in the egg] after the period of deterioration.[24]

Such is the process of the deterioration of this wondrous chosen nation in exile, prior to settling into our destined possession and resting place. This last phase [of exile] is especially difficult but in direct and consistent proportion to that which will follow. It has been said, when they [the Jewish people] decline they sink into the dust and they rise,[25] as it is written: "He has levelled it with the dust,"[26] and it is further written: "For our soul is bowed down to the dust . . . Arise for our help [and redeem us for Your mercy's sake]."[27]

I have learned of another reason as to why the Holy One, blessed be He, brings upon us terrible suffering and persecutions prior to the advent of our Messiah, may he come speedily in our time. . . . This [I came across] in the text *Tzofnat Pa'aneah* of our Rabbi Yosef Gikatilla,[28] [a commentary] on the Haggadah of Passover relating to the passage, "Blessed is He who keeps His promise to Israel":

Indeed we must meticulously and accurately pursue the reason for the exile in Egypt. It is a profound mystery. However, God chose the offspring of Abraham. If he had did not immediately placed them in exile, it would have been impossible for them to receive the Torah. For if they had multiplied and prospered without going into exile, they

---

24 Temurah 31a. [The author brackets the citation within the Emden text.] The young bird is considered to be ritually clean since the process of putridity within the egg takes place prior to development of the young bird. Following nature, Israel's process of redemption is also preceded by a form of deterioration. This assures perfect and pure redemption.

25 Paraphrase of Meg. 16a אומה זו משולה לעפר ומשולה לכוכבים. כשהן יורדין, יורדין עד לכוכבים עד עולין, וכשהן עולין, עפר. "This nation is compared to dust and it is also compared to the stars. When they descend, they sink into dust. When they ascend they soar to the stars."

26 Isa. 26:5.

27 Ps. 44:26–27. The plea for redemption is interpreted as a prediction of the eventual reality.

28 1248–c. 1325; major Spanish kabbalist, author of many influential works on kabbalistic themes and symbols, the most significant being *Sha'arei Orah* (Mantua, 1561).

would have become rooted in their Land and would have become successful there, receiving the Torah from God. Now how could they have been compelled to [leave their Land] to enter the desert and have enforced upon them certain dietary, sexual and other restrictions to which they were not accustomed? Even now, having accepted the Torah, some among us have trouble fulfilling certain of its demands. All the more so in regard to the prohibitions of the 613 commandments, incumbent upon all future generations, is there a greater task for man with his temptations? God therefore exiled them to Egypt where they were enslaved. They were not permitted to leave. They were in servitude among the nations.[29] God then sent for Moses saying: "Inform the people Israel: either you accept the 613 commandments and then I will redeem you, otherwise remain where you are. . . ." Thus the exile of Egypt resulted in the receiving of the Torah—a good and glorious reward directed to us from Him, Who is blessed. . . .[31]

So too should be explained the suffering as a prelude to the coming of the Messiah. It is well-known that this final redemption will be eternal. No further exile and subjugation will follow. The Holy One, blessed be He, does not want to lose even one Jew to other nations, as it is written: "And you [children of Israel] shall be picked up one by one,"[32] and "neither will one be rejected and kept banished."[33] Now, should redemption take place in a setting of goodness, tranquility and calm among the nations, many of our Jewish brethren would never consider leaving. What would they lack here in exile? They are well-to-do, prominent, and fill important posts among the nations; such as the Rothschilds and Jewish barons who have achieved fame and have been elevated to positions of officialdom and aristocracy. What is their link to the Messiah and Eretz Yisrael? They have their own

---

29 Our text: "Servitude in Exile."

31 *Perush HaHaggadah, Zofnat Pa'aneah* (Venice, 1602), 8 (unpaginated).

32 Isa. 27:12.

33 Variant of II Sam. 14:14 לבלתי ידח ממנו נדח "So that no one may be kept banished." The pleas of the widow of Tekoah to King David (II Sam. 14) on behalf of the banished Absalom has since been transformed into the traditional expression of faith in Divine compassion. See below, 151, n. 119.

Messiah. Jerusalem is right here. They need not seek a better Messiah than the one they already have here [in exile].[34]

Blessed be the Lord. Come and see[35] how our subject is treated in the Midrash of our sages, of blessed memory, in [their interpretation of] the verse "Then he sent out the dove."[36] The dove is the symbol of Israel.[37] Like the dove who could not find a perch,[38] so Israel will not find rest in exile, as it is written: "Nor shall your foot find a place to rest."[39] Like the dove who returned to the ark, so is Israel destined to return to their Land from exile and from the yoke of the nations. These [nations] are compared to water, as it is written: "Ah, the roar of many peoples that roars like the sea (Is. 17). . . ."[40] The subject is also repeated in the *Midrash Lamentations* I,[41] on the verse "She lived among the nations, but found no rest."[42] "Rabbi Shimeon ben Lakish said:[43] Had she found rest, she would not have returned. . . . "[44] The *Torah Temimah*[45] comments [on Lamentations 1:3]: "This is its meaning: She lived contentedly among the nations, and would never have given any thought to return to Eretz Yisrael. However, she was frustrated, because 'she found no rest.'"

ALAS, THE CLEAR AND ACCURATE MEANING OF THIS CHERISHED TEACHING HAS BEEN SOUNDED THROUGHOUT THE AGES, EVEN TO THIS

---

34 The author again refers to the response of the Worms Jewish community during the period of Ezra's return to Jerusalem (*EHS*, 64). See below, 28–29, n. 77.

35 Cf. Gen. 24:31.

36 Gen. 8:8.

37 Several analogies in the Talmud and midrash include CantR. 1:63; Ber. 53 b.

38 Gen. 8:9.

39 Deut. 28:65.

40 Verse 12, continuing the dove (Israel) and sea (nations-exile) theme.

41 Paragraph 30.

42 Lam. 1:3.

43 Cited by R. Yudan.

44 The author cites a similar text from GenR. 33:8.

45 Popular commentary on the Pentateuch and Scrolls by talmudic scholar R. Baruch HaLevi Epstein. See above, p. 48, n. 70.

VERY DAY.[46]

The views of our sages of blessed memory are now on record. The mystery of exile and the hardships of the decrees which have constantly been our lot are designed to arouse us from our slumber in exile. This is the voice of our Beloved. This refers to the Holy One, blessed be He, who knocks[47] at the portal of our hearts, to stimulate within us a desire and longing to return to our Holy Land, neglected for almost two thousand years. We have instead compromised for a nominal and tenuous life of calm among the nations, thereby rejecting the glory of God and the splendor of our nation and Holy Land. We have sold the birthright of Israel for a portion of lentil stew of the nations.[48]

God, therefore, weeps, as it is explained in Hagigah,[49] because the glory of Israel was withdrawn from them and given to the nations. (I do not have before me the Talmud and am unable to cite the page or the text. I work without texts. . . .)[50]

. . . [Israel in exile, indifferent to its destiny] has become reality in our time. So many of our people have assimilated and been absorbed into

---

46 *Torah Temimah*, Lam. 1:3 (vol. V. following Deuteronomy), n. 62. The capitals appear in the *EHS* edition only, likely designed by our author for emphasis.

47 Cf. Song 5:2. Also CantR. 1:2 יבא דודי: זו השכינה "Let my beloved come" (Song 4:16): This refers to the Shekhinah."

48 A caustic reference to Gen. 25:29–34. Whereas Esau had exchanged his precious birthright for momentary physical satisfaction, it was now the descendants of Jacob who rejected their heritage for the delusion of tranquility among the nations.

49 Hag. 5b interprets Jer. 13:17 ["For if you will not give heed, my inmost self must weep," because of your arrogance מפני גאותן: אמר רב שמואל בר יצחק: מפני ׳מפני גוה׳י. של ישראל שניטלה מהם ונתנה לעובדי כוכבים. "What is the meaning of [the expression] 'Because of your arrogance'? R. Samuel ben Isaac said: For the glory [the positive meaning of *ga'avah*] that has been taken from them and given to the nations of the world." גוה (*geivah* = arrogance) is interpreted as the tragic loss of national glory and dignity over which the Almighty weeps, rather than the conventional Divine warning of retribution for the people's "arrogance."

50 Sources from the biblical, rabbinic and Hasidic literature are presented (*EHS*, 66–67) to reinforce the author's thesis that Israel has forsaken its own Land in the process of "making itself at home," in alien societies. Therefore, redemption is necessarily more painful, especially for the most deeply assimilated elements. It will be the hostile environment of the exile which will remind them, at times involuntarily, of their Jewish inheritance.

the society of nations. They no longer identify with their fellow Jews or consider themselves the children of the living God. Now there appears this evil one[51] and issues the decree of racial laws.[52] The intensive search for the source of their ancestry spanned as many as three generations until they exposed their identity as offspring of Abraham, Isaac and Jacob.

Thus was realized the revelation of the prophet: ". . . and instead of being told, 'You are not My people,' they shall be called 'Children of the Living God'!"[53] Namely, they had descended to such a level that everyone thought of them as "You are not My people." Therefore, the Holy One, blessed be He, in His goodness saw to it that "they shall be called 'Children of the Living God'!"[54] The prophet had these [thoroughly assimilated Jews] in mind [when he declared]: "and you shall be picked up one by one [O Children of Israel]."[55] Similarly, our rabbi from Apt[56] taught: Even relentless villains will be sifted and

---

51 Adolf Hitler.

52 Reference to the restrictive anti-Jewish Nuremberg Laws (adopted at the National Socialist Convention in Nuremberg, September 15, 1935) specifically the "Law for the Protection of the German Blood and of the German Honor," and the subsequent regulation to the Reich Citizenship Law of November 14, 1935, which defined "who is a Jew." Hungary adopted a similar, though less extreme "Definition of a Jew" bill on May 4, 1939, under the proto-Fascist regime of Count Pal Teleki, a devout Catholic, and a nationalist-chauvinist. On August 2, 1941 a more extreme "Definition of a Jew" bill was made, modeled after the Nuremberg Law, under the premiership of Laszlo Bardossy, who continued and intensified his predecessor's anti-Jewish policies. With the occupation of Bohemia and Moravia by the Nazis on March 15, 1939, anti-Jewish legislation, including racial definitions according to the Nuremberg Laws, was applied. For a detailed analysis of the complexities of the laws, see R. Hilberg, *The Destruction of the European Jews* (Chicago, 1967), 43–53. R.E. Braham, *The Policies of Genocide: The Holocaust in Hungary*, vol. 1 (New York, 1981), 147–56, 194–99.

53 Hos. 2:1. See also Hos. 1:9.

54 The author views the forced reemergence of the Jewish soul, saved from the depths of assimilation as a miraculous, beneficial phenomenon. Though the newly "discovered" Jew is now clearly in physical danger, it is much preferred to the certain spiritual annihilation.

55 Isa. 27:12. To redeem this type of Jew is the most difficult task of all, requiring that these "shall be picked up one by one."

56 R. Abraham Yeshoshua Heshel of Apt (1755–1825), disciple of R. Elimelekh of Lizhensk, was a renowned Hasidic leader known as the *Ohev Yisrael*, "Lover of

removed from the depths of the *kelipot* by the Holy One, blessed be He,[57] "neither will one be rejected and kept banished."[58]

I also looked at the text *Malbushei Yom Tov* of the holy Zidachover[59] who cites R. Menahem Mendel of Rimanov.[60] Accordingly, the second son in the Haggadah [of Passover] i.e. the evil son, will also benefit from the *tikkun* [restoration] of the final redemption. Due to his love for Israel this holy person refused to refer to him as a villain [*rasha*], but rather "the second son." Note to what extent one should love a fellow Jew. Not even a relentless villain, such as the second son in the Haggadah, was to be referred to as a "villain." (This should be an example for all those who tend to apply to others the expression *rasha*.). . . I further noted in the *Bnei Yessaschar*[61] in [the portion of] the seven [weeks of] consolation,[62] in the name of the kabbalists, that during the final redemption even the unrepenting villains will benefit from *tikkun* and they will all be redeemed.[63]

Israel," for his emphasis on *Ahavat Yisrael*, the title of his volume of commentary on the weekly portion and festival texts.

57   *Ohev Yisrael* (Zhitomir, 1863), 92b. The Rabbi of Apt interprets *MPs.* 107:4. כשם שהזוהבי הזה פושט את ידו ונוטל הזהב מן הכור, כך הקב״ה הוציא את ישראל מיד מצרים מכור הברזל. "Just as the goldsmith reaches out in order to remove the gold from the furnace, so the Holy One, blessed be He, removed the Israelites from Egypt, the iron furnace." The villains of Israel are part of the bedrock of exile and have to be excavated forcibly from the alien and impure environment.

58   Variant of II Sam. 14:14.

59   R. Yissakhar Dov of Zhidachov (d. 1923) grandson and disciple of R. Isaac, founder of the Zhidachov dynasty. *Malbushei Shabbat VeYom Tov* (Munkatch, 1927) is a collection of Hasidic commentary on the weekly portion.

60   Major Hasidic leader (d. 1815), disciple of R. Shmelke of Nikolsburg and R. Elimelekh of Lizhensk. The commentary on the "Four Sons" and the selection cited is on p. 51b.

61   R. Zvi Elimelekh of Dinov (d. 1841) was the author of the popular volume of hasidic *Torot* (Discourses), *Bnei Yessaskhar* (Zalkowa, 1846), organized according to the Jewish calendar and festivals. See also below, 263, n. 889.

62   The seven weeks following *Tishah B'Av* during which consolation passages are read on each successive Sabbath from Isa. 40, 49, 54, 51, 54, 60 and 61.

63   *Bnei Yessaskhar* (Zolkiew, 1850), 64b . . . נחמו נחמו עמי וגו' נחמו נחמו בגי' יצחק שאמרו רז״ל אשר ב״ב תהי' הגאולה ע״י מליצת יצחק . . . כי שם ג״ק כנגד ד' בנים דברה תורה, ד' פעמים ב״ן בגימ' יצחק, שאפי' הבן הרשע שורשו בקודש ועתיד להיכלל בקודש "'Comfort, O comfort My people, etc.' *Nahamu, nahamu* is equal to יצחק [Isaac] in gematria . . . since our rabbis of blessed memory said the redemption will come speedily in our own time by means

I also found a passage in *Pesikta Rabbati* on the verse:

"Arise, shine":[64] Said the Holy One, blessed be He, to the Messiah: Due to the sins of these [the wicked], your tongue will eventually [cleave to your palate.][65] [Do you wish it thus?] He replied: Master of the universe, with the joy of my soul and the happiness of my heart I shall assume them (namely, to assume all the suffering to which the Holy One referred[66]), so that not even one Jew will be lost.[67] Furthermore, on the verse: "Rejoice greatly,"[68] the Messiah declares that even "those who mocked him" and did not believe in his coming, will be forgiven so that they not perish. . . .[69]

I further discovered a passage in the volume *Netiv Mitzvotecha* of our rabbi the kabbalist R. Isaac of Komarno[70] ("The Path of Faith," the sixth column, the letter Yod),[71] where he relates from the *Sefer HaHezyonot* of Rabbi Hayyim Vital[72] [the following]:

---

of the idiom 'Isaac'. . . . There as well the Torah made reference to the Four Sons, since four multiplied by ם [ben = 52] adds up to יצחק [Isaac] by means of gematria. Even the evil son is rooted in holiness and will eventually be included in holiness."

The numerical equivalent (gematria) of נחמו נחמו (*nahamu, nahamu*) (Isa. 40:1) [2 x 104] [208] and 4 x ם [4 x 52] imply the prophecy of the redemption because of the merit of Isaac. All segments of the Jewish community represented by the four sons, including the villain are rooted in sanctity and worthy of redemption.

64 Isa. 60:1.

65 Cf. Ps. 137:6.

66 The phrase in the brackets is the author's insert into the midrash text.

67 *Pesikta Rabati*, "*Kumi Ori*," chapter 36, Meir Ish Shalom ed., (Tel Aviv, 1963), 161b.

68 Zech. 9:9. גילי מאד (*gili me'od*) vs. גילו מאד (*gilu me'od*) in our text.

69 *Pesikta Rabati*, Gili Me'od, chapter 34, *op. cit.*, 159b. זה (זכ׳ ט:ט) צדיק ונושע הוא׳ משיח שמצדיק דינו על ישראל כשיושב עליו כששחקו עליו כשיושב בבית האסורים . . . אלא שמצדיק עליהם את הדין ואומר להם כולכם בני הלא אתם. "'He is just and victorious' (Zech. 9:9) This refers to the Messiah who defends the Jewish people when they [the wicked Jews] mocked him when he sits in prison . . . indeed he defends them declaring to them 'you are all my children.'" The author expands on the readiness of the Messiah to take upon himself suffering in order to prevent the loss of even one Jewish soul. *EHS*, 78.

70 R. Isaac Judah Jechiel (Yitzhak Isaac) Safrin, 1806–1874. Founder of the Komarno Hasidic branch of the Zhidachov dynasty and authority in kabbalah.

71 *Netiv Mitzvotecha* (Premishlan, 1884), 22.

72 *Shivhe R. Hayyim Vital (Sefer HaHezyonot)* (Lemberg, 1862), 21–22. The version

"He [R. Hayyim Vital] asked his master the Ari[73] of blessed memory, how was it possible for him [the Ari] to refer to him [R. Hayyim Vital] as a very exalted soul? Why the least significant of the earlier generations would be surely [in the category] of a *tzadik* and *hasid*. He could never measure up to one of those. To this the Ari replied: You should know that the greatness of one's soul is not in accordance with the acts of a person as it appears to others. Rather [the quality of the soul] is determined by He who searches the innermost heart, the Almighty, in accordance with the times and the particular generation. One's smallest act in this generation is equivalent to a number of mitzvot in former generations, since the *kelipot* and evil in our times have grown infinitely stronger. . . . Now if in the times of the Ari the *kelipot* became so intense, what shall we say of our own bitter age? Clearly we should embrace anyone who is called Jewish! He should be the object of our love and concern. After all, his actions must be seen in the face of evil temptations and suffering. I swear to you by eternal life, that the *reshaim* in this country, and especially in the Germanic countries, no longer have their free will. They have acted under compulsion as would a captive child in the hands of gentiles. They do not speak with knowledge.[74] Yet they all would at any given moment be prepared to spill their blood freely for the sanctification of the great Name. They would do so with love, joy and dance. (These are his sacred words.)[75]

This is the truth. He would, within his limited grasp of Judaism, indeed be prepared to sacrifice his soul. Were he to grasp more [of the meaning of Judaism] his acts of martyrdom would be greater yet. Note, therefore, my brethren, the clear stipulation of this sacred, divine person,[76] who directed us to embrace anyone identified as a

---

in our text is a free paraphrase of R. Isaac Judah Jechiel of Komarno. R. Hayyim Vital (1543–1620); disciple of R. Isaac Luria (1534–1572) and chief exponent of Lurianic kabbalah in Safed.

73   Acronym for Ashkenazi R. Isaac Luria.

74   Cf. Job 34:35 לא בדעת ידבר. "[Job] does not speak with knowledge."

75   R. Isaac Judah Jechiel Safrin of Komarno, *Netiv Mitzvotecha*, 22. A phenomenal display of recall if this passage, almost identical to the original, was recorded from memory.

76   R. Isaac Judah Jechiel Safrin of Komarno.

Jew and who consequently suffers with the [Jewish] masses. It is a mitzvah to give them credit and to encourage them with love. Study his words carefully for he was known for his Divine inspiration. . . .[77]

> Certainly this generation is beloved by God. They will be drawn near during the redemption. We are not permitted to reject them. On the contrary, because of all the suffering which we have encountered in exile in recent times from which the sinners of Israel were not exempt, because they too suffered in the name of Israel, since they now recognize the falsehood which founders of Reform have long ago bequested to them; since they would gladly return to us with all their hearts; since they have lost their way and have become estranged from us; [for all these] it is incumbent upon us to extend our hands to them and draw them close to us with brotherly love.[78]

Rabbi Yissakhar Dov of Belz[79] the divine and holy person of blessed and sacred memory, may his merits protect us, expressed himself in a similar fashion. This occurred in the year 5674[80] at the outbreak of World War I. He escaped from his prominent residence to the city of Ratzfert[81] in the country of Hagar.[82] During that period I still lived in the holy community of Bosermin[83] near Ratzfert. For almost his entire

---

77 The returning exiles in the period of Ezra, those who were idol worshippers were given a reprieve since the environment in which they developed shaped their habits. *EHS*, 69.

78 The author proceeds to extol the value of *teshuvah* [repentance, *lit*, return] in anticipation of, and following redemption. The *Midrash*, Rashi, and Maimonides and R. Eliyahu (author of *Shevet Musar*), are cited to demonstrate the efficacy of *teshuvah* for all Jews, including the unrepenting *rasha* [wicked person].

79 The third in succession of the important Hasidic dynasty of Belz in Galicia (1854–1927) and grandson of its founder R. Shalom Rokeah (1779–1855). During his Hungarian sojourn (1914–1921) he attracted many new devotees to the Hasidism of Belz. This may have served as the source of conflict between R. Yissakhar Dov and R. Hayyim Eleazar Shapira (1872–1937), grandson of the founder of Munkatch dynasty of hasidism. (R. Yissakhar Dov lived in Munkatch from 1891–1921.)

80 1914.

81 Ujfeherto, app. 20 km northeast of Hajdubözöreny.

82 באַרץ הגר (*Be'Eretz Hagar*) i.e., Hungary or Magyar region.

83 Hajduböszöreny in northeast Hungary.

stay I found refuge under his wings[84] and drew close to him and to his family, visiting freely. . . . From every part of the country they came to welcome him. The leading sages of the time, distinguished statesmen and great men of God visited with him. Principal among them was the holy patriarch R. Moshe David Teitelbaum, descendent of the prominent dynasty, grandson. . . .[85] and outstanding disciple of the author of *Yitav Lev*. He was a magnificent orator and preacher. He presented the following plea before our rabbi of Belz:

> The Jewish people in almost every part of the globe are in a state of distress. They suffer time and again. The only remedy is for the entire community of Israel to awaken and repent. It would be appropriate that such a penitent movement be led by a *tzadik* of his generation, such as himself [R. Yissakhar Dov]. Should he indeed agree to lead such a revival movement, he would thereby surely influence this generation to return to the Father in Heaven. In this fashion they would achieve the redemption for which the entire community of Israel has waited for so long and with so many difficulties. He pleaded with him for almost an hour, punctuating his remarks with persuasive arguments. Only he [R. Yissakhar Dov] could undertake such a responsibility. When he concluded his remarks, our Rabbi responded briefly and to the point as follows: "HAS THE LAPOSHER RABBI NOW CONCLUDED HIS ARGUMENTS THAT WHEN THE MESSIAH WILL COME, JEWS WILL REPENT IN ANY CASE? THE MAJOR TASK IS NOW FOR JEWS TO LOVE ONE ANOTHER. ONE MUST LOVE EVEN THE MOST INCORRIGIBLE JEW AS ONE WOULD HIMSELF. HEARTS MUST BE UNITED. EVERY DIVISIVE CAUSE MUST BE REMOVED FROM OUR HEARTS. THE REDEMPTION OF ISRAEL IN TIMES OF MISERY IS DEPENDENT ON THIS ALONE."[86]

---

84   Ps. 91:4 באברתו יסך לך "He will cover you with His wings."

85   Grandson of R. Yekuthiel Judah of Sighet (1808–1883), the author of *Yitav Lev* (1875); an important link in the Teitelbaum dynasty of the Hasidim of Galicia and Hungary.

86   The small capital letters are the author's. The quote appears as a mixture of Yiddish and Hebrew. The plea for *ahavat Yisrael* (love of Israel) may also have been in response to the emerging strife among certain hasidic dynasties cited above. At the same time the author cites the teaching of R. Yaakov Yitzhak, the "Seer of Lublin," who pleads with God to perform a miracle on behalf of Israel in times of distress

These were his sacred words which emanated from his innermost heart. . . . Note Rashi on the verse: "He thought: Surely they are My people, children who will not play false. So He was their Redeemer." (Is. 63:8) This is Rashi's commentary:

"'Surely they are My people." Though it is clear to me that they will betray Me, nevertheless they are My people. They are to me as "Children who will not play false." See also Rashi on the verse "The people took to complaining":[87] *The* people [*Ha'am*] implies "the wicked;" when they are worthy they are referred to as "*My* people". . . . Consequently it is a mitzvah to love them and to draw them near with affection. In this manner we shall achieve redemption. Therefore, the verse concludes: "So He was their Redeemer."[88]

This supports the statement of our Rebbe of Belz. . . .[89]

Nevertheless, we must ask the following: Have not we, in our generation, been witness to all these phenomena in great quantity? Furthermore, we are in the era of the End of Days, at the close of the sixth millenium.[90] We do not as yet sense a spirit of purity from the beyond with which we are to be inundated by the Almighty. Despite the intense suffering of recent days which has softened the heart of

---

which would unite the Jewish people as in the days of Purim. *EHS*, 73.

87 Num. 11:1. Rashi distinguishes between the impersonal העם (the people) and עמי (My people).

88 Isa. 63:8.

89 In a prodigious display of scholarship, our author presents numerous sources in support of the rabbinic values of mutual trust; finding merit in the behavior of others; and the drawing near to Judaism of recalcitrants with love and affection. It is the task of Satan to accuse the Jewish people. It is implied that those who find fault with other Jews are in league with Satan. (*EHS*, 73–74). The involved treatise endeavors to reconcile an opinion of Maimonides which ostensibly contradicts the statement of the Rebbe of Belz. (Is repentance a prerequisite for the Messiah or a consequence of redemption?) (*EHS*, 74–75).

90 Much of messianic speculation revolves around millenarian chronology (Ps. 90:4). Expectations intensified during the sixth millennium in anticipation of the millennial Shabbat and the final redemption. See Sanh. 97a; AZ 9a. תנא דבי אליהו: שֵׁשֶׁת. אלפים שנה הוי עלמא, שני אלפים תוהו, שני אלפים ימות המשיח, ובעונותינו שרבו יצאו מהם שיצאו. "The *Tanna DeBei Eliyahu* teaches: The world is to exist six thousand years. In the first two thousand there was barrenness; two thousand years the Torah flourished; and the next two thousand years is the Messianic era, but because of our many inequities, years [of the sixth millenium] have already passed"

every Jew, Elijah, who is to arouse us to repentance, for which we are surely prepared, has not come.

The answer is to be found in our sacred Torah, in the portion of *Nitzavim*.[91] "And the Lord your God will bring you to the Land which your fathers inherited and you shall occupy it . . . Then the Lord your God will open up[92] your heart and the hearts of your offspring to love the Lord your God with all your heart and soul, in order that you may live."[93] Note the *Or HaHayyim* commentary: "After he opened his heart to love the Lord with all his heart and soul, you will not find a superior form of repentance."[94] Now the verse first specifies our entry into the Land and its occupation as our inheritance from our forefathers. Following this, the Lord will open our hearts and project upon us a spirit of purity from above, which in turn will direct our hearts to Him. However, this is impossible as long as we are in an alien land. The spirit of purity would then necessarily be prevented from reaching us. All of us have before us the holy task to strive to come back to our Holy Land by means of His agents and the causes which have been designed [for this purpose] by the Cause of all Causes. . . .[95]

It is explained in the words of the prophet Ezekiel (chapter 36):

I will take you from among the nations and gather you from all the countries, and I will bring you back to your own land. I will sprinkle pure water upon you, and you shall be pure. [I will cleanse you] from all your uncleanness. . . . And I will give you a new heart and put a new spirit into you: I will remove the heart of stone from your body and give you a heart of flesh; and I will put My spirit into you. Thus I will cause you to follow My laws and faithfully to observe My rules. Then you shall dwell in the Land which I gave to your fathers, and you shall

---

91   Deut. 29:9–30:20.

92   In the sense of release, to free, to allow the heart to be sensitive and appreciate.

93   Ibid. 30:5–6.

94   *Or HaHayyim*, Deut. 30:6.

95   The Divine Spirit will inspire repentence only in Eretz Yisrael interpreting Maimonides in *Hilkhot Teshuvah* 7:5 and in Sanh. 1:3.

be My people and I will be your God.[96]

Hence this explicit text in Scripture indicates that only following our return to the Land of our fathers shall we be worthy and will God open our hearts so that we may live and serve Him with our entire heart and soul. . . .[97]

I have now seen the holy *Or HaHayyim* commentary on the portion of *Tzav*[98] which is strikingly identical to the teaching of our rabbi the Hatam Sofer. It refers to the verse: "And he shall remove his garments and clothe himself in other garments; and carry [the ashes] outside [the camp to a clean place]."[99] The first garments[100] represent the justice which will be meted out to those who have caused us harm. And now He will confer benefits and take us out from exile. Doing so, He will clothe [us with] garments representing goodness. He will not delay the ingathering of the exiles until such time when the doors of evil will be destroyed. Rather He will gather the dispersed here and now. He will remove us from the camp of evil people to the purity of Eretz Yisrael. . . .[101] The Holy One, blessed be He, will be compelled to hasten our removal from these evildoers prior to their destruction, the eventual final redemption and the coming of the redeemer.

Hence such prescient persons as our rabbis the *Or HaHayyim* and the Hatam Sofer predict in identical fashion that with God's marvelous concern, and following much suffering we will be brought to Eretz

---

96 Ez. 36:24–28.

97 Our author (*EHS*, 77) presently cites the Hatam Sofer (*Derashot Parah*, 5562 [1802], *op. cit.*, vol. 1, 208b [416]) as further evidence that Eretz Yisrael will be returned to the Jewish people by way of suffering, prior and conditional to final redemption. Ez. 36:35–36, Zech. 2:8 and Ber. 5a are presented by the Hatam Sofer as supportive sources.

98 Lev. 6–8.

99 Lev. 6:4

100 Which are to be removed. The passage Lev. 6:1–6 is interpreted within the context of Israel's long suffering exile ("all night") and the ultimate redemption ("until morning"). Israel has made the ultimate burnt sacrifice on the "fire (Torah) of the altar."

101 *Or HaHayyim, op. cit.*, part 2, 9b.

Yisrael. It is clear and obvious that these prophecies refer to our own generation. . . .[102]

We may now return to my original point. All of these plagues with which we are inflicted are for the sole purpose of stimulating us to return to our Holy Land. In this respect, I heard a beautiful interpretation in the name of our teacher, a man of God, the scholarly and holy R. Bunim of Pshyshkha[103] on the verse: "Draw me, we will run after you."[104]

He explained it thus: An animal may be acquired by two kinds of *meshikha*.[105] One possibility: if he [the prospective owner] calls her and it follows after him.[106] The second: he strikes it with a stick and it runs before him. With either of the two he acquires it by means of *meshikha*. Which of the two does the animal prefer? Certainly *meshikha* by means of calling [is preferred], where the animal does not suffer. . . . So it is with us and the Holy One, blessed be He, with regard to our being called to return to Eretz Yisrael. If we heed to the voice which calls in the name of the Holy One for our return to Eretz Yisrael, then it will resemble the *meshikha* of it [the animal] being called and following [the owner]. We would not suffer. We would go of our own free will without any outside compulsion. God would lead us and we would follow. . . . This would not be the case if we disregard the call to return to our Land of our own accord. . . .

---

102   The *Or HaHayyim* and JT *Sukkot* are cited to demonstrate the extreme severity of the ultimate exile in comparison to the exile in Egypt. The author in Budapest echoes the 18th century Hayyim ben Moshe Attar in Morocco: "Happy is he who was not compelled to see the bitterness and subjugation of Israel." (*EHS*, 78)

103   1775–1827, leading disciple of and successor to R. Yaakov Yitzhak of Pshyshkha (Przysucha), the founder of the Pshyshkha hasidic dynasty and teacher of R. Menahem Mendel of Kotzk, R. Yitzhak of Vorki, R. Hanoch of Alexander and R. Yitzhak Meir of Gur.

104   Song 1:4. The editor was unable to trace the *drush* [homiletic commentary] among the writings attributed to R. Simha Bunim, *Kol Simha* (Breslau, 1859).

105   *Lit.* "pulling," one of the modes of taking legal possession, by drawing the object towards oneself. The present discourse refers to BB 75b and Kid. 22b where the two variants of *meshikha* are described.

106   Our text reads: "He calls her and she follows." קורא אותה והיא הולכת אחריו. The Talmud text reads: קורא לה והיא באה "He calls her and she comes."

Therefore, we request of God: "Draw me, and we shall run after you," that is to say, acquire us by means of the *meshikha* [107] which calls us and we follow. The call comes from You alone through the righteous of each generation. Hence, we would not be acquired with the *meshikha* of the stick, which would have compelled us to run before Him, and He would follow. . . . [108] The events in our time have shown that everyone now wishes to run to Eretz Yisrael, if they would only be permitted to do so "even those who were always opposed to the *aliyah* movement. This type of departure however, is like that of being struck with a stick. "It runs before him." [109] Had they heeded the call of the *tzadikim* they would be drawn after them in the spirit of "Draw me and we shall run after You. . . ." [110]

There is [a lesson] in the *Tikkunei Zohar Hadash* appended to the *Zohar Hadash* (80b) [111] on the verse: "I the Lord will speed it in due time." [112] It has been established: "If they are worthy, I will speed it; if not, [the Messiah will come] in due time. [113] One ought to know what is meant by the 'time' of 'the Lord'." [114] [After all] there is a *time* and there *is* a time. [115] This is the hidden meaning of *Kohelet*: "A time to weep and a time to laugh." [116] As soon as it is time for weeping,

---

107 משכני (*moshkheni*) and משיכה (*meshikha*) derive from the same root. (משך, draw, pull).

108 Contrary to the pattern in Song 1:4.

109 BB 75b and Kid. 22b.

110 Our author supplements sources from the Midrash of Psalms and *Kapot Temarim* on *Rosh HaShanah*, which relate the suffering of Israel to its neglect of Eretz Yisrael. (The author actually refers to *Yom Teruah* on RH 30a by R. Moshe ben Shlomo Ibn Habib (c. 1654–1696), who is also the author of a commentary on *Sukkot, Kapot Temarim*. Our author's reference is cited in *Yom Teruah* (Karlsruhe, 1766), 11a. EHS, 79–80.

111 The passage was located in the Brody (1876) edition, 172b–73a (344–45). The text of our author is a variant of the Brody version.

112 Isa. 60:22.

113 Sanh. 98.

114 Likely, in the time designated by God. בעתה (*be'itah*) in Isa. 60:22 is subdivided to produce בעת ה' "In the time set by the Lord."

115 The ambiguity of "in due time" is now addressed by the Zohar.

116 Eccl. 3:4.

because Israel is oppressed, the time for our redemption will be at hand. This is why it is written: "It is a time of trouble for Jacob, but he shall be delivered from it."[117]

. . . And when Moses saw the oppression and poverty of Israel it was written: "and behold a boy was crying."[118] Yet what does the verse indicate immediately following the crying? "She took pity on him."[119] This is redemption. . . .

There is no doubt that we have drawn near to these very times. One may hear the voices of weeping in the corners of Jewish homes which are filled with great horror, may God have mercy. This holds true even more so for our fellow Jews in Poland, Slovakia, and the other European countries. The destruction, the murders, the massacres, the cruelties, [directed against] infants and the aged, the annihilation of great communities once filled with scholars, authors and pious schoolchildren who were flowering amidst the study of Torah—this is known to all. When the destruction ceased they were expelled to a distant country, without clothes and bereft of all their belongings. "O my heart, my heart [grieves] for those who were slain."

"O my suffering, my suffering for those who were slain."[120] Has there ever been a time when the need to weep is greater than now? [121] Also in accordance with the words of the Zohar whereby weeping

---

117 Jer. 30:7.

118 Ex. 2:6.

119 Ibid. The Zohar identifies "she took pity" with the Shekhinah and the attribute of Mercy. Further, suffering foreshadows weeping which is "prayer in the truest sense" effecting a change in the Divine attribute of Judgment (din). Zohar, II, 19b–20a. אמר רבי יהודה:הלכך גדולה צעקה צעקה מכולן שצעקה היא בלב . . . צעקה וזעקה דבר אחד הוא וזה קרובה להקב"ה יובר מתפילה ואנחה . . . האי צלותא שלימתא דהיא בלבא ולעולם לא הדרא ריקנא. . . . רבי יצחק אמר: גדולה צעקה, שמושלת על מדת הדין של מעלה. "R. Yehudah said: 'Crying is superior to all [supplications], since it emerges from the heart . . . crying and outcry are one and the same. It means more to the Holy One, blessed be He, than prayer and sighing. . . . The complete prayer which emerges from the heart will never be rejected. . . .' R. Yitzhak said: 'Superior is the outcry which controls Divine Justice.'"

120 From the Nahem prayer of the afternoon service for the Ninth of Av. Jer. 4:19. The new JPS translation of מעי "my suffering" is preferred over "bowels" or "entrails."

121 If weeping indeed can bring about a change in the Divine plan, then now is "a time to weep."

reflects a state of oppression and poverty, then this too has been realized in our time. The assets of Jews have disappeared. Woe to those who witnessed the plundering of Jewish possessions in the streets of Slovakia.[122] Even the clothing and household articles of Jews were taken. A regulation was enforced whereby a gentile coming upon a possession of a Jew could acquire it upon request. Thus the Jew was stripped bare, and the following verse could have applied to us: "'For the oppression of the poor for the sighing of the needy, now will I arise,' said the Lord,"[123] has materialized in our own day. The Jews were left destitute. We had hardly time to absorb [the plunder of our movable possessions] when the evil rats took our homes and fields while we were still living there. Then they robbed us of our very lives. We were expelled, not to a place of our choosing but rather to a distant land to die by starvation.[124] What I have described here is but a drop in the ocean of undeserved cruelty directed at us because we are the offspring of Abraham, Isaac and Jacob. . . . Our poverty and oppression is of the kind described by the prophet Zephaniah: "But I will leave amongst you a poor and distressed people and they shall find refuge in the name of the Lord."[125] Similarly the verse in II Samuel 22 [is appropriate]: "The poor people you shall redeem."[126] As

---

122 From the time of President Benes' resignation on October 5, 1938, and the subsequent establishment of an autonomous Slovakia as a satellite of Nazi Berlin (March 14, 1939), the economic state of Slovakian Jewry deteriorated radically. A detailed accounting of expropriations, dispossessions, plunder and the loss of all economic independence of the Jewish community prior to the final destruction (1940–1941) is presented in Livia Rotkirchen, *The Destruction of Slovak Jewry* (Jerusalem, 1961), 9–19 (Hebrew), XI–XIX (English). The misfortunes of Slovakian Jewry were compounded by the pro-Nazi President Dr. Josef Tiso, a Catholic priest, and his energetic Minister of Interior Sano Mach, who also commanded the notorious Hlinka Guard, the Slovak equivalent of the SS. See also Raul Hilberg, *The Destruction of the European Jews* (Chicago, 1967), 458–73; Gerald Reutlinger, *The Final Solution* (London, 1968), 415–25.

123 Ps. 12:6. The verse is reversed in this text.

124 For details of deportation procedures see Rothkirchen, *op. cit.*, XXII–XXVI (English), 21–43; 57–217.

125 Zeph. 3:12.

126 II Sam. 22: 28.

it is written in the Zohar, *Beha'alotkha*[127] 153a,[128] concerning "the final exile" which will take place in poverty,[129] he meant to say: As it is written "But I will leave among you a poor people, etc."[130] and in order to fulfill the verse: "The poor people you shall redeem."[131] The wealthy will refuse to be charitable, claiming that their tax burden is already too heavy. They lie, having hid their wealth within their homes. . . .[132] [However] those who have been compassionate and virtuous will not have to undergo a difficult process of refinement (during the period of the pangs of the Messiah)[133] and would not be purified by means of lukewarm water, such as the ordinary [*benoni*] person, and certainly not by means of hot water, by which the *reshaim* [evil doers] will be purified.[134] Concerning them [the *reshaim*] it is written: "Everything that can tolerate fire, shall be made to go through fire [and it shall be clean]."[135] So indeed is the current situation. There are numerous

---

127   Corresponding to Num. 8–12.

128   Cited as 157a.

129   The Zohar text: ובגלותא בתראה לית מיתה אלא עוני "During the final exile there will be no death, only poverty."

130   Zeph. 3:12.

131   II Sam. 22:28. Signaling the beginning of the final exile which will take place in conditions of poverty.

132   The selfish wealthy in times of need do not fulfil the second half of Zeph. 3:12 "and they shall find refuge in the name of the Lord."

133   Brackets inserted by the author into the the freely rendered Zohar text.

134   The Zohar transposes the Passover ritual cleansing requirements for utensils which have absorbed various degrees of leavened matter (*hametz*) (Pes. 30) to the ethical and psychological realm of people. During the messianic period they too will be cleansed by various degrees of suffering in keeping with the ethical standards of each person. Leaven and unleavened matter symbolize the opposing evil and positive inclinations. Zohar, II, 40b. וישא העם את בצקו טרם יחמץ [שמות יב:לד] וכתיב: שאר לא ימצא בבתיכם [שם, שם:יט] אוקימנא בין חמץ ומצה בכמה דוכתי דא יצר רע ודא יצר טוב. "'So the people took their dough before it was leavened' [Ex. 12:34]. It is also written: 'No leaven shall be found in your houses' [Ex. 12:19]. . . . In a number of places distinction between leavened and unleavened bread is identified as the [distinction between] evil and good inclination [in human beings]."

135   Num. 31:23. The spoils of war, especially the wealth enumerated in verse 22, is transposed by the Zohar to the *rasha* who is devoted to the accumulation of the spoils of life at the expense of others. They will have to suffer the most difficult of refinement processes in order to be cleansed.

wealthy [among us] who were in a position to help revive unfortunate souls among our brethren. They did nothing. Eventually they lost their wealth at the hands of Esau the evil one, as it happened in Slovakia. For them the words of the Zohar were realized. "Everything that can tolerate fire shall be made to go through the fire," the fire of exile.[136]

[On the other hand] let us acknowledge our gratitude to our Jewish brethren in America. Were it not for the support of their "Joint,"[137] when they were still able to send relief to us prior to the outbreak of the war, we would have starved. When their support ceased due to the war, the state of some of our brethren declined badly. In Poland there were deaths due to starvation. And, nevertheless, they are prepared to send relief even now, without delay. May the Almighty remember them for the good and [due to their merits] may they be saved from every kind of suffering and distress. The verse "You shall be established through righteousness [you shall be safe from oppression]"[138] may be applied to them, [as well as] "Great is charity, in that it brings the redemption nearer. ..."[139]

Yet you may claim: How is it that our fellow Jews in America and England live in a state of calm, tranquility and dignity, as they always have? They are not exposed to even the slightest cleansing which is to be the fate of all of Israel during the pangs of the Messiah prior to

---

136 Our author may be offering an ironic commentary on the Zohar. The apparent wealth accumulated in exile does not pass the litmus test of Num. 31:23. The gold is, therefore, destroyed in the very process of purification. It is in reality only an image of wealth when it is consumed for selfish purposes without concern for the unfortunate.

137 Joint Distribution Committee, also referred to in the literature as the American Jewish Joint Distribution Committee (JDC). The organization was formed on November 27, 1914, by American Jews of German background to assist Jewish refugees and poor in wartime Europe. The "Joint" continued its work with the Jewish needy between the wars and was especially devoted to relief work in Russia. Activities reached a peak during and after World War II, and concentrated on the rescue, relief and rehabilitation of survivors of the Shoah.

138 Isa. 54:14.

139 BB 10a. The author cites from the volume *Tehillah LeMoshe* (The Prayer of Moses) based on midrash passages of R. Moshe Teitelbaum (1759–1841), the Admor of Uhel, disciple of Yaakov Yitzhak, the Seer of Lublin, linking the acts of charity and mutual good will in times of crisis to the eventual redemption. *EHS*, 81–82.

the redemption.[140] We realize, however, that there are many influences at play with regard to exile. Thus with reference to our fellow Jews in the United States and the other [free] countries: Although the suffering which has befallen us has not actually touched them, to a certain extent and in a modest fashion they are affected. They share in our suffering, they weep and mourn together with us. Their esteem among their gentile neighbors is damaged. Imagine their feelings when their gentile neighbors read in the press or listen to the radio about our degradation. Is it possible that their own esteem is not degraded when their neighbors react saying: "See what is being done to their brethren! . . ." Certainly this [vicarious degradation] should be considered at least a modest form of cleansing, though by no means as severe as our own [plight].

At least with this [moderate cleansing-suffering] they will fulfill their obligation for some form of cleansing [necessary] during the pangs of the Messiah. The Almighty, Who knows the exact time for the End of Days, will also evaluate their [participation in the redemption process]. In any event we have certainly arrived at the moment of redemption, (as indicated earlier by the Zohar).[141] All that is yet necessary is for us to initiate our own awakening which will then be culminated by God on our behalf. . . .[142] Above all, we must awaken to return to our Holy Land. This is the purpose of all that has ensued, as I have already elaborated. Then shall be realized the sacred verse:[143] "And the children of Israel went forth defiantly." Amen, may this too be echoed by God.

This concludes the first chapter. May the Lord watch over us as

---

140 As background to the author's response two sources (the Maharal of Prague and the Maharam of Padua) (1473–1565) are introduced (*EHS*, 82–83) pointing to the profound complex interrelationships and influences of exilic conditions upon Jewish life everywhere, known only to the Almighty.

141 See above, 12-13, n. 54 and 57.

142 In a gloss [*EHS*, 83–84] the author expands upon a teaching of R. Yaakov Yitzhak of Lublin (*Zichron Zot, Tetzaveh*), the final, permanent redemption will be "masculine" in character, unaccompanied by the birthpangs of the Messiah ("feminine" in character). The masculine attribute, however, requires the initiative of the people.

143 Ex. 14:8. This verse appears in the scripture reading of the week (*Beshalah*, Ex. 13:7–17:16) during which this first chapter was completed.

His precious possession.[144] May we be privileged to build Zion and
Jerusalem distinguished as "foremost,"[145] the second day in the week
of "and the children of Israel went forth defiantly," in the year 5703,[146]
the capital Budapest, may she be spared.

144   *Lit,* "as the apple of His eye."

145   *Lit,* "first," ExR. 15:2. וציון נקרא ראשון שנאמר: (ירמיה יז:יב) 'כסא כבוד מרום מראשון
מקום מקדשינו'. "And Zion is called 'foremost' as it is written (Jer. 17:12): 'O Throne of
Glory foremost exalted, our sacred shrine.'"

146   Corresponding to 12 Shevat 5703 (January 18, 1943).

CHAPTER TWO

CONCERNING THE REDEMPTION OF
ISRAEL: REDEMPTION AND
DELIVERANCE

In the book of Kings it is written: "For the Lord saw the very bitter plight of Israel, helpless and abandoned, no one to aid Israel. And the Lord resolved not to blot out the name of Israel from under heaven; and He delivered them through Jeroboam son of Joash."[1]

The *Midrash Eliyahu Rabba*[2] comments on this verse:

> . . . and the Lord resolved . . . What was Jeroboam's merit in this event? Was he not an idolator? [Yet God chose him] because he refused to accept the slander regarding the prophet Amos. Here is a generation that worships idols, and the leader of the generation worships idols, nevertheless, "the Land which I promised[3] to Abraham, Isaac and Jacob, saying, to your offspring I will give it," give it to him [Jeroboam] because he refused to accept slander. What He did not give [as possession] to Joshua the son of Nun or to David, King of Israel,[4] was given to him, as it is written: "and He delivered them through Jeroboam son of Joash."[5]

---

1 II Kings 14:26–27.

2 At the close of chapter 17. The text here erroneously cites *Tanhuma*.

3 Deut. 34:4. Our author quotes אשר אמרתי לאברהם "which I promised to Abraham" from the midrash text.

4 *Vs.* the midrash "or as a possession to the previous kings of Israel."

5 The *Eliyahu Rabba* text elaborates upon Jeroboam's refusal to accept slander against the prophet Amos. Cf. Pes. 87b. מפני מה זכה ירבעם בן יואש מלך ישראל להמנות עם

Thus when it is the intent of the Supreme Will to redeem Israel in a time of great distress, He will help even by means of the very wicked such as our idolator; as long as he possesses a positive human trait of love and a sense of solidarity [with his fellow men] which would lead him to refuse to listen to slander. And what the greatest *tzadikim* were not privileged to receive, such as Joshua the son of Nun and King David, was given to him [Jeroboam], though he and his generation were not worthy of it in their own right. . . .[6]

Our master the Maharal wrote in his volume *Netzah Yisrael* that all of the promises of the Holy One, blessed be He, as expressed by His prophets are in no way conditional; [they will be fulfilled even should we not fulfill His will, Heaven forbid. (He elaborates upon this point.[7])

Likewise, our teacher Rambam taught in his *Iggeret Teiman*:[8]

The Almighty assured us that He will refrain from despising all of us completely though we may anger Him and violate His commandments as it is written (Jer. 31):[9] "Thus said the Lord: 'If the heavens above could be measured and the foundations of the earth below could be

---

מלכי יהודה? מפני שלא קבל לשון הרע על עמוס. "Why did Jeroboam the son of Joash king of Israel merit to be counted together with the kings of Judah? Because he did not respond to the slander against Amos."

6 It was only in the days of Jeroboam that the northern portion of Solomon's kingdom, which had been lost, was restored (II Kings 14:28). R. Ovadiah Sforno (Italy, 1475–1550) in his commentary on Gen. 35:11 explains Divine acts which transcend human rationale whereby redemptive rewards are directed to people not considered "worthy" by ordinary standards. [*EHS*, 85–86.]

7 The Maharal refers to this principle throughout the *Netzah Yisrael* volume. כי השי"ת בחר בישראל בעצם ולא בשביל מעשיהם הטובים שלא לומר דוקא כאשר הם עושים רצונו שלו אז השי"י בחר בהם ולא כאשר אין עושים רצונו של השי"י. ולפיכך כתיב יהייתי להם לאלהים' קודם ואח"כ והמה יהיו לי לעם' כלומר מה שהשי"י בחר בישראל הוא קודם ואף כי ישראל אינם מקבלים אלוקותו. "God chose Israel for intrinsic reasons and not due to their virtuous deeds, so it should not be said that only when they fulfill the will of God are they chosen by Him, and not when they reject the will of God. Therefore, it is written first (Ez. 37:17): 'I will be their God' and it is followed by 'and they shall be My people.' That is to say: The selection of Israel came first even though Israel does not accept God's authority." (*op. cit.*, 22 a. See also 60a).

8 Kapah edition (Jerusalem, 1972), 26. וכן בשרנו והבטיחנו יתרומם שמו כי מן הנמנע לפניו יתעלה לשנוא את כללותינו ואף על פי שמרדנו בו והמרינו מצותו אמרה 'כי אמר ה' אם ימדו שמים מלמעלה וגו. See below, 258-259.

9 Verse 36. Our text reads "(Isa. 31)."

fathomed, only then would I reject all of the offspring of Israel for all that they have done,' declares the Lord."

Our holy master in [his work] the *Noam Elimelekh*[10] agrees with Maimonides: ". . . [Israel] is flawless and perfect since the collectivity of Israel constitutes *tzadikim* as it is written: 'Your people shall all be righteous.'[11] Even though there may be elements who commit sin, yet the totality [of Israel] always endures in its state of sanctity. There is neither a demonic nor evil spirit embodied within them. Their image is engraved Above. . . ."[12]

The manner in which redemption shall be manifested—whether by means of a revealed extraordinary miracle, or by means of a miracle embodied within a natural course of events—will depend upon our acts and conduct. If we conduct ourselves in accordance with Torah, observing the mitzvot to their fullest, then we shall be deserving of redemption by extraordinary means through a revealed and conspicuous miracle, beyond the course of nature. If Heaven forbid, we do not comply with the will of God, then redemption will appear by means of a miracle embodied in the natural course of events by a natural process.[13] This interpretation is found in Sanhedrin 98:

> R. Alexandri said: 'R. Joshua studied two contradictory verses. It is written: 'Behold, with the clouds of heaven there appeared one like a son of man!'[14] Elsewhere it is written: '[Behold, your king comes to you. . .] humble and riding on an ass.'[15] If they are meritorious he will come 'with the clouds of heaven,' if not, 'humble and riding on an

---

10   R. Elimelekh of Lyzhansk or Lizhensk (1717–1787) among the early masters of Hasidim, a leading disciple of R. Dov Baer of Mezeritch and among the founders of Galician Hasidism. His major work *Noam Elimelekh* (Lwow, 1787; Sklov, 1790) is a collection of sermons on the weekly portion in the Hasidic style.

11   Isa. 60:21. See also below, 258-259; 269.

12   *Noam Elimelekh* (Sklov, 1790), 86a. Israel's image, like the heavens above, is indestructible. *EHS*, 96.

13   Such process being considerably more difficult as opposed to the former, which is swift and does not require human effort.

14   Dan. 7:13.

15   Zech. 9:9.

ass. . . . '''[16]

Midrash Tanhuma[17] on the portion of *Devarim*[18] states:

Why is it written: "The arid desert shall be glad" (Isaiah 35:1)? In order to teach you that the Holy One, blessed be He, does not reveal His Presence and His Goodness all at once, since you would be unable to endure [its intensity]. You would all perish. [What does the Holy One do?] He reveals Himself [to His people] gradually.

The Zohar in the portion of *Beshalah*[19] teaches:

When the community of Israel shall be restored to her place, then the Holy King shall return to Zion [to be reunited one with the other].[20] It is the community of Israel which must be initially restored[21] to its place. Only then will the Holy King return to Zion. . . .[22]

Unlike many of our people who imagine and fancy that the Messiah will come to Israel suddenly, like a flash flood, from darkness to brilliant light[23] all at once, these genuine sages explain the gradual ascent [of Israel] from one stage to a higher stage, until the ladder of Bet El,[24] they reach the highest level, to which they then will have

---

16   Sanh. 98a. Since Israel does not merit the swift and effortless form of redemption, it is now in their best interest to partake in the evolving natural process of redemption. This will permit gradual adjustment to a new untested reality, though that be a praiseworthy experience, not unlike the diver whose ascent from the depths of the sea must necessarily be gradual. The author proceeds to cite supporting sources which rationalize the natural process [*EHS*, 87–88].

17   *Devarim* 2, Buber edition (New York, 1946), 1.

18   Deut. 1:1–3:22.

19   Ex. 13:17–17:16.

20   Zohar, vol. 8, Sulam edition (Jerusalem, 1951), (250), 72.

21   In preparation for the return of the Holy King.

22   This thesis is supported with references to JT Yoma 3:2, *Keli Paz* (Venice, 1657) of the 16th century Syrian rabbi and commentator R. Shmuel Laniado (commentary on Isaiah), and *Shtei Yadot* (Amsterdam, 1726) of the 17th century Polish kabbalist R. Abraham Hazkuni (commentary on the Pentateuch).

23   Cf. the Passover Haggadah, the *Lefikhakh* prayer for redemption. See also Isa. 9:1.

24   Ref. to Gen. 28. For the numerous symbolisms and allusions to redemption in

become gradually adjusted. An abrupt ascent [on the other hand], from one extreme to the other, is far from being realistic. The Jewish people would be unable to cope with the massive dose of benevolence, comparable to the patient who is recovering from a serious and perilous illness. He cannot immediately absorb a host of foods and other mundane luxuries. He is yet weak. It may also be compared to one who has lived in a dark house. He could not enjoy sudden exposure to brilliant light. . . .[25] This is the reason why our prophets referred to our righteous Messiah as *Tzemah* [26] as it is written: "I am going to bring My servant the branch" (Zech. 3).[27] "I will raise up a true branch of David's line"[28] (Jer. 23). Further we include in our prayers:

"Speedily cause the offspring (*tzemah*) of your servant David to flourish. . . ."[29] Therefore, the Messiah is also called *Tzemah* since his prestige and that of Israel will rise gradually as would a plant [*tzemah*] of the earth. Consequently, all of these [sources] demonstrate that our future redemption will evolve naturally. That is to say, it will appear as a miracle disguised in a natural setting. It will require a period of time to allow the natural process to take its gradual course. . . .

All that I have presented thus far is genuine and drawn from the pure wells of our rabbis from the Talmud, the Midrash, the Jerusalem Talmud, the Zohar and leading scholars, such as Maharal and Yavetz,[30] endowed with the Holy Spirit. . . .

Now we are able to grasp the sermon of the Hatam Sofer delivered in the month of Elul 5580.[31] It seems from the opinion of Maimonides

---

the Jacob's ladder episode, see GenR. 68–69.

25 The gradual, natural form of redemption will be necessary, since the People of Israel will not desire miraculous redemption due to their own merit. The merit of the Fathers [Patriarchs] will enable the gradual form of redemption [*EHS*, 99].

26 Lit. "branch," suggesting gradual organic growth.

27 V. 8. See also Zech. 6:12.

28 Jer. 23:5. See also Jer. 33:15 and Isa. 11:1.

29 From the daily prayer service, the "Eighteen Benedictions."

30 See above, 31, n. 95, also 302, below.

31 1820.

in Sanhedrin, first chapter[32] that Israel will be reunited in Eretz Yisrael prior to the coming of the Messiah, even without the rebuilding of the Holy Temple.[33] In the work *Shvilei Emunah* authored by the grandson of the Rosh[34] (The tenth "Path," in chapter one) it is written: "The Midrash teaches[35] that prior to redemption many Jews from the four corners of the globe will voluntarily settle in Eretz Yisrael. And they shall vigorously pray on the Temple Mount and the Creator, blessed be He, will respond and hasten the epoch of redemption."[36]

---

32   The editor could not trace the reference although the passage would be consistent with Maimonides in his *Perush HaMishnayot Sanhedrin*. (Chapter 10): אמנם ימות המשיח הוא זמן שתשוב המלכות לישראל ויחזרו לארץ ישראל "Indeed, the Messianic era will usher in the return of Israel's kingdom when they [the Jewish people] will return." The reference to "Chapter One" may be linked to Maimonides' elaboration upon the laws of conferring Rabbinic authority (סמיכת זקנים) [*semikhat zekenim*] in Eretz Yisrael. ויראה לי כי כשיתהי הסכמה מכל החכמים והתלמידים להקדים עליהם איש מן הישיבה וישימו אותו בראש ובלבד שיהא זה בא"י . . . והקב"ה יעד שישובו כמו שנאמר ואשיבה שופטיך כבראשונה ויועציך כבתחילה אחרי כן יקרא לך עיר הצדק' וזה יהיה בלא ספק כשיכון הבורא יתברך לבות בני אדם ותרבה זכותם ותשוקתם לשם יתברך ולתורה ותגדל חכמתם לפני בא המשיח להרמב"ם ממסכת סנהדרין, פרק ראשון, ד"ה 'סמיכת זקנים.' "I believe that there will be a consensus of all the sages and students who will reach out to someone in the academy and appoint him as chief [magistrate of the Sanhedrin]. This will have to take place in Eretz Yisrael. . . . The Holy One, blessed be He, bears witness that they will return, as it is written (Isa. 1:26): 'I will restore your magistrates as of old, and your counselors as of yore. After that you shall be called City of Righteousness. . . .' This will no doubt occur when the blessed Creator will secure the hearts of humankind. He will increase their merits and their desire for God and Torah. Their wisdom shall prosper, [all this] prior to the coming of the Messiah as it has often been expounded in Scripture." (Commentary of Maimonides on the *Mishnayot* of the Tractate Sanhedrin, chapter 1, *Semikhat Zekenim*.)

33   Hatam Sofer, *Derashot* (vol. 2), *op. cit.*, 360b(720).

34   R. Asher ben Yehiel (c. 1250–1327) among the great talmudists of his time and leader of Ashkenazic Jewry. His grandson, R. Meir ben Yitzhak Eldabi, a scholar and kabbalist, settled in Jerusalem where *Shvilei Emunah* a work on religious belief and ethics was composed (1360).

35   Possible reference to *Tanh. Noah* 11. מסרת אגדה היא שאין ירושלים נבנית עד שיתכנסו הגליות. "The tradition indicates that Jerusalem will not be rebuilt until all the exiles have returned."

36   *Shvilei Emunah* (Riva di Trento, 1559), 122b. תוב במדרש כי יתנדבו הרבה מישראל תופסי תורה וחסדים ואנשי מעשי לבא לדור בארץ ישראל ולהתישב בירושלים ע"ה איש איש כפי נדבת לבו וננצה בו רוח טהרה והכשר חיבת הקדש מארבע פינות העולם, אחד מעיר ושנים ממשפחה למען היות לו ניר [עיין א' מלכים יא:אֹלו] ויתד נאמן בהר הקדש, ועל זה נאמר [ירמיה ג:יד] ולקחתי אתכם אחד מעיר ושנים ממשפחה' כאשר יתייישבו שם החסידים ההם ירבו להתפלל בהר הקדש בירושלים וישמע הבורא ית' שועתם ויקרא קץ הגאולה "It is written in the Midrash [it is not certain which

The *gaon* and *tzadik*, our R. Hillel of Kalameo[37] in his work *Teshuvot Bet Hillel,* paragraph 31, quotes this [*Shvilei Emunah* text]. He is also very enthusiastic [concerning the *aliyah* of Jews which would precede redemption] in a letter to the *gaon* R. Zalman Spitzer of Vienna,[38] [requesting of R. Spitzer] that he speak to Baron Rothschild concerning his hoped—for financial support and involvement [in the *aliyah* venture]. This kind of a project is dependent upon wealthy Jews. (A comparable situation is described in *Midrash Rabba, Toledoth.*[39]) During the period of R. Joshua ben Hananiah, the emperor permitted *aliyah* to Eretz Yisrael and the building of the Temple. R. Joshua ben Hananiah assigned two very wealthy Jews to defray the costs [of the venture]. The *gaon* and *tzadik* adds: "Is there any pious Jew who would refuse to share in this mitzvah. . . ."[40]

---

midrashic source is intended] that when a multitude of Jews committed to Torah and good deeds will offer to settle in Eretz Yisrael and Jerusalem the holy city, everyone in accordance with the promptings of his heart, inspired by a pure motive and sacred love, emanating from the four corners of the earth, one from every town, and two from every family, so that they may be a lamp for Him (cf. I Kings 11:36) and a firm support on the Holy Mountain, as it is written (Jer. 3:14): 'I will take you, one from a town and two from a family.' When these pious people will settle there, worshippers on the Holy Mountain in Jerusalem will increase and the blessed Creator will respond to their supplications and He will declare the final redemption."

37   R. Hillel Lichtenstein (1815–1891), Hungarian rabbinic leader at the forefront of Orthodox opposition to Reform; student of Hatam Sofer.

38   R. Binyamin Solomon Zalman Spitzer (1826–1893), rabbinical leader of Orthodox Jewry in Austria, fierce opponent of Reform, pupil of the renowned scholar R. Moses Schick. The letter was written September 1876 to the head of the Frankfurt branch, most likely to Mayer Karl Rothschild (1820–1886), who followed his pious uncle Amschel Mayer. One can only speculate as to why the request was not made of Ferdinand James, head of the Rothschild Vienna branch.

39   GenR. 64:10 (29). Reference to the aborted attempt at rebuilding the Temple during the reign of Hadrian. The wealthy Pappas and Lulianus families provided the returning exiles with "silver, gold and all their needs." When Hadrian was no longer in need of the good will of the Jews, he abruptly withdrew permission for the restoration. Our author cites the Midrash as evidence of the keen involvement of the wealthy in restoration and redemption. The Midrash presents the story as evidence of the unreliability of the nations. Temporary periods of benevolence are dictated by policies of self-interest. The source of this interpretation is the qualifying רק טוב "have always dealt kindly. . ." in Gen. 26:29, which depicts the tenuous relationship between Abimelekh and Isaac.

40   *Teshuvot Bet Hillel* (Satmar, 1908), 23–24. Our author presents sources from Rashi and the Mishnah on Ps. 69:36–37 and 70:1 to demonstrate the prerequisite of

I support the reasoning of Hatam Sofer in his exposition of the
Book of Ruth: "The consequence of our wickedness is dispersion and
exile. Had the Temple been destroyed and had we remained in Eretz
Yisrael, it would not have been as painful, as it is written in Maimonides,
The Laws of Fasting:[41] 'With the murder of Gedaliah ben Ahikam, the
glowing embers of Israel were extinguished and because of our sins
we were dispersed. . . .'"[42] Therefore, the ingathering of Israel in
Eretz Yisrael must precede the genuine redemption in order to remove
ourselves from the consequences of our wickedness and enter an
intermediate stage of misfortune—the destruction of our Temple.
However, Israel will be restored to its own place, and being gathered
in Eretz Yisrael there is hope for its ultimate destiny. . . . Permit me
to add to his sacred words,[43] and to explain how the initial ingathering
is at all possible without the prior rebuilding of the Temple; given
the limitations of exile, and the inability of Eretz Yisrael to absorb
the entire Jewish nation all at once, until such time when the Land
will shed its skin[44] which would permit her to gather in all of her
children. As is known, our sages taught: "Eretz Yisrael is compared to
a deer. . . ."[45] It, therefore, seems to me that the gathering of Israel
into the midst of Jerusalem and Eretz Yisrael will serve as a center for
all of the Jewish people so that even those who remained in exile will
necessarily direct their eyes and hearts towards it. They too will be
linked to this center with every strand of their souls. By means of
Eretz Yisrael they will all become united so that they would no longer
be considered dispersed. This is not the reality at present. Israel is a

---

aliyah for redemption. *EHS*, 90–91.

41   *Rambam, Hilkhot Taanit* 5:2.

42   Hatam Sofer, *Derashot* (vol. 2), The Book of Ruth, *op. cit.*, 299 (597).

43   That is, those of Hatam Sofer.

44   See the author's further discussion (below, 95-96) on the ability of Eretz
Yisrael to adjust its size to the needs of the ingathered.

45   למה ארץ ישראל נמשלה לצבי? לומר לך מה צבי זה אין עורו מחזיק בשרו אף ארץ ישראל, אינה
מחזקת פירותיה. "Why was Eretz Yisrael compared to a deer? To teach you that as the
skin of a deer cannot contain its flesh, so cannot Eretz Yisrael contain its produce."
ואתן לך ארץ חמדה, נחלת צבי "I gave you a desirable land, the heritage of the deer." Ket.
112a, based on Jer. 3:19.

dispersed flock of sheep,[46] lost among the nations with nothing which would unite one Jew with another. They are like nearly-dismembered limbs dangling from the body, neither linked to the individual and certainly not with the [Jewish] totality. . . We are all as abandoned fish in the sea. As we have witnessed during the past number of years, even the lowest and most common scoundrel has felt free to do with us as he wishes; commit against us depravities and murder without having to account to anyone for his actions. . . Such [anarchy] could not be possible if we were to found, with the help of God, a center in Eretz Yisrael which would raise our glory with honor before all the nations of the earth. We too would be considered a distinguished nation. As it is taught in the exposition of *Midrash Song of Songs* of the verse "Attribute to the Lord, you families of people, attribute to the Lord glory and strength."[47] "When You shall indeed bring them, do not bring them in shame but with glory and strength."[48] Thus the individual who remains in exile would not be irresponsibly abandoned.

Anyone considering acts of violence against us must understand that he will be accountable to someone for his acts. He will be held responsible and, therefore, should refrain from acting towards us with hostility. [The ingathering] would also cause the hearts of Jews to be reunited, even those in exile. Peace will reign among us. Thereby we shall attain, with good hope, the final redemption, speedily in our time, Amen. . . .[49]

These are among the permanent attributes of Eretz Yisrael [with regard to boundaries]. At times she contracts and at times she expands, all in accordance with the prevelant needs of Israel at any given

---

46   Cf. Jer. 50:17: שה פזורה ישראל "Israel are scattered sheep."

47   Ps. 96:7.

48   CantR. 4:18. A plea for redemption with honor. The Jews in the diaspora with an organized center in Eretz Yisrael could conduct their lives with dignity prior to their redemption.

49   Authorities are invoked (R. Isaac Abravanel (1437–1508), R. Yaakov ben Shlomo Ibn Habib (c. 1445–1515), R. Menahem Azariah Fano (1548–1620) who describe the ability of Eretz Yisrael, albeit a limited physical entity, to asborb the entire Jewish people. Indeed, the redemptive process adapts itself to the degree of initiative of the Jewish people. The greater the return of Jews to their Land, the greater the absorbtion potential of the Land.

moment. Note the comments of R. Joseph Shaul[50] in the Mishnah tractate Avot: "And no person said to another: 'The place is too confining for me to lodge overnight in Jerusalem.'"[51] [It seems to me] this is the reason why Eretz Yisrael is referred to as *Eretz Tzvi*.[52] The meaning is as follows: Just as a person when making a garment for a child will provide for folds which can be expanded as the child grows, similarly, with regard to the Land. When Israel does not reside in its Land, it folds.[53] This is evidence that Eretz Yisrael belongs to Israel. When they are settled and people inhabit the Land, it will assume the size of its population.

"When they made their pilgrimage [during the three festivals of *Pesach*, *Shavuot* and *Sukkot*,] it would expand even further. It was not at all confining for people [who wished] to lodge overnight. This was a great miracle."[54]

The teachings of our scholars[55] are actually expounded in *Midrash Rabba* on the verse "When the Lord your God shall expand your border":[56] Is it possible that the Holy One, blessed be He, can expand Eretz Yisrael? R. Isaac said: "When one examines a scroll, one cannot estimate its length or breadth. But when it is unrolled its actual size becomes apparent." So it is with Eretz Yisrael. The greater part of it consists of mountains and hills. [How is this known?] It is written:

But the Land you are about to cross into in order to possess, is a land

---

50 R. Joseph Saul HaLevi Nathanson (1810–1875), leading Polish halakhic authority.

51 Avot 5:5. Sufficiency of space for lodging, even during the peak pilgrimage periods, is enumerated as one of ten miracles associated with the Temple.

52 The splendid or glorious Land, as in Dan. 8:9, 11:16, 11:14, Jer. 3:19. Lit. "The Land of the Deer" (See previous discussion of analogy, above, 31, n. 94 and Ket. 112.)

53 I.e., contracts. It cannot absorb an alien people.

54 *Bet Shaul* [on the Order Nezikin] in *Mishnayot Nezikin* (Vilna, 1921) 2 [in rear of volume].

55 Concerning the capacity of Eretz Yisrael to expand and contract in accordance with Israel's needs.

56 Deut. 12:20.

of hills and valleys. . . .[57] It is a land . . . on which the Lord your God always keep His eyes and looks after. . . .[58] How do we know that the Holy One, blessed be He, straightens [the terrain]? As it is written: "Every valley shall be lifted up, every mountain and hill brought down; rugged places shall be made smooth and mountain ranges become a plain."[59]

Only then will the full extent of Eretz Yisrael become known.[60] Thus all of the teachings of our rabbis are incorporated in this midrash: When Israel will be "straightened" out the true extent of its unlimited size and dimensions will become clear. All will depend upon the resident Jewish population, relative to which [the Land] will expand or contract at any given time. Therefore the present smallness of our Land will not hinder our ingathering when God wills it. It will unroll in its breadth and width, as would a scroll, in accordance with [the needs of] our settlement. Those who will settle upon her will not feel confined. Study as well the *Tashbez*,[61] who remarked upon this miracle in his own time on the festival of *Shavuot*.[62] Note as well the Hatam Sofer on *Yoreh Deah*, Responsa 234.[63]

---

57 וגבעות (*ugeva'ot*) vs. ובקעות (*uveka'ot*) in the Deut. text.

58 A variant of Deut. 11:11–12.

59 Isa. 40:4.

60 DeutR. 4:11.

61 Responsa of Rashbaz, R. Shimon ben Zemah Duran (1361–1444), North African authority in the fields of halakhah, philosophy, poetry and science.

62 *Tashbez* (part 3, Responsa 201, 2) (Lemberg, 1891), 32. שלא אמר אדם לחבירו צר 'יר לי המקום' כי בבית הכנסת שבירושלים הם צריכים לאנשי המקום כל השנה ומתמלאת פה אל פה בעת התקבץ שם חג השבועות החוגגים יותר מג' מאות איש כלם הם נכנסים שם ויושבים רווחים, כי עדיין היא בקדושתה, וזה סימן גאולה שלישית. "So that no one would say to his fellow: 'This place is too small for me.' In a synagogue in Jerusalem they relied upon the native populace throughout the year. But when more than three hundred pilgrims celebrated the festival of *Shavuot* [in this very synagogue] they all were able to enter and be comfortably seated, since it [Jerusalem] is still in a state of sanctity. This is our omen of the third redemption." The demand for space in Jerusalem, and its ability to accommodate its pilgrims and residents attests to the permanent sanctity of the city, and is evidence of the advent "of the third redemption."

63 New York, 1958, 96a–97b. The Hatam Sofer surveys the halakhic literature defining the relative preference of residing in Jerusalem above other cities in Eretz Yisrael because of its inherent sanctity. The author expounds upon the characteristics

[Even] as I clearly respond throughout to all the arguments of our master and rabbi, the author of *Minhat Elazar* of Munkatch. . .[64] (I too was in his circle.) I am also aware that his premises were based upon a form of miraculous and wondrous redemption. Those who took matters into their own hands were considered to be deniers of the [true] redemption which will be miraculous. These arguments are maintained in all of his works. . . .

Without detracting from his revered status, I must respectfully indicate that he viewed all things from a meritorious perspective based on his [lofty] standards.[65] Yet, in truth, this last generation, due to our many transgressions is "not worthy." Redemption is, therefore, destined to be disguised in the natural process. . . .

It is worth adding that had our rabbi, the author of *Minhat Elazar*, been with us to witness all these terrible decrees and acts of murder which have befallen us, Heaven help us, he too would acknowledge that we should abandon the lands of exile, return to Eretz Yisrael which had provided us [in the past] with royalty, and not wait for the call to the Messiah. Consider the volume *Zayit Ra'anan, Yitro*, section 292, of our rabbi the author of *Magen Avraham*,[66] in which he comments on [the *Midrash*] of R. Nathan on the verse "of those who love Me and keep My commandments":[67] "They who live in Eretz Yisrael and

---

of natural redemption, drawing on the Rashi commentary on Isa. 60:22, as developed in Sanh. 98a. *EHS*, 94.

64   R. Hayyim Elazar of Munkatch, descendant of the Bnei Yessaskhar, R. Zvi Elimelekh of Dinov, and leader of the Munkatch-Shapira dynasty from 1904 to his death in 1937. Though a zealous opponent of all forms of political Zionism, he nevertheless opposed the emerging ultra-Orthodox Agudat Israel movement (founded in Katowice in May 1912, to counteract political Zionism among other objectives), possibly viewing it as conflicting with his own local community concerns. See Avraham Fuchs, *Yeshivot Hungaria*, 497–505 and above, 73, n. 79; below, 327, n. 1288.

65   Which would have justified sudden, miraculous redemption. See *Minhat Elazar* 133–34; 93, n. 1.

66   R. Abraham ben Hayyim Gombiner (c. 1637–1683) Polish halakhic authority and author of the classic commentary *Magen Avraham* on the *Shulhan Arukh, Orah Hayyim* 1692. *Zayit Ra'anan*, a commentary on the *Yalkut Shimoni* collection of *midrashim*, was published in Dessau (1704) and in Venice (1743).

67   Ex. 20:6; Deut. 5:10.

sacrifice themselves for all the mitzvot."[68] To this the author of *Magen Avraham* added: "'They who live in Eretz Yisrael,' because in Eretz Yisrael they were exposed to harsh decrees and could have sought refuge outside the Land. Nevertheless, they chose to sacrifice themselves by living in Eretz Yisrael. This is not so when we encounter harsh decrees outside the Land. He forfeits his life if he does not leave for another country. . . ."[69]

Now, in the wake of all these harsh decrees in the lands of exile, having the opportunity to flee to Eretz Yisrael, where the authorities permit us to enter,[70] is there any doubt that our rabbi would not have agreed to this? . . .[71] This is the text from the closing paragraph of the *Kuzari:* "Man deserves blame when he does not seek to bring positive acts to any fruition.[72] Merely to direct one's intentions to the Holy Land is not sufficient. When action and intention are integrated, then you may expect reward. . . When the people will be aroused with their love for this sacred place [Eretz Yisrael], then the object of their desire shall be speedily[73] realized. The reward will be great, as it is written: 'You will now arise and have compassion for Zion; it is time to favor her, the appointed time has come; for your servants

---

68 *Yalkut Shimoni* I:292 (According to Oxford MS 2637 = Hyman-Shiloni ed. [Jerusalem: Mosad Harav Kook, 1977, 454]). Saloniki 1521–6 edition (our author's text) ונותנים נפשם על כל המצוות *vz.* ומוסרין נפשם על כל המצוות (Oxford MS), both versions signify: "They sacrifice themselves for all the *mitzvot.*"

69 *Zayit Ra'anan* (Venice, 1703), 21a.

70 Possible reference to the British government's relative relaxation of immigration policy to Palestine in the summer of 1943. Refugees from the Holocaust would be guaranteed entry via Turkey. However, as Katzburg indicates, this did not represent a significant change in policy since the White Paper quota of Jews permitted entry had not yet been filled. In any event this arrangement was cancelled by High Commissioner Viscount Gort in November of 1944. Nathaniel Katzburg, "*Mediniyut Ha'Aliya shel Britannia Bimey Milhemet Ha'Olam HaShniya,*" in *Nisyonot U'Fe'ulot Hatzalah BiTkufat HaShoah,* ed. Gutman (Jerusalem, 1976) 152, 165 (n. 8).

71 Sources supporting the necessary initiatives of settlement and rebuilding as a prelude to redemption, at times compelled by hostilities in exile, are introduced. (Ramban on Deut. 12:5; *Ahavat Yonatan* (Prague, 1766), 99b, a work of homiletics by R. Jonathan Eybeshutz (*EHS*, 95).

72 *Kuzari, op. cit,* 5:27, 333–334 (Schocken 1967 edition).

73 ינחנו הענין המיוחל vs. ינחץ הענין המיוחל

hold her stones dear and they have compassion for her dust.[74]

This means that Jerusalem can only be rebuilt when Israel's intense yearnings will bring her to embrace her stones and dust..."

He further expounds in the second part, which praises those who live in Eretz Yisrael: "You fall short of the duty prescribed by your Creator by not attempting to make it your objective, your home in life and death, though you pronounce, 'Have mercy on Zion, for it is the home of our life,'[75] and though you believe that the Shekhinah will return there. . . . By right the precious souls of man should have returned there . . . [after all] your forefathers preferred to live there rather than in their place of origin.[76] This they did even when the Shekhinah was as yet not revealed and the Land was inhabited by forces of obscenity. . . nevertheless they had no other desire than to uphold it [and not to abandon it] even during times of famine save for God's commandment."[77] Thus we have a clear opinion from this "Godly personage."[78] Even if, Heaven forbid, Eretz Yisrael becomes inhabited with forces of obscenity, it is still preferred to live there than anywhere else. This should serve as an example for those in our own day who drape themselves in piety and slander the Land claiming it does not meet their religious standards.

I found an old volume of commentary on the Order of Festivals,[79] based on both the close reading of the text, homiletics, allusions, and esoterica.[80] (Since the title page is missing I cannot identify the sacred

---

74 Ps. 102:14–15.

75 Blessing recited following the *Haftarah* reading from the prophets on the Sabbath and festivals.

76 Our author cites the *Kuzari*: בוחרים לדור בה יותר מכל מקומות מולדתם ובוחרים הגרות במקומותם אזרחים משהיו יותר בה "They prefer to reside there rather than in all their places of origin. They prefer residence there rather than in their previous places of citizenship."

77 *Kuzari* 2:23, *op. cit.*, 92–93.

78 R. Yehudah HaLevi.

79 One of six major divisions of the Talmud.

80 The author utilizes the mnemonic acronym פ*ר*ר*ד*ס (*pardes*) which began to be utilized in the Middle ages to denote four kinds of biblical interpretations:

    1) *Pshat* פשט—the literal or close reading of the text.

    2) *Remez* רמז—allusions or allegorical interpretations, also utilizing gematria

source of this work. It is evident that the author was a great personage, a kabbalist and among the distinguished scholars of an early generation.[81])

In the first part, ninth paragraph of the *Sefer HaBrit*[82] [the author] is much embittered over the undue duration of exile with no positive signs in sight for its conclusion. He elaborates remarkably upon the insincerity of our prayers which are supposed to [were they properly directed] redeem the Holy One, blessed be He, from exile. This is our failure.

Our mitzvot are not performed with conviction, namely to restore the Shekhinah to its original stature and thereby to hasten the end.[83] He adds that we should not place our hopes, prayers and merit in the hands of prominent people, trusting that they will bring the redeemer. Those who seem important are not always in fact so. He says, furthermore, that though we pay much lip service to the coming of the Messiah, it is merely an external gesture performed without sincerity. The individual much prefers to complete the building of a home or to conclude a business transaction, four to five years in the making, and to enjoy the benefits here. This is the actual reason for the long duration of the exile. Therefore, it is incumbent upon every Jew, though he may not be learned or observant, to direct all his efforts to redeem the Holy One and the Shekhinah from exile.[84]

(numerical word play).

    3) *Drash* דרש—homiletical interpretation.

    4) *Sod* סוד—esoteric and mystical interpretation.

81   This passage is evidence that our author was not always without sources as suggested in the text. See above, 63, n. 18. This work was likely composed under various conditions. The anonymous source is presented as further evidence for the gradual evolvement of redemption which gives Israel the opportunity to be a catalyst for the process of *tikkun olam* (restoration of the world).

82   Bruenn, 1797. A popular work on world geography and the natural sciences, integrated with Jewish thought and ethics, by the writer and traveler Pinhas Elijah b. Meir Horowitz (c. 1765–1821).

83   *Sefer HaBrit* (Vilna, 1904), 49b–50a (98–99).

84   The historic exile causes abnormality in the cosmos and in the functioning of the Divine Sefirot according to Kabbalah (G. Scholem, *Kabbalah*, Jerusalem, 1974, 165.) To pray for the redemption of the Shekhinah from *galut* is central to the Hasidism of Mezeritch. פירוש, יאל תעש תפילתך קבע׳ ר״ל אל יתפלל אדם על עסקי צרכיו, רק

We are now confronted with the following question already raised by renowned masters. After all, we have been praying [for redemption] ever since the destruction [of the Temple], to this very day. We have fulfilled the verse: "[They] will seek the Lord their God and David their king"[85] and the holy Temple. In our prayers all three are included.[86] Why then have we not been answered? We "have not come [as yet] to the designated haven."[87] We do not discern any kind of "a good omen."[88] Yet R. Shimon ben Menassiah said: "The Jewish people will not be shown a good omen until they repent and seek" all three.[89] Surely we have stated this all along three times daily, and have nevertheless not been shown any good and beneficial omen!

With the help of the Almighty, I will attempt to explain. In the tractate Niddah 70b [it is stated]:

"[Three[90] were concerned with matters of worldly conduct.][91] What must a person do that he may become wise?" [He replied to them] "Let

---

יתפלל תמיד בשביל השכינה שתגאל מגלות. "The meaning of 'Do not make your prayer into a routine experience' [Avot 2:13; Ber. 4:4] suggests that a person should not pray for his own personal needs. He should always pray for the redemption of the Shekhinah from its exile." *Maggid Devarav LeYa'akov of the Maggid Dov Baer of Mezeritch* (ed. R. Schatz Uffenheimer) (Jerusalem, 1976), 25. R. Teichthal takes issue with the author of *Sefer HaBrit* who seems to foreclose redemption in the event that Israel does not repent. Numerous sources are introduced as evidence that redemption is not dependent upon repentance (*EHS*, 97). Our author examines the factor of comprehensive and properly directed prayer of the totality of Israel, of present and previous generations, as a critical factor. The motif of the sixth millenium is again developed via extensive citation (Zohar, Ari, Maharsha, the liturgy) pointing to the period of redemption which is indeed at hand (*EHS*, 96–100).

85   Hos. 3:5. See above, 23.

86   Reference to the fourteenth and fifteenth benedictions of the thrice daily *Amidah* service of the liturgy. ולירושלים עירך ברחמים תשוב; את צמח דוד עבדך מהרה תצמיח "Have mercy, Lord, and return to Jerusalem, Your city. Bring to flower the shoot of Your servant David."

87   Deut. 12:9. אל המנוחה ואל הנחלה [עד עתה] כי לא באתם "Because you have not yet come to the alloted haven and settlement."

88   Rashi, Hos. 3:5. See above, 23.

89   Cf. *Yalkut Shimoni* II, 106. א״ר סימון בן מנסיא: אין ישראל רואין סימן גאולה לעולם עד שיחזרו ויבקשו שלשתם.

90   Of twelve questions addressed by the Alexandrians to R. Joshua b. Hananiah (Nid. 69b).

91   שלשה דברי דרך ארץ.

him devote time to study." They replied: "Indeed many did so but to no avail." "Then let them pray for mercy from Him, the Source of wisdom, as it is written: 'For, the Lord gives wisdom; from His mouth come knowledge and understanding. . . .'[92] What does this mean? One without the other is not sufficient."[93] "Let him engage much in business." They replied: "Indeed many did so, but to no avail." "Then let them pray for mercy from Him, the Source of wealth, as it is written: 'Silver is Mine, gold is Mine.'[94] What does this mean? One without the other is not sufficient."[95] "What must a person do that he may have male children?" He replied to them "Let him marry a woman worthy of him. . . ." They replied: "Indeed many did so, but to no avail." "Then let him pray for mercy from Him, the Source of children, as it is written: 'Behold, children are a heritage from God.'[96] What does this mean? One without the other is not sufficient."[97]

Thus with regard to three varied but essential elements upon which man is dependent, our sages teach us that prayer without effort and effort without prayer is not sufficient. You may apply this to every human and wordly endeavor. Were one to pray in order to achieve a goal, without investing any effort at all, he may achieve prayer, but his goal will never be achieved. . . .

With regard to the excerpt from the Talmud "What must a person do that he may have male children? . . ."[98] I am reminded of a story told to me by an aged *hasid* of R. Eliezer of Komarno.[99] The holy *Rebbe* was attended by an elderly bachelor. Though he was of limited

---

92 Prov. 2:6. Our texts cites the variant כי יתן חכמה מפיהו "For the Lord grants wisdom."

93 Study and prayer represent human potential made possible through one's own efforts and diligence, as well as human limitations for which one must seek compassion from God.

94 Hag. 2:8. Our text's variant לי הכסף והזהב "Silver is Mine and gold is Mine."

95 See n. 93 for the application of the parable.

96 Ps. 127:3.

97 Nid. 70b–71a.

98 Ibid.

99 Died 1898; son of R. Isaac Judah Jehiel Safrin, founder of the Komarno hasidic dynasty.

intelligence, he was a God-fearing person. He was called Peretz Gab-bai.[100] They asked this Peretz: "Why do you not marry a woman?" He replied: "Why do I need a woman? Do I lack anything being with the *Rebbe*?" They replied: "But a man is in need of children!" He retorted: "Children? I will submit a *kvittel*[101] to the *Rebbe* and I will have children!" When they related Peretz's words to the *Rebbe* he laughed, exclaiming: "That is the kind of image one acquires—like that of a Peretz—when one relies completely on the *Rebbe*."[102] We learn from this that one without the other is insufficient. Prayer [in this instance] not accompanied by the marrying of a woman, is inade-quate. One cannot emulate a Peretz Gabbai who relied on the prayers of the *Rebbe* and would not marry a woman![103]

In the sacred volume *Bet Elohim* of the Mabit (colleague and member of the court of the *Bet Yosef* [Rabbi Yosef Karo])[104] the 18th chapter, "The Gate of Prayer,"[105] [R. Moshe ben Yosef Trani] examines all of the prayers of pious men and women recorded in the Torah. When he came upon the prayer of Jacob he wrote as follows: "The prayer of Jacob is as it is written 'He came upon [*vayifga*] a certain place'[106] and *pegia* means only prayer.[107] We learn from this that it was our ancestor Jacob who arranged the evening prayer. Now the evening prayer is voluntary,[108] since he did not originally intend to pray there. As an

---

100   The attendant of a hasidic rebbe. In this instance, the term may have been applied in jest.

101   Yiddish for a written petition of the hasid to his rebbe.

102   In the original text the latter portion of the story appears in Yiddish.

103   As additional material is introduced emphasizing the futility of prayer which is not accompanied by personal effort (*EHS*, 103–104), the author once again describes his difficulty in recalling text sources away from his study and library. וכעת אי אפשר לי לציין על הספר והמקום שאני כותב כעת בלי ספרים מחמת גולתי שברחתי מחדר הורתי מחמת המציק "Presently it is impossible for me to cite the source and page. I write without the benefit of a library ever since I took flight from my study due to the tormentor" (*EHS*, 103).

104   See above, 14, n. 58.

105   *Sefer Bet Elohim, op. cit.*, 23a–27b.

106   Gen. 28:11.

107   "Coming upon" Ber. 26b; Ta'an. 7b, 8a, Sot. 14a, Sanh. 95b, *Mekhilta Beshalah* 34; *Tanh. Beshalah*.

108   Unlike the morning and afternoon services which are obligatory. Ber. 27b.

afterthought he contemplated: 'Is it possible that I shall have passed through the place where my fathers prayed and not have prayed too?'[109] He immediately resolved to return and pray. Therefore, it was ruled that it [the evening prayer] be voluntary. The 'intention' of our ancestor Jacob in his prayer at this site is associated with our [current] final exile. The Egyptian exile and our subsequent redemption is linked to Abraham our ancestor. The Babylonian exile and the subsequent redemption is linked to Isaac. This exile and our subsequent redemption is linked to Jacob. As I wrote in my essay concerning the concealed End, *Geulat Olam* (I am sorry that I did not have the opportunity to obtain this work),[110] When Jacob declared: "It is possible that I shall have passed through the place where my fathers prayed and not have prayed too?" he referred to Bet El, that is, Jerusalem.[111] They prayed for the rebuilding of Jerusalem and the Temple, and their prayers were accepted, as reflected in the First and Second Temples. Jacob too wished to pray for the rebuilding of Jerusalem and the future Temple. Therefore, his prayer coincided with the setting of the sun,[112] an allusion to the long exile. . . ."[113, 114]

Nevertheless, had he not assumed his own initiative and returned [to Jerusalem—Bet El from Haran], there would have been no response from Heaven. Further, aside from his [Jacob's] stimulus to return, it was expected from the Above that he fulfill some action towards that

---

109 Reference to Jerusalem. See Rashi, Hul. 91 b. שהתפללו בו אבותיי האי בית אל לא הסמוך לעי הוא אלא ירושלים ועל שם יהיה בית אלהים קראו בית אל והוא הר המוריה שהתפלל בו אברהם והוא שדה שהתפלל בו יצחק . . . אלא לא כאברהם שקראו יהר' ולא כיצחק שקראו ישדה' דכתיב ילשוח בשדה' אלא כיעקב שקראו יבית "'Where my fathers prayed.' This is not the Bet El near Ai but rather the reference is to Jerusalem, since there will be established the House of God [the Temple] they called Bet El. This is also the Mount of Moriah where Abraham prayed. This is 'the field' where Isaac prayed. . . . But unlike Abraham who referred to it as 'Mountain,' nor like Isaac who named it 'Field' as it is written: '[And Isaac went out] to meditate in the field,' (Gen. 24:63) it will be as referred to by Jacob who referred to it as 'House'" (Gen. 28:17, 19).

110 *Lit.*, "Redemption of the World," which was unavailable to the author. The editor, too, could not locate this work of R. Moshe ben Yosef Trani.

111 See above, n. 109.

112 Gen. 28:11 .f

113 Zech. 14:7 See above, 20, n. 21.

114 *Sefer Bet Elohim*, 24b.

goal. Indeed only when he returned to Bet El from Haran was he privileged with a response from Above in the form of the contraction of the Land. . . ."[115] This all alludes to our own time. We are currently in the final stage of exile, as demonstrated by our rabbis. Wishful thinking alone is not sufficient to invite a corresponding response from Above. We must wish to return to our Land and, as well, begin to take some practical steps [towards this objective]. Then, as was the case with our father Jacob, the response from Above will be forthcoming. The Land will act in response to us. Through us the Lord's purpose might prosper.[116] However, if we simply wait for miracles and wondrous spectacles without making any efforts of our own, our expectations will be in vain. Heaven awaits our initial response. . . .[117] I noted the following in the sacred volume *Avodat HaGershuni* [whose author[118] was] a colleague of the Shakh:[119] "We must take the initial step; since were the Almighty to do so, we could not possibly synchronize our action to coincide with His. Should we begin first then God will accurately direct His actions to coincide with ours. . . ."

Note what is written in *Ahavat Yehonatan*,[120] on the weekly portion of *Balak*.[121] The very act of return to Eretz Yisrael is the essence of repentance. "When despite the many hardships they will neither aban-

---

115   קפצה לו הארץ "The land sprung towards him." The "contraction" symbolized the mutual reciprocity of man's combined will and action to which God responds. Hul. 91b. כה יהיה דעתיה למיהדר קפצה ליה ארעא, מיד ויפגע במקום' "As soon as he decided to return, the land sprung towards him; at once 'he came upon the place' (Gen. 28:11)."

116   Cf. Isa. 53:10. וחפץ ד' בידו יצלח "And through him the Lord's purpose might prosper" vs. חפץ ד' יצליח בידינו "The Lord's purpose might prosper through us."

117   Support for the simultaneous action of people and God is introduced by the author via *MPs.* on Ps. 85:4 (*EHS*, 106).

118   R. Gershon Ashkenazi (d. 1693) a leading rabbinic authority in Poland, Moravia and Austria. Outspoken opponent of the Sabbatean movement; author of the collection of *Responsa Avodat HaGershuni* (Frankfurt, 1699). The editor was unable to trace the text in the 1861 Lemberg edition.

119   R. Shabbetai b. Meir HaKohen (1621–1662), rabbinic authority distinguished for his commentary on the *Shulhan Arukh*, *Siftei Cohen* (Cracow, 1641).

120   *Op. cit.*, 59b. See above, 99, n. 71.

121   Corresponding to Num. 22:2–25:9. The commentary is on the reading of the Prophets for the Balak portion, corresponding to Mic. 5:6–6:8.

don God nor their possession of the Holy Land, may it be speedily rebuilt and reestablished, this will represent the very essence of their repentance. This is so, since repentance must take place in the same circumstance and manner [which produced that which necessitates repentance]. After all, their sin during the [First] Temple period was their descent to Egypt, as it is written: 'Woe to them that go down to Egypt [for help].'[122] Many great sins emerged from this policy. Therefore, it is destined that their future repentance will come about by their not abandoning their possession."[123] Now behold how in our own time even those who were most found wanting have directed their attention towards returning to their possession and are dedicating themselves to that objective. They do not seek another land. . . .

The Holy One, blessed be He, must surely consider this as worthy of repentance. When they do not fulfill the [other] commandments of the Torah, it is due to their deficient background and [should be considered] as a "child captive among the gentiles"[124] as explained by our teacher Maimonides in the laws of "Rebels."[125] Yet their very *aliyah* will certainly be considered as repentance. . . .

Note what is written in *Midrash Talpiot*,[126] in the entry *Galut*. He

---

122 Isa. 31:1. The northern kingdom invited disaster by turning to Egypt for assistance against its powerful neighbor to the north. The prophets' warning about horses which may cause a kingdom to be lost went unheeded. See also Isa. 30:2–3. Reference may also be to Hezekiah's pro-Egyptian policy and his revolt against Sennacherib in 703–701 B.C.E.

123 The overreliance on Egypt rather than on the Almighty, according to the prophet, was tantamount to losing political independence—hence the "abandonment" of their Land.

124 כתינוק שנשבה בין העכום Reference to a person who may not be responsible for his actions due to mitigating circumstances in his environment. Shab. 68; Shav. 5a; Ker. 3b. See below, 165.

125 *Mishneh Torah, Sefer Shoftim, Hilkhot Mamrim* 3:3. הרי הוא כתינוק שנשבה ביניהם וגדלוהו. "He is like a child captive among those who reared him."

126 (Lemberg, 1875, 77b). Encyclopedic work, in alphabetical order of 926 entries (numerical value = תלפיות (*Talpiot*) by the rabbi and renowned preacher R. Eliyahu ben Avraham Shlomo HaKohen of Smyrna (d. 1729). Only the first part to the letter *khaf* was published in Smyrna, 1736. He is best known for his *Shevet Musar*, a classic collection of ethical sermons and novellae (Constantinople, 1712).

cites the *Zohar Hadash*:[127]

> Michael, the ministering angel responsible for Israel asked: "Master of
> the Universe, when will Israel be redeemed from the exile of Edom?
> You have indicated, after all, that following much suffering they would
> be redeemed." Replied the Holy One, blessed be He: "Let Sammael
> who oversees Edom debate this with you."[128] Argued Sammael: "You
> indicated that Israel will remain in exile until they repent. At the present
> they are wicked, etc." Said the Holy One, blessed be He, to Michael:
> "You should have taken note of the beginning of the statement: 'Return
> to the Lord your God [and obey Him].'[129] Only then is it written: 'For
> the Lord your God is a compasssionate God.'"[130] Replied Michael:
> "Master of the Universe, is it without reason that You are called
> Compassionate? Should You not be compassionate even when they
> may not be worthy?" Responded the Holy One, blessed be He: "I
> already gave My Word that they will not be redeemed until they repent
> before Me. Though it may be no larger than the eye of a needle, I will
> expand it into a large passage."[131]

We see therefore how God is prepared to redeem even were
repentance to be as slight as the "eye of the needle. . . ."[132]

---

127   A free rendering of the *Zohar Hadash* (43 b) passage by R. Eliyahu ben Avraham
Shlomo HaKohen.

128   Sammael is synonymous with Satan. Michael and Sammael assume the role of
defender and prosecutor respectively in rabbinic tradition. ExR. 18:5. כך מיכאל וסמאל
עומדים לפני השכינה מקטרג והשטן ומיכאל מלמד זכותן של ישראל. "Thus Michael and Sammael
appear before the Shekhinah. Satan accuses and Michael [the angel] defends the
Israelites." See below, 157, n. 156.

129   Deut. 4:30.

130   Ibid. 4:31. Supporting the argument of the prosecution.

131   Cf. with CantR. 5:2. אמר הקב"ה לישראל: בני פתחו לי פתח אחד של תשובה כחודה של
מחט ואני פותח לכם פתחים שיהיו עגלות וקרנות נכנסות בו. "Said the Holy One, blessed be
He, to the Jewish people: 'My children! Make for me an opening for repentance the
size of a needle and I shall make for you the openings through which wagons and
vehicles could enter.'"

132   Though the return to the Land is interpreted as only a small expression of
repentance, this initiative will stimulate God to "open up" the hearts of the nonobservant
leading to their complete "return." Their long sojourn in exile has only affected their
outer appearance. The Jewish soul remains pure and seeks to return to its source.

Take note of *Midrash Yalkut [Shimoni] Eikha* commenting on the verse:

"When the House of Israel dwelt on their own soil, they defiled it [with their ways and deeds]."[133] Said the Holy One, blessed be He: "If only my people would dwell in Eretz Yisrael even were they to defile it."[134]

In this vein, [we apply the *midrash*] in our own time. They have dwelt so long among the gentiles, that they are not aware of the implications of their transgressions, being victims of circumstances. They cannot be compared to the transgressors at the time of the second Temple. Further, they love the Land and will only accept the Land of their fathers. They are prepared to die for her. Many have given their lives for her. We heard of the Jewish defenders against the Arab uprisings who sacrificed their lives, exclaiming prior to their death: "No matter; it is good to die for our country."[135] Take note of Hatam Sofer citing the tractate Sanhedrin[136] in his Responsa: "A Jew who is killed by a gentile, is a *kadosh* [sacred martyr] though he may have been a transgressor and *rasha*."[137] Surely those who gave their

---

They are to be encouraged, and drawn close, since they are precious before God (*EHS*, 107–109).

133 Ez. 36:17.

134 *Yalkut Shimoni* II, 1038 .

135 Reference to Joseph Trumpeldor (1880–1920), Russian-Jewish war hero, pioneer of military defense of the Yishuv. He died defending Tel Hai in the Upper Galilee on March 1, 1920. His legendary last words are quoted by our author in bold print.

136 47a. The responsum cites Sanh. 48a.

137 *She'elot uTshuvot, Hatam Sofer, Yoreh De'ah*, responsum, 333 (p. 137, 1958, N. Y. edition). The case relates to a Jew killed by gentiles in 1811. Hatam Sofer refers to the victim as *kadosh*, citing in support Sanh. 47a, where the inhabitant transgressors of the "condemned city" (Deut. 13:13–19) achieve forgiveness by their very death. ביום עש"ק שופטים תקע"א לפי"ק הביאו לכאן איש קדוש איש הנהרג בידי עכו"ם רוצח ונקבר ביום א' שלאחריו ושמו ר' דוד בר"י שאכרלס ז"ל הי"ד . . . דנהרג בידי עכו"ם נתכפר לו מיד . . . ומחויב לקוברם בקבר אבותיהם לפי כבודם. ח"ס, יו"ד, תשובה שלג. "On the day before the holy Sabbath [Friday] of the [weekly] scripture portion of *Shoftim* [Deut. 16:18–20:9] in the year 5571 [1811] they delivered here the body of a holy martyr who was murdered by a gentile murderer. He was buried the following Sunday. His name was David the son of Judah [Joseph?] Shachrels, may his memory be a blessing, may God avenge his blood. . . for anyone killed by a gentile is forgiven immediately. . . It is an obligation

lives for our Land [are *kedoshim*]. See *Sifrei Zuta* on the portion of *Beha'alotkha*,[138] paragraph 33:

> R. Shimon said: "Behold the attractive character of Eretz Yisrael. All others who go to war are at first enthused. Yet when they approach the moment of battle they collapse [in fear]. But the Jewish people do not respond thus. When they approach Eretz Yisrael their feet carry them aloft, as one says to the other: 'Should we enter Eretz Yisrael and die at once; is it not worth our while to enter the very place which was promised to our Fathers by God?'"[139]

Such was the very response of the *kedoshim* who were killed in the battle against the Arabs, as described by R. Shimon.[140] Is there any doubt that they are worthy of the world to come? Though one may not realize it,[141] the Jewish soul thirsts to return to its source. Our sages have confirmed this: "For whoever lives in the Land of Israel may be considered to have a God,"[142] that is to say, though he may not consciously seek the Divine, yet his innermost soul craves [to return to God].[143]

Hatam Sofer comments in his volume of sermons for the days of *Sefirah*[144] on the verse: "I have gone astray, like a lost sheep; look for your servant, for I do not forget Your commandments."[145]

---

to bury them in their [Jewish] ancestral grave in accordance with the dignity that is their due." (Hatam Sofer, *Yoreh De'ah*, responsum 333)

138 Corresponding to Num. 8–12. The Midrash expounds Num. 10:33.

139 *Sifrei Zuta, Beha'alotkha*, 33 (Jerusalem, 1947), 52–53.

140 Ibid.

141 The religious significance of dwelling in Eretz Yisrael.

142 Ket. 110b.

143 The qualifying דומה (*domeh*) "is compared to," is the basis of our author's original interpretation. He introduces the "interlocking" concept of every element which constitutes the totality of Israel (כלל ישראל). Every Jew, irrespective of motive or degree of religious observance, may contribute a particular mitzvah towards the totality of mitzvot, thereby fulfilling the prophecies of Zech. 3:9–10 and Hos. 3:5. (*EHS*, 110.)

144 The period of forty-nine days between *Pesah* and *Shavuot* during which the Omer is counted. Hatam Sofer, *Derashot*, vol. 2, 290b.

145 Ps. 119:176.

Now on the basis of what we have learned in Baba Kama 118 [we may deduce the following]: If a man stole a sheep from the herd and returned it,[146] he will not fulfill the positive commandment of "returning" [the article to its owner][147] until he has expressly notified the owners [of their loss and restoration]. . . . Rabbi Hisda explains this as necessary to alert the owners of animals who have learned the habit of running out into the fields. . . .[148] It is further explained in the Jerusalem Talmud[149] that if the herd is led by an adult billy goat or a shepherd's pipe ["pandora"], or any other object [of note] whereby the stolen animal would recognize its herd, then the mere restoration is sufficient. In such an instance, although, the sheep tends to wander, it would nevertheless return to its original herd, since it has become accustomed to points of reference. So it is with us. Though Jews have necessarily sinned because of the evil impulse[150] and the subjection of foreign powers,[151] and have tended to wander into the fields, departing from the paths of Torah, as sheep gone astray, nevertheless do not ever suggest that restoration is difficult, Heaven forbid.

"For I have not neglected Your teaching."[152] Given the slightest

---

146 Mishnah, BQ 118a.

147 Ex. 23:5; Deut. 22:1–4.

148 ואנקטי נגריברייתא "They have learned to wander outside." Mere restoration would not be sufficient since the owners would not be aware of the animal's wandering habits and would not take any special caution.

149 JT BQ 10:8. תיישא רבא דמרין אית, פנדורא דמרין אית חוטרא, דמרין אית. "There are [sheep] led by a shepherd's staff, those by a shepherd's pipe and those [trained to follow] an adult billy goat." It is puzzling as to why our author cites the *Shulhan Arukh, Hoshen Mishpat* (likely, *Hilkhot Genevah,* 356), attempting to reinforce the Yerushalmi when the Hatam Sofer cites only the Yerushalmi. *Hoshen Mishpat* makes no reference to either the תייש [billy goat] nor the פנדורה [shepherd's pipe].

150 *Lit.,* "the yeast in the dough," שאור שבעיסה.

151 Cf. Ber. 17a. רבון העולמים, גלוי וידוע לפניך שרצוננו לעשות רצונך,ומי מעכב? שאור שבעיסה ושעבוד מלכויות. "Master of the Universe, you are fully aware that we want to comply with Your will. What prevents [us]? The evil impulse and our subjugation to foreign nations."

152 Ps. 119:153. Resolution of the stray sheep parable. The Torah, like a shepherd's flute, is a point of reference for the Jew, though he may have gone far astray. One must never despair from restoring the lost Jew to his people. The latent spark may be hidden from the individual, but it could be ignited at any moment. Illustrating the retrievability of lost souls, our author cites the Abravanel commentary on Isa. 66:20–21.

reminder we recall the heyday of our youth, "leaning on her beloved,"[153] blessed be His Name. . . .[154]

Note what is taught in the first chapter of Berakhot[155] concerning Isaiah the prophet who spoke to Hezekiah the king saying:

"Set your affairs in order, for you are going to die and not live. . . .[156] You shall die in this world and not live in the world to come. Asked Hezekiah: "What is the meaning of all this?"[157] Replied he: "Because you did not try to have children." Said he: "I had reason, because I saw by the Holy Spirit that the children issuing forth from me would not be virtuous." Replied he: "Since when are the secrets of the All-Merciful your affairs? You should have fulfilled that which you were commanded and allow the Holy One, blessed be He, do that which pleases Him."[158]

This is relevant to our discussion. Since every Jew is obligated to fulfill the mitzvah of settling in Eretz Yisrael and of helping to rebuild our Holy Land, it is incumbent upon him to declare: "What has been entrusted to me by the Holy One, blessed be He, I must fulfill; what God eventually wishes to bring about is His affair." And as Hezekiah could not exempt himself from the mitzvah of procreation, claiming that his offspring would be unworthy, so too one is not permitted to

---

The verse "And from them likewise I will take some to be priests and Levites," is applied to the forced converts of the Inquisition in Spain and Portugal. ואמר שמאותם ב״י שיבאו מהארצות הרחוקות שהיו מעורבים בגויים ונשקעים בתוכם גם מהם יקח להיות כהנים ולויים ולא יחושו אם נמכרו לעבדים ונעשו גויים ע״י האונס . . . . "He [Isaiah] meant to indicate that from these very Jews who were assimilated among the gentiles He will take those who will be priests and Levites. . . . They will not be concerned whether they were sold into slavery or were forcibly converted." Don Isaac Abravanel (1437–1508) the great Sefardic classical biblical commentator could count his grandfather and grandson among the forced converts. Both subsequently returned to Judaism (*EHS*, 112–113). See below, 114, n. 165.

153   Song 8:5, portraying the relationship of resolute love between the people of Israel and their Creator.

154   Hatam Sofer, *Derashot*. See above, 109, n. 137.

155   10a.

156   Isa. 38:1; II Kings 20:1.

157   That I should be punished thus.

158   Ber. 10a. See below, 282, n. 1012.

excuse himself from the mitzvah of rebuilding the Land by claiming that his efforts will not be adequate, Heaven forbid. Surely it is the command of the Creator which is being fulfilled.[159]

In all of his wonderful works our teacher Maharal, when he wishes to draw the attention of the reader to some extraordinary idea, will comment as follows: "There is no doubt that significant events do not occur by chance. They are the result of Divine Providence."[160] This point is emphasized frequently for those who have studied his sacred works, to which I have devoted myself; they will be made aware of this extraordinary phenomenon present during our entire history in exile. The student of this history will observe the constant cycle of instability. We are unable to rest our feet for too long in any given place. Though we may live for a while in security and peace, it is not long before the increasing jealousy and hatred of our gentile neighbors becomes apparent. They eventually take our money and property, all that we own. They compel us to leave the country bare, without any means. Thus we wander from nation to nation; from the frying pan into the fire. . . . This is precisely the situation which we find ourselves at this very moment in almost all of the European nations. We find

---

159 The tragedy of the spies, the aborted entry into Eretz Yisrael (Num. 13–14) and Israel's destined "permanent weeping for future generations" (NumR. *Shelah* 16:20. לדורות בכיה לכם אקבע אני לפני, חינם של בכיה בכיתם אלא. "But since you wept for nought before Me, I shall cause you to weep for generations") are the consequences of second guessing the Almighty, and a lack of confidence and faith in His superior judgment. This theme is the focus of text cited by our author from *Tosafot ben Yehiel* a commentary on the *Midrash Tanna DeBei Eliyahu* (Jerusalem, 1906), by Akiva Yosef Schlesinger (1837–1922) among the leading forerunners of modern religious Zionism who settled in Eretz Yisrael in 1870 and helped found Petah Tikvah in 1878 (*EHS*, 112). See below, 235. The participation of all elements of Jewry is a concomitant of the prerequisite for the necessary gradual evolution of the final redemption (*EHS*, 113–115). See above, 92, n. 35.

160 *Gevurot HaShem* (London, 1954), 85, 95. See below, 120, n. 202. שהיה לומר וא"י
דבר זה במקרה שהרי מדבר זה בא הגאולה שעל ידי זה ברח [משה] למדין ונשא בת יתרו ונגלה לו
השכינה. ואיך תהיה הגאולה במקרה? שאין דבר יותר חשוב כמו גאולת ישראל. ואיך תהיה על ידי דבר
במקרה? זה לא יתכן. "It is impossible to say that this occurred by chance. After all, redemption was the result! Because of this occurence he [Moses] took flight to Midian, married Jethro's daughter and was exposed to the revelation of the Shekhinah. How, therefore, is it possible for redemption to occur by chance? Nothing, after all, is as essential as the redemption of the Jewish people. Could such an event, indeed, occur by chance? It is impossible!"

ourselves amidst such enormous cruelties, which neither our tongue nor our pens are able to recount. As R. Shimon b. Gamliel said in Shabbat 13, "For if we came to record them, we would be inadequate."[161]

What has befallen us presently is not unique. History repeats itself.[162] Nevertheless, it never occurred to us in times gone by, when we were compelled to abandon our dwelling place, that we should acquire a new community and settlement in our Holy Land. It was only during these recent decades in which a movement arose for the purpose of purchasing land in Eretz Yisrael, and to make them fertile to plant gardens and orchards and to build homes. Tracts of land which had lain as wasteland for two thousand years and were useless; and which were no more than swamps and mud basins, breeders of diseases, are being transformed into places worthy of settlement. From its inception, despite obstacles and delays which everywhere confronted these pioneers, Eretz Yisrael is becoming a productive land, commercially viable, and a towering center[163] as well. Many thousands turn to her from every corner of the world. She has become "beautiful in her panorama, the joy of all the earth."[164] Why did all this not occur to them during the numerous expulsions in times gone by? . . . Among them were great personalities such as the Abravanel.[165] Why did they not think of acquiring land in Eretz Yisrael and transforming it into a modern settlement? Note the letter of Don Isaac Abravanel to the *gaon* the Prince of Pisa[166] (from a manuscript in the British Museum)[167] in which he cries out against the bitter fate of the Jewish people.

Take heed and see how we have had no peace nor rest from the time

---

161   13b. אף אנו מחבבין את הצרות, אבל מה נעשה שאם באנו לכתוב אין אנו מספיקין.

162   Yiddish in *EHS* source.

163   ולתל תלפיות (*U'letel Talpiot*) [An elevated tower of beauty.] See Ber. 30a on the verse in Song 4:4

164   Ps. 48:3.

165   See above, III, n. 152. Expelled from Spain in May 1492, and forced to flee Naples in 1494.

166   Yehiel b. Isaac da Pisa (d. 1490), the most prominent of the distinguished da Pisa family of loan bankers in Italy during the Renaissance.

167   British Museum Ms. Add. 27, 129.

when our city [Jerusalem] was destroyed, our Temple laid waste and Judah sent into exile. Because of the malice of Edom and the Ismaelites,[168] and *Hagrites*[169] we have always been the objects of incrimination.

If it happened that we benefit from a day or two of respite,[170] it would not be long before we again would be pounded with the rumble of fear emanating from the east, west, north and south, consuming the remnant of Israel, stripping their skin in the process.[171]

[When this letter was written] he still lived among royalty in Portugal. Why did he not consult with this great prince[172] in order to create projects whereby land would be acquired in Eretz Yisrael for the purpose of settling it anew. This would have served the ingathering of the persecuted exiles who were being banished from place to place. They never even discussed the current model [of pioneering and settlement]. Did they lack material resources? They were still at the pinnacle of their wealth. Since the time of the Abravanel it has also not occurred to anyone [to engage in practical settlement]. . . .[173]

Now, following this long exile, can these present efforts to rebuild the Land anew; to prepare it so that it will absorb its children; to build homes and acquire fields for agriculture; to make it suitable for settlement—is all this mere chance, Heaven forbid?[174]

I am fully aware, my children, that my words will arouse difficult questions. If indeed the current rebuilding in the Holy Land is an

---

168 Christianity and Islam in post-biblical context.

169 Cf. Ps. 83:7. "Moab" in the original Ps. text is deleted in our text.

170 Cf. Ex. 21:21 אַךְ אִם יוֹם אוֹ יוֹמַיִם יַעֲמֹד. "But if he survives a day or two."

171 Letter of Isaac Abravanel to Yehiel ben Isaac da Pisa in *Sefer Ha'Atzamim*, copied and published by R. Menashe Grossberg (London, 1901), 34–40.

172 Yehiel ben Isaac da Pisa.

173 Our author briefly describes the unsuccessful venture of Don Joseph Nasi (1524–1579), prominent statesman of Marrano origin, who obtained concessions from the Sultan to establish a viable community in Tiberias (1558). Numerous political intrigues in the Tiberias area and in Constantinople prevented him from realizing his projects. [*EHS*, 116–17].

174 Our author reviews sources and text previously cited. See above, 52-53, 57-58, 89-94, which demonstrate the prerequisite of settlement for messianic redemption. [*EHS*, 117–119.]

indication of the approaching end and the beginning of redemption, how are we to explain the considerable number of pioneers who unfortunately violate the Sabbath and commit transgressions, Heaven forbid? They seem to behave like people of other nations. How is it possible that the Creator of the entire world would signify the beginning of redemption by way of their acts?

Is it not within our tradition: "Reward is brought about through a person of merit [and punishment through a person of guilt]?"[175] My dear children: Your question seemingly has much merit. Nevertheless, heed my words well. Who is able to comprehend the meaning of the acts of the One of perfect understanding? Behold the God of the universe. All that occurs on this earth derives from Him. From the innermost depth of His deliberations He sets into motion intricate processes whereby His decrees are fulfilled in the world below. He knows and understands why He chose precisely these [instrumentalities] to initiate the beginnings of redemption and designated them as favorable portents.

I will demonstrate with a clear passage from tractate Hullin 63[176] concerning unclean fowl: Raham,[177] refers to a vulture [shrakrak].

> Asked R. Yehudah: "Why is it called raham? Because when raham comes, mercy comes upon the world." (Rashi explains: rahamim [mercy] refers to rain.) R. Bibi the son of Abaye said: "Provided it perches upon something and cried 'shrakrak' (Rashi explains: "When it chirps it sounds like 'shrakrak.'") There is a tradition that if it settles upon the ground and whistles, the Messiah will come at once, for it is said: "I will whistle to them and gather them [for I will redeem them]."[178] Rashi comments upon the verse in Zechariah 10: "'I will whistle to them', as one might whistle in order to draw the attention of someone who has lost his way,

---

175 Shab. 32a; NumR. 13:17. How can these pioneers, transgressors, serve as the Divine instrument for the reward of initiating redemption?

176 Hul. 63a.

177 Lev. 11:18; Deut. 14:17. Various translations relate raham to the eagle or vulture family (Jastrow). Others translate "bustard," of the Otididae family of game birds. (JPS Torah, 1962.)

178 Zech. 10:8.

'and gather them' in time for the eventual End." For a brief moment I was stunned by this teaching of our sages. The prophet predicts that the signal for the eventual End of Days and the redemption would be given by an unclean fowl. This is reiterated by the Talmud. . . . Would it not have been more appropriate for the signal to be given by a clean fowl and that "reward be brought about by someone of merit"?[179] Actually the truth is as Job said, "will you fathom God by means of examination?"[180] Is there anyone able to account for His acts? God understands the way of wisdom.[181] Why would He indeed choose as His instrument *this* particular creature? "Since when are the secrets of the All-Merciful your affairs?". . . .[182]

Questions of this kind concerning the acts of the Almighty are better not asked. His ways are beyond ours; His plans are not our plans.[183] It is sufficient that they are the agents of the Merciful One. Therefore, remain silent. Do not interrogate our God! A hint to the wise is sufficient.[184]

If you wish, I am prepared to demonstrate further that the builders of the Land, who seem to you as the wicked of Israel, Heaven forbid, are actually the harbingers of redemption, as suggested in Talmud Hullin cited previously. Our sacred teacher in his volume *Noam Elimelekh*[185] compares the wicked of Israel to the unclean fowl mentioned in the Torah. . . .[186]

---

179 Hul. 63a.

180 Job 11:7, interpreted as follows

181 Cf. Job 28:23.

182 Ber. 10a.

183 Cf. Isa. 55: 8–9.

184 A harsh response to the Orthodox leadership who rejected any cooperation with the Zionist endeavor on the grounds that its movers and activists were "transgressors of Israel."

185 R. Elimelekh of Lizhensk. See above, 89, n. 10.

186 Probable reference to the positive attributes of the eagle (*Noam Elimelekh*, *Vayikra* 48a) and the raven (ibid. *Ki Tavo* 84b). The unclean fowl are associated with *kelipah* (ibid. *Devarim* 78b) which envelops and entraps the holy spark. The process of *tikkun* and redemption is to release the "clean" or sacred core, stripping the *kelipah* of its "unclean" shell. Our author alludes to the challenge of "stripping" the secular

(Note *Bekhor Shor* on Baba Kamma[187] and *Torat Hayyim* in the chapter of *Helek*[188] commenting according to the Kabbalah. Since I am presently without books, in exile in the capitol, hidden in the remote part of a home, I am unable to cite the source referred to.) (While on the subject, I will comment as to why the Talmud emphasized "When it settles upon the ground [and whistles, the Messiah will come at once. . . .]"[189] This is related to the commentary of *Midrash Exodus Rabba* upon the verse" 'And they will rise up [and leave] "from" the Land.'[190] Whenever Israel is at its lowest ebb it will rise, for see what is written 'And they will rise up from the Land.'[191] Similarly, David said: 'For our soul is bowed down to the dust; our belly clings to the earth,'[192] at that very moment [David explains]: 'Arise and help us and redeem us for the sake of Your goodness."'[193]

This is the intent of the Talmud "When it settles upon the ground": When Israel's glory will have been severed and ground down, then, it seems to me, the Messiah will come.

Now, my children, aside from allaying your concerns as to how it is possible for the Holy One, blessed be He, to initiate redemption by

---

builders of the "unclean" exterior, allowing their "sacred" core to be fully released, exposed and elevated. This is possible only by encouraging and joining in their task. Thus *tikkun* and redemption take place simultaneously on two interacting levels, in the Land and in the individual Jew.

187 *Bekhor Shor* (Zolkiew, 1733) BQ 120b, by the distinguished Talmud scholar in Poland, R. Alexander Sender ben Ephraim Zalman Schor (d. 1737), a small collection of novellae on various Talmud tractates. Elaborating upon the verse in Ben Sira 13:15 cited in BQ 92b, the *Bekhor Shor* quotes the Ari: The segregationist thrust of this commentary would seem to run counter to the integrative and unifying approach of our author.

188 *Sefer Torat Hayyim* 32a (Prague, 1692) on Sanh. 108b. It is difficult to identify the relevant passage. Possible reference to the legendary phoenix bird who was blessed with long life. In Sanh. 108b the bird is blessed with eternal life because it sacrificed its own comforts for the sake of others (Noah). The connection between impure birds and their role in redemption may have been the intention of the author.

189 Hul. 63a.

190 Ex. 1:10.

191 ExR. 1:9.

192 Ps. 44:26.

193 Ibid. 44:27.

means of those who transgress His will and by means of those who lack even a semblance of Judaism, Heaven forbid, the Almighty enlightened me with another reason which I wish to share within my finite understanding. I will preface this with a passage from Sanhedrin 97b commenting on the verse "Though he be delayed, wait for him":[194] Should you claim: "*We* look forward [to his coming] but *He* does not," therefore, the verse exclaims: "Surely the Lord is waiting to show you forgiveness; indeed He will arise to pardon you."[195] (Rashi comments: "The Lord Himself awaits and desires the Messiah.[196] But since we await him and He does likewise, what delays [the coming of the Messiah]?. . . The attribute of Divine Justice delays it.[197] In the literature of the Kabbalah it is expounded that when the Almighty, blessed be He, wishes to achieve something of extraordinary significance to both the upper as well as lower world, he then chooses to conceal it in a variety of garments, even to the extent of draping it in unseemly forms. Further, it is purposely encased in ugliness so that the prosecuting judges and accusers would be unaware of its significance.[198] Were it in fact proclaimed openly this would immediately invite the intervention of the accuser. The attribute of Justice would impede [the redeeming action]. . . .[199] Likewise it is written in the sacred volume *Noam Elimelekh, Vayeshev:* "If someone intends to break up the power of an object, he must do so employing

---

194   Hab. 2:3.

195   Isa. 30:18.

196   The actual Rashi commentary on "The Lord is waiting" אלא יחכה וימתין עד בא קיצה. "He will await and look forward to his coming until the end of days."

197   Sanh. 97b.

198   Cf. ibid. 97a. ג׳ באין בהיסח הדעת, אלו הן: משיח מציאה ועקרב. "Three come unexpectedly. They are: the Messiah, a lost object, a scorpion."

199   Supporting sources introduced include the *Maggid Mesharim* commentary of R. Joseph Karo on Gen. 45:5. The sacred objective may assume a profane guise in order to enable the holy forces to enter into the unholy realm and to conquer the *kelipah* from within. In this fashion Joseph justifies his descent into Egyptian exile. "Now, do not be distressed or reproach yourselves." Similarly this explains the emergence of King David, the Redeemer, from Ruth the Moabite. The camouflage permitted David to contend with the "other side" (*Sitra Ahra*). To break the enemy from within, instrumentalities of the enemy are to be employed. *Maggid Mesharim, Vayigash* (Lemberg, 1840), 23b. [*EHS*, 121].

a similar object."[200] This corresponds to the teaching of the *Maggid Mesharim*. . . .[201]

Observe what is written in the eighteenth chapter of *Gevurot HaShem* by our teacher Maharal of Prague.[202] I will cite his sacred words at length since they illuminate contemporary events in Eretz Yisrael, namely, the paradox of reaching a lofty Divine purpose by means of much materialistic and mundane endeavor. Heaven forbid that they [the pioneer—toilers] be rejected and interfered with. On the contrary, we must draw near to them as much as possible and support them. This is precisely the will and purpose of God. It is destined from on High that from these very toilers will emerge a marvelous and most lofty handiwork which is linked to our great future and the ascending glory of our sacred nation as reflected in the prophecy of our sacred prophets.

> You must understand why the intrinsic Divine character of this Holy Kingdom of Israel emerges from within a profane kingdom. That indeed a kingdom with a godly temperament evolved in this fashion is alluded to in the verse: "I have brought fire from out of you."[203] That is to say, the expulsion of sacred substance, symbolized by fire, emerging from within the godly system of the profane, consumes everything in its wake.[204] A similar process takes place with premature fruit encased in its peel [*kelipah*] until it is ready to emerge fully mature. It then rejects its outer layer, as does anything with an inner more exalted core. . . . Such was the [process of] maturation of Moses our teacher, may he rest in peace, when he was [raised] in Pharaoh's court. There as well the

---

200   *Noam Elimelekh, Vayeshev* 19b.

201   See n. 199. Additional examples are cited from *Noam Elimelekh, Korah* 69a (Abraham's origins from Terah), and the Alshich and *Iggeret Shmuel* commentaries on Ruth the Moabite. Here as well, the camouflage theory is emphasized.

202   A philosophic and homiletical treatise on the Exodus from Egypt and a comprehensive analysis of the Passover festival (Cracow, 1582).

203   Ez. 28:18.

204   The purposeful implant of the sacred within the profane achieves the desired destruction of the profane in the process of emergence and eruption. See the paradoxical application of this principle among the Sabbatean radicals as discussed in G. Scholem "The Holiness of Sin," *Commentary* 51:1 (January 1971), 57.

inner divine character of Moses was compelled to emerge from its material frame, otherwise, his intrinsic [Divine] substance could not have been distinguishable. This concept is most profound, and familiar to those who study such phenomena. . . So it is with the Messiah who lingers in the kingdom of the Edomites. . . ."[205, 206]

Thus it is actually Satan who is forever awaiting us in ambush and insistent on delaying redemption. When the Land is rebuilt and the Shekhinah is raised from the dust, this represents the fall and the destruction of the *Sitra Ahra* (the other, impure side). Now if the initial stage of rebuilding [the Land] had been attempted by the *Haredim*[207] and the God-fearing, it would have been obvious to all concerned [that the objective was] to build a city of God. Imagine if among the pioneers of the movement to build and make the Land fruitful, were the likes of our rabbis of Belz,[208] Shiniva [Sieniawa],[209] Gur,[210] and Munkatch,[211] and other great *tzadikim* of this generation, how could they have avoided detection by the attribute of Justice and the *Sitra Ahra*, knowing that their very objective [if realized] would have broken their power forever and signaled their destruction! . . . They would have certainly intervened and delayed them. . . .[212]

---

205 Cf. Sanh. 98 a. והיכא יתיב? אפיתחא דקרתא "Where does he sit? At the gates of the city," and Rashi and Vilna Gaon readings of בפתחא דרומי "At the gates of Rome" and the related Maharsha commentary.

206 *Gevurot HaShem* (Lemberg, 1859 edition), 31b. Additional sources heretofore introduced are again amplified in the following chapter. These focus on the gradual, natural forms of redemption. *EHS*, 123.

207 Reference to the ultra-Orthodox, *lit*. "the fearing ones."

208 See above, 73, n. 79.

209 R. Yehezkel Shraga Halberstam (1811–1899) most prominent of the sons of R. Hayyim Halberstam, founder of the Galician hasidic dynasty of Zans. His works were collected in the posthumous volume *Divrei Yehezkel* (Shiniva, 1906).

210 Likely reference to R. Avraham Mordechai Alter (1866–1948) great grandson of R. Yitzhak Meir Rothenberg Alter, the founder of the Gur (Gerer) hasidic dynasty. See below, 189, n. 396.

211 See above, 73, n. 79 and 98, n. 64.

212 Our author attributes such "delaying" strategies to the failure of the rebuilding projects of R. Joshua b. Hananiah (See above, 93, n. 40) and Don Joseph Nasi (115, n. 173), the camouflage of the Persian Emperor Cyrus as the instrument of the second return (516 B.C.E.) and the "strategic" delays of the returned exiles during

Note that all my reference to the builders of the Land as *resha'im* [wicked ones] were merely the terms devised by the zealots who refer to them as such. I meant to indicate that even according to their frame of reference, they err.[213] As I demonstrated, they [the apparently wicked] also serve as the agents of the Almighty. I personally, however, cannot accept this assumption. In my opinion they are not wicked at all. They are the true descendents of Abraham, Isaac and Jacob. They are the proven seed [of the people Israel]... May this serve as a lesson to those who with impunity transform a Jew into a *rasha* and refer to him by such a designation. They [who rebuild the Land] are all the beloved seed of God, blessed be He. May He inspire them from Above with a genuine spirit, to refine their hearts, to draw them near to His blessed service, all these due to the merit of dedicating their lives to the mitzvah of settlement. Amen, may it be Your will....[214]

It is taught in the *Tanna DeBei Eliyahu Rabba*, first chapter:[215]

"To guard the way,"[216] this refers to proper behavior.[217] The "Tree of Life,"[218] —this teaches that "proper behavior" precedes the "Tree of Life." Now the "Tree of Life" is actually Torah, as it is written "It is a tree of life to those who grasp hold of it."[219]

The rabbi, *gaon* and *tzadik* comments on this passage:[220]

"This teaches that 'proper behavior' precedes the 'Tree of Life.'" This has need of explanation. What kind of *derekh eretz* (proper behavior) is

---

the period of Ezra. (CantR. 5:4). (*EHS*, 125) The advantage of redemption in natural guise is now clear. It will not be recognised by the accusers. [*EHS*, 128].

213   Since even the wicked serve a valuable role in the redemption process.

214   The need to camouflage redemptive acts by means of questionable agents is well documented (*EHS*, 126–128).

215   1:1.

216   Gen. 3:24.

217   *Lit.* "the way of the land," דרך ארץ (*derekh eretz*), i.e., proper behavior in earning a livelihood and settling the land, subsequently to be related to the Land, דרך המביא לארץ "The path which leads to the Land."

218   Gen. 3:24.

219   Prov. 3:18.

220   R. Akiva Yosef Schlesinger, *Tosafot Ben Yehiel, op. cit.*, 2a.

inferred here? As it is defined in the *Yalkut*:[221] "There [Adam and Eve] were driven out from the Land, this refers to Eretz Yisrael"[222]

It may also be implied that one must not accept the opinion of the spies who rejected the Land,[223] by claiming that Torah precedes Eretz Yisrael. They, therefore, asked not to enter Eretz Yisrael but rather to remain in the desert in order to study Torah with Moses our Teacher, since Torah was reserved only for those who partook of the manna.[224] Our text, therefore, teaches us that "the way of the Land" [*derekh eretz*] is actually the way which leads to the Land, and this takes precedence over Torah, as it is written in the *Sifrei* [*Re'eh*][225] that "settlement of Eretz Yisrael outweighs the entire Torah."[226] He further states that the spies erred when they refused to enter Eretz Yisrael, concerned that when residing in the Land their sins would be considered to be more severe than if they resided outside the Land.[227] By this very act they, in fact, sinned, since this equated them with the nations of the world, who refused to take upon themselves the responsibility of Torah. Israel, however, exclaimed in great faith: "We will do and obey . . ."[228] "If one

---

221 *Yalkut Shimoni* I, 34.

222 Probable reference to: הראה לו חורבן בית המקדש "He disclosed to him the destruction of the Temple." ibid. See also *Tanh. Genesis* (Buber ed.) 25 שבשבילו חרב בית המקדש. "This was the cause of the destruction of the Temple."

223 Num. 13–14.

224 R. Schlesinger introduces irony into his midrash-commentary, which he considered to be of contemporary significance. It was after all, Moses who pleaded to be permitted to enter the Land (Deut. 3:23–27). See above, II 7, n. 159. See *Mekhilta, Beshalah*, 56. מכאן היה רבי שמעון בן יוחאי אומר: לא נתנה תורה לדרוש אלא לאוכלי המן "This compelled R. Shimon bar Yochai to say: 'The interpretation of Torah was restricted to those who ate the manna.'"

225 On Deut. 12:29. *Sifrei* 90.

226 וירשתם אותה וישבתם בה, ושמרת לעשות את כל החוקים האלה ואת המשפטים (דברים יא:לא-לב) אמרו: ישיבת ארץ ישראל שקולה נגד כל המצוות שבתורה. "'When you have inherited and settled in it, take care to observe all the laws and norms. . . .' They taught: Settlement of Eretz Yisrael outweighs the entire Torah." The verse in Deut. 11:31 prefaces the commandment of settlement to the observance of the other mitzvot (*Sifrei*, 90). See below, 145, n. 87; 166 and 267.

227 Due to the sanctity of the Land.

228 Ex. 24:7. The unconditional acceptance of Torah by Israel was linked to their eventual entry into the Land. The spies had now rejected this act of faith.

comes to cleanse himself, he is helped."[229]

Thus we need not be concerned if we sin in the process of our settling [the Land], since "he who comes to cleanse himself will be helped from Above. . . ."[230]

It seems to me that just as the End is obscure and hidden without benefit of predictablity, likewise the essence and character of redemption, how it will begin or terminate, how it will proceed, all this will also be obscure and hidden. As it is written in the *Derashot HaRan*, towards the close of the eleventh homily:[231]

> We have as evidence the redemption from Egypt. At the very time of their own redemption, in the midst of extraordinary acts and events, they were unable to comprehend their origin until it was revealed to them by the Almighty Himself, blessed be He.[232] Surely we will be even less informed concerning the future redemption. This is why Maimonides stated[233] that "redemptive events will not be made known until the moment they occur. . . ."[234]

---

229 Shab. 104a; Yoma 38b. The Almighty assists those who act honorably. *Tosafot ben Yehiel, op. cit* 1b.

230 Our author continues to develop the theme of the "gradual" and "natural" process of redemption. Such a process would include a transitional period of partial foreign rule in Eretz Yisrael. During this period, the Temple would be rebuilt with the approval of the other nations. Unlike the First and Second Temples built and rebuilt by Solomon and Zerubavel-Cyrus, the Third Temple will be the product of the entire Jewish people. These evolutionary steps would lead to the full redemption and the establishment of the Davidic Kingdom. Sources from Isa. 44, the Jerusalem and Babylonian Talmud, and their commentaries, Saadia Gaon, Maimonides, Nahmanides, Radak, R. Bahya ben Asher, Meir Loeb ben Yehiel Michael, Abravanel and R. Ephraim Zalman Margulit (*Shem Efraim*, commentary on Rashi, 1760–1828) are introduced to support this form of redemption. [*EHS*, 131–2].

231 Volume of twelve sermons (Constantinople, 1533) by R. Nissim ben Reuben Gerondi (Ran c. 1310–1375); among the foremost rabbinic scholars in Spain.

232 Most likely a reference to the passive and ambivalent attitude of the people throughout the Exodus, until the climax and revelation described in Ex. 14:31. וירא ישראל את היד הגדולה אשר עשה ד' במצרים וייראו העם את ד' ויאמינו בד' ובמשה עבדו. "And when Israel saw the wondrous power which the Lord had wielded against the Egyptians, the people feared the Lord; they had faith in the Lord, and in His servant Moses."

233 *Iggeret Teiman, op. cit.*, part 3, 151-177.

234 *Shneym-Assar Drushim L'harav Rabbenu Nissim*, (Jerusalem, 1959) 42 (83). Hence,

At the beginning of this winter, on the fourth day of the week of
Vayeshev[235] in the year 5703[236] while in exile,[237] circumstances compelled
me to return to Bosermin[238] my former community.[239] I was able to
visit my former student, my friend, scholar, *hasid* and noted man of
wealth, our teacher R. Abish Rothman. During winter days in my
youth, when I lived in the home of my father-in-law, of blessed
memory, the *gaon* and *tzadik*, our teacher R. Yaakov Yosef Ginz,[240]
head of the Rabbinical Court [in Bosermin], I studied with him daily
and diligently lessons in Talmud and the *Tosafot* commentaries. He
[R. Abish], in turn, became a distinguished leader in his community.
He was an ardent *hasid* of the great *gaon*; prince of Torah; the sacred
light; master of both the revealed as well as the esoteric tradition;
expert in the study of Zohar; the holy and glorious R. Aharon Yeshayahu
Fish,[241] of blessed and sacred memory; head of the rabbinic court in
the holy community of Hades;[242] among the great disciples of our
rabbi of Komarno; who conferred upon him the statue of *rebbe*. I had
the privilege of making his acquaintance. We enjoyed basking in the
warmth of Torah during his annual winter visits to Bosermin. It was

---

any manifestations of redemption, no matter the quarter from which it emanates nor
the form which it assumes, must be welcomed and nurtured (*EHS*, 133).

235   The portion of weekly scriptural reading from Gen. 37:1–40:23.

236   December 23, 1942.

237   Budapest.

238   Hajduboszoreny in northeast Hungary.

239   It is possible that with the more ambivalent policy of Hungary towards Germany
during M. Kallay's assumption of political leadership (10, 3, 1942) the inhibition of
movement of Jews within the country was temporarily reduced. See, L. Rotkirchen
Toldot Yehudei Hungaria (Jerusalem, 1976), 109; Reutlinger, *The Final Solution*, 449–54.
See also below, 231, n. 672.

240   Distinguished rabbinic personage in Hungary (d. 1925), author of *Harei Besamim*
(Song 8:14) (Warsaw, 1931) a commentary and homilies on *Midrash* passages in
accordance with the weekly readings of scripture.

241   *Tzadik* and ascetic (d. 1928); distinguished disciple of R. Yaakov Moshe Safrin
(1861–1929) of the Komarno hasidic dynasty. Father-in-law of R. Eliezer Schapira of
Munkatch.

242   Hajduhadhaz in Northeastern Hungary; one of several towns with the prefix
Hajdu by which the general area NNW of Debrecen is known.

his habit to visit his *hasidim* and admirers in different communities, during the various Sabbaths in the calendar. It is impossible to describe his piety and simplicity beyond his recognized qualities of scholarship and common sense. He was able to distinguish between authenticity and falsehood. He was truly a great man among the giants. . . . At the time Abish repeated to me a conversation which he heard from the very lips of this sacred person. It concerned the nascent Zionist movement which was attempting to proceed with the rebuilding of Eretz Yisrael when many of the great sages attacked them.[243] He, however, responded as follows:

> Leave them be. We truly have no idea how redemption will come about. The Zohar[244] is ambivalent as to whether redemption will be preceded by the rebuilding of Jerusalem and the ingathering of the exiles, or whether it will take place without our assistance. Since we do not know the will of the Almighty, and are witness to those who enthusiastically wish to rebuild though they may be the most unsatisfactory among Israel, who will dare to obstruct them in their work! Perhaps it is the Will of God that the rebuilding will be done by this kind of people! Are the secrets of the Almighty your affair?[245] The Prime Mover and Planner knows how to shape events. Therefore, leave them be. . . .

I have learned from an authentic source who heard the following from the sacred lips of the godly person, the *gaon* in matters revealed and hidden, the Admor of Vizhnitz,[246] the master and rabbi, the holy

---

243　*Lit.* "stoned them."

244　Zohar I, *Midrash HaNe'elam, Toldot,* 139a. דתנן: בית המקדש קודם לקבוץ גלויות. ק״ג קודם לתחיית המתים, ות״ה הוא אחרון שבכלם. "It was taught: The Temple will precede the ingathering of the exiles. The ingathering will precede the resurrection of the dead. The resurrection will be the final stage." See also Zohar I, 134a. But note Zohar III, 221 ואכנס לון קב״ה לבנייהו בארעא. וביתא אתבני על ידא דבר נש, ובגין כך לא אתקיים. "And God brought their children to the land, and the house was built by human hands, and, therefore, it did not endure." Here man's initiative is negated.

245　Ber. 10a. בהדי כבשי דרחמנא למה לך? "Of what affair are the secrets of the All-Merciful to you?"

246　R. Yisrael Hager (1860–1936) grandson of R. Menahem Mendel the founder of the Vizhnitz hasidic dynasty. Author of *Ahavat Yisrael* (Grosswardein, 1943) and

R. Yisrael who lived in Grosswardein. He refused to participate in attempts to outlaw the Zionists. He believed that their rebuilding of the Land was decreed by Heaven, since the *biryonim*[247] were responsible for the destruction of our Land and Temple. Therefore, these were to rebuild in order to make amends for what they had originally destroyed. . . .[248]

Note, therefore, how two great people with keen insight recognized the power from Above which motivated the acts of these builders.[249]

It is appropriate at this time to relate a wonderful story told to me by my colleague the outstanding *gaon*, the holy and glorious Rabbi Yisrael Weltz[250] *dayan* [rabbinical judge] and teacher in the assembly of God-fearing congregants in the capital city. When the Malbim[251] published his commentary on the Book of Daniel[252] he was criticized by the outstanding scholars of his time for calculating the End of Days at the conclusion of his commentary.[253] They sent him a

---

Or Yisrael (Aradea, 1938). He founded a major yeshiva in Grosswardein (Nagyvarad, SE Hungary).

247   Reference to zealot bands active during the fall of Jerusalem. They are portrayed as the catalyst for the tension and violence within the city which led to its ultimate destruction. See Git. 56a and Rashi: אנשים רקים ופוחזים למלחמה "Irresponsible people, itching for war" and the Maharsha: והם פריצי ישראל שהיו בהם כמפורש ביוסיפון והם מתוך שנאתו זה את זה גרמו להם החורבן והגלות שלא היו רוצים ליכנע לרומים. "They were among the violent Israelites as described by Josephus. Because of mutual enmity and their refusal to give way to the Romans, they caused the destruction [of the Temple] and exile."

248   The modern-day, secular-oriented *halutz* (pioneer) makes amends for the destruction of the *biryonim*. The two are considered by the Vishnitzer to be linked spiritually.

249   Citing sources from Daniel, the Malbim and Zohar, our author digresses to affirm that the mystery of redemption will be revealed during the redemptive process which evolves rapidly with the close of the sixth millennium. (*EHS*, 134.)

250   See above, 10, n. 42.

251   R. Meir Loeb ben Yehiel Michael (1809–1879), scholar and noted Biblical commentator.

252   *Veyaveah Lakez* [Hab. 2:3] (1868).

253   אנו כותבים את הדברים האלה בחשוון שנת התרכ״ח, ולפי החשבון שעלה בידינו זמן הגאולה ירחק עוד שישים שנה. "We write these words in the month of *Heshvan* [*Marheshvan*] in the year [5]628, [1868]. According to our calculation, the time of redemption is off by 60 years." ibid. (Jerusalem Pardes edition, 1957), 727. He proceeded to predict the date of redemption to fall in the period of 1913–28. Some saw the Balfour Declaration (1917) as a "sign" of the beginning of the redemption.

reprimanding letter. How dare he go counter to the warning of the sages: "Blasted be the bones of those who calculate the End. . . ."[254] In response to the many inquiries on the subject he came forth with the following public declaration (the original is housed in the museum of Prague):

My dear colleagues and friends: I will tell you a story which took place in the vicinity of Bucharest, an area under my rabbinical jurisdiction. A wealthy tannery merchant had an only son. At his Bar Mitzvah he delivered [as was the custom] a fine scholarly presentation.[255] In order to reward his beloved son for his scholastic efforts in general, and his public discourse in particular, which everyone appreciated, he offered to have his son accompany him on a long and arduous business trip to the Leipzig fair. "You will enjoy the journey as much as I enjoyed your *pshetel*." The son was overjoyed with his father's plan. His mother and the servants helped with preparations for the difficult and lengthy journey of approximately three to four weeks. Obviously, the itinerary would include dangerous mountain roads. When it was time for the husband and son to leave, a tearful farewell from wife and mother was in order. Prayers were expressed for their safety, that the Almighty would help them return without mishap. After the father and son had settled into their carriage and were two hours into their long journey, the son turned to the father asking how much longer it would take to reach Leipzig. Upon hearing the question the father became quite piqued, and confronted the son with an angry look. He [the father] did not respond and sat brooding. The son also remained silent, preferring not to repeat the question. Following three to four weeks of travel, the father inquired of the coachman: "Moshe, tell me, how much longer to Leipzig?" "With God's help we will arrive in the city in an hour and a half." When the son heard the father's question to the coachman, he was puzzled indeed. "Father, I do not understand. Why were you upset

---

254   Sanh. 97b. תיפח עצמן של מחשבי קיצין "Blasted be the bones of those who calculate the End" *vs.* our text תיפח רוחן של מחשבי קיצין "Blasted be the souls of those who calculate the End."

255   Referred to in Yiddish as a *pshetel*, a modest interpretative discourse.

and angry with me when I asked about the travel time remaining till Leipzig? Now I heard you ask the very same question!" The father responded with a smile: "My son, both your initial as well as current question is unreasonable. Your first question was asked when we hardly set forth on our voyage. You should have known by the extent of our preparations and your mother's tears at our departure that we were not about to leave for a mere few hours. Certainly we were about to leave for a long and difficult journey. I was therefore justified in being angry in response to your question about Leipzig after only two hours journey. But now that we are so near to Leipzig it is time to inquire as to our arrival time.

This is the story, my friends! Our arduous path during two thousand years of bitter exile has followed the identical pattern. It is obvious why our sages, of blessed memory, would not allow people to engage in calculating the End. From the extent of the weeping and the preparations prior to the exile it was quite evident that its duration would not be limited to a mere day or two. Indeed, when he perceived the destruction [of the Temple] and the exile, Jacob our Patriarch was shaken and frightened, as it is described in the *midrash*.[256] Therefore, it was as yet inappropriate to calculate the End.[257] On the contrary, had they realized [at the outset] the extent [of their exile], who would have been able to tolerate all the sufferings? In fact, as it is explained in the Zohar when R. Shimon bar Yohai perceived the actual duration of exile he wept: "Woe to the lingering exile! Who will be able to tolerate it?"[258] Now, however, that we are within hailing distance of Leipzig it is proper to inquire as to the distance yet to be covered to

256 GenR. 69:1, on verses 28:10, 12, 16. מלמד שהראה הקב״ה ליעקב בהמ״ק בנוי וחרב ובנוי. ויירא. ויאמר: מה נורא המקום הזה "This teaches that the Holy One, blessed be He, displayed for Jacob the Holy Temple, built, destroyed and rebuilt. Shaken, he said, 'How awesome is this place!'" See also ibid. 65: 17, 19, 68:19.

257 Ibid. 96:1. למה היא סתומה? מפני שבקש יעקב אבינו לגלות את הקץ ונסתם ממנו. "Why is it [the preceding Biblical portion, separated by a space in the midst of a line] closed? Because Jacob wanted to reveal the End [of Days] and he was prevented from doing so."

258 *Zohar Hadash* (Loverno edition), *Balak* 67b; *Ozar HaZohar*, vol. 1 (Jerusalem, 1976), 177a.

Leipzig. A word to the wise! . . .

The *Midrash* comments on the verse "He spread a net for my feet."[259] "R. Abba ben Kahana said: 'If you see benches in Eretz Yisrael filled with Babylonians, you may expect [to hear] footsteps of the Messiah.' What is the reason? Because it is written: 'He spread a net for my feet.'"[260] I saw the *Torah Temimah* commentary on this verse: *Para*[261] is sounded as *Paras*.[262] The Babylonians, these are the Persians. (Not exactly, but these are equated since they were both locations for our exile.) The term *leraglai*[263] symbolizes the Messiah, based on the verse "How welcome on the mountain are the footsteps of the herald [announcing happiness, heralding good fortune.]"[264] Thus "if you see benches in Eretz Yisrael filled with Babylonians," that is to say if you will see the footsteps of the exiles ascending from Babylonia to Eretz Yisrael, this is proof that the Almighty, blessed be He, has calculated the imminent End and signals us accordingly. . . . Perhaps additional evidence is to be found in Ketubot 110b–111a:[265] "[R. Yehudah said]: Whoever goes up from Babylon to the Land of Israel transgresses a positive commandment, for it is written: . . . 'I have sworn you, O daughters of Jerusalem . . . do not arouse or stimulate love [to ascend to Eretz Yisrael] until it please.'"[266] In other words, until God wills it so. Such a sign will be apparent with a general awakening to return. This will be God's appointed time; when you shall see many *olim* fill the benches of Eretz Yisrael, these indeed represent the footsteps of the Messiah. The "footsteps of the herald" will then already be implanted at the gates of Jerusalem. It is also possible that the term

---

259 Lam. 1:13.

260 LamR. 1:43.

261 "He spread" פרש.

262 "Persian" פרס.

263 "for my feet." (Lam. 1:13).

264 Isa. 52:7 The term רגלי "footsteps" appears in the context of redemption, the "mountain" being Jerusalem.

265 The *Torah Temimah* commentary on Lam. 1:13.

266 Song 2:7.

reshet[267] evolved from *yerushah*.[268] That is to say, the Messiah's footsteps approach because of Israel's [uncontested] inheritance.[269]

As certain evidence in our own times for the dawning of redemption we point to the influx of so many of our Jewish brethren to Eretz Yisrael from every corner of the globe in their thousands and tens of thousands.[270] Likewise, the wars which took place in our time, from the year 5674 ...,[271] having as yet not actually ceased, flaring up here and there, only to erupt on a worldwide scale larger than ever, also point to the dawning of redemption, as it is said in the tractate *Megillah*: "War is an omen of the dawning of redemption."[272] The *Midrash Rabba, Lekh* confirms this:

If you see nations who provoke one another [to war] you may anticipate the footsteps of the Messiah. [How may we know this?] We know this from Abraham. During his time there erupted warfare between the kings. Consequently it was Abraham who was redeemed.[273] (Note the source. I do not have the Midrash before me.)[274]

It seems to me that all this[275] and what is taking place in our own

---

267 "Net," רשת Lam. 1:13.

268 Inheritance ירושה of the Land.

269 *Torah Temimah* commentary on Lam. 1:13.

270 Immigration to Eretz Yisrael between the decade 1933–1943 amounted to 260,674, and during the previous decade (1922–1932) 110,826. See annual immigration tables, *Jewish Encyclopedia*, vol. 9, 533.

271 1914.

272 Meg. 17b. Cf. מלחמה נמי אתחלתא דגאולה היא "War also signifies the beginning of redemption."

273 GenR. 42:7. Cf. אם ראית מלכיות מתגרות אלו באלו צפה לרגלו של משיח. "If you witness that nations provoke one another, you may expect the coming of the Messiah." Reference to the war of the four kings against the five kings (Gen. 14:1–27) followed by God's promise to Abraham: "Your reward shall be very great." (ibid. 15:1.)

274 Additional evidence is adduced from a Kabbalistic work, *Brit Menuha* (Berdichev, 1807), 24, which demonstrates the relationship between major strife and confusion among the nations, and redemption. (*EHS*, 137.)

275 Evidence in the sources presented which underscore the strife-among-nations correlation with the dawning of redemption.

day is reflected in the prophecy of Haggai (2).[276] "For thus said the Lord of Hosts: 'In just a little while longer I will shake the heavens and the earth, the sea and the dry land; I will shake all the nations. And the precious things of all the nations shall come [here], and I will fill this House with glory,' said the Lord of Hosts." This too supports the teaching of the kabbalist previously cited. . . .[277] All this adds up to a significant manifestation of the approaching redemption; and it is occurring here in our own time—the wars, the chaos in the world, and the many who are directed to Eretz Yisrael. Thus we can readily see that we are practically in Leipzig.[278] May the Almighty, blessed be He, quickly provide our deliverance and redemption, speedily in our day. Amen.

I have now completed this chapter, divided into twenty-one sections reflecting the good omen "Truly (akh), God is good to Israel,"[279] speedily in our own time, this fourth day in the week of [the weekly portion] Mishpatim,[280] in the capital city, the year Geshet el HaKodesh,[281] speedily in our time. Amen.

---

276 Hag. 2:6–7.

277 See above, n. 274.

278 Reference to story related above, 132–133.

279 Ps. 73:1 אך טוב לישראל The numerical value of אך (a'kh') is equivalent to twenty-one. The original text is divided into twenty-one sections within the second chapter. These were not marked in this edition.

280 Corresponding to Ex. 21:1–24:18.

281 Num. 8:19. בגשת בני ישראל אל הקדש. (The full intended citation of the verse: ". . . That there may be no plague among the people of Israel in case the people of Israel should come near [begeshet] the sanctuary." The letters גשת (g'sh't') numerically signify 703, the abbreviation of the year 5703. It was common practice to integrate remnants of scriptural references with positive inference into a numerological pattern which also signified the year of publication. The date of the completion of the second chapter was Wednesday, February 3, 1943, exactly one month following the beginning of the project.

THE THIRD CHAPTER:
SETTLEMENT AND CONSTRUCTION

Prior to devoting this chapter, with the help of the Almighty, to the mitzvah of settling and reconstructing the Land, I will offer words of preface.

PREFACE[1]

Why indeed is it necessary that we first begin building the Temple, following which the Temple Above will descend upon the Temple below?[2] This coincides with the teaching of our rabbi the *Shelah*[3] in his homily on the weekly portion of *Tetzaveh*:[4]

> I will begin with that which is well-known. There is the *deveikut* [attachment] of the Holy One, blessed be He, to us, and of us to Him. But we are the cause of the great *deveikut* which He activates on our behalf due to the stimulus [from us] below which arouses a great response from Above. This will clarify a passage of Rashi in *Mishpatim* on the verse: ". . . and to bring you to the place which I have prepared":[5] "My place[6]

---

1 The major portion of the preface to the third chapter is devoted to sources espousing the rebuilding of the Temple as an essential element in redemption, and the requisite of involvement of all the masses (*EHS*, 139, 142). See also 292, n. 1079.

2 The initiative below will trigger the desired response from Above. (See above, 25, n. 58).

3 See above, 26, n. 65.

4 Ex. 27:20–30:10.

5 Ex. 23:20.

6 The text in the *Shelah* and *EHS* reads מקומו (*mekomo*) "His place" *vs.* the Rashi

in which I have long since established the seat of My glory. This is one
of the verses which [implicitly] states that the Temple Above is positioned
exactly opposite the Temple on earth."[7]

[The Rashi text] is problematic. [Which Temple] is actually dependent upon which? Certainly the smaller one[8] is dependent upon the
larger one.[9] The text should have stated: "The Temple on earth is
positioned exactly opposite the Temple Above."[10] We have a further
difficulty with [an implied contradiction between] the opening and
closing parts of the [Rashi] text. [At first] it is stated "My place to
which I have long since established the seat of My glory," suggesting
that the Temple Above was already established.[11] But this is followed
by "the Temple Above is positioned exactly opposite the Temple on
earth," as if the Temple below was established first, Heaven forbid![12]
The text, however, is to be understood as follows: the Temple Above
was certainly created first. The Almighty, blessed be He, then commanded the construction of a Temple on earth based on the secret
specifications of the Temple Above. Due to the merits of worship in
the Temple on earth, the inspiration drawn from the Temple Above
was made possible. This inspiration cannot descend from Above until
a stimulus originating below ascends upwards. The descent of this
[Divine] inspiration meets that which emanates from below. The required stimulus from below represents the preparatory foundation[13]
upon which the emanations from the Temple Above will descend.
This is the meaning of the teaching of our rabbis: "Although fire
descended from Heaven[14] it is nevertheless a religious precept to
bring also some ordinary fire,"[15] since the ordinary fire from earth

---

מקומי (*mekomi*) "my place."

  7 Rashi on Ex. 23:20.
  8 On earth, below.
  9 In heaven, above.
 10 Not the reverse, as stated in Rashi.
 11 As expected.
 12 Negating the superiority of the Temple in Heaven.
 13 כסא והכנה *lit.* "throne and preparation."
 14 Lev. 9:24. ד ותצא אש מלפני "Fire came forth from before the Lord."
 15 Eruv. 63a. מצוה להביא מן ההדיוט "One must bring from the ordinary fire" in

stimulates the spiritual fire from Above."[16] However, when we will be privileged to experience the final *tikkun*, we will also merit witnessing the descent of the very substance of the Temple Above which will come to rest on the Temple below. Not merely its Divine emanations will descend, as was the case during the first two Temples. It will indeed descend in its entirety. Then the Creator of all that which is Above will make His abode among those below. This is after all the ultimate purpose of Creation ....[17]

It is obvious that prior to the rebuilding of the Temple the Jewish people will necessarily have to be ingathered. ....[18] Those who neglect such efforts will be severely punished, as I documented previously in the name of *Ezrat Kohanim*.[19] The root of all the misfortunes which have now befallen us is our neglect of Eretz Yisrael which the Almighty observes at all times and from everywhere.[20] Furthermore, we have besmirched and insulted those who have undertaken the task of her reconstruction. If we do not change our attitudes, our misfortunes will further undermine us, Heaven forbid. These misfortunes and shameful calamities actually represent a substitute for the exhortations of the prophets. They entreat, urging us to awake from our idle slumber. We came upon the *Midrash Tanhuma, Behar*, paragraph 3,[21] concerning Elimelekh and his sons.[22] The following is the commentary

our text. The bringing of ordinary fire is adduced from Lev. 1:7 ונתנו בני אהרון הכהן אש על המזבח "The sons of Aaron the priest shall put fire on the altar." See also Yoma 21b and 53a.

16 *Shenei Luhot HaBrit, op. cit.,* 328a–328b.

17 The harmonic resolution of the Divine integrating with man as reflected in Ex. 25:8; 25:45–46; I Kings 6:13; Zech. 2:14–15; 8:3 climaxing in: כה אמר ד'. שבתי אל ציון ושכנתי בתוך ירושלים ונקראה ירושלים עיר האמת והר ד' צבאות הר הקדש. "Thus said the Lord: I have returned to Zion, and I will dwell in Jerusalem. Jerusalem will be called the 'City of Faithfulness', and the mount of the Lord of Hosts, the 'Holy Mount.'"

18 Neglect of such ingathering or the minimizing of the efforts of the nonobservant will invite Divine retribution (*EHS*, 143–4).

19 Commentary on the mishnaic tractate Middot (Warsaw, 1873–7) by R. Yehoshua Yosef Feinberg.

20 Cf. Deut. 11:12.

21 Zundel edition (Jerusalem, 1970), part II, 43b; paragraph 8 in the Buber edition (Jerusalem, 1964), Leviticus, 54a.

22 Ruth 1:1–5.

on the verse: "They settled there about ten years":[23]

> During these ten years the Holy One, blessed be He, admonished them
> in the hope that they would repent and return to Eretz Yisrael.[24] When
> they did not repent, He struck at their cattle and camels. When they
> still refused to repent, forthwith "they died."[25] The repeated warnings
> from the Almighty, blessed be He, did not emanate from the prophets.
> . . . Rather the calamities were sent [as warning signals] instead of
> prophets for the purpose of having them repent. How were they to
> repent? Merely by returning to Eretz Yisrael.[26] Since they neither re-
> pented nor felt the need to repent they were punished—at first by
> losing their fortune, and eventually their lives. . . .[27]

We find support in the commentary of Nahmanides on the very
verse utilized by the Talmud to demonstrate that Eretz Yisrael was

---

23 Ibid 1:4

24 The sages are highly critical of Elimelekh and his sons, leaders of their
community for abandoning Eretz Yisrael during a period of need. RuthR. 1:4 ולמה
נענש אלימלך?‏ . . . אלימלך היה מגדולי המדינה ומפרנסי הדור, וכשבאו שני רעבון אמר: עכשיו כל ישראל
מסבבין פתחי, זה בקופתו, וזה בקופתו. עמד וברח לו מפניהם. "Why was Elimelekh punished?. .
. Elimelekh was among the great notables and benefactors of his generation. When
the years of famine drew near he said: Presently all of Israel will be pounding at my
door, everyone with his own [alms] basket. He broke away and fled from them." And
Yalkut Shimoni II, 599. וכן היה ר' שמעון בר יוחאי אומר: אלימלך, מחלון, וכליון גדולי הדור היו,
ומפני מה נענשו? שיצאו מארץ לחוצה לארץ. . . ‏'ושם האיש אלימלך'‏ . . . דאפילו מי שיש לו זכות אבות
אינה עומדת לו בשעה שיוצא מארץ לחוצה לארץ. "And thus said R. Shimon bar Yohai:
Elimelekh, Mahlon and Khilion were great notables in their generation. Why then
were they punished? They left Eretz Yisrael and went abroad. . . . 'The man's name
was Elimelekh'. . . . Though one may be blessed with the merits of one's fathers, this
will be of no value if one leaves Eretz Yisrael and goes abroad."

25 Ruth 1:5.

26 "Repentance" תשובה (teshuvah) and "to return" לשוב (lashuv) are etymologically
related.

27 Citing Nahmanides, Deut. 28:33 (within his commentary on Deut. 28:42), the
author admits that the periodic "good life" of Jews in exile may reflect God's compassion
for His people. However, the current calamities and upheavals must necessarily serve
as warning signals for the abandonment of *galut* (exile) as in the case of Elimelekh
and his sons. If Abraham sought God's protection when compelled to leave famine-
stricken Eretz Yisrael for Egypt (Gen. 12:10 and GenR. 40:1, expounding upon Ps.
33:18), surely when the reverse is true, the Jew should abandon the disastrous exile
for Eretz Yisrael which beckons. (*EHS*, 145–46)

given [to the Jewish people] through suffering,[28] as it is written: "That the Lord your God disciplines you just as a man disciplines his son."[29] This verse is followed by: "For the Lord your God is bringing you into a good land."[30] Nahmanides comments as follows: "At first [the Lord disciplines you] with afflictions in the wilderness, then the trial with the manna, so that the advantages of the Land and its fruits will be pleasant to you [by comparison]."[31] . . . Our master Nahmanides thereby instructs us to recognize in the essence and content of suffering the stimulus which should direct us to ascend to our Holy Land. . . .

And now, after all which has transpired in the lands of exile, do we still in this day and age require additional instructions from Heaven, that it is indeed the wish of our King, the Holy One, blessed be He, that we return to the Holy Land? This, in fact, is the purpose [of our sufferings], so that we shall be unable to exist any longer among the nations. He has withdrawn any promise [of protection] from *galut*. He does not wish us to dwell any further here in *galut*. Let us take this as encouragement to return our glory to the Land.

Seek to comprehend what is written by our rabbi in the volume *Ahavat Yehonatan*,[32] in his commentary on the weekly reading of the

---

28 Ber. 5a: תניא: ר׳ שמעון בן יוחאי אומר: שלש מתנות טובות נתן הקב״ה לישראל וכולן לא נתן הבא והעולם ואי׳ תורה, הן: אלו יסורין. ע״י אלא. "It has been taught: R. Shimon bar Yohai says: "The Holy One, blessed be He, gave Israel three precious gifts, and all of them were given only through suffering. These are: the Torah, the Land of Israel and the World to Come."

29 Deut. 8:5.

30 Ibid. 8:7.

31 Nahmanides (Ramban), Deut. 8:5. Our text mistakenly cites שתעכב "which will delay" vs. שתערב לפניך טובת הארץ ופרותיה (*shete'akev* vs. *shete'arev*).

32 R. Jonathan Eybeschutz (see above, 21, n. 32), *Ahavat Yehonatan*, *op. cit.*, *Haftarat Et'hanan*, 3a. וזהו פירושו דכנסת ישראל צווחה באלה ובשבועה אם תעירו ואם תעוררו . . . את האהבה נגד קבוץ ישראלי באם שהכל נועדו יחדיו לילך לירושלים וכל האומות מסכימים אפי״ה צווחה שחלילה שתלך שמה כי הקץ סתום ואולי אין עתה הזמן האמיתי. "And the following is the interpretation: The Congregation of Israel calls out to the Jews with a 'promise and oath' not to stimulate or awaken the love [of the Divine]. That is, even if everyone will agree to proceed together to Jerusalem and the nations will agree, under no circumstance should she [Israel] proceed, since the End is concealed, and perhaps the proper time is not appropriate." See below, 257-259.

Prophets linked to the portion *Et'hanan*,[33] and the verse: "I enjoin you, [daughters of Jerusalem . . . that you do not stimulate or awaken [My] love until she please]:[34] "The Congregation of Israel implores those [who plan to settle] not to return to Eretz Yisrael despite the approval of the nations, since the time [of redemption] is concealed." Now all the opponents have documented their opposition to this lofty and sacred idea of the rebuilding of the Land based upon this interpretation.[35]

From what I have written earlier it is clear that the *Ahavat Yehonatan* is justified in the event that we have no sign from Heaven that the Almighty desires us to abandon the lands of exile; that is to say, when the Jewish world community lives in peace and tranquility . . . but this is certainly not the case in our era when the [following] words of the prophets have been applied to us in reverse:

> "The remnant of Jacob shall be among the nations [in the midst of many peoples] like a lion among the beasts of the forest, like a young lion among the flocks of sheep, trampling wherever it goes, mangling its prey, with no one present to deliver."[36]

On the other hand, the nations have permitted us to return to our sacred Land.[37] Is there still any doubt that it is the will of the Almighty, blessed be He, that we return to Eretz Yisrael? I am certain that had our master the author of *Ahavat Yehonatan* shared our lives with us in our present exile, and beheld what we are experiencing in this bitter exile, he too would urge us: "My fellow Jews, the time has come that we ascend to Zion and to the Land of our fathers. This is the will of God. What we are experiencing in exile has not come about by random

---

33   Deut. 3:23–7:11; Isa. 40:1–26.

34   Song 2:7, 3:5. The slumber of love symbolizes exile, as in Isa. 51:17. התעוררי ירושלים קומי התעוררי "Rouse, rouse yourself! Arise, O Jerusalem!" See below, 257.

35   I.e. the interpretation of Jonathan Eybeschutz in *Ahavat Yehonatan*.

36   Mic. 5:7.

37   Probable reference to the Balfour Declaration of November 1917, and the subsequent waves of immigration to Palestine of 388,000 Jews between the years 1920 and 1943. See *Encyclopedia Judaica* 9:533 "Table 1: Immigration, 1882–May 14, 1948."

chance. It is the finger of God directing us to leave exile for the inheritance of our fathers. . . ."[38]

Thus, now in our own time, when the stepmother, namely, the diaspora, does not respect us, and on the contrary humiliates us,[39] giving Jacob over to despoilment[40] and depositing a yoke of iron upon our necks,[41] all will admit that it is best we return to the mother, namely, Eretz Yisrael. . . .

The Preface [to the Third Chapter] is Concluded

With the help of the Almighty I will now discuss whether the religious precept of building and settlement of the Land applies as well when [the Jewish people are] in exile. The view of Nahmanides in *Sefer HaMitzvot* is well-known:[42] To take possession of the Land and "not to leave it for any other nation but ourselves," is a positive biblical precept valid also in our own day. [His view] is based on the verse (Numbers 33):[43] "And you shall take possession of the Land and settle in it, for I have given the Land to you to possess it. You shall apportion the Land 'which I gave to your Fathers by oath.'"[44] Thus, according to a detailed analysis of Nahmanides it [the acquisition of the Land] is a positive biblical precept for all time, included in the 613 precepts.

---

38 Our author amplifies this thesis with quotations from the JT Berakhot, the *Hatam Sofer, Likutei Haver ben Hayyim* (by R. Hezekiah Feivel Plaut, 1818–95, student of the Hatam Sofer), and *Divrei Yehezkel* (R. Yehezkel Shraga Halberstam [see above, 121, n. 209]). In each source the tolerance towards exile was premised on the assumption of security and tranquility, which permitted the Jew to develop in "study and worship." These conditions no longer pertained. (*EHS*, 148).

39 As opposed to the parable of the respectful stepmother who is favorably compared to the demeaning mother (Eretz Yisrael) which seemed to be the rationale for R. Kahana's departure from Eretz Yisrael to Babylonia. JT Ber. 2:8.

40 Cf. Isa. 42:24. ‏מי נתן למשיסה יעקב?‏ "Who was it gave Jacob over to despoilment?"

41 Cf. Deut. 28:48 ‏ונתן עול ברזל על צוארך‏ "He will put an iron yoke upon your neck," and Jer. 28:14, ‏עול ברזל נתתי על צואר כל הגוים האלה‏ "I have put an iron yoke upon the necks of all those nations."

42 *Sefer HaMitzvot* (Maimonides), Part 2, *Mitzvat Aseh Leda'at HaRamban: Mitzvah 4*

43 Verses 53–54.

44 ‏אשר נשבעתי לאבותיכם‏ in our text is not part of Num. 33.

The author of *Megillat Esther*[45] explains the contrary reasoning of
Maimonides in not including it among the 613 precepts: This precept
was in effect only during the Temple period, as long as they were not
exiled from their land. Following their exile, however, this mitzvah is
no longer in force until the coming of the Messiah. He [the author of
Megillat Esther] supports Maimonides' reasoning with the ruling of
Tosafot in Ketubot[46] who cite R. Hayyim[47] as follows: "It is not a
mitzvah." All the authorities who followed the Tosafists,[48] however,
rejected the view of R. Hayyim as a matter of halakhah [law].

   Note the *Shelah*, *Shaar Ha'Otiot*,[49] confirming that they [the opinions
of R. Hayyim] were a minority view, untenable and not to be considered
as legal precedent. The Maharit,[50] as well, second part, [*Yoreh De'ah*]

---

45   Commentary by the Spanish-Italian 16th-century scholar R. Isaac Leon ibn
Tzur (Venice, 1592), in which he consistently defends Maimonides against arguments
raised by Nahmanides.

46   Ket. 110b. הוא אומר לעלות וגו' אינו נוהג בזמן הזה דאיכה סכנת דרכים. והיה אומר רבינו
חיים דעכשיו אינו מצוה לדור בא"י כי יש כמה מצות התלויות בארץ וכמה עונשין דאין אנו יכולין ליזהר
בהם ולעמוד עליהם "'He wishes to ascend [to Eretz Yisrael], etc.' This [ruling] does not
apply in our day due to the danger on the roads [to travelers]. And R. Hayyim added
that presently there is no commandment to reside in Eretz Yisrael since there are a
number of mitzvot linked to the Land [which we cannot observe] as well as a number
of prohibitions which we cannot avoid or clearly understand."

47   The 12th century French Tosafist R. Hayyim b. Hananel HaKohen, outstanding
pupil of R. Tam. See E.E. Urbach *Ba'alei HaTosafot*, vol. 1 (Jerusalem, 1980) 124–128,
and note 13 p. 126 expressing doubt as to the authenticity of this Tosafist source
cited in our text.

48   School of Talmud scholars in Germany and France who developed the analytical
and critical commentary and glosses, particulary in response to the Rashi commentary,
from the close of the 11th century to the 14th century.

49   *Shenei Luhot HaBrit*, op. cit., 77b. וכל המצות התלויות בא"י נוהגות גם אחר החורבן
מדאורייתא (לפי ר' יוחנן) "All of the mitzvot linked to Eretz Yisrael are to be performed
according to Biblical authority after the destruction [of the Temple] as well. (According
to R. Yohanan)"

50   Responsa of the scholar R. Joseph b. Moses (1568–1639) of Safed and Jerusalem
She'elot U'Tshuvot Maharit, vol. 2 (Tel Aviv, 1959), 54–55. ועוד דעיקר הטעם משום קדושת
ארץ ישראל ומצות ישיבתה הוא אפילו בזמן הזה בחרבנה כמ"ש הרמב"ן ז"ל בפי' המצות . . . ומ"ש בתוי
דאין מצוה לדור בא"י, הגהת תלמיד היא ולא דסמכא היא כלל. "Further, the major reason [for
the commandment of settlement] is the inherent sanctity of the Land. The mitzvah
of its settlement is operative even in our time though it is destroyed, and noted by
Nahmanides, of blessed memory, in his commentary on the mitzvot. . . . With regard
to the statement in Tosafot that residence in Eretz Yisrael is not a mitzvah, this
represents a gloss of a student and lacks all authority."

paragraph 28, elaborates on this matter and rules according to Nahmanides. Similarly all of the distinguished authorities who followed the *Megillat Esther* reject his [R. Hayyim's] views as baseless and without validity.[51] There is no need to elaborate further on a matter which has been resolved for some time. In the year 5658[52] an anthology of mitzvot related to settlement in Eretz Yisrael was published in Vilna by the distinguished scholar of Dvinsk (Dinaburg).[53] It is a superb and extraordinary work devoted to a critique of the position of *Megillat Esther*, which challenges his explanation of Maimonides' exclusion of this mitzvah [of settlement] based on the fact that the mitzvah was not in force at all times. He effectively refutes his thesis from beginning to end with valid documentation from the Talmud and from Maimonides as well.

[According to R. Blumberg] Maimonides too considers [settlement of Eretz Yisrael] as a biblical precept in our time and for all time. He did not include it among the 613 precepts, however, since it did not meet any of the criteria which Maimonides established for inclusion.[54] There are a number of such mitzvot in the Torah which did not merit inclusion, such as settlement, since they, as well, did not meet the fourteen criteria of Maimonides. . . . Many of the greatest scholars of the time indicated their approval of [R. Blumberg's] works, which were included in the printed edition. . . .[55]

---

51 See concise statement by the *Pit'he Teshuvah* commentary on *Shulhan Arukh*, *Even Ha'Ezer* 75:5 (gloss 6) וכן מבואר [יישוב א״י] של זו מצוה . . . לקיום שוים הזמנים כל וא״כ ואחרונים הראשונים הפוסקים מכל . . . "Hence all periods [in history] are equal with regard to the performance of this mitzvah [of settling the Land]. This is the consensus of all the earlier and later authorities."

52 1898.

53 R. Yonah Dov Blumberg of Dvinsk (b. 1852) scholar and author of *Kuntres Mitzvat Yeshivat Eretz Yisrael* (Vilna, 1897).

54 These criteria or principles designated by Maimonides as שורשים (*shorashim*) are listed at the beginning of the volume *Sefer HaMitzvot, op cit.* 6a–75b. The English translation is available in Maimonides, *The Commandments*, translation, Ch. B. Chavel (London/New York, 1967), vol. 4, 359–425.

55 Printing written approvals הסכמות (*haskamot*) from contemporary authorities is a time honored tradition in Judaica publications. In this instance, Rabbis Shlomo Cohen of Vilna, Hayyim Berlin of Volozhin, Moshe Shapira of Riga, and Shmuel Mohliver of Bialystok published their *haskamot* and letters of support which are

I am also amazed at the *gaon*, the author of *Megillat Esther* who thinks that Maimonides was of the opinion that during the period of exile the mitzvah of settling the Land is not operative, and in fact is prohibited. . . . But note, in fact, what Maimonides has to say in his *Sefer HaMitzvot* concerning the positive Biblical precept of sanctifying the new month, Mitzvah 153.[56] He indicates that all our calendrial calculations [for ritual purposes] transacted in exile have no validity and cannot be relied upon.

> For argument's sake, let us say that Eretz Yisrael no longer had any of its inhabitants. (Heaven forbid that we should ever reach this stage, since He promised never to destroy all of our national remnants).[57] No religious court would be able to function [without a resident population]. Neither would a court outside the Land, though authorized and commissioned in Eretz Yisrael, be permitted to declare: "This is our calculation." This procedure would be invalid[58] since it is forbidden except under the circumstances mentioned above, as we explained, to calculate the months and the leap years from outside the Land since "from Zion shall go forth Torah."[59, 60]

I have quoted him completely in order to demonstrate his views on the primary importance of settling the Holy Land. From the text of our teacher we learn the extent of the dependence of our entire sacred nation upon the settlement of the Land. Thus, if there is the

---

included in the volume *Kuntres Mitzvot Eretz Yisrael, op cit.* 6–8. Our author also questions the interpretation of the *Megillat Esther* based on the concept of ירושה (*yerushah*) "inheritance," which in legal terms assumes a validity without limits in time also according to Maimonides (*EHS*, 150–151).

56   *Sefer HaMitzvot, op. cit.,* 132a–135b.

57   As in Isa. 6:13 "וכאלון אשר בשלכת מצבת בם זרע קדש מצבתה . . . . and the oak of which stumps are left even when they are felled: Its stump shall be a holy seed." See also Ps. 94:14 and I Sam. 12:22 as cited below, nn. 66 and 67.

58   לא יועילו כלום "It will not be helpful" *vs.* לא יועילנו כלום "It will not be helpful to us."

59   Isa. 2:3.

60   *Sefer HaMitzvot, op. cit.,* 132b–135b. The "circumstances mentioned above" relate to the requirement that the calendar be established by the Sanhedrin in the Holy Land.

possibility that Jews would not inhabit the Land, Heaven forbid, it would prove to be fatal for the entire nation. . . . This staggers the imagination. Yet it is so because, in my opinion, Eretz Yisrael is in fact the very heart of the nation as explained in the sacred text *Or Ne'erav* of the saintly R. Cordovero cited earlier. . . .[61] Thus, every link of the Jewish people with the Holy One, blessed be He, is precisely by way of Eretz Yisrael. . . .[62] Therefore our sages declared: "He who lives outside the Land may be regarded as if he has no God. . . ."[63]

The *gaon* R. Blumberg[64] interprets the Midrash on Ruth as follows:[65]

One verse says: "For the Lord will not cast off His people, neither will He forsake His inheritance,"[66] whereas another verse says: "For the Lord will not forsake His people for His great Name's sake."[67] [The latter verse refers to outside the Land. The former verse refers to the Land.] Outside the Land He acts for the sake of His great Name,[68] but in Eretz Yisrael He acts for the sake of His people and His inheritance.[69]

This coincides with the view of Maimonides[70] that the national status of the Jewish people is validated by their very presence in Eretz Yisrael. God therefore acts in Eretz Yisrael for their sake alone. Outside the Land this is not so since the existence of the Jewish [nation] is not linked to His action for His Name's sake alone.[71] In this fashion he[72]

---

61   See above, 48, n. 65 and 66. Eretz Yisrael represents the heart, the vital organ of the Jewish people. *EHS*, 152.

62   See above, 43, n. 37.

63   Ket. 110b. The author expresses his excitement in discovering the kindred soul. R. Yonah Dov Blumberg and the volume *Kuntres Mitzvat Yeshivat Eretz Yisrael* (cited previously). See above, 141, n. 53.

64   R. Yonah Dov Blumberg, *Kuntres, op cit.* 56a (III).

65   RuthR. 2:11.

66   Ps. 94:14.

67   I Samuel, 12:22. *EHS* reverses the order of the verses.

68   The *Midrash* cites Isa. 48:11 as a supporting text.

69   Close of *Midrash* citation in *Kuntres* 56a (III).

70   Cited above, 141–142.

71   This bracketed passage is added by our author amidst his paraphrase of the *Kuntres* source.

explains why Maimonides did not include the positive commandment
of settling the Land among the 613 mitzvot, though this mitzvah is
biblically ordained. This is so since the Fourth Principle in the *Sefer
HaMitzvot* sets aside any mitzvah in which are included all the other
mitzvot of the Torah.[73] Since the settlement of the Land is a mitzvah
of such magnitude that it consists of all the mitzvot, includes the
entire Torah, the setting of the festivals and the New Moon, and all
related precepts which are dependent upon the Land, as Maimonides
himself asserts[74] [citing] "From out of Zion shall come forth Torah,"[75]
it is, therefore, not included in the calculation of mitzvot which are
particular [rather than comprehensive] in nature. (Note the *Or Ha-
Hayyim* on the portion of *Nitzavim*[76] who indicates also that settling
the Land is an all-embracing and not an individual mitzvah.[77]) Similarly,
Nahmanides in listing his eighth mitzvah regarding the precept "You
must be wholehearted with the Lord your God,"[78] explains the reason
why Maimonides did not include this precept in his listing of the
mitzvot: it too is all-embracing.[79] It is, therefore, essential that every
Jew carefully study his work[80] and be enlightened as to this significant
mitzvah so that henceforth one will not minimize the precept of
settling the Land. . . .[81]

---

72   R. Blumberg.

73   *Sefer HaMitzvot, op. cit.,* 38b השורש הרביעי: שאין ראוי למנות הצוויים הכוללים התורה
כוללה "The Fourth Principle: [A mitzvah] which is not to be included [in the count]
because it is all inclusive." See above, 141, n. 54.

74   Ibid. 135b.

75   Isa. 2:3.

76   Deut. 29:9–30:20 and specifically the commentary on Deut. 30:11–14.

77   יולא מעבר לים היא וגו' פי' כמו שאירע למשה שהגם שעלה לשמים והוריד התורה נמנעו ממנו
. . . השגת קיום מצותיה התלויות בארץ שהם כמה וכמה כמעט רובי התורה "Neither is it beyond
the sea' . . . In other words, as it indeed occurred to Moses who went up to heaven
and brought down the Torah. This prevented him from fulfilling the mitzvot which
were linked to the Land. There are so many in number—practically the majority [of
mitzvot] in the Torah."

78   Deut. 18:13.

79   *Sefer HaMitzvot,* "Mitzvot Aseh L'da'at HaRamban," *op. cit.,* 172a.

80   *Kuntres Mitzvat Yeshivat Eretz Yisrael* by R. Yonah Dov Blumberg.

81   Our author provides supplementary documentation supporting settlement as

I am also astounded at the holy *gaon*, the author of *Minhat Elazar* who insists that one may not cooperate at all with the builders of the Land in our time since they do not, unfortunately, live in accordance with the Torah. He believes that it is preferred that they have the Land all to themselves to do as they wish, rather than that we participate with them with our own resources and our own spirit. I cannot fathom why this [the latter] should be so! I could understand such an attitude if we were to cease and desist from any involvement in building, for then they too would remove themselves for the scene. In that event it may be justified to sit and do nothing[82] rather than build and violate a precept, Heaven forbid.[83] (Though in my humble opinion this is not clear at all. As I cited above[84] from the tractate Sanhedrin,[85] the Holy One, blessed be He, prefers the rebuilding of the Land, though it be by means of transgression, Heaven forbid.[86] If the option before us is one of observing the positive precept of settlement by means of transgression, Heaven forbid, otherwise settlement would not take place at all, it may be proper to rule that the precept of settlement takes precedence, since it outweighs all other mitzvot in the Torah,[87] as

---

central to the very existence of the Jewish people and to the complete observance of Torah. In challenging the Rebbe of Munkatch who did not consider settlement as a mitzvah for all time (*Minhat Elazar*, vol. 5, Responsa 12, 5b–8a), and who vehemently opposed the Zionist as well as the ultra-Orthodox *Agudah* program concerning Eretz Yisrael, *EHS* invokes the activist opinions of the *Responsa Bet Yehudah Responsa* (Livorno, 1746), written by Judah Ayash, an 18th-century scholar who lived in Algeria and Eretz Yisrael, R. Joseph Saul HaLevi Nathanson in *Responsa Yosef Da'at* (Lemberg, 1879), *Pe'at Shulhan* (Safed, 1836) by R. Israel b. Samuel of Sklov (d. 1839 in Eretz Yisrael). He was a noted talmudic scholar and outstanding pupil of the *Gaon* of Vilna, the Maharit (see above, 140, n. 50) and the Mabit in defense of Nahmanides and the *Responsa Avnei Nezer* (Pietrokov, 1914) by R. Avraham Bornstein (1839–1910), noted scholar and head of the rabbinic court of Sochaczew, and son-in-law of R. Menahem Mendel of Kotzk. (*EHS*, 156–157).

82 The rabbinic שב ואל תעשה (*shev ve'al ta'aseh*) is employed.

83 As specified above, by the *Minhat Elazar*.

84 See above, 49, nn. 73–77.

85 102b.

86 As was the case with King Omri. See I Kings 16:23–26.

87 *Sifrei, Re'eh*, Deut. 12:29. מעשה בר' יהודה בן בתירא ור' מתיא בן חרש ור' חנינא בן אחי
ר' יהושע ור' יונתן שהיו ויוצאים חוצה לארץ והגיעו לפלטום וזכרו את ארץ ישראל זקפו עיניהם וזלגו
דמעותיהם וקרעו בגדיהם וקראו המקרא הזה: ויירשתם אתה וישתבם בה, ושמרתם לעשות את כל
החקים' (דברים יא: לא-לב) וחזרו ובאו למקומם, אמרו: ישיבת ארץ ישראל שקולה כנגד כל המצות

explained by our rabbis. Further, the very existence of the nation is dependent upon the settlement of the Land. As it is well-known, the principles of talmudic law determine that an important and significant positive commandment may prevail over the [prohibition] of a combined positive and negative transgression.[88]) However, the facts are that they continue to build despite us, as they have now done for some time even without the participation of the pious. Why then should our noncooperation be deemed preferable over a policy of physical and spiritual involvement in their task? In this fashion, at the very least, a spirit of Torah and holiness will be infused into the acts of rebuilding since we will be able to develop some sphere of influence. Perhaps with the involvement of the God-fearing they will, with the help of God, act completely in accordance with the Torah. On the other hand, if the pious stand aside leaving all the initiative to others, then surely they will not act in the spirit of the Torah. So much of past evidence indicates that the renunciation by the *Haredim* of the rebuilding movement ever since the renaissance of the Zionist enterprise has had little influence upon events. Truly, the absence of Torah in their [the Zionist] endeavors is to be lamented. But what have the *Haredim* accomplished by withdrawing from this sacred task? Would it not have been preferred to join with the builders, no matter who they may be, in order to contribute their influence and sanctity to this project? Then the Land would have taken on another appearance entirely: an appearance of holiness and a spirit of purity. As it is well-known, a small amount of light penetrates a large chamber of darkness. I cannot, therefore, comprehend the logic of the holy *gaon*. . . .[89,90]

שבתורה. "When R. Yehudah b. Betera and R. Mathya b. Heresh and R. Hanina b. Ahi and R. Yehoshua and R. Yonatan went abroad and they arrived at Puteoli, they remembered Eretz Yisrael. They lifted their eyes, wept, rent their clothes and read the following verse: (Deut. 11:31–32) 'You will inherit it and you will settle it; take care to observe all the laws.' They returned to their original location, declaring: 'The settling of Eretz Yisrael is equal to all the mitzvot in the Torah.'"

88 Pes. 59a and related Tosafot אתי עשה דפסח.

89 The Rebbe of Munkatch.

90 Our author elaborates upon the futility of efforts of the devout Jew who breaks off participation in the redemptive process because of the presence of the

Thus it has been with regard to the rebuilding of our Holy Land. Since the awakening of this [Zionist] movement, the devout and pious have disengaged themselves from any involvement and have in fact opposed it. Reckless elements took matters in their own hands, relentlessly seeking to obtain their objective of rebuilding [the Land]. The will of the Lord prospered in their hands.[91] They toiled and struggled until they succeeded. Now, since the devout kept aloof from any involvement, should anyone be at all surprised that the rebuilding was accomplished in a secular fashion? It is certain that had we all participated, the spirit of Torah and piety would have significantly penetrated this program from the very outset. Now, of course, that a beautiful settlement [in Eretz Yisrael] is an accomplished fact, because of the reckless elements, they now are considered the masters of the Land. After all, this represents the fruit of their labor. The ruling of the Hatam Sofer[92] has been substantiated. In any event we are aware that the approach of the Hatam Sofer and his pupil, the Maharam Schick, does not correspond to that of the holy *gaon*, the author of *Minhat Elazar*. The ruling in all cases is according to the Hatam Sofer and the Maharam Schick, namely, the devout and the pious are not permitted to remove themselves from acts of building.[93] On the contrary, a sacred task has been allotted to them to participate in the sacred project from here on in. They must help unite all the elements, joining hands together with the pioneers, in this sublime enterprise

---

nondevout. Yet it is imperative to involve the totality of Israel in the return to the borders of Zion if the Lord is to fulfill the covenant with our ancestors. The views of the Hatam Sofer and his pupil the Maharam Schick (1807–1879) are invoked. (*EHS*, 159–60).

91 Cf. Isa. 53:10 וחפץ ה׳ בידו יצלח "And through him the Lord's purpose might prosper."

92 See above, n. 90.

93 Reference to discussion in the responsa of the Maharam Schick, *Orah Hayyim* (Satmar, 1904), no. 70, 21a, emphasizing the futility and negative consequences of a policy of isolation of the devout from the masses. Such policy precludes any contact with the ordinary and recalcitrant Jew to the detriment of the entire Jewish nation. The responsa deals with the question of preaching Torah in the "language of other nations." The positive ruling is justified on the basis of utilizing the tools of the majority environment in order to counter the assimilationist forces of the environment.

in order to strengthen it in every way.

As it is cited in the *Midrash Shoher Tov*, chapter 18: One verse[94] employs the term *migdol*,[95] the other[96] *magdil*.[97] "This is so since redemption for this nation shall not appear at once, but gradually, as suggested by the term *magdil*, namely it [redemption] will gradually manifest itself before the people of Israel."[98] When the reckless elements will take note that the devout do not disengage from them, but in fact wish to join with them, then they too will draw near and abandon their negative views. After all, they too are descended from Abraham, Isaac and Jacob and rooted in holiness. Note the introduction to the *Tanya*[99] who taught that even the most recalcitrant of Jews grasp at the letters of the Torah and the Torah [within them] binds them to the Lord, blessed be He.[100]

Their souls yearn to return to their source, as I indicated previously.[101] Then we will surely complete the task of rebuilding and God's Name will be sanctified because of our acts.

Note the volume, *Notzer Hesed*, a commentary on the tractate *Avot*[102] by our saintly Rabbi of Komarno,[103] expounding upon "Stay away from a bad neighbor; do not latch on to the wicked"[104] he comments: "The *Tanna*[105] does not say 'stay away from the wicked,' as he does

---

94 II Sam. 22:51. *EHS* reverses the order of the verses in the Midrash.

95 "He is the tower [of salvation]," suggesting the final complete redemption.

96 Ps. 18:51.

97 "Great [deliverance]. . . . He provides for His King," suggesting a process.

98 MPs. 18:36 (269) Vilna, 1891, 162.

99 Authored by R. Shneur Zalman of Liadi. See above, 3, n. 2.

100 וכל שישים רבוא כללות ישראל ופרטיהם עד ניצוץ קל שבקלים ופחותי הערך שבעמינו ב"י כולהו מתקשראן באורייתא ואורייתא היא המתקשרת איתן להקב"ה. "And all of the 600,000 Israelites in sum total, as well as individuals down to the most humble and unpretentious of Jews among our people, all attach themselves to the Torah; it is then the Torah which attaches them to the Holy One, blessed be He." Introduction to *Tanya*, Vilna, 1937, 6.

101 See above, 110.

102 Lvov, 1856; and Jerusalem, 1912.

103 R. Isaac Judah Jechiel Safrin. See above, 71, n. 70.

104 Avot 1:7.

105 Nittai the Arbelite, ibid. אבל אל תרחיקהו דלמא יעשה תשובה על ידך, שתקרב אותו או

with regard to the bad neighbor. He limits himself to 'do not latch on,' that is to say, Heaven forbid that you stay away from the wicked. On the contrary, it is a mitzvah to draw him near to you. By doing so you are able to influence him to the good."

Surely, "do not latch on" to him, namely, [do not] become sincerely convinced [of the propriety of his ways]. Yet, by all means, do not reject him.

This is applicable to our own situation.

I will relate to you what was told to me yesterday, Monday, the portion of *Emor*,[106] 5703,[107] here in the capital while visiting the great *gaon*, the holy flame, our teacher David Meisels, the senior [rabbinic] judge of Ohel[108] and the author of the responsa, *Binyan David*.[109] He is hospitalized at the Varos Meyer Hospital.[110] May the Almighty heal him quickly so that he may return to his sacred work until the coming of the Messiah, speedily in our day. Now on this past Sabbath of the intermediate Passover festival[111] I was invited to preach in the local *Hevrat Shas Yere'im*[112] synagogue, which was crowded on this occasion. I inserted in the sermon the matter of rebuilding our Land, which, considering what has befallen us, is now incumbent on all of us. We have no other option except that we all rebuild our Land upon its

---

שלא ילך ויחריב העולם. על כן הנכון לקרב הרשעים. "However, do not reject him since through your efforts he may repent. Bring him near so that he should not destroy the world. It is proper then, to bring the wicked near. . . ." *Notzer Hesed* (Jerusalem, 1912), 2b.

106 Weekly reading of scripture Lev. 21:1–24:23.

107 May 10, 1943.

108 Satoraljaujhely, city in the north eastern Hungarian district of Zemplen near the Czechoslovakian border.

109 Ohel, 1931.

110 Reference to the Varosmajor hospital and rest home of the Orthodox community in Budapest situated along the western bank of the Danube River. (The editor is grateful to Professor Natanel Katzburg for this information.) See below, 237.

111 April 24, 1943.

112 An important Orthodox synagogue in Budapest attended by many scholars. Synagogues which devoted specific hours to the regular study of Talmud would often append the designation *Hevrah Shas* to their name, *lit.*, [study] group of the Six Orders (ש״ס, *Shas*) of the Talmud.

ruins.

I proceeded to preach on this subject with considerable passion. Many were upset with me.[113] This reached the attention of this *gaon*[114] who reacted as follows: "In reality, it has turned out we were in error in withdrawing from the movement to build the Land (Yiddish)." These were the very words of this great *gaon*, a leader of his generation. And he said further: "A great many of our Jewish brethren would have been saved had we all been involved in the rebuilding of our Land and not feuded among ourselves." He then burst forth weeping, for some of his children as well who were trapped in Slovakia.[115]

---

113   For supporting the Zionist enterprise.

114   R. David Meisels.

115   The author proceeds to underscore a major principle in his dynamic and existentialist philosophy of the halakhic process, relevant to the debate at hand. Only those involved in the contemporary life struggle, in the here and now, are in a position to participate in the legal discourse. Those no longer active in the affairs of this world "be it even Moses or the angels," are not in the position to rule on matters which concern the present generation. Consequently, rabbinic attitudes and rulings on the Zionist question which may have been appropriate in previous generations are not necessarily valid in the present. R. Levi Yitzhak of Berdichev (*Kedushat Levi, Likutim*, 108b) and the Mabit are introduced as evidence for this position.

מי יכול להבחין זאת באיזה מדה צריך זה העולם להתנהג שיופסק הלכה כמותו? מי שהוא בחיים והוא
בזה העולם הוא יודע באיזה מדה צריך זה העולם להתנהג אבל מי שאינו חי אינו יודע כלל באיזה מדה
צריכה לזה העולם להתנהג בה. . . והשגות אלו לא ניתנו אפילו למרע"ה כיון דנפרד נפשו מגופו. . . ונפשו
אינו יכול להשיג עניני עוה"ז ואפילו המלאכים אינם משיגים בעניני עוה"ז ויידע ענינינו תמיד בכל דור
ודור יכול לקבוע ההלכה לפי ענין הדור בכל עת המצטרך משא"כ צדיק שכבר נסתלק מזה העולם ואינו
יודע מצב הדור אינו יכול להכריע ההלכה כפי אותו הדור. . . יען שהצדיק אשר החמיר אינו עוד בעוה"ז
והוא אינו יודע כעת ענינם הנצרכים אל העולם כי נפרד מאתנו אז אין הלכה כמותו א"כ לפי"ז בזמנינו
שנעשה השערורריה הגדולה בישראל ואין מקום עוד להשאר בגולה פשיטא דאין לחוש לדברי הגדולים
שהיו נגד הישוב ורק ההלכה כאלו הגדולים שהיו בעד הישוב כי השעה צריכה לכך ואולי אם היו בחיים
הגם הם בעצמם היו מסכימים לכך ודוק אתנו והיו רואין מצבנו עתה. (*EHS*, 161–4)

"Who is in a position to determine what should be considered as the proper policy to pursue? One who is alive in this world can know the proper policy to pursue. But one who is not alive [i.e., one who is dead] is not aware of the the proper policy to pursue. . . . Such insights are not made available even to Moses our Lawgiver because his soul is detached from his body. The angels as well do not have insight into worldly affairs. . . . Only those who are always involved [in human affairs] in every generation can determine the norms for that generation as the need arises. This cannot be achieved by a *tzadik* who has left this world and does not know regarding the situation of this particular generation. . . . Therefore, the *tzadik* who [at one time] interpreted the law in a stringent manner will not have his ruling accepted [at a later time] since he has already lost contact with his generation and is ignorant concerning contemporary realities. Hence, in the face of the great horror which faces

This should teach us that even the greatest scholar and the most pious of men should not be overly confident when he chooses to oppose the movement to rebuild the Land, believing that he does so only for the sake of Heaven. He certainly could not be as learned and as pious as the tribal chieftains sent by Moses.[116] Nevertheless they betrayed their mission due to self-interest.[117] The opposite also is true.[118]

Thus we see that the Almighty persuaded the Israelites to dispatch scouts to Eretz Yisrael for their benefit. This [mission] would serve the purpose to arouse their longing and desire for this good Land.

Thus they will be proven worthy of entering and claiming the Land. What we have discussed thus far will now be clearer. There is no doubt that the Holy One, Who alone is interested in our welfare, without rejecting or banishing any soul,[119] that He inspired our Jewish brethren to long for and desire only the Land of our forefathers.

Jews in our own time and there is no longer a place for us in exile, it is obvious that we can not respond to the teachings of our great scholars who have always objected to the settlement [of the Land of Israel]. We can only respond to those great leaders who favored settlement since this is the call of the hour. Perhaps if they [the leadership which opposed settlement] were alive with us today and had personally witnessed our predicament, they would now agree as well. Ponder carefully." Countering the views of the Munkatcher Rebbe, our author returns to the theme of redemption by natural means. Such redemption was made necessary since the Jewish people in the diaspora forfeited a miraculous redemption by their refusal to return to Eretz Yisrael during the period of Cyrus and Ezra (*EHS*, 164–5). The readiness of nations to permit our return to the Land (i.e., the Balfour Declaration) is God's way of directing the people Israel to correct the error committed in the period of Cyrus (ibid. 166). The wealthy who refused to participate in rebuilding the Temple, thus obstructing redemption, again come under criticism (ibid. 167; cf. 81).

116 To scout the Land. Num. 13:1–15. See also NumR. *Shelah* 16:4 שנאמר: אנשים' בני אדם צדיקים הם . . . אעפ"כ בני אדם גדולים היו ועשו עצמן כסילים . . . מכאן שהיו צדיקים בפני ישראל ובפני משה . . . ראויים הם . . . שנא' כי דור תהפכות המה' שנתבררו צדיקים, ונתהפכו. "As it is written: 'men.' These were righteous people. . . . Nevertheless, these great leaders made fools of themselves. . . . They were indeed righteous before the people Israel and Moses . . . they *were* worthy . . . as it is written (Deut. 32:20): 'For they are a treacherous breed.' They were selected as being righteous people and they acted treacherously.'

117 See above, 26–27, nn. 63–64.

118 The nonpious and uneducated may fulfill unprecedented achievements with their selfless devotion to *binyan Eretz Yisrael* (building the Land of Israel).

119 Variant of II Sam. 14:14. Cf. above, 66, n. 33.

They are prepared to give their lives for this [cause] despite their many years of exile during which they were under the influence of other nations. For this alone they are deemed worthy of acquiring the Land and settling in it. Then certainly one good deed will bring in its wake yet another.[120] Eventually, when many Jews have settled there, the Lord will purify their hearts and they shall return to His service, may He be blessed. ...

And this is the meaning of the verse in Ezekiel 20[121] "And I will bring you into the wilderness of the peoples." *Midbar* [wilderness] is derived from *dibbur*[122] [speech] as indicated in *Exodus Rabba*, chapter 2:[123] "The word *midbar* can only mean *dibbur*, as is written: 'and your speech [*u'midbarekh*] is beautiful.'"[124]

---

120 Avot 4:2. מצוה גוררת מצוה "for one mitzvah generates another." The fulfillment of the solitary precept of *Yishuv Eretz Yisrael* will draw with it others. This will signify the eventual return of the secular settlers to the way of God. Our author, citing Maimonides (*Hilkhot Teshuvah* 7:5) notes the significance of a single important precept which reflects repentance, and the process of redemption (*EHS*, 169). In this vein note Yoma 86b. אמר רבי יונתן: גדולה תשובה שמקרבת את הגאולה שנאמר: ובא לציון גואל ולשבי פשע ביעקב (ישעי' נט:כ) מה טעם ובא לציון גואל משום דשבי פשע ביעקב "R. Yonatan said: Great is repentance, because it brings redemption closer as it is written (Isa. 59:20): 'He shall come as a redeemer to Zion, to those in Jacob that turn back from sin.' What is the reason that 'He shall come as a reeemer to Zion?' because of those 'that turn back from sin.'" *Repentance* and *return* are employed synonymously. The potency of performing but one mitzvah, is further demonstrated. The alarming prophecy in Isaac's belated blessing to Esau (Gen. 27:40), והיה כאשר תריד ופרקת עלו מעל צוארך "But when you grow restive, you shall break his yoke from your neck," would not be realized as long as Israel continues to observe at least one of the precepts in the Torah (*EHS*, 171). The concern of other nations for the "Jewish problem" is viewed as a certain sign that the natural process of redemption by political means was at hand. This process was predicted in the *midrash*, Abravanel and R. Yehudah Alkalai's (1798–1878) *Minhat Yehudah* (Vienna, 1843), cited in *EHS*, 171–2, and contemporarized by the Balfour Declaration and the subsequent public debate in the international arena.

121 20:35.

122 Following the root דבר (*d'v'r'*).

123 *Vs.* 20 in *EHS*, 172.

124 Song 4:3. Cf. the play on words in ibid. 3:6 מי זאת עלה מן המדבר "Who is she that comes from the desert?" and the parallelism of כחוט השני שפתותיך "Your lips are like a crimson thread" in 4:3. The significant "speech" between God and Abraham reflected in the "covenant of the pieces" (Gen. 15) would preceed Moses' entry into the wilderness. The "speech" of the nations in their parliamentary assemblies also signifies redemption.

That is to say, "I will bring you to the stage of the nations' speeches." They will talk among themselves and discuss the long duration of our exile. I have heard that his excellency the Cardinal of Hungary had wisely expressed himself before the king and ministers as follows: "We have never before heard or seen anyone in captivity for a period of eighteen hundred years as is the case with these unfortunate Jews, who have suffered under kings and ministers. Nevertheless they behave properly and virtuously. . . ."

Unlike this solitary kind priest who spoke kindly of the Jewish people one hundred years ago,[125] when the Jewish problem was not yet a burning issue, today many parliaments turn their attention to solving it [the Jewish question] so that we may ultimately benefit. . . . All this is profoundly mandated by the Creator of the entire universe. . . . Thus it is written: "[Kings shall tend your children], their queens shall serve you as nurses,"[126] that is to say, all the powers will agree to nurse us with milk and honey, as it is written, "You shall suck the milk of the nations, suckle at royal breasts,"[127] "they shall bow to you."[128] That is to say: The Holy One, blessed be He, will direct events in a dignified yet mundane fashion, employing political events.[129]

"And lick the dust of your feet,"[130] this means that the nations too shall accompany God on this day and enter Eretz Yisrael. There they shall live and engage in commerce, with love and in brotherhood and friendship "and you shall know that I am the Lord. Those who trust in Me shall not be shamed."[131] This is cited from the master in his

---

125   The identity of the archbishop is not certain. The serious interest of the nations in a Jewish homeland in prewar Europe may have been viewed by the author more in hope than in reality.

126   Isa. 49:23.

127   Ibid. 60:16. The *EHS* quotation should read ושד מלכים תינקי "You shall suckle at royal breasts."

128   Ibid. 49:23.

129   Namely, the world's rulers will serve as instruments in the grand divine design for Israel's redemption.

130   Ibid.

131   Ibid.

volume, section 19.[132]

My dear readers, note well the words of this *Sefardi* master, great human being, scholar, and disciple of the *tzadik*, rabbi and author of *Pele Yo'etz*,[133] which has been widely acclaimed everywhere. He cites the leading scholars, including *Yafe To'ar*,[134] among the great early masters, who all believe that the return of Eretz Yisrael will be achieved by natural means and the ordinary political process. Their [Jewish] problem will become a concern for the other nations.

He wrote this at a time when it [the Zionist question] was not yet an issue in the world's parliaments. Now that the Jewish question is indeed a burning issue before the nations can we ignore this phenomenon?[135] Any intelligent person must surely admit that this is the era which our prophets had in mind when they foresaw the time of any redemption brought about by causes initiated by the Prime Mover. . . .[136]

I also cite evidence from our teacher Maimonides that one is not to rely on miracles alone. Rather we must do all we possibly can by natural means, then we shall be assisted by Heaven. In his correspondence to the sages of Marseilles, he expressed his opinion about astrology which he considered nonsense and a mere waste of time. He then goes on to say: We lost our kingdom, our Temple was destroyed, our exile was extended and we have come hither due to the sins of our fathers. [They sinned] because they were immersed in the literature

---

132   R. Yehudah Alkalai, *Minhat Yehudah* (Vienna, 1843), 14.

133   R. Eliezer Papo, died 1824. *Pele Yo'etz*, published in two parts (Constantinople, 1824 and Bucharest, 1860) is devoted to rules of ethics and morality.

134   Commentary on *Genesis Rabba* (Venice, 1597), *Exodus Rabba* (Venice, 1597) and *Leviticus Rabba* (Constantinople, 1648) by the late 16th century Ashkenazi rabbi of Constantinople, R. Shmuel ben Yitzhak Jaffe.

135   Possible reference to the Bermuda Conference on Refugees, April 19–30, 1943, and the Evian Conference of July 1938. Neither conference proved effective in dealing with the desperate situation of refugees caught in the web of destruction.

136   *EHS* continues to vehemently lash out at those who preach redemption by supernatural means. Quoting extensively from the *Minhat Yehudah* he terms these futile efforts as a hidden form of "desecration of the Name of God" (חילול השם בסתר) *EHS*, 175–6.

of astrologists.[137] They erred in believing that this literature contained wisdom and was of great value. **They did not engage in military training, nor did they conquer territory.**[138]

They believed that the astrologers would help them. Therefore the prophets [of blessed memory] referred to them as fools and idiots since they led others into a useless void. They could not save them[139] . . . These are the sacred words of our master Maimonides. He blamed our fathers for the destruction of our Land and our Temple because they neglected the art of warfare and the conquest of land. They simply wasted their days and depended upon this [system of astrology]. Now why did he not accuse them of neglecting the study of Torah or [neglecting] the performance of good deeds? Because he wishes to indicate that [in certain situations] this would not be sufficient.[140] This coincides with the views of Nahmanides in a number of his commentaries on Scripture. . . .[141] The Rashba as well rules accordingly in Responsum 419.[142] Yet we take note of the Midrash[143] on the weekly scripture *Pekudei*[144] commenting on the verse, "Unless the Lord builds the house, its builders labor in vain on it. . . ."[145]

One should not conclude from this that man should remain inactive and rely only upon God to build [the house]. Rather it [the verse] intended to convey the idea that when man works and toils he should not depend exclusively upon his own efforts lest he toil for naught.

---

137 The Maimonides text adds here דברים אלו הם עקר ע״ז כמו שביארנו: "These practices represent the fabric of idol worship, as we have explained."

138 The bold type appears in the *EHS* text.

139 Maimonides, *K'tav Teshuvot LeHakhme Kehal Ir Marsilei [Marseilles]* in *Kovez Teshuvot HaRambam V'Igrotav, Igrot HaRambam* (Leipzig, 1859), 24–26.

140 Likely ועי״כ דזה לחוד לא מהני vs. להוד (*lehud* vs. *lehod*).

141 See above, 46, n. 54 (*EHS*, 49).

142 Most likely Responsa 418, which attacks at length occult beliefs, including astrology, which would in fact deny the principle of freedom of choice, *She'elot U'Tshuvot HaRashba*, vol. 1, Responsum 418 (Bnei Brak, 1958), 154–74.

143 *Tanhuma HaKadum VeHaYashan, Pekudei* (Buber Edition).

144 Ex. 38:21–40:38.

145 Ps. 127:1. To rely exclusively on one's own resources, without any relationship to the divine and the sacred, is doomed to failure.

Truly, this is confirmed in the first chapter of Yoma, in the Jerusalem Talmud.[146] During the Second Temple they [the Jews] were engaged in Torah and mitzvot. It was not due to the absence of the merit of Torah and mitzvot that the Land and Temple were destroyed. It must be concluded, as is the opinion of Maimonides[147] that they relied on nonsense.[148] They did not become involved with natural causes of events upon which the Land is dependent, such as military arts and conquest. . .

Certainly he did not imply that we learn the military arts and conquer territory while in exile. This is not within our ability to achieve considering the dispersion of our forces among the nations. This we should have done while we were all united in our Land. . . He did, however, intend for us to use other natural means available to us, such as petitioning the rulers to extend their benevolence and terminate the exile which hangs over us. We could [also] acquire land by means of purchase. (This point is expanded upon by the *gaon* and *tzadik* our teacher R. Zvi Kalisher[149] in his volume *D'rishat Zion*.[150] Other scholars elaborated upon this subject. Evidence is presented from the Jerusalem Talmud, Moed Katan 2:4, that the purchase of land from them [the gentiles] is equivalent to [military] conquest.[151]

146　JT Yoma 1:1 (4b). אבל בשני מכירין אנו אותם שהיו יגיעין בתורה במצות ובמעשרות וכל וסת טובה היתה בהן, אלא שהיו אוהבין את הממון ושונאין אלו לאלו שנאת חינם שהיא שקולה כנגד ע"א וגילוי עריות ושפיכת דמים. "But [in regard to the] Second commononwealth, we recognise that they toiled in the study of Torah and were meticulous in the observance of mitzvot, and tithes. They were imbued with good habits but had a lust for wealth. This led to mutual senseless hatred which is equivalent to the combined [sins of] idol worship, incestuous relationships and murder." The meticulous observance of the mitzvot did not evidently bring about a change in values which should have prevented an overly materialistic society and the resultant senseless hatred. Similarly, in order to achieve national redemption the people will be compelled to assume political and military initiatives in order to acquire and preserve the Land. The practice of mitzvot and the study of Torah by themselves will not suffice.

147　See above, 155, n. 139.

148　Reference to astrological forecasts described as תהו ובהו (chaos).

149　1795–1874. Rabbi, scholar, and student of R. Akiva Eiger, early advocate of modern Zionism, based on applying religious activist-redemptive elements for settling Eretz Yisrael, as opposed to the accepted view of a supernatural miraculous redemption.

150　Lyck, 1862. I could not locate the reference.

151　According to Resh Lakish it is permitted to purchase land in Eretz Yisrael

To redeem the Land from their possession is a mitzvah as noted by the Ribash[152] in section 101.[153]

(Note as well the elaboration in *Kuntres Yeshivat Eretz Yisrael* by the great *gaon* our teacher Yonah Dov Blumberg of the holy community of Dvinsk, published in Vilna in 1897.[154] These all speak of natural efforts without relying on miracles alone. Then the help will come from Heaven. He will bring us to our Land and put an end to our exile. Without our action, however, we will bring upon ourselves the injunction of Maimonides: "This is the cause of the long exile and our having come to this stage." In other words, we can only blame ourselves for the long exile. We have reached the stage where we are at anyone's mercy, as fish in the sea. Anyone is at liberty to do with us as he wishes. Our blood is being spilled like water, because of our many sins. May God grant us the insight to recognize the truth. May He stimulate every Jew to desire and return to the bosom of our mother[155] and to actively work towards this goal. May He open the eyes of those blinded by Samael,[156] with fabricated and unfounded

---

from a gentile even on the Sabbath (though in a modified form, שינוי) because of the mitzvah of settling the Land. Evidence is presented that Jericho was conquered on the Sabbath.

152 R. Isaac ben Sheshet (1326–1408), leading Spanish authority on halakhah.

153 ואחרי שלדברי מצוה מותר ולחלל את השבת] . . . והתירו שבות דאמירא לכותי במלאכה דאורייתא . . . אין ספק שהעליה לארץ ישראל מצוה היא . . . שהרי העולה על דעת להתישב נקרא עוסק במצוה. . . . ועשה ק"ו מהקונה שדה בא"י שכותבין עליו אונו ואפי' בשבת והתירו שבות. . . . דאדרבה הקונה שדה מן הכותי היא מצוה גדולה. "And in the interest of the mitzvah [of building the Land] it is permitted [to violate the Sabbath by telling a gentile scribe to write a deed even on the Sabbath] . . . there is no question that the settling in Eretz Yisrael is a mitzvah . . . since one who contemplates settling is considered to be involved in a mitzvah. . . . One may extrapolate from the case of one who acquires a field in Eretz Yisrael for whom a purchase contract is written [by a gentile] even on the Sabbath, permitting the violation of rest. . . . On the contrary, one who acquires a field [in Eretz Yisrael] from a Cuthean performs an important mitzvah." *She'elot uTshuvot Ribash*, Jerusalem, 1993, responsum 101 (94).

154 See above, 141, n. 53. The secular 1897 (*vs.* possible 1898) date is cited in the volume.

155 See above, 8, n. 34; 33–36; below, 199–203, 206, 236.

156 Satan, the Angel of Death, who stands to the left (hence שמאל, *Sama'el*) of Israel in order to accuse the Jewish people before the heavenly judge. The Hebrew abbreviation ס"ם (*s'm'*) also alludes to poison סם (*Sam*). See above, 108, n. 128.

arguments. On the contrary, [to these] our sages, of blessed memory, take the opposite view.

The *gaon*, the godly man of *kabbalah*, our teacher R. David Lida[157] in *Ir Miklat*[158] expounds upon the verse, "But the Land must not be sold beyond reclaim,"[159] as follows: "Our teacher, R. Hayyim Shabbetai,[160] wrote that with the redemption of the Land is linked our own redemption and with its bondage is tied our own servitude."[161] Nahmanides in *Sefer HaMitzvot*, commandment 227,[162] cites the Jerusalem Talmud, *D'mai*[163] obligating us never to allow our Land to be subjugated to the nations. He summarizes as follows: It seems from these opinions that it is clearly a prohibition to subjugate the Land to the nations.[164] We are not permitted to leave it for them. Just as we are forbidden to sell our bodies [by means of outright purchase] to the nations . . . and as we are commanded to redeem them [in the Jubilee],[165] as explained in the verse: "For it is to Me that the Israelites are servants."[166] We were, therefore, cautioned not to transfer the possession of Land into their hands. The reason given is similar to that of the slave. Since the Land is in fact His, He does not wish to have others settle there. We must, therefore, return. Since we do not seem to be anxious about releasing the Land from their hands, we

---

157   R. David ben Aryeh Leib of Lida, 17th century Lithuanian rabbi and commentator. While serving the Amsterdam community, he was accused by the Sefardi rabbis of being a follower of Shabbetai Zvi, an allegation vehemently denied by his Polish colleagues.

158   Dyhenfurth, 1690. A commentary on the 613 commandments; reference is to the 334th commandment.

159   Lev. 25:23.

160   Abbreviated in our text מוהרמ״ש, 17th century Salonica chief rabbi and author of numerous responsa.

161   *Ir Miklat* (Jerusalem, 1959), 41a.

162   *Sefer HaMitzvot L'HaRambam Im Hasagot HaRamban*, ed. H. D. Chavel (Jerusalem, 1981), 347–348.

163   JT *Demai* 5:8 (23a).

164   In the Ramban text.

165   Lev. 25:47–55 commands the family of a Jewish slave in the service of a resident alien to redeem him in the Jubilee year.

166   Ibid. verse 55.

ourselves are oppressed measure for measure. Should we, however, attempt to release the Land from their hands, we will [also] merit our own freedom. . . . .[167]

The Maharsha further adds in Berakhot 6[168] in connection with the mitzvah of gladdening the bridegroom and bride [on their wedding day]. "R. Nahman b. Yitzhak said:[169] 'It is as if he had restored one of the ruins of Jerusalem,' as it is written: 'For I will restore the fortunes of the Land as of old. . . . '"[170] The Maharsha in *Hiddushei Aggadot* writes: "This represents the very existence and settlement of Eretz Yisrael."[171] That is to say, if they will fulfill the obligation of settling Eretz Yisrael then the Lord proclaims that "I will restore the fortunes of the Land as of old. . . ."[172]

We may, therefore, better understand the relationship between redemption and the required affection for our Holy Land. The redemption will be brought nearer in proportion to the degree of affection. Observe what is written in the volume *Even Shlomo*[173] of our

---

167 *EHS* (178–180) reinforces the principle of speeding redemption by means of active involvement in rebuilding the Land. Kings David and Solomon are presented and portrayed as exemplary models in the rabbinic literature. (Ta'an. 15a–15b; and related commentary of Maharsha). The author reiterates the thesis of the *Baal Mishnat Hasidim* (above, 31, n. 97) that the task for rebuilding the Land was deliberately left to the Jewish people as part of the design of redemption.

168 6b.

169 Regarding one who participates in this mitzvah.

170 Jer. 33:11. The verse opens with: "The sound of mirth and the sound of gladness, the voice of the bridegroom and the voice of the bride, the voice of those who cry, 'Give thanks to the Lord of Hosts, for the Lord is good, for His kindness is everlasting' as they bring thanksgiving offerings to the House of the Lord. . . ." Thus, the connection of the restoration theme with the joy of a wedding.

171 The growth of Eretz Yisrael will be enhanced by the mitzvah of raising new families.

172 Jer. 33:11. The author elaborates on the motif of "the merits of the fathers" and its relationship to the "merit of the Land," introduced earlier in the volume (above, 5, *EHS*, 181–182). This theme is expanded via kabbalah symbolism in *Otzrot Yosef* of R. Yosef Engel (above, 50, n. 78–79), the Midrash and Rambam (*EHS*, 182, 183)

173 Shmuel Malzan (ed.) *Even Shlomo* (Vilna, 1889) 11:9, 50. A collection of principles on proper ethical behavior, education of children, methods of study and prayer, death and redemption, by R. Eliyahu, the Gaon of Vilna. אבל קץ האחרון לא תליא

rabbi the *Gaon* of Vilna,[174] of blessed memory. He wrote that the future redemption is not dependent upon our repentance but rather upon the merits of our Fathers. This we declare thrice every day "who remembers the good deeds of the Patriarchs and graciously brings redemption to their children's children."[175] Thus [redemption] is dependent upon the merit of the Fathers, and the merit of the Fathers is in turn, dependent upon the degree to which we hold our Land in esteem. I was, therefore, correct in indicating that everything is dependent on the affection for the Land. May the Almighty inspire us to devote ourselves to the sanctity of our Land to rebuild it for the sake of His blessed and glorious Name. May we then merit the complete redemption speedily in our day.[176]

In *Midrash Rabba,* the portion of *Mas'ei*[177] there is [cited]:

Said the Holy One, blessed be He: "Eretz Yisrael is My favorite above all else. Why so? Because I sought it out [for them]. . . ."[178] to inform you that none are considered as beloved[179] as is Eretz Yisrael." Said the Holy One, blessed be He, to Moses: "Indeed the Land is My beloved," as it is written: ". . . it is the Land which the Lord your God looks after always."[180] "And Israel is My beloved," as it is written "But it was because the Lord loved you . . . [that the Lord freed you with a mighty hand and rescued you from the house of bondage]. . . ."[181] Said the Holy One, blessed be He: "I will bring in My beloved Israel to the Land[182]

בתשובה אלא בחסד. "The final redemption is not dependent upon repentance but upon good deeds."

174   The Vilna Gaon (1720–1797) among the most exceptional of scholars and community leaders in recent Jewish history.

175   From the daily liturgy the *Amidah* prayer in *Daily Prayer Book* (ed. Philip Birnbaum) New York, N.Y., 1949, 83–84.

176   The author reintroduces the theme of God's interdependent affection for both Eretz Yisrael and the people Israel (See above, 49–50).

177   NumR. 23:7.

178   Based on Ezek. 20:6.

179   חביבה *vs.* חביבות in our text. Singular *vs.* plural of the term *haviv.*

180   Deut. 11:12.

181   Ibid. 7:8.

182   ארץ (*Eretz*) *vs.* ארץ ישראל (*Eretz Yisrael*) in our text.

which is My beloved," as it is written: " . . . when you enter the land of Canaan."[183] Now the Maharal[184] has already elaborated in his writings[185] that the Divine love for Israel is not dependent upon other factors. Whether one fulfills His will, or not, Heaven forbid, His love is never removed from them. This is confirmed in Maimonides' *Iggeret Teiman* and by our rabbi the author of *Noam Elimelekh* in Deuteronomy.[186] Accordingly, therefore, the Lord, may He be blessed, always desires for His favorite children to enter the Land, since they remain His favorites always. Only if they are good, however, will they enter by means of a revealed miracle. If, Heaven forbid, they are not worthy, then their entry will be by natural means—as I have elaborated previously.[187]

Further [note] the Midrash commenting on the verse: "This is the land that shall fall to you as your portion":[188]

What is the meaning of "to you"? For you it is deemed worthy. This may be compared to a king who had male and female servants. He would [nevertheless] marry his males to female servants from another

---

183   Num. 34:2.

184   See above, 44, n. 39.

185   *Netzah Yisrael.* Tel Aviv, 1955, 21. בין כך וכך קרוים בני [עפ"י" קדושין לו] ודבר זה אין כי . . . שינוי לו בכל חטא חטא אשר יעשו תהיה החטא מה שהוא. . . . אבל בודאי על ישראל בכלל שם בנים. כי החטא הוא לפרטיה בלבד הם החוטאים אבל שיכוח בשביל הפרט שם בנים מן כלל ישראל, דבר זה אי אפשר. "In either case they [the people of Israel] are referred to as 'children' [according to Kid. 36a). This status does not undergo change even should they be guilty of iniquities of any sort. . . . Certainly the totality of Israel assumes the designation 'children.' The concept 'sin' relates to individuals only. One cannot conceive that the status of 'children' should depart from the totality of Israel."

186   *Noam Elimelekh Devarim,* 88a. אך שהתיקון לזה הוא במה שכולל עצמו עם כללות ישראל. כי יש עולם הנקרא כל ישראל והעולם ההוא שלם בלי שום פגם. כי הכללות ישראל הם צדיקים, כמו שכתוב יעמך כולם צדיקים' [ישעיה ס:כא] ואם כן אף שהפרטים חוטאים לפעמים, אבל הכללות הם תמיד קיימים בקדושתם ואין שטן, ואין פגע רע בהם חלילה. The rectifying [*tikkun*] of this situation [the process of sinfulness] can come about by the joining of the individual with the totality of Israel. There exists a world called 'All-of-Israel' (*Kol Yisrael*). This world is unimpeachable, without a fault. The totality of Israel [*Klal Yisrael*] is righteous. As it is written [Isa. 60:21] 'And your people, all of them righteous.' Although there are individual elements who sin at times, the total aggregate always exists in a state of sanctity. There is neither an indictment nor a negative flaw, Heaven forbid."

187   See above, 89–90.

188   Num. 34:2.

estate. Then the king came to his senses and reconsidered: "My male servants are mine. My female servants are mine. It would be best, after all, if I marry my male servants to my female servants." Similarly, the Holy One, blessed be He, declared: "The Land is Mine," as it is written ["The earth is the Lord's"][189] and it is [further] written; "For the Land is Mine."[190] Israel is Mine, as it is written: "For it is to Me that the Israelites are servants."[191] It is best that I bequeath My Land to My servant—what is Mine to what is Mine. Therefore it is written: "This is the Land that shall fall to you as your portion."[192]

One may question as to the need for the previous parable of our sages, of blessed memory.[193] It would have been sufficient to have simply indicated that the identical term "mine" [li] is linked to [both] Eretz Yisrael and the people Israel.[194] There is a further difficulty as to why the Midrash was compelled to cite the verse: "For it is to Me that the Israelites are servants."[195] The verse in connection with the giving of the Torah should rather have been cited: "[Indeed, all the earth is Mine], but you shall be to Me [a kingdom of priests and a holy nation]."[196] Why would the verse describing Israel's servitude be cited?[197] One may interpret this as follows: the Midrash had difficulties with the phrase "[This is the Land]. . . that shall fall to you as your portion,"[198] for it implies that the "Land" would "fall to you" of its own volition. It should have been stated "This is the Land which you shall take possession of." [After all,] taking possesion is linked to [the people] Israel and not dependent upon the Land. Therefore the [sages

---

189   Ps. 24:1. Cited in the *Midrash* text and omitted in *EHS*, 184.

190   Lev. 25:23.

191   Ibid. 25:55.

192   Num. 34:2.

193   The parable of the *Midrash* regarding the king who had male and female servants.

194   Ibid.

195   Lev. 25:55.

196   Ex. 19:5–6.

197   Suggesting an inferior and demeaning status.

198   Num. 34:2.

introduced the] parable in order to anticipate the difficulty in relationship to the king and his children. . . We are familiar with the teaching of our sages: When they fulfill the will of the Omnipresent they are called "sons"[199] before the Omnipresent, and when, Heaven forbid, they do not fulfill His will, they are servants.[200] It is clear that when the people Israel fulfill the will of the Omnipresent, there is no doubt as to their receiving the Land. It may be compared to the grafting of one grape vine with a [similar] grape vine.[201] However, if, Heaven forbid, the will of the Omnipresent is not fulfilled and they assume the status of servants, one might have thought that the Holy One, blessed be He, would match the Land to any [group of] servants, namely, to the nations of the world. Therefore, the Midrash presents the parable in order to indicate that even when Israel behaves as servants, the Holy One will match Israel with the Land of Israel. . . .

Thus the Midrash was insistent on utilizing the verse "For it is to Me that Israelites are servants"[202] . . . as opposed to the verse in connection with the giving of the Torah,[203] since this [verse] refers to the time when they will obey Him, as it is written there: "Now then, if you will obey Me faithfully."[204] This also satisfactorily explains why it is written: "[This is the Land] that shall fall to you as your portion,"[205] and it is not written: "[This is the Land] which you shall take possession of." The [latter verse] would have indicated they were worthy of taking possession on their own merits. Then the process of possession would be linked to Israel since they would deserve it. This is true only when they do His will.

Therefore, the Torah was compelled to state: "[This is the Land] that shall fall to you [as your portion]." Namely, the Land shall fall to you due to the readiness and [positive] attitude of the Land and not

199   As in Deut. 14:1 *vs.* Lev. 25:55.
200   Paraphrase of BB 10a. Cf. Kid. 36a.
201   As in Pes. 49a. This is deemed a proper and acceptable match.
202   Lev. 25:55.
203   Ex. 19:5–6.
204   Ibid.
205   Num. 34:2.

due to the worthiness of your deeds, indicating: "It is preferred that
[the Land] fall to you rather than to other servants," as in the parable.
This is how our sages and the Torah demonstrate the will of the
Creator Who desires that Israel shall always dwell in our Holy Land,
even when they do not obey the will of the Omnipresent, Heaven
forbid, and are not worthy in their own right.

I came upon a similar idea in the interpretation of the Midrash in
the verse in Lamentations: "Whenever I thought of them":[206]

"If only My children were together with Me, even though they upset
Me!"[207] [As proof text] it is written: "Oh, to be in the desert at an
encampment for wayfarers!"[208] Said the Holy One, blessed be He: "If
only My children were together with Me as they were in the desert
when they complained against Me."[209]

Note this well![210] Further they quoted:[211]

When the House of Israel dwelt on their own soil they defiled it [with
their ways and their deeds].[212] Said the Holy One, blessed be He: "If
only they were to be My people in Eretz Yisrael though they defile
her."

This Midrash is puzzling. How can the Holy One, blessed be He,
expect us to be His people in Eretz Yisrael although we defile her!

---

206   Lam. 3:20.

207   LamR. 3:18. God's longing for His people transcends His anger. Their dwelling
in Eretz Yisrael, though undeserved, provides the common place of God with His
people. Variant reading: בני עמי (b'nei ami) "The children of My people" vs. בני עימי
(banai imi) "My children together with Me."

208   Jer. 9:1.

209   The Midrash inverts the close reading of the text. The Jeremiah text describes
God as seeking to distance Himself from His treacherous and dishonest people. The
Midrash homiletically restates the verse as follows: "If only My people were again
with Me, in the desert camp following the Exodus. The term מלון (malon) "hostel" is
utilized to suggest מלינים עלי (melinim alai) "though they complain."

210   The author again develops the motif of cleansing the "unclean" who dwell in
Eretz Yisrael. EHS, 185–189.

211   LamR. 3:18.

212   Ezek. 36:17.

After all, the Land cannot tolerate those who defile her, as it is written: "So let not the Land spew you out for defiling it [as it spewed out the nation that came before it.]"[213] . . . However, there is no difficulty at all. Obviously, the higher and lower courts functioned when the Jewish people lived on their land.[214] In every city, courts were in session, as described in Sanhedrin.[215] They guided and taught the Jews. Every Jew developed in the spirit of Torah. They knew the laws and legislation of Torah. Then, if someone violated the precepts of the Almighty, he clearly was cognizant of the specific violation. . . .

When they were dispersed among the nations, however, without teacher or prophet, "they mingled with the nations and learned their ways."[216] Most of our Jewish brethren, because of our many sins, do not have a proper understanding of the value of the Torah's commandments. This is especially so among those who were educated among the sages of the nations and were left bereft of the light and energy of Torah. There are countries and localities where Torah has been completely forgotten, because of our many sins. These people simply have assumed the status of a child captive among the gentiles.[217] Therefore,[218] it is proper that this commandment should be inoperative among the 613 biblical commandments of the Torah. The rule which would have demanded that the Land reject them [the impure][219] is inappropriate. Although they defile her, Heaven forbid, the Land adores them, since they [behave in violation of the commandments] without conscious intent. The Land awaits their return to a full appreciation of our holy Torah resulting from God's projection of the

---

213 Lev. 18:28. The author digresses in order to laud the wisdom and perceptiveness of the sages with regard to the meaning of this verse.

214 The Great Sanhedrin, composed of seventy-one judges, sat in the Temple Mount area in Jerusalem. The lower (or *lit.* "smaller") courts, lesser Sanhedrins of twenty-three judges, were located throughout Eretz Yisrael (Sanh. 1:1, 16b).

215 Ibid.

216 Ps. 106:35.

217 See above, 107, nn. 124 and 125.

218 Since these Jews are blameless, having had no Jewish education.

219 As per Lev. 18:28.

Pure Spirit upon them from Above, when He will remove from them
the heart of stone.[220]

Furthermore, according to Maimonides (The Laws of Repentance),
the Holy One, blessed be He, does not evaluate the merits according
to our calculations, but according to His own considerations.[221] He
knows how to evaluate one virtuous act in such a way that it can tip
the scales of many acts of wrongdoing. Hence, those who devote
themselves to the settlement of the Holy Land, which outweighs the
entire Torah [in its importance], as explained in the *Sifrei* (the portion
of *Re'eh*),[222] may earn the merit which will counter all transgressions;
especially when these efforts are made with great dedication. . . .

I have already demonstrated at the outset[223] that rebuilding the
Land is very much desired and considered proper before Him, blessed
be He. It does not matter who it is [who builds], as long as the
building is a preparation for settlement.

It now is appropriate to submit additional evidence[224] from *Midrash
Rabba*,[225] the portion of *Vayetze*:[226]

> R. Yose the son of Hanina said: "Names have been associated with four
> [combinations] of characteristics.[227] There are those with ugly names
> and ugly deeds. There are those with ugly names and fine deeds and
> those with fine names and ugly deeds. [Examples of] those with ugly
> names and fine deeds—these are the families of the exile: 'the sons of

---

220 Cf. Ezek. 36:26. The author documenting from the classical sources, assigns
to the nations the role of שומרי המקום, "the guardians of the place," until the permanent
return of the Jewish people to their Land.

221 *Yad HaHazakah, Hilkhot Teshuvah* 3:2. ואין שוקלין אלא בדעתו של אל דעות והוא
היודע היאך עורכין הזכויות כנגד העונות "Decisions are made only on the basis of Divine
calculations. Only He knows how to evaluate virtuous acts in juxtaposition to acts of
wrongdoing."

222 Deut. 12:29. See above, 145, n. 87.

223 See above, 49–54.

224 That the rebuilding of Eretz Yisrael is desired by the Almighty.

225 GenR. 71:3.

226 Gen. 28:10–32:3.

227 *EHS* reads ארבע מידות בשמות "Four characteristics are evident in names" *vs.*
ארבע מידות נאמרו בשמות "are mentioned in connection with names" in the Midrash.

Bakbuk, the sons of Hakupha, the sons of Harhur.[228] They were privileged. They went up [to Eretz Yisrael] and rebuilt the Temple."

This Midrash is also cited in the portion of *Shelah*:[229]

"Those with ugly names and fine deeds—these are the families of the exile: 'the sons of Barkos, the sons of Sisera, the sons of Thamah.'"[230] ... In the Book of Ezra it is written: "The following were those who came up from Tel-Melah, Tel-Harsha, Cherub, Addan and Immer.[231] And it says further: 'They were unable to tell whether their father's house and descent were Israelite.'"[232] Rashi comments:[233] "Since they lost contact with their origins and were not sure if they were descended from Israel."[234] Our teachers of the Midrash describe those who ascended from exile during the period of Ezra as having ugly names while performing fine deeds. They were ugly, gentile names. For instance, Sisera[235] was the name of a gentile.[236] Some were in such a low state that they could not trace their Jewish ancestry.

There is further evidence of their poor spiritual state by virtue of the gentile names cited in the verse [as in Ezra and Nehemiah]. I will attempt to demonstrate the accepted use of gentile names by Jews from our own situation in exile. I will, however, preface this with the

---

228 These are listed among the captive exiles who returned from Babylon to Jerusalem as Temple servants, as described in Ezra 2:51 and Neh. 7:55. Their names sound harsh to the ear yet they pioneered in rebuilding the Temple.

229 Num. 13:1–15:41, NumR. 16:10.

230 Ezra 2:53; Neh. 7:55.

231 Ezra 2:59; Neh. 7:61. Both the original *EHS* text and the Jerusalem edition (1983) omit "and Immer." The spelling אמר (*Immer*) is confused with ואמר עד (*Ve'amar od* "and he said further") which follows and was likely the source of error in the original, and copied in the subsequent Jerusalem edition.

232 Ibid.

233 *EHS* paraphrases Rashi.

234 Actual Rashi text in Ezra 2:59: הם נקראו אסופים שנאספו מן השוק כי לא הכירו אב ואם ולא נודע אם מישראל הם. "They were referred to as *asufim* because they "were gathered" from the market place not able to identify father or mother, and whether they were Jews."

235 Ezra 2:53, Neh. 7:55.

236 Judges 4:2. ושר צבאו סיסרא והוא יושב בחרשת הגוים "His army commander was Sisera, whose base was Haroshet-HaGoiim."

teachings from the teachings of the Rosh[237] on the tractate Gittin.[238]

He indicates that in exile, it was customary to add a gentile name to the sacred name given to every Jew, to be used when engaged in transactions with them [the gentiles] . . . When he associates with Jews, however, he utilizes the sacred name only. The gentile name is not employed. On the contrary, it would indeed be an embarassment for him if they refer to him by his gentile name while among Jews. Further, imagine if this would occur while in the presence of a *tzadik*, perhaps the *tzadik* of his generation, why this would be most disgraceful! Let us for a moment imagine if a *tzadik*, a rabbi of the statute of the Rebbe of Belz, or any other prominent *tzadikim*, were to convene an assembly on behalf of the Jewish people. Let us further imagine that every participant were requested by the *tzadik* to approach him and introduce himself so that he may get to know those who will participate with him. He will ask his name. Each will respond: "I am Shimon the son of Moshe; I am Yaakov the son of Levi," and so on. But should one respond to the question, "what is your name?" "Herr Rabbi, I am Franz," "I am Heinrich," "I am Adolph," or similar gentile names, why, this would evoke laughter and ridicule from those assembled, since as far as the great *tzadik* is concerned, he is not Franz, or Heinrich, or Adolph. He is only Moshe, Shimon, and Avraham, or any other Jewish name.

It is, after all, the tradition of Jews who have grown up in a religious and pious environment that among Jews one is referred to by his Jewish name—certainly in the presence of a famous *tzadik*. It would be disgraceful were he to identify himself as a gentile. Yet were someone to appear who was educated in a place where Judaism was forgotten, Heaven forbid, totally under the influence of the nations, such as in Bohemia, Moravia, and similar places devoid of Jewish education—such a person would be completely ignorant of any sacred name. During

---

237   R. Asher ben Yehiel (c. 1250–1327) among the foremost commentators on the Talmud.

238   Rabbenu Asher (*Rosh*), Gittin, chapter 1, 11b, paragraph 11 . בעא מיניה ריש לקיש מר׳ יוחנן: עדים החתומים על הגט ושמותיהם כשמות פרסיים מהו? וגו׳ "Resh Lakish inquired the following from R. Yohanan: 'Witnesses signed upon a divorce document with names which sound Persian, what is their status? Etc.'"

his entire life he would be identified only by a gentile name. . . . Such a person could not understand why merely mentioning his name to the Rebbe would result in laughter. What sin did he commit? . . .[239] All this reflects the low state of his spiritual condition, which is terrible indeed.

Such was the situation of the returnees from exile during the Second Temple period, as it is written: "These are the people of the province who came up from among the captive exiles [whom King Nebuchadnezzar of Babylon had carried into exile to Babylon, who returned to Jerusalem and Judah, each to his own city, who came with Zerubbavel, Jeshua, Nehemiah, Seraiah, Re'elaiah, Mordechai, Bilshan, Mispar, Biguai, Rehum, Boanah].[240] These were the *tzadikim* of their generation under whose leadership they[241] went up to Eretz Yisrael. They asked everyone for his name in order to record their names on a list of returning *olim*. Certainly they would provide their sacred names given to them and not their gentile names. It would not be proper to use their gentile names before these *tzadikim*. Yet there were those among them who were in such a lowly spiritual state that it did not occur to them that using a gentile name before a *tzadik* would be disgraceful . . . Therefore, the verse concludes: "They were unable to tell whether their father's house and descent were Israelite. . . ."[242] Nevertheless, these very people were described by our sages, of blessed memory, in the Midrash as having deeds which were considered beautiful by the Creator of the universe though their names were ugly. . . .[243] How can this generation with so many faults be described as one with fine deeds?

---

239 The author employs the first person to emphasize the incredulity of the very assimilated Jew who cannot comprehend that his gentile name should be a source for laughter.

240 Ezra 2:1–2.

241 The returning exiles.

242 Ezra 2:59.

243 The author continues to elaborate upon the sinful behavior of the returnees from exile in the time of Ezra. They intermarried with gentile women, desecrated the Sabbath, imitated the abhorrent practices of other nations, and engaged in theft and promiscuity (*EHS*, 191, 192).

Wherein lies their beauty? One is greatly astonished at this!

Necessarily, therefore, we are forced to conclude that in the very action of their *aliyah*, the building of the Land, and subsequently the Temple, was represented their beauty and loveliness . . . though, except for this, they violated almost every precept in the Torah, Heaven forbid. . . . Yet we note in the Book of Ezra[244] that twenty years following the building, Ezra undertook to remove the foreign women from their midst. He sat weeping, tore the hair from his head,[245] cursed and did what he had to, until he succeeded in purifying and cleansing them from their grave transgressions. However, during their *aliyah* he refrained from any intervention. He merely gathered all those who wished to come, without questioning their motives, though he was keenly aware of their abhorrent acts. Nevertheless, he did not reject them but welcomed them wholeheartedly. He realized that much manpower was needed to achieve the rebuilding of the *yishuv*.

The more who participated, the faster it would be completed. Perhaps he was given to understand, by means of the Holy Spirit, that their acts are beautiful and desirable before the Lord, be He blessed. He, therefore, did not inquire into the background of anyone who offered to assist.

They declared in the Talmud (Avodah Zarah 26a): "Come and see the difference between the robbers of Babylonia and the bandits of Eretz Yisrael." Note the commentary of Rashi.[246] The *gaon* R. Solomon Kluger, of blessed memory,[247] in his volume *Avodat Avodah*,[248] cites the verse: "Indeed it shall be said of Zion, 'Every man was born

---

244 Chapter 9.

245 Ibid. verse 3.

246 The disciples of R. Akiva, having outwitted the bandits, receive the latter's compliments, and praise from their master. The bandits in Babylonia, having been fooled by an identical device, heap scorn upon R. Menashe and his master R. Yehudah: AZ 25b–26a. Rashi explains the purpose of these midrashim להודיעך שבחה של ארץ ישראל "To sing the praises of Eretz Yisrael."

247 See above, 62, n. 9.

248 *Avodat-Avodah, op cit.* 53a.

there.' He, the Most High, will preserve it."[249] The focus of his teaching:

There is a distinction between *hutz-la'aretz*[250] and Eretz Yisrael. In Eretz Yisrael the Almighty benefits even from the wicked who live there. The previous verse is to be understood in this vein. The psalmist distinguishes between *hutz-la'aretz* and Eretz Yisrael. He declares, "Glorious things are spoken of you, Oh City of God, *Selah*."[251]

The Almighty attaches importance only to those who acknowledge Him. But those who do not acknowledge Him, the wicked, do not provide Him with glory or satisfaction. This is his lesson: Come and see the difference between Eretz Yisrael and *hutz-la'aretz*—thus "I mention Rahab and Babylon among those who acknowledge Me."[252] For the sake of those who acknowledge and know Me I will be mindful of their location. "Philistia, and Tyre, and Cush"[253] he is important to Me because "*he*[254] was born there", namely, he who acknowledges Me, was born there. The localities of those who do not acknowledge Me, however, do not concern me at all. However, "it shall be said of Zion, 'Every man,'"[255] both the righteous as well as the wicked. For both, the locality is of concern to Me since they were all born there. Accept this as evidence that the Holy One, blessed be He, will renew her [Zion] again to her original state.'[256]

Now, who dares in our day to characterize these *olim* as "ugly" or, Heaven forbid, "wicked," or to castigate their efforts in rebuilding the Land with great dedication, causing her to flower, and to speak of

---

249 Ps. 87:5.

250 Territory outside the Land of Israel.

251 Ps. 87:3.

252 Ps. 87:4.

253 Ibid.

254 Ibid. Italics by editor for emphasis. It is the individual person who determines God's relationship to Him in *hutz-la'aretz*.

255 Ps. 87:5.

256 The special relationship of God to Eretz Yisrael which operates irrespective of the character of its inhabitants attests to its eternal redemptive qualities. This entire interpretation is almost a verbatim quotation from *Avodat Avodah*, 53a.

them with derision and insult? After all, they fulfilled the great positive commandment of "You will occupy and settle in it"[257] and the resulting explicit as well as latent consequences [of this commandment]. And as I have demonstrated in the introduction of this book[258] (see also 17 above[259] and my citation of the Maharam Hagiz[260] and *Hesed L'Avra-ham*[261] concerning the punishment for those who slander the builders of Eretz Yisrael) and reiterate with utmost conviction, that their deeds are beautiful before the Holy One, blessed be He, and their reward is great indeed. If only my reward could be included with theirs! One need now but ask of them to walk in the path of the Lord from this day on, for all is to be accomplished in the spirit of Torah and in accordance with the instructions of our great *tzadikim* and Torah scholars. We will yet achieve this [goal] with the help of God, if we will draw them near to us with an attitude of love, affection and respect for them. Words spoken softly by wise men are heeded.[262]

---

257   Deut. 11:31, and *Sefer HaMitzvot LaRamban Vehasagot HaRamban* (Jerusalem, 1981), 244–46. מצוה רביעית "the fourth precept." See below, 214, n. 571 and n. 574.

258   See above, 49–54.

259   In the section devoted to הסכמות *haskamot*, [*EHS*, 2–20], expressions of ac-knowledgement of, and consent and support for R. Zvi Hirsh Kalisher's classic works, which called for the rebuilding of Eretz Yisrael by natural means, and additional rabbinic documentation of the active human dimension of bringing forth redemption.

260   Reference to R. Moshe Hagiz (1672–1751) scholar of halakhah and kabbalah; author of numerous works including *Sefat Emet* (Amsterdam, 1697; Vilna, 1876) a volume devoted to the sanctity of Eretz Yisrael, its virtues and the mitzvah of settlement. *EHS* cites 51b from an early edition unavailable, but the passage may be found in the Vilna 1876 edition (32b).

261   A major work on the principles of kabbalah, and especially the teachings of Moses Cordovero, by the kabbalist R. Avraham ben Mordechai Azulai (c. 1570–1643). Our author cites from *Hesed L'Avraham* 33a (*Ma'ayan* 3, *Nahar* 12) (Amsterdam, 1685), with minor changes. The original reads: ידוע שכל מי הדר בא"י נקרא צדיק הגם שאינם צדיקים כפי הנראה, שאם לא היה צדיק היה מקיא אותו הארץ כדכתיב יותקיא הארץ את יושביה. וכיון שאינה מקיא אותו בודאי נקרא צדיק אעפ"י שהוא נראה בחזקת רשע. "Know, therefore, that one who lives in Eretz Yisrael is referred to as a *tzadik*, even though they might not appear as *tzadikim*. Were it otherwise, the Land would have spewed them out as it is written [Lev. 18:25] 'And the land spewed out its inhabitants.' And since it does not spew him out, he is surely referred to as a *tzadik* although he is presumed to appear as an evil person."

262   Eccl. 9:17 דברי חכמים בנחת נשמעים *vs.* דברי חכמים בנחת ישמעו in our text (The present *vs.* the future tense).

This should be done without denunciation nor raising our voices against them. Only then will they subject themselves to the expectations of Torah and piety.

We will indeed succeed to purify them just as Ezra was able to draw them near to Torah and sanctify them. [This will occur] after they realize that they have been made welcome and not rejected. Here is the truth in all its clarity for those who wish to see the truth.

Now note Rashi on the verse in Song of Songs, "The mandrakes yield their fragrance":[263]

> The baskets of both the good figs and the bad figs, as it is written: "The Lord showed me two baskets of figs. . . ."[264] One basket contained very good figs . . . the other basket contained very bad figs."[265] These [latter] represent the sinners of Israel. Presently both [the good and bad] emit their fragrances.[266] They all seek Your Presence.[267]

All this alludes to the acts of *aliyah* and the subsequent rebuilding of the Second Temple. Similarly, it is related to the efforts of *aliyah* and rebuilding in our time. . . .[268]

The prophet exclaimed: "Raise your voice with power, O herald of joy to Jerusalem [raise it, have no fear]. Announce to the cities of Judah: Behold your God."[269] The latter is not clear at all. It is but an

---

263 Song 7:14 and Rashi commentary.

264 דודאי *duda'ei* in the Jeremiah context about to be cited translates "baskets" in the Song of Songs דודאים (*duda'im*) reads "mandrakes." Rashi, homiletically integrates the two verses ignoring the variant meanings of דוד (*dud*) "basket" *vs.* דודאי, דודי (*dude, dudaei*) "mandrakes."

265 Jer. 24:1–2.

266 As a symbol of their love for the Creator. The mandrake is the fruit often associated with stimulating love.

267 Cf. Ps. 105:4.

268 The author documents the deep hatred between the Babylonian Jews and the returnees to Eretz Yisrael. The former refused to participate in the return during Ezra's period since they claimed that the returning population was of such negative character that they would in no way associate with them. Our author blames this intolerant and standoffish attitude of diaspora Jewry as the reason why the Jewish people were not privileged to witness the full redemption in their own time (*EHS*, 194).

269 Isa. 40:9.

abrupt phrase which suggests some relationship between "your God" and "the cities of Judah."

The term "Behold" also points to some kind of unique departure. Yet the verse concludes abruptly. . . .

I will preface [my explanation] with the commentary of our master the *Or HaHayyim*[270] on the familiar verse, "But you who clung to the Lord your God, are all alive today."[271] His commentary is based on the ruling of Maimonides Laws Pertaining to the Foundations of the Torah, sixth chapter,[272] concerning the seven appellations [of the Divine] which may not be erased. He ruled: prefixes to the Divine may be erased. Suffixes such as *kha*[273] as in *Eloke kha*[274] or *khem*[275] as in *Eloke khem*, these are not to be obliterated. These suffixes are considered [as sacred] as the rest of the letters of the Holy Name. The Holy Name consecrates them. These are the words of Maimonides.[276]

This is what he [Moses] intended to say in the declaration "[But you] who cling to the Lord" that is, since His name, the Name of God, blessed be the Lord, is unique, no letter may be appended or linked at the close [of the Name], only at its beginning;[277] as in "to God."[278] These [prefixed] letters are not sacred and may be erased. If this is so, then the clinging of Israel to God[279] will be performed in a manner whereby God does not sanctify Israel. Therefore, the verse

---

270   See above, 9, n. 37.

271   Deut. 4:4.

272   Section 3. Maimonides summarizes the laws pertaining to the sanctity of the various appellations for the Divine, specifically the prohibition not to destroy or erase suffix appendages to certain names for God; these laws are based on Deut. 12:3–4.

273   Your.

274   Your God.

275   Your (plural).

276   Our author now cites the *Or HaHayyim* commentary on Deut. 4:4.

277   The linkage at the end of a Divine appellation conveys to the letter or combination of letters a sacred status which it may not deserve.

278   Editor's quotation marks כגון לה׳ או בה׳ (As in "to God" or "with God").

279   The prefixed בה׳ "to God" in Deut. 4:4

concludes with *Elokekhem*.[280] This is to indicate that this clinging to
the Divine is not the type whereby letters are added at the beginning,
but rather at the conclusion. These consist of *khem* of *Elokekhem*, and
are as sacred as the main letters of the Divine Name. Now I have
noted a marvellous point in the holy book *Tzeror HaMor*[281] by the
grandfather by marriage of our rabbi the *Bet Yosef*,[282] R. Abraham
Saba,[283] who was among the exiled from Spain.[284] In the weekly portion
of *Matot*[285] he comments upon the sanctity of Eretz Yisrael which
follows closely [the sanctity of] the Holy One, blessed be He . . . This
is the meaning of the verse concerning Caleb son of Jephunneh,
"because he remained loyal to the Lord,"[286] namely, "followed after
Me," in the literal sense . . . Since Eretz Yisrael is joined immediately
behind the Divine, it is sanctified just as are the suffixed letters of the
Divine Name, indeed as *khem* in *Elokekhem*.[287]

Now, according to this interpretation, the intention of the prophet
has become quite clear when he declares: "Announce to the cities of
Judah: Behold your God [*Elokekhem*]."[288] Namely, the following is to
be announced to the cities of Judah: They actually represent the
Divine Name of "your God." Just as the suffixed letters are like the

---

280 "Your God," as a suffixed appendage.

281 See above, 29, n. 83.

282 R. Joseph Karo (1488–1575) author of the authoritative *Bet Yosef* and *Shulhan
Arukh* codes of halakhah. R. Yitzhak Saba, father-in-law of R. Joseph Karo (the
father of the first of his three wives), was the son of R. Abraham Saba. See *Bet Yosef,*
Tur Orah Hayyim 425.

283 See previous footnote.

284 In the year 1492.

285 Num. 30:2–32:42. See *Tzeror HaMor, op. cit.,* 126. כי קדושת השם היא הראשונה,
ואחריה קדושת הארץ. "The sanctity of God is foremost, followed by the sanctity of the
Land."

286 Free rendering of JPS: *The Torah,* Deut. 1:36. Literally, "because he followed
after Me." The loyalty of Calev to God expressed itself in his readiness to settle Eretz
Yisrael despite the objections of the ten tribal leaders and the people. The Divine-Eretz
Yisrael relationship is also alluded to in Song 1:4, and developed by R. Abraham ben
Jacob Saba in the *Tzeror HaMor* commentary (see above, 29, n. 83).

287 See above, n. 280.

288 Isa. 40:9. See above, 173–174.

letters in the Divine Name and are so sanctified, similarly the cities of
Judah, which are immediately linked to the Divine Name[289] and are
also sanctified. . . .

This then represents the unique departure of the prophet and his
special use of "Behold". . . .[290]

It is clear why the prophet chose [the phrase] "The cities of Judah"[291]
rather than of "Eretz Yisrael." This is because the beloved status of
Eretz Yisrael is conditional on its being inhabited and settled, as it is
written in *Midrash Tanhuma* (the portion of *Re'eh*):[292]

> Beloved is Eretz Yisrael since it was chosen by the Holy One, blessed
> be He. You will note that when the [Holy One, blessed be He,] created
> the world, He allocated the countries to the respective princes of nations.
> He chose Eretz Yisrael . . . He selected Israel for His portion, as it is
> written: "But the Lord's portion is His people, Jacob His own allot-
> ment."[293] Said the Holy One, blessed be He: "Let the people Israel who
> have come into My portion settle the Land which is assigned to My
> portion."[294] Therefore the Holy One, blessed be He, delayed Israel in
> the desert for forty years. When the nations heard that Israel will enter
> Eretz Yisrael they proceeded to destroy and decimate everything. The
> Holy One, blessed be He, however, wished for Israel to enter a land
> fully built and developed with homes, fields, trees and gardens. When
> they [the Canaanites] returned[295] and repaired everything [originally
> destroyed], the Holy One, blessed be He, then told Moses to bring
> them in.[296]

That which makes Eretz Yisrael beloved to God is its very settlement

---

289   As in the previous interpretations of Deut. 1:36 and Isa. 40:9.

290   See above, 173.

291   Isa. 40:9. Cities suggest population, settlement, community.

292   Paragraph 8, expounding upon Deut., 12:29.

293   Deut., 32:9. Cf. discussion of this verse above, 160–164; 43, n. 37.

294   *Tanh. Re'eh* 8.

295   To Eretz Yisrael believing that the Israelites would not really enter and would
remain permanently in the desert.

296   *Tanh. Re'eh* 7.

by Israel. If it remains desolate, however, and unworthy of settlement, it is also unworthy to be attached to God. Without such linkage the Divine cannot sanctify it. Thus ruled the *Taz*[297] (*Yoreh Deah*, 2764) that inconsequential letters attached to the Name are not sanctified.[298]

Therefore, the prophet declared: "Announce to the cities of Judah [Behold your God!]"[299] He emphasized "to the cities," that is, cities which are populated and worthy of settlement. So it was with the tribe of Gad and Reuven who exclaimed:

"We will build [here sheepfolds for our flocks and] towns for our children."[300] The term "towns" indicates their potential for settlement. They will deserve to be linked to the Holy One, blessed be He. Then truly the Divine will sanctify them with the holy Name. . . .[301] With this point one can better understand the words of *Midrash Rabba*, the portion of *Kedoshim* :[302]

R. Judah the son of R. Simon opened [the discussion]: " Follow only the Lord your God."[303] Now is it really possible for an ordinary person of flesh and blood to follow the Holy One, blessed be He?[303] However, ever since Creation, the Holy One, blessed be He, is concerned first and foremost with planting, as it is written; "And the Lord God planted a garden [eastward] in Eden.[304] So shall you be concerned first and

---

297   R. David ben Shmuel HaLevi (1586–1667) leading rabbinic authority on halakhah in Poland. *Taz* are the initials of the four divisions of his major work *Turei Zahav*, a commentary on the *Shulhan Arukh* code of law.

298   276:9 (7) וכתב איזה אות אחריו שאין לו שום פירוש, ומשמעות אין בו קדושה ולדברי הכל נמחק. "And if one adds another letter to it [the Divine Name] which has no meaning, it carries no sanctity and all would agree that it may be expunged."

299   Isa. 40:9.

300   Num. 32:16.

301   The argument for settlement of Eretz Yisrael as the essential requirement for the special relationship between the Land and the Divine, is now completed.

302   Lev. 19:1–20:27. LevR. 25:3.

303   Deut. 13:5.

303   The original *Midrash* cites Ps. 77:20 as proof text: "Your path was in the sea; your route in the great waters and your trail was not known."

304   Gen. 2:8.

foremost with planting when you shall enter the Land, as it is written; "When you will enter the Land you shall plant [all kinds of trees]...."[305]

The implications are as follows: When a Jew comes to our Holy Land, when he cultivates the holy earth by planting trees and vegetation, when he builds homes and is involved in similar activities required for the settlement of the Land, the Land is thereby sanctified by him with the holy [Divine] Name, though this may not have been his intention at all. This is reflected in the Shakh,[306] *Yoreh De'ah* paragraph 276, who rules that every [Divine] Name, though written without [sacred] intentions, may not be erased.[307] So ruled all the great later halakhic authorities in their responsa. . . .[308]

This [concept] is also implied in the verse in Psalms 102:"You will surely arise and have mercy on Zion; it is time to be gracious to her; the appointed time has come. Your servants take pleasure in its stones and they cherish its dust. The nations will fear the Name of the Lord and all the kings of the earth Your glory."[309]

The Maharsha in tractate Ta'anit[310] expounds upon this verse. When one becomes attached to and craves the stones and dust [of Zion], one brings closer the time of redemption. By this is meant its rebuilding

---

305   Lev. 19:23. The concept of *imitatio dei* enunciated in *Sifrei, Ekev* 49 (i.e., man is called upon to emulate God's ethical characteristics of compassion) is expanded to include productive efforts in Eretz Yisrael. *EHS*, 196. See also Sot. 14a.

306   R. Shabbetai ben Meir HaKohen, 1621–1662, authority on halakhah, author of commentary on the *Shulhan Arukh*

307   *Siftei Kohen, Yoreh De'ah* 276:12. וכן שם של קודש שלא נכתב לשם קדושה מותר למחקו לצורך תיקון דווקא. . . . ואם הרבה שמות נכתבו שלא לשמן בס״ת אסור למחקן אע״פ שהוא לצורך תיקון. "And further, a holy name which was not written for a holy purpose, one is permitted to expunge but only for the purpose of correcting. . . . Should many names have been written in a Torah scroll without purpose, one is prohibited from expunging them even for the purpose of correction."

308   See *Gilyon Maharsha, Yoreh De'ah* 276:9. דגם בלא נכתב לשם השם כל שצורת שם עליו יש בו אסור מחיקה. . . . "although it was not written with intent [as a Divine Name] any appearance as such prohibits erasure." See also *Sefer HaTashbez*, vol. 1, Responsa 176.

309   Ps. 102: 14–16.

310   Maharsha, Ta'an. 15a.

and settlement.[311] Therefore, the verse concludes with "The nations will fear the Name of the Lord." This is to say: by means of construction the Land is sanctified with the holy Name, with the Name of the Lord. All the rulers of the world will see the glory of the Lord upon her . . . Amen, may this indeed be His will.

In order to grasp the magnitude of the mitzvah of working the land in our Holy Land, one which surpasses practically all others, I will cite the words of our holy master the Hatam Sofer, whose teachings and legal opinions are disseminated daily in schools everywhere. The quotation from his novellae on the tractate of Sukkah 36[312] reads as follows:

> Said the master: A dark etrog[313] (citron) is invalid. Yet we learned elsewhere: A dark etrog is valid, one which resembles a dark [etrog] is invalid?[314] Abaye said [in agreement with this second version]: When we also studied the Mishnah [in reference to the invalid dark etrog][315] we interpreted this to mean one which resembles a dark etrog. Raba said: There is no contradiction:[316] one concerns ours;[317] the other refers to theirs.[318]

---

311 Stones and dust are not the mere object of aimless veneration, but rather the very raw materials by which the Land is rebuilt. The Maharsha text, however, seems to emphasize God's personal intervention in rebuilding the Land and thus revealing His glory unto the nations.

312 36a. *Hiddushei Hatam Sofer al Seder Moed, Lulav HaGazul.* New York, 1954.

313 The citron, one of the four species linked to the Sukkot festival as directed in Lev. 23:39–40. אתרוג כושי "a dark etrog" denotes either a citron from the land of Kush (Ethiopia) or a very dark-colored citron.

314 If its native color is dark, the citron is considered valid for use. If the discoloration is due to external factors, it becomes invalid. The alternate reading: "An Ethiopian etrog is valid; one which resembles an Ethiopian etrog is invalid."

315 Suk. 34b.

316 Between the divergent texts in which the first invalidates even the native dark etrog, while the other permits its use.

317 A native dark etrog may also be invalid as in our Mishnah if utilized in Eretz Yisrael where the etrogim are of a light yellow or green color.

318 The *beraita* which permits the dark etrog refers to the Babylon communities [Rashi commentary] or to the Ethiopian communities, where the traditions included the native darkly colored etrog.

The Hatam Sofer comments as follows:

We interpreted this to mean one which resembles a dark etrog.[319] I heard the following from my teacher and rabbi the Hafla'ah[320] of blessed and righteous memory, concerning the controversy between R. Shimon bar Yohai and R. Yishmael in the tractate Berakhot.[321] R. Shimon bar Yohai believes: If a person is to plow during the plowing season and sow during the sowing season, what time will remain for [the study] of Torah? It is best that he study Torah and then his work will be completed by others. R. Yishmael reasons: Conduct yourself in accordance with the expectations of the world, as it is written: "You shall gather in your new grain. . . ."[322] During the plowing time, he shall plow. When he can free himself from his chores then he shall study Torah. They interjected, "Many did as suggested by R. Shimon bar Yohai and they failed. Those who followed [the advice of] R. Yishmael succeeded. . . ." He explained: The reasoning [related to their failure in following the advice of R. Shimon] is that they acted as if they were R. Shimon bar Yohai. They were not actually R. Shimon bar Yohai. (This is to say, they merely imitated R. Shimon bar Yohai.[323]) Surely when one acts on behalf of God Who examines one's intentions and knows one's thoughts one certainly must succeed. However, they act like R. Shimon bar Yohai, imitate him, but do not actually possess his qualities. Therefore, they did not succeed. What is mentioned here concerning the "dark etrog," refers to a *tzadik* who acts in an unusual fashion similar to the Ethiopian, whose skin is unusual. He is considered valid.[324] But one

---

319   Suk. 34b.

320   R. Pinhas HaLevi Ish Horowitz (1730–1805), rabbi and scholar in Frankfurt, author of the three-part *Sefer Hafla'ah* (hence his designation), teacher of R. Moses Sofer, the Hatam Sofer.

321   35b.

322   Deut. 11:14.

323   The bracketed section appears in Yiddish.

324   In order to validate, and in a sense, justify the unusual approach of R. Shimon bar Yohai which would permit the study of Torah without requiring a sharing in the physical responsibilities of working the Land of Israel, one would have to acquire the native characteristics of R. Shimon. This would be analagous to the native texture of the dark etrog.

who resembles the "dark etrog," and wishes to imitate R. Shimon bar Yohai is invalid. In fact, such efforts[325] were indeed unsuccessful. To this point [we have cited] the teachings of the rabbi;[326] elegant words from a wise man. Henceforth, his humble pupil, yours truly, will add a few words. It seems to me, R. Yishmael restricted the verse "You shall gather in your grain"[327] to Eretz Yisrael when the majority of Jews lived there.[328] Working the land is in itself a mitzvah related to the settlement of Eretz Yisrael, thereby extracting [from her soil] her sacred fruit. For this purpose the Torah commanded, "You shall gather in your new grain." [To illustrate:] And Boaz "will be winnow**ing barley on the threshing floor tonight,"[329] fulfilling the commandment.[330] [It is] as though one might claim: "I will not wear the tefillin since I am involved in the study of Torah."[331] Similarly one cannot claim: "I will not gather in my new crop since it conflicts with the study of Torah."[332] It is possible that other crafts which involve the building up of the world are also included in the mitzvah.** However, when we are dispersed among the nations due to our many sins, he who engages in the settlement of the world causes destruction in the realm of devotion to God.[333] (See his responsa, part 2, paragraph 138 and the *Shelah* at the conclusion of the laws of Sukkah.)[334a] In such an instance

---

325   To study without earning a living.

326   R. Pinhas HaLevi Ish Horowitz, author of *Sefer Hafla'ah*.

327   Deut. 11:14 discussed in Ber. 35 b.

328   See Tosafot בזמן שאתה משמט Gitin 36a.

329   Paraphrase of Ruth 3:2. הנה הוא זורה את גורן vs. בועז זורה גורן השעורים הלילה השעורים הלילה.

330   Of settling the Land.

331   The setting aside of the various disciplines and routines of the ritual in the interest of study is not acceptable. *Tefillin* are the pair of phylacteries worn upon the forehead and hand during the weekday morning services, containing verses based on Ex. 13:16, Deut. 6:8, 11:18.

332   The theoretical claims appear in bold type in the *EHS* original.

333   Involvement in the secular affairs of other nations and countries would be at the expense of the study of Torah.

334a   *She'elot uTshuvot Hatam Sofer* (vol. 2), *Yoreh De'ah* (179) Responsa 138, 51. ואולי בבונה בית אבנים שלא לצורך להרחיב לו משכנות בח"ל ולהתייאש מן הגאולה בכיוצא באלו הרי בנינו סכנה ואינם מצוה מצוה להגן . . . כי היכי דאיכא מצוה בארץ ישראל טפי מדקלי משום ישוב א"י.

R. Yishmael would admit to R. Shimon bar Yohai (one should not engage in the affairs of the world, but only in Torah).

In this respect we rely on the opinion of R. Nehorai at the conclusion of the tractate Kiddushin:[334b] "I abandon every trade in the world and teach my son Torah only." This is in reference to territory outside the Land of Israel. . . . One concerns ours; the other refers to theirs.[335] Namely, for Babylonian Jews [referring to those outside of Eretz Yisrael], it is proper to conduct oneself according to R. Shimon bar Yohai and not to engage in development of land but devote oneself to the study of Torah. For the Jews in Eretz Yisrael this approach is invalid since the development of Eretz Yisrael must be realized by Jews. These are his sacred words.[336]

These teachings stagger the imagination. This is the degree to which our master esteemed the working of the Land . . . comparing the development of agriculture in Eretz Yisrael to the positive commandments of *tefillin*[337] which a Jew is instructed to fulfill daily. Without fulfilling the positive commandments of *tefillin*, one is not considered to be a Jew.

He is among those who descend [into *Gehinom*] and not among those who ascend [from *Gehinom*] as explained in the Tractate Rosh HaShanah.[338] Therefore, shame shall cover those who ridicule the

---

"Perhaps when one unnecessarily builds a house of stone in order to expand his habitation outside the Land, thereby [indicating that he is] despairing of redemption, with such efforts he places his abode in danger and one is not required to defend it . . . but it is a preferred mitzvah (to build homes) in Eretz Yisrael because of the [mitzvah of] settling *Eretz Yisrael*" *Shenei Luhot HaBrit* (vol. 2), *Masekhet Sukkah*, *Amud HaShalom* 78b. אודיע מה שבליבי היה בוער תמיד כשראה ראיתי בני ישראל בונים בתים כמו "I מבצרי השרים עושים דירת קבע בעולם הזה ובארץ הטומאה . . . וזה נראה ח"יו כהיסח הדעת מהגאולה will indicate that I would consistently be furious when I witnessed Jews building homes [in *hutz la'aretz*] as if they were palaces of the nobility, thereby creating a permanent residence in this world in impure lands. . . . This implies, Heaven forbid, the ignoring of Redemption."

334b Kid. 82a.

335 Suk. 36a.

336 Conclusion of the lengthy quotation from the Hatam Sofer.

337 See above, n. 331.

338 17a. פושעי ישראל בגופן מאי ניהו? אמר רב: קרקפתא דלא מנח תפילין "What is meant by 'wrongdoers of Israel who sin with their body'? Rav said: This refers to the cranium

positive commandment of settling the Land with fictitious and forced arguments; these are null and void in the face of the teaching of the Hatam Sofer of blessed memory. One should not pay any attention to them at all.

"Who put wisdom in the *tuhot*?"[339] What is meant by *batuhot*?[340] *Batavaya* (comments the author of *Matnat Kehuna*:[341] "A specie of fowl."); "Who gave understanding to the *sekhvi*?'" (Job 38).[342] This refers to a rooster. Levi said: In the Arabian region they call the rooster *sakuya*[343] while the chicks are yet young. The mother hen gathers them under her wings, keeps them warm and hoes the path before them.[344] When they develop and one [of the chicks] wants to draw near to her, she pecks him upon the head saying: "Go out and peck in your own filth." Thus it was with the Israelites in the desert during forty years. The manna descended [from Heaven],[345] the well sprang forth,[346] the quail was abundant,[347] and the clouds signifying the Presence of the Lord surrounded them,[348] the pillar of cloud guided them.[349] Now when the Israelites entered the Land, Moses said to them: "Everyone shall carry forth his own hoe and engage in planting," as it is written: "When you enter the Land you

---

which does not put on the phylactery [*tefillin*]."

339 Job 38:36. The author continues to develop the concept of *Yishuv Eretz Yisrael* via citations from LevR. 25 referred to above, 178 and n. 305.

340 מי שת בטחות חכמה. Translated by JPS *Writings* as "hidden parts,"but following one meaning in the parallelism of Job 38:36 with שכוי (*sekhvi*), טוחה (*tuhah*) would refer to some form of fowl or wildlife.

341 R. Yissakhar HaKohen Berman, 16th century commentator on the midrash, and student of R. Moshe Isserles.

342 Job 38:37. For the purpose of the *EHS* interpretation, שכוי (*sekhvi*) is read as "rooster" although the term is not clear.

343 Related to שכוי. See discussion in the Mirkin edition of *Midrash Rabba* (Tel Aviv, 1973) vol. 8, 65.

344 Pecking in search of food.

345 Ex. 16:4.

346 Num. 21:16–18.

347 Ex. 16:13; Num. 11:31–32.

348 Numerous references in Scripture, e.g., Num. 9:15–23.

349 Ex. 13:21; Ex. 14:19; Num. 14:14.

will plant. . . ."[350]

Note as well Rashi's commentary on the verse "Therefore the tribe Levi did not receive any hereditary share along with their brethren. Their portion is with the Lord."[351] Rashi adds:

Since they were selected for the purpose of serving the altar[352] and did not have time to plow and sow. . . .[353]

In *Midrash Tanhuma*, the portion of *Kedoshim*[354] comments on the verse, "When you enter the Land and plant. . . ."[355]

Said the Holy One, blessed be He, to the Israelites: "Although you will find the land full of all that is good, do not be tempted to say: 'We shall relax, we will not plant.' Rather be careful with the task of planting since it is written: 'You will plant any tree for food.'[356] As you entered and found saplings which were planted by others, so shall you plant for your children." A person may not claim: But I am old! How many years do I still have to live? Why shall I take the initiative and toil for others [since tomorrow I will die]? Therefore, a person should not abstain from planting. Rather, as he found [that which others planted before him], so shall he increase [the produce] yet further—though he may be old. Said the Holy One, blessed by He, to the Israelites: "Take a lesson from Me. Do I depend upon saplings?" [Yet] Scripture indicates: "'The Lord God planted a garden in Eden in the east."[357]

Midrash Rabba, "Genesis ," chapter 64[358] expounds upon the verse: "Do not go down to Egypt; stay in the Land [which I point out to

---

350 Lev. 19:23.

351 Deut. 10:9.

352 In the service of the Temple.

353 The hereditary portion of the Land required people dedicated to production, a condition which the Levites could not fulfill.

354 Lev. 19–20.

355 Lev. 19:23.

356 Ibid.

357 Gen. 2:8. Conclusion of *Tanh. Kedoshim* 8.

358 Paragraph 3.

you.]"[359]

Create a living community[360] by planting, sowing, establishing new settlements."[361]

One also notes in the *Midrash Tanhuma, Re'eh*,"[362] expounding upon the verse: "Trust in the Lord and do good, live in the Land and remain loyal. . . ."[363]

["live in the Land"][364] create a living community in the Land,[365] sow, plant . . . "remain loyal"[366] see the loyalty of the forefathers.

[Midrash] Rabba[367] and *Tanhuma*[368] further interpret the verse: "Live in the Land"[369] make a place for the Shekhinah in the Land.[370] This

---

359   Gen. 26:2.

360   שכונה (*shekhunah*) playing on the imperative שכן (*shekhon*) in Gen. 26:2, suggesting a creative, productive society.

361   Likely intent of הוי נציב (*havei netziv*) as in the traditional blessing recited when seeing a new settlement built in Eretz Yisrael. ברוך . . . מציב גבול אלמנה "Blessed are Thou . . . Who establishes the homestead of the widow." Cf. Prov. 15:25. Alternate interpretation of the *Matnot Kehunah:* Trees in the process of pruning, or strengthening.

362   Deut. 11:26–16:17. *Tanh. Re'eh,* 11.

363   Ps. 37:3.

364   Again the play on the expression שכן ארץ "live in the Land."

365   Employing the rendering of the *Yalkut* שכונה בארץ "A neighborhood, community in the Land."

366   Ps. 37:3. Puzzlingly, the *EHS* edition transposes רעה with ראה. ראה - אמונה ראה. אמונתן של אבות "Observe the faith of the Patriarchs" *vs.* ורעה אמונה "Pursue faith." The Jerusalem 1983 *EHS* edition adopts the misplacement of the letters ignoring the רעה אמונתן of the Midrash. רעה in the Midrash suggests "follow," "pursue," "watch" (Ibn Ezra) which makes the ראה - רעה transposition unnecessary. The *Yalkut* rendering also maintains the רעה reading. (*Yalkut Shimoni* I, 892.)

367   GenR. 64:3.

368   *Tanh. Re'eh* 11.

369   Ps. 37:3.

370   *EHS* again emphasizes the activist redemptive theology which has become the central theme of this volume. The *Etz Hayyim* commentary, on the *Tanhuma* alluded to, suggests this in subtle fashion: ר"ל שכון ארץ' פי' שכן השכינה בארץ וזה יהיה כשתעשה אמונה אז האמונה שכן השכינה בארץ. "That is to say: 'Live in the Land' (Ps. 37:3) implies, implant the Shekhinah in the Land. This is the result of faith. Faith will cause the

was interpreted by the commentaries as follows: if the sowing and planting are conducted with faith [in the Almighty] and in the spirit of Torah, then surely, the Shekhinah will dwell in the Land.

This is the very intention of *Midrash Rabba*[371] commenting upon the verse: "When you enter the Land and plant any tree for food."[372]

> This is the reason for the verse "she is a tree of life to those who grasp her."[373] . . . Said R. Huna in the name of R. Benyamin the son of Levi: "The parable is one of a king who requested of his son to leave and engage in business. Replied he: 'Father, I fear the robbers on the highways. On the sea [I fear] the pirates.' What did the father do? He carved a niche in a stick, inserted an amulet and gave it to his son. He said: 'Take this stick and you will not have to fear any creature.'"
>
> Similarly said the Holy One to Moses: "Tell the Israelites: 'My children, occupy yourselves with Torah and you need not fear any nation.'" Had it been written "She is a tree of life to those who toil on her behalf," the enemies of Israel could never rise up [against you], only against those "who grasp her."[374] Had it been written "he who will not study [the terms of this teaching]"; the enemies of Israel could never rise up. However, it is written "[cursed be] he who will not uphold the terms of this teaching."[375]
>
> "Shimon the brother of Azariah said in his name."[376] But Shimon was greater [in scholarship] than Azariah. (Why was Azariah named?) Since it was Azariah who engaged in business ventures and supported Shimon, thereby the teaching was quoted in his name. [Similarly,] in the place

---

Shekhinah to dwell in the Land."

371   LevR. 25:1.

372   Lev. 19:23.

373   Prov. 3:18. The feminine refers to the Torah, which is feminine in Hebrew.

374   The passive commitment of Prov. 3:18 is not as sufficient a defense against Israel's enemies as would be the active toiling of a nation for its ideal.

375   Deut. 27:26. The Jewish people will be tested in the sphere of action אשר לא יקים "who will not uphold" rather than the less demanding sphere of study אשר לא ילמד "who will not study [them]."

376   Sot. 21a. In talmudic designations the son is usually identified together with his father. Rashi explains the sibling designation as a tribute to Azariah who supported Shimon's studies, sharing in his reward.

[in Scripture]: "And of Zevulun he said: 'Rejoice, O Zevulun on your journeys and Yissakhar, in your tents.'"[377] But, was Yissakhar not greater than Zevulun? However, since Zevulun removed himself from study and engaged in trade, thereby he supported Yissakhar, providing him with [material] reward for his toil [in study]. This is why the verse[378] bears his name, as it is written: "And of Zevulun he said: 'Rejoice, O Zevulun on your journeys and Yissakhar in your tents.'" R. Tanhum said: "Whoever sets forth upon a journey and is not prepared to do battle,[379] the result will lead to his falling in battle. The tribe of Zevulun, however, whether prepared or not will enter battle and be victorious. Thus it is written: 'Of Zevulun, those ready for service, able to man a battle-line . . . giving support wholeheartedly.'[380] Whether they were prepared or not, they could enter [battle] and be victorious."[381]

Thus concludes the Midrash.

It appears that in the Midrashic interpretations of the verse, "When you enter the Land,'[382] there are contradictions. At first this verse was interpreted as Moses instructing the Israelites to engage in planting and preparing the Land upon entering Eretz Yisrael. Then the verse was interpreted in terms of [the necessity for] the study of Torah.[383] We must, therefore, conclude that they were both necessary in the Land—Yeshivah students engaged in Torah study, and the tillers of the Land. One will support the other.[384] Thus it was with King David

---

377 Deut. 33:18.

378 Ibid.

379 One who does not anticipate the expected and unexpected dangers during journeys in one's life will ultimately fall victim to these dangers.

380 I Chron. 12:34 בלא לב ולב is translated as "giving support wholeheartedly." The Midrash treats the passage literally. The tribe of Zevulun will succeed irrespective of their state of preparedness or state of mind.

381 The lesson of Zevulun, emphasizing a balance of pragmatism and ideals, will be applied to the contemporary setting.

382 Lev. 19:23.

383 See above, 184.

384 The author again cites Sanh. 49a (see above, 57) demonstrating the necessary interaction between study (King David) and the art of warfare (Yoav ben Zeruyah).

who said: "Half will go into battle and half will guard the baggage...."[385]

This should be our course as well. We should prepare certain individuals who will serve as the backbone of study and religious devotion. (Because of our many sins we have as yet not been worthy of the rebuilding of the Temple,[386]—may it be His will that we be worthy of it speedily in our own day, Amen.) Integrated with them will be others assigned to develop the Land. Then our Land shall become "the most desired of lands."[387] This most desired of lands will then succeed in our hands. It will be an everlasting foundation from which shall spring forth the total redemption and the coming of the son of David, speedily in our own day. . . .

I had indicated previously[388] that when our teachers, the authors of the Midrash interpreted the verse, "When you shall enter the Land,"[389] with two contradictory views—first that they [the Israelites] devote their efforts to cultivating the earth and planting trees and also to the study of Torah—they indicated that both are valid.

In this vein I noted the words of our rabbi, the holy *Or HaHayyim*, interpreting this verse,[390] "When you shall enter the Land and plant any tree for fruit." Three precepts are recorded here:

> 1. to enter the Land, as it is stated, "Everyone ascends to Eretz Yisrael";[391]

---

385   A liberal interpretation of the events described in I Sam. 30. David's band of warriors, who initially set out against the Amalekites, is diminished by two hundred men who were too weak to carry on with the battle (Ibid. 30:10). These were left behind to guard the supplies but shared equally in the spoils of battle. The "guarding of the baggage" is equated by the *Midrash* to the study of Torah. *EHS* cites Maimonides to support the symbolic relationship necessary for the development of the Land between scholars and ordinary working populace in society (*EHS*, 20).

386   Following the destruction of the Temple, the Almighty remains accessible through commitment to study (Meg. 16b) and the observance of the mitzvot by the Jewish people. (Ber. 8a).

387   Mal. 3:12.

388   See above, 183–184.

389   Lev. 19:23.

390   Lev. 19:23.

391   Ket 13:11. The priority given to the act of settling in Eretz Yisrael is reflected in a series of laws favoring the party who prefers to immigrate to or refuses to

2. to plant fruit trees which improve to the Land; and

3. to mark the years of *orlah*.[392]

The verse, "When you shall enter the Land" (with emphasis on the Land)[393] suggests a rejection of the material appetite [for territory].[394] Rather, the objective to entering the Land (the specific) is to appreciate and desire the Holy Land, chosen by God, the place of the Mountain of the Lord. . . .[395]

I obtained a volume of correspondence of our Rabbi of Gur,[396] *Osef Mikhtavim* (Collected Letters), where I noted the following:[397]

> This is indeed my opinion—the precept of settling Eretz Yisrael, which our sacred Torah commands us to fulfill, is not at all dependent upon a specific period in time, but only upon [one's] ability and [the proper use of] opportunity. Therefore, one must exploit the present opportunity and to toil with the utmost means [to achieve this objective].

If the [*aliyah* of] pious Jews will increase, so will their influence. This will protect the sanctity of the Land. And he himself repeated this: **The influence of pious Jewry will increase. The settlement of the Holy Land will be in the spirit of the sacred written and oral tradition.**[398, 399]

Thus we have the opinion of our devout Rabbi of Gur, may he live

---

emigrate from Eretz Yisrael.

392 During a tree's first three years of life it was forbidden to eat its fruit. During the fourth year, its fruit could be eaten in Jerusaelm. Only in the fifth year was its fruit permitted to all. Lev. 19:23–25.

393 The author injects this observation into the *Or HaHayyim*'s commentary.

394 As opposed to the usual quest for the acquisition of territory among nations.

395 See Gen. 22:14; Ps. 24:3; II Chron. 33:15. Generally interpreted as the mountain upon which the Temple was to be built, i.e., Mt. Moriah; *(Har HaBayit,* the Temple Mount).

396 R. Avraham Mordechai of Gur, son of the revered Sefat Emet, and great-grandson of R. Yitzhak Meir of Gur, founder of the Gur hasidic dynasty. See above, 121, n. 210.

397 *Osef Mikhtavim* (Warsaw, 1936), 63.

398 The bold type appears in the original text.

399 Ibid. 65.

a long and good life, that the precept of settling our Holy Land is not linked to any specific time, but rather is dependent on ability alone. (It is likely that he disputed the opinion of the *Megillat Esther*, cited above,[400] which linked this precept to the messianic period and not to the period in exile.) . . .[401]

In the summer of 5703[402] I spent a number of weeks in the city of Bekescsaba[403] with my family. There I met my dear boyhood friend, R. *Gaon* Nathan Zvi Brisk, the senior judge of the holy community of Nadisalanta,[404] may he live a good and long life. (He is the son-in-law of the *gaon*, the author of *Bet Naftali*,[405] who in turn was the son of the *gaon*, the author of *Kol Aryeh* of blessed memory.)[406] He shared with me the sacred volume *Akh Pri Tevuah*[407] of the holy Rabbi of Liska[408] of blessed memory, [commenting on] the weekly portion of *Vayehi*.[409] He cites the volume *Nahal Kedumim*,[410] which equates "Eretz

---

400 See above, 140, n. 45.

401 The *Megillat Esther* opinion would not consider settlement in Eretz Yisrael necessary prior to the advent of the Messiah. The author again buttresses the activist schools of Nahmanides, Rashbaz, R. Shimon ben Zemah Duran (1361–1444), Maharam Schick, and other authorities on behalf of the precept of *Yishuv Eretz Yisrael* (settling of the Land of Israel), *EHS*, 204. See also above, 140-144 for a similar line of argumentation in response to the *Megillat Esther* opinion.

402 1943.

403 Town in southeast Hungary, in the Danube-Tisza region.

404 R. Nathan Zvi ben Yehoshua Brisk (1883–1944) was killed at Auschwitz together with his brother Mordechai, who was also a well-known Transylvanian rabbi and scholar. Nadisalanta (should read Nagyszalantao), on the Romanian-Hungarian border is more commonly known as Salanta.

405 R. Naftali HaKohen Schwartz, Hungarian rabbinic scholar and author of the responsa *Bet Naftali* (Pecs, 1899).

406 R. Abraham Judah HaKohen (1824–1883), Hungarian rabbi, pupil of the Hatam Sofer and author of the responsa *Kol Aryeh* (Brooklyn (1967).

407 Volume of homilies on the Pentateuch (Munkatch, 1898).

408 R. Zvi Hirsh Friedman of Lesko (1798–1874), a scholar and disciple of the hasidic master, R. Hayyim of Zanz.

409 Gen. 47:28–50:26.

410 *Nahal Kedumim, Vayehi* (Warsaw, 1899), 15b, edited by R. Hayyim Josef David Azulai (1724–1806), born in Jerusalem; international traveler, scholar and kabbalist, known by his acronym Hida.

Yisrael" with *Tet Lev.* [411] Namely, if every Jew will concentrate [his efforts] in residing in Eretz Yisrael, our righteous Messiah will come.

I shall bring proof supporting the words of these holy teachers who wrote of redemption as being conditional upon our concerted efforts to return to Eretz Yisrael, from that which I cited previously, [412] from the Talmud, chapter *Gid HaNashe*, [413] and from the Rashi commentary on the Torah[414] where the sages of blessed memory asked: "If he had not decided to return[415] would he have been restrained by Heaven from returning?"[416] Our sages of blessed memory have already written: This event [in the life] of Jacob[417] was in anticipation of the final redemption for which we wait daily. From the moment he decided to return, and indeed did return, the miracle occurred. So it shall occur with us if only we set our minds to living in Eretz Yisrael. Our redemption is dependent upon our return to Eretz Yisrael and we, too, shall be the recipients of miracles as was our father Jacob of blessed memory.

This clarifies the verse in Ezekiel (7:2), "You, O mortal: Thus said the Lord God to the Land of Israel: Doom! Doom is coming upon the four corners of the Land. Now doom is upon you!"[418] The simple interpretation of this verse is clear and based upon this last teaching: When Israel will attempt to bring the Land of Israel to the End, to redeem her from the impure.[419] Accordingly, the "End is upon you,"[420]

---

411 In gematria the numerical value of תת לב "pay attention," "take care," "concentrate"—832—is identical to ארץ ישראל (Eretz Yisrael).

412 *EHS*, 104–105.

413 Hul. 91 b.

414 Gen. 28:17.

415 To Jerusalem; specifically to the Temple site in order to pray at the very place at which Abraham and Isaac prayed before him (See Rashi Gen. 28:17).

416 Surely not, since this was a desirous act.

417 The premature setting of the sun (Gen. 28:11) will be reenacted in reverse during redemption (i.e., rising prematurely as in Mal. 3:20) GenR. 28:12.

418 Ezek. 7:2–3.

419 קץ (the end) in the Ezekiel verse refers to the ultimate punishment of doom brought down upon the Land by the Almighty because of Israel's sins. *EHS*, however, translates קץ (*ketz*) as end or finality in the sense of redemption. The "impure" may

is intended [to read] as signifying that the end is in your hands. As long as you devote your efforts to this purpose you will achieve it. You will also benefit from Divine assistance. All depends upon the degree of devotion of Israel to this purpose.

My friend also quoted his father, the *gaon*, the *tzadik*, our teacher, Rabbi Yehoshua, of blessed memory who served as chief judge of the rabbinic court of the holy community of Tisadada.[421] (I knew him in my childhood. He was world renowned as a magnificent *tzadik*, a man of virtuous deeds. Many went to him to inquire of God[422] with petitions.) He was the disciple of the holy Rabbi of Lisk[423] who informed him that he sent funds to Eretz Yisrael in order to purchase a parcel of land. For he believed that every Jew must attempt to help settle our Holy Land with Jews and to develop housing to sow fields and plant vineyards.

I would humbly like to add the following from the commentary of Rashi on the verse in Isaiah 59: "He shall come as redeemer to Zion."[424]

"As long as Zion is desolate, the redeemer can not yet come."[425] Thus we are committed to rebuild our Land in order to hasten our redemption.

Note the Jerusalem Talmud (at the close of the chapter *Haya Kore*),[426] which describes Eretz Yisrael as the mother of Israel. Similar references are made towards the close of the Jerusalem Talmud Ketubot[427] and

---

refer either to Jews who do not appreciate the sanctity of the Land and abuse her (as in a close reading of the Ezek. 7:2–3 text) or to the foreign nations who had sent Israel into exile.

420   Ezek. 7:3 הקץ עליך. Colloquially, "it is up to you."

421   Town in northeast Hungary, approximately 55 km from the border of prewar Slovakia, though *Pinkas Hungaria* (*op. cit.*, 319–320) lists the Jewish population at 175, the area was densely populated with neighboring Jewish communities.

422   Cf. לדרוש את אלהים "to inquire of God." I Sam. 9:9.

423   R. Zvi Hirsh Friedman (1798–1874), hasidic master and scholar.

424   Isa. 59:20.

425   Rashi, Ibid.

426   Chapter two of tractate Berakhot (2:8). See above, 8, 33–36 and below, 199–203, 206, 236.

427   Most likely a reference to 13:11, which emphasizes the preference of Eretz Yisrael over other localities.

Mo'ed Katan, chapter 3, rule I: "He abandoned the bosom of his mother (Eretz Yisrael) and embraced the bosom of an alien woman (the lands of the diaspora). The lands of exile he describes as a "step-mother." It seems to me that the reason [for this characterization] I discovered in the volume *Otzrot Yosef*[428] composed by the *gaon*, the teacher of all diaspora Jewry, R. Yosef Engel of blessed memory.

He states in the name of the kabbalists that Eretz Yisrael corresponds to the sphere of *malkhut*.[429] *Malkhut* in turn corresponds to the mother of Israel. These kabbalists interpret the verse "Because of your crimes was your mother dismissed,"[430] as reference to the Shekhinah.[431] As it is written by our sages of blessed memory (Megillah 29):[432] "[It has been taught: R. Shimon bar Yohai said:] Come and see how beloved are Israel in the sight of God. Everywhere Israel was exiled, the Shekhinah went with them."

As is well-known, the Shekhinah is also identified with *malkhut* and *malkhut* is the mother of Israel;[433] therefore, the verse declares: "Because of your crimes was your mother dismissed."[434] It is now clear why the

---

428 See above, 50, n. 78–79.

429 *Otzrot Yosef,* (Vienna, 1928), *Ma'amar Levanah,* 6, 12. נודע כי גם א"י עניינו ג"כ בספירת מלכות שלמעלה. ודע כי עפ"י יסוד חכמת האמת הנ"ל כי ירושלים עיר הקדש היא בחי' ספי' המלכות והנה כבר ידעת כי ספי' המלכות נקראת אמן של ישראל. "It is known that Eretz Yisrael also is linked to the sphere of *Malkhut.* Be aware that based upon the Doctrines of Truth [the Kabbalah] Jerusalem, the Holy City is in the category of *Malkhut.* You are surely aware that the sphere of *Malkhut.* is referred to as the mother of Israel." *Malkhut* is correspondingly associated with *adamah* (earth) and the Messiah. S.A. Horodetsky, *Torat HaKabalah Shel Rabbi Moshe Cordovero* (Jerusalem, 1951), 155. Gershom Scholem, *Kabbalah* (Jerusalem, 1974), 166, 334. See below, 50, n. 80, 239.

430 Isa. 50:1.

431 Zohar I, 27b. (Yoma 96), ועל גילוי עריות גלו ישראל ושכינתא בגלותא ודא איהי ערוה דשכינתא. "Because of incestuous sexual offenses Israel was exiled and the Shekhinah is in exile. This in itself is the shame of the Shekhinah." The Zohar identifies the exiled mother in Isa. 50:1 with the Shekhinah in exile. See also Zohar III, 253b, *Ra'ya Mehemna,* where the mother bird who is sent away (Deut. 22:7) due to the sins of Israel is identified as the Shekhinah. See also *Otzrot Yosef, op. cit.,* 7.

432 29a. See also above, 53, n. 100. נודע בהתחלות החכמה כי ספירות המלכות נקראת שכינה. "It is acknowledged as the very basis of wisdom that the sphere of *Malkhut* is referred to as Shekhinah."

433 *Otzrot Yosef, op. cit.,* 12.

434 Isa. 50:1.

Jerusalem Talmud describes Eretz Yisrael as the mother of Israel.[435]

This interpretation of the Jerusalem Talmud allows me to explain the Midrash on the verse: "Your sons and daughters shall be delivered to another people."[436] Do not read *l'am aher*,[437] but rather *le'em aher*,[438] namely, your sons and daughters will be delivered to lands of exile which for us are like "another mother" (commonly referred to as a stepmother).[439] They shall become totally devoted to her and to her alien spirit, to the extent that she indeed will become a substitute mother, while they will altogether forget the Land which is their genuine mother. "And your eyes shall strain for them constantly."[440] You will be compelled to observe their upbringing[441]—for you delivered them to another mother. That is to say, you agreed to educate them as would an alien mother and indeed they developed in the manner of a foreign mother's upbringing. Hence, their entire objective was to serve only the lands of exile. As it is confirmed by Solomon in the Song of Songs: "They made me guard the vineyards."[442] [Upon this verse] they comment in the Midrash:

> Out of deference to the nations. "My own vineyard,"[443] this refers to the Holy One, blessed be He, "I did not guard." What was the result?[444]

---

435   Shekhinah, *malkhut*, the exiled mother, and Eretz Yisrael are all interrelated.

436   Deut. 28:31 See Yev. 63a, Ber. 56a.

437   "To another people" לעם אחר.

438   "To another mother" לאם אחר.

439   In Yiddish (*shtiffmutter*). See above, 8, 33–36, and below, 206, 236.

440   Deut. 28:32.

441   In an alien culture.

442   Song 1:6.

443   Ibid. The midrashic interpretation is cited in *Yalkut Shimoni* I, 982. לא זזו מנתבאין נביאות שקר עד שהגלו אותי מארצו. שמוני נוטרה את הכרמים לכבד את האומות, וכרמי שלי׳ זה הקב״ה לא נטרתי. "They did not cease and desist from revealing false prophecies and consequently I was exiled from His land. Watchmen for the vineyards were assigned [but in order] to pay homage to the nations. 'My own vineyard,' this refers to the Holy One, blessed be He, "I did not guard.'"

444   The Jerusalem *EHS* edition erroneously transposes מה היה (the past form) into מה יהיה (the future form), *EHS*, 207 *vs.* Jer. *EHS*, 203. The author's emphasis is precisely upon the historic realization of the biblical prophetic warning, which justifies the מה היה reading.

"But you shall be helpless."[445]

You will have nothing to show for all your efforts on behalf of the lands of exile. Everything will be taken from you. You will remain bare and stripped of all possessions.

What befell our people in Europe we have, because of our many sins, witnessed in our own day.

Therefore, child of Israel, be it known, that from this day onwards you will never again attempt to seek a place of rest except with your genuine mother, namely, Eretz Yisrael. After all the suffering which has befallen us, and all the pain caused us by our own[446] stepmother, the lands of exile, only Eretz Yisrael, our genuine mother, can comfort us. As it is written by the prophet (in Isaiah 66):[447] "As a mother comforts her son, so will I comfort you; you shall find comfort in Jerusalem." We shall no longer express confidence in our stepmother, the lands of exile, by remaining here. So much of their resources did our parents and forefathers and their offspring invest in her [their adopted home in exile]. They built for us palaces, mansions, and salons, for they all believed: "This is my resting place for all time. Here I will dwell for I desire it."[448] Thus we became entirely distracted from our true mother, the Land of Israel.

Note our rabbi the Shelah[449] [commenting] towards the conclusion of the tractate *Sukkot*[450] and the Hatam Sofer, *Yoreh Deah*, 138[451] who greatly complained against those who became totally involved in the diaspora, by building for themselves homes and castles and by investing all their silver and gold in diaspora property, thus enriching and expanding the borders of the stepmother. They neglected to strengthen

---

445 Deut. 28:32.

446 "Our own" not included in Jer. *EHS*, 203.

447 Isa. 66:13.

448 Ps. 132:14. The resting place intended for Zion, chosen by the Lord, is ironically transferred by the Jew to exile.

449 See above, 26, n. 65.

450 See above, 181, n. 333.

451 Ibid.

the border of the widow,[452] the border of our righteous Matriarch
who weeps and sheds tears on our behalf.[453] It never occurred to them
to consider her in some transaction which might be of benefit to her.
Their only concern and desire was to enhance their own lucrative
income. Each person's only wish was to build an expansive home with
a courtyard of marble, a permanent fixture, one which would serve as
an inheritance for his children and grandchildren who will have been
born in an alien land. He was only anxious to perpetuate his own seed
and to live a full life in exile. Thus hundreds and thousands of years
were lost to us in exile. All of our energy and blood we gave to our
stepmother. Now we have received from her, in appreciation for all
of our care on her behalf, a stick with which she has proceeded to
whip us cruelly without mercy and compassion. She has wounded our
entire body, from head to toe without a spot which remained
unblemished.[454] She proceeded to expel us with vehemence. She took
our wealth from us, compelled us to leave her home naked and bereft.
So many of our fellow Jews in the thousands and tens of thousands,
died horrible deaths at the hands of our stepmother. Shall we now
express our trust in her by returning to her once again? What guarantee
do we have that after a few decades she will not again act towards us
in this manner? In fact our history has demonstrated that these acts
recur in cycles throughout the years.

   Thus far we have not learned from our past, that we can no longer
trust the lands of exile. Because of all this which has happened—never,
never! Never shall we ever return to our stepmother. Rather we will
rise and ascend to our genuine mother. We will dedicate to her all of
our energies, from now and forever. We will rebuild her walls and
reconstruct her ruins. "Let us be strong and resolute for the sake of
our people and the cities of our Lord, and God will act kindly"[455]

---

452   Cf. Prov. 15:25.

453   Referring to the Matriarch Rachel as in Jer. 31:15, 16 or *Petihta* LamR.,
Petihta, 24.

454   Cf. Isa. 1:6.

455   II Sam. 10, 12. This verse is integrated into the *EHS* exhortation with a
variant עמנו יעשה הטוב והי׳ "and the Lord will act kindly with us," *vs.* the biblical והי׳
בעיניו הטוב יעשה "and the Lord will do what He deems right."

with us in showing "a sign of favor, that my enemies may see and be frustrated."[456] They taught in the *Midrash* (cited in *Kol Yaakov*[457]): "From the time of the destruction of the holy Temple, scholars have been fated to study amidst suffering, poverty and distraction in order that they might pray for the coming of the Messiah."[458] The interpretation of this *Midrash* seems consistent with that which I heard from my brother-in-law, our teacher R. Moshe Klein, may he live a good and long life, rabbi and performer of righteous acts in the holy community of Grosswardein.[459] The *gaon* R. Meir Shapira, of blessed memory,[460] the chief justice of the [rabbinic] court of the holy community of Lublin, visited Hungary in order to discuss with the key leaders of his generation the matter of resettlement and building the Land, since, as it is known, there was opposition to this. Following all of his arguments and presentation of evidence, he could still not persuade them to cooperate. He then spent a Shabbat with a [hasidic] *rebbe*, a leader [of the community] in that country.[461] He noted the custom to eat fish twice at the third meal.[462] One was eaten prior to the time of candle lighting[463] and the other, following the candle

---

456 Ps. 86:17.

457 The *Midrash* will be employed to demonstrate the negative aspects of study as self-indulgence, isolated from the needs of society and community. See *Seder Eliyahu Zutah*, 4.

458 מאותו שעה נגזרה גזירה על ישראל שילמדו אותה מתוך צער ומתוך השעבוד ומתוך הטלטול ומתוך הטירוף ומתוך הדחק ומתוך שאין להם מזונות. בשכר אותו הצער עתיד הקב״ה לשלם להן שכרן לימות המשיח ולעולם הבא. "From that moment it was decreed that Israel will be fated to study [the precepts of Torah] amidst suffering, amidst servitude, during wandering, in a state of frenzy and deprivation, lacking nourishment. As reward for these afflictions, the Holy One, blessed be He, will bestow upon them their bounty in the messianic era and in the world to come." See also *Yalkut Shimoni* I, 392.

459 The German and Yiddish for Oradea, a city in Transylvania, Western Romania, under Hungarian rule between 1940–1944.

460 1887–1934. Polish rabbinic authority, pioneer in Yeshivah education, founder of the *Yeshivah Hokhmei Lublin*, leader of *Agudat Yisrael*.

461 Hungary.

462 In Jewish tradition the *seudah shelishit* is partaken of at twilight, Sabbath afternoon, between the late afternoon (*minhah*) and evening (*ma'ariv*) service.

463 I.e., before Sabbath ended and it was still forbidden to light candles.

lighting.[464] Those eaten prior to candle lighting were referred to as *finstere fisch*,[465] those following candle lighting *lichtige fisch* .[466] Said the Rebbe of Lublin: "Now it is clear to me why you oppose *aliyah* and the rebuilding of the Land. As long as you continue to consume *lichtige fisch*, you can afford to do without Eretz Yisrael. Unfortunately, most of Israel eat only *finstere fisch*, and you are unaquainted with their suffering."

Now after what has befallen us on the European continent, when all of us have tasted *finstere fisch*, we should certainly agree to this.[467] The fact that in Hungary one can still find individuals, especially among the *rebbe'im* (hasidic rabbis), who oppose this, indicates that they have not yet tasted what most of Israel has already experienced. May God spare them this. This is the intent of the *Midrash*, "in order that they might pray for the coming of the Messiah. . . ."[468]

And as I now write these words, when we are yet in the very midst of exile's suffering, surrounded with fear and panic on all sides, we must listen to the "camp of the Hebrews,"[469] and the shouts which emanate from every quarter, to return to the Land of our claim, "to rebuild the walls of the city,"[470] and to raise our Holy Land "from the heap of dust."[471] But we should be apprehensive, that after those [hostile] decrees will abate, with God's help, [the Jews] will return to their original strongholds in the lands of exile. As it is explained in

---

464   After the Sabbath meal.

465   Dark or gloomy (Yiddish).

466   Bright or radiant fish (Yiddish). Possibly to symbolize the redemptive process of מחושך לאור גדול [from the Passover liturgy], "From darkness to a great light."

467   To turn to *aliyah* and rebuilding Eretz Yisrael.

468   See above, 197. The religious leadership which does not experience the suffering of the people cannot anticipate or initiate the redemptive process. The author proceeds to cite sources (Maimonides, R. Zvi Elimelekh of Dinov) which suggest that one who returns to Eretz Yisrael for a second time, following a temporary stay in the diaspora, functions on an even higher and more sacred plane than during the first contact with Eretz Yisrael (*EHS*, 209–10).

469   Cf. מחנה העברים I Sam. 4:6.

470   ולבנות את חומת העיר Cf. Neh. 3:33, 4:11 .

471   מערמות עפרה Neh. 3:34.

the tractate *Derekh Eretz Zuta, Perek HaShalom*:[472]

Evil decrees come and go, they are ever renewed by the enemies of Israel. [The world remains forever.[473]] Israel remains forever. He will not leave them and they will not be abandoned. You are not finished and will not be destroyed, as it is written: "For I am the Lord—I have not changed, and you are the children of Jacob—you have not ceased to be."[474]

. . . A decree is likely to cease.[475] Surely there will come a period of rest and respite for Israel. They will readjust to their original state and will remain here in exile. Furthermore, should they come upon a good enterprise or lucrative income, they will console themselves with various pretexts in order to tie themselves once again to their stepmother. They will continue to betray their genuine mother, Eretz Yisrael. They will make a mockery of themselves, believing that their stepmother will continue to be kind to them. They will regress to their former ways and forget about Eretz Yisrael.

I then heard the following interpretation of the *Baal HaTurim*,[476] on the weekly portion *Va'erah*,[477] from my dear friend, the *gaon*, rabbi, saint, our teacher Yisrael David Margoliot Schlesinger,[478] who served as head of the rabbinic court in the holy community of Szolnok,

---

472 The concluding chapter.

473 Not included in *EHS* text.

474 Mal. 3:6. Both the *Derekh Eretz Zuta* and the supporting Malachi text are brilliantly introduced by the author as representing the two-edged sword of Israel's enduring qualities. They overcome their sufferings and their enemies "evil decrees come and go" yet revert to their old stubborn ways, as reflected in the balance of Mal. (3:7–9).

475 Cf. Ket. 3b, גזירה עבידא דבטלא "A decree is likely to cease."

476 Jacob ben Asher, one of the major Spanish *halakhic* authorities of the Middle Ages (c. 1270–1340). Though his fame rests on his code of law *Arba'ah Turim* (upon which Joseph Karo based his own *Bet Yosef* code) his vignette commentary on the Pentateuch, *Perush HaTorah l'R. Ya'akov Baal HaTurim* (Constantinople, 1500), continues to be a popular companion to Pentateuch study.

477 Ex. 6:2–9:35.

478 Noted rabbi and teacher in the Hungarian communities of Szolnok and Budapest. Settled in Holon, Israel after the Holocaust and died in 1961.

and presently is rabbi of the hasidic bet-hamidrash[479] Linat HaTzedek
in Budapest:

"And the thunder stopped."[480] "And they stopped building the city."[481]
That is to say: As long as thunder, the noise and the cries in response
to the difficult decrees were still abounding, everyone is enthusiastic
about building the holy city. Once the thunder stops and the decrees
abate, however, then they cease, once again, to build the city. They will
return to their original place and become enamored of their state in
exile, as in days past.

These were his words.[482] The words of the wise are precious.
Therefore I say: Our fellow Jews in this generation who have gone
through this trying period must be reminded and cautioned as to
what is written in the seventh chapter of Sanhedrin, the fourth mishnah:

He who has intercourse [with a male or[483]] with a beast, and a woman
who mates with a beast, (both) are to be stoned.[484] If the person has
sinned, how has the animal sinned? But because the person was enticed
by it [the animal], Scripture orders that it be killed by stoning.[485] Another
reason: The animal should not pass through the streets and people will
say: "This is the animal on account of which so and so was stoned."[486]

---

479 A modest house of study and prayer.

480 Ex. 9:33, following the plague of hail in Egypt.

481 Gen. 11:8, when God confounded the speech of men who built the city called
Babel. The *Baal HaTurim* connects both the Genesis and Exodus episodes. The *kolot*
(Ex. 9:23, 28, 29, 33, 34) are interpreted as the cries of the Egyptians who under the
pressure of the plagues, similar to the confounded men in the Babel story, ceased the
building of the city (i.e. the garrison cities built with Hebrew slave labor; Ex. 1:11).
The "city" now represents Zion. The desire to build is keenest when the noises of
suffering "thunder" are most intense.

482 R. Yisrael David Schlesinger.

483 Deleted in *EHS*.

484 Absent in the *Mishnah* text. "Both" refers to the person and the animal.

485 Lev. 20: 15, 16.

486 Sanh. 7:4.

We have clear evidence from the Talmud[487] and Maimonides[488] that the sword with which the condemned are executed may no longer be utilized, even though it served the purpose of fulfilling the command [mitzvah] "Thus you will sweep out evil from your midst."[489] But since it was the instrument by which a person was killed, no further benefit may be derived from it. Surely, if the execution entailed a transgression [averah], the instrument would certainly be prohibited from further use.

Now, how much more so must we not reap any benefit from these countries who were the instruments of so many misfortunes of the Jewish people in our time. How can we dare pass through those countries and say: In such and such a place were murdered, burned, stoned, spoiled and kidnapped so and so? There is not a family in Israel which has not had one of its members ensnared by their traps—a father or brother, a son or a daughter, in the hundreds, thousands and tens of thousands, as is well-known the world over. Such being the case how can one nevertheless look upon these places? Is there actually a person who is so lacking in refined emotion that he is still able to fraternize with these places which have heaped upon us shame and contempt, and created for us grievous misfortune on a scale never experienced in all of our history? This and more must concern and arouse the survivors in these countries of exile.

It is also well-known that when a person is killed or maimed, in that very place there remains an impact, and an evil spirit hovers over it waiting to ambush a person's soul. Note the *Yalkut*[490] *Mas'ei*[491] commentary on the verse: "For blood pollutes the land."[492] Says R.

---

487 Sanh. 45b; AZ 62b. אחת אבן שנסקל בה, ואחת עץ שנתלה עליו, ואחד סייף שנהרג בו ואחד סודר שנחנק בו, כולן נקברין עמו. "The stone with which he [the condemned] was stoned, the gallows on which the body was hanged after stoning, the sword with which he was beheaded or the cloth with which he was strangled, are all buried with him."

488 *Hilkhot Sanhedrin* 15:9.

489 Deut. 13:6; 17:7; 19:19; 21:21; 22:21, 24; 24:7.

490 *Yalkut Shimoni* I, 788.

491 Num. 33:1–36:13.

492 Num. 35:33. כי הדם הוא יחניף את הארץ.

Yoshaya: "[The verse contains] an abbreviation [*notarikon*]—'anger will settle upon the land.'"[493] This is, therefore, the reason for the mishnaic teaching[494] that any accessory to a man's misfortune should be stoned and ostracized.[495] How many thousands, tens of thousands of evil spirits hover over these countries wherein our Jewish brethren have been maimed and suffered disaster in our own time? According to this *Midrash*[496] all of these countries are infested with the spirit of anger due to the bloodshed of many thousands which transpired there. How can we still remain here? This was the reason why our ancestors refused to return to Spain after the exile,[497] although the persecutions in that country subsided.

Therefore, let him not deceive himself, nor allow his heart to be tempted[498] by means of some lucrative business enterprise which he will establish here. Nothing good will come of it. An evil spirit will hover over it. It will eventually be his misfortune, God forbid. I have already made my views known concerning the few who remained in areas where there had been almost total expulsion of the Jewish people. Actually, these were individuals who remained there in order to make money by exploiting special privileges and playing the market. They did indeed hoard wealth, but in the process forgot the purpose of these plagues which were thrust upon us by the Creator of the universe—namely, to stimulate the children of Israel to abandon the lands of exile, and to crave to return to the Land of our forefathers....

They tend to forget. Their minds are dull and therefore they do

---

493　יחניף (*yahanif*) "will pollute" is seen as a contraction for יחון אף "anger will settle." The biblical context of murder is expanded by the *Midrash* to include the permanent contamination of the site of the murder which must be forever ostracized.

494　Sanh. 7:4.

495　Lev. 20:15, 16.

496　See above, n. 490.

497　May 1492. There is no recorded evidence by rabbinic authorities of a formal *herem* [excommunication, banishment] against Jews residing in Spain. Jewish communities were not formally recognized by Spanish governments until December 1968. The editor is grateful to Dr. Yomtov Assis, Hebrew University, Jerusalem, for this information.

498　Cf. Deut. 11:16; Job 31:9, 27.

not understand.[498] They follow others who are engaged in large business ventures which come their way during periods of instability and speculation. I cautioned them that they will not succeed, that it was "idle futility."[499] I cited [for them] *Midrash Rabba*, the weekly portion of *Bo*[500] chapter 13,[501] concerning the plague of locusts:[502]

> What is the meaning of "not a single locust remained?"[503] R. Yohanan said: "When the locusts arrived the Egyptians were delighted. They exclaimed: 'Let us collect them, and fill up barrels!' Said the Holy One, blessed be He: 'Evil people! You rejoice with the very plague which I have brought upon you?' Immediately, the Lord caused a shift to a very strong west wind which lifted the locusts.[504] What is the meaning of 'not a single locust remained'? Even those in the pots and barrels which were pickled flew away."

Similar [will be the fate] of these people who rejoice in profitable ventures of market speculations made possible by the catastrophies in our time; to them, as well, the Holy One, blessed be He, exclaims: "You dare rejoice with the very plague which I have brought upon you?" I swear by your very lives, nothing shall remain in your hands! All of it will vanish with the wind! So too will be the future of those engaged in postwar speculation. Nothing will be gained. The only [possible] consequence of the sufferings which we have endured is to abandon exile—to rise and return to the cities of Zion and to settle them. Only then shall we succeed, prosper and achieve tranquility and calm forever. May this be the will of the Lord. . . .

Let no person imagine and suggest: when governments will return to normalcy after the war there will remain in Europe only a fraction of our Jewish brethren. [They will rationalize] "because of our many

---

498 Cf. Isa. 6:10.

499 רעות רוח. A favorite expression in Eccl. 1:14, 2:11 *et al*.

500 Ex. 10:1–13:16.

501 ExR. 13:6.

502 Described in Ex. 10:12–20.

503 Ex. 10:19.

504 Ibid.

sins, the great mass of our Jewish brethren were lost and destroyed in the hour of the war. Those few who will remain will engage in profitable ventures among the gentiles. They will not fear the jealousy directed against them by the gentiles. Envy, after all, is caused by the mass of the Jewish people. The few who remain, a handful here and there, can surely not be the cause of envy among the gentile neighbors." I cannot imagine that any Jew who would say or even think thus. First of all let me ask: who appointed him[505] the successor, one who would inherit the masses of Jews killed in sanctification of the Name? Further, who is the person of pure heart who would want to build upon the spilt blood of Jews and exploit all this for his own benefit? Does he actually believe that the only consequence of all this spilt blood was that he could build his house upon this blood and thereby raise his fame? Not so! Never! The object of the Jewish tragedy is explained in the *Midrash Shoher Tov*, section 17 (to which I referred previously):[506] so that Israel will ask to return to Eretz Yisrael. . . . If we rise and ascend to Zion we will redeem the souls of the children of Israel who were killed sanctifying the Name of God. [By sanctifying] their lives [they] caused us to return to the domain of our forefathers. If we will be worthy of a large ingathering in Eretz Yisrael, and if the Almighty will direct our hearts to live and worship Him sincerely . . . then we will merit that those destroyed, who died or were murdered because of [conditions in] exile, will rise first from the dead. This is explained in the Ritba,[507] Ta'anit at the close of the first chapter.[508] Similarly, it is noted in *Ikarei HaDat*[509] in the name of *Teshuvat HaRadbaz*.[510]

---

505   The Jew who remains in Europe in order to engage in business ventures.

506   MPs. 17:4. See above, 22, n. 37.

507   R. Yom Tov ben Abraham Ishbili (Seville) (c. 1250–1330) a major Spanish scholar of Talmud and author of the novella *Hiddushei HaRitba*

508   Actually the concluding chapter 30b. *Hiddushei HaRitba, Ta'anit* (Jerusalem, Mosad HaRav Kook, 1975), 195–96; based on Dan. 12:12.

509   *Ikarei HaDat al Yoreh Deah*, section 36:66 (Florence, 1806) 121–122, by R. Daniel ben Moshe David Terni, a late 18th century Italian rabbinic authority, poet and musician.

510   R. David ben Shlomo Ibn Abi Zimra (1479–1573), rabbinic authority and kabbalist in Egypt and Safed. *She'elot uTshuvot HaRadbaz* vol. 3 (Fiorda, 1781), 644, 43b.

It is acknowledged, therefore, that in abandoning these countries of exile and returning to Eretz Yisrael, not only do we redeem the souls of our Jewish brethren who were murdered and fell here in exile because they compelled us to return to the domain of our forefathers, but we hasten their resurrection. Hence, their martyrdom was actually not in vain. . . .

It is well-known from [the writings of] the holy Ari[511] that the reason for the [martyrdom of] the "Ten Martyrs of the Empire"[512] was in order to render weak the power of the *kelipot* (shells)[513] by sanctifying the Name of God with death.

Similarly, these martyrs in their hundreds and thousands, in our time, have weakened the *kelipot* which had prevented us [in the past] from returning to our Holy Land. Now the gate is open for entry into our Holy Land. The prophet Nahum[514] indeed prophesied: "The gates of your Land have opened themselves. . . ."

However, if we abstain from doing so, God forbid, and we allow our hearts to be tempted and continue to remain here in exile, then not only will we have transgressed against the will of our Creator, we will also be guilty for all of the Jewish blood which was shed in vain.

Therefore, my brethren and friends, take to heart these words which I have written here. Then will the Exalted One be praised above and below.[515] Amen, may it be His will.

I noted in the daily newspapers here a statement quoted in the name of a wise and pious person, [Franklin Delano] Roosevelt, the President of the United States of America. He said that it would not be sufficient to merely restore the favorable conditions which existed

---

511 Hayyim Vital, *Etz Hayyim*, vol. 1, *Sha'ar Vav* (6) *Sha'ar T'L'* 130–133.

512 For the various sources describing the martyrdom of the *Asarah Harugei Malkhut* (the Ten Martyrs under Roman rule) during the Hadrianic persecutions in Eretz Yisrael following 135 CE. See the *piyutim* אלה אזכרה (*Eileh Ezkerah*) "These Shall I Remember" in the Musaf liturgy of Yom Kippur and ארזי הלבנון (*Arzei HaLevanon*) "Cedars of Lebanon," in the Tishah B'Av "Kinot" service. Also Ber. 61b; Men. 29b; A. Jellinek, "*Midrash Eileh Ezekerah*," in *Bet Midrash* vol. 2 (Jerusalem, 1938), 64–72.

513 See above, 33 n. 107.

514 Nah. 3:13.

515 In heaven and on earth.

prior to the war. Rather, after this terrible war, mankind expects a future which exceeds all previous positive standards. Now how shall we Jews respond, after all of the sacrifices which we have made? Shall we indeed be satisfied with the *status quo*?

It is written in the weekly portion *Vayelekh*:[516]

> When My anger will flare up against them, and I will abandon them and hide My countenance from them, they shall be ready prey; and many evils and troubles shall befall them. And they shall say on that day, "Surely it is because our God is not in our midst that these evils have befallen us." Yet I will surely keep My presence hidden on that day because of all the evil they have done.[517]

The commentators all inquire: Since Israel confessed to their wrongdoing, acknowledging that all this befell them because God was not in their midst, why then did God put forth His wrath? Indeed, He intensified His hiddenness, as it is written: "Yet I will surely keep My countenance hidden. . . ."[518] I read in the volume *Yad Yosef*,[519] authored by the scholar R. Yosef Zorfati of blessed memory,[520] who lived in the year 5377,[521] the following appealing thought: Indeed we discover that Pharoah repented and in fact declared: "[I stand guilty this time.] The Lord is in the right and I and my people are in the wrong."[522] His repentance, however, did not endure beyond the time in which the plague struck him. During the period of respite Pharoah reverted to his former self, so that he had to be beaten again and again. So it is with us. If repentance is limited to "that day"[523] only, while the suffering is yet with us, yet as soon as it passes on,

---

516   Deut. 31:1–30.

517   Deut. 31:17–18.

518   Ibid. 18. The reinforcing הסתר אסתיר is emphasized.

519   Venice, 1616.

520   Yosef ben Hayyim Zarfati, 17th-century scholar, physician and author of *Yad Yosef* homilies on the Bible.

521   1617.

522   Ex. 9:27. Verbal acknowledgment of guilt is a central feature of repentance. Maimonides *Hilkhot Teshuvah*, 1:1, 2:2, 2:5.

523   Deut. 31:17.

things return to their usual pattern, then repentance is not actually repentance at all. On the contrary, God will reveal His anger, Heaven forbid! When the suffering is over and we forget all which befell us, and we do not fulfill our vows to return to our homeland, and we reconcile ourselves to remain here—then God's wrath will pour down upon us from an intense hiddenness.

In the *Midrash, Yalkut Eikha*[524] they said:

> Said R. Simlai: "What is the meaning of the verse, 'How long will you fools love folly?'[525] Said the Holy One, blessed be He: 'It is common in this world, when a person eats [food with] stench (which is offensive) for two or three days, it becomes disgusting to him. Yet you who have engaged for a number of years in idol worship, as it is written: '"Out!" you will call to them.'[526] 'Dung' will you call it.[527] Yet your souls do not become disgusted. . . .'"[528]

The Holy One, blessed be He, reprimands and confronts Israel: "You have lived among the nations for some time. You have become their servants. Yet this fails to disgust you. Should not this lifestyle to which you have been subjected revolt you as would disgusting filth, exclaiming 'Out!'? You should have craved for, and returned to the home of your fathers, the Land of your Patriarchs, to live among yourselves, your fellow countrymen, with your family, your brethren, the children of your mother, within your mother's bosom." The Holy One, blessed be He, expects this from us. That is why He is discontented with our own lack of dignity to which we have become accustomed in exile among the nations. . . .

I recalled the story of a Jewish villager who approached one of the great *tzadikim* of his generation so that he might pray for his [the

---

524 *Yalkut Shimoni* II, 998.

525 Prov. 1:22.

526 Isa. 30:22. The prophet predicts Israel will banish the idols in disgust: צא תאמר לו.

527 A play on words צואה תאמר לו "dung you call it."

528 Despite Israel's recognition of the abomination of idol worship, they are not repelled by their own acts and continue to wallow in their depravity.

peasant's] welfare. He gave him a written petition.[529] The *rebbe*
responded with *"Brakhah V'hatzlahah."*[530] Exclaimed the villager: "No,
Rebbe! I am not in need of a *brakhah*.[531] I need *hatzlahah*."[532] The
rebbe could not understand his words and asked: "Why don't you
want to receive blessings?" Replied the villager: "Rebbe, I own an inn
which is patronized by people who recite blessings, but from them I
cannot earn a living.[533] Only from people who do not recite blessings
do I earn a living."[534] This villager was, then, convinced that all of his
sources of income were linked to neighboring gentiles. These attitudes
and characteristics served to estrange him from his fellow Jews.

Similar to the villager as an individual is the sad state of affairs with
our unfortunate people. So accustomed have they been to nurse at
the breast of a strange mother that they are convinced there is no
other way. God, blessed be He, protests against the Israelite nation
and this state of affairs, exclaiming: "How many years have you been
in the habit of behaving thus without reacting in disgust!" God, blessed
be He, then convinces us by means of wordly events that if we do not
recoil from them, they will be disgusted with us, until we change our
ways in the lands of exile—until we learn to live in fraternity with our
fellow Jews, to live without jealousy, hatred and competition in our
Land. Amen, thus declares the Lord.

Furthermore my brethren, consider and study well the history of
our lives in exile. Inevitably, after difficult times came periods of ease
and freedom. Yet these days of relief lasted but a few decades, when
the troubled periods returned. . . . Therefore, do not trust, or allow
your hearts to turn to the smiling faces which will gaze upon you
after these difficult times are gone. Do not believe that you will enjoy

---

529 A *kvittel* (*Yid*) or *pitkah* (*Heb.*) given to the rebbe by the hasidic petitioner is a
tradition in early hasidic lore orginating in the schools of applied or practical *tzadikism*.
See Aaron Wertheim, *Law and Custom in Hasidism* (Hoboken, Ktav, 1992), 244–248.

530 "Blessings and success."

531 Blessing.

532 Success.

533 Pious but poor Jews.

534 Well-to-do gentiles. This interchange appears in Yiddish in the original.

immunity forever.[535] Rather plan and set out to return to the home of
your mother. Under her wings you will enjoy an everlasting and
secure resting place,[536] with God's help.

If only our forefathers in previous generations would have responded
[to the call]! Had they been stirred by the great *geonim* in the year
1864,[537] then we, their descendants, would not have been the victims
of the suffering during this troublesome period. But they chose to
disengage themselves entirely. I refer to the fact that they removed
themselves from any attempts at intervention with heads of state so
that they could live an independent national life in the land of their
forefathers. They preferred to live in the lands of exile in exchange
for lentil stew[538]—some business and a lucrative income. Thus they
could continue to live among the fleshpots.[539] In this manner, and in
other ways, was their appetite fulfilled. They no longer have any
connection with Eretz Yisrael, with this sacred nation. This has always
been the attitude of our ancestors in exile. As a result we, their offspring,
have come to this pass.

The prophet Jeremiah had this in mind in his elegy: "Our fathers
sinned and are no more; we remain to bear their iniquities."[540] They
sinned by eliminating themselves from efforts at creating an
autonomous way of life for themselves in their sacred Land, like
every other nation. They acted as if they were no longer in this world
at all,[541] as if they were not an independent nation with rights to live

---

535 Cf. Prov. 27:24. Alternative reading: "Do not be certain that you will enjoy
abundance forever."

536 Cf. Gen. 8:9.

537 Reference to various supporters of Zvi Hirsh Kalisher (1795–1874) in response
to the revised edition of *Derishat Zion* (1865). In this work Kalisher sets forth the
basic premise of religious Zionism: Redemption would be brought about by natural
means (the return of a working, productive people to its Land), and only then would
the supernatural miraculous redemption follow.

538 Reference to Gen. 25:34. As Esau lightly traded away his birthright for
immediate but temporary satisfaction, so have the Jewish people forsaken their treasured
legacy in exile for momentary material benefits.

539 Reference to בשבתנו על סיר הבשר "When we sat by the fleshpots" (Ex. 16:3).

540 Lam. 5:7.

541 Suggested by ואינם "and are no more" (Lam. 5:7).

in its own land. They were content to be the remnants[542] among the
nations. What is the consequence of all this? We hear their iniquities,[543]
and pay with the suffering which we presently endure. . . .

So my brethren, my friends, let us please make certain that we too
should not become victim to the identical sin of the preceding
generations, so that our children subsequently will not bewail and
repeat the same elegy, "Our fathers sinned and are no more; we
remain to bear their iniquities." Therefore, from now on we have no
other recourse but to devote all of our efforts to return to our Holy
Land, all of us united. Then we, our children and grandchildren will
receive the full blessing of God until the end of generations to come.
Emerging from all this will be the coming of the son of David,
speedily in our times, Amen.

In this fashion I propose to interpret the *masorah* .[544] There are four
instances of *halokh*:[545] "journeying by stages ," "diminishing by stages,"
"receding by stages," "becoming richer by stages." Thus, if we will be
satisfied with "journeying by stages" in exile as has been the case until
now, the consequence will be one of "diminishing by stages." As it is
well-known, the exile constantly diminishes us. Painfully we have
seen with our own eyes and in our time to what degree the difficult
exile depreciates us, due to our many sins. This would not be so if we
"gradually return"[546] to our Holy Land, then we will "become greater
by stages."[547] Our nation will become greater both in quantity and
quality, spiritually as well as materially. By our acts the Name of
Heaven will be sanctified, since in enhancing the nation we also enhance

---

542   Cf. Ex. 26:12 שרח העודף "the overlapping excess."

543   The author continues to apply Lam. 5:7 to the argumentation at hand.

544   *Masorah* refers to the ancient tradition and system by which the elaborate task
of transmitting biblical text was achieved. See *Encyclopedia Judaica*, vol. 16, cols.
1401–82. In this context the author will interpret four variations of the term הלוך
(*halokh*) which appear in Gen. 12:9, 8:5, 8:3 and 26:13.

545   The term הלוך appended suggests a steady, gradual process.

546   The intent of הלוך ושוב in Gen. 8:3 is one of recession (i.e., the flood waters
receded). Our author, however, isolates the term in order to focus on ושוב (*vashov*);
hence, to return.

547   Gen. 26:13.

His Holy Name, may it be blessed and elevated, as it is expressed in Torah, the prophets, and the scriptures[548] in numerous places. With the help of God, this will be recognized and will be clear.

Further note, my brethren, what is written in the Torah:

> Remember what Amalek did to you on your journey after you left Egypt; how, undeterred by fear of God, he surprised you on the march when you were famished and weary and he cut down all the stragglers in the rear. Therefore, when the Lord your God grants you safety from all your enemies around you, in the Land that the Lord your God is giving you as a hereditary portion, you shall blot out the memory of Amalek from under heaven. Do not forget![549]

In view of events and the difficult exile which have occurred in our time, one may interpret the text in *Midrash Leviticus Rabba*.[550] The term *Mitzrayim*[551] need not refer to the Egyptian exile alone. Every misfortune which has befallen us in exile has been called *Mitzrayim*, formed by *meytzar -yam*.[552]

We have seen this in our day. When a Jew is beset by misfortune, God forbid, and he wants to extricate himself from his confinement, an Amalek appears and blocks his path, preventing him from any act [of self rescue].

Refer to the Maharsha, Ta'anit 15[553] and his interpretation of David's verses in chapter 102:[554] "I am like a great owl in the wilderness,

---

548 Likely references to the numerous passages in scripture where the degradation of Israel would be interpreted by the nations as a defeat for the God of Israel. The elevation of Israel, on the other hand, surely is an expression of glory of God. See Ex. 7:4–5, 15:11–15; Num. 14:13–16; Ezek. 36, 39: 25–29; Ps. 79:3–13.

549 Deut. 25:17–19.

550 13:2 ‏כל המלכיות נקראו על שם מצרים על שם שהיו מצירין לישראל‎ ‏א"ר יוסי ב"ר חנינא:‎ "R. Yosi the son of Hanina said: 'All the empires are referred to as *Mitzrayim* [Egypt: the root in Hebrew *m'tz'r*] because they afflicted (*metzirin*) Israel.'"

551 Egypt.

552 *Lit.*, "A sea of misfortune." See below, 300, n. 1124.

553 15a, cited as 17 in the original.

554 Ps. 102:7, 9.

an owl among the ruins. All day long my enemies revile me." David the king recounts the hardships which shall befall Israel in exile. There are birds called *kos* and *ka'at*. [555] They dwell in the desert or desolate locations not populated by humans. When they are in trouble they cry for help but there is no one who listens to them. So it is with us in exile. When violence and injustice is directed against us we cry for help. But there is no one who listens to us. And yet when we approach the ministers of justice to register complaints before them regarding the robbery committed against us, not only do they not respond with help, they insult and punish us. This is [the meaning of] the verse, "I am like a great owl in the wilderness," [556] compared to a *ka'at* in the wilderness and a *kos* among the ruins, which no one listens to. Moreover, "my enemies revile me." [557] Our own eyes have confirmed this during the troubled period that has befallen us presently.

Therefore the verse informs us: "Remember what Amalek did to you on your journey after you left Egypt." [558] The intent [of the verse]: At the very time when you were in a state of misfortune and wanted to flee from the troubled area, an Amalek caught up with you along the way, interfered with your progress on your way and prevented you from any action. Thus you were caught in misfortune. Remember also the cruelty: "And he cut down all the stragglers in the rear." [559] He displayed no compassion in his cruelty towards us, the weak and the ill. "And you were famished and weary," [560] from the weight of misfortunes which they brought upon you. And "he was undeterred by fear of God" [561] to the extent that he did not refrain from causing you unlimited evil and misfortune.

But remember what I nonetheless assure you: "When the Lord

---

555   Mentioned in Ps. 102 : 7. These may be unidentified night birds. Some interpret them as pelicans (Jastrow) and vultures.

556   Ps. 102 : 7.

557   Ibid. 9.

558   Deut. 25:17.

559   Ibid. 18.

560   Ibid.

561   Ibid.

your God grants you safety from all your enemies around you."[562] That is to say, all things come to an end. These afflictions from your enemy will also come to an end. Then you will remember to direct your energy and your manpower only "into the land that the Lord your God is giving you as a hereditary portion."[563] Namely, you dare not think of staying longer here in exile. Rather, make the effort to return to the land of your fathers. In this way, "you shall blot out the memory of Amalek from under heaven..."[564]

Therefore, the verse concludes: "Do not forget!"[565] That is to say: I know your weak disposition. You forget quickly all of the hardships which they have inflicted upon you during difficult days. Easily, and in response to the slightest gesture of affection on their part, you are reconciled and appeased—this, in order for you to retain the meager, scanty and limited earnings which were yours prior to the decrees enacted against you. So what if they will offer you a good and lucrative income! It is likely you will forget all that they inflicted upon you. You will be reconciled and continue to live among them. You will once again forget your portion and inheritance. Therefore the verse exhorts: "Do not forget!" what they inflicted upon you. Do not ever become reconciled to them. Rather, return and grasp the inheritance of your fathers, for *this* is the will of God. Therefore have all of the sufferings befallen you—so that you will be aroused, as I have written previously.[566] Note this carefully!

Again I chanced upon the sermons of the Hatam Sofer[567] in his eulogy for R. Yeshayahu Berlin,[568] of blessed memory, and his

---

562 Ibid. 19.

563 Ibid.

564 Ibid.

565 Ibid.

566 Especially in the first chapter, although references to the relationship of suffering to Eretz Yisrael are among the central features of this work.

567 Hatam Sofer: *Drashot Me'Avinu Moshe Sofer*, vol. 2 (Jerusalem, 1974), 306 (611).

568 Noted 18th-century rabbi, scholar and author (1725–1799), known for his critical emendations to the Talmud.

interpretation of the verse: "He subdues for us peoples, sets nations at our feet. He chose our heritage for us, the pride of Jacob [whom He loved]."[569] "As it is, however, the entire Torah is based on the assumption of free will [i.e., the Torah is to be observed with our positive choice][570] and not upon compulsion." Nahmanides[571] on the portion of *Mas'ei*[572] comments on the verse, "And you shall take possession of the Land and settle in it,"[573] which is an explicit positive commandment to settle the Holy Land.[574] Now if we are not in a favorable position on this earth, we will be unable to fulfill this mitzvah except under duress.[575] Our free choice to perform the will of God will not be evident. However, when our conditions among the nations will be favorable, and we will choose to live only in it [the Holy Land], then we shall fulfill this positive commandment out of choice. . . .

In the *Midrash*[576] our sages taught:

"Israel did not know; My people did not understand."[577] "Israel did not know"—this refers to the past. "My people did not understand"—this refers to the future.

The intent is rather obvious, in my opinion. This prophet reproaches Israel for quickly forgetting the sufferings which it has endured, instead of studying the past, so as to better understand the future. They should learn from the troubled days and years which they experienced when confronted with difficult decrees, when their skin was stripped

---

569   Ps. 47:4–5.

570   Comment of *EHS* upon the *Hatam Sofer* text.

571   *Peirushei HaTorah LeRabbenu Moshe Bar Nahman*, ed. Hayyim Dov Chavel, vol. II (Jerusalem, 1960), 338. See discussion above, 172, n. 257.

572   Num. 31:1–36:13.

573   Num. 33:53.

574   Nahmanides includes this precept in his *"Hasagot"* to Maimonides' *Sefer HaMitzvot* as the fourth in the series of positive commandments which Maimonides did not include. *Sefer HaMitzvot LaRambam VeHasagot HaRambam.* op. cit., 242–46.

575   They will be compelled to return to Eretz Yisrael during persecutions.

576   *Yalkut Shimoni* II, 387.

577   Isa. 1:3.

from them, and when the verse "you shall sow your seed to no purpose,"[578] was realized.

Seemingly without precedent, they were violated and trampled upon. This past they should have known, in order to anticipate the future and not to place confidence in future events. They have quickly forgotten all of this, and act as if they do not know. Consequently, they give no thought to the future. This was the prophet's cry, "Israel did not know"—the past; "My people did not understand"—the future [implications], that these events can repeat themselves, Heaven forbid, as proven by current events. In plain language: The tragedy of the Jewish people lies not in the sad events which befall it, but in that they refuse to learn any lesson from them. Therein lies the real tragedy.[579]

In the Sefardi version[580] of the Additional service on the New Moon it is written: "May this month mark the conclusion and end of all our suffering; may it signal the beginning and commencement of the redemption of our lives."[581] There is considerable redundancy: first, "The conclusion and end of all our suffering" and "the beginning and commencement of the redemption of our lives," are essentially the same. After all, the end of our suffering implies the beginning and commencement of life's redemption. Conversely, if one's life is redeemed then in any event suffering would end. Why, then, both expressions? Second, what is the significance of "conclusion and end?" They seem to be one and the same. Third, what is the meaning of "beginning and commencement"? These also are redundant! Certainly these expressions were not composed unthinkingly. There must be an appropriate meaning hidden here.

The Almighty enlightened me and allowed me to understand the

---

578   Lev. 26:16. The *EHS* text reads וזרעתם לריק כחכם "You shall waste your strength" *vs.* וזרעתם לריק זרעכם "You shall sow your seed to no purpose."

579   This passage appears in Yiddish.

580   Regional differences are factors in the development of Jewish liturgy. The Sefardi variants were traditions developed by Spanish and Portuguese Jewries. The Ashkenazi versions were adopted by Jews of Western and Eastern Europe, although hasidic traditions often incorporate Sefardi variants.

581   Alternate reading נפשנו, "our souls."

deep meaning of this prayer. [It provides insight into] what we have
experienced in recent years. From time to time we lived side by side
with our gentile neighbors in Europe in peace and tranquility, in
security and confidence without any obstacles between us. Then,
suddenly they were transformed into our enemies. They treated us as
foes, assailed and assaulted us until the nation of God was despoiled
and plundered. The prophecy of Isaiah had come true for us:[582] "It is
a people plundered and despoiled: All of them are trapped in holes,
imprisoned in dungeons. They are given over to violence, with none
to rescue them; to despoilment, with none to say 'Give back!'" Note
[the] Rashi [commentary].[583] This very thing has repeated itself in our
time. Our belongings have been taken from us. We have been flogged
with a variety of cruel beatings. We have been expelled to a wasteland.[584]
Our words are insufficient and cannot contain all that has been done
to us in this frightening and bitter exile. Unimaginable acts have been
perpetrated against us. We have arrived at the very nadir of humiliation
and exile. We search intensely for an answer. Why has this befallen
us? Why are we considered less than other nations in the world?
Every nation is privileged to live a pleasant life on this planet. We
have been robbed of such a privilege. It is clear to all that our lives
are worse than those of animals on this earth.

Something else amazes us. It is known that much of European
Jewry, unfortunately, have become totally assimilated among their
gentile neighbors—in spirit, language and behavior. They abandoned
the covenant of their Fathers. One would have imagined that this
should have resulted in a mutual relationship, harmony and love.
After all, similarity gives birth to love. Yet we witness the opposite.
On a bitter day they pursue us to [the path of] destruction without
discriminating between those who are very observant in the ways of

---

582   Isa. 42:22.

583   Rashi's commentary places emphasis on the phrase והוא עם בזוז "It is a people
plundered" in Isa. 42:24. In the process of being despoiled Israel fails to relate
punishment to a cause, or to search for meaning. ולא ישים על לב כל זה לומר למה קראתנו
זאת. מי למשיסה יעקב. "No one will care enough to ask: 'Why has this occurred to us?
Who was it gave Jacob over to despoilment [Isa. 42:24]?'"

584   Cf. Lev. 16:22: ארץ גזרה "An inaccessible wasteland."

our holy ancestors, and rebellious Jews who have assimilated. They are all the same in the eyes of the enemies.

They are familiar with the teaching of our sages of blessed memory: "A Jew who sins remains nevertheless a Jew."[585] This seems amazing. One must also wonder at our own long history of exile. How is it possible for our Jewish brethren to allow themselves to be humiliated, to be plundered and killed, when these acts in our time repeat themselves. Our Jewish brethren live in exile a few decades among the nations in peace and tranquility and then persecutions erupt once more. So it was in Spain.[586] They benefitted from many years of calm and then came plunder and exile. So it was in Germany and in old Austria.[587] And thus it has been with us in almost every European country. Now, why have we not achieved the standard enjoyed by other nations—to live securely for many years on their own land in comfort and tranquility without ever being interrupted by evil periods?

Perhaps, my brethren, you will claim that this is all a decree from Heaven, part and parcel of the exile which has been fated for us until the Messiah will come speedily in our day. [Therefore] we need not

---

585 A variant of Sanh. 44 a: אמר רבי אבא בר זבדא: חטא ישראלי (יהושע ז:יא) אף על פי שחטא ישראל הוא -. "'Israel has sinned!' [Jos. 7:11]. R. Aba bar Zivda said: "Although he [Achan] sinned, he is still an Israelite.'" The Talmud refers to the strong Jewish roots which will resist a hostile and tempting environment. Hence, "A myrtle, though it stands among reeds, is still a myrtle, and it is so called (Sanh. 44a)." This nonlegal statement takes on legal connotations in the 11 th century, i.e. a Jew cannot voluntarily reject his Jewish identity [in relation to certain *halakhot*]. See Menahem Elon, *HaMishpat Ha'Ivri*, vol. 1 (Jerusalem, 1973), 146. *EHS* transforms this teaching into an ironic "justification" of anti-Jewish persecution, irrespective of the Jews' formal relationship with Judaism.

586 *EHS* employs the Yiddish *Shpanien* in referring to the mass expulsion of the Jews in 1492 following their creative "Golden Age" in Spain.

587 Probable reference to the marked contrast of the early Jewish settlement in Germany—the relatively calm period of the 10th and beginning of the 11 th century—with the brutal wave of persecutions which marked the 11th through the 16th centuries, punctuated by the expulsion of Jews from Mainz (101 2), the massacres of the first Crusade (1096), the required wearing of the "Jewish" badge, the first blood libels (13th century) and the Black Death (plague) massacres (1348–50). Similar patterns of privileges and protection followed by restrictions, persecutions and expulsions characterized the history of Jews in Austria from the 12th through the 18th centuries. See *Encyclopedia Judaica* articles "Austria," vol. 3, pp. 887–906; "Germany," vol. 7, pp. 457–504, and related bibliographies.

do anything about it! Let it be known, my brother, that I do not
agree with you. Take note of Nahmanides [his commentary] on the
portion *Ki Tavo*, [588] who takes the opposite view from your own. On
the contrary, the verse, [589] "Yet, even then, when they are in the land
of their enemies [I will not reject them or spurn them so as to destroy
them]," teaches the promise of exile, in order to assure us that as long
as we remain in exile we will dwell in peace and tranquility. We will
earn a comfortable livelihood and benefit from all of the privileges of
other peoples, perhaps more so. [590] Refer to [the Nahmanides
commentary]. Therefore, Heaven does not necessarily decree such
things. On the contrary, from the teaching of Nahmanides, we learn
that we are to blame ourselves for all of this. [591] We have, therefore, to
determine why and how.

But, "pay attention and listen" to my words, [592] and "you will be
able to solve the problem." [593] Understand that the individual consists
of two parts—the body and soul, each of which must be sustained
with food and nourishment, the body with material food and soul
with spiritual nourishment. Included in the spiritual food is the proper
system of how to live upon this earth, the [proper use] of intelligence
and knowledge in the [right] measure and emphasis. For if he will
take more than the body requires, the body will be destroyed, its life
terminated. The spirit and intelligence of man feed his acts with
prudent judgment for the benefit of body and soul. So shall the body
and soul live in cooperation. One should not transfer the dimension
of one to the other, but utilize them both equally in one's lifetime.

---

588   Deut. 26:1–29:8.

589   Lev. 26:44. The author proceeds to summarize Nahmanides' lengthy teaching
on Deut. 28:42. Exile, as explicitly promised by Scripture, is not endless and need not
paralyze the Jew in an attitude of fatalism. Favorable conditions will prevail which
will permit the Jewish people to renew their covenant with God by actively removing
themselves from exile and returning to their homeland. Suffering will be considered
a sign to speed the end of exile.

590   Nahmanides (c. 1195–1270) is likely drawing from the exile experience of the
Jews of Spain.

591   Exile and redemption are determined by man's will and action.

592   Cf. Deut. 27:9. הסכת ושמע.

593   Eccl. 8:1 ותבין פשר דבר.

Only then will he succeed in living a long and pleasant life. . . .

As it is with the individual, so it is with a nation in its totality. The nation as well is dependent for its existence upon two facets—the physical and the spiritual. The physical life of a nation consists of the material, namely, economic considerations, commercial considerations, agriculture work—all that is necessary for the life of a people. Spiritual life represents the spirit of the people, the soul of the nation. Every country places great value in stimulating endeavors regarding these aspects of its national life. In accordance with the growth of the spiritual and intellectual character of the country, so shall its material strength grow strong. We have daily proof of this in our time. A country which is highly developed in the intellectual domain, in particular, "science and technology," is also highly developed materially. Accordingly, the knowledge of a country reflects its vital life, as the relationship of the soul to the body . . . Consequently, if the nation does not place any value in enriching itself in its spiritual domain, if it concentrates all of its efforts in the physical and material [domain], in order to enrich its capital assets and wealth, it has no reason to exist and will be doomed to destruction. Sooner or later, its material wealth to which it devoted all of its energies will also disappear, as the history of mankind has repeatedly demonstrated.

Now, as I have already indicated earlier,[594] when the situation in exile will become difficult God will remove from us the promise of exile, discussed above,[595] as a sign that He wishes us to abandon the lands of exile and return to our Land. The initiative [to return] we must make. God will hopefully complete the task for us. As with an individual who cannot achieve perfection of the soul without tranquility, so the nation in its totality without a dwelling place cannot devote itself to spiritual concerns. Our sages of blessed memory explicitly stated in the first chapter of Hagigah:[596] "Since Israel has been exiled from its dwelling place, there is no greater neglect of the

---

594   In the original *EHS*, 145, and our text 218, especially n. 589.

595   Nahmanides' contention that the Jewish people will not be harmed in exile, based on Lev. 26:44.

596   5b, interpreting the triple appearance of the word "tears" in Jer. 13:17.

study of Torah."[597]

Now we may interpret the prayer discussed above.[598] There are deliberate differences in the nuances of the language. I will preface my remarks by highlighting these nuances.

There is a distinction between the terms *sof*[599] and *ketz*.[600] *Sof* indicates the termination of an event which began at a specific time. Thus, the suffering in our time began in a specific year and ended also in a specific year.[601] So the year wherein suffering is concluded is termed as the *sof* of the sufferings begun earlier. It is conceivable, however, that this very event could repeat itself, as it did once before. The term *ketz*, however, indicates that this event will come to a permanent end. It will never, ever recur. As it is written at the conclusion of the book of Daniel[602] "at the end of days." There are numerous such references in Scripture.[603]

So it is with terms *tehilah*[604] and *verosh*.[605] These as well are different concepts. *Tehilah* implies beginning; and *rosh* suggests preeminence and distinction,[606] referring to the prominent aspect of an act. When there are two purposes to one's efforts, which of the two is preeminent? This is the meaning of *rosh*, such as the head which is the predominant member of the body. . . .

Accordingly, we may well understand the text of the prayer [of the

---

597   Exile distracts one from study.

598   225.

599   Conclusion, סוף.

600   End, קץ.

601   The *Sho'ah* in Europe seemed to the inside observer to develop in stages, persecutions interrupted by brief periods of calm, which raised the hopes of the victims. The diaries are replete with reaction to this phenomenon which was fed by the hope and desperation of the victims.

602   12:13, לקץ הימין, suggesting finality.

603   The cataclysmic events described in Ezek. 7:1–6 which employs the term and its variant six times in order to stress the inevitable finality of the destruction. See also Lam. 4:18.

604   Beginning, תחילה.

605   Preeminence, ראש (*lit.* head).

606   The author employs קרן "horn" as a synonym for ראש, suggesting strength, honor and preeminence as in Ezek. 29:21; Ps. 132:17.

new moon] mentioned previously. We pray to the Lord, blessed be He, that "this month may mark the conclusion and end of all our suffering." Namely, it is not sufficient that we have arrived at a conclusion [*sof*] of the sufferings which have befallen us, since these may even recur, though for now they are concluded. We therefore pray that these sufferings also come to a final end [*ketz*], and that they not recur. Consequently, we conclude with "[may it signal] the beginning and preeminence of the redemption." By this it is meant that the prayers which you recite to put a final end to sufferings, that they not return. [These prayers] are dependent upon you yourself and what you consider to be your best efforts. When you again resume your efforts the day following the conclusion of the suffering, will you still devote the major portion [of your actions] to the material and mundane? Then you will have no assurance that the sufferings, God forbid, will not return. In fact, very likely, after a few years they will return, as events in history have taught, since the soul of the nation is absent [in guiding your actions]. And if, nevertheless, you labor only on behalf of the body, the body without the soul has no future and is destined for destruction, God forbid. However, if you consider the redemption of your soul as important [*rosh*] and essential, the redemption of your soul, namely, that all your efforts will be for the redemption of your soul and the soul of your people, which consists in the building of our Holy Land, then the soul of our people will be redeemed. When our people will dwell in Eretz Yisrael, which "will be built and established"[607] in a spirit befitting its purity and sanctity and in accordance with Torah, then you may rest assured that our sufferings will come to a final end.

Now, we conclude [the *Rosh Hodesh Musaf* blessing for the new moon with] "the beginning and commencement of the redemption of our lives," so that the beginning of our efforts, after the suffering has passed from us and we have rest from our enemies, will be directed to the redemption of our souls. Unlike our actions in the past, this shall become the *preeminent* and major focus of our efforts. [Until now] we

---

607 Cf. Num. 21:27 תבנה ותכונן.

limited ourselves to the comforts of mundane and material pursuits. These alone were the focus of all our energies. For these we abandoned our Torah, our heritage, the sanctity of our people and our Holy Land. On behalf of a disjointed and degraded life in the lands of exile, our attention was diverted [from the Holy Land]. Naturally, the result was destruction and annihilation, Heaven forbid.

However, we must devote our major effort to the redemption of our soul, which is, first and foremost, the attempt to return to our Holy Land—because Eretz Yisrael is the very heart of our nation (as I indicated earlier in the name of the divine kabbalist, our teacher, R. Moshe Cordovero,[608] and Maimonides in *Sefer Ha-Mitzvot*). No creature can exist without a heart. When we acquire the heart of the Israelite nation, then we shall attain the soul of our holy people. It will give us vitality and eternal life. This will bring our sufferings to an end forever. This seems to me to be the meaning of this prayer. This interpretation rings true and clear....

Of utmost importance should be the attempts of the pious and God-fearing parties among our people who must make the effort to return to our Holy Land. They should not wait for the call of the prophet, as cited earlier in the name of Nahmanides[609] of blessed memory. When they shall effect a large ingathering of "those who fear the word of God,"[610] we shall strengthen and enhance the sanctity of the Land. We shall then assure the observance of Torah and the commandments in the Land, as mentioned above in the name of our rabbi, the man of God, the Rabbi of Gur, may he live a good and long life. . . .[611] The timely message which is conveyed to us should

---

608   See above, 48, n. 65.

609   On the verse in Deut. 12:5. ובספרי "תדרשו" דרוש על פי הנביא יכול תמתין עד שיאמר לך נביא, ת"ל "לשכנו תדרשו ובאת שמה" דרוש ומצא ואח"כ יאמר לך נביא. "In the Sifrei [it is explained]: 'You shall seek.' Seek as directed by the prophet. You might [wrongly] interpret this to mean: Wait for the word of the prophet. Hence, the verse teaches: 'Seek the site; there you are to go.' Seek and you will discover, and only then will the prophet address you." *EHS* text, 95.

610   מהחרדים על דבר ד'. Variant of Isa. 66:5.

611   See above, 189, n. 396.

be understood. The "time of love" has arrived[612] when we return to our dwelling place, "our hereditary possession."[613] We have no longer any business here [in exile]. . . .

The prophet Ezekiel[614] speaks to us: "When I passed by you and saw you wallowing in your blood, I said to you 'Live in spite of your blood.' Yea, I said to you, 'Live in spite of your blood.'"[615] It seems that the prophet in his Divine inspiration directed his insight into our exile and what has occurred to us in the kingdoms of Europe in our time. We toiled with the sweat of our brow, and we contributed all of our efforts to all of life's endeavors, in the intellectual, economic and business [spheres]. The Jew was involved with both body and mind in the flourishing of life here in Europe, helping it reach the summit. The net result was the realization of the verse: "You shall sow your seed in vain, [for your enemies shall eat it]."[616] They consume the products of our toil while we are trampled upon without protection from the torrent of punishments which come thundering upon us, due to our many sins.

Consequently, the prophet calls out to us in anguish: "When I passed by you and saw you wallowing in your blood,"[617]—in your own blood which you gave to the lands of exile. *Damim* has a twofold meaning—money and actual blood,[618] your money and the blood of your toil. Yet with all this, you are trampled upon the soil, "you were completely naked and bare."[619] And I say to you, see to it that from

---

612 Ezek. 16:8 עת דודים God's covenant with Israel is portrayed as an act of supreme compassion and love, forged on a background of rejection and abandonment by the nations from the time of Israel's birth.

613 Cf. Num. 32:32 אחוזת נחלתינו.

614 Mistakenly cited as Isaiah.

615 Ezek. 16:6.

616 Lev. 26:16.

617 Ezek. 16:6.

618 בדמיך "in your blood" is given the additional interpretation "with your money" from דמים (*damim*).

619 Ezek. 16:7 The *EHS* Jerusalem edition mistakenly amends the original text to ואתה עירום ועריה *vs.* ואת עירום ועריה of Ezekiel which our author cites accurately. *EHS Jer.* ריט [219] *vs. EHS* רכה [225].

now on you will live within your own blood. In your own blood you will live![620] Namely, you will return to your land and estate. To it alone will you contribute your *damim*.[621] Then *you* will control your life; no one else will.[622] If indeed you invest your energy and toil in our Holy Land, you will build a home in Eretz Yisrael, you will dwell within it for the length of your days. Your children will continue to live there after you. If you have planted a vineyard in Eretz Yisrael, it will be you who shall dedicate it. It will be you and not strangers who will benefit from it. And so with all other productive enterprises in your Land. You and your children will be the benefactors; you will not toil in vain.[623] I therefore implore you and say to you: Do live with your own blood! Do live with your own blood! Realize this for it is the truth. . . .[624]

Let us learn from [the action of] Jacob our Father. Although he was still gripped by the fear of Esau,[625] he yet attempted to rescue his possessions so they would not fall into the hands of Esau, as it is written: "he sent across all his possessions."[626] Rashi explains, citing the midrash: "The cattle and movable possessions [he sent across] by transforming himself into a bridge [over the stream], taking some from here and placing them there."[627] Jacob always acted as a bridge. A bridge has two pillars; one on each bank of the river. Similarly, Jacob our Father always stood with one foot on the bank of the river, which was Eretz Yisrael. With the other he stood on the same bank with his brother Esau. This permitted him to transfer all of his

---

620   Paraphrasing Ezek. 16:6.

621   Your blood and material resources. See n. 618 above.

622   A free rendering of ואז אתה חי ולא אחר in the context of the text which follows.

623   According to Lev. 26:16.

624   Invoking the Hatam Sofer (*Derashot*, 7 Av, part 2) on Deut. 1:6–8, the author reaffirms the responsibility of the Jewish people to stake their just claim to Eretz Yisrael which was established in the covenant between God and His people at Sinai. When Israel toils for others at its own expense, it invites the punishment of a degrading reliance on others (*EHS*, 325–326).

625   Gen. 32:8.

626   Gen. 32:24.

627   Rashi on Gen. 32:24 based on GenR. 76:9.

possessions to Eretz Yisrael, to rescue them so that they would not fall into the hands of Esau. Jacob never stood with both feet on the same side with Esau. Rather, with one foot he stood on the other side, which was Eretz Yisrael. With the other foot he stood in the impure environment . . . But had he stood with both feet in the land of Esau[628] he would not have succeeded in preventing his possessions from falling into Esau's hands. . . . So it with his offspring. Were our minds and hearts not completely set upon our lands of exile, we would not be standing here with both feet, totally forgetting our Holy Land. We would not have lost our possessions to Esau. Woe to the Jewish wealth in the European countries which has been lost to Esau! How much of our Holy Land we might have redeemed and rebuilt with this wealth! . . . We were overly complacent in our dwelling place in exile . . . We did not follow the example of Jacob our Father who stood in exile with only one foot . . . Therefore, to our sorrow, we have come to this pass!

This is the intent, it seems, of *Midrash Lamentations*:[629] Had we been deserving[630] we would read [the text in Scripture] "no one will covet your Land."[631] Since we were not deserving we [are compelled to] read, "The foe has laid hands on everything dear to her."[632] Had we been indeed worthy of always bearing in mind the Land of Israel not to settle in the lands of exile, we would be reading "no one will covet your Land." Then even our dwelling here [in exile] was considered Eretz Yisrael, as explained in *[Sefer] Haredim*[633] and *Sefer HaHayyim*

---

628 Synonymous with the lands of exile.

629 Variant of LamR., *Petihta*, 11.

630 The LamR. text reads: "Had you been deserving."

631 Ex. 34:24.

632 Lam. 1:10.

633 A manual on spiritual and ascetic behavior arranged according to the mitzvot. Among the major works of the 16th-century kabbalist R. Eleazer ben Moshe, author of the popular poem *Yedid Nefesh*. Likely reference to *Sefer Haredim* (Constantinople, 1757), 56: וצריך כל איש ישראל לחבב את א״י ולבא אליה מאפסי ארץ בתשוקה גדולה כבן אל חיק אמו "Every Jew must care for Eretz Yisrael and to return to her with great longing, as would a child to the embrace of the mother."

[written] by the brother of the Maharal, of blessed memory,[634] which I will cite subsequently.[635] They would not have been able to control our possessions. Since we have not been worthy, having referred to the lands of exile as "[This is my resting place for all time;] here I dwell, for I desire it,"[636] standing here with both our feet, unlike Jacob our Father, may he rest in peace, we unfortunately cite: "The foe has laid hands on everything dear to her." For they have taken everything from us, as we ourselves have seen in our times, due to our numerous sins. It is all true and clear. May this be a lesson for us. From this day let us not stand here in exile with both feet, but with one foot only. With the second foot we should always be in Eretz Yisrael. May our eyes and hearts always be there. God will then bless us. Amen, may it be His will.

Note *Midrash Rabba*,[637] the portion of *Aharei*:[638]

> He who exceedingly covets money, but possesses no land, of what use is it to him? . . . It is written, "All the pilots of the sea shall come down from their ships and stand on the ground."[639] Is it not obvious that they stood upon the ground?] But [to teach you] when one's vessel sinks into the sea and he has property on land, then he stands.[640] If he does not have property, there is nothing more foolish."[641]

R. Joseph Pachanovsky, the *gaon* and *hasid*, from the distinguished family of our R. Hayyim of Pabjanice, writes in his volume *Pardes*

---

634   R. Hayyim ben Bezalel (c. 1520–1588) scholar and pietist, the elder brother of the Maharal of Prague (R. Judah Loew).

635   *EHS*, 261.

636   An ironic transposition of Ps. 132:13–14 wherein it is the Lord who chooses Zion as His everlasting resting place, כי בחר ד' בציון אוה למושב לו . . . זאת מנוחתי עדי עד, פה אשב כי אותיה. "For the Lord has chosen Zion; He has desired it for His seat. This is My resting place for all time; here I will dwell, for I desire it."

637   LevR. 22:1 The full midrash is cited here in order to illuminate the brief *EHS* selection cited outside the brackets.

638   Lev. 16–18.

639   Ezek. 27:29.

640   When catastrophe strikes at sea, the only alternative is to seek land!

641   Land represents stability, and provides its owner with a sense of security, purpose, and hope in times of catastrophe.

Yosef:[642]

As long as Israel does not return to its land, and will not dwell everyone under his own vine and under his own fig tree,[643] his wealth and business will be for naught. Note the volume *Shelom Yerushalayim*, section 7,[644] of the holy rabbi, our teacher the Admor[645] R. Yisrael of Kotzk,[646] which was reprinted,[647] who elaborates upon this point. In the responsa *Avnei Nezer,*[648] *Yoreh Deah*, Part II, section 454 and 455 there is a reponsa related to the above. Similarly, section 457.[649]

This is the quotation from the *gaon*, the illustrious *hasid*, cited above.[650] (I have no idea what has happened to him. May the merit of his study, righteousness, piety and good deeds support him during this period of calamity. . . .)[651]

---

642   Lodz: 1930, vol. 1, 77. Noted rabbi in Lodz (d. 1930), author of *Pardes Yosef*, an anthology of commentaries related to Rashi and Nahmanides on the Pentateuch.

643   Cf. I Kings 5:5.

644   *EHS*, 227 has misprinted "section 200" סיי' ר'י and is thus transferred to the Jer. ed. of *EHS*, 222. See especially pp. 43, 36, 47.

645   Acronym of אדוננו מורנו "our master, our teacher" appended traditionally to hasidic leaders.

646   R. Hayyim Yisrael Morgenstern (1840–1906) grandson of the renowned Menahem Mendel of Kotzk; rabbi in Pilov and author of *Shelom Yerushalayim* published in 1886 which defended his plan for agricultural settlement of religious Jews in Eretz Yisrael.

647   Pietrakov: 1925.

648   See above, 144, n. 81.

649   282–295 Tel Aviv, 1958 edition. Responsa devoted to the laws of settling Eretz Yisrael; especially paragraphs 14, 18 and 20. ממילא הדרים בא"י ומתפרנסים ממעות חו"ל לענ"ד שממעטים המצוה [של ישיבת א"י] ואינו ברור כלל אם יקיימו המצוה. (י"ח) אבל זה ברור (כ') דעיקר המצוה בתכלית השלימות הוא להיושבים בא"י ומתפרנסים מהשפע שמא"י. "In any case, those who reside in Eretz Yisrael and are supported by funds from abroad, fulfill the mitzvah [of settlement in Eretz Yisrael] in only a limited way in my opinion. It is not at all clear if they actually fulfill the mitzvah. (18) It is clear, however, the full significance of the mitzvah is realized when the settlers in Eretz Yisrael earn a living from the [potential] abundance offered by the Land (20)."

650   I.e., the author of *Pardes Yosef*, Yosef Pachanovsky.

651   The author in a brief digression returns to a major theme of the volume: the travesty of rejecting the nonobservant Jew. Citing from the talmudic literature, the Geonim, Radbaz and *Pardes Yosef*, R. Teichthal builds support for the principle of *kiruv* (bringing the alienated Jew closer to his roots) and thereby maintaining *ahdut*

In the [commentary of the] portion of *Kedoshim*,[652] the *Pardes Yosef* cites text from the Haggadah [of Passover]: "'Not only one [tyrant][653] rose up against us to destroy us. . . .' The intent of *lo ehad bilvad* ['not only one'] refers to the fact that we are not one [united] among ourselves. This alone is cause to destroy us, God forbid."[654] Then the Lord, blessed be He, will bring our hearts closer, one to another, and unity shall reign in Israel. Amen, may this be His will.

While involved here in the process of publishing this volume, I was compelled to leave the capital for a particular reason.[655] With the help of the Almighty, I found an opportune moment to return [to Slovakia]. There I visited a community, a fine community blessed with God-fearing laymen steeped in Torah study, a house of study and prayer with *hasidim* and men of good works. During the few weeks I lived there, I chose to pray in a *klois*[656] of *hasidim*, since there I found amicable company. The rabbi and *gaon*, the head of the [rabbinic] court, may he live a good and long life, honored me with an invitation to preach in the synagogue. Only one *hasid* who had heard my discourses in the capital and of my efforts and battles on behalf of *aliyah* to our Holy Land, most passionately attempted to prevent me from preaching. He was apprehensive that I would expound upon this noble concept and proceed to document the great obligation which we must assume on its behalf. Satan succeeded in preventing me from preaching on my first Sabbath there. The leaders of the community, however, again asked me to preach and I responded to their request. On the third Sabbath I preached before a large assembly. I spoke about the state of our holy nation during these times in the

---

Yisrael (the unity of the Jewish people) (*EHS*, 228).

652   Lev. 19:1–20:27.

653   I.e., the Pharaoh.

654   *Pardes Yosef, op. cit.*, part 3, 236b. ובהגדה ישלא אחד בלבד עמד עלינו לכלותינו לא אחד בלבד, מה שלא יש אחדות בינינו, זה גורם לכלותינו.

655   The author left Budapest a number of times on various missions during the period late October 1942–February 1944. See biographical notes of R. Hayyim Menahem Teichthal, the son of the author, in *Mishneh Sakhir*, nonpaginated preface (Jerusalem, 1974), 8–9. See also above, 125, n. 236.

656   Yiddish, for a small prayer and study room.

countries of Europe with such emotion and outpouring of the heart, that all those present wept. The thrust of my discourse was that we have no other alternative to being restored from this bitter exile, except—when the Lord will set us free from this bitter exile—to return to our Holy Land. Upon every Jew rests this sacred responsibility, to make the utmost efforts to leave the lands of exile and return to the bosom of our mother, which is Eretz Yisrael. This was the intention of the Almighty, bless His Name, in bringing us presently to this bitter exile—so to arouse us from the slumber of exile, and for us to desire and long to return to the estate of our fathers. I also shared with them the words of our sacred rabbi, the devoted servant of the Lord, R. Eliyahu of Greiditz,[657] of blessed memory, cited in the work of the *gaon* and *hasid* the author of the volume *Nefesh Hayah* (which I cited earlier):[658]

> The fact that the greatest of *tzadikim* [righteous] are also among those opposed to mass settlement of Eretz Yisrael, is only because of the increase of the *kelipot*,[659] Heaven forbid, who wish to delay this,[660] since they, the *kelipot*, are aware that their destiny is at stake."[661]

If this holy *gaon* expressed himself thus, during a quiet period for Jews, how much more so [is this position valid] when the violent storms of exile strike us in repeated waves? Can we be comforted by anything other than our precious Land? Nevertheless, we find even now those who refuse and oppose her. Can the human mind possibly account for such a thing, unless it can be explained by the increase of the *kelipot*, Heaven forbid? . . .[662]

These words aroused this *hasid* against me with a zealous passion.

---

657 See above, 33, n. 106.

658 *EHS*, 9.

659 See above, 33, n. 107.

660 The abandonment of the lands of exile.

661 The unholy forces in the universe are dependent upon the impurities inherent in exile for their own existence.

662 The author laments the loss of his people in exile, pleading for the return of the scattered remnant "to the precious Land of our desire." *EHS*, 229.

Thus on a subsequent Shabbat, which also coincided with a *yartzeit,*[663] he prevented me from leading the *Musaf* [additional] service on the Sabbath since he was the *gabbai*[664] of the *Bet HaMidrash* [the small prayer-study congregation]. He indicated that someone else had prior claim. Eventually it became evident that there was no truth to this. This was simply an emotional response of opposition to my discourse. In fact, many clashed with him over this matter. (Indeed on the following Sabbath, which coincided with the blessing of the new month of *Av,*[665] they honored me by inviting me to bless the new month and lead the congregation in the *Musaf* prayers. This I accepted. He, however, had already succeeded [in preventing my leading the prayers].)

The following Monday morning, in the week of the portion *Matot-Mas'ei*[666] good tidings arrived in the synagogue concerning changing developments in the world.[667] There was joy and happiness among Jews[668] because we recognized in this news the beginning of the

---

663　The anniversary of someone's death; in this context likely the death of a close relative. Accordingly, the man observing the *yartzeit* leads the services in the synagogue.

664　An unpaid lay elected official of the congregation who, among other tasks, distributes the honors, especially the leading of the services and being called to the Torah reading.

665　Probably July 28, 1943. The 3rd chapter of *EHS* was written between February and September 1943.

666　Num. 30:2–36:13. This reference and further remarks below are puzzling. The week of Sunday July 29–Saturday 6 August coincides with the portion of *Devarim,* i.e., Deut. 1:1–3:22. Since the volume was completed on November 18, 1943, references to July 1944 are out of the question. Neither could this refer to July 1942, since the author did not arrive in Budapest until late October 1942. See *Mishneh Sakhir, op. cit.,* paginated p. 8 of biographical preface.

667　Possible reference to three major setbacks to the enemy in late July 1943. On the Italian front, the Axis forces were suffering heavy losses. Mussolini was deposed as premier of Italy on July 25th. Late July also witnessed some of the most massive Allied bombardments of major German cities, especially Hamburg and Berlin. Third, a major summer offensive by the Russians especially in the Orel Salient occured on July 26th. Late July led to a general retreat by German armies on the eastern front. Any of these developments could signal a change in fortunes to the beleaguered Jews in Slovakia and Hungary.

668　Cf. Est. 8:17.

redemption. None of the services held that day included the *tahanun*[669] due on this festive day. At that moment we felt the joy exactly of the Jews in the days of Mordechai and Esther.[670] After the various prayer services were completed, we remained in the *Bet HaMidrash* and discussed the events. I stood amongst a group of elderly people and young ones as well, truly God-fearing and imbued with a genuine hasidic spirit, a seed blessed by the Almighty[671] and the image of God reflected upon their faces. I said to them: "Now that the redemption which approaches has begun, every Jew must recognize his obligation to God and to his holy people by leaving this impure land and seeking to return to our Holy Land. Only then will this bitter exile which swept over us, not have been in vain. But if we remain in this atmosphere among the nations, all this will have been without purpose and to no avail. To this, one of the listeners replied: "It is not so! The *rebbe* does not agree on the matter of Eretz Yisrael." He said further: "The reason that our fellow Jews in Hungary have been saved[672] is due to their not being involved in the movement to build the Land."

Our heart truly pains us as we have to listen to so many fools who speak, saying that the Holy One, blessed be He, is compassionate with our fellow Jews who dwell in Hungary because they rejected the movement to build the Land and did not cooperate on its behalf. May the Almighty spare us from such opinions! Go see the extent of their obstinacy. With such people one should not argue at all. Solomon

---

669 Penitential prayers recited immediately after the repetition of the *Shmoneh Esrei* benedictions, but deleted on the Sabbath, festivals and joyous events. The author may have erred as to the exact day in the week of July 28th. Monday, August 1, 1943, would have coincided with the new month of *Av*, where the *tahanun* prayers would have been omitted in any event.

670 See n. 667, above.

671 Cf. Isa. 61:9, 65:23.

672 The Germans invaded Hungary in mid-March 1944, more than seven months after this episode occurred. Further, from March 9, 1942 to March 17, 1944, Hungary was led by Prime Minister Miklos Kallay, who pragmatically began to draw nearer to the Allied cause in 1943 and provided some protection to the Jewish population. See above, 125, n. 239. This was interpreted by the anti-Zionist factions as a reward for their efforts. For a less favorable evaluation of Kallay, see Bela Vago, "Germany and the Jewish Policy of the Kallay Government," in Randolph L. Braham (ed.), *Hungarian Jewish Studies*, 2 (New York, 1969), 183–210.

referred to them [when he remarked: "Do not answer a fool in accord with his folly [else you will become like him]."[673] Yet the young men [among the spectators] agreed with him, claiming that there are many sinners in Eretz Yisrael and one must not have contact with them. Similar arguments were presented, and I was unable to convince them of my position in spite of the counterarguments which I presented. They were united [in their opposition] because their *rebbe* was opposed to it. To this I responded: "True, your *rebbe* is a great man among giants. Be aware, however, that the Rebbe of Gur[674] is no less a great *gaon* and a sacred man of God, credited with many thousands of scholars and pious people under his influence. He taught: if many of the pious and God-fearing would gather in Eretz Yisrael, they would thereby reinforce the sanctity of the Land.

I have now heard that the holy *gaon*, our R. Yosef Hayyim Sonnenfeld of blessed memory,[675] rabbi of Eretz Yisrael, also stated this to the *gaon*, the *tzadik*, our teacher Fishel Sofer Sussman of blessed memory,[676] chief judge of the rabbinic court of the Jewish community here:[677] if many of the God-fearing will gather there, they will [by that act] strengthen the sanctity of the Land. He said the following: "You shall share in the goodness of Jerusalem.[678] It is not sufficient to be on the outside criticizing the Land and its inhabitants. One must enter and strengthen the sanctity of the Land.[679] Therefore your arguments are not valid." Nevertheless, they could not be persuaded to change their

---

673   Prov. 26:4.

674   See above, 121, n. 210 and 189, n. 396.

675   1849–1932, a great scholar and rabbi of the Orthodox community in Jerusalem, especially active in the Old City; pupil of R. Abraham Sofer and opponent of R. A.I. Kook on the issue of separation of the Orthodox community from Zionist and non-Orthodox bodies.

676   Ephraim Fishel (Viktor) Sofer Sussman (1887–1942), chief judge of the rabbinic court in "Pest" from 1914.

677   Budapest.

678   Ps. 128:5.

679   Fishel Sofer Sussman, *Eileh Mas'ei* (Budapest, 1927) 13–14. The volume records his visit to the Holy Land, May 3–June 1, 1926.

mind. . . .[680]

So I have shown you that there is nothing new under the sun.[681] My fate has been no different from that of my predecessors, including those greater and better than I.[682] Why, therefore, should I be surprised if in our own time are to be found those who speak against me for my commitment to the sacred task? Nevertheless, I shall not be dissuaded from my work, having found support and help from our rabbis past and recent, referred to above. May my hope provide me the strength so that I may find other courageous allies who will declare in response to my work: "Be encouraged!" and who will, with God's help, offer support to my efforts and acknowledge the great significance of all this. Especially [is this necessary] in view of the growing power of the *kelipah* which is diverting the hearts of the *tzadikim*, convincing them to abandon the positive [aspects of this program]. . . .

When I once appeared before the assembled and presented a discourse here in Congregation Linat HaTzedek, I explained the meaning of what King David of blessed memory exclaimed in Psalms 51:[683] "May it be Your will to favor Zion; may You build the walls of Jerusalem. Then You will desire sacrifices of righteousness, with burnt offerings and complete burnt offerings; then shall they offer bullocks upon Your altar." This is difficult considering the text in the tractate *Shevu'ot,*[684] which attaches no importance to the size of offerings made before Heaven. "It is the same whether one gives much or little as long as he directs his heart to [his Father in] Heaven."[685] If so, why is

---

680 The author proceeds to offer Biblical documentation of selfish motives which interferred with the settlement of the Land (i.e., the spies in Num. 13 : 1–33, Num. 14:1–45 ; and Joshua in Jos. 11:18 based on the midrash in NumR. 22) in comparison to the selfless love of Moses for his people and Land. (*EHS*, 231–32).

681 Eccl. 1:9.

682 The author documents the struggles of scholars and religious leaders, e.g. the 14th-century author of the volume *Kaftor Vaferah*, Estori Yitzhak ben Moseh HaParhi, R. Yonah Dov Blumberg of Dvinsk (referred to above, 141 , n. 53.), R. Yisrael Yehoshua Kutner, in his support reference to the volume *Drishat Zion* of R. Zvi Kalisher (see above, 156, n. 149).

683 Verses 20–21.

684 15a *vs.* 14 in *EHS*.

685 Ibid. מלמד שאחד המרבה ואחד הממעיט ובלבד שיכון את ליבו לאביו שבשמים. The

it written, "then shall they offer bullocks upon Your altar,"[686] as if wishing to bribe [the Almighty], Heaven forbid, with large offerings the size of bullocks? Let us first see, however, the words of our holy Rabbi of Lublin,[687] the righteous of blessed memory, commenting on the verse:[688] "Only with the following will Aaron enter into the sanctuary; with a young bull for a sin offering."

It is acknowledged that the very existence of the Jewish people was dependent upon the service of the high priest in the holy of holies.[689] If he properly fulfilled his task, then they would progress and succeed in every endeavor. If, on the other hand, Heaven forbid, there was some fault or defect [in the service of the high priest], then this could cause a decline. Therefore, Satan and members of his entourage lie in ambush in order to encourage some fault in his tasks. [Consequently] the high priest was compelled to attach a sword to his thigh and to reinforce the soldiers in order to defeat the *sitra ahra*.[690] For this purpose he required much strength. It is known that the strongest among animals is a young bull. This is the meaning of the verse:"Only with the following will Aaron enter into the Sanctuary; with a young bull for a sin offering."[691] For a sin offering—that is to say in order to defeat [the domain of] sin which "lurks at the door,"[692] in order to cause the *tzadik* to fail in his task.[693] Therefore, Aaron was compelled to enter the sanctuary with the strength of a young bull."

As I indicated earlier, whenever Jews devoted themselves to the

---

problem of the size of an offering is introduced by way of the verse in Neh. 12:31. ואעמידה שתי תודות גדולות "I appointed two large thanksgiving [choirs and processions]."

686   Ps. 51:21.

687   R. Yaakov Yitzhak HaHozeh MiLublin. See above, 12, n. 52.

688   Lev. 16:3.

689   The annual rite of the high priest on Yom Kippur is described in Lev. 17.

690   *Lit.*, "the other side"; kabbalistic term for the domain of Satan and the demonic forces; see above, 119, n. 199.

691   Lev. 16:3.

692   Cf. Gen., 4:7.

693   The Mishnah anticipates this concern and describes the precautions taken. Yoma 2a. See also *Midrash HaGadol*, Leviticus, *Aharei Mot* (Jerusalem, 1975), 464–65.

restoration of Zion from the dust and to rebuilding the Land, they encountered opposition. Many obstacles were placed in their path. The person perfect in faith, however, must take courage. This was the intent of King David of blessed memory: "May it be Your will to favor Zion; may You build the walls of Jerusalem."[694] Namely, when the Almighty will wish to rebuild Zion and Jerusalem, stimulating people to act accordingly, and Satan will oppose this with obstacles, "then You will desire,"[695] that is to say, God will want "sacrifices of righteousness, burnt offerings and complete burnt offerings."[696] As a burnt offering and a complete burnt offering is totally consumed upon the altar,[697] so it is necessary for the people who dedicate themselves to the building of the Land to do so with their complete strength and soul. As with the complete burnt offering, their devotion to the task must be total. "Then shall they offer bullocks upon Your altar."[698] By this is inferred the need to join the work with the strength of a young bull in order to defeat all of those who delay and interfere with this sacred work, which is as precious in the eyes of God as the altar. Then it will be considered as if their work was [fulfilling the requirements of] a complete burnt offering. Note this well.

In the volume *Shimru Mishpat*[699] of the kabbalist, the *gaon* R. Akiva Yosef,[700] of blessed memory, the author of *Lev Ha'Ivri*,[701] I read the author's description of what occurred to him when he was active on behalf of developing settlement in Eretz Yisrael. These are his words:

---

694   Ps. 51:20.

695   Ps. 51:21.

696   Ibid.

697   Lev. 1:9.

698   Ps. 51:21.

699   Jerusalem, 1914. Discourses and poetry supporting the plans for the develpment of an autonomous religious community in Eretz Yisrael.

700   R. Akiva Yosef Schlesinger. See above, 113, n. 159.

701   Pub. 1865. Commentary on the ethical will and testament of his teacher R. Moshe Sofer, the Hatam Sofer. Volume 2 includes learned polemics against assimilationist and anti-Orthodox groups in the wake of the 19th century emancipation movements.

And when I was involved with the matters of settlement in Eretz Yisrael for the purpose of finding in Eretz Yisrael a place for the Lord, an abode for the Mighty One of Jacob,[702] I crossed the borders of Eretz Yisrael. Doing so I rode upon my donkey from Za'anan (the name of the place)[703] to Jerusalem, "may it be rebuilt and reestablished speedily in our own days."[704] When I crossed into the territory of [the tribe of] Benjamin I pondered upon it (as in *imru bilvavchem*)[705] and my heart pounded. It seemed as if an elderly distinguished man approached me and told me: So you want to provide settlement in Eretz Yisrael for sinners and abominable individuals, for licentious people and rebels? I was taken aback. I stared at him incredulously, exclaiming: "It seems that you are in reality the prince of Edom.[706] Previously you were an old and foolish king. Presently there is no longer a king in France. You remain merely an old fool. And it is written: "Do not reply to a fool in accordance with his folly, [else you will become like him.]"[707] I rode on singing a melody.

(Note the text[708] where he indicates that he composed a melody in enthusiasm of the sacred project of settling Eretz Yisrael so that he would not despair due to those villains who persecuted and pursued him.)

As I indicated previously,[709] this was also my reponse to the arguments of certain narrow-minded *hasidim* here in Hungary who claimed that our Jewish brethren who lived in Slovakia and Poland were the victims of the wrath because they were involved in settlement and building of the Land, while those who lived in Hungary were necessarily saved

---

702   Cf. Ps. 132:5; Gen. 49:24.

703   Possibly Za'anan or Zanan, in the territory of Judah. See Jos. 15:37, Mic. I:11.

704   Abbreviated (תובב״א) תבנה ותכון במהרה בימינו אמן.

705   Ps. 4:5.

706   Possible reference to the angel who wrestled with Jacob and according to GenR. 77:2, symbolic of obstruction.

707   Prov. 26:4.

708   Schlesinger, *Shimru Mishpat, op. cit.*, 43b.

709   See above, 228–232.

because they refused [to cooperate in this venture]. Woe to the ears
who hear this! Woe to the generation who have become so stupid
and who were developed and educated in such a futile fashion which
permits them to pass such perverted judgment against thousands and
tens of thousands of Jews who were killed sanctifying the holy Name.
They also degrade the value of the commandment to settle in Eretz
Yisrael which our sages of blessed memory elevated and compared[710]
to the entire Torah.[711] To all this, one can only respond: "Do not
reply to a fool in accordance with his folly,"[712] as stated by the wisest
of all men,[713] and may God forgive them.

During the summer of 5703[714] while living here in the capital,
there was an unusually oppressive heat wave. I spent a few weeks in
the Arta Sanitarium hospital, also known as Varos Meyer,[715] to enjoy
some fresh air. It is located on a mountain where the air is clean. On
the Sabbath of the [weekly] portion of Re'eh[716] I was urged by colleagues
to deliver timely words of admonition in keeping with the blessing of
the new month of Elul,[717] and the premessianic suffering which we
have presently endured. Two scholars, sons of saintly fathers, insisted
that I not refuse, since I had originally declined to accept this honor,
for reasons of my own. They persisted, however, and I could no
longer decline. Prior to ascending [to the pulpit] to preach, these two

---

710 *EHS* Jerusalem edition properly replaces "compared" (והשווה) with "degraded"
(ושפלוהו) in the original.

711 *Sifrei* on Deut. 12:29 section 28. מכאן אמרו: שקולה מצות ישיבת א"י כנגד כל המצות
שבתורה. "They hereby concluded: The mitzvah of settling Eretz Yisrael is equal to all
the mitzvot in the Torah." Though the midrash does not explain the reason for the
equation, it may be tied hermeneutically to the previous verse: "You will dispossess
them and settle in their land" (Deut. 12:29). "Be careful to heed all the commandments
that I enjoin upon you" (Deut. 12:28). See also *Sifrei* on Deut. 11:18, which links the
performance of the commandments to the Land of Israel.

712 Prov. 26:4.

713 Solomon.

714 1943.

715 See above, 149, n. 110.

716 Deut. 11:26–16:17. The date was Saturday, August 28, 1943.

717 The month devoted to spiritual preparation for the High Holy Days. In 1943,
the month of Elul was commemorated on August 30th and September 1st.

scholars stipulated that I not raise issues pertaining to the settlement of Eretz Yisrael.

I responded to one of them, acknowledging his Torah scholarship that he occupied a position of rabbinic authority in a large Godly community, that he acted piously towards his Maker, that he was righteous and innocent, consistent in his sincerity both inside and outside his home. I said to him: "I know that you speak to me sincerely in requesting that I not refer to Eretz Yisrael in my discourse. [See below]* Yet I will argue whether you are actually justified in your refusal to listen to a public discourse which stresses devotion to the Land and which is of the highest priority." I told him that I will prove for him that this talk is all a plan of the Satan,[718] Heaven forbid. For who is a greater authority than the author of *Tzemah HaShem LiTzvi*[719] who was among the great disciples of our rabbi R. Beer.

*[The following aside appears in *EHS* 235–36 below the regular narrative.] Should the Torah not garb itself in sackcloth[720] [upon hearing such objections]? Shall Eretz Yisrael not be upset at this affront to its honor, as indeed would a mother whose children insult her. So it is when one is prohibited from raising one's voice in public in order to encourage those who support her [Eretz Yisrael] and raise her from the dust as we are commanded by the Holy One, blessed be He, and as I have shown above, citing at length the teachings of our sages of blessed memory, those sublime souls of previous and recent generations. Yet these pious people in our time put her to shame and degrade her to the extent that one is not permitted to publicly expound [on the virtues of] the settlement of the Land. And if by chance one will courageously speak up[721] and will not be afraid to tell the truth, then they will prohibit [people] from listening to his exposition. More than once have I heard them say that because of those who were involved in the settlement of

---

718 מהס״ם from Sammael, i.e., the devil, Satan, the Adversary; see Isa. 4:2.

719 Reference to R. Zvi Hirsh of Darborna. Hasidic master (d. 1802), a disciple of R. Dov Ber, the Maggid of Mezeritch and teacher of R. Menahem Mendel of Kossof. The first edition of the volume was published in Berdichev in 1828.

720 Cf. Jer. 4:8.

721 *Lit,* "if one will set his face like flint." Cf. Isa. 50:7.

the Land were thousands and tens of thousands of our Jewish brethren punished. Is this not an insult against our sacred Torah? Does this not cause grief and anguish to the holy Shekhinah which represents [the sphere] of *malkhut*,[722] as does Eretz Yisrael, the mother of Israel?[723] Woe unto the ears who hear this! Even to pronounce such words is a geat sin in its own right. Now should not anyone who is the least bit intelligent compare this to the episode of Joshua and Caleb[724] who did not fear, telling the truth in public against the entire congregation? This included the tribal chiefs who removed themselves [from the sanctity of leadership] by preventing Israel from ascending to Eretz Yisrael, as cited by the *gaon*, and kabbalist R. Akiva Yosef of blessed memory[725] in the commentary on *Tanna DeBei Eliyahu*, based on the *Zohar*. There the spies claim that "here in the desert we have the manna and are not distracted with the need to earn a livelihood. We have the time and conditions to devote to study and worship." This would not be so if they enter the Land and be compelled to engage in working the Land. This would distract from devotion to God. So Joshua and Caleb resisted them responding vehemently: "If the Lord is pleased with us, He will bring us unto that Land . . . only you must not rebel against the Lord . . . but the Lord is with us."[726] Yet what follows! "The whole community threatened to stone them."[727] It is described: "The Presence of the Lord appeared in the meeting tent [to all the Israelites]"[728]—and as Rashi comments, the cloud descended in order to save them,[729]—so will it be at all times when someone will defend the honor of the Land and will

---

722 See above, 50, n. 80; 193, n. 429.

723 See above, 8, n. 34

724 Num. 13:1–14:45

725 See above, 113, n. 159.

726 Num. 14:8–9.

727 Ibid. 10.

728 Ibid.

729 Rashi states: הענן ירד שם. "There the cloud descended." Based on the midrash: מלמד שהיו זורקין אבנים והענן מקבל "This teaches us that the cloud intercepted the stones which were thrown!"

not be swayed by the arguments of those who intrigue. To them[730] is
the verse addressed: "Do not respond to a fool according to his folly
[lest you become like him as well]."[731]

He was a holy person and awesome. His great stature is reflected in
his sacred volume.[732] He comments on the weekly portion of *Va'Era*, [733]
referring to the verse: "The Israelites would not listen to me; how
then should Pharaoh heed me, [a man of impeded speech!]"[734]

This is what he has to say: This [logic] is difficult [to accept]. After all,
the Israelites did not listen because "their spirits [were] crushed by
cruel bondage."[735] But Pharaoh, who was not burdened by all this,
should have listened to him. One may explain: Actually this mission [of
Moses] to the Israelites was needless, since surely they wanted the
Lord, blessed be His name, to redeem them. Why then was it at all
necessary for anyone to be sent? But this was the situation: It is written:"[So is] the word that issues from my mouth, it does not come back
to me unfulfilled [but] performs what I propose, achieves what I sent it
to do."[736] Nahmanides in the weekly portion of *Lekh [Lekha]*[737] comments:"Every good decree which emanates from the mouth of the Holy
One, blessed be He, must be similarly duplicated here below[738] in such
a manner that it cannot be obstructed by any agent who might desire to
do so."[739] It was clearly known to God that the Pharaoh would not
listen to these words. Then God's words would have come back unful-

---

730   The defenders of the Land.

731   Prov. 26:4 This completes the author's digression.

732   See above, 238, n. 719.

733   Ex. 6:2–9:35.

734   Ex. 6:12.

735   Ex. 6:9.

736   Isa. 55:11.

737   Gen. 12:1–17:27.

738   On this earth.

739   R. Zvi Hirsh's paraphrase of Nahmanides' comments on Gen. 12:6. ודע כי כל
גזירת עירין כאשר תצא מכח גזירה אל פועל דמיון תהיה הגזרה מתקיימת על כל פנים. Concerning
all decisions of "the guardian [angels, see Dan. 4:14]," know that when they proceed
from a potential decree to a symbolic act, the decree will in any case be effected.

filled. Consequently God saw to it that the Israelites would be told of the redemption first. Surely they would heed Moses' message of redemption. With their [positive] response they would duplicate a similar act which would compel Pharaoh to heed these words as well. Therefore Moses was taken aback when the Israelites did not respond to his effort at duplication. "How then should Pharaoh heed me?"[740]

Thus you can see when Moses came to Israel, the time for their redemption had come, as explained in the *Midrash Song of Songs* on the verse: "My beloved knocks [let me in, my own, my darling, my faultless dove!]"[741] Moses exclaimed to the Israelites "The time of your redemption has come."[742] Nevertheless, since "the attribute of Divine Justice[743] wished to delay [redemption]"[744] as it is known, Moses was first compelled to stage a symbolic act in order to subvert all the antagonists and obstructionists. This was accomplished by Moses speaking to the Israelites about redemption. They would then heed his words and accept them, as the verse eventually indicates.

"Then Moses and Aaron went and assembled all the elders of the Israelites. Aaron repeated all the words that the Lord had spoken to Moses . . . . and the people were convinced. When they heard that the Lord had taken note of the Israelites and that He had seen their plight, they bowed low in homage."[745] And the Israelites were indeed redeemed from the bondage in Egypt. This was all achieved because the Israelites listened to Moses as he related to them the subject of redemption. This symbolic act prevented the antagonists and

---

740 Conclusion of approximate citation by our author from *Tzemah HaShem LiTzvi* on Ex. 6:12.

741 Song 5:2.

742 The midrash describes the knocking of the beloved (God) upon the gates of redemption, dependent upon the readiness of Israel to but slightly open the gate of repentance. פתחי לי פתח אחד של תשובה כחודה של מחט ואני פותח לכם פתחים שיהיו עגלות וקרונות נכנסות בו. CantR. 5:3. "Open for me a slot of repentance the size of a needle, and I will uncover for you gaps through which wagons and coaches will enter."

743 *Midat hadin* as opposed to the attribute of Divine Compassion [*midat harahamim*].

744 See Sanh. 97b: מדת הדין מעכבת.

745 Ex. 4:29–31.

obstructionists from nullifying the decree of the Holy One, blessed be He. And the word which issues from His mouth shall not return unfulfilled. . . .[746]

On Monday of the portion of the weekly reading of *Eikev*[747] during the summer of the year 5703,[748] I went in the company of my colleague, the renowned *gaon* and outstanding scholar, the honorable teacher and rabbi, Yisrael Weltz,[749] senior *dayan*[750] of the local Jewish community, in order to welcome the great Rabbi of Belz, *tzadik* of our generation, may he live a good and long life, our teacher and rabbi, the godly and saintly Reb Ahrele.[751] May the Lord help him. May the crown sparkle forever upon him who has graced this capital city following the difficult and dangerous events which he experienced because of the sins of this generation. Because of the Lord's compassion for him he arrived here, having escaped from the decrees of Poland, a firebrand plucked from the flames.[752] Before proceeding to a private audience [with the *rebbe*][753] we greeted his younger brother, the holy

---

746   The author draws the analogy with contemporary events. The "due time" (Isa. 60:22) has come for redemption. As in Egypt, *midat hadin* delays the final event. Public response of Jews to discourses on redemption and matters related to the rebuilding of Eretz Yisrael will similarly nullify the destructive plans of the modern obstructionists (*EHS*, 237–40).

747   Deut. 7:12–11:25.

748   August 16, 1943.

749   See above, 10, n. 42.

750   Rabbinic judge.

751   R. Aaron Rokeach (1880–1957), the fourth Admor of the Belz hasidic dynasty founded by his great-grandfather R. Shalom of Belz (d. 1852). The rebbe arrived in Budapest on May 23, 1943 following a harrowing escape from the Bochnia workcamp near Cracow. See Bezalel Landau and Nathan Ortner, *HaRav HaKadosh MiBelz* (Jerusalem, 1967), 100–24. The farewell message of the rebbe, presented by his brother R. Mordechai before a huge throng the day (January 16, 1944) prior to their departure from Budapest to Eretz Yisrael, has been the subject of intense debate because of its assuring and optimistic message that Hungarian Jewry would not suffer the fate of their martyred brothers in Europe. See the polemical "*HaRabanit MeStropkov al Havtahat HaRabbi MiBelz Ushtei Hashkafot Sotrot al Lekah HaGzerot*," by Mendel Peikach in *Kivunim* 24 (August 1984), 59–72.

752   Cf. Zech. 3:2; Amos 4:11.

753   The privilege of meeting the hasidic master in private ביחידות is referred to by the author as לפני ולפנים, *lit.* "in the innermost interior."

gaon R. Motele,[754] the senior judge of the [rabbinic] court of Bilgurei, may he live a long and good life. I knew him from my early youth during the calm and peaceful years before World War I. During the months of Elul and Tishrei[755] and when they resided in Ratzfert,[756] I used to sit in the shadow of the inner sanctum of the holy R. Yissakhar Ber,[757] may the righteous be remembered as a blessing, may his merit protect us and all of Israel. This holy personage discussed with us the terrible current events concerning our brethren in Poland which he personally witnessed, and how he was rescued by God by means of marvelous miracles. One subject led to another, and the discussion turned to Eretz Yisrael. Yisrael Weltz, mentioned earlier, told him that I am involved in this and in the process of writing a book on the subject. He[758] then proceeded to relate that the holy rabbi, the Rabbi of Israel, the divine personage, the Maggid and Admor of Trisk,[759] of blessed memory, wrote in his sacred work *Magen Avraham*[760] [Shield of Abraham], commenting on the weekly portion of *Va'erah*,[761] that the future redemption will take place by natural means.[762] Therefore, we must prepare all that is necessary to achieve this process. The Lord will then successfully complete the task for us. I regret that I do not have this sacred volume in my possession to actually see his

---

754   1902 –1949.

755   Approximately September and October, the period of the High Holy Days.

756   See above, 73, n. 81.

757   The grandson of R. Shalom of Belz and father of R. Aaron. He died in 1927.

758   R. Mordechai Rokeach.

759   R. Àvraham Twersky (d. 1887), grandson of R. Nahum of Chernobil (the Russian city—later the scene of the nuclear disaster) the founder of the Chernobil hasidic dynasty and pupil of the Baal Shem Tov.

760   Lublin: 1887, devoted to discourses on the weekly biblical reading of the Sabbath and holidays.

761   Ex. 6:2–9:35.

762   On Ex. 6:7 "And I will take you to be My people, and I will be your God" והלשון ילקחתי׳ היא נגד גאולה רביעית לבוא בב״י . . . אבל גאולה העתידה יהיה איה״ש עפ״י דה״ט [דבר הטבע]. "The expression 'And I will take you' refers to the fourth redemption of the Jewish people which will come quickly in our days . . . but this future redemption will, God willing, take place by natural means."

sacred words, but I trust the veracity of the holy rabbi...[763]

I will now direct my words to the *golus Yid*.[764] Especially to you, the *golus Yid*, who are so attached to the clods of earth in the lands of exile in which you live from the time of your expulsion. [So much so are you attached] that should you be beaten a full day with terrible blows and should he who beats you but let up for a moment, you are prepared to be appeased at this very place. You do not consider the morrow, at which time the blows will return. There is an instant "tomorrow," and one which arrives in time to come.[765] In this fashion, have you spent your days and years absorbing repeated blows during two thousand years in exile. And still you have not learned from the past in order to recognize the future. It appears to me that this was the intent of our sages of blessed memory when they declared in the midrash on the verse "Israel does not know, My people take no thought:"[766] "Israel knew not in the past, and My people take no thought with regard to the future."[767] Thus the prophets lament the limited perspective of people in exile. They do not learn from the past and fool themselves [in believing] that the future in exile will be better. They, therefore, do not consider returning to the estate of their forefathers. Since *they* do not care, neither does Heaven assist them in returning them to the Land. As I indicated previously[768] in reference to Jacob our Father, if he had not insisted on returning [to

---

763 R. Mordechai Rokeach. There follows a lengthy digression describing the exceptional qualities of the Maggid of Trisk as they emerge from the hasidic folklore *EHS*, 241–44. The author summarizes previously cited sources which emphasize the consequences for those who denigrate Eretz Yisrael as did the spies sent by Moses during Israel's sojourn in the desert. Like the mistaken spies, the detractors of Eretz Yisrael will not be privileged to taste its fruits and benefit from its rewards. *EHS*, 244–245.

764 *Lit.*, "Galut Jew," Yiddish for the Jew with an exilic mentality, about to be depicted by the author.

765 *Tanh.* 13 on the verse "And when tomorrow, your son asks you saying" (Ex. 13:14). See also *Mekhilta, Bo*, 28.

766 Isa. 1:3.

767 *Yalkut Shimoni* II, 387.

768 See above, 104–106.

pray for Israel's redemption], Heaven would not have assisted him.[769] This suggests how we should respond in exile, as our rabbi the Mabit, of blessed memory and the words of our rabbi the Hidah, cited previously,[770] direct us to do. Namely, our return to the Land depends only upon dedication to this [task]. And from the positive, one hears the negative.[771]

As it is said, "The greatest tragedy of the Jewish people is their inability to learn the lessons of the bitter and tragic events which they have endured. Therein lies the Jewish tragedy."[772] "Israel knew not in the past, and My people take no thought with regard to the future."[773] A word to the wise.

I am further astonished at you, *golus Yid*. Your eyes are so covered that you do not see what is going on around you. You observe how your brothers are beaten and tortured with blows and oppressive suffering. Yet you are not at all moved. You see the blood of your brothers spilled upon the earth like water and you are not terrified because you believe that fortune will yet smile upon you. You think that these things will not come upon you and take effect since you live in a secure place. You believe yourself to be immune thinking, "I shall be safe."[774] May your words come true and may it be God's will.

However, *golus Yid*, be silent and listen![775] Open your eyes, and note that your brothers who sustained this calamity of the sword and destruction, whose possessions were plundered,[776] they too lived in a safe place and secure dwellings, just like yourselves. Eventually their fortune turned for the worse, Heaven forbid.

This was their fate. What is the source of your brazen confidence

---

769 *Lit.*, Since he *cared*, Heaven did not intervene to stop him.

770 Ibid.

771 *Sifra, Eikev* 11:18; NumR. 9:47.

772 The text within quotation marks appears in German with Yiddish-Hebrew characters.

773 *Yalkut Shimoni* II, 387.

774 Cf. Deut. 29:18.

775 Cf. Deut. 27:9.

776 Cf. Est. 3:13; 8:11.

that you will be spared presently to the extent that you do not fear
and your heart does not display concern for the suffering of your
friends? Can we not demonstrate that you do not really share in his
suffering? After all, when you are approached to contribute from
your own pocket to relieve the suffering of the victims you give what
your heart permits. But analyze the extent of your contribution. Does
it approximate the suffering of the victims? Is it compatible with your
ability to give in accordance with what you have been blessed with by
God? Therefore you have not fulfilled your obligation with your gift.
This is all due to your lack of brotherhood and love for Israel which
would have given you the ability to truly empathize with your suffering
brother, as in the case of Moses our teacher. "He saw an Egyptian
beating a Hebrew, one of his kinsman."[777] Is not "one of his kinsman"
superfluous [in the verse]?[778] Further, the beginning of the verse
mentioned "he went out to his kinsfolk." But the verse teaches us that
Moses felt the pain of the Egyptian beating of the Hebrew as if he
actually was one of his brothers. Therefore he exposed himself to
danger in order to save the oppressed from his oppressor, without
consideration of the consequences. This is the Jewish dimension of
rescue. So should it have been in our own time, on behalf of those
who escaped from their place and country of hell to another country,
to save their lives and those of their household, "from the fowler's
trap,"[779] like "an antelope caught in a net,"[780] which was thrown over
them in their country. Instead of reaching out to them with compassion
and great concern, they [the refugees] were cooly received and treated
as a burden, with the exception of a few individuals who truly dedicated
themselves to the rescue of their escaping brethren. However, the
leaders and those who sit in high places remained cold [to their
plight], as if the matter was of no concern to them. They showed
contempt and lack of feeling for the suffering of Israel. Furthermore,
during this era of suffering directed against all of Israel in the countries

---

777   Ex. 2:11.

778   איש עברי "a Hebrew" already suggests מאחיו "one of his kinsman."

779   Cf. Ps. 91:3 מפח יקוש.

780   Cf. Isa. 51:20 כתוא מכמר vs. ומתוא מכמר.

of Europe, when Israel has been decreed as open to plunder and abandoned in life and property, when one would expect an all-out effort, we painfully witness instead that the rich and able celebrate "peacefully in their citadels."[781] They do not move from their places even the slightest. They do not genuinely share in the pains of Israel.[782] . . .

It seems clear that, with the help of God, the intention of Rav[783] was to teach the following: Whenever others are in distress, and someone has his health and wealth spared, that person should not declare "I have peace of mind. What do I care about the problems of others?"[784] See [the tractate] Ta'anit, chapter 1. When the community is indeed immersed in difficulties and an individual is spared, should this person declare, "I have peace of mind," and not feel the distress of the community? Ministering angels place their hands upon his head and curse him [saying] that he will not be privileged to see the period of consolation of that community. Note the citation.[785] (I have no volume of Talmud before me to provide the citation.) Rav taught similarly. Though one is not directly involved with the troubles of others, he nevertheless is expected to empathize with their travail to the extent that he is in fact one of them. He is prepared to sacrifice his soul, body and wealth for them. . . . He will do all in his power, and even beyond that in his power, to rescue them. He will not be

---

781   Cf. Ps. 122:7 שלוה בארמנותם vs. ששלוה בארמנותיך. שלוה בארמנותיך.

782   This powerful condemnation of the privileged Jewish classes of Budapest for their indifference to the plight of their fellow Jews in late 1943 is only matched by the vigorous accusations in the desperate letters of R. Michael Dov Ber Weissmandel of Nitra, recorded in his classic *Min HaMetzar* (Jerusalem, 1960), against the indifference of the Jews in the free world to the fate of their brethren in the Holocaust. Their indifference is contrasted with the selfless dedication of Moses the lawgiver in responding to the plight of his brethren in slavery, despite his protected privileged position in the court of the Pharaoh (*EHS*, 247–48).

783   Cited by R. Bardela the son of Tavyuma in Hag. 5a interpreting Deut. 31:17.

784   A free rendering of Ta'an. 11a אל יאמר אדם אלך תניא אידך בזמן שהצבור שרויין בצער. לביתי ואכל ואשתה ושלום עליך נפשי. "Another [Baraita] taught: When the community is in distress one should not declare: 'I will retire to my home, I will eat and drink and all will be well with me!'"

785   Ibid.

concerned with his own safety. He would respond as if he himself
were in distress.

Said Rav: "He who is not within the 'concealed Face'!⁷⁸⁶ namely, he
who does not feel part of the concealment of the Face from others, or
identifying himself with them in their travail, and he who is not
included in 'they shall be ready prey,'⁷⁸⁷ namely, when the gentiles
plunder another's assets, and he who sees or hears of this and does
not react as if the gentiles were plundering his own assets, he is not
one of them, he is not one of the seed of Israel."⁷⁸⁸ The religious
standards of Moses our teacher, of blessed memory [were of this
dedicated kind]. He placed himself often in a situation of danger.
Whenever he saw one of his Hebrew brethren in trouble, he related
to him as one would to his own brother, his own flesh and blood. He
therefore knew no bounds with regard to his dedication to the rescue
of the children of Israel. This is how every Jew should act.

As our sages of blessed memory taught in *Midrash Rabbah Leviticus*⁷⁸⁹
on the verse "Israel are scattered sheep":⁷⁹⁰ Israel is compared to
sheep. Just as when sheep (who are sensitive by nature) are beaten on
one part, the entire body responds, so the people of Israel. When an
Israelite is beaten the entire people respond to him.⁷⁹¹ This is the
correct way for Jews [to respond].

While involved in community affairs I was honored by the good
leaders of the community, in the city of Be'ke'scsaba,⁷⁹² to present a

---

786   The concealing of God's goodness and mercy from His people הסתר פנים as in
Deut. 31:17.

787   Ibid.

788   Hag. 5a.

789   4:6.

790   Jer. 50:17.

791   Our author deviates from the parable as it actually appears in the Midrash.
למה נמשלו ישראל לשה? מה שה הזה לוקה על ראשו או באחד מאבריו וכל אבריו מרגישין, כך הן
ישראל. אחד מהן חוטא וכולן מרגישין (italics ed.) "Why is Israel compared to a lamb? Just
as a lamb, when its head or one of its limbs aches all the other limbs react, so it is
with Israel. One of its members sin and all the others are affected."

792   City in the Bekes district on the Romanian-Hungarian border. Following the
German occupation of the area in the Spring of 1944 most of the 2,500 Jewish
residents were murdered in Auschwitz. *Pinkas HaKehillot: Hungaria* (Jerusalem, Yad

discourse in the synagogue on the previous weekly Scripture reading of *Korah*.[793] I explained the Masoretic tradition[794] of the double use of the term *padoh*.[795] First [in the context of]: "but you surely shall have the first-born of man redeemed."[796] The second [instance]: "A brother certainly cannot redeem a man, or pay his ransom to God; the price of life is too high and so one ceases to be forever."[797] One should carefully investigate the language of the verse. "But you surely shall have the first-born of man redeemed."[798] It should have read: "[You surely shall have our first-born son redeemed], as it is written in the weekly portion of *Bo*.[799] But it seems to me, as it is clear, when we see one of our Jewish brethren in difficulty, may God have mercy, and we have the opportunity to save him, then we are compelled to so do. The verse in Scripture clearly states: "You shall not stand idly by your neighbor's blood."[800] In these times, however, the suffering which we have endured is more complex than those of former times. Presently there is a decree prohibiting any assistance to those who escape in order to save their lives. Severe punishment is in store for anyone who extends a helping hand. Such a decree complicates the suffering for the fugitive. Not only was he compelled to abandon everything and make one's escape, he also faced the prospect that none would be prepared to offer him safety in their home. Where shall he go, away from his personal travail? But as it is surely known, nothing in this world occurs by chance. It is not without purpose that the Holy One, blessed be He, permitted such a decree. In fact this very thing emanates from Heaven. Let no man imagine, however, that Heaven approved

---

Vashem, 1975), 180–82.

793 Num. 16:1–18:32. Likely reference to Shabbat, July 3, 1943.

794 The accepted fixed biblical text in its external form in Jewish tradition.

795 Redeemed, in absolute infinitive form. The author links the two occurences of this form in the Pentateuch.

796 Num. 18:15.

797 Ps. 49:8–9.

798 I.e., "Your first-born son" rather than the "first-born of man," an apparently unnecessarily cumbrous locution.

799 Ex. 10:1–13:16.

800 Lev. 19:16.

this decree in order to exempt the Jewish person from rescuing his comrade. Not at all! Absolutely no! The contrary is true. Heaven wished this [to come to pass] in order to heighten [the challenge of the] test, and so that the rescue will be performed with genuine self-sacrifice. As we know, when severe Divine Justice is loosed in the world, it will not be nullified and silenced except by means of self-sacrifice. Therefore, God brought it about in this manner. The decree which was enacted [purposely] prohibited assisting refugees in order to fulfill the precept with absolute self-sacrifice. But it was not at all intended to exempt them [from fulfilling their responsibility]. It is also known that any repetition of an expression [in Scripture] directs [the reader] towards an intensified commitment, even to [fulfill the mandate] one hundred times. As an example of the interpretation of our sages of blessed memory of [the expression]: "Drive away the mother" [*shale'ah teshalah*][801] and additional examples.

It is also well-known that Israel is referred to as the "first-born,"[802] since they are the first-born among the nations. This is the intention of the Masoretic text: "But you surely shall have the first-born of man redeemed,"[803] to indicate that Israel is the first-born among "man" (*adam*).

As we know, the nations of the world are called "man."[804] Do not believe that Heaven caused this decree prohibiting the rescue of refugees from another country in order to exempt you from this obligation.

---

801   The echoing of the root שלח (*sh'l'h*) emphasizes the precept of driving away the mother bird prior to removing the fledgling or eggs from the bird's nest. Deut. 22:6–7. Additional instances of reduplication in Scriptural expressions in Lev. 19:17; Ex. 23:5; Deut. 22:4; Ex. 22:25; and Deut. 15:14 are similarly interpreted in BM 31a.

802   Ex. 4:22 כה אמר ד' בני בכרי ישראל "Israel is my first-born son." Shab. 89b. See also ExR. 19:8 for the relationships of redemption of the Jewish people and the "first-born" status of the Messiah.

803   Num. 18:15.

804   Tosafot in AZ 3a, s.v. כהנים, discusses various opinions as to the application of the epithet "man" (האדם) to idol worshipers, based on the interpretation of Ezek. 34:31. See also BM 114b and Tosafot in Yev. 61. ור"ת מפרש דיש חילוק בין אדם להאדם דעובדי כוכבים בכלל האדם נינהו. "And Rabbenu Tam explains that there is a difference between the word *adam* and *ha'adam*, and idol worshipers are included within the term 'man.'"

Certainly not! On the contrary! "You shall surely redeem."[805] You have a double obligation to redeem him, even though such rescue involves personal risk to you. Thus the *S'M'A'*[806] in paragraph 420[807] cites the Jerusalem Talmud and rules that a person must place himself in a possible state of danger in the event that his fellow Jew is in certain danger. If he does not do so because of concern for himself, lest he too be confronted with danger, the second verse teaches us "a brother cannot redeem,"[808] that is to say, when you will not redeem your brother, claiming it is not permitted by the authorities, and consequently your brother will be trapped in an antelope's net[809] then "man will not pay his ransom to God"[810] and you will be responsible for his blood. If, however, you redeem him with genuine self-sacrifice then "the redemption of their lives will be valued"[811] to such an extent by God, may His Name be blessed, that all of Israel's suffering and decrees will be consigned to oblivion. This is the meaning of "one ceases to be forever,"[812] namely, the decrees will cease and desist forever.

The Book of Esther leads us to a similar conclusion when Esther declares: "Now I have not been summoned to visit the king [for the

---

805 Num. 18:15 תפדה פדה namely, the reduplication of the root פדה (*p'd'h'*) indicates urgency.

806 Acronym for *Sefer Me'irat Einayim,* a major commentary on the *Hoshen Mishpat* section of the *Shulhan Arukh* by R. Joshua Falk (c. 1555–1614).

807 Actually paragraph 426:1. דבירושלמי מסיק דצריך אפילו להכניס עצמו בספק סכנה עבור זה. "The Jerusalem Talmud concludes that one must even expose himself to possible risk [in order to save a life]."

808 Ps. 49:8. A homiletical departure from the close reading of the text. See above, 249.

809 See above, 246, n. 780.

810 The author brilliantly shifts the *etnahta* pause of the trope from אח לא פדה יפדה איש "No man will be able to redeem even a brother," in Ps. 49:8 to אח לא פדה יפדה "A brother will not redeem another," reflecting the realities of the Holocaust, resulting in איש לא יתן לאלהים כפרו [therefore,] "man will not be able to make payment [reciprocate] to God."

811 Free reading of ויקר פדיון נפשם.

812 Ibid. וחדל לעולם.

last thirty days]."[813] Mordechai became angry with her.[814] He understood from her statement that in order not to endanger herself she
refused to violate the law and intervene on behalf of Israel.[815] In
response, he said to her: "On the contrary, if you keep silent [in this
crisis, relief and deliverance will come from another quarter while
you and your father's house will perish]."[816] Do not believe that you
are safe. Quite the contrary may be true. To this she responded: "Go,
assemble [all the Jews. . . .] and if I am to perish, [I shall perish]."[817] I
have now reconciled myself to take my life in order to save Israel.[818]
This is the connotation of *avad'ti* [I already perished] long ago.[819] My
wish is only for the restoration of Israel. In the discourse[820] I expanded
[upon this theme]. Examine it carefully.

Unfortunately,[821] here we do not in fact discern [such devotion].
Our critique is directed at the majority. There are always exceptions
to the rule, thank God, who devote themselves and contribute their
assets towards rescuing Israel. But these individuals have not emerged
from the upper echelons of the people—those who live in palaces of
kings and are the perennial occupants of seats of authority and rule.
They sealed their [sources of] affluence[822] and blocked their funds.
They always discovered pretexts to avoid commitments on behalf of
suffering Israel. . . .[823]

---

813   Est. 4:11.

814   Ibid, 4:12–14.

815   See ibid. 4:11. אשר כל איש ואשה אשר יבוא אל המלך אל החצר הפנימית אשר לא יקרא
אחת דתו להמית. "[All . . . know] that if any person, man or woman, enters the king's
presence in the inner court without having been summoned, there is but one law for
him that he be put to death."

816   Ibid, 4:14.

817   Ibid, 4:16.

818   The author interpolates Esther's intentions into the narrative.

819   The term אבדתי (*avad'ti*) appears in the first person, past tense—indicating
that she has in fact already forfeited her life on behalf of her people.

820   See above, 249–250.

821   *Lit.*, "due to our many sins."

822   *Lit.*, "their fat."

823   Citing Ps. 80:9 and Hul. 92a the author compares the worthy leadership of
Israel to the branches of a vine which share their fruit with others, and for whose

This is all a result of exile which has transformed you into a *golus Yid*. I refer to the life which has shaped you into a person apart and separated from the goup. In exile you do not function as a people.

Translated into German:

"In exile you do not conduct yourself as a people whereby you consider yourself a member of the holy Jewish people."[824] You do not feel part of the dispersed Jewish people, separated from the nations.[825] You regard yourself a citizen of the region in which you reside. You are a citizen only when you are a resident and where you conduct your civil affairs. By this I wish to indicate that you do not at all consider your obligation to your holy people, the Jewish people. You consider only the commitments which you have made with your fellow citizens among whom you reside. There you devote yourself with all your heart and soul. As a result, you separate yourself and become detached from the majority of holy people. You have become an isolated and solitary individual in your place of exile. . . . You have exchanged the world of eternity for the ephemeral. The domain of the holy nation is enduring and eternal. Your separate and isolated world, however, is transient, coming into existence and perishing overnight.[826] There is so much evidence in our time which attests to this fact. Overnight, all your successes earned in exile were lost. And so has the *golus Yid* been presently transformed into a betrayer of his people and his genuine possessions.

We do not refer to the ordinary Jew. His only aspiration is his trade and livelihood, with which he is totally involved. He is neither aware of, nor feels any part of the eternal people, the Jewish people, to which he has responsibility. We witness daily the readiness of such a person to fulfill his municipal, national and social commitments in his place of residence. But should he be approached on behalf of the assemblage of Jews, he becomes tight-fisted. Even when he contributes, it is done grudgingly, without any sense of duty. Is there any greater

---

sake the nation will be delivered in time of need (*EHS*, 250).

824 The original German appears in Hebrew characters (*EHS*, 250).

825 Cf. Est. 3:5.

826 Cf. Jonah 4:10.

treachery? Yet even some of our own fellow Jews, those of our brethren who are observant of the Torah and men of good deeds, isolate themselves from the total nation, the Jewish people. They have no attachment and affinity with the masses since their outlook is limited to the narrow circle within which they move.

Let us take the example of the *hasid* who is totally devoted to his rebbe and fellow *hasidim* who move within the shadow of this rebbe. His world is limited to the small area of his daily concerns. Beyond this Sabbath boundary[827] he does not care. He is not at all concerned with the totality of the Jewish people dispersed and isolated in the world. And should he be requested to contribute something towards the welfare of the totality of Israel, he will respond meekly with the greatest reluctance. Yet within his own circle, money is no object. Similarly, let us probe the righteous Orthodox Jew who never fails to frequent the house of worship morning and evening. He is among the dominant participants in the "Talmud study circle."[828] In fact his world is the Talmud study circle. Outside this circle is beyond his ken. With his involvement in Talmud study he is convinced that he has fulfilled his obligations and mission on behalf of Torah and the Jewish people. . . . Is such a person in fact not isolated and separated from the totality of the Jewish people? . . . It is, therefore, not surprising that he cannot become upset by the misfortune of his fellow Jew, far from his own place of residence, with whom he has never had any contact. It is so obvious and clear.

When the Jew was emancipated in Europe during the last century, benefiting from citizenship equal to the other citizens of the land, profiting equally from the best these countries had to offer, able to perform freely to his heart's content, to live wherever he desires, to engage in intellectual pursuits in his native language and the like—these

---

827   The limits within which movement was permitted on the Sabbath, based on rabbinic interpretation of Ex. 16:29 and Num. 35:5. See Eruv. 51a. Thus תחום שבת (Sabbath boundary) is also an expression for moving within a limited isolated area.

828   חברת ש״ס. The *Shas* circles devoted to daily and weekly study of Talmud of laymen and scholars alike, were a standard feature of Jewish community life in Eastern Europe. ש״ס=ששה סדרים (*Shishah Sedarim*) representing the six orders into which the large body of Talmud literature is divided.

privileges provided the final impulse which severed him from the mass of the Jewish people. This was the cause of his absorption and assimilation into the people amongst whom he lives. [All this is diametrically opposed to the sentiment expressed in the following verse:] "Indeed, it shall be said of Zion, 'Every man was born there.'"[829] Those people born therein are exemplary[830] in every way—in spirit, intelligence and leadership ability. Since then [in exile] the ties with the totality of the Jewish people have been severed. They [the emancipated European Jews] have nothing in common with them. Prior to their emancipation, when they still lived in ghettos, they were not so alienated. Polish rabbis were acceptable in the communities of Hungary, Germany, Bohemia and Moravia.

This was not so after the Jews were freed and emancipated. A Polish rabbi was no longer eligible to serve in Hungary, Germany or Moravia. They [Jewish communities] were now divorced and detached one from another, as distant from East to West. This was the consequence of assimilation of gentile ways which also made its mark upon the Jew devoted to Torah and *mitzvot*. We used to see and hear how·in Germany and even in Hungary a Jew from Poland was considered inferior—"a Polish Jew." In Germany they would refer to him as "Ost-Jude." This epithet was sufficient to classify him in the lowest of rank. Even among the genuinely pious rabbinic scholars one could detect an attitude of disparagement towards the Polish Jew, as if he emerged from another nation and not from his own [Jewish] people. . . . Hence the truth in the designation, *golus Yid*. He has provoked what has befallen us.

---

829 Ps. 87:5.

830 The homiletical play on the words ציון (*Zion*) and מצויינים (*metzuyanim*) "exemplary and of high quality," a variant on the exposition of *Sifrei* Deut. on 26:5, cited in the Passover eve Haggadah text. While the *Sifrei* commentary refers to the self-discipline of the Jews who maintained their distinct identity while enslaved despite the cultural surroundings of Egypt, our author links מצוין (*metzuyan*) to ציון (*Zion*). The exemplary and high quality of Jewish life can only be achieved in Zion and not in the precarious environment of exile.

Our rabbis taught in *Midrash Rabba* on the portion of *Vayehi*[831] where Jacob says to his sons: "Come together that I may tell you what is to befall you in days to come," [832]

> He, [Jacob] said to them: "Become a united community,"[833] as it is written:[834]"And you, O mortal, take a stick and write on it: 'Of Judah and the Israelites associated with him.'" (It is written *havero*[835] and sounded *haverav*.[836] It is written *havero*, [that is to say] the Israelites were forced into a united group[837]—prepare yourselves for redemption. What follows [in the verse]? "I will make them a single nation in the Land."[838]

Thus for the quotation from the Midrash. I will supplement what is further written in the verse following: "And I will cleanse them and they shall be My people, and I will be their God."[839] Hence, by virtue of their all uniting into one group, the Lord will direct towards them a purifying spirit from on high. They will, therefore, be worthy of being a people to God, and for the Lord to be their God.

Midrash Ecclesiastes[840] further comments on the verse "And a time for sowing:"[841]

> As it is written:[842] "Bring them close to each other [so that they become one bundle][843] joined together in your hand." And what verse follows?

831　Gen. 47:28–50:26.

832　Ibid. 49:1.

833　Warning them against dissension and controversy. רבנן אמרי: צוה אותן על המחלוקת. "The sages urged: Enjoin them to reject dissension." GenR. 98:2.

834　Ezek. 37:16.

835　*Lit,* "his friend" in the singular.

836　*Lit,* "his friends" in the plural.

837　Suggested by the use of the singular in the root חבר (friend).

838　Ezek. 37:22.

839　Ibid. 23.

840　EcclR. 3:10.

841　Eccl. 3:7.

842　Ezek. 37:17.

843　The text in brackets does not appear in *EHS,* 252.

"Thus said the Lord God: I am going to take the Israelite people from every quarter, and bring them to their own Land. And I will make them a single nation in the Land."[844] This is the meaning of the verse "And a time for sowing."[845]

Thus far the text of the Midrash. . . .[846]

Our many sins have been the cause of the decline of Israel's honor and the disgrace of our people. We have fallen to the lowest standing. All this because the Jewish people are torn into shreds and divided into fragments. This is how I described before you the *golus Yid* . . . . So also has the kabbalist and God-fearing scholar, our rabbi and teacher, R. Judah Loew of Prague, of blessed memory, affirmed in his volume *Netzah Yisrael*.[847] Jerusalem and the holy Temple are the center which unites and assembles the totality of Israel. They fashion them into one people. The Second Temple was destroyed because Israel was not united; they were not worthy of this place. If we will correct this matter and become united, we will be worthy of redemption and the place which unites us as a people. I have already referred previously[848] to the Talmud [Sanhedrin] the chapter of *Helek*.[849] The *gemara* inquires: "Since both we and God wait [for redemption] (note that God as well waits for redemption) who delays it? The [Divine] attribute of Justice delays!" Similarly, the Midrash (on Song of Songs) interprets the verse "Do not arouse nor awake my love, until she will wish for it."[850] "Until the [Divine] attribute of Justice will wish it."[851] That is to say,

---

844 Ezek. 37:21–22.

845 Eccl. 3:7, suggesting the connecting together of disunified parts.

846 This latter section does not appear in the Ecclesiastes Midrash. The author supplements this with passages from *Tanh. Nitzavim* (Deut. 29:9) 1 and Talmud Men. 27a to document the requisites of unity prior to redemption.

847 See above, 44, n. 39.

848 See above, 119.

849 Sanh. 97b.

850 Song 2:7, 3:5. See above, 137–138, nn. 32 and 34.

851 CantR. 2:18. מה ׳עד שתתחפץ׳, מלכות של מעלן, לכשתתחפץ מדת הדין מאליה, אני הוא מביאה בקולי קולות ולא אתעכב. "What is the meaning of 'until she will wish for it'? [Reference is to] the Kingdom on High. When the attribute of [Divine] Justice will independently arrive at a decision, I will hasten her [redemption's] coming, without delay."

until such time that the attribute of Justice who delays for us the redemption, will wish it. . . .

Our teacher[852] has commented in the volume *Noam Elimelekh* on the verse:[853] "And he brought Him all these, and cut them in two, placing each half opposite the other; but he did not cut up the birds," in relation to the covenant of the pieces.[854] These are his words:

> Namely, he placed one opposite the other. "The birds,"[855] an allusion to Israel, "he did not cut up."[856] That is to say, the merit of the sum total of Israel can never be challenged. "Even the wicked among them are saturated with *mitzvot*."[857]

Thus the text [of the *Noam Elimelekh*].[858]

In fact the words of the *Noam Elimelekh* which characterized the totality of Israel as a state of consistent holiness without any trace of blemish are also found in the sacred volume *Netzah Yisrael* of our rabbi the Maharal of Prague.[859] There he also writes that they are firmly bound to the Divine with love which will never be detached. Similarly, I came across a passage in *Iggeret Teiman* of Maimonides:

> In addition He brought us good tidings and the Almighty strengthened us in [declaring] that He will refrain from ever rejecting us as a group though we may anger Him and violate His commandments. As Jeremiah (31:36)[860] wrote: "Thus said the Lord: [If the heavens above could be measured, and the foundations of the earth below could be fathomed,

---

852   R. Elimelekh of Lizhensk.

853   Gen. 15:10.

854   Gen. 15.

855   Ibid. verse 10.

856   Ibid.

857   Cf. Ber. 57a. אפילו ריקנין שבך מלאים מצות כרימון "Even the empty among you are filled with mitzvot like [the pits in] a pomegranate."

858   *Lekh Lekha* (Tel Aviv, 1973), 13. The author reiterates R. Elimelekh of Lizhensk's teaching on the flawlessness of the totality of Israel, cited above, 89.

859   *Netzah Yisrael*, chapter 11, Tel Aviv, 1955, 40–46. See also above, 44, n. 39. The Maharal distinguishes between the incorruptible and constant merit of the community of Israel and the changing, sinful possibilities of the individual.

860   The *EHS* text reads Isa. 31:25.

only then would I reject all the offspring of Israel for all that they have done—declares the Lord.]"

These are his precious words.[861]

Following all the discussions which I presented herewith, everyone would understand the point which I have made previously: Our entire redemption and destiny is tied to the one condition that we remain united and consolidated within one complete entity; that we unite within ourselves people representing every sector from among us, from those on the extreme right to those on the extreme left. [This is to be done] until all of Israel becomes a unified perfect whole. Then we will conquer the Divine attribute of strict Justice. We will silence the Adversary [Satan] so that he cannot scheme against us,[862] as indicated earlier. Then [the verse] "And the Israelites departed with boldness,"[863] will come to fruition on our behalf, speedily in our day.

Truly, I realize that everyone would be astonished and would ridicule me, saying: You are correct. Upon the unity of all of Israel rests our redemption. How is it possible to remedy all of this? Who is capable of bringing them all together? How can one include and gather all of Israel from the four corners of the earth and forge them into one flock with such different points of view and features? Indeed, this difficulty was raised by our rabbi (the author of) *Hafla'ah* [864](commenting) at the close of Ketubot[865] on the eventual unification of all of Israel in our time, which was forestalled due to the differences

---

861 Kapah edition (Jerusalem, 1972), 26. See above, 88, n. 8. The author again supplements the theme of the flawlessness of Israel citing Jer. 6:30 and Ezek. 22:18 (where Israel is referred to as "rejected silver," and "dross") against Zech. 4:2, where Israel is likened to a "candelabrum all of gold" (*EHS*, 254).

862 Cf. ותגער בשטן לבל ישטינני "Rebuke the adversary, that he may not accuse me," from the הנני (*Hineni*) personal prayer of the *hazzan* prior to the Musaf service on the High Holy Days.

863 Ex. 14:8. Their exit from the exile of Egypt was done not out of fear but with confidence.

864 The extensive commentary on the tractate of Ketubot by R. Pinhas HaLevi Ish Horowitz (1730–1805), whose Hebrew initials form the Hebrew title of the commentary.

865 112b.

in views among them.[866]

Our sages of blessed memory have instructed us saying: "Do not underrate the importance of anything."[867] Even the ordeal of the abnormal periods which we have endured teach us that events which people had believed to be unrealistic, proved to be very real. And things which no man even believed were possible in this world were eventually realized. Similarly, incorporating all of Israel into a unified whole is a likely possibility and is not contrary to its natural inherent tendency, as I shall proceed to relate with the help of the Almighty.

I read in the lucid writings in *Netzah Yisrael* of our rabbi the Maharal of Prague of blessed memory, chapter one,[868] who presents us with a principle. Natural law demands to be taken seriously. Its existence is strong and durable. It does not veer outside its natural boundary fixed by the Creator of the universe. It will not operate within a sphere not related to its natural orbit. Eventually it returns to its natural state. That which is foreign to its natural properties will not endure. Nature is eternal. Consequently, since the Jewish nation, more so than others, was endowed by the Holy One, blessed be He, with the natural attribute of unity, its dispersion would be unreal. As our sages of blessed memory have taught:[869] With regard to Jacob it is written: "'All the persons'[870] who came with Jacob [to Egypt]."[871]

---

866   *Hafla'ah* (Jerusalem, 1961) on Ket. 112 b. ר"ל אף שגם בעת ההיא יהיו קטנים וגדולים בדעת אבל כולם יודעים את ד' ויהי' להם ידיעה גדולה באמיתות הבורא ואז וה' אהבה נפלא אחדות גמורה. "He indicated that during that time [the epoch of redemption] the great and the simple will retain their reason, but all will be keenly aware of God and the truth of the Creator's ways. This will usher in a period of extraordinary love and absolute unity."

867   Avot 4: 3.

868   *Netzah Yisrael* (Tel Aviv, 1955), 4–5. The "natural law" of Israel in its Land is presented thus: וזה כי אין ספק כי גלות הוא שינוי ויציאה מן הסדר. שהש"י סידר כל אומה במקומה הראוי לה וסידר את ישראל מקום הראוי להם שהוא ארץ ישראל. "There is no doubt that exile represents a departure from, and mutation of, the normal order of things, since God arranged for nations to be ensconced in their appropriate location. Israel was also placed in a location befitting it—that is, Eretz Yisrael."

869   LevR. 4:6.

870   כל הנפש suggests the singular. In fact, the Midrash employs a different verse than that cited by our author: "The total number of persons that were of Jacob's issue." Ex. 1:5 also employs the singular form of נפש (*nefesh*).

Concerning Esau it is written: "'And all the persons'[872] of his household."[873] Regarding Jacob, unity[874] is a matter of nature. This is not so in the case of Esau. We observe this [idea] as well at the time of the giving of the Torah [at Sinai]: "And Israel 'encamped' there."[875] "As if [they were] one person with one heart."[876] From their very inception as a people the Creator marked them as one nation. Therefore, to conceive Israel as dispersed is baseless, outside the boundaries of reality, and without the possiblity of existence. And as all elements which have shifted outside their natural orbit eventually return to their origins, so shall the dispersed and divided elements of Israel return to their place as a united entity. Thus, this [phenomenon of division and dispersion] cannot be attributed to sin and wrongdoing. Eventually, the dispersion of Israel will be acknowledged as unreal.

Observe the interpretation of our sages of blessed memory in the *Midrash* on the verse[877] "And He said to Abram: Know well[878] [that your offspring shall be strangers in a land not theirs]": "Know that I shall disperse them. Know as well that I shall gather them."[879] That is to say, from the very dispersion you will know that I shall gather them in....

Exile itself is clear proof of redemption, since it is a departure and

---

871 Gen. 46:26.

872 כל נפשות, i.e., the plural.

873 Gen. 36:6.

874 Suggested by the singular form of נפש.

875 Ex. 19:2. ויחן, the singular form.

876 Rashi on Ex. 19:2 based on the *Mekhilta DeRabbi Yishmael* (op. cit., Yithro, 70), כל מקום שהוא אומר ויסעו ויחני, נוסעים במחלוקת וחונים במחלוקת, אבל כאן השוו כולם לב אחד. לכך נאמר ויחן שם ישראל נגד ההר. "Wherever the text reads 'they journeyed ... they encamped,' it refers to their journeying in a state of dissension and encamping in a state of dissension. Here, however, they were all compared to a united organism. Therefore, it is said: 'Israel encamped [the singular form] there in front of the mountain.'"

877 Gen. 15:13. Both *EHS* and the Jerusalem edition read: ויאמר ה' אל אברם "And the Lord said to Abram." vs. ויאמר לאברם "And He spoke to Abram."

878 The reinforced form of ידע תדע "know well" is interpreted by the Midrash.

879 GenR. 44:21. שאני מכנסן "I shall bring them in" of the Midrash vs. *EHS* שאני מקבצן "I shall gather them."

a deviation from [the natural] order. The Almighty, may He be blessed, designated an appropriate habitation for every nation. He allocated a place for Israel—Eretz Yisrael.[880] Exile is a deviation and departure from the natural habitat. Hence, from exile we may understand redemption. . . .

He[881] wrote as well that the root *g'a'l*[882] (for redemption) contains identical letters [as *galah*, "to go onto exile"] with the exception of the *alef* in the center of *g'a'l* and the *heh* at the end of *g'l'h*'.[883] Each contains its special meaning. The root *g'a'l* suggests that the Almighty, blessed be He, will redeem them from the four corners of the earth, uniting them in their dispersion, so that they remain united.[884] Therefore, it is written with an *alef* which indicates unity. Similarly, every unifying element in the universe is positioned in the center. The extremities are divided. This teaches us that only with the merit of unity will the Lord gather them from the dispersion of exile. The word *galah* includes the *heh*, because the letter *heh* points to the dispersion in the four corners [of the earth], in all directions, as well as the center. What is dispersed is scattered everywhere, which would include the four corners and the middle. The middle and four corners add up to five, represented by the letter *heh*. . . .[885] Accordingly the *heh* appears at the end of the word and not in the middle, to indicate that departure into exile is also departure from the natural order. It is also a departure and change from the proper place [of the Jews] which is Eretz Yisrael, the center of the world.[886] [The state of exile] will not forever remain so. Consequently, there yet remain some

---

880 See above, 40, n. 23.

881 The Maharal of Prague, *Netzah Yisrael, op. cit.,* 4–5.

882 גאל.

883 גלה.

884 The letter א (*alef*) in גאל [for redemption] represents the central singular unifying factor—reflecting אחד, אחדות [unity].

885 The numerical value of ה (*heh*) is five.

886 See *Tanh. Kedoshim* (Leviticus) 10. כשם שהטבור הזה נתון באמצע האיש כך א״י נתונה באמצע העולם. "As the navel is situated in the center of the person, so is Eretz Yisrael placed in the center of the world."

elements of unity even in their exile. The [fifth] element is situated amid the four united elements and connects the four dispersed elements to itself. The center always unites and connects each thing. This indicates that there is yet a unifying force within Israel in their exile. They have not completely disintegrated. With this unifying force in progress they will unite even more. . . .[887]

In this context we can better understand the sacred and divine teaching of our R. Menahem Mendel of Premishlan,[888] the disciple of the Baal Shem Tov, cited in the sacred treatise *Igra Depirka*[889] of our teacher R. Zvi Elimelekh, of blessed memory, (letter *dalet*) who writes as follows:

I was told a powerful story about the saintly, holy rabbi, our teacher, R. Mendel of Premishlan. The story is recounted thus:

They[890] were participating in a festive meal when he [R. Mendel] gave coins worth four pfennigs to the servant for five pfennigs worth of drinks. The servant paid no attention to the currency, being certain that they were worth five pfennigs. When he went to the cashier he was told that the coin was worth only four pfennigs. The messenger returned, informing the rabbi of the discrepancy. The rabbi began to argue with the messenger, insisting that it must be a five-pfennig coin. The messenger persisted and the matter turned into a quarrel. The disciples of the rabbi suggested to the servant-messenger that he concede to the rabbi (since they realized that this was not an uncalculated incident). The messenger cooperated, stating: "Let it be in accordance with the master." Then the rabbi rose in prayer reciting the following: "May it be Thy will that all of mankind acknowledge and recognize in the German language that a *"Vierer ist ein Funfer."*[891] This is what I heard. I

---

887 The גאולה (*ge'ulah*) "redemption"—גולה (*golah*) "exile" dialectic is further developed by the author via Zech. 4: 1–2 and LevR. 32: 7 (*EHS*, 258).

888 First generation adherent of Hasidism (b. 1728) and a member of the inner circle of R. Israel Baal Shem Tov, the founder of the movement.

889 Volume of hasidic and *kabbalistic* discourses by R. Zvi Elimelekh Shapira of Dinov (Zolkiew, 1861). Non-paginated letter ד. See above, 70, n. 61.

890 R. Mendel and his disciples.

891 A play on words. The literal meaning: A four-pfennig coin is worth five.

believe this refers to the unity of God according to the *Zohar*:[892] "God consists of four realities. When these are evoked the Divine is established." Fathom this incident and study the extent to which the *tzadikim* will go and the message which they bring. You will be astonished.

This concludes the words of the *gaon*, the master in Israel in [the volume] *Igra Depirka* .

[In my opinion these words allude to the ideas of our teacher the Maharal [in his interpretation] above, that the letter *dalet* [ד] refers to Israel's exile and their dispersion throughout the four[893] corners of the earth. The letter *heh* [ה] refers to solidarity and redemption. The solidarity which was sustained in *galut*, if fully realized, will bring about redemption.[894] This may help us understand the teaching of the Zohar: "God consists of four realities. When these are evoked the Divine is established." Note, for this very thing did the *tzadik* pray may there emerge "five" from "four."[895]

Note his lengthy exposition on this subject.[896]

Therefore, Israel is allotted the name Rachel because it is written: "Rachel is weeping for her children."[897] And it is explained in the *Midrash*[898] that Israel is named after Rachel. Therefore, the woman is called "home." As R. Yosi said: "All my life I have never called my wife,

---

Vierer also sounds almost exactly like *Führer*—leader. Thus, the Leader, the Almighty who fills the four corners of the universe with His Glory, assumes a fifth unifying dimension—the unifying stroke which transposes the *dalet* (ד = 4) into *heh* (ה = 5). *Heh* is an abbreviation representing the Almighty.

892   See above, n. 884.

893   The numerical value of *dalet* being four.

894   See above, n. 887.

895   See above, n. 891.

896   The theme of Israel's unity and its relationship to redemption according to the Maharal. *Netzah Yisrael, op. cit.,* 4–5. See below, 352.

897   Jer. 31:15.

898   GenR. 71:3. תאני רשב"י: לפי שכל הדברים תלוין ברחל לפיכך נקראו ישראל על שמה - ירחל (ירמיה לא:יד) מבכה על בניה.' "R. Shimon bar Yohai taught: Because everything is contingent upon her, Israel is known as Rachel—'Rachel weeps for her children.' [Jer. 31:14] We learned that Israel is named Rachel, as it is written: 'Ephraim is a dear son to Me' [Jer. 31:19]." See also GenR. 82:11.

'my wife' . . . but my 'home'. . . ."[899] And since Rachel was the homemaker[900] for Jacob. . . . and whoever is referred to as "home" embodies and unifies all, just as one's home embodies and unifies all. Consequently, Israel is named for Rachel since she inspires unity. Israel is endowed with [the potential] strength necessary for its unity, although it has not been realized. Thus, Rachel, the inspiration for Israel's unity, requests compassion until the time when Israel will be completely gathered into their Land. To this [request] the Holy One, blessed be He, responded: "Restrain your voice from weeping, your eyes from shedding tears,"[901] for due to Rachel, the ingathering power of Israel, the Jewish people will return from exile. Therefore, "your children shall return to their territories."[902] This is what we wished to explain.[903]

These are the words of the kabbalist master, the saintly scholar, our rabbi the Maharal of Prague, who spoke with Divine inspiration. May his merit protect me and all of Israel. Amen. . . .[904]

I express my heartfelt gratitude to the Almighty that following the study of this subject upon which depends the redemption of Israel, He enlightened me and inspired me with a marvelous and proper design as to how the entire sacred Jewish people may actually become unified as one group. The idea is to select one mitzvah from the

---

899 Yoma 1:1, Git. 52a, Shab. 118b and Rashi והיא עיקר הבית. "Basically she *is* the home."

900 A play on words inspired by GenR. 71:3. The verse ורחל עקרה (Gen. 29:31) clearly indicates: "But Rachel was barren." R. Yitzhak and R. Abba in the midrash invert the root עקר ("k'r") from the destructive "uprooting," or "remove" to עיקר (*ikar*) meaning "root", "essence," and "important," hence רחל היתה עיקרו של בית "Rachel was the essence of [Jacob's] home." See below, 368.

901 Jer. 31:15.

902 Ibid.

903 *Netzah Yisrael, op. cit.*, 4–5.

904 *EHS* proceeds to summarize the Maharal's theme of natural unity inherent in Israel's character, latent in exile but to be realized in Eretz Yisrael as the final chapter in Israel's redemption. Israel would have to initiate such efforts. The Almighty will then contribute Divine assistance and help complete the process towards solidarity. The author supports this principle of human Divine partnership by citing Shab. 104a. הבא ליטהר, מסייעין אותו. "If one comes to purify himself, he is helped" *EHS*, 259–260.

commandments of the Torah which would be observed by all of Israel, from the youngest to the oldest. This mitzvah would serve as the common thread which would bind us into one body and people within the Land. The entire Jewish people will become a unified group, complete in body and spirit, in holiness and purity. As explained previously[905] the collective Israel is always in a state of holiness. Neither impediment nor evil forces are present. I also referred previously[906] to Maimonides and the Ran, as well as the devout kabbalist, our teacher R. Shalom Sharabi of blessed memory, who was cited in the work *Pele Yo'etz* to the effect that with commitment to one commandment one achieves complete repentance which may result in redemption. As it is written in the first chapter of Kiddushin:[907] "Everyone who performs one mitzvah is well rewarded, his life is prolonged and he inherits the Land." If this is the case with the individual, so much more so when many perform the mitzvah. Its effect is infinitely great and it can bring about all of the above mentioned results.[908]

I was aware that many would ask which of the Torah's commandments would be selected by the totality of Israel? I will respond in accordance with the Ran in his discourses cited above, who noted that the mitzvah by which one can merit the world to come would have to be of great significance and equal it [in value] to many commandments. Note this in the source. Similarly, in our situation. In order to gather the totality of Israel into a central organism, we too must select a mitzvah which is superior to and more important than the other mitzvot in the Torah. Then the question will be asked: Is there a scale which can distinguish between one commandment and another? Is it not [written]: "She does not chart a path of life"?[909] On the other hand, it is written: "Measure the course you will walk

---

905   See above, 89.

906   See above, 152, n. 120; *EHS*, 169.

907   39b.

908   Leading to unity and redemption.

909   Prov. 5:6; i.e. one should not exploit the mitzvot as a means of selecting preferences and priorities in life.

and all your ways will prosper."[910] (In fact our sages of blessed memory in Moed Katan[911] made reference to this contradiction.) Necessarily, wherever our sages of blessed memory pointed to a superior mitzvah among mitzvot, we are permitted to be selective [in its favor]. Now in *Sifrei*, the weekly portion of *Re'eh* and *Tosefta* in Avodah Zarah, the fifth chapter specifically designates the mitzvah of settling Eretz Yisrael as corresponding to all of [the commandments in] the Torah.[912] (According to the Ramban in *Sefer HaMitzvot*, it [the commandment of settling Eretz Yisrael] is included among the 613 commandments. Most of the early and late legal authorities concur with him. I have already demonstrated previously[913] that Maimonides as well establishes biblical authority [for this commandment], though he does not list it among the [613] commandments.) Therefore, let us choose this mitzvah of settling the Land, whereby every Jew in this world will collaborate in its realization. Thereby we will emerge as a united people in the Land. The unity of the Jewish people will be built. Then the potential of Israel's unity, which had heretofore remained latent, will emerge as reality. Then will we be privileged to witness the final redemption, as described previously. We will be privileged to welcome the great future prophesied for us by our sacred prophets. . . .[914]

Understand, my brethren, and do not take my words lightly. Only

---

910   Prov. 4:26; suggesting a degree of discrimination in selecting the kind of commandments to be observed.

911   9a. The text resolves the contradictions as follows: A mitzvah which can also be observed by others may compel one to select a commandment which cannot be observed by others. Yet certain mitzvot must by their very nature, be selected by all, i.e. charity, and, according to our author, so too the mitzvah of settling Eretz Yisrael which unites all of Jewry.

912   See above, 127, n. 226; 145, n. 87.

913   See above, 143–144.

914   The author continues to elaborate upon the theme of Eretz Yisrael as a catalyst for the unity of the Jewish people. Supportive documentation is presented from *Sefer Haredim* (See above, 225, n. 633) and II Sam. 7:23. Jews who remain outside the Land but unite with their brethren in Eretz Yisrael in support of its rebuilding also contribute significantly to the process of Jewish unification. (R. Hayyim ben Bezalel the author of *Sefer Haredim* and the Mabit are cited.) *EHS*, 261–62. Even the wicked who help establish Eretz Yisrael are partners in the unifying cause of Israel. (ExR. 20:10; *EHS*, Foreword, 17.)

in the complete unity of Israel can redemption be realized. Such
unity can come about only in the manner which I have previously
suggested—to unite and weave together the entire nation under the
banner of settling the Land and its rebuilding. All of our rabbis'
teachings document this, as I will show with the help of the Almighty.

There is [a passage] in the *Pesikta*[915] (in the section "At that Time")
based upon what the Holy One, blessed be He said: "At that time, I
will search Jerusalem with lanterns" (Zephaniah).[916] This refers to the
period of redemption:

> Israel responded:[917]"Master of the Universe, is this the extent of the
> esteem (which you promised to us)? Is it sufficient for you to search for
> Jerusalem with lanterns? What of the promise of the prophets made to
> us: 'No longer shall you need the sun for light by day [nor the shining
> of the moon for radiance by night], for the Lord shall be your light
> [everlasting].'[918] Further it is said: 'Arise, shine, for your light has dawned:
> the Presence of the Lord has shone upon you.[919] And [now] you say, 'I
> shall search Jerusalem with lanterns.'[920] (In other words, he complained
> to the Holy One, blessed be He, who was searching Jerusalem with
> lanterns. After all, He had promised more.) Said the Holy One, blessed
> be He, to them: "What you perceive is not so. Just as I displayed for
> Zechariah the form of the lampstand, as it is written in the verse: 'Here
> is a lampstand all of gold,'[921] this refers to the Assembly of Israel, 'Every
> part of you is fair, my darling. There is no blemish in you.'[922] Similarly,
> Moses was instructed: 'You shall fashion a lampstand of pure gold.'[923]

---

915   *Pesikta Rabati*, ed. Meir Ish Shalom (Tel Aviv, 1963), 29b.

916   Zeph. 1:12.

917   To God's promise to seek Jerusalem.

918   Isa. 60:19.

919   Isa. 60:1.

920   Suggesting a relationship much less than promised in Isa. 60. How can God's
full radiant Presence be compared to mere lanterns?

921   Zech. 4:2.

922   Song 4:7. The connecting term between the two verses is כולה-כולך (*kulah-kulakh*).

923   Ex. 25:31.

This refers to the Assembly of Israel."

To this point the text [of the *Pesikta*].[924]

[But] it is not clear. What is the nature of the response of the Holy One, blessed be He, to the complaint of Israel which claims You promised that You will be unto us as a light while You subsequently come with lanterns? It will be understood, however, in view of my previous comments concerning the lampstand as the symbol for Israel's unity.[925] Redemption for Israel will not be possible unless it stands united. The Divine attribute of Justice will hinder [redemption]. When they are united, no one will hinder nor cause harm, since within its totality Israel is flawless.[926] This is the meaning of the appearance of the lampstand in the book of Zechariah and the verse: "Here is a lampstand all of gold."[927] This refers to the Assembly of Israel. Precisely when they are assembled in unity, then they shine as flawless gold. Likewise with the lampstand of Moses: "And you shall fashion a lampstand of pure gold,"[928] namely, Israel shall be made of pure gold. . . .

In this vein the Holy One, blessed be He, responds to Israel: "Certainly, I will be a Light unto you. You will not need another source of light. Yet I cannot accomplish this, appearing before you with My Light until you will have been completely united into one alliance. . . ." Such as was the response of the Almighty: "I will not appear, as you might believe, with mere simple lamps in order to find you. Rather I intend [to appear] with the lamps to which I referred—in accordance with the appearance of the lampstand of Zechariah and Moses which reflects the assembly of Israel gathered and thoroughly united. Then, 'Every part of you is fair, my darling. There is no

---

924   The author cites an identical passage from the *Yalkut Shimoni* II, 516.

925   *EHS*, 298 based on Zech. 4:2; LevR. 32:7; and Sforno on Num. 8:2–4. The six candles turn to the Almighty in unity through the seventh candle in the center. וירוממו את שמו יחדיו "They shall exalt His Name together [united]."

926   See above, 89, 258–259.

927   Zech. 4:2.

928   Ex. 25:31.

blemish in you.'[929] Surely I will then be for you a Light and declare
unto you: 'Arise, shine, for your light has dawned. The Presence of
the Lord has shone upon you.'"[930] This seems to me the interpretation
of these words. With the help of the Lord [this explanation] is clear
and correct. . . .[931]

Realize as well that we are compelled to marshal the totality of
Israel around this mitzvah, in order to compensate for an old debt
which has been a burden upon us from days of yore, from the very
time that we became a people. Due to this liability we are in exile.
We were thus oppressed for thousands of years, compelled to shed
great tears of lamentation upon alien land. I am about to explain with
God's help.

I will introduce for you the *Midrash Yalkut* [*Shimoni*], the weekly
portion of *Shelah*,[932] as follows:

> "The entire community broke into loud cries and the people wept that
> night."[933] This refers to the verse: "The words of a querulous man are
> bruising" (Proverbs 26).[934] R. Eliezer the son of R. Yosi the Galilean,
> taught: "The words of a querulous man are bruising (deadly)."[935] And
> so it was with them.[936] When they [the spies] returned from exploring

---

929 Song 4:7.

930 Isa. 60:1.

931 The author documents the potential power of even a partial unity, as proven
during the period of Ezra's return to Zion. Though he had to contend with problematic
and dubious elements among the returning population (Ezra 2:59), the sense of unity
of purpose (3:1) helped the returnees to overcome these enemies who obstructed
their return (8:31). The redemption would have been final and complete had all of
Israel responded to Ezra's call for return (*EHS*, 263–64).

932 Num. 13:1–15:41. *Yalkut Shimoni* I, 244.

933 Num. 14:1.

934 Verse 22. Likely association of נרגן (*nirgan*) "querulous" with ותרגנו באהליכם
"you sulked in your tents." in Deut. 1:27.

935 Prov. 26:22. כמתלהמים ("bruising") becomes the focus of the play on words
כמת להם—they wept "as if in mourning"—directed at the community in the desert
which had no confidence in the Almighty. Another interpretation of כמתלהמים is
"frivolous" from להא-להה (Arabic). See Prov. 26:18. The actual reading of the *Yalkut*
is: כאדם שיש לו מת והוא צווח ובוכה "As if in mourning—he grieves and cries."

936 The demoralized spies.

the Land they proceeded to disperse themselves among all the tribes, each to his respective tribe, flinging himself into every corner of the house (in other words, he hurled himself into every nook and cranny of the house).[937] His sons and daughters approached him and asked him: "Why are you so grieved?" While yet standing he collapses before them exclaiming: "Woe unto you my sons, daughters, and daughters-in-law. Oh, how the Amorites will mock you! How they will dominate you! Who will be able to look into their faces! I know what I saw!" Immediately sons, daughters and daughters-in-law broke into tears. When the neighbors heard the story they also wailed. And so it was transmitted to each family until the entire tribe wept.

Every tribe then wept for the other until they totaled a mass of six hundred thousand who raised their wailing voices. How is this known? From what we read: "The entire community broke into loud cries."[938]

(Evidently, the expression in the verse, "the entire community" is problematic for the Midrash. Therefore, this is explained: The entire community joined as one, united in their wailing and crying together with the spies. This was due to the threat and panic created by the spies in their respective tribes and homes. . . .)

Here is evidence that the spies, who were the elders of the Israelites, and had been given a vote of confidence by the entire people, were sent on a mission to explore the Land in order to speed the entry into the Land and to inherit and settle the Land of our fathers. They were unfaithful and betrayed the trust given to them by all of Israel. Thus Moses responds and censures [Israel]: "And when the Lord sent you on from Kadesh–Barnea, saying 'Go up and occupy the Land that I am giving you,'"[939] (he indicates that the sole purpose for sending the scouts will be[940] to ascend to and occupy the Land.) Eventually, "You

---

937 Feigning hysteria.

938 Num. 14:1. The author continues to quote the *Yalkut* elaboration of the response of a people turned purposely into a hysterical mass by ten demoralized leaders who had lost confidence and perspective (*EHS*, 265).

939 Deut. 9:23.

940 The original edition is marked י (*yod*), likely referring to the future יהיה "it will be." The Jerusalem edition mistakenly amended this to the past היתה "it was."

flouted the command of the Lord your God. . . . [you did not put trust in Him and did not obey Him]."[941]

Observe, my brethren, how they employed modern methods to win over the masses, what one refers to as "propaganda. . . ." They accomplished this because they did not spare any efforts in entering the homes of every one of six hundred thousand people with their agents and emissaries of their agents. They proceeded to upset the occupants of these homes until they all, the entire mass, wailed to the heavens with an enormous cry. That is why the Israelites claimed: "Our kinsmen have taken the heart out of us,"[942] since they sulked in their tents. Moses confirmed this: "You sulked in your tents."[943] David also said:"They grumbled in their tents."[944] "They rejected the desirable Land."[945] Note the emphasis on "their tents," namely, since they grumbled in everyone else's tent they succeeded in rejecting the desirable Land for the entire congregation. . . .

They were the cause for the bitter exiles which we have endured for some two thousand years. We experience exile to this day without the end in sight. On the contrary, it has escalated daily until it has reached the current state in which we find ourselves.

This has all been pressed upon us due to the evil transaction—as this sin of the spies is called in the *Midrash* cited previously[946]—for this evil transaction of yesteryear. The Holy One, blessed be He, declared: "By your lives, eventually this [debt] will be collected." Thus far, this debt has not been repaid. Therefore, we must tolerate all which befalls us. In the Midrash of Lamentations it is also written: "Israel has transferred a degrading debt to its [future] generations

---

941 Ibid.

942 Deut. 1:28.

943 Ibid. 27.

944 Ps. 106:25.

945 Ibid. 24.

946 *Yalkut Shimoni* I, 244. יותשא: כשם שאתה ורעה. יותשא: ליויתם מלוה רעה. יותשא' - אמר להם הקב"ה: אומר 'כי תשה ברעך', חייכם שסופכם ליפרע. '"They raised [their voices in sobbing]': said the Holy One, blessed be He: 'You have become involved in a bad debt.' As it is written 'When you make a loan transaction to your neighbor, pay it; I swear, you will eventually have to make amends.'" The midrash involves a play on the word ותשא and תשא. See next note.

[with their weeping.]"[947] Consequently, as long as we do not repay this debt, Heaven forbid, we cannot expect that our status will improve.

Now the *Magen Avraham*, section 494,[948] in discussing the laws of *Shavuot* provides the reason for our remaining awake during the night of *Shavuot*.[949] It is in order to rectify the flaw of our forefathers when they slept during the night at the transmitting of the Torah [in the desert]. Now if for such a minor blemish our rabbis instituted a process of correction, how much more so must we correct a major failure upon which hinges our entire life, our dignity, the glory of our Lord, blessed be He, the glory of our sacred Torah, the glory of the kingdom of the House of David and the glory of our sacred Land. It is, therefore, as clear as the light of day for all who are prepared to admit to the truth that we have no other option in extricating ourselves from the grim situation in which we have been placed for these two thousand years, because of a bad debt which we have assumed, until we are able to correct [this matter] and liquidate this liability. When [the burden of] this promissory note will be lifted from us, we will, with the help of God, courageously leave this bitter and sick exile. We shall reestablish the glory in our sacred Land and the children will return to their borders,[950] speedily in our day. Amen. . . .

And so it is with *Tikkun Leyl Shavuot*,[951] which compensates for what we should have long ago accomplished: to have been alert the entire night,[952] to prepare ourselves with the ornaments of a bride in anticipation of the appointed day at which time the Holy One, blessed be He, was to enter into the covenant of betrothal and marriage with

---

947 LamR. 1:24. יתשא חובי בישא או זפיתון לדירא. ותשא (*vatisah*) in Num. 14:1 is transferred to תשה (*tasheh*) in Deut. 24:10.

948 *Magen Avraham, Shulhan Arukh, Orah Hayyim* (vol. 2), 494.

949 The early tradition of all night study (*Tikkun Leyl Shavuot*) in anticipation of receiving the Torah anew in every generation may have its source in *Pirke DeRabbi Eliezer* 49 describing Moses waking a slumbering people: עמדו משנתכם! כבר בא החתן ומבקש את הכלה ולהכניסה לחופה. "Awake from your slumber! The groom has arrived to seek his bride and to lead her to the wedding canopy."

950 Cf. Jer. 31:16.

951 See n. 949 above.

952 Prior to receiving the Torah on Mt. Sinai.

the community of Israel under the canopy represented by the moment of revelation at Mount Sinai.[953]

And since we presently compensate every year for what we failed to do then,[954] similarly we must correct the failure of the spies and those of every generation who were responsible for the bad debt which was incurred and which we are compelled to pay to this very day. Then our promissory note will be torn asunder, and with the help of God we will be worthy of the great and wondrous redemption which all of Israel has been so anxiously awaiting. . . .[955]

My dear brethren, you must surely become aware of what our sages of blessed memory noted in the Midrash:[956] "In the same manner which the righteous provoke,[957] so do they provide the remedy." Therefore, to the extent that our forefathers [the spies] undermined the enthusiasm of the Israelites for Eretz Yisrael, so are we obligated to stimulate them and to ignite within them the fire of desire for Eretz Yisrael. Just as they succeeded in convincing the entire congregation united as one party to be opposed to Eretz Yisrael, so must we galvanize all of Israel into one party in support of Eretz Yisrael.[958] Just as the generation of the spies applied themselves energetically to propaganda (and they developed an entire propaganda machine and recruited people to propagate lies about Eretz Yisrael),[959] what we presently

---

953   See *Pirke DeRabbi Eliezer* 41, *Pesikta DeRav Kahana* 1:3. See also *Yalkut Shimoni* II, 279.

954   At Sinai.

955   The author again refers to the *Maggid Mesharim* text cited previously (*EHS*, 167–69). According to R. Joseph Karo's interpretation, the generation of Israelites in the desert was not worthy of entering the Promised Land. The scouting expedition of the leading representatives of the twelve tribes [Num. 13] was to serve as a catalyst for arousing the enthusiasm of the timid Israelites in preparation for entry into the Land which was promised to their forefathers. This plan, which backfired, was to become a burden on the Jewish people throughout the generations (*EHS*, 167–68).

956   *Tanh. Beshalah* 24 מתקנין הן בו מקנטרין שהן במה הצדיקים וכן *EHS* vs. דצדיקים במדה מתקנין הם במדה בה שמקלקלין.

957   *Vs.* the *EHS* "spoil."

958   Missing from the *EHS* Jerusalem text.

959   The section enclosed in round brackets appears in Yiddish.

refer to as the Propaganda Ministry,[960] we too must establish a propaganda apparatus which will penetrate into every Jewish home and turn every Jewish soul to support of Eretz Yisrael. In this manner we shall repay this bad debt, the mortgage deed will be torn up, the damage will be repaired, the accuser will disappear, the advocate will be victorious, the day of deliverance will come and we will be privileged to see the fruition of the verse: "Let the heavens rejoice and the earth exult,"[961] for joy shall reign both in the upper as well as the lower spheres. Amen, may this be His will.

Observe [what is written in] the tract *Bet Rabbi*,[962] devoted to our rabbi, the author of the *Shulhan Arukh HaRav* and the volume *HaTanya*. They learned [lessons] from the war in his time—the war of Napoleon against the Russian Empire,[963] and from the contemporary practice among warring nations who establish propaganda ministries with the specific task of winning the masses over to their cause. We must also realize that in order to convince the masses of this sacred and lofty idea, one must especially assign distinguished people who are well endowed with genuine understanding, keen perception, and a reverence for God. These talents should enable them to enlighten the holy nation to their obligation with respect to the settlement of Eretz Yisrael. They must arouse a longing and yearning to raise the dignity of the Land and uplift her from the dust.

I also came upon [a passage] in *Tanna DeBei Eliyahu*, chapter eight,[964] from which one may ascertain that one is permitted to learn from

---

960 Possible ironic reference to the Ministry of Popular Enlightenment and Propaganda conceived by Hitler for Paul Joseph Goebbels as early as August 5, 1932. See William L. Shirer, *The Rise and Fall of the Third Reich* (New York, 1960), 166–67.

961 I Chron. 16:31.

962 The chronicles of R. Shneur Zalman of Liadi by R. Hayyim Meir Heilman, *Bet Rabbi* (Jerusalem, 1970), 90–91.

963 By 1812, the Bonaparte-Czarist confrontation reached such proportions that it was identified as the wars of Gog and Magog and precursor of the messianic era by some hasidic leaders. R. Shneur Zalman of Liadi supported the Russian cause, in opposition to R. Menahem Mendel of Riminov and the Maggid of Koznitz. See Simon Dubnow, *Toldot HaHasidut* (Tel Aviv, 1975), 318–19, 329. See also *Bet Rabbi*, *op. cit.*, 90, n. a.

964 *Tanna DeBei Eliyahu* (vol. 1) (Jerusalem, 1959), ch. 8, 146.

them[965] and their traditions. (This is in addition to my previous reference to *Bet Rabbi*).[966] It is explained how Elkana[967] made preparations
to ascend[968] with a large assemblage and with much fanfare.

"The size of the nation reflects on the glory of the king."[969]

> He [Elkana] said to the Israelites: Note the ways of the Canaanites and
> idol worshipers and how they applied themselves to their strange gods,
> though they are hollow and worthless. Surely, then, it is essential for
> you to apply yourselves and ascend before the Ark of the Covenant of
> God, the Eternal One, may His name be blessed forever. He urged
> them to ascend together with him. When they ascended with him they
> made certain to camp out in the streets of the city in order to publicize
> [the event].

Observe the lengthy text[970] describing his efforts at convince the
Israelites to ascend with him as a celebrating throng, thus to pay
homage to the King of the world. The Holy One, blessed be He,
appreciated this and rewarded him with Samuel the prophet. . . .[971]

I know for certain that had we originally dedicated ourselves in this
fashion to educate the people regarding the great value of developing
affection and love for the Land, for this alone we should be privileged
to be redeemed. As [his] patron angel wrote to our teacher the *Bet
Yosef*:[972] [Had we developed a proper attitude towards Eretz Yisrael]
we[973] would not have been in this situation whereby ordinary innocent
people, even scholars of Torah, could believe that it is forbidden to

---

965   The non-Jewish nations.

966   See above, n. 962.

967   The father of Samuel. I Sam. 1:3, 21.

968   To Shilo, the center of community worship during the period of the Judges.

969   Prov. 14:28.

970   *Tanna DeBei Eliyahu, op. cit.*

971   The Elkana in I Chron. 15:3, 23 is curiously also associated with *aliyah* to
Jerusalem as the Levite guardian of the tent which housed the Ark of the Covenant
being returned by King David to the Holy City.

972   *Maggid Mesharim, 'Shelah'* (Jerusalem, 1960), 116.

973   In the wake of the sin of the biblical spies and the subsequent cool attitude of
Jews in the diaspora towards the settling of the Land.

speak with affection in public on behalf of the Land and that we may not listen to such discourses. Further, statements were made which jarred every ear, [namely] that our brethren in the other countries took the brunt [of the Jewish tragedy in Europe] because they supported the resettlement of the Land, while those who lived in Hungary were saved because they distanced themselves from such affairs.[974] I myself heard simple people, ordinary laymen, God-fearing folk, who walk the honest path, and *hasidim*, learned men, become agitated when speaking against those who cherish the Land and prejudge them unjustly. They were not aware that they fell into the very sin of the spies. Thus they further magnified their old debt, unaware that they thereby intensify the anger of God, Heaven forbid. May the good Lord forgive them for this deed.

Only out of ignorance do they speak thus; they are not aware of the consequences of their acts. They simply lack knowledge on this important subject. Therefore, they must be informed and taught the significance of all this, to redress an old mistake and to teach them to yearn for and cherish our Land. One must not, Heaven forbid, arouse any hatred and animosity against the settlers. Hence, we will conciliate the Lord and merit the final redemption, speedily in our own day. . . .[975]

---

974 The rapid destruction of Hungarian Jewry began following the entry on March 19, 1944 of German troops, after these lines were written. See above, 231; 236–237.

975 The author summarizes the "propaganda" motif. In order to compensate for the sins of their ancestral leaders who were guilty of inciting the people against entering the Land, the current leaders now bear the responsibility for encouraging unconditional love for the Land and its settlement and hastening the final redemption. The burden of guilt for exile rests upon the community leaders who have the ability to shape public opinion. The *Or HaHayyim* commentary (Lev. 25:25) is paraphrased: דמנהיגי ישראל שבכל דור עתידין ליתן את הדין עבור שאנו עוד שוהין בגלות. "The leaders of Israel in every generation will eventually be held accountable for the fact that we are yet in exile." *EHS*, 270. The Jewish people have already endured the *hevlei Mashiah* (The pangs or pains of the Messiah). Their suffering compensates as acts of repentance. What now remains is the physical return of the people to the Land, preceded by a movement which would arouse their longing to return. The entire process of return and redemption would thus follow a natural course, a cardinal argument of the author (*EHS*, 271).

[With regard] to my volume of responsa *Mishneh Sakhir*,[976] volume two, which I had printed[977] in 1939–40. (It is still stored in the Katzburg printing plant in the city of Tirna. May God grant me the privilege to remove it from there, together with the imminent salvation of Israel. It pains me to think of this book in which I invested so much effort until it was printed. In quantity it contains one hundred and fifty pages. Qualitatively, it includes two hundred and fourteen responsa[978] based upon the four sections of the *Shulhan Arukh*. Almost all [the responsa] deal with practical issues.)

[In the introduction] I explained the verse in Ezekiel 33:[979] "Now, O mortal, I have appointed you a watchman for the House of Israel; [and wherever you hear a message from My mouth, you must transmit My warning to them. When I say to the wicked, 'Wicked man, you shall die,'] but you have not spoken to warn the wicked man against his way, he, that wicked man, shall die for his sins but I will demand a reckoning for his blood from you." I clarified that the term *damo*[980] has two meanings: real blood, as well as money,[981] as I am about to explain—with the help of God.

I shall preface my remarks from *Midrash Rabba* in *Eikha*[982] on the verse "[Bitterly she weeps in the night,] her cheek wet with tears."[983] With her priests, as it is written: "[Everyone] must give the shoulder, the cheeks and the stomach of the animal to the priest."[984] This is

---

976   For description of vol. 1, see below, 397, n. 3. See also *Mishneh Sakhir*, vol. 1 in the biographical essay (nonpaginated) by his son Hayyim Menahem (Jerusalem, 1974).

977   Evidently, the second volume was printed by the Katzburg publishing firm during 1939–40. Its distribution may have been delayed due to events in Eastern Europe and/or financial difficulties.

978   Responsa to contemporary legal questions based on and reflecting the four volumes of the *Shulhan Arukh*.

979   Verses 7–8.

980   "His blood," Ezek. 33:8.

981   Related to דמים (*damim*).

982   *Midrash Lam.* 1:26.

983   Lam. 1:2.

984   Deut. 18:3. Jerusalem weeps together with her priests, her spiritual leadership. The connection is established via the term לחיה (her cheeks) in the Lamentations

most puzzling. Was there nothing else over which to weep during the destruction of the Land[985] but for these unsubstantial gifts which were given to the priest?[986] I am baffled. Yet this *Midrash* is fittingly explained in the introduction to the volume *To'ar Moshe* devoted to the laws of ritual slaughter by the *gaon*, the author of [the volume] *Mata Dirushalayim* of Pressburg:[987]

> It is written: "This then shall be the priests' due[988] from the people. . . . Everyone must give the shoulder, the cheeks and the stomach to the priest."[989] One should note the use of the term *mishpat*[990] of the Torah in relation to the priests' tributes. We shall see that the Torah informs of a law which carries a mutual obligation on both sides—the priests on behalf of the people, and the people on behalf of the priests. In their role as priests of the Lord, they are instructed to teach the nation of the Lord the ways of Torah and the commandments, as it is written:[991] "They shall teach Your norms to Jacob [and Your instructions to Israel]." After this[992] they were consoled by law in compensation for their services. On the other hand, once the gifts of priesthood were presented in payment for instruction and care on behalf of God's people, and should the priests not perform as expected of them, then God's people are entitled to make a judgment against them, as it is written in the verse:[993]

---

passage והלחיים (the cheeks) and the gift obligations of the people for the priests who served God in the Temple.

985 Described in the opening passages of Lamentations.

986 With the destruction of the Temple. The biblical commandments related to the priestly services were terminated.

987 R. Moshe Aryeh Leib Liteh Segal Rosenbaum, pupil of Hatam Sofer, rabbinic court justice in Pressburg and author of *To'ar Moshe* (Pressburg, 1872), a treatise, on the laws of ritual slaughter. The selection cited is taken from the second preface of the volume.

988 משפט הכהנים. *Lit*, "the rule related to what is due to the priests."

989 Deut. 18:3.

990 Law, instruction, statute. But also, punishment, judgment.

991 Ibid. 33:10. The passage represents the blessings of Moses to the tribe of Levi. The priests descended from Levite origins.

992 Num. 18:21.

993 Isa. 3:14. Again the use of the term משפט (*mishpat*) "charge."

"The Lord will bring this charge against the elders and officers of His people. 'It is you who have ravaged the vineyard; that which was robbed from the poor is in your houses.'" Since they do not watch over the people of God, their portion and gifts are, in fact, objects of plunder in their possession. Well-known is the explanation of our sages of blessed memory of the verse: "[Gone from fair Zion are all that were her glory,] her leaders were like stags [that found no pasture; they could only walk feebly before the pursuer.]"[994] They pressed their heads into the ground and did not censure the Israelites.[995] They took absolutely no interest in them. Consequently, they forfeited the Land. Note that when the Land was operating routinely and the people acted in arbitrary fashion without any safeguards applied by the priests who were supposed to instruct them, they [the people] did not object to their silence. On the contrary they were thankful. But once the Land was destroyed and they experienced the suffering and bitter exile which befell them, they bewailed the priests who did not see to it that they walked in the path of God. They claimed: We from our side fulfilled our responsibilities towards them. We presented them their due, but they did not fulfill their obligation towards us. That is why our sages[996] of blessed memory interpreted: "Bitterly she weeps [in the night], her cheek wet with tears"[997] for her priests, as it is written: "Everyone must give the shoulder, the cheeks and the stomach to the priest."[998] Namely, we fulfilled our instructions with regard to them. But they did not respond to their obligation towards us. Accordingly, all the gifts received from us are in fact stolen goods. They are the source of our bitter fate, and the destruction of the Land. They willingly accepted our gifts, but they did

---

994   Lam. 1:6.

995   *Midrash Lam.* 1:34 describes the behavior of the stags during a heat wave. They turn and bury their face into each other, ignoring all else. Similarly, the leaders of Israel ignore their own flock in time of iniquity and crisis. מה אילים הללו בשעת שרב הופכין פניהם אלו תחת אלו, כך היו גדולי ישראל רואין דבר עבירה והופכין פניהם ממנו. "Just as the stags at a time of hot weather will turn their faces underneath one another [ignoring all else], so the leaders of Israel would turn a blind eye to transgressions which they witnessed."

996   LamR. 1:26.

997   Lam. 1:2.

998   Deut. 18:3.

not know how to look after us so that this misfortune would not befall us. Therefore, it is not us, but they who must cry and grieve.[999]

Likewise, I discovered the following in the sacred volume *Bet Aharon* of our holy, awesome and exalted teacher, R. Aaron of Karlin[1000] of blessed memory, who wrote a letter of rebuke to the rabbis and teachers entrusted with judicial responsibilities who were receiving rewards from the community and enjoying the benefits from the public trust. He wrote as follows: "If you will violate the trust given you in the course of your holy work it is as if, Heaven forbid, you would pocket funds earmarked for holy purposes, and fill your bellies with that which is consecrated for higher purposes, which is prohibited for pleasure and dedicated to God."[1001] These are his words in brief. He greatly expanded upon this rebuke. Such is the meaning of the words of the prophet: "His blood I shall demand from you."[1002] We have here a double meaning:[1003] Actual blood-responsibility for the Jewish blood spilled, Heaven forbid—this the prophet will demand from you, as I indicated earlier in my volume[1004] based on the *Tanna DeBei Eliyahu*. It also refers to money—he will demand the money from you and the gifts which you received, though you did not look after the community. Consequently you possess stolen goods. Note this well. . . .[1005]

As long as this is not accomplished we blame the Holy One, blessed be He, in vain for the protracted exile. It is futile to appear in houses of prayer and study with the prayer: "Our Father, our King, with Thy

---

999   Conclusion of the *To'ar Moshe* text.

1000   See above, 13, n. 57.

1001   In a lengthy letter, R. Aaron of Karlin severely rebukes pious Hasidim who violated the holy Sabbath by publicly circumventing strict restrictions placed against business transactions. *Bet Aharon* (Brody, 1873), 296.

1002   Ezek. 33:8.

1003   Of the term דמו (*damo*).

1004   *EHS*, 14–15.

1005   The author returns to the theme of national unity as indispensable for redemption (*EHS*, 272).

great compassion, cancel all of our liabilities."[1006] As long as there yet
remains in place the document of liability, one in which we expressed
antipathy towards the precious Land,[1007] as it is written: "They rejected
the desirable Land. . . . They grumbled in their tents."[1008] According
to the Midrash,[1009] Israel obligated itself to a faulty debt, which stands
to this very day. How then are we able to pray for the cancellation of
our debt when we must yet arrange payment and correct [the situation]
as I have indicated? It is analogous to the debtor who requests the
creditor to destroy the debit document in his possession. How is he
expected to do this? Certainly not! So it is in our instance. We therefore
ask of the Almighty to turn the heart of every Jew towards the truth
and accept our arguments contained herein, since they are based on
the masters of truth, upon the teachings of our sages of blessed memory,
and the Midrashim whose words are truth and justice. Note this well.

I was aware that these meek folk who withdrew[1010] had good intentions, but they were fearful that association with people who had
abandoned the path of Torah would be detrimental to their children.
To them I say the following: Though their intentions are acceptable,
their acts are not acceptable for a number of reasons. The first I
already noted earlier.[1011] As the prophet [Isaiah] cautioned Hezekiah
the king, "You should have acted as you were commanded. Are the
secrets of the All-Merciful your affair?"[1012] So in our situation. Since
you are obligated to build and settle the Land, which is a positive
biblical commandment, everyone is obligated to unite as one man.
This cannot be accomplished intermittently. What you are commanded
must be done. Why delve into the secrets of the All-Merciful? Further,

---

1006 From the *Avinu Malkeinu* liturgy of the High Holy Days and fast days: אבינו
מלכנו מחוק ברחמיך הרבים כל שטרי חובותינו.

1007 Reference to the biblical episode of the spies.

1008 Ps. 106:24, 25.

1009 LamR. 1:24.

1010 From involvement in the rebuilding of Eretz Yisrael.

1011 See above, 113 and 116–119. The resettlement of Eretz Yisrael by the
nonobservant is part of the Divine will and message and therefore must be supported.

1012 Ber. 10a. A variant of Isaiah's response to King Hezekiah, who refused to sire
children since he foresaw the birth of the evil Menashe. See above, 113.

one [fulfillment of a] commandment leads to another.[1013] No Jew will be harmed by participating in this far-reaching mitzvah whose value is unlimited. On the contrary, the sanctity of the Land will be enhanced if the majority of the God-fearing would participate, as I indicated earlier, citing the holy Rebbe of Gur, may he live, and Nahmanides.[1014]

I wish to cite another clear proof text from Scripture that the arguments [of the pious] are in error, with the very emergence of the light of our righteous Messiah, who was descended from Ruth the Moabite who requested of Boaz: "Spread your robe over your hand-maid, for your are a redeeming kinsman."[1015] And he indicated that there is a redeeming kinsman closer in relation.[1016] "Stay for the night. Then in the morning, if he will act as a redeemer, good! Let him redeem. But if he does not want to act as a redeemer for you, I will do so myself. . . ."[1017] "Meanwhile, Boaz had gone to the gate and sat down there. And now the redeemer whom Boaz had mentioned passed by and he called: 'Come over and sit down here, so and so!' And he came over and sat down. . . ."[1018] "Boaz continued: 'When you acquire the property from Naomi and from Ruth the Moabite, you must also acquire the wife of the deceased, so as to perpetuate the name of the deceased upon his estate.' The redeemer replied: 'Then I cannot redeem it for myself, lest I impair my own estate. You take over my right of redemption [for I am unable to exercise it.]'"[1019] And so Boaz proceeded, taking Ruth [as his wife] and bringing forth from her our righteous Messiah.[1020] Rashi explains the verse "'Lest I impair my own estate'[1021]—'my offspring,' as [in the verse] 'Sons are the

---

1013   Avot 4:2.
1014   See above, 190, n. 401.
1015   Ruth 3:9.
1016   Who would be obligated to take the widowed Ruth as a wife and perpetuate the family name.
1017   Ibid. 3:13.
1018   Ibid. 4:1.
1019   Ibid. 4:5–6.
1020   King David. Ibid. 4:17–22.
1021   Ibid. 4:6.

provision of the Lord'[1022] you will impair my offspring."[1023]

Now this redeemer was a "pious soul."[1024] He was afraid to marry Ruth and thereby to bring forth the light of the Messiah lest he thereby impair his offspring.[1025] He therefore responded: "Then I cannot redeem it for myself lest I impair my own estate."[1026] Scripture is critical of him, as Rashi explains the verse: "'So and so'—His [the redeemer's] name is not specified, because he refused to redeem," though he did cite a reason "lest I impair my own estate."[1027] Nevertheless, Scripture faults him, for he did not act properly. When it is a question of revealing the light of the Messiah, "one should not be a fool and appear with pietism."[1028]

Now it is said in the name of our holy rabbi, R. Naftali of Ropshitz,[1029] who was known for his clever remarks, that a proper Jew must be at once "good, pious and wise."[1030] One without the others is not sufficient. One who is exclusively good is an adulterer.[1031] To be pious only, is to be a fool. To be clever alone, is to be skeptic. To be good and pious and clever is the proper course of a Jew. These were his words.[1032] "A wise man's talk brings him favor."[1033] They are worthy of a kiss.[1034] In fact this idea is stipulated in Tosafot in the first chapter of Avodah

---

1022   Ps. 127:3. The term נחלה "estate" assumes offspring.

1023   Rashi on Ruth 4:6.

1024   The author uses the Yiddish איין פרוממער—with a critical connotation—perhaps "pietistic."

1025   By marrying a convert of Moabite origin.

1026   Ibid. 4:5–6.

1027   Ruth was perceived as a foreigner with possible biblical sanctions directed at those considering intermarriage (Deut. 23:4; Neh. 13:1).

1028   The section in quotes appears in Yiddish. The author presently inserts an addendum, appearing as an elaborate footnote in the original.

1029   Hasidic master (1760–1827), pupil of the Hozeh of Lublin, the Maggid of Koznitz and R. Elimelekh of Lizhensk.

1030   In Yiddish.

1031   Deriving personal pleasure from being good without the broader moral religious motives behind the act. The mere adherence to good conduct can be self-indulgent.

1032   R. Naftali of Ropshitz.

1033   Eccl. 10:12.

1034   Cf. Prov. 24:26.

Zarah 20b,[1035] citing the Midrash: [1036] "One should be wise, humble, and God-fearing—one without the other two is not sufficient." This Midrash is also cited in the great work *Or Zarua,* at the beginning of the volume (*Drush Aleph-Bet,* no. 44). [1037] Note it. These are the very conclusions of our Rabbi of Ropshitz.

Now Boaz followed the approach of our holy rabbi[1038] in that he was not concerned with "lest I impair my own estate." Though he was God-fearing and intelligent, he was also aware of the teaching of the *Hovot HaLevavot* [1039] quoted previously[1040] concerning the subject of caution—do not be overcautious. Act as you were instructed. The Holy One, blessed be He, will do His part. Beware that when it concerns the unveiling of the Messiah's radiance one should not take a pietistic attitude.[1041] Since he [Boaz] fulfilled his part, he was privileged to reveal the light of the Messiah.

The same holds true for the building of the Land. Since it is commanded to rebuild the Holy Land and to uplift it from the mounds of dust, it is prohibited to obstruct the construction with pietistic caution, Heaven forbid! One is implored to join in building with anyone and to be concerned with the sacred restoration in the Land,[1042]

1035   Cited as 18b in *EHS.*

1036   Variant in *Derekh Eretz,* chapter 7. ג' דברים שקולין זה בזה - חכמה, יראה, ענוה. "Three concepts are equal in importance: wisdom, reverence [for God], humility." Tosafot in AZ 20b has the variant reading: שלשה דברים שקולים זה כזה: יראת חטא, חכמה, ענוה . . . דלא סגיא להא בלא הא. יראה בלא חכמה וחכמה בלא יראה ושתיהם בלא ענוה וענוה בלא שתיהם. "Three concepts are equal in importance: fear of sin, wisdom, humility. . . . One is not complete without the presence of the others. Reverence without wisdom, wisdom without reverence, both without humility and humility without both [wisdom and reverence.]"

1037   *Or Zarua LaTzadik* (Lublin, 1929). Anthology of assorted works by the hasidic master R. Zadok HaKohen of Lublin (1823–1900), including treatises on the forms of the Hebrew alphabet.

1038   R. Naftali of Ropshitz.

1039   The popular 11th-century classic of ethics and ways of piety composed by R. Bahya ben Yosef ibn Paquda in the Arab vernacular and translated into Hebrew by Yehudah ibn Tibbon.

1040   *EHS,* 15. Reference to the consequences of excessive hesitancy and caution.

1041   This sentence appears in Yiddish.

1042   Yiddish.

and the Lord will assist us as I have indicated. Certainly one should not abstain from and hinder restoration, Heaven forbid. This is not the act of an intelligent person. A hint to the wise.

I have already referred previously to the views of the *Havot Yair* (172)[1043] in reference to R. Zeira's comments concerning the Babylonian [Jews]: "These Babylonians are fools."[1044] [This opinion was] due to his love for Eretz Yisrael. Here we see the extent to which it pained R. Zeira that they did not all return[1045] with Ezra, thereby impairing the [process of] eternal redemption. R. Zeira was a most earnest person, never was there a smile upon his lips. [The tractate of] Niddah 23,[1046] describes the extent to which R. Jeremiah attempted to make him laugh, yet never did. On the slightest pretext he fasted extensively as described in Baba Metzia.[1047] Surely, he would never engage in excessive talk, especially in sharp words which would dishonor others by referring to the Babylonians as fools. But this was my point. He was so distressed that these Babylonians did not ascend to Eretz Yisrael at the time of Ezra—which was to have been the final redemption. Yet due to pietistic contentions[1048] they did not return and thus they brought about this result. He, therefore, refers to them as fools. When confronting momentous challenges such as *aliyah* to the Land, one should not appear with foolish and frivolous notions. Observe [what is written in] the close of [the tractate] Ketubot,[1049] noting the extent to which R. Zeira passionately loved the Land. Note it well! . . .

Hence, we should not at all respond to the argument of the "pious

---

1043 *Sefer She'elot uTshuvot Havot Ya'ir* (Lemberg, 1896), responsa nos. 152, 76. The work of R. Ya'ir Hayyim ben Moshe Shimshon (1622–1714), authority in halakhah and philosophy, who served as rabbinic judge in Worms.

1044 Ned. 49b; Betza 16a.

1045 *Lit.*, "ascend."

1046 23a *vs.* 24 in *EHS.* See Rashi there and Ber. 31a. אסור לאדם שימלא שחוק פיו בעולם הזה. "One should not fill his mouth with laughter in this world."

1047 85a.

1048 Yiddish.

1049 112a. R. Zeira, unable to obtain a boat crossed hastily into the Land by means of a precarious rope bridge.

ones." Rather we should proceed to cherish our sacred Land and to surrender ourselves to her. Consequently, we will have a hand, with the help of the Lord, in uncovering the light of the Messiah, speedily in our day. Amen.

I have already cited at the outset of this book[1050] the message of our rabbi of Israel, R. Yehoshu'ele Kutner of blessed memory, in a communication to R. Zvi Kalisher,[1051] not to take to heart the arguments of the opponents since they do not speak with understanding.[1052] The holy and divine *gaon* R. Eliyahu of Greiditz went even further, with regard to the opponents who were under the influence of the *kelipot*,[1053] Heaven forbid. Likewise, the *gaon* and kabbalist R. Akiva Yosef, the author of *Lev HaIvri*, expressed similar views as I have indicated previously.[1054] A third related opinion [explains their action] suggesting they are still under the influence of the [biblical] spies who were fearful about entering the Land since this would harm their own interests,[1055] as described earlier in detail.[1056]

In summary, whoever has any brain in his skull, and whoever has true faith in the Almighty and in His Land, can never reject with any argument and in any fashion, the uplifting of the dignity of our Land. Should someone nevertheless appear with such arguments, these would represent the claims of Satan and his group. May the Almighty save us from their opinions. The *Ya'avetz* in his *siddur*[1057] rejects the claims

---

1050 *EHS*, 3.

1051 In the *haskamah* (statement of acknowledgment and support) of the renowned scholar R. Yehoshua Kutner to R. Kalisher's classic in religious Zionism, *Drishat Tzion* (1864). See above, 156, n. 149.

1052 Cf. Job 34:35.

1053 See above, 33, n. 107 and 229, n. 661. The use of מסימת עינים (*mesimat einayim*) may possibly have been intended as אחיזת עינים "deception." Namely the opponents served the fraudulent purposes of the *kelipot.* In either case, the *kelipot* exist by means of *galut.* It is in their interest to sustain and prolong the exile of Israel.

1054 See above, 235, n. 701. The opponents are described as old fools.

1055 They feared that in Eretz Yisrael they could no longer continue in the role as leaders [of a] people in the desert.

1056 See above, 26–27; 239–240.

1057 See above, 30, n. 91.

[of those who oppose rebuilding the Land] because of the sinners who reside there. What alternatives confront us here outside the Land? Note the source.

This certainly is valid today when we witness what has befallen us and the fate of the centers of Torah in Poland, Lithuania and Hungary. Do we still have any possessions or assets here? We are perceived by them [the non-Jews] as outsiders. They have destroyed our capital,[1058] our bodies and our entire life. Consequently, any intelligent person and genuinely God-fearing soul will come to the realization that we have nothing further to desire from any nation here. What remains now for all of us is to return to the possessions of our forefathers. This is clear and as authentic as Torah. Those who dispute these [facts] challenge the truth and Torah. Note this well!

My brethren, I shall illustrate this point in another manner. I will relate to you an incident which happened to me when I escaped from hell's country[1059] in order to save my bare soul. I was unable to take with me any parcel with my belongings. I rescued only [a pair] of *Rashi tefillin*.[1060] The *tefillin* of *Rabbenu Tam* I was compelled to leave behind. The complexity of the escape was such that I could not bring along a thing. But the *Rashi tefillin* I could not abandon. I could not bring myself to be separated from them because their worth to me is greater than any possession in the world. They are priceless. I had acquired them during my youth, prior to World War I. I had them inscribed by the renowned scribe and pure *tzadik* R. Hayyim Sofer of

---

1058   Compare with Gen. 31:14–15.

1059   From Nitra, Slovakia to Budapest, most likely between October 25–28, 1942. See above, 22, n. 34.

1060   The phylacteries (*tefillin*, likely derived from תפילה, "prayer") are worn at morning weekday prayer based in the tradition upon the verses in Ex. 13:9, 16; Deut. 6:8–9; 11:18. The expanded biblical context of these verses are inscribed in separate small parchment scrolls contained in the four compartments of the *tefillin* worn on the head (תפילין של ראש). (The phylactery worn on the hand [תפילין של יד] contains all of the inscribed material on one scroll.) Rashi and his grandson, the tosafist Rabbenu Tam (1100–1171), differ in their opinion of the order and position of the four scrolls in the תפילין של ראש. In order to fulfill the tradition of both scholars, many pious Jews supplement *Rashi tefillin* with those of Rabbenu Tam. See *Shulhan Arukh, Orah Hayyim* 34:1–2.

Munkatch of blessed memory.[1061] Therefore, they are very important to me. I will not move even an inch without them. Thus, when I came to the capital[1062] I had neither *Rabbenu Tam tefillin* nor *tallit*.[1063] I hereby express thanks to my friend, rabbi, *gaon*, a pure *tzadik*, offspring of revered ancestry, our teacher R. Yisrael David Margoliot Schlesinger, rabbi of the local house of study Linat HaTzedek. Through his efforts I received from the distinguished personage and God-fearing man, our teacher R. Hayyim Mordechai Stern, may his radiance continue to shine, *Rabbenu Tam tefillin*, which were very beautiful and elegant and which revitalized me. Now I possessed these two pair of *tefillin*, but I still lacked a *tallit*. I will now compliment my affluent friend Wolf Reichman, may his radiance shine forth, who furnished me with a *tallit* with which to pray. So the Almighty provided me with two pair of *tefillin* and a *tallit* with which to pray. But all was not yet complete for I still needed a sash[1064] for prayer. The Almighty helped me also in this regard. I have here a former student who used to study at our Yeshivah.[1065] He gave me a *gartel* for prayer. I still did not have the complete set. After having brought together all of the religious articles mentioned, I was still in need of a small prayerbook. I now express my thanks to my friend and pupil, outstanding Torah scholar and God-fearing teacher and rabbi, Zalman Leib Klein,[1066] may his light shine forth, one of the active members of the Talmud study circle here in the capital. . . .

Nevertheless, whenever I wished to pray in the morning, I was

---

1061   He was the personal scribe of the father of the Munkatcher Rebbe, R. Zvi Hirsh Shapira (1850–1913), and wrote a Torah scroll for his son and successor R. Hayyim Eleazar Shapira (1872–1937).

1062   Budapest.

1063   Prayer shawl.

1064   The *gartel* [Yiddish] is the woven waistband worn by *hasidim* during prayer and other ceremonies as part of the ritual to prepare oneself with care for prayer. The sash separates the upper body (the intellect and spirit) from the lower (the material and physical) and serves as an aid to internalize the verse in Isa. 11:5: "Justice shall be the girdle of his loins, and faithfulness the girdle of his waist." See Aaron Wertheim, *Law and Custom in Hasidism* (Hoboken, Ktav, 1992), 113–114.

1065   Likely the Moriah Yeshivah in Piestany, Slovakia.

1066   Kelman in the Jerusalem edition of *EHS*.

anguished and troubled due to these religious objects. Never did I ever have them together at one time, so that I could pray without interruption. At times the *Rashi tefillin* were missing, on other occasions, the *Rabbenu Tam tefillin*. When both were at hand, my prayer shawl was lacking—or the *"gartel,"* or perhaps the prayerbook. Daily, this was my situation. With difficulty did I ever have these handy at one time. This was because I did not possess a *tallit* bag[1067] wherein all of the sacred items could be stored together without their being dispersed in all directions. Then my friend and pupil Reb Zalman Leib had pity on me and also gave me a *tallit* bag into which I gathered all of the ritual paraphernalia together.

I was pleased and delighted . . . I contemplated on the extent and significance of this *tallit* bag and how it has the ability to gather and unite, so that never is there anything lacking or separated. The *tallit* bag indeed gives meaning and value to its contents so that they might fulfill their tasks at the time that they are needed. Yet, following intense contemplation on the significant endowment of this *tallit* bag, I arrived at the conclusion that despite its considerable capacity to bring together, it does not in any manner change any of the objects within it, for the better or worse. I never noticed that any one of these sacred articles either decreased in sanctity or was in any way exchanged for another. I always found the *Rashi tefillin* as they were. They were never interchanged for those of *Rabbenu Tam*, or the reverse. Neither were the *tefillin* transformed into a *gartel*, or prayerbook or prayer shawl, or the reverse.

The account of this *tallit* bag has an application for Israel in exile. We [also] have among ourselves different kinds [of Jews]. There are those on the high level of holiness, as are the *Rashi tefillin*. Then there are those similar to the holiness of *Rabbenu Tam tefillin*. And those of the kind comparable to the *tallit*. And those on the level of the *gartel*. And those on the level of the small prayerbook. These [latter] are the simple people. They are simple Jews, likened to the simplicity of the small *siddur*. There are those of limited worth, but

---

1067   Bag which contained the prayer shawl and the *tefillin.*

are nevertheless Jews. Now all of these classes should amalgamate into one group, as exemplified by the four species[1068] and as explained in the poetic liturgy of Sukkot[1069] and in the Midrash.[1070]

Further, we need one another, as explained so well by our rabbi of Zans[1071] in his work the *Divrei Hayyim* [commentary] on the Torah[1072] (addenda to the weekly portion, *Re'eh*).[1073] It may be compared to the body and its many interrelated parts upon which life is dependent. These are organs such as the hands and feet. One can live without hands and feet. Now can the head indicate to the feet or hands: I no longer wish to have any contact with you since I can live without you? Certainly not! This is similar to any of the arguments whereby a relationship is severed because one is inferior to the other. Certainly one can live without hands and feet. But what kind of life is it, Heaven forbid? Nevertheless, the truth is that the head has need for the feet since all the power of support lies in the legs and the ability for work lies in the hands. They complete the full stature of man. Now man is complete. So it is with a nation. There are people with superior intellect and perfect understanding, and those with limited knowledge and an inferior set of values. Yet all are necessary for the nation. One complements the other. They must be united into one

---

1068 The citron, palm branch, myrtle and willow branches of the Sukkot (Tabernacles) festival. Lev. 23:40.

1069 Likely the אקחה בראשון "I shall take on the first day . . ." *piyyut* of the morning service of the first day of Sukkot. וכמו הם אגודים אלה באלה, כן תלויים אלה באלה "And just as they are bound together, so are they [the wicked] tied to them [the merit of the righteous]." The unity in diversity motive is also alluded to in the אאמיר אותך סלה "I will always praise you" *piyyut* רחמם בנשאם אגדות "Have compassion for them when they take the bound species" and the אכתיר זר תהילה "I will crown You with [my] prayer of praise" segment גדתי ארבע, למספר רובע "I have united four [species] in accordance with [Israel's] four camps", both of the *Sukkot* morning liturgy.

1070 LevR. 30:11. אלא אמר הקב"ה: יוקשרו כולם אגודה אחת והן מכפרין אלו על אלו ואם עשיתם כך אותה שעה אני מתעלה." "Declared the Holy One, blessed be He, however: 'Let them all be bound together, and one will atone [for the sins of] the other. If they do so, I will at that moment be exalted.'" See below, 359–360.

1071 See above, 27, n. 70.

1072 Brooklyn, New York (1962), 230 with some variation in text.

1073 Deut. 11:26–16:17.

federation. These are the words of our rabbi.[1074]

(Note Maimonides in the introduction to the Order [in the Talmud] of Zeraim which I cited earlier).[1075] For this reason the Almighty established wicked people in Eretz Yisrael—in order to create for the righteous a community in which wasteland would be reclaimed. But due to our dispersion among the nations, it is impossible to gather us into one federation. We always have a shortcoming. This is our weakness. Consequently everyone dominates and harasses us. Among ourselves we are split and splintered, as I described previously when portraying the *golus Yid*.[1076] Therefore, if we correct this longstanding defect, we will, with the help of the Almighty restore unity among us and bring together the sum total of Israel into one circle and thereby fulfill the commandment of settling the Land. This community will constitute the large *tallit* bag of the holy nation which will gather into one place all of dispersed Israel in the world. . . .

Therefore, I call upon you people, Jewish people from every corner of the earth, from minor to adult, man and woman, young and old, all of you rise and respond, stand and be alert[1077] to enter this covenant of rebuilding the Land. May no one exclude himself. (Actually, according to the tractate Horayot, page 3, a majority would be sufficient.)[1078] Let us proceed to rebuild our Land by means of our total participation.[1079] That is why both the First and Second Temples were not sustained, because there was not complete participation. Therefore, if we will all now become involved, we will bring to it an

---

1074   R. Hayyim of Zans.

1075   *EHS*, 201.

1076   See above, 255–257.

1077   Cf. היום יכתב "Today it will be written" segment from the Yom Kippur morning liturgy.

1078   The discussion in the Babylonian Talmud Hor. 3a focuses on the relative culpability and responsibility of the majority, the minority, the individual, and the court in following an erroneous court decision. Particularly pertinent is the teaching of Rav Assi: ובהוראה הלך אחר רוב יושבי ארץ ישראל "In legal opinions he was influenced by the majority of the populace in Eretz Yisrael."

1079   Veiled reference to the negligible participation of the Jewish people who remained in the diaspora when Ezra returned to Eretz Yisrael to rebuild the Second Temple. See Yoma 9b.

everlasting impact and the Almighty will be with us, as it is written in Scripture (Haggai 2): "Be strong, all you people of the Land, says the Lord, and act! For I am with you, says the Lord of Hosts . . . and My spirit is still in your midst. Do not fear!"[1080] We will then merit the final redemption with the establishment of the kingdom of the House of David, because it came about by means of uniting the totality [of the people]. There would be no adversary or evil affliction. . . .

At the outset of this volume,[1081] I preached to the current settlers and builders of the Land.[1082] I shall now augment my message and address them once again. I have already demonstrated how the light of Israel's salvation is linked to the involvement of the totality of Israel in the holy task of building and settling the Land. The involvement of the God-fearing and the devout, as well as the participation of the masses of Israel [is necessary]. No matter who they might be, the desired result cannot be achieved by one without the other. One should know and understand that without the [participation of the] devout, the cities of Zion will not be built. Only with the Divine Spirit can the cities of Judah be constructed. And if a portion of the multitude succeeded in the initiative of rebuilding the Land, let them not believe that it was the exclusive product of man's efforts. Rather it was all accomplished with the help of the Almighty and the Cause of all Causes who induced them specifically to be the agent through whom beginnings were accomplished, as I have explained at length earlier.[1083] Thus the support of the Almighty will still be necessary in order to enhance and develop this work still further until its ultimate completion. Without the Divine support, Heaven forbid, the entire entity can come to naught.

Above all, I am here to arouse the masses who have come to the Land and engage in agriculture, who build walls and erect houses and [work in] other building trades related to settlement. These [activities]

1080   Hag. 2:4–5.

1081   See above, 54–58.

1082   To the nonobservant and secular pioneers.

1083   See above, 116–117.

are purely material in nature, akin to farming and settlement outside
of Eretz Yisrael known as "land culture."[1084] This is how they were
trained and educated outside the Land, within the culture of the
nations of the world. It is as the Midrash comments on the verse in
Song of Songs: "'They made me guard the vineyards; my own vineyard
I did not guard.' 'They made me guard the vineyards'—to enhance
the nations. 'My own vineyard'—this is the Holy One, blessed be
He—'I did not guard.'"[1085] This is a lesson and a clear rebuke to our
Jewish brethren in exile who contributed all their spiritual resources
to the cultures of the nations of the world. Thereby they exalted and
elevated them to the pinnacle [of cultural achievements] among European countries. Most of these European nations who reached the
ultimate in culture did so only because of the contributions of Jews
who contributed all of their spiritual energies to them. Yet, instead of
being grateful to them, and being properly rewarded within their
culture, they [the Jews] were deprived of their rights. They were
excluded from any benefits. Yet others benefited from their toil. Such
is the fate of our Jewish brethren who have withdrawn from guarding
the vineyard of the Lord of Hosts and proceeded to guard the vineyards
of the nations. At the very least they surrendered themselves to the
culture of the nations. When they arrive in the Land and continue
with the kind of work to which they were accustomed abroad, they
must be informed that though such labor is regarded abroad as materialistic, in the Holy Land it is considered spiritual devotion. Every
enterprise and act directed towards labor of the Land, such as plowing,
sowing, the planting of trees, the building of homes, the paving of
roads, and similar activities necessary for the settling of the Land is
deemed a mitzvah. It is likened to one who is engaged with [the
mitzvah of] *tefillin*, the lulav palm, the sukkah tabernacle and the
balance of instrumentalities related to the fulfillment of the command-

---

1084 Yiddish or German. The author may have been referring to the often
misunderstood version of the Socialist Zionist "secular" philosophy of A. D. Gordon
(1856–1922) sometimes described as "the religion of the physical labor of the land," a
communion with nature, soil and soul, to paraphrase Hertzberg. See Arthur Hertzberg,
"Aaron David Gordon," *The Zionist Idea* (New York, 1971), 369–386, especially 370.

1085 *Yalkut Shimoni* II, 982.

ments.[1086]

Were I not afraid of my colleagues and more so of my teachers who would mock me, I would express my original idea. Just as our sages of blessed memory stated in the tractate Sukkah 46[1087] and Menahot 42[1088] "One who assembles a lulav palm or a sukkah for himself recites the *Shehehiyanu* [Thanksgiving] blessing.[1089] Similarly, one who begins to work the Land of Eretz Yisrael for himself or for the first time builds a home for himself, should also recite the *Shehehiyanu* blessing. And perhaps [it should be recited] when the act is not a personal one (here one should distinguish between sukkah and lulav)[1090] and the settlement of the Land involves [as an essential part of the commandment] the preparation of the Land suitable for settlement. Consequently, it [the act] need not necessarily be limited to one's personal benefit. It may [at the same time] benefit others since it also benefits him. I will be brief with my argument; but see further Tosafot in the tractate of Sukkah where it is questioned why some mitzvot have the *Shehehiyanu* blessing linked to them and others not. [Tosafot] conclude that whenever a mitzvah is related to joy the blessing is recited. Where there is no joy, the blessing is not recited. In our case there is certainly joy. Surely it is appropriate to recite the *Shehehiyanu* whenever one begins working and rebuilding the Land. Presently, I am only commenting [for discussion]. One should not issue a ruling and certainly not apply [this suggestion] until the outstanding authorities of the generation will consent. Note this well!

1086   The author again refers to the legal rulings of the Hatam Sofer, Rashbash and Tashbaz: Settlement of Eretz Yisrael is a positive biblical commandment (*EHS*, 281, and above, 51–54; 178–190).

1087   46a. העושה לולב [סוכה] לעצמו, אומר ברוך שהחיינו וקיימנו והגיענו לזמן הזה "One who waves a lulav palm for himself (as in the case of one who builds a sukkah for himself) recites: 'Praised are you . . . for granting us life, for sustaining us and for helping us reach this day.'"

1088   42a.

1089   See above, n. 1068. According to Tosafot, Suk. 46a, s.v. העושה סוכה לעצמו "One who builds a sukkah for his own use . . . ," the thanksgiving blessing is limited to occasions of personal joy, as in the case of one who builds a sukkah for himself. In actual practice, the blessing is recited when one begins to use it for its ritual purpose.

1090   Where the act by its very nature becomes a personal, private mitzvah.

In any event, all those who work the earth in Eretz Yisrael will now understand that their labor is not physical but spiritual in nature. Their every activity on behalf of the rebuilding of Eretz Yisrael reflects the spirit of our God. Perhaps this was the meaning of Isaiah the prophet when he declared: "Announce to the cities of Judah: Behold your God!"[1091] Note that in addition to the difficulty with this verse (discussed previously)[1092] concerning the intent of the phrase "Behold your God!" one may add the idea which I have presently noted. Upon every activity on behalf of the "cities of Judah"[1093] rests the sanctity and spirit of "your God," since every act is considered a mitzvah as any other in the Torah. Further, the Land is thereby sanctified with the holiness of the Almighty.[1094] Now since every laborer must readjust himself emotionally, mentally, intellectually and perceptually to this holy and superior task, he is expected to reject the alien notion of labor brought with him from outside the Land. He is to be sensitized to its spirituality. Then he may be certain that the Almighty will send him help from the sanctuary.[1095] "He will bless" their efforts.[1096] The settlement will increase, expand and multiply until we achieve the aim of the complete redemption, speedily in our own day. Amen.

It is therefore necessary that they [the settlers] draw close to the God-fearing people in order to learn from them. The outstanding scholars of their generation should serve as their model for conduct in the spirit of the Torah. You shall walk inspired by this new spirit of Torah. You will fulfill the mission for which you came to build and stimulate the Land. You will act as you did abroad,[1097] except that

---

1091   Isa. 40:9.

1092   See above, 175–176. The author questions the abrupt conclusion of this verse.

1093   The Jerusalem edition mistakenly amends the original "cities of Judah" (ערי יהודה), which was faithful to Isa. 40:9, to "Judean Mountains" (בהרי יהודה).

1094   In addition to the intrinsic sanctity of the Land, the Jewish people, in fulfilling God's commandment to rebuild the Land, increase its holiness.

1095   Cf. Ps. 20:3.

1096   Cf. מי שברך (Mi Sheberakh) prayer at the conclusion of the Sabbath morning service.

1097   You will continue to be productive in your own land as you contributed to

there will be a turn for the better. There you acted in an alien fashion befitting the spirit of the nations. Here you will behave in the spirit of Torah and Lord of Hosts. You will see for yourselves that through you the Lord's purpose will prosper.[1098] All of the blessings related in the books of the prophets shall come upon you.[1099] As I cited (at the close of the foreward to this book)[1100] the comment of Rashi on [the verse[1101]] in the portion of *Zot HaBrakhah*:[1102] "Silver and gold from all the lands will flow to Eretz Yisrael," if the Land will conduct itself in the spirit of the Torah. Our Holy Land will be built and established at a tempo so rapid that we ourselves will be amazed at how much its borders will have expanded within a brief period. The Almighty will assist us with every task, and angels from heaven will come to our aid, as it is related in *Midrash Ecclesiastes*.[1103]

It is the story of R. Hanina the son of Dosa who noted that his fellow townsmen were bringing contributions and voluntary offerings to Jerusalem. [He said: "Everyone is offering contributions to Jerusalem] and I do not offer a thing." What did he do? He went out to the wasteland of his city. Seeing a rock, he chipped, chiseled and polished it. (Note the *Matnot Kehuna* commentary:[1104] "*Veshivevah*—an expression meaning 'breaking' as it is written in the [Talmud] chapter 'R. Akiva said.'[1105] *Umirkah*—it [the rock] was made smooth and polished as it is

---

other lands.

1098   Cf. Isa. 53:10.

1099   Cf. Deut. 28:2.

1100   See above, 57–58.

1101   Deut. 33:25.

1102   Deut. 33:1–34:11.

1103   EcclR. 1:1.

1104   On EcclR. 1:1, explaining ושבבה (*veshivevah*). The *EHS* text erroneously cites מ״יר vs. the מ״כ abbreviations for the commentary.

1105   The ninth chapter in the tractate Shabbat (87a). The *Matnot Kehunah* utilizes an indirect paraphrase of both the Talmud and Rashi commentary on the term "breaking" שמשבבין. In the context of the discussion, Moses enumerated to the Israelites at Sinai the punishments for violating the commandments. This might have "broken" their spirit, or discouraged them from accepting the Torah.

cited *Tamrukei nashim.*")[1106] He [R. Hanina ben Dosa] then said: "I have
vowed to bring it [the rock] to Jerusalem." He needed to hire porters.
By chance, five men happened upon him. He said to them: "Will you
take this stone to Jerusalem for me?" Said they to him: "Give us fifty
sela coins and we shall take it up to Jerusalem." He was ready to pay
them, but did not have it at hand. He dismissed them and they went
their way.

The Holy One, blessed be He, then summoned five angels in the
guise of men. He said to them: "Will you take this stone for me?" They
responded to him: "Give us five *sela* coins and we shall take up your
stone to Jerusalem, provided you will personally assist us." He then
participated [in hauling the stone] with them. They found themselves
standing in Jerusalem. He wanted to pay them their due, but could not
find them. He entered the "Chamber of the Hewn Stone"[1107] and inquired
about them. He was told: "It seems that the ministering angels [of
God] brought up your stone to Jerusalem."

These are the words of the midrash. This midrash is also to be
found at the beginning of *Midrash Song of Songs*.[1108] Now it seems
strange that having with him five *sela* coins to cover the cost of labor
he would not have given the sum instead to purchase a goodwill
offering [for the Temple].[1109] For five *sela* coins he surely could have
purchased an animal for the goodwill offering. But he wished to
demonstrate [with the gift of a stone] that anyone who contributes to
the building of a city or its repair is as welcome before God as a burnt
offering or sacrifice. He, therefore, specifically chose to bring up to
Jerusalem a stone which is linked to the walls of the city. He was then
assisted by Heaven, as indicated by the ministering angels who carried

---

1106   Est. 2:12, *lit.* "cosmetic polish" from the root מרק (*m'r'k'*). This concludes the
Matnot Kehunah commentary on EcclR. 1:1, interjected by the author.

1107   The לשכת הגזית the rectangular chamber located in the southeastern corner of
the Temple Mount, presumably named so because of its construction. It is best
known as the meeting place of the Sanhedrin high court.

1108   CantR. 1:4 A variant of the Kohelet midrash.

1109   Since the offerings of others in the first instance compelled him to seek some
appropriate gift for the Temple.

the stone. Now why did they request of him to personally lend a hand in carrying the stone since they were in any event lifting it? How did his participation contribute? Were they dependent upon him?

It seems to me that the answer lies in a passage I read in a text which cites the holy *gaon*, R. Yeshayahu Muscat of blessed memory, chief judge of the rabbinic court of Praga near Warsaw,[1110] commenting on what our sages[1111] of blessed memory taught. The ark carried its bearers.[1112] Nevertheless, the Almighty commanded that it be borne [by others], because He preferred the awakening [to originate] below.[1113] As it is written in the Zohar:[1114] "With the awakening below will come the awakening Above." These are his words.[1115] The angels[1116] also wanted him to be personally involved in the awakening below. Then assistance from Heaven would follow.

And so shall it be, my friends! If your labors will be completely performed in the spirit of Torah and tradition, guided by Torah scholars and leaders, I am confident in the presumption that the Lord "will send you help from the sanctuary and sustain you from Zion."[1117] And as it is interpreted in the *Midrash*:[1118] "From the sanctification[1119]

1110 1783–1868. Scholar and hasidic leader. Outstanding pupil of the Maggid of Koznitz.

1111 Sot. 35a.

1112 When the Israelites crossed the Jordan into the Holy Land. The Ark as an independent object in motion is derived from the phrase ויעבר ארון ד' "The Ark of the Lord . . . advanced" (Jos. 4:11).

1113 With man.

1114 Among the oft-repeated formulas of the Zohar. See Zohar I on Gen. 11:31. דהא כיון דאתער בר נש אתערותא בקדמיתא כדין אתער אתערותא דלעילא. "Since the person initially stimulates a response [in the human sphere], a [similar] response is triggered in the upper spheres." See also above, 24–25 and below, 312, n. 1200.

1115 R. Yeshayahu of Praga.

1116 Who assisted R. Hanina ben Dosa.

1117 Ps. 20:3.

1118 MPs. 20:5.

1119 Homiletical reading of ישלח עזרך מקדש *Lit.*, "May He send you help from the Sanctuary."

of your actions and the distinction of your actions"[1120] you will make progress in your sacred task. You will benefit from the habitat of good fortune. All the blessings described in the portion of *Behukotai*[1121] and *[Ki] Tavo*[1122] will be fulfilled. The Lord will affirm for us: "I am the Lord your God who brought you out from the land of *Mitzrayim* [Egypt]"[1123] (namely, from a land in which we were in a state of distress and need)[1124] "to be their slaves no more, who broke the bars of your yoke and made you walk erect."[1125] May this be His will. Amen.

Thus far in this chapter I have expounded upon the subject of rebuilding and settlement of the Land by carefully explaining this mitzvah. I have surveyed the subject in all its aspects. I have confirmed with convincing and compelling evidence that the obligation of the mitzvah is incumbent upon everyone at all times. No individual may absolve himself from this [obligation]. We have an even greater commitment in our present times to emerge and awake from our slumber and idleness. For anyone who has eyes can see, and who has ears may hear that now is the appropriate time for an awakening. One will have heard and seen what has occurred to us during these difficult days and the calamities of the past four years against us which have come to pass, which historians will describe as "The Calamities of 1940–43", similar to the Crusader calamities known as the "Calamities of 1096."[1126] Speech cannot describe them. The pen is unable to depict them in writing. Everything occurs in accordance

---

1120 *Midrash* interpretation of ומציון יסעדך *Lit.*, "and sustain you from Zion." The actual reading of the *Midrash* text: מקדוש מעשים טובים שבכם... מצויינים במצות שלכם.

1121 Lev. 26:3–27:34, specifically, 26:3–13.

1122 Deut. 26:1–29:8, specifically, 28:1–14.

1123 Lev. 19:36; 25:38; 26:13.

1124 *Mitzrayim* (מצרים) represents a combination of מיצר (*meytzar*) "distress" and ים (*yam*) "sea." See above, 211, nn. 550 and 552.

1125 Lev. 26:13.

1126 The devastation of Jewish communitites in the Rhine and Bohemia areas of Europe by waves of Crusaders between May and July 1096; especially Speyer, Worms, Mainz, Cologne, Regensburg, Metz and Prague.

with the Supreme will, because of our many sins.[1127]

As I explained the *Midrash* in Lamentations: "They asked R. Yehoshua, the son of Levi: 'Where is God?' He replied: 'In a large metropolis in [the Empire of] Rome.'"[1128]

Both the question and response are a puzzle. Is it indeed proper to ask "Where is the Blessed One?" Where is He not? Further, why was this of particular concern during the period of R. Yehoshua ben Levi?[1129] What prompted such questioning? In addition, how are we to understand his response "In a large metropolis in [the empire of] Rome"? Does not His Glory fill the entire universe?[1130] The interpretation, however, is as follows: It is known that the period of R. Yehoshua ben Levi was one of regular calamities for Israel. The destruction of the Temple[1131] was still felt. Israel suffered extensively from difficult and cruel misfortunes. They then approached him in bewilderment inquiring "Where is the Holy One, blessed be He? Why is He silent in the wake of what has befallen Israel?" We have heard similar echoes in our time, when they asked: "Where is the Jewish God? Why is He silent in response to all this?"[1132] In this fashion they questioned R. Yehoshua ben Levi. Accordingly, he replied: "In a large metropolis in [the empire of] Rome." This is its meaning: Since all of the [evil] decrees emanated from Rome, the seat of the advisors of the empire and the source of the calamites against Israel, he explained to them: Do you actually believe that these decrees were

---

1127 This most difficult of theological positions in the wake of calamity is now explained via the text in the JT Ta'an. 1:1.

1128 A variant of JT Ta'an. text: אמר ר׳ שמעון בן לקיש: ״אלי, מאיכן נזדווג לי משעיר?״ אמר רבי יהושע בן לוי: ״אם יאמר לך אדם: ׳איכן הוא אלהיך?׳ אמור לו: ׳בכרך הגדול שבאדום.׳ מה טעמא? ״אלי קורא משעיר״ [ישי כא:יא] "Said R. Shimon ben Lakish: *"Eli"* [*Lit.*, "to me"] my God [homiletical reading], wherefrom in "Seir" [Rabbinic for Rome] shall I be united with You?' Said R. Yehoshua ben Levi: "If someone will ask you: 'Where is your God?' Tell him: 'In a large metropolis in [the Empire of] Rome.' On what basis? *'Eli* calls [to me] from Seir (Isa. 21:11)." According to the *Korban Ha'edah* commentary, JT Ta'an. 1:1. Isa. 63:1 is also interpreted in this vein.

1129 R. Yehoshua ben Levi lived in Eretz Yisrael c. 200–250 CE.

1130 Cf. Isa. 6:3.

1131 70 CE.

1132 This question is phrased in Yiddish.

issued without the knowledge of the Holy One, blessed be He? Not
at all! Rather He, so to speak,[1133] was also present in the assembly of
the ministers [of the empire] when the evil decrees were enacted. It
was all accomplished with His agreement, because such were His
plans. In this fashion I responded as well to the many who asked me
[similar questions] when I was still in the country of hell:[1134] "Where
is the Jewish God, blessed be He?" I replied: "He is in the ministry of
the enemy, and agrees with their actions. The reason for His approval
is cited by R. Yonatan in his work *Ahavat Yonatan*[1135] in commenting
on the reading from the prophets[1136] for the weekly portion of
Eikev[1137]—to arouse them to go to Eretz Yisrael. Also our R. Yaakov
Emden[1138] in his Siddur noted: When Eretz Yisrael is ignored calamites
befall Israel, as I have elaborated previously at great length and there
is no need to repeat.

At the very least, the time is ripe in our own day for an awakening
to commit ourselves to the Land of our desires. Therefore, my brethren
and friends—Arise! Awaken! Be counted! Unite! "Let us be strong
and resolute for the sake of our people and the Land of our God,"[1139]
for the sake of our Torah, all of us united as one, of like mind on
behalf of the Land of God. The opportunity has come for all of us to
go up and bring others, since our redemption is at hand, as one may
see from all the indications which have been revealed in our time.
Everyone should hasten and support with his own resources the mitzvah
of *aliyah* and reconstruction. . . .[1140]

1133   "So to speak," כביכול (*kiv'yachol*) is common rabbinic parlance, employed to
moderate daring anthropomorphic descriptions of the Divine.

1134   Slovakia. The author escaped from Slovakia to Budapest in the fall of 1942.

1135   See above, 99, n. 71.

1136   Isa. 49: 14–51, 3, especially 49:19. כי חרבתיך ושממתיך וארץ הרסתיך "As for your
ruins and desolate places and your land laid waste."

1137   Deut. 7:12–11:25.

1138   See above, 30 and nn. 91, 92 and 95 for the relevant passage.

1139   II Sam. 10:12.

1140   The example of King David is cited. He fasted in order to contribute the
resources saved for the building of the Temple in Jerusalem. (JT Peah 4:2) Our
author would be content if the modern Jew would forgo fasting but merely reinvest

Apart from all this, let every Jew contemplate what became of all the silver and gold and assets of Israel from previous centuries to this very day [earned] in the countries of exile! How all of it has been wiped out and fallen into the hands of Esau! They did not have the insight and understanding to transfer these assets to Eretz Yisrael in order to acquire fields and construct homes which would have remained in Israel's possession forever. As noted by the Ribash[1141] in his Responsa no. 101 and 387: The mitzvah of settling Eretz Yisrael is not of a provisional nature.[1142] It is perpetually applicable. It is binding upon all of Israel so that the Holy Land would not be absorbed by malevolent elements. See the source.

The exiled [Jews] should have learned from [the example] of Jacob our Father. When he confronted Esau in combat, his concerns were not to allow his wealth and resources to fall into Esau's hands. He succeeded in doing so by turning himself into a bridge by placing one foot on the banks of the river on the side of Eretz Yisrael and the other he placed on the side of the evil Esau which was outside the Land. I explained previously[1143] that this description is not to be taken literally but figuratively. It is to teach us that via this [personal] bridge he transferred all his possessions to Eretz Yisrael. He never stood with both feet on the same side as Esau. One foot was always firm in Eretz Yisrael. His eyes and his heart were in Eretz Yisrael. This enabled him to gradually transfer his assets to Eretz Yisrael. Had he stood with both feet, here, outside the Land, his attention would have been diverted away from Eretz Yisrael. That would have meant the end. Esau would have benefited from all of his efforts.

---

the resources spent on luxuries for the rebuilding of the Land (*EHS*, 285–86). The bringing of redemption cannot be limited to select individuals but must be the result of the collective efforts of the entire people (*EHS*, 286–88).

1141 R. Isaac ben Sheshet Perfet (1326–1408), rabbinic authority in Spain, and author of an important collection of responsa (Constantinople, 1546).

1142 *She'elot uTshuvot Ribash* Jerusalem, 1993, responsa 101 (p. 94), 387 (p. 505). וכן אין לומר שאין העליה מצוה כי אם הישיבה שהרי עולה על דעת להתיישב נקרא עוסק במצוה (סי' ק"א). "One should not assume that the mitzvah of *aliyah* is valid only with [actual] settlement. Rather even one who contemplates settlement is considered to be involved in the mitzvah" (responsum 101).

1143 See above, 224–225.

This is precisely what is now happening in our own day to the assets of the Jews. At one time these were remarkably substantial. It has all vanished because of the many sins whereby we stood with both our feet here in exile and we lost sight of Eretz Yisrael. Therefore, the fruits of our toil were seized before our very eyes.

This is to teach us a lesson, never again to settle down here permanently with our entire being. One foot must always be positioned in Eretz Yisrael. Then we will succeed with the help of the Lord to transfer our resources there. We will invest our surplus assets in the rebuilding of our Land. Our wealth will grow and multiply for our sake and that of our children, for the benefit of our holy nation and the sanctification of His Name, may it be blessed and exalted.

The obligation will be especially incumbent upon us when we shall find respite from our enemies and when this bitter exile will have abated. We will then direct our attention to Eretz Yisrael and enhance its glory with the acquisition of fields and the building of homes. We learn this from Jacob our Father, as it is written: "And Jacob came in peace to the city of Shekhem, which is in the land of Canaan. . . . And he purchased a parcel of land [where he had spread his tent]."[1144] Rashi explains: "[This may compare to] a fellow who says to his friend: 'That man escaped by the skin of his teeth,[1145] and returned in peace.'"[1146] "And he purchased a parcel of land." Note the commentary of Ibn Ezra who wrote as follows: "A 'portion[1147] of the Land.' In this manner the verse informs [us] of the great virtue of Eretz Yisrael. A portion acquired [in Eretz Yisrael] is as important as a portion in the world to come."[1148] Nahmanides also cites this [Ibn Ezra commentary].[1149]

1144   Gen. 33:18–19. Jacob parts company with his brother Esau following their reconcilliation. He then journies to Sukkot and settles in Shekhem.

1145   *Lit,* "from between the teeth of two lions" מבין שני אריות.

1146   Rashi commentary on Gen. 33:19.

1147   Abraham Ibn Ezra focuses on the root חלק (h'l'k') of חלקת השדה (*helkat hasadeh*) signifying "portion," "share."

1148   Ibn Ezra commentary on Gen. 33:19.

1149   Nahmanides commentary on Gen. 33:19.

The learned books thereby teach that in the possession of the Land we become members of the world to come, thus interpreting "And your people, all of them righteous, shall possess the land 'for all time.'"[1150] The *Midrash* explains that Jacob after being saved from Esau thought as follows: "I will fulfill a mitzvah considered important in the eyes of the Holy One, blessed be He, more than all others." He then acquired a parcel of land in Eretz Yisrael.

We must also follow this example. Thanks to God's compassion we have survived and escaped by the skin of our teeth—"complete,"[1151] at least physically.

We also confirmed this in the *Midrash* on Psalms, section 17,[1152] in reference to the plague, Heaven forbid, in the time of David, when God the prophet explained to David that the punishment [of the plague] was because [the people] did not demand the building of the Temple.[1153] With the cessation of the pestilence David immediately approached Ornan and purchased from him a place for the building of the Temple. And it is written in First Chronicles:[1154] "And David gave to Ornan for the place six hundred shekels of gold by the weight." In the Book of Samuel (towards the end):[1155] ["So David bought the threshing floor and the oxen] for fifty shekels of silver." Note [what is written in the tractate] Zevahim 116[1156] where Rabba questions the discrepancy[1157] between the verses.

Rashi, commenting upon Chronicles, writes as follows: "'six hundred

---

1150   Isa. 60:15 לעולם (*le'olam*) is taken as the bridge between the idea of possession of Eretz Yisrael and the world to come.

1151   שלם (*shalem*) Gen. 33:18. The cataclysmic destruction of Hungarian Jewry following March 19, 1944, was as yet unforseen by the author.

1152   MPs. 17:4.

1153   The text in II Sam. 24:13–15 links the plague which decimated 70,000 Israelites to David's sin of numbering the population. According to the *Midrash*, David violated the injunction of Hos. 2:1: "The number of people of Israel shall be like that of the sands of the sea, which can not be measured or counted."

1154   I Chron. 21:25.

1155   II Sam. 24:24.

1156   Zev. 116b.

1157   Of five hundred and fifty shekels.

shekels of gold by the weight.' In [the Book of] Samuel it is written: 'for fifty shekels of silver.' How is this? He collected fifty shekels from each tribe which adds up to six hundred shekels, so that all of Israel would have a share [in the altar]." These are his [Rashi's] words.

Hence, David wanted to give recognition to all of Israel at the very moment of purchasing the site [upon which the Temple would be built] in order to appease the Lord for that sin in having delayed the demand for the Temple.

Notice this *Midrash* on Psalms which reasons by inferring a major point from one which is minor. If they were punished during the period of David—when there was as yet no Holy Temple—for failing to demand its construction, certainly we, who already had the Temple, but lost it because of our sins, would certainly be punished, Heaven forbid, for neglecting the demand for construction of our Holy Temple, as in the parable of the father who repeatedly thrashes his son. The son eventually asks of his father: "Why do you beat me so often?" The father replied to him: "Why do you not follow my instructions?" For this reason they [our sages] established that we pray three times every day concerning our return to our Land and to rebuild the Holy Temple.[1158] Accordingly all these beatings which we endure in exile are due to the neglect of returning to our Land.

Therefore, when these terrible beatings which we have endured in our day will cease, we will have to emulate David. Without delay we are to proceed and acquire land and a site for the construction of our homestead so that we will not be punished once again, Heaven forbid.

Furthermore, in the hope that with the help of the Almighty, the

---

1158   The 10th, 14th and 17th of the 19 blessings of the *Amidah* liturgy recited morning, noon and night during every weekday, are concerned with the return of the people and God's Presence to the Holy Land. But the *Midrash Psalms* cites the following: 1. The Festival introduction to the priestly blessings: אנא רחום, ברחמיך הרבים וגו׳ "Please, Compassionate One, restore Your Presence to Zion your habitat with great compassion. . . ." 2. The 14th blessing of the *Amidah* liturgy: בונה ירושלים "Praised are You, Lord Who rebuilds Jerusalem." 3. The third blessing in the Grace after Meals: ובנה ירושלים "May You rebuild Jerusalem, the Holy City. ." The *Midrash* speaks of *three* relevant prayers *every* day. Our author speaks of *three* prayers recited *thrice* daily which could refer to the *Amidah* liturgy. The editor could not locate the source for the *EHS* variant.

nations after the war will permit the Jewish nation to return to the Land of our inheritance and to possess it, then surely the obligation will fall upon all of Israel. It will be a collective and not an individual enterprise. See the Responsa Rashbash, the son of the Tashbaz, who expertly explained the positive commandment of settling in Eretz Yisrael.[1159] There he indicated that the mitzvah of ascending [to Eretz Yisrael] is incumbent upon individuals and not upon the sum total [of the Jewish people] since we are sworn "not to storm the ramparts"[1160] against the wishes of the nations. Note the source. Consequently, in the event that the nations will allow us to ascend to, and possess, Eretz Yisrael then this mitzvah resumes its previous status which is binding on the sum total [of the people]. So, in addition to the efforts of every individual, we note the obligation of the entire group, as we learned from David the king, of blessed memory and as I indicated previously.[1161]

In the *Midrash*[1162] and *Tanna DeBei Eliyahu*[1163] they noted that the

---

1159 *She'elot uTshuvot HaRashbash*, responsa 1–3. (Jerusalem, 1968), (Photofacsimile of Livorno 1741 edition). אין ספק שהדירה באי״י היא מצוה גדולה בכל זמן, בין בפני הבית בין (תשובה ב) שלא בפני הבית. "Undoubtedly residence in Eretz Yisrael is an important mitzvah at any time whether in the Temple era or without the Temple." R. Shlomo Shimon Duran (c. 1400–1467) North African authority of the renowned Duran family of scholars, son of R. Shimon the son of Zemach Duran, known as the Tashbaz.

1160 שלא יעלו ישראל בחומה "To employ massive force or violence." An alternative reading: כחומה (kehomah) "as a wall"—do not attack together as if you were a wall. This is R. Zeira's reading of Song 2:7 cited in Ket. 111a.

1161 See above, 302.

1162 *Yalkut Shimoni* II, 234. מה נשתנה הושע בן אלה שגלו עשרת השבטים בימיו? אלא עד עכשיו היתה עבודת אלילים קשורה ביחיד [ירבעם] וקשה לפני הקב״ה להגלות את הצבור בעון יחיד. כיון שבא הושע בן אלה וביטל כל המשמרות כלן ואמר 'כל מי שיעלה לירושלים יעלה,' ולא אמר 'הכל יעלו לירושלים,' עליו הוא אומר: 'ויעש הרע בעיני ד' . . .' מפני ששמט קולר מצוארו ונתנו בצואר הרבים. "How was it different in the era of Hoshea ben Elah during which the ten tribes were exiled? Up to that period idol worship was limited to an individual [i.e., Jeroboam]. Hence, it was difficult for the Holy One, blessed be He, to exile an entire community because of the sins of one individual. When Hoshea ben Elah arrived, however, and he abolished all the guards [who blocked the way to Jerusalem], declaring: 'All who wish to ascend to Jerusalem may do so.' He did not say: 'All should ascend to Jerusalem.' Of him it was said: 'He did what was displeasing to the Lord' [II Kings 17:2], because he removed responsibility from his shoulders and transferred it to others.'"

1163 *Tanna DeBei Eliyahu Zuta* 9:2 (Jerusalem, 1962), 64.

exile [of the ten tribes] did not begin until the time of Hosea the son
of Be'eri. [This was so] because prior to that time the kingdom of
Jeroboam forcibly prohibited the [ritual] pilgrimages [to Jerusalem].[1164]
Therefore, the onus [for this transgression] was exclusively upon
him.[1165] (Even so during this period [of Jeroboam's reign] those devoted
to the Lord exposed themselves to danger in order to make the
pilgrimage, as described in Ta'anit 28.[1166] They shall be remembered
forever.)

No longer was this so in the time of Hosea. The guards were
abolished. They now had permission to make the pilgrimage but did
not do so. They all sinned and, therefore, were all exiled. This is
[related in] the *Midrash*. Likewise it is so in our times. The
government[1167] has granted permission to settle. The obligation rests
upon the masses. It is a communal and not an individual enterprise to
be supported by the resources of the community.

I am inclined, with the help of God, to teach those who make
contributions towards the rebuilding of our Holy Land, to declare
when they set aside [their contribution]: "I hereby make this
contribution for the purpose of building our Land and thereby fulfill
the positive commandment of settling the Land as charged by the
Creator of all the universe and thereby to reestablish His foundation
in the upper spheres."[1168] In this fashion the contribution will be

---

1164   Since this would signify loyalty to the kingdom of David and threaten Jeroboam's
rule. See I Kings 12:27.

1165   The masses had no choice; they could not be faulted.

1166   Ta'an. 28a. A description of families who disguised their baskets in order to
smuggle their first fruits to Jerusalem during the pilgrimage festival when this was
forbidden by the ruling powers.

1167   A likely reference to the Balfour Declaration of November 1917, by Arthur
Balfour, British secretary of state for foreign affairs, in a letter addressed to Lord
Rothschild which promised British support for the establishment of a national
homeland for the Jewish people in Palestine. The declaration was immediately approved
by President Woodrow Wilson and incorporated into the British Mandate instrument
in August 1920; approved by the League of Nations Council in July 1922, and
implemented on September 29, 1923, when the Mandate became official. Walid,
Ahwed Khalidi, "Palestine," *Encyclopedia Brittanica*, vol. 17 (1967), 168–69.

1168   The perfection of the upper world is dependent upon *tikkun* in the world
below; a major concept in mystical theology. See above, 50, n. 81; 299, n. 1114.

endowed with a sanctity from on High, and evil forces[1169] will be unable to harm the building efforts. . . .[1170]

One should know, however, that my recommendation in no way interferes with the essence of the mitzvah of settlement. Anyone who simply works and labors, even without the above declaration and without any elevated purpose, fulfills this positive commandment. This was the meaning of the teaching of the *Or HaHayyim* which I cited previously.[1171] We are certain that wherever an act has been realized, the intent is irrelevant. Even a mitzvah which has come about by means of a transgression is not impaired if the act has been fulfilled and can no longer be repeated, as taught by the Rashba in Yevamot 103.[1172] Certainly a choice mitzvah should be properly performed as I have indicated: to praise He Who rules above and below. Amen, may this be His will. Note it well.

I have taken notice of [the passage in] *Drishat Zion*[1173] which found difficulty with Nahmanides' interpretation[1174] of the words of Isaiah:

"Thus declares the Lord God who gathers the dispersed of Israel: 'I will gather still more to those already gathered.'"[1175] And he[1176] explained:

1169 *Lit.*, "the other side."

1170 The author documents the importance of introducing every mitzvah with a dedicatory statement to the Almighty, with sources from Karo's *Maggid Mesharim*, "*Terumah*" (Jerusalem, 1960, 68); the Zohar (Vilna, 1922), 50a, b. and the *Shenei Luhot HaBrit* (Shanghai, 1947) vol. 1, 44a. ונראה בעיני שלא די כשאומר בשם ה' אני עושה זה במלאכה גשמיות, רק יאמר בלשון שאומרים בעשיית מצוה שהלשון הוא: 'לשם יחוד קב"ה ושכינתיה ע"י ההוא טמיר ונעלם.' כך יאמר גם כן בכל מלאכה ופעולה." It seems to me that it is not sufficient to invoke the Lord's Name when performing a mundane act. Rather one should employ the formula used when performing a mitzvah, as follows: 'For the purpose of unifying the Holy One, blessed be He, and the Shekhinah, via the hidden and Holy Spirit.' Thus should one declare prior to the performance of any act."

1171 See above, 188–189; *EHS*, 203.

1172 See above, 54, n. 107 and n. 108.

1173 Zvi Kalisher, "*Drishat Tzion*," in Yisrael Klausner (ed.), *HaKetavim HaTzioniyim shel HaRav Zvi Kalisher* (Jerusalem, 1947), 41–42.

1174 "*Ramban: Shir HaShirim*," Hayyim Dov Chavel (ed.) *Kitvei Rabbenu Moshe ben Nahman*, vol. 2 (Jerusalem, 1964), 514.

1175 Isa. 56:8.

1176 Nahmanides. ופירש "and he explained" in Kalisher *vs.* ופרוש "and the explanation" in *EHS*, 292.

First He will gather in many of the dispersed of Israel, but not all. Following the war of Gog he said: "I will gather still more to those already gathered." A second ingathering will follow those already assembled previously. This refers to "the lost [exiles] who are in the land of Assyria."[1177] They are the ten tribes who will be gathered once more. He now questioned this very Nahmanides commentary on Song of Songs which specifies that the ten tribes will be assembled first.[1178] He states: both are correct. For is it conceivable for a great mass of people to be gathered in from the lost [exiles] in the land of Assyria only to come to a desolate and ruined land? No doubt they will be preceded by those who will bring forth food from the earth. Subsequently all the others will follow to a Land full of the Lord's blessing,[1179] wilderness having been transformed into farm land,[1180] complete with fields and vineyards in the possession of Israel. Thus it is explained in Hosea: "As I was about to restore My people's fortunes[1181] Judah as well[1182] reaped a harvest [of misfortunes] for you."[1183]

   This is the text of the verse and it is difficult to comprehend. It will best be understood with my approach. The verse speaks of Ephraim,[1184] namely, the ten tribes referred to throughout the chapter.[1185] And it is written: "Come let us turn back [to the Lord]. . . . [In two days He will make us whole again]. On the third day [He will raise us up]."[1186] Rashi explains: "With the building of the Third Temple, He will raise us up."[1187] This is followed by a long reprimand declaring: "What can I do

---

1177   Isa. 27:13.

1178   *"Ramban: Shir HaShirim"*, *op. cit.*, 514. וזהו: 'נאום ה' אלהים מקבץ נדחי ישראל' אלו עשרת השבטים. "This is the meaning of: 'Thus declares the Lord God Who gathers the dispersed of Israel.' These are the ten tribes."

1179   Cf. Deut. 33:23.

1180   Cf. Isa. 32:15.

1181   To gather them in from exile.

1182   In addition to Israel's Northern Kingdom.

1183   Hos. 6:11.

1184   The Kingdom of Israel.

1185   Hos. 6.

1186   Hos. 6:1–2.

1187   Rashi on Hos. 6:2.

for you, Ephraim?. . . ." Subsequently he returns to the original idea having declared "On the third day He will raise us up . . . and He will come to us like rain."[1188] He responds to Ephraim: "As I was about to restore My people's fortunes, Judah as well reaped a harvest for you."[1189] Prior to the arrival of a large mass of people Judah will prepare the harvest for you. He will establish for you an inhabited Land. Then will come the great ingathering. Then without doubt will arrive the Messiah son of Joseph who will rule over Jerusalem. This will be followed by Gog. Because of him the great Name will be sanctified and there shall be one Lord with one Name.[1190] They will all be endowed with a common speech to serve Him with one accord.[1191] Amen.

These are the words of the *gaon* R. Zvi Hirsh Kalisher, of blessed memory, in the volume cited.[1192]

This then is the original contribution of the *gaon* of blessed memory: [The tribe of] Judah will return prior to the other tribes in order to prepare the land.[1193]

In any event we see how Judah is first in all endeavors. He will also be first to return to the Land at the time of redemption. We who are descended from [the tribes of] Judah and Benjamin must therefore be the first to accept the obligation to build the Land. The ten tribes will subsequently be revealed and the ingathering shall be complete. And so shall the Lord declare, speedily in our own day, Amen. After the Lord will expand our borders and will bring us peace from our neighbors who surrounded us like attacking bees and who stung us with great cruelty, God will avenge us. Then we will all be able to turn together to this task. Then, bless the Lord, we will realize the

---

1188 Hos. 6:2–3.

1189 Hos. 6:11.

1190 Cf. Zech. 14:9.

1191 Cf. Zeph. 3:9.

1192 See above, n. 1173.

1193 The author proceeds to submit his own evidence based on Scripture, the *Yalkut Shimoni* II, 561) and *Tanhuma* (Num. 14) that the tribe of Judah is the forerunner for major events. ואף כשיבא המבשר, יהודה מתבשר בתחילה. "And when the forerunner [of the Messiah] will arrive, it will be Judah who is announced first."

vision of the prophet Nahum: "The gates of your Land have opened" (Nahum 3).[1194] We will not be tempted by the freedom which was given to us here once more. We will not exploit it in order to remain [in exile], Heaven forbid, as we have done in the past. Otherwise the oppression of the nations will recur, Heaven forbid.

As the prophet indicated (Amos 6):[1195] "Ah, those who are so happy about *Lo-davar*,[1196] who exult, 'by our might we have captured Karnaim.' But I, O house of Israel, will raise up a nation against you, declares the Lord [the God of Hosts], who will harass you." These are the words of the prophet. Hence the oppression of the nations is entirely due to our contentment with our lot here in exile. We prided ourselves as strong, possessing horns[1197] to gore them in the west, north, south and east. The Lord then proved to us that we rejoiced over something worthless and our sense of grandeur evaporated like a dream. Let us, therefore, learn from our experience and know how to utilize our newly-won freedom in order to create great movements from all of us in order to ascend to Zion with song and everlasting joy.[1198] And the Lord will fulfill His statement declared by His great prophet: "Then the Lord was roused on behalf of His Land and had compassion upon His people" (Joel 2).[1199] Amen, may it be His will. . . .[1200]

1194   Nah. 3:13. It is clear that the author removes the verse from its context, namely the destruction of the Assyrian empire and its city Ninveh, the symbol of violence and evil. The partial verse is projected upon the gates of Eretz Yisrael, which will open anew to its people.

1195   Amos 6:13–14.

1196   The classical commentaries translate *lo-davar* literally "worthless," or "meaningless." *JPS New Translation* based on II Kings 14:25, II Sam. 9:4–5; 17:27 identifies it as a town east of the Jordan. The author, of course, follows the traditional commentary.

1197   The literal translation of *karnaim* in Amos 6:13, but referred to as a town captured by Jeroboam. See *JPS New Translation*.

1198   Cf. Additional (Musaf) Service for Rosh Hodesh and Festivals. והביאנו לציון עירך ברינה, ולירושלים בית מקדשך בשמחת עולם. "And restore us joyously to Zion, Thy city, and in everlasting joy lead us to Jerusalem, the site of Thy sanctuary."

1199   Joel 2:18.

1200   The author introduces into the third chapter a major essay entitled "Essay on the Temple of the Lord." This section returns to the theme of human initiative as a prior requirement for ultimate redemption. Sources from Ezra (6:16) with the

Since I am presently marking the 23rd day in the month of *Elul* in the year 5703,[1201] with the "festival day of the full moon"[1202] fortunately upon us, I conclude this chapter with the discourse which I delivered last *Rosh HaShanah* and subsequently recorded in my notes on the Fast of Gedaliah.[1203] [This discourse was delivered in the holy community of Nitra following my exile from Pishtian[1204]] in the midst of *Elul* in the year "You return man to dust,"[1205] when the cruel ones

---

commentary of Malbim, and Ezekiel (chapter 4), are introduced to demonstrate the necessity of building the Third Temple by human hand prior to its completion by the Almighty. מדברי קדמונים אלה נראה שאם שהבנין שלעתיד יהיה בידי שמים, עם כל זה מתחילה נהיה אנו בונים בית המקדש בידינו ואח״כ ירד הבנין המקוה שבידי שמים. "From [our] forebearers we learn that although the future Temple will be determined by Heaven, nevertheless we are expected to assume the initiative and to build the Temple on our own. Thereafter will the anticipated edifice descend as determined by Heaven" (*EHS*, 294). Conflicting sources from the Talmud (*BQ* 60b) and the Zohar are reconciled. The Almighty purposefully utilizes the stones of the destroyed First Temple (which was exclusively built by human effort) in order to demonstrate the partnership between God and man necessary in endeavors of redemption. והנה לפי דברי הזהר (פרשת פקודי הנ״ל) יבנה המקדש מאבנים שהיו מעשה ידי אדם, ולא מעשה הקב״ה כביכול עצמו. "And behold, according to the Zohar (II, 183–187) the Temple will be rebuilt from manmade stones and not from the Holy One, blessed be He" (*EHS*, 294). This lengthy discourse employs an involved *pilpul* technique. Numerous sources which reflect the miraculous initiative of the Almighty in the final redemption are introduced as a foil for the many sources which strongly defend the human initiative. (*EHS*, 294–305). The "Temple" theme is discussed earlier in the preface to the third chapter; See above, 133–135.

1201 September 23, 1943.

1202 יום הכסה (*Yom HaKeseh*): Rosh HaShanah, the Jewish New Year. See Ps. 81:4.

1203 צום גדליה (*Tzom Gedalyah*): one of five public fast days in the Jewish calendar in addition to Yom Kippur. It occurs on the day following *Rosh HaShanah* and marks the murder of Gedalyah ben Ahikam, the last Jewish governor assigned by Nebuchadnezzar to govern the Jewish remnants in Judah. The death of Gedalyah terminated the last vestige of Jewish independence after the destruction of the First Temple.

1204 Piestny or Piestany in western Slovakia, a town of 12,000 prior to the Holocaust of whom approximately 1,800 were Jews. The author directed the local "Moriah" Yeshivah Talmud Academy and served as the spiritual leader of the community. The Yeshivah functioned until the winter of 1942, with the intensification of the expulsions from Slovakia. Nitra, approximately 30 miles southeast of Piestany served as a temporary haven prior to the author's escape into Hungary. *Mishneh Sakhir*, vol. 1 (biographical preface) *op. cit.*, unpaginated. Avraham Fuchs, *Yeshivot Hungaria Bigdulatan U'v'hurbanan*, vol. 2, ch. 8 (from galley proofs).

1205 Ps. 90:3. תשב (*t'sh'b'*) [return] = 5702 or 1942.

abased us to the dust; when I and my family escaped in the dead of
night, bare without possessions, to this community.[1206] We remained
there until after the [*Sukkot*=Tabernacles] holidays. From there the
Almighty helped me escape to this place.[1207] May the Almighty, blessed
be He, protect us with His wings[1208] until redemption will come to all
of Israel, speedily in our own day. Amen.

We pray to the Almighty during the High Holy Day services:
"Lord, grant honor to Your people . . . Grant joy to Your Land and
gladness to Your city. May the glory of Your annointed servant David
blossom."[1209] I saw a commentary [on this text] in an old *mahzor*:[1210]

> "Israel was exiled only after it rejected the following three: the kingdom
> of Heaven, the kingdom of David and the Holy Temple. . . ."[1211] R.
> Shimon ben Menasya taught: Israel will not be shown any good omen
> [of redemption] until they repent and request all three.[1212] That is why
> it is written "Lord, grant honor to Your people" by means of "they will
> seek the Lord."[1213] "Grant joy to Your Land and gladness to Your city."
> This refers to the [rebuilding of the Holy Temple]. "May the glory of
> Your annointed servant David blossom." This refers to the [reestablish-
> ment of the] kingdom of David.

Thus far the citation of the commentary.[1214]

After two thousand years among the gentiles, having intermingled

---

1206 Nitra. The escape was camouflaged by means of a hired ambulance. *Mishneh
Sakhir, op. cit.*, n. 68.

1207 Budapest.

1208 Cf. Ps. 91:3.

1209 From the *Amidah* of the High Holy Day services.

1210 The High Holy Day and festival prayer book.

1211 The *Yalkut* text (*Yalkut Shimoni* II, 106) has the variant. בשלשה דברים עתידים
למאוס: במלכות שמים, ובמלכות בית דוד ובבנין בית המקדש. "The following three will eventually
be despised [by the Jewish people]: the kingdom of Heaven, the kingdom of David
[the Messiah?] and the building of the Temple."

1212 Ibid. Again the variant: אין ישראל רואין סימן גאולה לעולם עד שיחזרו ויבקשו שלשתם
"Israel will never see the signs of redemption unless they express regret and petition
for all three."

1213 Hos. 3:5.

1214 From the *Mahzor*, which is not documented by the author and is unknown to
the editor.

among the nations and adopted their ways, the present realities indicate that a majority no longer have any idea about the nature of Judaism. One cannot expect them to change and to request the Kingdom of Heaven and the kingship of David. The fact that they seek the Land of Israel, however, incorporates all three [ideals]. I have already noted this previously at length.[1215] Our rabbis of blessed memory have also intimated: "Whoever dwells in Eretz Yisrael is akin to one who has God."[1216] [Further] the kingship of David and the kingdom of Heaven are one and the same, as the kabbalists have known. Now that we have seen the degree of their dedication to Eretz Yisrael, as I have demonstrated before,[1217] they seek all three [ideals], even without their being aware of this. (I have for some time reached this conclusion on my own, but now I have seen the volume *Minhat Yehudah*, which I noted previously,[1218] in paragraph 17,[1219] and he also writes in this fashion. He quotes the Zohar:[1220] "The Holy One, blessed be He, is not proclaimed King save in Eretz Yisrael." Accordingly, when our sages of blessed memory called for their quest of the kingdom of Heaven, they referred to a return to Eretz Yisrael in order to proclaim the Holy One, blessed be He, as King.[1221] This is the initial requirement for our total restoration.)

One may also add the following in reference to the teaching of the *Pesikta*, chapter 40,[1222]

"Sing joyously to God, our strength; raise a shout for the God of

---

1215 *EHS*, 103–04.

1216 Ket. 110b.

1217 See above, 106–110.

1218 See above, 152, n. 120.

1219 *Sefer Minhat Yehudah, op. cit.*, 13b.

1220 Zohar III, 276a. קב"ה כד איהו לבר מאתריה, לאו איהו מלך "When the Holy One, blessed be He, is away from His home, He is not King." The Zohar concludes (Ibid.): כגוונא דאבא, אינון בנוי. לאו אינון בני מלכים עד דיהדרון לארעא. "As the Father, so the children. They will not come into being as princes until they return to Eretz Yisrael."

1221 The concern for the welfare of God over consideration for man is characteristic of pietistic and mystical literature. See Rivka Schatz Uffenheimer, *HaHasidut Kemistikah, op. cit.*, 43, n. 5 & 43.

1222 *Pesikta Rabbati, Harninu* 39 (Vienna, 1880 ed.) 165b.

Jacob."[1223] R. Tanhum the son of R. Abba commenced: "No sin is in sight for Jacob."[1224] Why did Bilam refer to Jacob and not to Abraham or Isaac? Because he perceived within Abraham the impurities of Ishmael and the children of Ketura.[1225] From Isaac [he perceived] the impurities of Esau and his clans.[1226] Jacob, however, is entirely holy as it is written: "All these were the tribes of Israel twelve in number."[1227] Accordingly he [Bilam] did not mention any of the Patriarchs except for Jacob. "Raise a shout for the God of Jacob."[1228] Thus the text in the *Pesikta*.

Yet, there are difficulties. Is it not so that presently, due to our many sins there are also numerous impurities among the offspring of Jacob? Why is Jacob singled out? But as we shall see everything stems from the roots. Because the roots are wholesome, even the defects of some of the branches are considered inconsequential since they feed from the fluids of the roots. They will blossom anew. Would the roots be impaired, this could not happen. The healthy organism would be consumed by the decayed.[1229] Since Jacob is completely holy and the roots are entirely good, he will rejuvenate all his offspring until the end of time and shall blossom forth once again. Above all, they must not be wrenched from their roots. Then will they be enabled to nurture new life from this root.

1223 Ps. 91:2.

1224 Num. 23:21.

1225 Gen. 25:1–5.

1226 Gen. 36. These descendents from Abraham and Isaac would eventually become enemies of the Jewish people or turn to idol worship. See *Yalkut Shimoni* II, 109. זמרן, שהיו מזמרים בתוף לע"ז ויקשן שהיו מקישין בתוף לע"ז. "Zimran [was so named] because they [his offspring] performed on the drum as part of idol worship. Yokshan, because they pounded on the drum as part of idol worship." See also Sot. 13a.

1227 Gen. 49:28. All of Jacob's progeny deserved his blessings. They were all righteous.

1228 Ps. 91:2.

1229 Based on דשדא תכלא בכולא "for the decay has spread over the entire [egg]" in Hul. 64b. This noted discussion in the Talmud discusses the status of the egg within which a blood stain is discovered. In the standard situation the blood may be discarded and the egg may be eaten. If the stain is found on the yolk, however, the entire egg is forbidden, for נתפשט הקלקול בכולה "the decay has spread over the entire egg." See the Rashi commentary.

This is the intent of Bilam: "As I see them from the mountain tops, gaze on them from the height."[1230] Namely, their roots are altogether good.[1231] Consequently: "No sin is in sight for Jacob, no woe in view for Israel,"[1232] since their transgression and wickedness are but temporary. The moment that they link up with their roots, they shall "blossom like the lily."[1233] Therefore, it is important that on *Rosh HaShanah* we link ourselves to our Patriarch Jacob of blessed memory. By these means we shall attract to ourselves his sanctity and rectify all of our blemishes of the past year and from the time we were born. This is then the intent of the verse: "Blow the horn on the new moon . . . for it is a law for Israel, a ruling of the God of Jacob."[1234] Now note carefully [the expression] "the God of Jacob." For it is he, Jacob, who is completely holy and we are rooted to him. We will continue to transfer life and sanctity from the root to the branches which will blossom once again. In this connection the *paytan* [the religious poet] wrote: "When there is no one to plead [our case in response to the accuser,] do speak on behalf of Jacob in matters of law and justice [and declare us not guilty, O King of justice."][1235] He underscores "on behalf of Jacob" because of the good roots by means of which all will be restored for the good. May the Almighty assist us in linking ourselves to Jacob our Patriarch, always and for all times, Amen.

It is further written in the *Pesikta*:[1236]

1230 Num. 23:9.

1231 Probable reference to the *Midrash* (NumR. 20:16) on this verse. Bilam prefers to destroy the Jewish people all at once by ignoring the branches and exorcising the roots. The healthy deep roots make this impossible. כך אמר אותו רשע: מה אני מקלל כל שבט ושבט הריני הולך לשרשן. בא ליגע מצאן קשים. לכך אמר: יכי מראש צורים אראנו.' "Thus said this evil one: 'Why should I bother cursing each tribe separately. I will tear out their roots. When he approached he found them to be hard. Hence, he declared: 'As I see them from the mountain tops [from the perspective of impervious rock].'" See also the *Etz Yosef* commentary on this *Midrash*: The parable of the "mountain" and "heights" refers to people rooted in the Patriarchs and Matriarchs.

1232 Num. 23:21.

1233 Hos. 14:6.

1234 Ps. 91:4–5.

1235 From the Musaf [Additional] service for the High Holy Days.

1236 *Peskita Rabbati, Harninu, op. cit.*, 165b.

There is another reason why Jacob was singled out from the Patriarchs. Our rabbis taught: "Man receives measure for measure."[1237] This may be compared to a king who had three friends and planned to build a palace. He invited the first [friend] and said to him: "Note this site upon which I plan to build a palace for myself." Replied this friend: "I always perceived this as a mount." He then invited the second friend who replied [to the king]: "I always perceived this as a field." The king left him. He then invited the third friend who responded: "I always perceived this as a palace." Said the king to him: "I swear that I shall build this very palace and shall name it for you." Likewise, Abraham, Isaac and Jacob were friends of the Holy One, blessed be He. Abraham referred to the Holy Temple as "mountain," as it is written: "On the mount of the Lord there is vision."[1238] Isaac called it a "field," as it is written: "See, the smell of my son is as the smell of the field."[1239] But Jacob called it "palace," as it is written: "How awesome is this place! This is none other than the abode of God."[1240] Exclaimed the Holy One, blessed be He; "You refer to it as an abode though it is not as yet built. I swear that I shall build it and name it for you: 'O House of Jacob! come, let us walk by the light of the Lord.'"[1241] Also "and the many peoples shall go [and say: 'Come let us go up . . .] to the House of the God of Jacob.'"[1242] Jeremiah as well, exclaimed: "I will restore the fortunes of Jacob's tents."[1243] Asaf the Psalmist also confirmed these expressions, as it is written: "Raise a shout for the God of Jacob."[1244]

To this point [we cite] the *Pesikta*.

1237 Meg. 12b; Sot. 8b.

1238 Gen. 22:14.

1239 Gen. 27:27. For the connection to the Temple see GenR. 65:19. ד"א: מלמד שהראה לו הקב"ה בהמ"ק בנוי וחרב ובנוי וגו'. "Another interpretation: This teaches us that the Holy One, blessed be He, made known to him the Holy Temple, as it appeared constructed, destroyed and rebuilt. . . ."

1240 Gen. 28:17.

1241 Isa. 2:5.

1242 Isa. 2:3.

1243 Jer. 30:18.

1244 Ps. 81:2.

I am inclined to comment on this latter *Pesikta* text. [1245] The two friends who initially referred to the site of the proposed palace as "mount" and "field" implied that in order to build a palace for a king, the [proposed] site must in its own right be prepared and ready to receive such a distinguished building. Thus, the first one said: "I always perceived this as a mount." The second said: "I always perceived this as a field." By this they indicated that a simple mount or field are not in themselves worthy of having the palace of a king constructed on their site. Such was not the case with the third friend. He stated: "I envision a palace. Namely, I do not confine myself to the present which indeed suggests a simple mount or field. I envision only the future. That is to say, the palace will sanctify the site. It will enhance it to such a degree that it will be worthy of the king's honor." This attribute was so appreciated by God that He chose to single out the name of Jacob in connection with the Temple. Hence, His house would bear his name, since it is the nature of Jacob to perceive a thing in its future state, though it may presently not be important in its own right. Since in its future state it will be worthy of sanctity, it assumes a state of sanctity in the present as well. Consequently, Jacob referred to the Temple as the "abode of God"[1246] even prior to its construction. . . .

And so it is with us. Despite our lack of merit due to the neglect of the observance of Torah and mitzvot throughout the year, and now being confronted with *Rosh HaShanah*, when we are obliged to take upon ourselves the yoke of the kingdom of Heaven, how are we able to refer to God as our King? We have not fulfilled His will during the days gone by. But in our resolve to obey Him and worship Him with complete sincerity, for this alone, namely, because of the [perspective of the] future, we are authorized to acknowledge His kingship. . . .

May it be His will that the year to come will be for our good, a year of redemption and salvation.

1245 בסו״ד = בסוף דבריו i.e., "latter text." Alternate reading: בסיעתא דשמיא i.e., "with God's help."
1246 Gen. 28:17.

These were the ideas of my discourse which I delivered last *Rosh HaShanah*. Hence we have before us two positive qualities by which the ordinary human being may be uplifted from his degraded state. The first is to tie one's roots to Jacob our Patriarch, who is completely sacred. From this source flow the creative waters which will activate within us new life abundant in holiness. The second characteristic is to apply the future in the present. Both these characteristics are evident among the modern pioneers of our Land, though they may be simple, ordinary and even religously deficient, Heaven forbid. For we have discovered that Jacob our Patriarch considered the settling of the Land to be more precious than all the wealth in this world.[1247] He did in fact transfer all his vast possessions (which were extraordinary in their scope) to Esau, saying: The "overseas holdings"[1248] are not worthy of him.[1249]

Jacob also dedicated his life in realizing the positive commandment of settling the Land, as it is explained in the *Midrash*.[1250] Today, these pioneers as well dedicate their lives out of love for the Land, as is well-known. Hence, they thereby link themselves to the roots of Jacob. This bond will also elevate them spiritually. Further, Jacob acts in terms of the future and the future has already been assured by our rabbis of blessed memory. I cited previously[1251] that which Maimonides and other authorities have written: Following the ingathering in Eretz Yisrael, God will convey to them a pure spirit so that they shall fulfill His will with sincerity.

It is, therefore, obvious that all of Israel is commanded to join them. The whole of Israel would thereby sanctify the Name of the

---

1247   The link to Jacob is thus not only with regard to the two desirable traits but with his own unique commitment to the Land.

1248   The possessions acquired outside the Land of Israel.

1249   The editor could not locate this citation. The Jerusalem *EHS* edition cites Gen. 50:5, Rashi and Sot. 13a and Rashi. These are tenuous and oblique references to Jacob's burial plot in Eretz Yisrael and do not relate to Jacob's transfer of possessions to Esau. In fact, see *EHS*, 226 and above, 224–225 concerning Jacob's efforts to prevent his possessions from falling into Esau's hand. See also Gen. 33:18, Rashi commentary and GenR. 69:5.

1250   See above, 9–11; 13, n. 59.

1251   *EHS*, 76; *EHS*, 188.

Almighty, as we recite in our holy prayers on the Days of Awe: "May they all be united into a common fellowship in order to sincerely fulfill Your will. We are always mindful that sovereignty is Yours. You are the Source of all might and power."[1252] That is to say, when all of Israel unites, they thereby enhance His might and power. Since He is the Sovereign of the universe He will in turn glorify us without limits.[1253] Amen, may this be His will. As noted by Nahmanides on the verse: "Then He became King in Jeshurun, when the leaders of the people assembled the tribes of Israel together."[1254] The *Midrash*: "When is the Almighty established in heaven? When Israel is united in brotherhood below."[1255]

Thus, we conclude the third chapter on the twenty-third day of *Elul*, in the year 5703,[1256] here in the capital of Budapest. May the Almighty respond to the verse: "[Come, let us turn back to the Lord: He attacked, and can heal us; He wounded, and He can bind us up. In two days He will make us whole again;] on the third day He will raise us up and we shall be reborn before Him."[1257] May this occur speedily, in our time. Amen.

SUPPLEMENT TO CHAPTER THREE

Someone approached me carrying an open book, asking me if I would mind being shown what is written in this sacred volume. I took it

---

1252 From the *Amidah* of the High Holy Day service.

1253 The reciprocity of the covenant will be realized. The unity below will reveal the unity above.

1254 Deut. 33:5.

1255 Nahmanides (*Perush HaRamban al HaTorah*; vol. 2, Deut. 33:5, Jer. ed. 1982, 494.) paraphrases NumR. 15:14, interpreting Amos 9:6.

1256 September 23, 1943. The summer and autumn of 1943 was a period during which great pressure was placed on the reluctant Kallay government to take strong anti-Jewish measures. See Raul Hilberg, *The Destruction of the European Jews* (Chicago, 1967), 521–25. See below, 325, n. 1278.

1257 Hos. 6:[1] 2. Reference to "the third day" is the positive link to the conclusion of the third chapter. "Two days," refer to the exiles of Egypt and Babylonia. The "third day" refers to the final redemption and the establishment of the Third Temple. See Rashi, Radak and *Metzudat David* commentaries on Hos. 6:2.

from him and noted that it was the *Divrei Yehezke'el*[1258] from our holy
Rabbi of Shineve, of blessed memory. He brought to my attention the
opinion of our saintly rabbi concerning the rebuilding and settling of
the Land. He does not agree to working the fields in Eretz Yisrael.
Rather [says the Shinever] one should concentrate on supporting the
settlement of the Land by increasing allocations of sacred *shekalim* to
those occupied with the study of Torah and devotion [to the Lord].
He will then enhance our glory and restore our fortunes speedily in
our day. These are his views at the conclusion of his collection [of
discourses].[1259]

I responded to him as follows: Understand what our teacher the
Hatam Sofer wrote in his *Hiddushim* [novellae] to the tractate Hullin.[1260]
These are his words:

> The main objective of students who study with their teachers is to
> properly correlate matters in their legal application by analogy. . . .
> Accordingly, when one introduces a new idea we have an expression in
> Yiddish: "*gleich*" or "*ungleich*," namely, "corresponds" or "does not cor-
> respond." The analogy is either valid or not valid. In the ensuing discus-
> sion profound and very subtle judgments are presented which attempt
> to distinguish between one law and another. In this fashion a number
> of difficulties are resolved. Consequently, what a student may perceive
> as similar will be described by his teacher and scholar to be incongruent.
> The student will be shown the gap between the two which represents
> the difference between two approaches originally perceived as identical.
> . . . Thus shall truth be taught.

These are sacred words which are applicable for us. The major
principle at work when attempting to apply an idea is to seek its
congruency in its application. It must be precise in its legal application,
in all aspects and particulars. Should there exist even minor differences,
even the most subtle, the results will be different and one can no

---

1258   See above, 139, n. 38.

1259   Krakow, 1922 (2nd ed.) 49a. The *Likutim* section is not included in the first
edition.

1260   Hatam Sofer, *Masekhet Hullin* (New York, 1957), 4b–5a.

longer learn one from another. Consequently, if students were not sufficiently alert, and perceived the two ideas to be similar, seeking to apply one to the other, the scholar will demonstrate to them the resulting inconsistency. Their initial judgment, either to prohibit or to permit [an act], will be ruled invalid.

Having prefaced my remarks with this major principle which guides legal rulings, I shall respond to the evidence from the sacred work[1261] which you presented in seeming contradiction to my position.

Be aware, my son, that the words of our Rabbi of Shinev are not new to me. I have alluded to them previously.[1262] I distinguished between [the situation in] his time and ours. The substance of our lives in present times cannot be compared to the period in which he, of blessed memory, lived. I noted the following: "What our sacred Rabbi of Shinev wrote at the close of his book *Divrei Yehezke'el* was relevant to his time when Jews lived peacefully in exile. This is not so in our time when our very lives hang in the balance. Our rabbi the Hatam Sofer, the author of *Ahavat Yehonatan,* and our Rabbi of Shinev would admit to this being a signal from Heaven that we should abandon the lands of exile and return to the Land which the Lord our God looks after.[1263] Presently this is His will." These were my words. I demonstrated that the situations were different. Therefore, one cannot apply lessons for ourselves. My position is clear in theory as well as application.

With the help of the Almighty I will add more proof concerning the veracity of our argument, from our sacred rabbi, the author of *Shnei Luhot HaBrit*[1264] in his commentary on Rashi in the portion of *Lekh Lekha.*[1265] He [Rashi] commented: "'[Go out] from your native land.'[1266] Had he not already gone out from there with his father and come as far as Haran? But He [God] said to him [Abraham] as follows:

1261 *Divrei Yehezke'el;* see above, 321–322.
1262 *EHS,* 148.
1263 Cf. Deut. 11:12.
1264 See above, 26, n. 65.
1265 Gen. 12:1–17:27.
1266 Gen. 12:1.

'Remove yourself yet further and leave your father's house.'"[1267] This is Rashi's commentary. The author of *Shnei Luhot HaBrit* adds:

> The Holy One, blessed be He, knew that Abraham observed all the biblical commandments in the Torah and all rabbinic injunctions as well. He certainly would have been very scrupulous in their observance. It is likely that he would have been meticulous in following the dictum of Rav Yehudah in the tractate Ketubot:[1268] "Anyone[1269] who goes up from Babylonia to settle in Eretz Yisrael violates a positive commandment as it is written: 'They shall be brought to Babylon and there they shall remain until I take note of them.'[1270] The events in Abraham's time all point to the future though they did not yet take place.[1271] The Almighty, therefore, commanded him to vacate his original quarters which were located in Babylonia and transfer to Haran which did not have the status of Babylonia.[1272] Once he resided in Haran the Holy One, blessed be He, said to him: 'Leave and continue further yet, since it is now permissible for you to go up to Eretz Yisrael.'" For Rav Yehudah prohibited only the ascent from Babylonia to Eretz Yisrael since it is written: "They shall be brought to Babylon and there they shall die." From other countries, however, one is permitted to ascend to Eretz Yisrael. One need not ask why was it permitted to go from Babylonia to Haran since this too shall have been prohibited by the verse "They shall be brought to Babylonia and there they shall die."

Now if it is prohibited to establish residence in Eretz Yisrael, would this not certainly apply to other countries? The reply: it was a matter of life and death. One may not rely on a miracle.[1273] Since he was hurled

---

1267   Rashi in Gen. 12:1.

1268   110b–111a.

1269   העולה כל vs. העולה "he who goes up" in *EHS*.

1270   Jer. 27:22. *EHS* cites the *Shelah* and the interesting variant ימותו ושם "and there shall they die" vs. יהיו ושם "and there shall they remain."

1271   Though the injunction implied in Jer. 27:22 could not possibly have had historic significance for Abraham, it took on a religious and a quasilegal meaning which is applied to contemporary situations by the *Shelah* and our author.

1272   Haran, in the northeastern corner of the area south of modern Turkey, is outside of Babylon, halakhically speaking.

1273   Pes. 64b.

into a fiery furnace,[1274] it was an omen for him [Abraham] to distance himself yet further in order for him to settle first in Haran and then to ascend from there to Eretz Yisrael. This is the end of the text.[1275]

Thus, although Abraham our Patriarch was aware of Rav Yehuda's stricture which prohibited leaving Babylonia for Eretz Yisrael and certainly for other destinations, nevertheless the Lord compelled him to leave Babylonia. He could no longer remain there since his experience with the fiery furnace had placed him in danger....[1276]

Now let us discuss our situation. We refer to the state of the Jews in European countries who have come under the influence of the infamous enemy. A danger, the likes of which has never yet occurred in exile, has materialized. There are those who have been executed. Others have been burnt to death. Yet others were stripped and compelled to stand in the nude. The multitude who have drunk from the cups of bitterness [1277] are too many to recall. Everyone has been marked for destruction, Heaven forbid. Because of our many transgressions, as we are aware, [the enemy] has succeeded in carrying out his schemes among the major share [of the Jewish population]. Only a minor remnant remains alive, and this due to a great miracle. This must be considered among the miracles performed by the Holy One, blessed be He, for His people Israel, since the enemy resented even this saving remnant which the Lord, blessed be He, miraculously rescued. They were always exposed to the danger of being caught in his net, Heaven forbid. Often our lives were in danger. I recall the fear and panic among the Jewish populace in this country, at the beginning of this summer when the enemy pressed his excellency the minister to immediately resolve the Jewish problem.[1278] We are aware of how he

---

1274   GenR. 38:19.

1275   *Shelah* text cited above, 323–324.

1276   The author proceeds to summarize the *Shelah* text: Danger outside of Eretz Yisrael is to be seen as a warning to abandon the place and seek the Land of Israel (*EHS*, 311).

1277   Cf. Isa. 51:17.

1278   Further reference to the strong efforts of Nazi Germany in the summer and autumn of 1943 to compel the hesitant Kallay government of Hungary to adopt

solves this problem. He sends them to a desolate land, referred to as "deportation," Heaven forbid. The consequences of deportations are known to us. . . .[1279]

Indeed, at this moment, even as I write these very lines, an atmosphere of fear and terror hovers over us as we witness all of the Admorim[1280] in our countries making efforts in the face of enemy danger to flee to Eretz Yisrael.[1281] They seem not to consider the demoralizing effect this has upon the Jews when the word spreads: "The *rebbes* are fleeing! What will become of us?" Note *Midrash Ruth*[1282] explaining the reason for Elimelekh's punishment, because he demoralized the Israelites when he fled in time of disaster.[1283] Our vehement hope is in the Lord, that He may rescue us [from disaster] also in the future. Yet we are all aware that we have more than once been exposed to danger to our lives, and God miraculously spared us. Hence, we must follow the example of Abraham our Patriarch, namely, to distance ourselves

---

stringent anti-Jewish measures. See above, n. 1256.

1279   The author describes the stalling tactics of the Hungarian government in response to German pressures for the deportation of the Jews. The deportation order, which might have been fatefully sealed with the stroke of a pen, was avoided. The dangerous situation, however, remained; hence further justification for imminent *aliyah EHS*, 312–13. For a further summary of Nazi pressure on Hungary during this period see Lucy S. Dawidowicz, *The War against the Jews*, 1933–45, *op. cit.*, 512–13. For documentation of the relevant discussions between Hitler and the Hungarian regent Horthy in Klessheim castle on April 17, 1943, see Raul Hilberg (ed.), *Documents of Destruction* (Chicago, 1971), 187–90.

1280   Acronym for אדונינו מורינו ורבנו "our master, our teacher, our rabbi" honorific title for hasidic rabbinic masters.

1281   The author refers to the controversial issue of the behavior of some rabbinic leaders during the Holocaust. A comprehensive and systematic critical study of the subject has yet to appear. The escapes of the Belzer, Gerer and Satmer rebbes have been described in materials of various degrees of authenticity and partiality, complicated by intense polemics. See Moshe Yehezke'eli, *Hatzalat HaRabbi MiBelz MiGey HaHarega BePolin* (Jerusalem, 1962); Bezalel Landau and Nathan Orner, *HaRav HaKadosh MiBelz* (Jerusalem, 1959); Mendel Paikaz', *"HaRabanit MeStrovnov Al Havtahat HaRabbi MiBelz, . . ." Kivunim* 24 (August 1984), 59–72.

1282   RuthR. 1:4.

1283   Elimelekh, a wealthy landowner, aspiring to leadership, וישם האיש אלימלך שהיה, אומר: יאלי תבא מלכותי "His name was Elimelekh for he used to claim: 'I will attain the monarchy'" neither anticipated the crisis nor eventually accepted responsibilities for the community. RuthR. 2:8.

from here and to proceed to Eretz Yisrael, since it is a matter of life and death and one may not rely on miracles. . . .

The statements of our Rebbe of Shinev[1284] were made at a time when Jews lived here in solitude and tranquility. They were not intended for difficult times such as those we have endured. See for yourself. You are aware and have heard what has happened to the sacred rabbi, the holy luminary, the unique saint, Reb Yeshayele Krakower,[1285] the youngest son of our Rabbi of Zans and brother of our Rabbi of Shinev, may his memory be a blessing. He was hidden in the city of Bochnia near Cracow together with a few hundred or a thousand other Jews. Here in the capital inquiries were made with regard to his rescue and bringing him here. All the wealth made available for his rescue proved futile. It was too late. They were all murdered sanctifying the Name of God.

Earth! Do not cover their blood[1286] nor the spilled blood of the remaining thousands and tens of thousands of Jews. May their merit permit us to exclaim: "Enough! to our suffering. . . ."[1287]

What I have stated here will suffice as a response to those who wish to besmirch me because of my present efforts on behalf of *aliyah* to Eretz Yisrael . [Those who criticize my present efforts do so because] in my letter which was printed in the volume *Tikkun Olam*[1288] published

---

1284 See above, 321–322.

1285 The Tchechiver Rebbe, R. Yeshayah Halberstam (1864–1943), was killed in the ghetto of Bochnia in the summer of 1943. He was the youngest son of the Rebbe of Zans and brother of the Rebbe of Shinev. See Menashe Unger, *Sefer Kedoshim* (New York, 1967), 198–201. According to *Eileh Ezkerah*, ed. Y. Levin, vol. 4 (New York, 1961), 166, the Rebbe was publicly burned to death in the Bochnia ghetto, enveloped in his *tallit*.

1286 Cf. Job 16:18.

1287 Citing *Or Hayyim* on Deut. 32:36, the author prays that for the sake of the righteous and the innocent the Lord will again "vindicate His people" and will exclaim: "Enough! to our suffering" (*EHS*, 313).

1288 Reference to the volume *Tikkun Olam*, published in Munkatch in 1936, authored and edited by Moshe Goldstein at the request of R. Hayyim Elazar Shapira, the Munkatcher Rebbe. The work is a massive polemic supported by letters and statements of major rabbinic and community leaders, vehemently opposing Zionist settlement efforts in Eretz Yisrael. The Orthodox *Agudat Yisrael* and *Mizrahi* movements especially came under harsh criticism. Among the 150 rabbinic leaders who lent their name to

by the Rebbe of Munkatch[1289] of blessed memory, I spoke against
aliyah. Now I have reversed my position. Our present discussion explains
this precisely. At the time that I wrote the letter it was a period of
peace and tranquility. There was no danger to life nor need to rescue
life. Now that the situation has changed so have the demands.

I have already indicated at the outset of this volume,[1290] that I had
never been able to grasp the profound meaning of this obligation.[1291]
Now that I have become engrossed in this duty[1292] and become convinced of my error I will proceed to do what many of our sages in the
Talmud did. They admitted: "My statements to you were in error."[1293]
Also among legal authorities we find that they changed their rulings
from previously expressed opinions. Note this well! May the Lord
bring us to His sacred mount,[1294] speedily in our time, Amen.

I have concluded these words on Tuesday evening, the seventh of
the Days of Repentance,[1295] in the year 5704[1296] here in Budapest the
capital, may it live and be protected.

Daily we recite: "I believe with utmost faith in the coming of the
Messiah. Although he may be delayed I shall nevertheless await the
day of his coming."[1297] Further, our sages taught in the *Midrash*:[1298]

---

this volume, by way of signators or supporting documents, was R. Yissakhar Shlomo
Teichthal. His letter of February 9, 1936, to the editors of the *Yidishe Tsaytung* in
Munkatch (reprinted p. 104–47) attacks the Zionist settlement efforts and the *Agudat
Yisrael* party for premature political involvement in Eretz Yisrael at the expense of
Torah study.

1289   See above, 98, n. 64.

1290   *EHS*, 17–18.

1291   The obligation to settle the Land.

1292   *Lit*, "after I lodged in the valley of the Law [halakhah]." See Meg. 3b.

1293   Eruv. 16b, 104a; Shab. 63 b et al. דברים שאמרתי לפניכם טעות הם בידי.

1294   Cf. Isa. 56:7.

1295   The seventh of the Ten Days of Repentance between Rosh HaShanah (the
Jewish New Year) and Yom Kippur (the Day of Atonement). Erroneously listed as
the fourth of Ten Days. The secular date: October 6 (evening) 1943.

1296   The Hebrew acronym אשדת (*Ashdot*) may refer to Deut. 3:17 and 4:49, and
allude to the state of decline of the Jewish people in Europe.

1297   From the daily morning liturgy, based on the Thirteen Principles of Faith of
Moses Maimonides. Paltiel Birnbaum (ed.), *Daily Prayer Book* (New York, 1977), 155.
Also, *Perush HaMishnayot LehaRambam*, "*HaYesod Shneym Asar*," following tractate
Sanhedrin.

One finds that our ancestors were redeemed from Egypt only due to the merit of their faith, as it is written: "And the people believed . . ."[1299] Similarly, we observe that the exiles will be gathered in as the reward for faith, as it is written: "From Lebanon, come with me, my bride."[1300] "And I will betroth you forever . . . and I will betroth you with faithfulness."[1301]

Thus the text in the *Midrash Yalkut* on the portion of *B'shalah*.[1302]

Nevertheless, you should know that faith without action is neither beneficial nor productive. This I saw in the remarkable volume *Yad Yosef*[1303] of the pious scholar R. Yosef Zarfati,[1304] rabbi of the holy community of Andrinopole in the year [in his second homily] 5377.[1305] In his homily for the second day of Sukkot he explains the *Midrash* commentary on "May this be written down for the final generation."[1306]

This refers to the generation destined for death. "That people yet to be created may praise the Lord."[1307] The Holy One, blessed be He, will create them anew. What must we, therefore, take? The lulav and etrog[1308] with which we shall praise the Holy One, blessed be He. Consequently, Moses urges the Israelites "On the first day you shall take."

Thus the *Midrash*.[1309]

1298 *Yalkut Shimoni* I, 240.

1299 Ex. 4:31.

1300 Song 4:8.

1301 Hos. 2:21–22. The allegory of God as the lover inviting His beloved (the Jewish people) to return from Lebanon (exile) וארשתיך לי באמונה. "And I will espouse you with faithfulness" is interpreted: "I shall betroth you because of your faithfulness."

1302 Ex. 13:17–17:16.

1303 Amsterdam, 1700, 284–85.

1304 Scholar, author and rabbi in Adrinople in the late 15th and early 16th centuries.

1305 1517.

1306 Ps. 102:19. The *Midrash* is drawn to the term אחרון "final." The *JPS New Translation* commentary reads "a coming generation."

1307 Continuation of Ps. 102:19.

1308 The palm branch and citron, two of the four species, of the Sukkot festival, as in Lev. 23:40.

1309 Lev. 23:40–47. MPs. 102:3. See also *Yalkut Shimoni* II, 855, which employs

He [R. Yosef Zarfati] asked: What is the connection between God's statement that He will create them anew and the question "What must we take?" Are we indeed obligated to "take" anything in order to be created anew? Also difficult is [the phrase of the *Midrash*:] "Consequently, Moses urges the Israelites 'On the first day you shall take.'"

Who is to say this is the reason for [Moses'] command?
He [R. Yosef Zarfati] explains:

These four species[1310] are intended to teach us the doctrine of repentance. Namely, we have free will which enables us to correct all of our sinful ways with complete repentance with reflection, speech and deed, as it is written in the verse: "[No,] the thing is very close to you, in your mouth and in your heart to act upon it."[1311]

This verse refers to repentance.[1312] These species[1313] allude to reflection, speech and deed as he[1314] described.

I summarize these briefly. This is the intent of the *Midrash*.[1315] It is a fact: the greatness of the power of repentance is in its ability to nullify [evil] decrees.[1316] That is why it is written: "May this be written down for the final generation."[1317] These are the generations destined for death due to their sins. When they repent the Lord will in the future create them anew. He then asked: "But what shall we take in order to confirm this belief in our freedom to repent?" And he replied:

---

the variant: ומה להם לעשות? ליטול לולבין והדסים ולהלל אותו. "And what should they do? To take the lulav [palm branch] and myrtle and praise Him."

1310   Cited in Lev. 23:40.

1311   Deut. 30:14.

1312   The commentaries (Sforno, Nahmanides, *Kli Yakar*) link this verse to the return-repentance themes in Deut. 30:2 ושבת עד ד' אלי "and you return to the Lord your God" and 30:10 כי תשוב אל ד' אלי "Once you return to the Lord your God" while 30:14 contains the three criteria for repentance: audible confession "in your mouth"; regret "in your heart"; resolve not to "act upon it" sin.

1313   Referred to in Lev. 23:40.

1314   R. Yosef Zarfati.

1315   See above, n. 1298.

1316   RH 17b. אמר ר' יוחנן: גדולה תשובה שמקרעת גזר דינו של אדם.

1317   Ps. 102:19.

"Any form of faith which does not include action cannot persevere and is useless."[1318]

Maimonides, in *The Guide to the Perplexed*,[1319] explained the purpose of the Sabbath as sustaining the belief in [constant] renewal.[1320] What must we henceforth take in order to underscore the faith in our freedom to repent? We must take the lulav and etrog in our hands to indicate that everything lies in our hands—reflection, speech and action. These are the tools of return.[1321] Consequently, Moses cautions the Israelites: "On the first day you shall take...."

Hence we can understand the verse: "Why do you cry out to me? Tell the Jews to go forward!"[1322] All the commentators ask: What should a Jew do in time of travail if not to cry to the Holy One, blessed be He? Rashi explains: "Tell the Israelites to go forward!" They need but go forward, since the sea is no obstacle. Due to the merit of their fathers, because of them and their faith in Me when they left [Egypt], it is worthwhile dividing the sea for them. The *Siftei Hakhamim* commentary adds [on Rashi]: "This is the intent [of Rashi]: By moving forward, the raising of the staff will be effective and divide the sea. This will not happen if they do not move forward. Though you raise the staff, the sea will not be split. . . ."[1323] Accordingly this is the meaning of, "Why do you cry out to Me?"—You believe that your prayer will be effective. Not so, unless "they go forward." These are his words:[1324]

This seems difficult to understand. Since they were possessed with faith why should Moses' prayer not be effective on its own? Moreover,

---

1318 Set in bold type.

1319 Chapter 66 (Schlossberg editions; London, 1851; Warsaw, 1904; reprinted without date, Tel Aviv), 260–63.

1320 As the Sabbath is a vehicle for physical and spiritual renewal, so is repentance a form of religious renewal.

1321 The term תשובה (*teshuvah*) refers to both repentance and return.

1322 Ex. 14:15.

1323 Without the initiative of the Israelites, the lifting of Moses' rod (Ex. 14:16) would be a meaningless gesture.

1324 The supercommentary *Siftei Hakhamim* by Shabbetai Bass (1641–1718) on Rashi, Ex. 14:15.

it is hard to understand the fearfulness of the Jews in Egypt, as it is written: "The Israelites caught sight of the Egyptians advancing upon them and they were greatly frightened."[1325] Yet, previously it was written: "and the Israelites departed boldly."[1326] Rashi explains: "With great courage and pomp." Now if they had already confronted the Egyptians with courage, why would they nevertheless be fearful of them? I noted this [question] in the discourses of the Ran (discourse no. 10) who discusses this issue. Note it there.[1327]

However, because of the emphasis of our illustrious scholars of the past that faith without action is not effective, the difficulty of this passage is resolved. From the time the Jews left Egypt to the moment when they were confronted by the pursuing Egyptians they were in no danger. Their departure and journey were all accomplished by miracles. They needed to take no initiative, only to respond with faith, since they were carried on eagles' wings.[1328] Since they were assisted by miracles throughout their entire journey, their exodus did not, of course, represent an act which could strengthen faith. The Holy One, blessed be He, therefore, provoked a confrontation with danger. In their rear were the Egyptians, to their side the desert with wild animals, and in front of them was the sea. The Lord then commanded that they proceed towards the sea while it was yet filled with water, as it is written: "And the Israelites went *into* the sea."[1329] Only thereafter did it become dry. Thus with their entry into the sea did they actively demonstrate their faith. Only then were they sufficiently worthy that the sea would divide before them. . . .

This is the intent of the *Midrash* with regard to the lulav: "What shall they take?"[1330] Faith must be supplemented by action. Here as

---

1325 Ex. 14:10.

1326 Ex. 14:8.

1327 A likely reference to the presence of fear in response to natural and supernatural phenomena. The Israelites' fright following the exodus is perceived in positive terms, lest their triumphant departure (described in Ex. 14:8) arouse the potential arrogance depicted in Deut. 8:14, 17. *Drashot HaRan* (Jerusalem, 1959), 10 (69).

1328 Ex. 19:4.

1329 Ex. 14:22.

1330 See above, 329–330.

well. Faith alone is not sufficient. They need but confront the sea and it will no longer threaten them. Without action, however, your prayer will be to no avail. . . . This holds true concerning the faith in the Messiah. Though all of us, old and young alike, believe in him to the extent that no force or occurrence in this world could in any fashion sway us from this belief, faith alone is insufficient. It must be supplemented with action on our part so that this faith will be sustained. . . .

This faith in the coming of the Messiah is relevant to us as well. Should we choose to refrain from action and prefer to await his coming, when he would swoop down and carry us off to Eretz Yisrael, [this attitude] would confirm that we have no faith at all. Such faith would be merely superficial and self-deceiving. One who acts upon this faith, however, testifies to such faith. This type of faith compels him to take initiatives which are self-motivated and which in turn strengthen his inner faith. Then will help come from Heaven.

Such we have witnessed during the first redemption in Egypt, which is considered the origin of all subsequent redemptions. The Lord asked "Why do you cry out to Me?"[1331] in prayer. Prayer at this moment will not help you at all. Rather "tell the Israelites to go forward."[1332] Though the journey in itself was dangerous, since they had no alternate route except by means of the sea with its turbulent waters, yet this very act of movement complemented for them their faith in redemption. Consequently the true redemption of the Holy One, blessed be He, followed in its wake. This must be our model as well, as recorded by the prophet: "I will show him wondrous deeds as in the days when you journeyed forth out of the land of Egypt."[1333] As it happened in Egypt, so must it occur with us as well. The Lord will display wondrous deeds for us. Amen, forever.

1331 Ex. 14:15.

1332 Ibid.

1333 Mic. 7:15.

CHAPTER FOUR

THE CHAPTER OF UNITY AND
PEACE:
THE SOLUTION OF ISRAEL

As it is explained in the introduction to the sacred volume *Ohev Yisrael* of our holy Rabbi from Apt,[1] of blessed memory, the numerical value of *Ohev Yisrael*[2] is identical to the numerical value of *takkanah*,[3] in order to teach that only it (the love of Israel for one another) can be the solution for Israel, none other.

The Midrash on Lamentations, section 3,[4] interprets the verse: "He has worn away my flesh and skin. He has shattered my bones."[5]

"He has worn away my flesh"—this refers to the community. "And skin"—this refers to the Sanhedrin.[6] As the skin protects the flesh so

---

1 See above, 69–70, nn. 56 and 57.

2 "One who loves Israel."

3 "Reconstruction, rehabilitation, remedy." אוהב ישראל (*Ohev Yisrael*) and תקנה (*takkanah*) both equal 555 in *gematria* numerology. אוהב ישראל בגמטריא תקנ״ה, פ׳ בעז״ה. "היא תקנה לכל נפשות ישראל להתקרב לדרך ה׳ כל אחד לפי דרכיו *Ohev Yisrael* in *gematria* numerology is 555 (*T'K'N'H*), namely, that with the help of the Lord, this [concept of genuine love for Israel] is a remedy for all Jewish souls to draw close to the ways of God, everyone according to his own way." Introduction to *Ohev Yisrael* (Zitomer, 1863), 2, by R. Meshulam Zusya of Zinkow, grandson of the author.

4 Paragraph 5.

5 Lam. 3:4

6 The High Court.

the Sanhedrin protects the Israelites. "He has shattered my bones"[7]—the bones of humans. They were powerful people.

These are the words of the Midrash, but they are astonishing. Why would our sages of blessed memory direct this verse towards the community and Sanhedrin, and the powerful, mighty people in Israel? What were their intentions?

Yet the Lord enlightened me as to their profound intent. It was to teach us how to relate successfully to a community, resulting in good fortune. What are the obligations of the leadership towards the people? How shall they lead and direct them in the path of truth so that they would achieve true perfection in all matters?

I shall begin with the interpretations of the verse[8] introduced at the outset of these remarks and similarly addressed by two personalities.[9] These are from the prodigious scholar, our teacher Shlomo Verga[10] (who was a chronicler living in Italy three hundred years ago) in his work *Shevet Yehudah*,[11] and the scholar, our teacher the Maharam Schiff[12] in his discourses on Deuteronomy (appended to the tractate Hullin).[13] Both focused on the verse: "He has worn away my flesh and my skin. He has shattered my bones."[14]

The verse is constructed in the reverse order. (When wounded) the skin is affected first, then the flesh and finally the bones. It should have

---

7 A play on words. עצמותי (*atzmotai*) "my bones" and עצומי (*atzumei*) "my mighty ones."

8 Lam. 3:4.

9 Literally, "Two prophets who prophesized identically." Sanh. 89a ואין שני נביאים מתנבאים בסיגנון אחד. "No two prophets prophesy in the same fashion."

10 R. Shlomo Ibn Verga, late 15th/early 16th-century scholar and historian, and author of *Shevet Yehudah*, a volume containing accounts and explanations of persecutions of the Jews throughout postbiblical times. He resided at various times in Spain and Portugal.

11 Published in 1554.

12 R. Meir ben Yaakov HaKohen Schiff (1605–1641), rabbinic scholar and leader of the Fulda community. Known for his *hiddushim* (novellae) on tractates of the Talmud.

13 Follows his *Hiddushei Halakhot* to the tractates of Zevahim in the Poryck, 1810 edition.

14 Lam. 3:4.

been written: "He has worn away my skin and my flesh, and broken my bones." Or it should have begun with the bones and moved outwards—the fractured bones (followed by) the wasted flesh and skin. They were compelled to explain the verse: the focus of the injury is centrally located, hence, the flesh.[15] At times the injury projects outwards and therefore (the verse) adds "and my skin," since [the damage] exits into the skin. Other times the damage intrudes into the bones, hence, "He has shattered my bones." Sometimes the damage is projected simultaneously outwards and inwards.[16]

These are his words. Yet the question remains: What was the intent of the lamenter whereby he chose to describe the wound in this fashion? . . .

It seems to me that he was particularly concerned regarding the verse which alluded to the reason that we were deprived of our Land, exiled, and had our Temple destroyed, though we were a powerful nation and we struck fear into the hearts of the [non-Israelite] inhabitants of the Land. In the words of the lamenter: "The kings of the earth did not believe, nor did any of the inhabitants of the world, that foe or adversary could enter the gates of Jerusalem."[17] But it was only the lack of unity among the Israelites which caused our destruction. Had we indeed remained united as one body undivided, no nation in the world would be able to wrest our Land from us. But the plague [of discord] broke out in our very midst. Dissension among Israel was caused by various feuding parties. What one built, the other destroyed. As our own recent history has shown, there exists no harmony among them. This is alluded to in the Talmud and the Midrash.[18] Consequently, the injury originates in the center—among the Israelites themselves—and enters into and exits from the source. Thus the very

---

15 Which is mentioned first.

16 *Shevet Yehudah* (Jerusalem, 1947), 114.

17 Lam. 4:12.

18 Probable reference to internal strife which brings destruction upon the community. See Git. 59b–60a; the famous dictum on senseless hatred in Yoma 9b; *Yalkut Shimoni* II, 1010; Pes. 49b; Sanh. 7a.

foundation in the heart of Israel is destroyed. This permitted the enemies from without to attack and conquer them. They were compelled to fight a war [on two fronts]—from within and without.

Hence, laments the prophet: "He has worn away my flesh,"[19] namely, the wound originates from within Israel. As it is noted in the verse: "Those who ravaged and ruined you, emerge from your very own."[20] Due to the lack of harmony within the Israelite camp the ulcer erupted, expanding internally and externally. This accounts for ["He has worn away my skin"][21]—which is situated outside [the body]. "He has shattered my bones"[22]—is [the damage] from within. Presently we comprehend the Midrash: "'He has worn away my flesh'—this refers to the community." Namely, the plague originated within the Israelite community torn into different factions and parties with their own systems and ideologies. Every faction fought on behalf of its own ideology. In response, the opposing factions battled for their positions. One was in combat with the other. The community was without authority and harmony. Instead, misfortune and darkness stirred within the Israelite camps. As a result, the enemy appeared from outside and destroyed everything.

This also is the meaning of the Midrash: "'And skin'—which refers to the Sanhedrin. As the skin protects the flesh, so the Sanhedrin protects the Israelites." That is to say, as leaders of people it was the obligation of the Sanhedrin to consolidate the entire Jewish people into a unified alliance. As the skin consolidates and protects all the bodily organs, so must the shepherds [of the people] attempt with all their might to unify the various parts of the people into one entity. . . . Then the Jewish people shall endure. They will flower and blossom to great heights. There will be neither foe nor affliction.[23] If the shepherds [of the people] will not set their minds to creating unity among them, then the ulcer will infect the community with

19   Lam. 3:4.
20   Isa. 49:17.
21   See above, nn. 7–8; 14–15.
22   Ibid.
23   Cf. I Kings 5:18.

ruinous consequences. It will consume and destroy everything. "'He has worn away my flesh'—this refers to community." Then follows "my skin." The Sanhedrin as well will be removed from their positions.

This will lead to, "He has broken my bones." "These are the mighty[24] among men." These were the great and powerful of the nations who were destined to benefit the people. They too will not be of help to their generation. This is exactly what occurred in our own time resulting in loss, destruction and exile. Because of the lack of unity among ourselves our fate has been an extended exile. Satan continues to stir up discord among us. The leaders will eventually have to give an accounting for their deeds since they failed to forge the Jewish nation into a unified entity. After all, as we know from our rabbinic sources,[25] this is the only remedy for our affliction.

This is the statement of our holy and divine R. Sheftel, the son of our rabbi the *Shelah*, in the volume *Vavei Ha'Amudim*,[26] at the close of chapter 27:

> Note the opinion of the tractate *Derekh Eretz Zuta* in the chapter [devoted to] *Shalom* [Peace]: R. Joshua ben Levi said: "The Holy One, blessed be He, said to the Israelites: 'You were the cause for the destruction of My house and the expulsion of My children. Let them pray for her [Jerusalem] peace and I will pardon them.' Why? 'Pray for the peace of Jerusalem.'[27] It is also written: 'Seek the welfare of the city.'[28] It

---

24 The root עצם (*e'tz'm*) is common to "bones" and "mighty."

25 GenR. 98:2. Citing Ezek. 37:16 and the distinction between the written חברו (*havero*) and the pronounced חבריו (*haverav*). נעשו בני ישראל אגודה אחת. התקינו עצמ[כ]ן לגאולה "The children of Israel merged into a unified whole. [Jacob urged them:] 'Prepare yourselves for redemption.'" See also *Yalkut Shimoni* II, 549, commenting on Jer. 3:18. ויבאו יחד מארץ צפון על הארץ אשר הנחלתי את אבותיכם: וכן אתה מוצא שאין ישראל נגאלין עד שיעשו אגודה אחת 'They shall come together from the land of the north to the Land I gave your fathers as a possession.' Hence, you will realize that the Israelites will not be redeemed until they become a unified entity."

26 Ex. 27:10. *Lit.*, "The Hooks of the Posts." *Sefer Vavei Ha'Amudim, Amud HaShalom* (Nuremberg, 1762), chapter 27, 44. (Appended to *Shenei Luhot HaBrit* [Furth, 1764]. Schocken Library, Jerusalem cat. no. 20883).

27 Ps. 122:6.

28 Jer. 29:7.

is also stated: 'May there be peace within your ramparts, serenity within your palaces.'[29] Further, it is written: 'For the sake of my kin and friends I pray for your peace.'"[30] Thus, peace is of such magnitude that the Holy One forgives us though we caused the destruction of the Holy Temple. Consequently, when one insists on dispute he rejects peace.

In addition to all the sins for which we are guilty and which resulted in the destruction of the Temple and exile from our Land, the very destruction of the Temple is a sin for which we are liable. This is the intention of the lamenting prophet: "The crown has fallen from our head; woe to us that we have sinned."[31] Now what is so original with this lament? Has it not already been written previously: "Jerusalem has greatly sinned."[32] Yet this is what I had in mind. When Jeremiah declares, "The crown has fallen from our head," he refers to the Holy Temple. He adds: "Woe to us that we have sinned." This is our sin as well since we were the cause of the destruction of the Temple.[33]

I encountered a midrash: "Any generation wherein the Holy Temple is not rebuilt it is as if they caused its destruction."[34] This is problematic. Why so? Our fathers sinned and are no more.[35] They were the cause of the destruction of the Temple. Why then should each generation be accountable as if they had destroyed it?

I reject Israel's complaints and contentions regarding the attributes of the Divine when they claim: "We have not yet been saved although we worship the Lord our God and adhere to His Torah. We have faith in Him. We observe His commandments." If so, "Why did the Lord do thus"[36] to us that we are evicted from the House of the Lord? What

---

29   Ps. 122:7.

30   Ibid. 8.

31   Lam. 5:16.

32   Ibid. 1:8.

33   See Ibn Ezra on Lam. 5:16: בית המקדש מקום השכינה "The Temple is the abode of the Shekhinah."

34   JT Yoma 1:1.

35   Cf. Lam. 5:7.

36   Cf. Deut. 29:23.

delays the Messiah?[37] The truth is that we cannot find any response. Further, we do find among ourselves senseless hatred, envy and evil gossip. These characteristics we tragically carry with us from the sin of the Second Temple, as they are described by our sages of blessed memory in the tractate Yoma:[38] "The Second Temple, [characterized] by the study of Torah, the observance of mitzvot and kind deeds, why was it destroyed? Because of the prevalence of senseless hatred."[39] . . .

Our rabbi, R. Be'er of blessed memory[40] spoke to his disciples before his death: "My children. You must remain united. Then you will be able to overcome every obstacle. You will go forward and you will not retreat, God forbid.[41] This [idea] is intimated in [the verse] 'He is One; who can dissuade Him?'"[42] These are his words.

This lesson is to be applied to our nation generally. A poet referring to Israel phrased it beautifully as follows:

My fortunate People! My pathetic People!
Fortunate when you are united. Pathetic when divided.
Soft when dispersed, strong when determined.
My fortunate People, my pathetic People!
Pathetic are the factions among you,
Who are a curse in your tents.
Fortunate are you when you are united,
For unity is a death blow to those who oppose you.
"Upon your factions[43] lay the slain ones."

---

37 *Lit.*, "the son of Jesse."

38 9b.

39 The *Vavei Ha'Amudim* text (above, n. 26) continues to expound upon the evils of senseless hatred, the tragic consequences of the Kamza and the Bar Kamza fiasco described in Git. 55b–56a, which led to the destruction of the Second Temple.

40 See above, 3, n. 2.

41 The quotation to this point is in Yiddish.

42 Job 23:13. Though the verse refers to God, the hasidic exegesis suggests that when people who walk in the path of the Lord are one and united, they can overcome any obstacle. This teaching assumes a variant form of *imitatio Dei*

43 Cf. II Sam. 1:19, על במותיך חלל. The term במה (*bamah*) suggests platforms for the many factions and splinter groups.

Destroy your forums and build your ramparts[44]
And gather your strength towards your own unity.
Then you shall be established firmly forever.[45]

I have also noted that all of my concerns expressed previously are
explained in the elegy of Jeremiah who lamented:

> The kings of the earth did not believe, nor any of the inhabitants of the
> world, that foe or adversary could enter the gates of Jerusalem. It was
> for the sins of her prophets, the iniquities of her priests (and Rashi
> adds: "Due to the sins of the false prophets did all this evil occur") . . .
> So they wandered and wandered again, for the nations had resolved
> "They shall stay here no longer." The Lord's countenance has turned
> away from them.[46]

The commentators[47] add: So they fought[48] as [used in the context]
"when men fight," since they fought one another. Therefore, their
status was shaken, their foundation weakened from beneath them.
"For the nations had resolved":[49] when the nations heard that they,
the Jews, fought one another and even kill each other, they exclaimed:
"They [we, the nations] will no longer fear[50] [the Israelites], namely,
at the outset they did not believe that they would be able to conquer
the Israelites since they were a powerful nation. Now they exclaimed:
"[We] shall no longer fear them,[51] (as in the use of the term, "Moab
was frightened.")[52] The Lord's countenance has turned away from

---

44   The former fragment, the latter defend.

45   The source of this selection is unknown.

46   Lam. 4:12, 13, 15, 16. The translation of 4:16 פני ד' חלקם "The Lord's countenance
has turned away from them" follows the parallel לא יוסיף להביטם "He will look on
them no more." In the context of the author's message the term חלקם (ḥilkam) may
infer division and strife resulting from competing claims as to Who is God?

47   See the *Lehem Dim'ah* (Venice, 1606) commentary of R. Samuel ben Isaac
Uceda, 16th-century Safed kabbalist and Talmud scholar.

48   כי נצו as in Ex. 21:22 וכי ינצו אנשים vs. "they wandered," as in יצאו (yatz'u).

49   Lam. 4:15.

50   The root גור "dwell" is transformed to its alternate meaning "fear."

51   Lam. 4:15. Alternate reading: "They shall stay here no longer."

52   Num. 22:3.

them."[53] By this is meant that the wrath of the Lord "has divided them,"[54] He has separated them and split them into many parts. Consequently their strength was removed from them. It was all because of "the sins of her prophets and the iniquities of her priests,"[55] namely the faults of the leaders who did not see fit to unite them into one cohesive alliance. A wise political observer had this to say: "The divisiveness of a people signifies its decline."[56]

See [what is written in] the first chapter of Jerusalem Talmud, Yoma:

> R. Yohanan bar Torta said: "We know that the First [Temple][57] was destroyed because of idol and star worship, because of incestuous relationships and murder. But during the Second [Temple] we know that they were diligent in the study of Torah and particular in the observance of the mitzvot [and tithes].[57] They were endowed with fine manners (They possessed every variety of good behavior).[58] On the other hand, they loved wealth and hated one another without cause. The sin of causeless hatred is more severe than these three grave transgressions."[59]

In the Jerusalem Talmud[60] you will note that the sin of envy during the Second Temple caused destruction exceeding that of the First Temple. With regard to the latter, the enemy destroyed only the roof. The walls remained intact. But, the Second Temple was destroyed together with the walls and foundations, as it is written: "Strip her, strip her to her very foundations."[61] The Jerusalem Talmud concludes: [62]

---

53 Lam. 4:16.

54 The literal rendering of חלקם (hilkam).

55 Lam. 4:13.

56 Source unclear. *The International Thesaurus of Quotations*, compiled by R.T. Tripp (New York, 1987), cites an Ashanti proverb: "The ruin of a nation begins in the homes of its people" (p. 423).

57 Appears in JT Yoma 1:1 (4b) but is omitted from *EHS*, 321.

58 The author's interjection.

59 JT Yoma 1:1 (4b). The Talmud text concludes: וקשה היא שנאת חינם שהיא שקולה כנגד ע"א וגילוי עריות ושפיכת דמים. "More serious yet is causeless hatred which is equivalent to idol worship, incest and murder."

60 JT Yoma 1:1 (4b).

61 Ps. 137:7.

"Any generation in which it [the Temple] is not rebuilt—assumes the blame as if it had a hand in its destruction." Hence, since in our time the devil continues to perform his dance of hate without cause, and mutual jealousies [continue to exist], the exile is thereby protracted and the rebuilding of the Temple delayed. It is regarded as if it had been destroyed in our time.

We can conclude from all this that when we see people who sow jealousy and hatred among their fellow Jews, causing discord by means of all sorts of pretexts, though they may devote their energies to the study of the Torah and are meticulous in the observance of the commandments—they wreck the entire structure of the Jewish people and destroy the very foundations upon which the Jewish people exist. They prolong exile. It was to them that King David referred when he said: "If the foundations are destroyed, what has the righteous man accomplished?"[63] Of what value and purpose is his righteousness and actions if with such efforts he destroys the very foundation upon which the structure and being of the Jewish people exist? May the Lord help in uniting us in mutual love and kinship. Then, no nation or people will be able to control us. Amen, may this be His will.

With the help of the Lord I have discovered a novel interpretation of the words of our sages[64] of blessed memory when they taught: As long as the Jewish people remain a unified group no nation or people will be able to subject us. [This is based on] the teaching of R. Bahya on *Vayishlah*[65] commenting on the words of Solomon: "Like a muddied spring, a ruined fountain is a righteous man fallen before a wicked one."[66] R. Bahya our teacher interpreted this verse as follows:

---

62 Ibid.

63 Ps. 11:3.

64 Variant of the unity theme appears in numerous rabbinic texts. See *Tanh. Shoftim* 18. גדול כוח השלום שבשעה שישראל עושין חבורה אחת אפילו עובדת כוכבים ביניהם אין מידת הדין נוגעת בהן. "The consequences of peace are enormous, for when Israel works in unison, the strict justice of the Divine is inoperative although idol worshipers dwell among them."

65 Gen. 32:4–36:1.

66 Prov. 25:26.

The manner in which the righteous man falls before the wicked one
compares to the muddied spring and ruined fountain. That is to say,
this spring which is currently polluted with clay and other debris will
eventually clear up. The waste will settle and clear waters will rise to
the surface. Similarly with the righteous man who falls before a wicked
one. Eventually he will be purified.[67] He will rise to the surface and the
wicked one will fall. The events [occurring] with the Pharaoh and the
Jewish people, as well as those related to Mordechai and Haman are
evidence in this regard.[68]

These are his words.[69] They are filled with charm since they emanate
from a wise man whose lips should be kissed.

I now supplement the words of our master, R. Bahya. The waters
will indeed become clear and the sediment will settle to the bottom
only if the well and the water's sources are in a clear calm and serene
state, positioned peacefully one with the other, not moving from
their place. But if the waters are active, moving from place to place
and in a state of turmoil, then they pollute themselves. The instability
and agitation among the segments of waters will cause the [impure]
silt which had already settled to the bottom to rise and create pollution.

This is exactly how it is with the Jewish people. When they live
peacefully among themselves then the wicked fall. But if there is
struggle, dissension and internecine warfare then the silt among them,
namely, the enemies of the Jews, will rise and pollute the spring,
Heaven forbid. This was the intent of Esther in her urging of Mordechai: "Go, assemble all the Jews,"[70] let them all be assembled with
love, affection and friendliness, then will they become pure and rise
to the surface. The wicked Haman will fall before the righteous.
They acted [upon her instructions]. This action brought immediate

----

67 Of impurities. Possible allusion to repentance.

68 Proof that the wicked eventually are defeated while the righteous are elevated
is drawn from the biblical accounts of the Exodus from Egypt and the scroll of
Esther.

69 A paraphrased section from *Rabbenu Bahya: Be'ur al HaTorah*, ed. Hayyim
Dov Chavel vol. 1 (Jerusalem, 1966), 274–75.

70 Est. 4:16.

results, for Haman began to fall. Thus Zeresh said to Haman: "Before whom you have begun to fall . . . you will surely fall"[71] further and deeper to the bottom, since due to the quiet of the waters they shall become clear and they will rise. This was the meaning of the statement of our sages of blessed memory: "As long as the Jewish people remain a unified group, no nation or people will be able to subject them." Then we shall benefit from the verse: "Seven times the righteous man falls and gets up,[72] but he who is wicked will fall by one misfortune.[73] This is consistent with the teaching of our R. Bahya. . . ."[74]

Our holy Rabbi of Zans,[75] may the memory of the righteous be blessed, used to frequently tell a precious parable. It concerned one who wandered lost in the vast desert for many days without being able to discover the correct path which would lead him to an inhabited community.

> As he wandered in confusion he saw an old man approaching him from the distance. He reacted with great joy, believing that this person would surely point him to a direct path leading out from this terrible wilderness. He asked him: "Wherefore do you come and where are you going?" He shared with him the problem of his long odyssey in this terrible wilderness, without success in finding a path to civilization. He asked him to show mercy and to guide him in the right paths[76] in order to save him from his dilemma. The old man responded by telling him of a similar situation. He too has been a wanderer in this wilderness, not merely for many days, but years, so that he is now an old man. To this day he has yet to find a path out of the vast wilderness. Thus his fate was no different. The only advice he would offer: Let us no longer

---

71   Est. 6:13.

72   Prov. 24:16.

73   A combination of Prov. 24:16 and 28:18.

74   Developing the theme of unity and citing the Hatam Sofer ("Discourses for the *Haftarah* of the Second Day of *Rosh HaShanah*"), the author places the responsibility for forging Jewish solidarity, especially in times of crisis, squarely upon the scholar and religious leader (*EHS*, 322–23).

75   See above, 27, n. 70.

76   Cf. Ps. 23:3.

wander on the same paths which we have taken until now since they have obviously not brought us to our desired objective. Rather they would have to seek a new path and do so by joining their resources since two are better off than one.[77] Then there may be hope that they will achieve their desired goal with the help of the Almighty.

These are the words of the rabbi.[78]

I apply these teachings to our own generation. We have been thrust into an iron furnace,[79] a furnace of fire. Because of our many sins, most of our fellow Jews in Europe have been destroyed in this iron furnace. The few who have survived are like a "brand plucked from the fire,"[80] a "people escaped from the sword."[81] It has now been demonstrated to us that the path along which we have wandered throughout the long exile, which has been littered with feud, discord, factions and hatred without cause, did not lead us to the place of our aspirations. On the contrary. It has led us to annihilation, Heaven forbid. In the responsa of the *Rema*[82] he attests to the destruction of a number of communities because of strife. Similarly, [this holds true for] many, many countries in which there existed a few thousand large and small holy communities. These are now deserted and destroyed. Zion's roads are in mourning.[83] This may all be blamed on the profusion of disputes among Jews. As it is written in the magnificent [volume] *Or Zarua*, "The Laws of Prayer," in a responsa of R. Hisdai, how contemptible is strife which destroys Jewish resources and causes

---

77 Cf. Eccl. 4:9.

78 R. Hayyim of Zans.

79 Cf. I Kings 8:57.

80 Cf. Zech. 3:2.

81 Jer. 31:1.

82 R. Moshe Isserles (c. 1520–1572) the great Polish rabbinic scholar, codifier, and philosopher, known by the acronym *Rema* His glosses on the *Shulhan Arukh* of R. Joseph Karo became the accepted ritual guidelines for European Jewry. The *EHS* reference is likely to Responsa No. 11, which discusses the priorities of peace and the consequences of strife. *Teshuvot HaRema LeRabbenu Moshe Isserles*, ed. Asher Sieff (Jerusalem, 1970) 92–98.

83 Lam. 1:4.

the banishment of God's Presence. Since God's Presence is absent there is no one to watch over Israel. Note it there.[84] (I do not presently have the volume with me.)

Our teacher, the *Noda' BiYehudah*[85] had communicated to the *gaon* R. Yitzhak Hamburger, of blessed memory, concerning this very point, namely: in this day and age there is no longer any controversy for the sake of Heaven.[86] If this was the situation in his day, which was still a generation possessed with knowledge, what are we to say who are orphans descended from orphans?

Consequently, we who are the remnant few of a people escaped from the sword have no choice but to comply with the admonition of our teacher the Hatam Sofer, cited previously,[87] namely, to arbitrate among ourselves in the interest of amity. [The objective] is to draw close to one another,[88] to strengthen unity among ourselves and to begin afresh with an entirely new life style. We must disengage from old traditions which caused discord among ourselves.[89] We must gather

---

84 *Or Zaru'a, She'elot uTshuvot, Hilkhot Tefillah* (Zhitomir, 1862), vol. 1, 11 5, p. 41 (21). The author of this well-known halakhic treatise is R. Yitzhak ben Moshe of Vienna (c. 1180–c. 1250), scholar and rabbi in Germany and France. וגנאי הוא המחלוקת שהוא מחריב את הגופים והממונות, והמסלק את השכינה עליהם, אין עליהם שומר. "Discord is disgraceful for it destroys substance and values and repels the Shekhinah. And when the Shekhinah is not in their midst they have no protector." See also: Shab. 33a; CantR. 2:16; *Shir HaShirim Zuta* 1 2, 1:6-7; Zohar I, 180 שכינתא לא שרייא אלא באתר חדוה "The Shekhinah does not dwell except in places of harmony."

85 R. Yehezkel HaLevi Landau (1713–1793), among the leading Eastern European *halakhic* scholars of the 18th century.

86 Argument and difference of opinion based on sincerity in the objective pursuit of truth. See Avot 5:17. *Noda' BiYehudah, She'elot uTshuvot, Yore De'ah* 1 (Prague, 1776), (30a in this edition) ויתן מקום לשלום. ואין לך גרוע מהמחלוקת. ובזמנינו לא שכיח מחלוקת לשם שמים והשטן מרקד ונא מאד שיעשה שלום. והעושה במרומיו שלום יברך עמו ישראל בשלום. "May he [the litigant] provide place for peace. There is nothing worse than discord. In our times discord for the sake of Heaven is rare. The devil is overjoyed. I beseech you greatly—make peace. And He Who makes peace in His universe will bless His people Israel with peace." The response was sent to R. Avraham Helm, the senior rabbinic *dayan* (judge) in the community of Emden and not as stated in the text, "Yitzhak Hamburger," who was chief rabbi of Prague (d. 1758).

87 See above, n. 74.

88 Cf. Ezek. 37:17.

89 A paraphrase in Yiddish follows: "We must begin life entirely new, a life of unity conducted with a collective purpose."

all the resources among the survivors of our Jewish people and forge them into a unified body with a united purpose. Then the Lord will help us rebuild the ravaged places,[90] and assist in establishing for us a permanent and firm existence in the world. No longer will we be the object of calumny among the nations, for the Lord will cause His Presence to dwell among us. He will protect us, as indicated previously[91] in R. Hisdai's responsa: "From the negative[92] one arrives at the positive."[93]

The reader should not respond to me, wondering: "How it is possible to bring together all of the disparate elements among the Jews? To this I reply: Did we not encounter such a state of affairs in the time of Mordechai and Esther who gathered all of Israel into one body? Did you actually believe that in the time of Mordechai, everyone thought alike? Then as well [as today] people were of different opinions. Many were assimilated [into the non-Jewish populace]. Observe what is written in the Midrash[94] describing how Mordechai pleaded with them [the Jewish people] not to defile themselves with the delicacies of the king. Although the attendance at the feast was not compulsory, eighteen thousand defiled themselves with prohibited foods. They paid no attention to the words of the upright Mordechai and behaved disgustingly. Thus you will understand that even in those times, there were differences of opinion. Nevertheless, when the massive decree of Haman was imposed upon the totality of Israel, all Jews without distinction, whether meticulous in the observance of Torah and mitzvot or sinners, Heaven forbid, understood that the only remedy to this misfortune is the complete reunification of all Jews, from the extreme left to the extreme right.

Hence I interpret the verse: "It is a time of trouble for Jacob, but

---

90 Cf. Ezek. 36:36.

91 See above, 349, n. 84.

92 Strife expels God's Presence.

93 Cf. Ned. 11 a מכלל לאו אתה שומע הן.

94 EstR. 7:18. According to R. Yishmael, 18,500 Jews responded to the king's invitation to feast at his table. Their undignified behavior was exploited by Satan, who argued for the destruction of the Jewish people before God.

he shall be delivered from it."[95] Similarly, we recite in our prayers:
"Deliver them from distress into redemption and respite." That is to
say, we may locate the remedy within the misfortune. The very path
of misfortune shall also be the path of redemption.[96] Just as misfortune
falls upon the entire Jewish community, so will remedy and respite
come about by all of us joining together for God's cause. Then respite
and redemption will come from God. Mordechai acted in this manner.
He succeeded in uniting [the people] by converging on the misfortune
of the generation. He was painfully concerned with the honor of
Israel. He devoted himself to what was taught in the Zohar, the
Talmud, and Midrash, namely, one must love and bring close every
Jew, even the most corrupt. They too are the children of Abraham,
Isaac and Jacob. He drew them near rather than rejecting them. With
the force of love which he displayed he succeeded in gradually in-
fluencing them until they returned to accepting the Torah anew.[97] As
it is written in the volume, *Eshkol HaKofer*,[98] interpreting the verse:
"For Mordechai the Jew . . . was popular with the multitude of his
brethren, he sought the good of his people."[99] He was involved with
them and sought to make peace among them. He assisted them and
spoke well of them. He influenced them with authentic views but
presented in a courteous manner, without shouting and harsh language.
. . .

In this chapter devoted to unity, it is my wish to simply reinforce

---

95   Jer. 30:7. From the *piyyut "Yisrael Nosha"* of the Italian poet Shafatya ben
Amitai recited during *selihot* (the penitential liturgy) of the third day prior to *Rosh
HaShanah* (New Year) according to the Polish-Jewish tradition. *Seder HaSlihot
Keminhag Hapolin*, ed. Daniel Goldschmit (Jerusalem, 1965).

96   The Jeremiah and *selihot* texts suggest this connection via וממנה "and from it"
and ומתוך "and from."

97   Likely reference to Shav. 39a and Shab. 88a, describing the revelation at
Sinai. The Jewish people are portrayed as receiving the Torah against their will. מלמד
שכפה הקב״ה עליהם את ההר כגיגית. "This teaches that the Holy One, blessed be He,
inverted the mountain over them as if it were a tub." However, in the days of
Mordechai they accepted the Torah willingly, based on the verse in Est. 9:27. This
apparently was due to the efforts of Mordechai.

98   Abraham Saba, *Eshkol HaKofer al Megillat Esther* (Drohobycz, 1903), 98.

99   Est. 10:3.

my earlier remarks and to demonstrate that this is the will of our Father in Heaven. As noted by our teacher the *Shelah*,[100] in the "Gates of Letters," under the letter *alef*,[101] that we the Jewish people are referred to as *Knesset Yisrael*,[102] because "we are all assembled and united in the mystical awareness of His Unity, may He be blessed."[103] One must, therefore, avoid quarrels and not cause dissension among Jews. "The greatest evil in the world is quarreling, which is more serious than idol worship."[104] As noted by our teachers of blessed memory,[105] the generation of Ahab was victorious in their wars although they were idol worshipers because they were united and lived together in harmony. But the generation of Saul[106] was defeated in war though they did not sin, because they were men of gossip and provoked conflict among themselves. . . . Our Sages also said: "In three instances the Holy One, blessed be He, was conciliatory in matters of idol worship but did not give way in matters of discord. . . ."[107]

Therefore, my brothers and colleagues, do not believe those who come to create dissension among a united Israel, claiming that it is impossible to unite all of the elements of the Jewish people into one tree[108] because of the danger this would pose for Judaism.[109] Even

---

100 *Shenei Luhot HaBrit*, Pt. 1, *Sha'ar Ha'otiyot* (*Ot Bet Briyot*) 44b (86) כי גדל חיוב
אהבת הריע הוא לכבוד אהבת הקב"ה. . . . ועל כן נקראים אנחנו כנסת ישראל, כי כולנו מכונסים
ומתייחדים בסוד אחדותו יתברך. "The obligation is great to love a fellow Jew for this love is reflection of the love for the Lord. . . . Therefore, we are referred to as the Assembly of Israel, because we are all assembled and united in the mystery of His Unity, may He be blessed."

101 Should read "the letter *bet*."

102 The Assembly of Israel.

103 *Shenei Luhot HaBrit*, op. cit., 44 b (86).

104 *Shenei Luhot HaBrit*, op. cit., 45 (87).

105 *Yalkut Shimoni* II, 213. דור של אחאב כולם עובדי עבודת אלילים היו וע"י שלא היו בהם
דילוטרין [בעלי לשון הרע] היו יוצאים למלחמה ונוצחים. "The generation of Ahab were all idol worshipers. Since there were no slanderers among them, however, they were victorious in warfare."

106 The *Yalkut* reads "David" instead of "Saul," citing Ps. 57:5 in support.

107 *Shenei Luhot HaBrit*, op. cit., 45 (87).

108 Cf. Ezek. 37:17.

109 In order to create consensus, intergroup dialogue would be necessary. The

should this be so and there be the slight possibility of danger, the Holy One, blessed be He, would prefer that they live in unity rather than in conflict.[110]

Actually, there is no danger at all. The contrary is true. If the pious are openminded, then they [the nonbelievers] will also draw close to us in a positive fashion. As I noted previously in the third chapter, paragraph 50, in the name of the author of *Pardes Yosef*[111] citing *Avot DeRabbi Natan*:[112] "Righteous and pious Jews emanated from many sinners in Israel who were drawn close to scholars." These teachings of our sages of blessed memory and of the *Shelah* are more valid to us than the isolationists among the devout, irrespective of stature and though they be distinguished personages.[113] I also cited[114] the teachings of the divine scholar, our teacher the Maharal whose voice echoes the Holy Spirit, [who taught] that the unity of Israel was embedded in nature. It is reinforced by our Matriarch Rachel.[115] May this subject of unity not become an obstacle and stumbling block, Heaven forbid. Specifically, our generation—which has entered the iron furnace,[116] from which those who escaped with the help of God have been cleansed and softened—can persuade them for the better.[117] The author of the volume *Shenei Luhot HaBrit* has previously indicated[118] that the unity of Israel reflects the Unity of God, blessed be He.

The *gaon* in the volume *Teshuvah MeAhava*, Part I, number 205,

---

fear of the influence of non-Orthodox ideologies upon the community is rejected by the author since factionalism is considered the greater danger.

110   *EHS*, 228.

111   See above, 227, n. 642.

112   *Avot DeRabbi Natan* 2:9 שהרבה פושעים היו בהם בישראל ונתקרבו לתלמוד תורה . . . ויצאו מהם צדיקים חסידים וכשרים. . . . "because there were many sinners among the Israelites. But they were attracted to Torah, and righteous, pious and proper people were descended from them."

113   This latter phrase appears in Yiddish.

114   See above, 264.

115   See above, 264–265.

116   Cf. Deut. 4:20.

117   The bonds of mutual suffering would have imbued the survivors with a renewed sense of unity necessary for the survival of the Jewish people.

118   See above, 351.

writes as follows: "If building the Holy Temple can only be achieved by means of discord, it is best that it not be built. . . ."[119] I have also noticed the responsa of *Mahariz Enzil,* may the memory of the righteous be blessed, who cites[120] our teacher the Maharal writing in his volumes:[121]

It is known that God's name is synonymous with peace.[122] His seal is Truth.[123] Now what is closer in proximity to one's own self—one's name or one's seal? Certainly everyone would agree that one's name is more closely identified with the self than one's seal. To such a degree His designation "Peace" is more important to the Master of the universe than His own seal of "Truth." Hence, one must often forgo truth which is only the seal of the Holy One, blessed be He, on behalf of Peace which is His Name. . . ."[124]

I discovered a text in a manuscript of a great scholar (whose name was not noted on the front cover, but from the manner of his writing one gathers that he was a great man) who interprets the verse "And the feebler [flock] went to Laban, and the stronger to Jacob":[125]

---

119 *Teshuvah Me'Ahava,* a collection of responsa which are among the major works of R. Eleazar ben David Fleckeles of Prague (1754–1826), scholar and noted preacher. The citation of *EHS* is not found in the 1809 Prague edition, part 1, no. 205, but rather in Responsa no. 61, p. 33 b. *JEHS* copied the *EHS* inaccuracy.

120 "*Hiddushei Halakha veAggadah,*" in *She'elot uTshuvot Mahariz Ensel* (Jerusalem, 1970), 94b. The author, R. Yekuthiel Asher Zalman Enzil Zusmir (d. 1858), was rabbi in the community of Staro in Volhynia.

121 Maharal, "*Netiv Shalom,*" chapter 1, *Netivot Olam,* 1836, 42.

122 LevR. 9:9. See also NumR. 11:18. א״ר יודין ב״ר יוסי: גדול שלום, ששמו של הקב״ה (שופטים ו:כ״ה) נקרא שלום, הה״ד: ויקרא לו ה׳ שלום.׳ R. Yudin said in the name of R. Yossi: "Great is peace since the Lord is known by the appellation 'Peace,' as it is written [Judges 6:25] '[So Gideon built there an altar to the Lord] and called 'God of Peace.'"

123 Shab. 55a. דאמר ר׳ חנינא: חותמו של הקב״ה אמת "Since R. Hanina said: 'The seal of the Lord is truth.'" See also Sanh. 64a.

124 The author, citing tractate Yoma 85b and the renowned 19th century R. Amram Blum, equates the purification of Israel by the Almighty to the cleansing of the impure in the ritual *mikveh* As the waters of the *mikveh* must be unified and calm in order to purify those who enter, so must the Jewish people be unified and calm if they are to be properly cleansed by God (*EHS,* 327).

125 Gen. 30:42.

As it is known, Jacob's quality is *emet* (truth), as it is written: "You will bestow *emet* to Jacob."[126] The letters which constitute *emet* are extremely separated one from another [in the Hebrew alphabet], as noted in the tractate *Shabbat*.[127] The *alef* and *tav* are the letters at either end, and the *mem* is situated in the middle. *Emet* connects them. This is to demonstrate that the quality of *emet* has the power to join together even the most extreme elements which are situated at a great distance from one another. Just as the *alef*, which lies on the right end, together with the *tav*, which lies on the left end, are joined together by the *mem* which is positioned in the middle of the letters.[128]

It is known that the letter *mem* is formed by the [letters] *kaf* and *vav*,[129] as explained in the *Bet Yosef*, Section 36.[130] These add up in *gematria* to the ineffable Name of God.[131] This is to suggest that when one desires to unite two extremes, the Almighty, blessed be He, assists. He wishes and longs for the uniting of extremes. Therefore, His seal is *emet*[132] Note [what is written] in the *Shelah Sha'ar HaOtiyot*: "*Emet* suggests unity."[133] As the poet has stated: "His seal is *emet*, to inform you that He is One."[134] This was the quality of Jacob the Patriarch—to join and link everyone and to unite even those who are distant. This is

---

126   Mic. 7:20.

127   See discussion in Shab. 55a, employing the first (א) (*alef*) and concluding (ת) (*tav*) letters in various wordplay. These letters also form the parameters of *emet* (אמת).

128   Including the suffix letters of the Hebrew alphabet, *mem* is the middle letter with thirteen letters on either side.

129   *Mem* can be divided graphically into *kaf* (כ) and *vav* (ו).

130   R. Joseph Karo's commentary on *Orah Hayyim, Hilkhot Tefillin*, describes in detail the calligraphic technicalities with which the letters of the phylacteries' texts are to be inscribed.

131   The numerical value of כ (*kaf*) and ו (*vav*) (which form the *mem* design of the letter) amounts to 26, which is also the numerical value of the sacred letters of the Tetragrammaton.

132   Since within the word *emet* the letters on the extreme ends of the spectrum are united. Unity, therefore, equals truth.

133   42b. אחדות אחד האמת.

134   Identity of the source not certain.

the explanation of "and the stronger [went] to Jacob,"[135] namely, to connect[136] and link everything together, since holiness resides in the domain of the individual.[137] Those who follow this path[138] are in the class of Jacob. This is the significance of "the stronger went to Jacob." They belong to Jacob. "The feeble ones,"[139]—those who prefer to cause dissension among the dedicated elements and cloak[140] their acts in piety—"they belong to Laban."[141] He too clothed himself in religiosity and attempted to act more piously than Jacob, as we observe when he declared to Jacob: "It is not the practice in our place [to marry off the younger before the older.]"[142] With such excess piety, he [Laban] caused destruction in the world, as the kabbalists have noted.[143] For had Rachel been immediately given to Jacob [as a wife], he would have sired from her twelve godly tribes and the world of *tikkun* would have come about instantly. Neither the Egyptian nor the other exiles would have occurred. This is the meaning of the verse: "My father was destroyed by the Aramean. He went down to Egypt."[144] Rashi has difficulty with this

---

135   Gen. 30:42.

136   From the root קשר (*k'sh'r'*), to link or connect. The biblical context according to Nahmanides, is the robust male attachment (hence the term קשורים, "linked") to the female which produces a stronger breed of flock. See Nahmanides on Gen. 30:41.

137   The initiative of a sacred act begins with the individual.

138   Who aspires to unify diverse and antagonistic elements, which is identified as a sacred act.

139   Literally, they were "tied" to Jacob.

140   Gen. 30:42.

141   A play on the word עטופים "covered," "wrapped." Nahmanides suggests "wrapped in hunger"; Rashi offers: "wrapped in wool," hence the females felt no need to seek the warmth of the males. Both interpretations explain the עטף (*a't'f*) connection to "feeble."

142   Gen. 29:26.

143   Since the source presently cited by author is unknown, the teaching attributed to the kabbalists is difficult to trace and is not alluded to in the Zohar, Nahmanides or *Ohr HaHayyim* commentaries.

144   Deut. 26:5. The term אובד (*oved*) is alternatively explained as: "wanderer" [as a fugitive] from Esau in Aram; or "destroyer," namely, Laban the Aramean caused Jacob's exile in Egypt. See Pes. 116a; the *Targum* on Deut. 26:5 לבן ארמאה בעה לאובדא ית אבא "Laban the Aramean wished to destroy my father." The Passover Haggadah

[verse]. How did he destroy him [Jacob]? With the explanation [of the kabbalists] the problem is surely clarified since in fact he destroyed him with his excess religiosity and caused the exile in Egypt. And this is the fate of all those who carry on with excess religiosity, creating discord among the devoted by couching their deeds in reverence and piety. They belong to Laban: "The ones who disguise themselves [the feeble ones] belong to Laban."[145] They cause destruction and harm to Israel, as did Laban.

These are words of the great man.[146] The words of the wise are filled with charm and their lips are worthy of a kiss.

I add to the teachings of this great man from the words of the Midrash on Psalms, section 18 [commenting] on the verse. "You have saved me from the strife of people."[147]

Said Ben Azai: "David said: 'I prefer to rule over the entire world and not to rule over two individuals who have cloaked themselves in sheets.'"[148]

The commentator, the *gaon*, our teacher Yitzhak Cohen, the son-in-law of the Maharal of Prague,[149] explains:

"Those who cloak themselves in prayer shawls and fringes," (these are his words) namely, *sheine Yidden*.[150]

It is indeed remarkable that King David would pray to the Holy One, blessed be He, to be rescued from those who cause strife among people, that is to say, from *sheine Yidden*. It is remarkable that he

---

צא ולמד מה בקש לבן הארמי לעשות ליעקב אבינו. "Go and see what Laban the Aramean wanted to do to Jacob our Father."

145   Gen. 30:42.

146   Of the anonymous author.

147   Ps. 18:44.

148   MPs. 18:44 (Warsaw, 1875), 54.

149   R. Yitzhak ben Shimshon Katz HaKohen (d. 1624), son-in-law of R. Judah Loew b. Bezalel of Prague, commentator on the Midrash to Samuel, Psalms and Proverbs.

150   *Lit.*, "beautiful Jews," a caustic Yiddish expression, for Jews who flaunt their piety. העטופים בטליתות ובציצית "who are wrapped in their prayer shawls and fringes" is the phrase of the *MaHari Kohen* commentary.

would prefer to rule over the entire world and prefer not to rule over those who cloak everything underneath a prayer shawl and fringes, namely, a pious cover.

Truthfully, these are in his [King David] eyes merely creators of strife among people. This [midrash] adds much credence to the teachings of this great man. In any event we take note that King David as well feared them and prayed that he be saved from them and their lot since they cause destruction and devastation in the Jewish world. . . [151]

Observe what is written in [the volume] *Midrash Pinhas*[152] from our teacher R. Pinhas'l of Koretz,[153] who was renowned for the Holy Spirit which dwelled in his house of study and who was privileged to meet Elijah. Note page 22b, where a disciple writes as follows: "During the last summer prior to his passing he declared that all discord among Jews must be set aside. There must be no strife as a result of any Jew. . . ."[154] One learns from this text that even the most inferior and disreputable ones are also considered Jews, as they cite in the tractate Sanhedrin 44:[155] "Israel, even though he has sinned, is still considered Israel."

Consider and remember from whom these words emanate: from *tzadikim* such as the Hatam Sofer[156] and our teacher R. Pinhas of Koretz, who were inspired with God's Presence (Shekhinah). One becomes a truly *sheiner Yid*, when conducting oneself as a *sheiner Yid*

---

151 The author takes care to note that not every pious Jew was included in David's prayers. Those who are genuine *"sheine Yidden,"* who would draw other Jews close to them rather than repel them and who would seek unity rather than strife, were not intended. Hillel the Elder is held up as a model for genuine piety (*EHS*, 328).

152 A collection of teachings of R. Pinhas Schapira of Koretz assembled by his disciples and published in Lwow, 1872.

153 1726–1791. A forefunner of the hasidic movements and colleague-disciple of R. Israel Baal Shem Tov.

154 Pinhas MiKoretz, *Midrash Pinhas* (Warsaw, 1876), 22b (44). The Jerusalem Edition reprints the 62b pagination mistakenly cited in *EHS*, 329.

155 Sanh. 44a. The actual text reads: אע״פ שחטא ישראל הוא.

156 See above, 348.

A word to the wise....[157]

Elsewhere I explained the teaching of Rashi on the portion of *Beha'alotkha*.[158] It concerns Aaron, who became discouraged when he was not included among the chieftains during the consecration [of the Tabernacle].[159]

> Said the Holy One, blessed be He, to him: "I swear that your [function] is more significant than theirs, since you kindle and repair the lamps."[160] This needs clarification. How was his function more significant than theirs? The Midrash adds: The Holy One, blessed be He, said to him:[161] Do not fear, you are ordained for more important tasks. The sacrifices[162] are observed when there is the Holy Temple. The lamps, however, are observed forever,[163] as it is written: "toward the front of the lampstand."[164] This is also difficult. How does [the phrase] "toward the front of the lampstand" suggest that they [the kindling of the lamps] are observed forever? It is difficult [to understand] since, in fact, the lamps were lit only when the Holy Temple existed.

With the help of God we will clarify [the difficulty]. I shall first introduce the midrash interpreting the verse: "On the day that Moses

---

157   Citing *Shivrei Luhot* (Safed, 1864); Ber. 8a, and *Yalkut Shimoni* II, 920 (God's preference for community prayer); and kabbalah numerology, unity is equated by our author with God's blessing and His ineffable Name (*EHS*, 329–30).

158   Num. 8:1–12:16.

159   Num. 6:1–7:89. Rashi's comments are based on *Tanh. Beha'alotkha* 6 and NumR. 15:5.

160   Rashi, Num. 8:2.

161   In the midrash, God asks Moses to inform Aaron, which is consistent with Num. 8:1–2.

162   Associated with the consecration festivities of the chieftains.

163   Nahmanides (Num. 8:2) suggests that the midrash refers to the Hanukah lamps which continued to be kindled following the destruction of the Temple. אבל לא רמזו אלא לנרות חנוכת חשמונאי שהיא נוהגת אף לאחר החורבן בגלותינו. "However, they allude to the Hanukah lamps of the Hasmonean [era] which are ritually observed after the destruction [of the Temple] during our exile as well."

164   Num. 8:2. The *EHS* citation is an paraphrase of NumR. 15:5 and *Tanh. Beha'alotkha* 6.

finished setting up the Tabernacle."[165] "R. Yehudah bar Simon said: On the day that the Tabernacle was set up, Moses entered and he heard a glorious, beautiful, exquisite voice. Said Moses: 'Let me hear what God, the Lord, will speak.'[166] Said the Holy One, blessed be He, to Moses: 'I speak peace to them, [I bear no grudge against the children],' as it is written: 'For He will speak peace to His people, to His faithful, if only they renounce their folly.'[167] Thereafter it is written: 'His help is very near those who fear Him, to make His glory dwell in our Land.'[168] When [shall this occur]? On the day that the Tabernacle was set up."[169] This entire midrash is extraordinary and needs clarification.

We shall clarify with the help of God.

It is naturally more difficult for someone to care for that which has already been created and which is functional than [to exert] the effort necessary to produce it in the first place. All beginnings involve labor and a harnessing of energy in order to overcome the obstacles and delays which hinder initiative. One struggles but completes his project, albeit by means of great toil. But greater yet is the difficulty in sustaining this project, so that it functions, is viable, and does not remain idle for long periods of time. This is especially so when the project is of great importance for the welfare of human beings, and its efficient operation will bring benefits to mankind, for whom the world was created. This [principle] we know from the laws of nature.

Now let us examine the following [text before us] concerning the building of the Tabernacle commanded by the Holy One, blessed be He, as it is written: "And let them make Me a sanctuary that I may dwell among them."[170] The purpose [of the sanctuary] was to create a center for Israel and that the Almighty may cause His Presence to

---

165 Num. 7:1.

166 Ps. 85:9.

167 Ibid.

168 Ps. 85:10.

169 *Tanh. Naso*, 25.

170 Ex. 25:8.

dwell therein. Thereby, He will be close to the people near to Him.[171] From there will emanate all kinds of plentiful rewards. By means of this center the Israelites will always be linked to and joined to their Father in Heaven. Certainly, an activity of such magnitude and worth, which would eventually establish firm ties between the Almighty and Israel, required great initial efforts of planning and preparation so that it would fulfill the majestic purpose for which it was destined. Every Israelite would contribute to the enterprise.

One man alone remained remote without making any contribution to an eminent enterprise of this kind. He was none other than Aaron, the high priest of Israel, a godly, holy and awesome person. Rightfully he was disappointed that he was not invited to join in such an important enterprise. He was most distressed, as if Heaven had had reason to reject him.[172] It was then that he was reassured by the Almighty Himself. He said to him: "Aaron, my son, you are ordained for more important tasks."[173] The matter is as I explained. Crucial to every enterprise is its maintenance, that it operate with regularity, ceaselessly, and for the purpose it was established. Now the function of the Tabernacle was to draw all of the people of Israel into one location and to join them to our Father in Heaven. It was necessary to select one person who would be responsible for the uninterrupted, constant functioning of this center, so that it would not be terminated, Heaven forbid. We know the Holy Temple was destroyed due to lack of peace among Israel. Causeless hatred, conflicts and discord festered until it was destroyed.[174] It was, therefore, essential that following the completion and consecration of the Tabernacle, and in order that it function in accordance with its purpose, peace among Israel must be

---

171   Cf. Ps. 145:18 and 148:14.

172   Indeed Aaron feared that his exclusion was due to his role in the Golden Calf episode. See *Tanh. Beha'alotkha* 6 and commentary on note 27 אוי לי שמא בשבילי אין הקב"ה מקבל על שהיה לי חלק בעגל. "Woe to me! Perhaps the Holy One, blessed be He, has not [accepted the participation of the tribe of Levites {whose head Aaron was} in building the Tabernacle] because I was involved in [making] the [golden] calf." S. Buber, *Tanhuma* (New York, 1946 edition).

173   *Tanh. Beha'alotkha* 6. NumR. 15:5.

174   See JT Yoma 1:1 (4a).

preserved. Mutual harmony imbued with love and fellowship would be necessary so that the Tabernacle could function.

Considering this, the midrash[175] mentioned above is clear. In fact, while the building of the Tabernacle is a most worthwhile enterprise, its maintenance is even more worthwhile. Yet, its endurance is not secure without peace. Discord often emanates from those who consider themselves men of piety and scholarship and who refuse to associate with the common folk.[176] This creates conflict and discord among Jews. In any event, peace is disturbed and the Shekhinah withdraws from Israel as it is written in the volume, *Or Zarua*, "The Laws of Prayer," in the responsum of our teacher R. Hasdai; note it there.[177]

Thus, the intent of this midrash is as follows: Truly, the Almighty was delighted with His children on the day that the Tabernacle was set up, because they established such a noble and distinguished structure and consecrated it with joy and great enthusiasm so that it was welcomed by the Master of all creation. Then Moses our teacher thought: Surely, without doubt, strength and joy are in His place,[178] and the Almighty has not been so joyous since the day of Creation. As they [the sages] said in the midrash:[179] The day of the setting up of the Tabernacle was as distinguished as the day of the Creation of heaven and earth. Then Moses thought: Let me hear what God will speak,[180] as if to say: the Almighty will certainly speak of His children Israel with pleasure. He would laud them for the delight derived from them. To

---

175 *Tanh.* and NumR. in *Beha'alotkha*

176 The text is probably corrupt in *EHS* On the basis of the author's thesis throughout the volume (see *EHS*, 68–69, 73, 86, 153–54, 160, 184, 253–54 and numerous other passages) the text should probably read:ועקר הפירוד נצמח עפ"י רוב שאלו מחזיקים עצמם לחסידים ותלמידי חכמים ואינם רוצים להתחבר עם ההמון פחותי ערך "Much of the dissension emerges because quite often those who consider themselves the pious and scholarly refuse to associate with the ordinary masses." See also following paragraph. The text in the Jerusalem edition is similar.

177 See above, 347–348.

178 Cf. I Chron. 16:27.

179 Cf. Sifra Shemini 3:15. For further connection of the completion of the Tabernacle to the Creation, see *Tanh. Naso* 11 and Shab. 87b.

180 Cf. Ps. 85:9. This section is a paraphrased recapitulation of the Tabernacle midrash.

hear Israel's praises from the Almighty would be his [Moses'] greatest happiness.

Yet the Almighty said to him: My beloved Moses: Be assured that I indeed derive satisfaction from My children. But there is one fear which hovers before Me. [I fear] for the ongoing endurance of this noble enterprise. Would that it may exist thus always. May it not be abolished, Heaven forbid, since the sustaining of existence is more important than its creation. For this I have only one recommendation, namely, that "I speak peace to them."[181] May there be only peace among them. Surely I harbor no ill will whatsoever against My children. [Their leader] should only convey peace to "his people" and "to his hasidim."[182] That is to say, peace must reign between the hasidim and the simple folk, who are referred to as "people." "If only they renounce their folly."[183] [This refers to] the evil inclination's foolish advice, claiming that it is impossible for men of good deeds to join together with the humble folk. This is a device of the evil inclination by which it introduces dissent and conflict into the Israelite masses.

"[His help] is very near those who fear Him."[184] In truth, everyone fears the Almighty. Even the uncultured are filled with good deeds like a pomegranate [is with seeds].[185] When they all dwell together in unity and peace, they will realize: "His help [will permit us] to make His glory dwell in our Land."[186] This lesson is also forever relevant for the future. With unity they will merit the dwelling of God's glory in our Land. . . . Observe [the teaching of] the holy *Or HaHayyim* on the weekly portion of *Ha'azinu*[187] and the verse: "He will say: Where

---

181   See above, 359.

182   The meaning of Ps. 85:9 is removed from the context of the Tabernacle *Midrash* and directed and inverted to the contemporary scene. חסידים is not read as "the faithful," but as the "hasidim" of the author's generation. It is possible, but not likely, that the author had in mind the broader spectrum of pious leaders.

183   Ps. 85:9.

184   Ps. 85:10.

185   Eruv. 19a; Sanh. 37a; Ber. 57a.

186   A homiletic paraphrase of the conclusion to Ps. 85:10.

187   Deut. 32:1–52.

are their gods, the rock in whom they sought refuge?"[188] He writes as follows:

> "And Israel asks: 'Where is their God?'"[189] True, their deeds were not virtuous. Nevertheless, they appear with a claim before the Almighty, alluded to by the expression *Tzur* [the Rock].[190] Though Israel does act wickedly and will transgress a portion of God's commandments, nevertheless their entire trust is in God. For Him they endure poverty and degradation, and are martyred while sanctifying His Name. They anticipate and await the Rock, their Redeemer.[191] He [Israel] says to Him: "In the Rock he seeks refuge."[192]

These are his holy words. During these difficult times we have seen with our own eyes the truth of our holy teacher's words. May his merit protect us and all of Israel.

Now let us return to the teaching of Rashi.[193] After the Holy One, blessed be He, revealed to Moses that although the building of the sanctuary is an awesome and noble enterprise, its continued existence is yet more exalted; and that although this existence depends upon peace among all the factions of the people of Israel, it was necessary to select one man who would be capable of maintaining peace among the people. Who was more qualified for this task than Aaron? His soul was focused on love and the pursuit of peace, as explained in Ethics of the Fathers.[194] Study the *Sforno* [commentary] on *Beha'alotkha*[195] in explaining the [function of] the lampholder. [The purpose of] its creation and light was to unify and join all the factions of the people. Those [lamps] on the right represent students of Torah which

---

188 Deut. 32:37.

189 The commentators disagree in identifying the subject of ואמר "He will say." Rashi suggests it is the Almighty who taunts Israel. Ibn Ezra, Ramban and Rashbam refer verse 37 to Israel's enemies or the taunting nations. *Or HaHayyim* takes the extreme interpretation. It is Israel who has claims against their own God.

190 Deut. 32:37.

191 Ps. 19:15; 78:35.

192 *Or HaHayyim* on Deut. 32:36.

193 See above, 358–359.

194 1:12.

195 Num. 8:2.

is designated as right.[196] Those on the left represent those involved
with worldly affairs. [Both] should be united in realizing the will of
the Almighty so that His plan will be achieved by all concerned.
Together they shall uplift His Name in accordance with their commitment as it is written: "All the people answered as one, saying: 'All
that the Lord has spoken we will do!'"[197] In other words, together we
shall complete His plan.

This is the significance of the *menorah*: to teach us about unity
directed towards one purpose. These are his words.[198] Therefore, the
Holy One, blessed be He, said to Aaron: "Your function is more
significant than theirs."[199] You will be the means by which the Tabernacle will continue to be sustained. In this manner you will grow in
strength, since the support of an enterprise is worthier than its initiation.
The intent of the midrash is reinforced when it adds:[200] And the Holy
One, blessed be He, said to Aaron: "The lamps, however, are observed
forever." That is to say, the inner meaning of the lamps, which point
to the unity of Israel, is eternal. The existence of the Israelite people
will always be dependent upon its inner unity. Examine and appreciate
this, for these teachings have been perfected with the help of the
Almighty.

These lessons are applicable to us in our own times. We are physically
and spiritually exhausted from the suffering and grief which has beset
us until we are on the verge of despair. As one hears from so many:
We are doomed to perish,[201] Heaven forbid! There is neither any
prediction of, nor hope for improvement of our situation.

It seems that King David in his supplication referred to our generation in the 85th chapter of Psalms. Note *Tosafot Yeshanim*[202] on the

---

196   See Ber. 62a.בל. מימינו אש דת למו׳: ימימינו בימין שנאמר [דברים לג:ב]: מפני שהתורה ניתנה בימין שנאמר "Because
the Torah was given with the right hand, as it is quoted [Deut. 33:2]: 'At His right
hand was a fiery law unto them'"

197   Ex. 19:8.

198   See above, 358–359.

199   Rashi, Num. 8:2.

200   *Tanh. Beha'alotkha* 6; and NumR. 15:5.

201   Cf. Num. 17:28.

202   *Lit.*, "Old Tosafot." A collection of previously unedited manuscripts belonging

tractate of Yoma,[203] stating that King David prepared the Book of Psalms in anticipation of the period during which Israel will be in exile. He prayed for them (I have already mentioned a number of times that while writing this volume I do not have with me the volumes by which I can accurately cite the source): "Return to us, O God, our Helper, revoke Your displeasure with us. Will You be angry with us forever, prolong Your wrath for all generations? Surely You will revive us again, so that Your people may rejoice in You. Show us, O Lord, Your faithfulness, grant us Your deliverance."[204] (As if to say, Master of the universe, "Hasn't the experience of our suffering been enough? It seems as if the anger and wrath will persist forever and in every generation. Has not the time come that You return and revive us, that You show us Your faithfulness and grant us Your deliverance?") To this David responds on his own: "Let me hear what God the Lord will speak; He will speak peace to His people, to His faithful, if only they renounce their folly. His help is very near those who fear Him, to make His glory dwell in our Land."[205] . . . .

I shall, therefore, raise my voice to those of our generation who have endured this terribly difficult iron furnace[206] and all of the sufferings of Job—perhaps we have withstood even more so—and yet no one can foresee or suggest a remedy for our plagues.

We must attempt this once to fulfill the clear teachings of our sages of blessed memory. They have taught us on numerous occasions that all our hopes are dependent upon the manner by which we create complete unity without dissension, as I have

---

to the Tosafot school commentaries on the Talmud of the 12th and 13th centuries.

203 Jer. ed. of *EHS* suggests the source may be Yoma 71a. ד"ה זה מקום שווקים "This means the place of markets". . . But compare MPs. 18:1: כל שאמר דוד בספרו, כנגדו וכנגד כל העתים נאמרו. "Whatever is discussed by David in his volume [Psalms] refers [not only] to himself, but also to all of Israel and for all times."

204 Ps. 85:5–8.

205 Ps. 85:9–10. The author reiterates previous lessons on the discord and the virtues of unity, including the teaching of R. Elimelekh of Lizhensk (above, 89), who distinguishes between negative attributes of individuals and the positive characteristics of these same individuals when they are an integral part of a people. *EHS*, 334–335.

206 Cf. Deut. 4:20.

documented previously, citing from the Midrash and the Talmud. Then we will see the validity of their instruction because we will achieve our aims. We will merit true redemption with the help of the Creator. Hence, we must fasten the total holy nation from end to end.[207] This central bolt which will link us from end to end will correctly be the enterprise of rebuilding and settling our Holy Land. Only this precept is capable of such a thing, as I have indicated in this chapter. Further, we are still responsible for an old debt which we must yet settle, as I have observed previously.[208] Then the Almighty will be pleased and consider us with compassion and relief, speedily in our time.

Heaven forbid that such an ingathering and solidarity should be the cause of any harm to the *haredim*.[209] Let us use as a model the structure of a large factory, referred to as *fabrik*.[210] It is encircled by a high wall. This wall is its unifying factor and inside [the factory] there are various kinds of rooms, alcoves and divisions, each with its own task related to the factory. The high encircling wall unites them for one purpose. They are all referred to as "the factory." So it is with the joining of all Israel to the sacred enterprise under discussion. [The Holy Land] is but a canopy which embraces all of us. On the inside, however, each room is free to act in accordance with its inclination, such as the education of children as prescribed by the Torah and received by us from our sacred fathers. But with regard to the rebuilding and settling of the Land, let us be united and linked together. Since, truthfully, for this task it is essential to gather together all of the resources of the nation. As it is written in Ezra:[211] "The entire people assembled as one man in Jerusalem." Further it is written: "We together will build it to the Lord God of Israel."[212] Ibn Ezra

---

207   Cf. Ex. 26:28.
208   274, 277.
209   The vigilantly pious Orthodox Jew.
210   Yiddish for factory.
211   Ezra 3:1.
212   Ezra 4:3.

comments: "'We together'—this refers to the totality of Israel ."[213] I have previously cited[214] the lesson of our teacher Maimonides in his introduction to the order of Zeraim.

> Men of intelligence are in need of the masses so that the Land will not remain desolate.[215] For this purpose the masses were created in order to provide a society for the intellect so that they do not remain solitary... After all, the Holy One, blessed be He, installed the wicked in order to eliminate desolation. This is what the sages intended when they taught: "What is the meaning of the verse: 'For this applies to all mankind?'[216] The whole world [and its creatures] was created in order to provide companionship for him [for a God-fearing man]."[217]

Hence, they [the masses] are beneficial. Surely, for the purpose of rebuilding [the Land] the merging of all elements is required, for they too shall enhance the glory of Heaven. . . .

Study the *Divrei Hayyim* text of our teacher of Zans,[218] may his memory be a blessing, from the supplement to the weekly portion of *Re'eh*.[219] He explains the midrash: "Everywhere, one borrows from the other."[220] Our teacher [R. Hayyim of Zans] explains the meaning of the lesson:

> So that the world may be linked as one. This is the reality with regard to human limbs. Were man not linked to his limbs, he would be motionless. The purpose of man is to employ limbs in such a manner,

---

213 Ibn Ezra, Ezra 4:3.

214 *EHS*, 201.

215 Intelligence and wisdom would remain unapplied in a cultural vacuum.

216 Eccl. 12:13.

217 Ber. 6b. The author concludes selected Maimonides' views from his introduction to the talmudic order of Zeraim.

218 See above, 27, n. 70.

219 Deut. 11:26–16:17. *Divrei Hayyim* (Szolyva edition, 1912), 11 5b–116a.

220 ExR. 31:15. The midrash underscores the strict prohibition in Ex. 22:24 against extracting interest for loans extended to the poor. All of God's creations "borrow one from the other," in fact are mutually interdependent for their existence. Neither God nor any of His creations extract interest for such "loans."

where some limbs are dependent upon others, while others reciprocate. Every intelligent person understands that the hands cannot arrogantly claim that they perform the tasks for all other limbs or organs [of the body]. They are all unified. Neither should the other organs be upset that they do not function as hands since hands as well have disadvantages in that they do not [on their own] possess intelligence. The brain alone contains intelligence. There is no place, therefore, for either a sense of inadequacy nor arrogance on the part of one in relation to the other, since they are all included in the unified totality. Some function as agents of performance; others, of intelligence.

In this manner is humanity perfected. Should either the organs of intelligence or motion or manipulation be absent, or the head attempt to fashion objects and the hands endeavor to think, then humanity would be inactive. Why does creation function in such a manner? Because it is the will of the Almighty. Neither is there a reason why the world was created the way it was. In the Jerusalem Talmud and the midrashim[221] it is recorded how He [God] seemed to consult with the heavenly court concerning each organ and how it would be created. Regarding all the beings of creation it was taught:[222] "[R. Joshua b. Levi said: 'All creatures of creation] were brought into being [with their full stature][223] with their full capacities and their full beauty.'"[224] So it is certainly the manner of creation among humans. Organs which are lacking [in certain attributes], must be supplemented by others. The world in general has been created thus.

---

221 JT Sanh. 1:1. אמר ר' יוחנן: לעולם אין הקב"ה עושה בעולמו דבר עד שנמלך בבית דין של מעלן "R. Yohanan said: 'The Holy one, blessed be He, never undertakes a task in His world unless first consulting with the heavenly court.'" The description of the creation of the human organism follows the principle of human unity reflected in a discussion on the creation as a single individual and consistent with *EHS*, 336 and the teaching of R. Hayyim of Zans. See the extensive midrash in Sanh. 38: דבר—נברא יחידי אדם' אחר—מפני צדיקים ומפני רשעי' שלא יהיו צדיקים אומרים אנו בני צדיק ורשעים אומרים אנו בני רשע. "'Man was created alone.' Another explanation: Because of the righteous and the wicked—so the righteous should not claim, we are descended from the righteous and the wicked will claim, we are descended from the wicked."

222 RH 11a.

223 Alternate reading in Hul. 60a.

224 Every particle and organism was created with its own purpose and capacity.

These are his[225] sacred words, expressed with wisdom and truth. And so it is in the history of a nation. People are mutually dependent. There are those who resemble the hands which perform all kinds of labor. Necessary, as well, are people who represent the brain of the head. They are the eyes of the community. When they combine, they become one nation forged together in every fashion. . . ."

The precepts of the four species[226] attest to this principle, as known from the midrash[227] of our sages of blessed memory. They teach that with the binding of the four species into one unit, we bind ourselves to the Creator of the universe. [Consequently] all of the decrees against us will be nullified. The Almighty will, in His great compassion, direct towards us a life of abundance and boundless blessing,[228] and [the verses], "He will set you high above all the nations of the earth. . . ."[229] shall be fulfilled for us.

The prophet (Zechariah 8)[230] said, moreover: "But what it sows shall prosper: The vine shall produce its fruit, the ground shall produce its yield, and the skies shall provide their moisture. I will bestow all these things upon the remnant of this people." The Midrash[231] expounds [based on this verse] the lesson that the Land's prosperity is dependent upon peace, since it is written: "There shall be a sowing of *shalom* (peace).[232] Appreciate this [interpretation]. It appears that the prophet preferred the expression *zera* [sowing] rather than, "My children of peace," in order to allude to the lesson of the *gaon*, the kabbalist, our Rabbi Hayyim,[233] the brother of the Maharal and colleague of the

---

225 R. Hayyim of Zans.

226 See above, 329–330.

227 LevR. 30:11.

228 Cf. Mal. 3:10.

229 See combination of Deut. 26:19 and 28:1.

230 Verse 12.

231 Possible reference to JT Pe'ah 1:1 (4a). יעל האדמה׳ (דברים יא:כא): זו הבאת שלום בין אדם לחברו. "'Upon the Land' (Deut. 11:21): This refers to the bringing of peace among people"; and the *Pnei Moshe* commentary: לפי שבשלום כולן הן מתיישבין ומתקיימין על האדמה "Since peace promotes settlement and stability in the Land."

232 Alternate reading of the opening lines of Zechariah.

233 See above, 226, n. 634.

Rema of blessed memory, in his work *Sefer Hayyim,* towards the close of [the chapter] *Ge'ulah Vishua* (Redemption and Salvation).[234] He writes:

> Since we have established that the Holy One, blessed be He, has made a promise to Israel that He will not destroy them, they are always referred to as *zera* [sowing], as in the verse "I will give 'to your offspring' [this whole Land of which I spoke], to possess forever."[235] The reason: As in the instance of certain onions and other vegetables which are unfit as edibles because they have become hardened in the earth, and nevertheless are not uprooted but remain so that they will germinate seed from which will sprout fruit for another year—similarly, the Almighty does not destroy this wicked generation, though they so deserve [to be destroyed], since from them will sprout offspring from their sacred ancestors. He expects that from the stock of the roots of a lowly generation will yet emerge perfectly righteous people who will be present during the period of redemption. Then "the Lord will rejoice in His works!"[236] and "On that day there shall be one Lord with one Name."[237] At that time exile will be transformed into redemption to be crowned with everlasting joy.[238] With the addition of the letter *alef*[239] which signifies the absolute unity of His Name, may it be blessed and exalted for ever and ever.

These are his sacred words.[240] Hence, though a generation is not worthy, Heaven forbid, the Almighty utilizes it as seeds for a future generation, a righteous generation. As it is taught in the Rashbam towards the close of [the weekly portion of] *Ethanan* :[241] A thousand sinning generations may pass, Heaven forbid, but eventually a righteous

---

234   R. Hayyim ben Bezalel Loewe, *Sefer HaHayyim, op. cit.,* 27b–28a.

235   Ex. 32:13 לזרעכם. *Zera* in the sense of offspring appears regularly in Scripture.

236   Ps. 104:31.

237   Zech. 14:9.

238   Cf. Isa. 36:10; 51:11; 61:7.

239   Which transforms גלה "exile" into גאל "redemption."

240   An accurate rendering of the *Sefer HaHayyim* citation; see above, 370, n. 234.

241   Deut. 3:28–7:11.

generation will emerge from them. Note it there.[242]

Likewise the generation of the ingathering of Israel to Eretz Yisrael will not be worthy of the description "Israel," since their Jewish identity will not be apparent. Nevertheless, they are important to God, and He will deliver them to their Land because He will utilize them as seeds. From them will develop generations endowed by God, who will be worthy of [the indwelling of] His Presence upon them.

The Almighty brought to my attention here the booklet *Eileh Mas'ei*[243] (which relates the journeys of the *gaon*, the *tzadik*, our teacher, Fishel Sofer Sussman, of blessed and saintly memory, chief rabbinic judge of the community here in the capital).[244] I noted there on page 32 a defense of the corrupt pioneers by R. Yosef Hayyim Sonnenfeld,[245] of blessed and saintly memory. The following is the text in Yiddish:

> This concerns the morally corrupt pioneers who reveal so much sacrifice, courage and endurance in order to work the Land. In this fashion they nevertheless display such love for the Land that one can expect that this drive and devotion for the Land will cause them to repent for the better.[246] (I refer you to what I wrote previously about these *halutzim* [pioneers] in the second chapter).[247]

In passing I will cite the response of the *gaon*, and *tzadik*, the rabbinic authority of the Land of Israel, our teacher R. Yosef Hayyim Sonnenfeld, of blessed and saintly memory. He replied to the *gaon* and *tzadik*, our teacher R. Fishel Sofer, concerning his question on

---

242 Rashbam, Deut. 7:9. אע״פ שחוטאין מאה דורות, צדיק אחד תעמוד צדקתו אף לדור אחרון של אלף דור שימצא תמים. "Though one hundred generations may sin, one righteous person's merit will survive even to the last generation so that a thousand generations will be considered innocent." The author cites the text of the standard editions; ed. Rosin has תיגמל "will be rewarded" in place of תעמוד "will survive."

243 Cf. Num. 33:1. The booklet describes the journey to Eretz Yisrael from May 10 to June 14, 1927.

244 Budapest.

245 1849–1932. Considered the first spiritual leader of the separatist ultra-Orthodox community (*haredim*) in Jerusalem.

246 Fishel Sofer Sussman, *Eileh Mas'ei* (Budapest, 1927), 32.

247 See above, 109–110.

the advisability of acquiring fields in Eretz Yisrael. The following was his response:

> With the help of the blessed Almighty, Jerusalem the Holy City, may it be rebuilt and reestablished speedily in our time. Amen! Friday, the eve of the holy Sabbath, the portion of *Emor*,[248] of *Matmonim*,[249] the year 686 according to the abbreviated count.[250]
>
> Greetings for life, blessing, peace and all that is excellent, pleasant and everlasting. To my dear eminent, distinguished friend whose fame brings him honor,[251] our teacher R. Fishel Sofer Sussman, may his light shine, and may he be privileged to appreciate the goodness of Jerusalem,[252] speedily in our own time.
>
> Following these greetings to the distinguished personage I welcome his sacred mission with: Be strong and resolute.[253] The gathering together of the righteous is a benefit to them and an advantage to the world.[254] May the Almighty be compassionate with His people and faithful. May we be worthy of the complete arousal[255] and imminent redemption for the sake of the people as well as the individual.
>
> Concerning the question, I maintain: certainly the time is ripe for people with means to awaken and respond to the sacred settlement in Eretz Yisrael. Though in the past the hearts of Israel the Holy people, have yearned for the Holy Land, it supported only a small remnant which had concerned itself with *aliyah*. Support for a broad holy set-

---

248 The weekly portion to be read on the following day (Sabbath): Lev. 21:1–24:23.

249 ל"א למטמונים. The expression for the 49 מ"ט days of counting מונים between the second day of Passover to *Shavuot* (Pentecost). The response was written on the 31st day of the *Omer* counting ל"א.

250 5686, i.e. 1927. The letter is dated in the Hebrew equivalent of April 30, 1926.

251 This ornate style is characteristic of the rabbis' lengthy introductions when writing to their esteemed colleagues. The reference to מחותני הרב וכו', חתנא דבי נשיאה which indicates relationship by marriage, is not clear and has been deleted in the translation.

252 Cf. Ps. 128:5.

253 Cf. Deut. 31:7; 31:23; Jos. 1:6 *et seq*

254 Sanh. 8:5.

255 Cf. Isa. 51:17.

tlement, however, was, it seems, not part of such an awakening. The *gaon* and *tzadik* the *Yavetz*[256] of blessed and saintly memory has reverently spoken [on this subject] in the preface to the *siddur* [prayerbook][257] as expected in a matter of sanctity, drawing attention and reproving. Even so, *Agudat Yisrael*[258] also gave its support, and the awakening of the great *geonim* of Poland,[259] may their light shine, made a powerful impact. The latter also made their contribution once they gave consideration to *aliyah* to the Holy Land by their representatives and closely studied the matter. May all the dedicated of the people[260] do likewise. Let them select intelligent people, wise in the ways of human affairs, who would [be assigned to] study the matter. Following this we shall consult with the sages in the Land. Likely [the stricture] "Do not stimulate [nor awaken my love] until she please,"[261] has already been realized.[262] It seems that on behalf of this object of desire,[263] there will come an awakening from Above and the Almighty, may He be blessed, will hasten redemption for His people, speedily in our own day. I look forward with joy to your visit to the Holy Land. I hereby close as I opened, with a blessing: may you achieve great success on behalf of Torah and its commandments, and worthy acts. May we soon see redemption. It is a petition from a soul which waits anxiously. I send greetings to [you] the esteemed honorable gentleman and to your father-

---

256 See above, 30, nn. 91–92; 302.

257 Ibid.

258 The political party founded in 1912 by a broad coalition of various Orthodox factions in Eastern and Western Europe. While it opposed political Zionism on the grounds of human intervention in Divine affairs, it gradually supported independent efforts of settlement and the establishment of segregated autonomous communities, which operated, until the establishment of the state, outside the organized Zionist enterprises.

259 See the documentation by the author in the introductory *haskamot* section of the volume (*EHS*, 2–20).

260 Cf. Judg. 5:9.

261 Song 2:7; 3:5. See above, 137–138, nn. 32, 34; 257, nn. 849–851.

262 The "oath" which had served as a prohibition against human initiated acts for redemption no longer applies.

263 The settlement of Eretz Yisrael. Probably a play on words: שהחפץ הזה "this desire" and עד שתחפץ "until she please."

in-law the *gaon* and holy sage,[264] may he live long and good days. Amen.

Humbly,

Yosef Hayyim Sonnenfeld

Following [this exchange of correspondence] the *gaon* R. Fishel Sofer traveled to the Holy Land and met this *gaon* and *tzadik* [R. Sonnenenfeld]. He inquired: "Then the rabbi agrees?" [He referred to the settling of the Land.] What a question! R. Sonnenfeld responded with concern: "I wish and request from you—Come and purchase property in the Holy Land and observe the laws of *shmitta*,[265] naturally, as the others observe it." He referred to Bnei Brak and the *Rebbe* of Gur,[266] may his light shine, and *Petah Tikva* and others.[267]

In addition I noted [that the author of] this pamphlet cited a favorite remark from this saintly *gaon* the Rabbi of Eretz Yisrael:[268]

> "May you see Jerusalem prosperous"[269]—one should always look at the good of Eretz Yisrael.[270] One must take pains not to become a spy. The spies were punished because they defamed Eretz Yisrael although not a Jew lived there [in Jerusalem]. Certainly [they would deserve punishment] now when a large community of Jews dwell therein.

These are his words.[271]

My compliments to my dear friend, the brilliant young rabbi, our teacher R. Eliezer Sussman, may he live a long and good life, who is

---

264   R. Koppel Reich (d. 1925), chief rabbi of Budapest.

265   The sabbatical year according to Ex. 23:10–11; Lev. 25:1–7, 18–22; and Deut. 15:1–11.

266   Bnei Brak was founded in 1924 by thirteen Orthodox families from Warsaw, and soon included two houses of study associated with the Rebbe of Gur (who himself acquired property in the *Yishuv* during his frequent visits and encouraged the project). See Avraham Tannenbaum, *Ha'Ish Shelo Nirta* (Bnei Brak, 1982), 10.

267   *Eileh Mas'ei, op. cit.,* 29.

268   Rabbi Sonnenfeld.

269   Ps. 128:5. A literal translation of וראה בטוב ירושלים.

270   The *Eileh Mas'ei* (p. 14) text reads: "Jerusalem" *vs.* "Eretz Yisrael."

271   *Eileh Mas'ei, op. cit.,* 14.

the son of the saintly *gaon*, our teacher R. Efraim Fishel Sofer of blessed memory, chief rabbi of this community, who reproduced from his father's manuscripts [a selection of] the eulogy which he delivered on behalf of our teacher, the *gaon* R. Hayyim Yosef Sonnenfeld, of blessed memory.

Now who will pity you, O Jerusalem? Who will console you[272] lovers of the Land? He was [devoted to Eretz Yisrael] without restraint or limits. He never vexed a soul. Above everything, he tormented himself over those who came and contaminated the Land by desecrating the holy Sabbath, partaking in prohibited foods, and eating leavened bread on Passover. He defended these people who went astray, insisting that the Land which they work with so much love will bring them back to the good [path] and cleanse their hearts. He would rebuke anyone who would as much as slander those who dwelled in the Holy City. He brought to my attention a text in the *Shulhan Arukh, Orah Hayyim* section 580, citing the author[273] who states: The 17th day of *Elul* is a fast day of the *tzadikim* [the righteous, virtuous], for on that day those who slandered the Land died.[274] The *Magen Avraham*[275] commentary asks: Is it not written: "When the wicked perish there are shouts of joy"?[276] Responded the *Shelah*: "Since they [those who slandered] were themselves *tzadikim*." Note, therefore,

Even The Righteous Can Become Spies.

These are the exact words which my dear friend[277] copied from this manuscript. . . .[278]

---

272 Cf. Jer. 15:5.

273 R. Joseph Karo.

274 *Shulhan Arukh, Orah Hayyim, Hilkhot Ta'anit*, 580:2. See Num. 14:23–45.

275 R. Avraham Gombiner; See above, 98, n. 66.

276 Prov. 11:10. Why then would *tzadikim* fast? Should this not be a day of joy?

277 R. Eliezer Sussman, son of R. Fishel Sofer Sussman.

278 The author restates the related themes of the unity and sanctity of God and the Jewish people in Eretz Yisrael as articulated in the *Tzeror HaMor* (*EHS*, 10) and *Netzah Yisrael* texts (see above, 272), as well as the lessons to be learned from the gentiles on the use of propaganda in forging unity during times of crisis and war, and in peace, as taught by the *Tanya* and *Tanna DeBei Eliyahu* (see above, 275–276). *EHS*,

Frankly, however, we need not learn [lessons of unity] from [the nations of the world]. Our holy teacher the author of *No'am Elimelekh* has already taught us:[279]

We should focus upon the positive characteristics of our fellow men and not upon their deficiencies and defects. We should relate to one another in an honest fashion. Whenever Israel is in distress, the primary task of the leader of that generation is to bring about peace among them [the factions] and to unite them in a common bond. Such a situation we encountered in the First Book of Samuel, chapter 7[280] when the Philistines went forth against Israel. Samuel said: "Assemble all Israel at Mitzpah and I will pray to the Lord for you. They assembled at Mitzpah and they drew water [and poured it out] before the Lord."[281] In the second chapter of Jerusalem [Talmud] Ta'anit the text reads: "R. Shmuel bar R. Yitzhak said: 'Samuel incorporated all of Israel.'"[282] This is puzzling. What is meant by "incorporated all of Israel"? The objective [of Samuel] was: To cloak all of Israel under one garment.[283] Namely, he merged them into a unified entity. This was his first step. As a result he achieved an Israelite victory over the Philistines.[284] This is also implied in Samuel's request: "Assemble all Israel [at Mitzpah]. . . . They assembled."[285] That is to say, they assembled and united one with the other. In addition it reads:[286] "Samuel took one rock . . . and named it *even ezer* [stone of help]." Namely, this is to demonstrate that only when we

---

340–341.

279   See above, 89, n. 10.

280   Verses 5–6.

281   As a symbol of Israel's submission to the Lord.

282   JT Ta'an. 2:7 (11). In the confession for Israel's sins (I Sam. 7:6), according to the JT Ta'an. text it was Samuel who united the people in their crisis. This is deduced from the seemingly superflous שם in the verse. ויאמר שם חטאנו לד "And there [*sham*] they confessed that they had sinned against the Lord". שם = שמואל (*Shm* = Samuel). See the *Korban HaEdah* and *Pnei Moshe* commentaries on JT Ta'an. 2:7.

283   As suggested by the term חלוק "garment" in the text לבש שמואל חלוקן של כל ישראל. "Samuel wore the garment of all of Israel."

284   I Sam. 7:10–14.

285   I Sam. 7:5–6.

286   I Sam. 7:14.

are transformed as if made of one rock are we instantly helped against the Philistines. This allusion is also evident with Jacob our Patriarch, as it is written: "Taking one of the stones of that place, [he put it under his head and lay down in the place]."[287] Our sages of blessed memory taught:[288] he took twelve stones and they all merged into one. Behold, Jacob foresaw the destruction [of the Temple]. He then realized that there is no solution to the cancer of exile unless they will be transformed as if made of one rock. As soon as they were thus transformed—"And the Lord was standing beside him."[289] He assured him [Jacob] His protection.[290]

Comprehend these words for they are sincere and authentic!

Following my drafting of these comments one of my friends brought to my attention a text, of our teacher the *Malbim* on the Pentateuch dealing with the weekly portion of *Vayetze*, [291] explaining the merging of Jacob's stones as a lesson for Israel's unity and as a condition for its redemption. I borrowed a Pentateuch with the *Malbim* commentary and I indeed found it [the text]. I was delighted that I am of the same circle.[292] I shall briefly reproduce his remarks and these are his words:

The Midrash taught as follows:[293] "R. Yehoshua ben Levi interpreted a verse concerning exile, 'Jacob left [Beersheva].'[294] That is why it is written: 'Gone from fair Zion are all that were her glory.'[295] Since exile came about due to the sin of senseless hatred[296] and they could not be redeemed until they would be united as one people, as it is written: 'Take a stick,

---

287 Gen. 28:11.

288 Free rendering of GenR. 68:13.

289 Gen. 28:13. The unity of God with man is linked to the unity among people.

290 Gen. 28:13–15.

291 Gen. 28:10–22.

292 שמחתי להיות בן גילו, *lit.* "I was pleased to be his coeval," hence under the same influence and with identical views. See Yev. 120a.

293 *Yalkut Shimoni* I, 119.

294 Gen. 28:10.

295 Lam. 1:6.

296 Yoma 9b.

etc. . . . Bring them close to each other. . . .'[297]—consequently he [Jacob] sought a sign. If the rocks, representing the tribes of the Lord, would merge into one rock. . . . Then he noted that all the rocks did indeed unite. Therefore, he took one rock." These are his words.[298] He foresaw that eventually they would unite into one entity and then they would be redeemed from their suffering. Therefore, he took one rock.[299] Note this.

The author declares: With this section,[300] marked with the letters *hai* I intend with the help of the Lord to conclude this book and especially this fourth chapter devoted to unity and peace among Israel. Our sages of blessed memory have already taught: "A sign is significant."[301]

Study the [text of] *Yavetz* our teacher, on the laws of blowing the ram's horn [on *Rosh HaShanah*] in his *siddur*:[302]

Something marvelous occurred in the [marking of the] sections in the *Tur, Orah Hayyim*: When discussing the laws of the blowing of the *shofar* [the number designation of the] section is equivalent [to *shofar*] in its numerical value.[303] Though the author did not plan it this way, nevertheless the truth was communicated to him from Heaven. This sign signaled support [from Above] because he wrote his work for the sake of Heaven. Anyone genuinely involved in an enterprise for the sake of Heaven is unexpectedly shown a good omen.

These are his sacred words. Note [a text] from this same *siddur* concerning "Conduct on the Eve of Sabbath," group 3, letter 17,

---

297 Ezek. 37:15–16.

298 *Torah Or*, gloss by Malbim, Gen. 28:17 (Jer., 1956 ed.), 106 (53b).

299 Symbolizing the unity and redemption to be.

300 Marked חי which reads "life" when reversed חי.

301 סימנא מילתא היא Hor. 12a; Ker. 6a vs. סימנא מילתא לטבא "A sign is of positive significance" *EHS*, 342. An omen, such as the numerical חי (*hai*) "life" is to be taken seriously as a sign from Heaven.

302 R. Yaakov Emden, *Siddur Bet Ya'akov, op. cit.*, 611.

303 שופר "shofar" in numerical value = 585. The laws of the blowing of שופר in *Tur, Orah Hayyim* [vol. II] begin with section 586 [through 597].

where he makes a similar point.[304] As I indicated earlier,[305] our teacher Rashba (in his preface to his volume *Torat HaBayit*) also pointed out that it is quite evident to anyone who can perceive, that one who is involved in work for the sake of Heaven is assisted according to his need. And so it is in connection with my book. I swear by Heaven that I never intended to complete my book with the expression *hai.*[306] When I subsequently designated the letters [to the sections of the book] I discovered that it would conclude with the word *hai.* For this I was overjoyed since I perceived it as support from Heaven for all that I have expounded in my book.

I shall elaborate. We have learned that the Men of the Great Assembly, among them some prophets and those endowed with the Holy Spirit, formulated the eighteen benedictions,[307] as explained in [the tractate] *Megilla* 17.[308] They concluded the eighteen benedictions with: "Endow us [and all Thy people Israel] with peace, goodness, etc. . . . . Praised be Thou, O Lord, Who blesses Thy people Israel with peace."[309] This is to intimate that the foundation for everything is peace. "There is nothing without peace." (According to Rashi[310] in [the weekly portion of] *Behukotai*[311]) The preceeding benediction reads: "Every living creature shall thank You always."[312] Why was the expres-

---

304 *Siddur Bet Ya'akov, op. cit.,* 306. In discussing the direct relationship between the appetites for food and sex, R. Emden cites *Tur, Orah Hayyim, Hilkhot Derekh Eretz,* section 240 = ר"ם (*r'm'*) = "lofty." The genuine and positively directed sex act is lofty and sacred, but when an object of lust and carnality, it is the reverse, hence, מ"ר (*m'r'*) = "bitter." Here as well the "omen" of the section is reflected in its numerological significance.

305 *EHS,* 260.

306 See previous nn. 300–301.

307 Which comprise the essential elements of the daily liturgy together with the *Sh'ma* trilogy.

308 Meg. 17b. See also Ber. 33a and Avot 1:1.

309 Conclusion of the *Amida* service. *The Authorized Daily Prayer Book*: Hebrew Text, English Translation with Commentary and Notes by Joseph H. Hertz, New York, 1961, 292.

310 Lev. 26:6. אם אין שלום אין כלום. "Without peace all is naught."

311 Lev. 26:3–27:34.

312 Hertz, *Prayer Book, op. cit.,* 291.

sion "Every living creature" preferred? To imply: If we desire life, its
cause must be peace. As it is followed by: "Endow us... with peace...
Who blessed Thy people Israel with peace." Then we shall be worthy
of life as indicated by the juxtaposition of the term *hayyim* [life] with
shalom [peace] in the blessing which follows.[313] In a similar manner it
is written: "I had with him a covenant of life and peace."[314] Hence
these two concepts are linked one to the other.[315]

The sage in every generation must transmit to the Israelites the
lesson that their only means of restoration is to cherish every Jew,
even the most deficient. (See *Tomer Devorah* of the saintly Cordovero [316]
in numerous sections emphasizing the great obligation and the recon-
structive implications when Jews cherish one another, even the lowly
and deficient among them, Heaven forbid. The volume *Mikdash Me'at*
commentary on Psalms[317] cites our teacher, the saintly Rabbi of Lublin,[318] may his merit protect us, that he has greater love for the wicked
who acknowledges that he is wicked, than for the righteous who
acknowledges that he is righteous.)

The prophet exclaims:[319] "[For the mourners] I will create comforting
words: 'Peace, peace to those far and near,' said the Lord, 'and I will
heal them.'" This verse is complicated:

> 1. It should have been stated: "To those *near* and *far*," since
> it is incumbent on one to first make peace with those near
> him, and then with those far from him.

---

313   ושלו וחיים ורחמים וברכה וצדקה "and righteousness, blessing, mercy, life and
peace."

314   Mal. 2:5.

315   The author constructs other gematria (numerology) combinations which show
the importance of *ahavat Yisrael, EHS*, 343. See also above, 335, n. 3.

316   See above, 21, n. 31. See chapter 1, 4th paragraph: ישראל כל חבריו עם האדם כך
יחד. כלולות שהנשמות מפני אלו עם אלו בשר שאר הם "As a relationship between man and his
friends, so all of Israel is tied intimately one to another since their souls are linked
together." (p. 5, Vilna, 1911 ed.) Also, ch. 1, paragraph 13: האבות. מבזה הבנים והמבזה
"One who degrades children degrades [their] parents."

317   A. Walden (ed.) *Mikdash Me'at al Sefer Tehilim.* (Warsaw, 1889), 290.

318   See above, 12, n. 52.

319   Isa. 57:19.

2. What is [the connection of] the continuation: "said the Lord, 'and I will heal them,'" with the foregoing?

But let me preface by quoting what I heard from my brother-in-law, the saintly *gaon*, our teacher R. Shlomo [Friedman], may he live a good and long life. (He is the son of the saintly *gaon* R. David Friedman of blessed memory, who was chief rabbinic judge of the sacred community of Zelem. He [R. Shlomo] served as rabbi in Baden, near Vienna. Presently he is among the refugees in Switzerland. May the Lord help him be witness to the imminent rescue of the Jewish people.) Our grandfather[320] was the saintly *gaon*, our teacher R. Menahem Katz, who was also known everywhere as R. Menahem of Prosnitz,[321] and chief rabbinic judge of Zelem. (He was among the most prominent students of our teacher the Hatam Sofer.[322] He studied with him for fifteen years in his youth and five years after his marriage. He was a person of great character. When he was with our teacher of Zans[323] he shared his meals with him.) When I was with my brother-in-law, the *gaon* R. Mordechai Rotenberg, chief rabbinic judge of the sacred community of Antwerp, I came across a manuscript from him [R. Menahem Katz], of blessed memory. It was a large folio filled with applied *kabbalah* which he had received from his teacher, the Hatam Sofer. It is noted there: "I received this from my teacher." I requested this folio from my brother-in-law, may he be well, but he refused. And now we have no idea as to his whereabouts, nor that of his family. May God have mercy upon him and all of Israel. Amen, may this be His will.

Prior to his[324] death he asked for the *hevra kadisha*[325] (since he had originally instructed them not to come near until he would call for

---

320 The father-in-law of R. David Friedman.

321 Ca. 1800–1891. Among the most prominent of Orthodox Hungarian rabbis in the second half of the 19th century.

322 The *EHS* pagination is manipulated to read דשׁמ׳ (*d'sh'm'*) (equivalent to 344) rather than שׁמ׳ד (*sh'm'd*) which would follow alphabetically, but means destruction.

323 See above, 27, n. 70.

324 R. Menahem Katz.

325 Members of the communal burial society. *Lit.*, "sacred society."

them). The entire community congregated about him. He blessed
them and appealed for peace. He commented on the rabbinic teaching:
"Great is peace, for the Name of the Holy One, blessed be He, was
erased for the sake of peace."[326] He explained that there are two kinds
of peace.

> 1. When there is no contact with the other and each goes
> his own way. Naturally, there is no conflict between them,
> but neither is there genuine peace, except in the negative
> sense.[327]

> 2. When they associate one with another and live together
> in love and friendship. This is genuine peace.

We now encounter the subject of the *sota*.[328] Owing to the husband's
suspicion of his wife, they had become alienated and are separated.
Due to the rubbing out of God's Name [in the water of bitterness],
they were reconciled and peace between them is restored.[329] Hence,
the teaching of our sages of blessed memory: "Great is peace." Note
the kind of peace which is considered superior and primary—the kind
which is even worthy of the blotting out of the Name of the Holy
One, blessed be He. Such a peace brings closer those who are distant.
They now live close in peace, harmony, and friendship when at first
they were separated. Such a peace is indeed great and sublime. These
are his sacred words.[330] With these dying words he passed from this
world. May his merit protect his offspring and all of Israel.

Now in *Hovot HaLevavot*[331] it is stated that human speech was

---

326 Hul. 141a; Shab. 116a. גדול שלום שבין איש לאשתו שהרי אמרה תורה, שמו של הקב"ה
שנכתב בקדושה ימחה על המים. Based on the laws of *sota* (a suspected adultress) and the
jealous husband, Num. 5:1–31, specifically verses 21–23.

327 The absence of hostility.

328 *Lit.* "the "straying" or "errant woman," accused by her jealous husband of
infidelity, as in Num. 5:11–31.

329 When the trial by ordeal cleared the wife of any wrongdoing.

330 R. Menahem Katz.

331 *The Duties of the Heart.* The classic work of ethical-religious doctrines by R.
Bahya ben Yosef ibn Paquda (c. 1050–1100). Vol. 1 (Jerusalem, 1965), 163–165. והלשון
קולמוס הלב ושליח המצפון. ולולא הדבור, לא היה לאדם צוות בחבירו והיה כבהמה. ובדבור יראה

created in order to bring together the separated. By means of speech people unite one with another.

Accordingly, the verse[332] "I will create comforting words" can be explained. Namely, the purpose of the creation of speech was to bring about peace. Therefore it is written further: "Peace, peace"—(the dual use of *shalom*, *shalom* emphasizes its primacy) "to those far"[332]—precisely for those who are far. That is, to bring close those who have heretofore stood afar one from the other and to reconcile them. Such is an exalted peace. It seems to me that this is the reason that the verse stated it ["to those far"] at the outset, followed by "and the near."[332] Do not be concerned that there is harm in making peace between extremes, since the Lord proclaimed: "and I will heal them."[332] You shall attend to your [duties] and God will attend to His tasks in healing them all spiritually and physically. Such seems the meaning of this verse to me. With the help of God this is the absolute truth of Torah.

So you see, my friends, it is the obligation of every Jew to intercede for the welfare of his people[333] and not to create friction among [those who should be] close allies. Upon this depends our redemption. I am pained, therefore, that we still have among us those who publicly arouse hostility and strife against the builders of the Land who are engaged with its settlement. They proclaim the sins of our sacred mother[334] as an abomination[335] in order to arouse animosity and enmity against her builders, claiming that they are heretics, sinners and apostates and that it is forbidden to associate with them. They create similar acts of alienation among the dedicated and prevent the rest of the nation from devotion to this sublime mitzvah, as I have explained

---

היתרון בין בני אדם ובו תהיה ברית כרותה בינהם ובין האלהים ועבדיו. "The tongue is the pen of the heart and a messenger of the conscience. Without speech man would resemble the animal, unable to establish amicable relationships with others. Speech marks the superiority of human beings, which [also] reflects the covenant between themselves, and between God and His devoted adherents."

332 Isa. 57:19.
333 Cf. Est. 10:3.
334 Eretz Yisrael.
335 Cf. Ezek. 16:2.

previously in detail.

To you people, Jews young and old, I call upon you unremittingly: Do not respond to such language, even should it emanate from a famous person, no matter how important he may be.[336] The truth does not support him. The Lord would not consider such a thing. I have already discussed previously in the second chapter,[337] the acts of these people, who are accused of being criminals and rebels, from which will yet emerge important and significant results. They will enhance and hasten the establishment of the House of David. I have documented the lessons of our teachers the Maharal of Prague, *Midrash Shmuel, Shach* and *Noam Elimelekh*,[337] all men endowed with the Holy Spirit: Great designs of holiness must evolve from secular elements and transgressors. These teachings of the holy masters are more trustworthy than those of the most famous personalities of our times. How can one compare them to these giants? On the contrary, every God-fearing person should be obligated to join these secular workers in this sacred enterprise. In this manner they will reinforce the sanctity of the Land, since a start has already been made in the secular domain.

Due to the merit of unity among all of Israel we shall be worthy of God's Presence. The Lord will establish His Shekhinah among us and will guide their [the settlers'] hearts towards a pure course as they will all return to worship Him in complete sincerity, as the prophet proclaimed: "I will remove that country's guilt in a single day."[338] And in this vein God said: "'Peace, peace to those far and the near,' said the Lord, 'and I will heal them.'"[339] Namely, you must be sure that peace free of strife will reign among you, even with those to whom you refer as transgressors. Let the enterprise of building the Land unite you. Only this mitzvah is able to create unity, as I have explained at length. Do not be concerned,[340] because "I will heal" their hearts with a pure spirit from beyond. And these who appear to be pious

---

336   This last phrase appears in Yiddish.
337   See above, 119–124.
338   Zech. 3:9.
339   Isa. 58:19.
340   About joining with the nonobservant.

and cry aloud for severance do not speak intelligently, as the saintly *gaon* R. Yehoshua of Kutna has explained at the outset of this volume.[341]

Do not be bewildered [asking]: Is it indeed possible for a renowned *tzadik* to speak irrationally? I will go beyond this as I cited previously[342] in the name of the guardian angel in [the volume] *Maggid Mesharim*, who revealed to our teacher the *Bet Yosef* that Moses selected the greatest and most able scholars to serve as scouts. Nevertheless, the author of the Midrash refers to them as "foolish emissaries" because they spread calumnies about the Land. Study the text in *Midrash Rabbah* and *Tanhuma*,[343] on the weekly portion of *Shelah*.[344] Surely these in our time are not superior to the spies in piety and Torah scholarship. Further, R. Zeira, who was very careful in his use of speech,[345] nevertheless referred to the Babylonian [Jews]: "These foolish Babylonians!" because they did not ascend [to Eretz Yisrael] in the time of Ezra [the scribe], although they were great scholars of the Torah (as I elaborated previously in chapter three).[346] Surely at the present time when so few of us remain, due to our many sins, and we are actually "people escaped from the sword,"[347] common sense demands that we embrace and reach out one to the other.

Let it be known, therefore, that all those who also resist *aliyah* at this time and oppose the settlement and reconstruction of the Land are identified with the faction of the spies; those who choose *aliyah* are part of Joshua's and Caleb's faction. Our teacher the *Ari*, of

---

341   *EHS*, 2.

342   *EHS*, 166–168. See above, 119, n. 199.

343   NumR. *Shelah*, 16:4. אעפ״כ בני אדם גדולים היו ועשו עצמן כסילים, עליהם אמר משה: יכי (דברים לב:כ) דור תהפוכות המה, בנים לא אמון בם.' "Although they [the spies] were distinguished leaders they behaved as fools. Moses portrayed them: 'For they are a treacherous breed, children have no loyalty in them.' (Deut. 32:20)" *Tanh. Shelah* 2. לפי שהיו שלוחים טפשים "Because they were foolish emissaries."

344   Num. 13:1–15:41.

345   Meg. 28a. שאלו תלמידיו את ר׳ זירא יבמה הארכת ימיסזיי אמר להם: . . . ולא קראתי לחברי בחניכתו. "R. Zera was asked by his disciples: 'How do you account for your good old age?' He replied '. . . nor have I called my friend by his nickname.'"

346   See above, 277; *EHS*, 165.

347   Jer. 31:2.

blessed memory, revealed to his disciple our teacher R. Hayyim Vital, of blessed memory: Whoever selects to fulfill a mitzvah on behalf of which a *tzadik* [previously] offered his life, the soul of the *tzadik* comes to assist in selecting this mitzvah. Well-known is the account of the author of *Midrash Shmuel* who entered the house of study and the holy *Ari* stood up before him; a word to the wise.[348] So it is with us. Joshua and Caleb endangered their lives for the sake of *aliyah* since the people were prepared to stone them to death,[349] [yet] they exclaimed: "Let us by all means go up."[350] If we dedicate our lives for *aliyah*, the souls of Joshua and Caleb shall come to assist us as well. This is as accurate and clear as the teaching of Moses received from the Almighty.

My dear friend the aged rabbi and upright *tzadik*, descendent of *tzadikim*, the *gaon* our teacher R. Yisrael David Margolit, may he live a good and long life, rabbi of the local Linat HaTzedek synagogue, brought to my attention the text in the Talmud of Avodah Zarah 54b: "For R. Yehoshua ben Levi taught: 'The conquest of Eretz Yisrael takes preference over the removal of idol worship.'" Rashi adds: "Following the conquest they will search them out and uproot them." It seems to me that this is the reason that Ezra [the scribe] did not dissuade his contemporaries from their detestable acts immediately upon entering the Land, but twenty years after the Temple was (re)built in Jerusalem, since he wished to avoid conflict and strife at a time that he was absorbed with the conquest and building of the Land. In this manner he fulfilled the teaching of R. Yehoshua ben Levi that the conquest of the Land takes preference over the removal of idol worship. And similarly the matter before us deserves the combined power of the sacred nation. Let us approach this sacred enterprise linked arm in arm. Then will our effort be considered worthy before the Holy One, blessed be He. He will complete it for our benefit, and from this shall emerge the final redemption, speedily in our time. Amen.

---

348 The legend in detail is recorded in Shlomo Shlumil ben Hayyim, *Shivhei HaAri* (Lwow, c. 1830), 6–7.

349 Num. 14:10.

350 Num. 13:30.

I have now come across a text of our teacher, in Responsa *Imrei Esh, Yoreh Deah*, section 101 as follows:

> One need not elaborate on the well-known virtue of settling Eretz Yisrael, as cited towards the end of the tractate Ketubot.[351] Nahmanides includes it among the 613 commandments. Hence, we must presently make certain that at least our Land will not become desolate, Heaven forbid. This commandment is incumbent upon all of Israel. They must excite their coreligionists to ascend to the place chosen by the Almighty.

These are his sacred words.[352] Hence he also notes that this mitzvah is the responsibility of all of Israel. It is a community enterprise as I have indicated all along.

These and similar teachings we are now obligated to transmit to the Jewish people. Then we will fulfill the [implications of the] verse: "The Lord spoke to Moses, saying: Speak to the Israelite people," which is directed to all the learned of our generation, who are obligated to inspire love for a fellow Jew, unity and peace. This will be a positive determinant for Jews whereby they will be worthy of life and peace.

Should someone ask: Who made you chief[353] that you raise your voice in addressing the Jewish people? I will reply to this with two responses: First, every scholar is permitted to speak out in order to address his generation. This is made clear by the great legal authority, our teacher the Mabit (who was a colleague of our teacher the *Bet Yosef*)[354] in his introduction to his work *Bet Elohim*:[355]

The sages in the Midrash interpreted the verse "This is the record of

---

351 Ket. 110b–11 2b.

352 *Imrei Esh* (Lemberg, 1852), 66. Responsa of R. Meir ben Judah Leib Eisenstadter (d. 1852), a pupil of the Hatam Sofer and among the leading rabbis in mid-19th-century Hungary.

353 Cf. Ex. 2:14.

354 See above, 13, n. 58.

355 Ibid.

Adam's lineage."[356] It is to teach that the Holy One, blessed be He, revealed to the first Adam every generation and its commentators, every generation and its scholars, every generation and its [community] leaders. The use of the expression *dor dor* [*vedorshav*][357] rather than *dor vedorshav*.[358] is to imply that the Lord will not leave His people in any given generation bereft of its commentators, scholars and community leaders or to decrease their numbers by one or two consecutively in every generation. No generation will ever be bereft of its leaders. In every generation, therefore, a person's learning must become his craft in order to demonstrate personally that he, as it were, is descended from Adam's lineage from his [generation of] commentators, scholars and community leaders. This does not imply arrogance, since in doing so he prepares himself to be worthy and to bring merit to others.

Note this source, since he elaborates on this matter. This is the first point.

I say further that you should study what was written in *Rambam, The Laws of Sanctifying the Moon*, 4:10: In intercalculating the leap year one departs from the norm. [Such a case] is comparable to [the court's deliberations regarding] capital offenses which require a majority of two,[359] since if one wishes to remove something from its usual pattern it takes on the status of capital offenses.[360] This is relevant to us, since we want to remove the Jewish people from their normal exilic pattern, which is a matter of a capital offense.[361] That the situation in exile is life-threatening is clear, as we have seen in our time.

With regard to capital cases we have a ruling that we commence with [the opinion of] the least eminent [of the judges].[362] Since I am

---

356   GenR. 24:2.

357   Every generation.

358   A generation and its commentators.

359   The rationale is offered by R. Obadiah b. David's commentary and not evident in the Maimonides text.

360   Homicide, murder and other capital crimes require stricter procedures than others.

361   The question of the Jew in exile is a matter of life and death.

362   Since if a guilty opinion is submitted first by the most learned or senior judges, the remainder of the judicial bench will be intimidated and a guilty verdict

certainly insignificant in this era I am delighted to speak first and offer my humble opinion on the restoration of the generation and its being rebuilt on its mound,[363] with the help of God. The eminent leaders of the generation will heed my words and accept the truth from he who speaks. Thereby they themselves will realize [the teaching]: "Happy is the generation in which the eminent people respond to the humble."[364] In essence all of the statements published in this volume are not of my own invention, but were drawn from the living well [of the Torah], the well which the princes dug;[365] these are the princes of Torah, our teachers the masters of the six orders [of the Talmud], the Midrash, the Zohar and our other sacred works. It is on the basis of their teachings that this book which I leave for you was formulated.

I am aware that not everyone will find the message which I have presented here pleasing. There are those who will be angry with me. However, before you raise your voice against me, permit me to mention the incident cited in the Jerusalem Talmud, Sanhedrin at the beginning of the second chapter[366] and Horayot at the beginning of the third chapter,[367] concerning Resh Lakish who ruled: "A *nasi*[368] who sins is flogged."

When R. Yehudah Nasi[369] heard of this ruling he was angered and he, Resh Lakish fled. Then R. Yehudah Nasi himself pursued him and asked: "Why did you see fit in saying what you did and abuse me so?" He [Resh Lakish] said: "Did you really believe that I would be frightened and inhibited by you and refrain from expressing an opinion in the

---

will become a certainty. See Sanh. 32 a and the relevant Rashi commentary.

363 Cf. Jer. 30:18.

364 RH 25b. אשרי הדור שהגדולים נשמעים לקטנים.

365 Num. 21 :18, and the relevant *Or HaHayyim* commentary.

366 JT Sanh. 2:1 (9b–10a).

367 JT Hor. 3:1 (11b–12a).

368 President of the Great Sanhedrin, the supreme court in the days of the Second Temple and during Amoraic times. The position was occupied by descendants of Hillel the Elder.

369 R. Judah ha-Nasi, son of Gamliel III was Nasi from 230–270 C.E. and grandson of Judah ha-Nasi.

instruction of the Torah?"[370]

Thus the Jerusalem Talmud text. I echo these sentiments. Because they are concerned with a blow to their prestige as a result of the issues raised in my book, which are based on the teachings of our sages of blessed memory, shall I refrain from conveying the instruction of the Torah? The messages which I communicated and published in my book are the absolute truth of the Torah. Anyone whose trademark is truth will admit to the truth. I am prepared to debate with anyone who wishes to challenge me in debate, but only on the basis of hala-khah,[371] and according to *Tosafot* at the beginning of the tractate Horayot[372] in its interpretation of the ruling of the sages of blessed memory: "One may not arrive at a legal ruling based on a previous practical experience";[373] also I previously indicated in the Second Preface,[374] citing R. Yosef ben Lev in the responsa of the Mabit section 116. Note and study this with care!

There are yet particulars related to this subject which are pent up within me. I will conclude for the present, however, since the contents of this book have already grown and swelled. My contemporaries, I will yet come back to you in writing and by means of discourse, with the help of God.

"And the speech of the wise is healing."[375] May the Lord bind up

---

370   See relevant *Pnei Moshe* commentary on JT Sanh. 2:1.

371   Jewish law as a basis for practice.

372   Hor. 2a, Tosafot, *"Hakha Maskinan"*: ה״פ :[ב״ב ק״ל] אין למדין הלכה על פי המעשה התם: אם יאמר לך אדם ראיתי מעשה שאירע בכה״ג שהורו כן, אין לסמוך על דבריו דשמא לא עיין היטב ושמא באותו מעשה היה קצת משונה. "One may not arrive at a legal ruling based on previous experience [BB 130b]. This was explained: If someone will claim—I witnessed an incident involving such and such a circumstance and they ruled thus and thus, it cannot be relied upon, since he may not have observed with accuracy, and the alleged incident may have taken place somewhat differently."

373   BB.130b. Tosafot in Hor. 2a explains this ruling as a caution to the misleading tendency to apply unlike situations in attempts to create legal precedents. Throughout the volume the author points to the unprecedented events of the pre-Holocaust and Holocaust period which require a different set of legal standards in urging Jewish settlement of Eretz Yisrael. See above, 98–99 327–328.

374   *EHS*, 30.

375   Prov. 12:18.

His people's wounds and heal the injuries it has suffered,[376] speedily in our time, Amen. May this be His will, Amen, Amen. Blessed is the Compassionate One who assists them.

I have concluded this work on Thursday evening prior to the holy *Shabbat* according to the order [of the weekly portion] "And your descendants shall seize the gates of their foes,"[377] in the year *Israel In Whom I Glory.*[378] As it is taught in the *Yalkut* [*Shimoni*] [commenting] on [the weekly portion of] *Tetzaveh,*[379] and in Jeremiah 31:[380] "Said the Holy One, blessed be He, to Moses: 'Moses, whatever you can do to praise Israel before Me, do praise! To acclaim them—do acclaim! Since I will eventually be glorified on account of them', as it is written: 'Israel in whom I glory.'" The expression, "Since I will eventually be glorified on account of them," clearly indicates that although they may not as yet be worthy of His being glorified on account of them, nevertheless, "I ask of you, Moses, do whatever you possibly can to praise Israel before Me, indeed proceed to glorify them." This clearly endorses all that I have written in this volume in the capital of Budapest, may the Almighty protect it, and "I am in the midst of exile!"[381]

May it be the will of the Holy One, blessed be He, to convert *galut* [exile] into *ge'ulat Yisrael* [redemption of Israel] with the addition of the *alef* which represents the unity of His Name, may it be blessed, as cited previously and attributed to our teacher the Maharal of Prague.[382] I also discovered this [idea] at the end of the volume, *Ge'ulah Vishuah* (Redemption and Deliverance) authored by our teacher R. Hayyim of blessed memory, the brother of the Maharal.[383] The word of the

---

376   Cf. Isa. 30:26.

377   Gen. 22:17, from the weekly portion of Scripture read in the synagogue on the following Sabbath (*Vayera,* Gen. 18:1–22:24), hence, Thursday evening, November 11, 1943. The verse chosen obviously reflects the prayers of the author.

378   Isa. 49:3. בך אתפאר = 704 (+1240) = 1943/4

379   Ex. 27:20–30:10. *Yalkut Shimoni* I, 376.

380   *Yalkut Shimoni* II, 315.

381   Cf. Ezek. 1:1. ואני בתוך הגולה.

382   See above, 260–265.

383   R. Hayyim b. Bezalel *"Sefer Geulah Vishu'ah," Sefer HaHayyim* (Jerusalem,

Lord is fulfilled on the testimony of two witnesses.[384] And the Lord in Whom we trusted, let us rejoice and exult in His deliverance.[385] Blessed is His glorious Name,[386] Who exists from eternity to eternity.[387] Amen, may it be His will, Amen and Amen.

It Is Completed. PRAISE THE LORD, CREATOR OF THE UNIVERSE.

Addendum to Fourth Chapter

In Isaiah 57[388] [it is written]: "[Your assorted idols] shall not save you when you cry out. They shall all be borne off by the wind [snatched away by a breeze]. But those who trust in Me shall inherit the Land and possess My holy mountain." The Midrash[389] comments on this [verse]: They taught: When they and their descendants will assemble [in prayer] and will deliver you from Esau. They shall be borne off by the wind—this refers to Esau. "But those who trust in Me shall inherit the Land and possess My holy mountain" this refers to Jacob. . . . This Midrash informs us that only when Jacob is assembled [in unity] will he be delivered from Esau. So it was and so will it always be. Only when Jacob and his offspring will be gathered and assembled together, will Esau be borne off by the wind. Then Jacob will inherit and possess the Land and His holy mountain. Amen, may it be His will, speedily in our time, Amen and Amen.

ואז מן גלות נעשה גאולת עולם על ראשם בהוספת האי המורה על יחוד שמו יתברך 115, (1968). "From the exile will emerge the great eternal redemption, with the addition of the *alef* [the addition of א (*alef*) to the root *g'l'h'* (exile)] creates *g'a'l* (redemption) which points to the unity of His blessed Name."

384   With God's unity, exile will be transformed into redemption, as documented by the Maharal and his brother. Cf. Deut. 19:15 and Isa. 40:8.

385   Cf. Isa. 26:3.

386   Cf. Ps. 72:19.

387   Neh. 9:5.

388   Isa. 57:13.

389   GenR. 84:1. Also the variant in *Yalkut Shimoni* II, 488.

APPENDIX

A Translation of the Original Hebrew Cover

"You shall find comfort in Jerusalem"

Isa. 66:13

"My help shall come from the Lord
who maketh heaven and earth"

Ps. 121:2

[This volume] anticipates our deliverance from this final exile, provided we comply with all that the Creator of the entire Universe, the Lord of our Fathers, asks of us in order to hasten redemption. All this shall be explained and rationally examined. The arguments will be confirmed by the perceptive sources which emanate from the pure well of our Holy Torah, our Sages of Blessed memory, the Babylonian and Palestinian Talmud, the Midrash, Zohar and other works of our sacred literature. Every Jew is entreated to meticulously study this entire volume, if indeed he value the honor of God, His sacred people and his self-respect. Then, with the help of God, I assure the reader that he will be enlightened as to the obligations which one has toward himself, to his entire sacred people, and for the sake of His great Name, be it blessed and uplifted, speedily in our own day, Amen.

[left vertical page frame]

"You Shall See And Your Heart Shall Rejoice, Your Limbs Shall Flourish Like Grass."

Isa. 66:14

[right vertical page frame]

"As A Mother Comforts Her Son,
So I Will Comfort You."

Isa. 66:13

"The Power Of The Lord Shall Be Revealed On Behalf Of His Servants, But He Shall Rage Against His Foes."

Isa. 66:14

This volume was written by the least among the families of Israel,[1] a former presiding judge in a respected post,[2] who resides currently in Budapest. He is the author of the Responsa *Mishneh Sakhir*[3] of which contains sections which are yet in manuscript while others have been published.

I began to prepare this manuscript for publication on the eve of the third day of the weekly portion *Va'erah*[4] in the year 5703.[5] This volume was written here in the capital, in the "Valley of Calamity"[6] suffering the terrible pangs of the Messiah[7] which have strangled us[8] during this Second World War. May the Lord grant me the privilege

---

1 Expression of humility. Variation of Mic. 5:1 צעיר להיות באלפי יהודה "Least among the clans of Judah."

2 The author served as head of the rabbinic court in the health resort community of Piestany in Western Slovakia and in the Kostolany area in East Slovakia. See the memorial page included in the preface of the 2nd edition (1969) published by the author and noted further.

3 "The Teachings of *Sakhir*." A variant of the author's given name and based on Deut. 15:18 כי משנה שכר שכיר עבדיך "For he [the Hebrew slave] has given you double the service of a hired man." Possible reference to the author as a loyal servant of the Lord. Volume 1 was published in Bardiow, Slovakia (1924), and republished in Jerusalem in 1974. The unpublished manuscripts were partly issued in *Mishneh Sakhir: Orah Hayyim*, Vol. 2 (Jerusalem, 1987).

4 Jewish calendric designations are supplemented by the titles of the weekly reading of the scripture. *Va'erah* consists of Ex. 6:2–9:35.

5 Monday evening January 4, 1943.

6 בעמק עכור. The calamitous events of the Holocaust are portrayed in association with Jos. 7:24–25; and 15:7 where the name first appears. In Hos. 2:17 the reference is to exile with the hope of redemption—the "Entrance of Hope" (פתח תקוה)—to which the author alludes below.

7 חבלי משיח. A major concept of Jewish eschatology which is treated in greater depth in the body of the volume, especially Chapter 1. Isa. 26:17 כמו הרה תקריב ללדת תחיל תזעק בחבליה, כן היינו מפניך ד' "Like a woman with child approaching childbirth, writhing and screaming in her pangs so are we because of You, O Lord" represents one of the possible scriptural allusions to pre-messianic suffering. See also Hos. 13:13, Jer. 49:24, 13:21, 22:23, Isa. 66:7 where the pangs are avoided. בטרם תחיל ילדה, יבוא חבל לה, והמליטה זכר "Before she labored, she was delivered, before her pangs came, she bore a son." The Midrash employs this verse to suggest the Messiah, the son of David, who will precede the appearance of Israel's adversary, Pharoah (GenR. 85:2 expounding the events in Gen. 38). The subject is discussed in the involved eschatological material in Sanh. 98b.

8 השתרגו "interwoven." Plays on the multiple meaning of "pangs" and "rope".

to complete this work in the Entrance of Hope.[9] May I soon behold Israel's deliverance and triumph,[10] when the Lord shall restore the exiled of Zion,[11] promptly, and presently, Amen.

---

9 פתח תקוה. See n. 6, above.

10 ובהרמת קרנם. *Lit.*, "and the raising of their horn," following Ps. 148:14, וירם קרן לעמו "He has exalted the horn of His people." Expression of restoration.

11 Ps. 126:1.

IN EVERLASTING MEMORY
Rabbi, Scholar, Author of this volume,
My Crown,[12] My Master, Father, Teacher, and Rabbi,
The Gaon[13]

RABBI YISSAKHAR SHLOMO,
the son of
RABBI YITZHAK TEICHTHAL

blessed be the memory of the righteous and holy.[14]
Senior Judge of the Holy Community
of Kostolany and Region[15]
Presiding Judge and Head of talmudical Academy in Piestny
(Czechoslovakia)
The author of *Mishneh Sakhir* volumes of Responsa[16]
Martyred on the tenth day of *Shevat,* 5705.[17]

---

12   The lament נפלה עטרת ראשנו "The crown has fallen from our head" (Lam. 5:16) referring either to the Temple or the Shekhinah, has been incorporated into personal memories when the head of a family has departed.

13   Title of excellence in rabbinic scholarly tradition.

14   "Holy" is appended in the event of martyrdom.

15   See 397, n. 2.

16   See 397, n. 3

17   January 24, 1945.

INDEX

A

adultery 382
agriculture 115, 182, 219, 294, 311
Agudat Yisrael 145, 197, 328, 373
aliyah 27, 29, 56, 79, 93, 107, 170, 173, 189, 198, 228, 286, 302, 328, 373, 385-386
American Jewry 83-84
Amoraim 19
amulet 186
angel (patron) 40, 41, 108, 247, 276, 297, 299, 385
Anger (Divine) 18, 88, 202, 206-207, 237, 277, 343, 365
Arabs 56, 109-110
Ark of Covenant (*Aron Hakodesh*) 25
Arrow Cross Fascist Party 18
assimilation 68-69, 169, 216, 254-256, 349
astrology 155

B

Balfour Declaration 127, 138, 151-152, 308
Bar Mitzvah 128
Bermuda Conference 154
blood (innocent) 157, 202, 204-206, 223-224, 246, 249, 278, 281, 327
business ventures 66, 186-187, 195, 203-204, 208-209, 219, 222

C

charity (to Jews in distress) 83
children 103, 104, 112, 150, 153, 160, 177, 184, 196, 204, 210, 224, 284, 304, 366,
369...of Israel...94, 161, 164, 186, 199, 204, 265, 273, 339, 350, 360, 361-362
commandment . 15, 38, 50, 52, 55, 66, 88, 98, 100, 107, 111, 130, 144, 158, 165, 166, 172,
181-183, 214, 222, 237, 266-267, 283, 294-295, 296, 307-309, 324-325, 340, 344, 363,
373, 387, see also *mitzvah*
conversion 39, 284
covenant 4, 42, 216, 273, 276, 292
Crusades 300

D

Definition of a Jew Bill (Hungary) 69
deliverance (see *Redemption*)
destruction (of European Jewry) 17-18, 21, 62, 78-81, 201-204, 217, 220-222, 245, 247,
281, 288, 302, 325-326, 339, 347,...of Temple...23, 28, 94, 102, 127, 129, 155, 197, 207,
301, 337, 339-340, 343

E

emanation (Divine)... 134-135
enemies 29, 35, 56-57, 186, 197, 199, 211-213, 216-218, 221, 223, 303-304, 326, 338,
343, 345
Eretz Yisrael...return to 10-16, 22-36, 67, 77-79, 84-85, 90, 92-95, 98-100, 106-132, 371,
384-388...merits of...3-10, 22, 222...as heritage...37, 41-58, 370, 393...geography
of...96-97...settlement and reconstruction (*tikkun*)................................. chapter 3, 367-369
evil 11, 18, 29, 34, 57, 63, 69-70, 72, 77, 82-84, 89, 111, 121, 199-203, 206, 212, 229,
234-235, 238, 266, 272, 287, 293, 302-303, 309, 339-344, 351, 362, (see also *Amalek,
kelipah, kelipot*)
exile .... 14, Second Preface, 44, 56, 62, 64-68, 74, 78, 83-85, 94-95, 98-101, 105-108,
113-115, 118, 126, 129-130, 137-142, 152-157, 167-169, 175, 191-199, 231, 244-246,
253-266, 270-273, 280-282, 291-294, 303-304, 307-315, 324, 329...result of
disunity...chapter 4

F

faith...supported by human initiative .... 123, 186, 235, 329-333, 340, 359, 363, 372...in
miracles...38...in Messiah... 328
famine 17
forefathers/mothers 39-40, 47, 77, 100, 104-105, 151, 185, 195, 202-205, 209-210, 217,
244, 273, 288, 329, 370, (see also *patriarchs/matriarchs* and Biblical names in Index)

G

gartel 289-290
gematria 354, 378, 380
ghetto 255
God (every page)
golus (*galut*) Jew 244-248, 255-257, 292
Great Assembly (Men of)... 379

H

Habad Hasidism 3,4

halakhah 18-19, 25-26, 140, 390
haredim 121, 146, 366
hasid 26-27, 72, 103, 125-126, 227-228, 229, 236, 254, 277, 362-363
Hasidism................................... 3, 49, 53, 103, 125-126…dynasty…53, 71, 74, 78, 126, 189
haskamot (rabbinic approval of a new publication) 141
hatred (causeless) 343-344
Hester Panim (The concealed Appearance of the Divine).........................63, 206-207, 248
Hevra Kadisha (Burial Society) 381
Hevra Shas Synagogue 149
Holy Spirit (*Ruah Hakodesh*)...................................4, 33, 91, 112, 170, 352, 357, 379, 384
honor 25, 95, 238-239, 257, 314, 350, 372
human initiative (on behalf of redemption) 25

I
idolatry 87-88, 207, 386
Ingathering (of Israel) (*kibbutz galuyot*) 94-95, 97, 115, 126, 204, 222, 265, 309-311, 320, 366, 371

J
Joint Distribution Committee.. 83
joy (of Land, "mother," Jerusalem).... 35-36, 58, 71-72, 114, 130, 173, 230, 275, 295, 312, 314-315, 361-362, 370, 373, 375
Jubilee 158
Justice (Divine attribute) 63, 119, 121

K
kabbalah 50, 53, 158-159, 172, 193, 222, 299, 358, 381
kelipah...................................... 33, 53, 70, 117, 120, 205, 221, 229, 233-234, 287
klois 228
kvittel (written petition) 104

L
labor (forced) brigades.. 18
leadership…(and those who "mislead")21-22, 26, 49, 87, 150, 169, 198, 229, 239, 246-248, 254, 280-281, 299, 336, 338-339, 343, 361-362, 376, 388-389
liturgy, see *prayer*

M
malkhut.. 193, 194, 239, (see also *Shekhina*)
manna 137, 183, 239

martyrdom (kiddush hashem) 42, 72, 204-205, 237

masorah 210

matriarchs 196, 264-265, 352

menorah.. 364

meshikha (form of acquisition) 78-79

Messiah ....7-8, 12-14, 20, 23, 32-33, 58-59, 83-84, 90-92, 98, 101, 116, 118-119, 121, 130-131, 140, 149, 190-192, 197-198, 217, 237, 283-287, 311, 328, 333, 341...birthpangs of...chapter 1

.... See also *redemption*

midbar (wilderness) 137, 152, 212, 310, 346-347

midnight vigil (*tikkun hatzot*).. 52

military preparedness 155-157

millenium 20, 36, 76

miracles (and non-reliance upon)..36, 38, 46-47, 89, 324, 327

mitnagdim 3

mitzvah (especially related to settling Eretz Yisrael) 19, 51, 53-54, 72-73, 75, 89, 93, 99, 101, 112-113, 122, 133, 139-142, 144-145, 149, 152, 156-159, 179, 181, 201, 214, 222, 255, 258, 265-270, 283, 294-296, 300, 302-305, 307-310, 319-320, 340, 343, 349, 383-387

morashah (Eretz Yisrael as Divine legacy to Israel).... 37, 40, 43-44, 45-48, 131, 143, 213-214, 307

"Mother" (of the Jewish People vs. stepmother) 8-9, 33-36, 192-194, 195-196, 199-203, 229, 238-239

murder (of Jews) 94-95, 98, 201, 204-205, 328

N

names of God 174-179

New Moon (Rosh Hodesh).. 144, 215, 221, 269, 314, 388

non-Jews (gentiles, nations) . 24, 28, 33, 44, 51, 55-56, 58, 72, 95, 107, 109, 115-116, 132, 137-139, 152-154, 156, 158, 163, 165, 167, 169, 176, 178-179, 181, 186, 195, 208-210, 214, 218, 222, 250, 255, 275, 297, 306-307, 325, 337, 339, 342, 344, 349...persecution by...17-19, 29-31, 66-69, 80-82, 113, 201, 204, 206-207, 211, 216-217, 221, 288, 294, 312, 313-315...angels of...40-41. See also *Exile*

Nürenberg Laws 69

O

oaths (3 oaths) 138, 307, 324-325

Operation Margaret 18

orlah (Lev. 19:23-25) 189

P

Passover.. 65, 70, 82, 149, 228, 375

Patriarchs 5, 160, 185, 207, 317-318

.... See also Name Index

peace (deceptive in exile; genuine in Eretz Yisrael).... 27, 95, 113-114, 138, 216-218, 226, 247, 304, 311, 323, 327-328, chapter 4

pioneers (criticism of by elements of Orthodox leadership; in their defense by the author) . 114, 116-117, 120-121, 147-148, 320, 371-372; see also *secular Zionists*

plunder (by other nations) 30-31, 113, 216

pogrom 18, 62

poverty 81-82

prayer (must incorporate effort) 103, 215, 210-221, 231, 306

procreation.. 112-113

propaganda 272-275

prophet ... 22, 33, 37, 63, 69, 76, 81, 87-88, 91, 112, 117, 120, 132, 135-136, 138, 154-155, 165, 173, 175-177, 195, 205, 209-211, 214-216, 222-223, 244, 268, 276, 282, 296-297, 302, 305, 312, 338, 340, 342-343, 369, 379-380, 384

punishment (in Jewish history and during the Shoah) 17, 23, 116, 172, 223, 249, 305, 326, 374

R

Rebbe .... 26-27, 104, 125-126, 198, 208, 231-232, 242, 374...escape of...326-327

Rebistve 27

redemption (restoration, deliverance, salvation) ..... 14, 20, 22, 25-26, 33, 58-59, 61-66, 70, 74-75, 80-81, 84, chapter 2, 138, 148, 154, 158-160, 178, 188, 191-192, 215, 221-222, 231, 241-242, 245, 252, 256-260, 262, 265-266, 268-269, 274, 277-278, 284, 286, 293, 296, 302, 312-314, 319, 326-327, 333, 350, 365-366, 370, 373, 377, 386, 391-392...by natural means...154-157, 243. See also *Messiah*

Reform (Judaism) 15

Reich Citizenship Law 69

repentance 74, 76, 106-108, 152, 160, 166, 206-207, 266, 328, 330

restoration (see *redemption*)

resurrection.. 204-205

retribution 63

revelation 38-39, 273-274

reward....................................... 50-51, 64, 99, 116, 172, 187, 266, 276, 294, 297, 329, 360

righteousness 30, 61, 63, 89, 91, 171, 191, 196-197, 227, 229, 233, 238, 274, 283, 292, 305, 344-346, 352, 370-372, 375, 380

ritual slaughter 279

Rosh HaShanah 20, 313, 317, 320, 378

Rosh Hodesh (New Moon) 215, 221, 388

S

Sabbath 149, 228, 230, 237, 254, 331, 372, 375, 378
salvation (see *redemption*)
Satan .... 75, 121; 238, 259, 287, 339. (See also *evil*, *kelipah*)
secular Zionists ...... 49, 107-127, 145-149, 151-152, 164-173, 231-232, 277, 370-371, 375, 383...socialists...56, 294. (See also *pioneers*, "*transgressors*")
Shas Talmud Study Circles 254
Shavu'ot 97, 273-274
Shekhinah 20, 24, 53, 100, 121, 185-186, 193, 239, 357, 361, 384
shemitta (Sabbatical year) 374
sin (transgression) 32, 46-47, 50, 54, 71, 94, 98, 107, 109, 116, 123, 145, 157, 165, 181, 188, 201, 203-204, 217, 223, 226, 242, 257, 278, 301, 304, 306, 308-309, 317, 330, 340, 342-343, 347, 357, 383, 385, 389
sitra ahra 121, 234
soul 48, 110, 148, 201, 218-222, 248, 386
sparks (holy) 12-13
spies (in the wilderness) 270-274, 282, 374, 385-386
starvation 81
suffering ... 6-8, 17-18, 20-21, 39, 59, chapter 1, 88, 108, 129, 137, 195, 206-207, 209-210, 215-216, 220-222, 234-238, 245-249, 280, 300, 350, 363-366, 376

T

Tabernacle (*mishkan*) 359-364
tahanun (penitential prayer) 231
tallit 289-292
tefillin 181-182, 288-290, 294
Temple .... 14, 22-24, 28, 92-94, 102, 105, 107, 109, 115, 124, 126-127, 129, 133-135, 140, 154-156, 167, 169-170, 173, 188, 197, 257, 292, 298, 301, 305-307, 310, 313-314, 318-319, 337, 340-341, 343-344, 353, 358, 360-361, 377, 386. (See also *destruction*)
tikkun (restoration) 51-53, 70, 101, 135, 273, 355
Tikkun Olam (the pre-Shoah Rabbinic statement) 327-328
Tisha B'Av 81
Torah ..... 5-6, 19, 26, 37-40, 44, 46-49, 51-58, 63, 66-77, 89, 104, 107, 111, 117, 122-123, 172, 186, 254-255, 276, 279, 288, 296-297, 299, 302, 324, 340-341, 343-344, 350, 363-364, 366, 373, 383, 385-386, 389-390...study of...18, 80, 125, 180, 182, 186-188, 219-220, 254
"Transgressors" (who in fact may actually initiate redemption) . 49-54, 57-58, 70, 81, 109, 116-117, 122, 172, 371, 384

Tzaddik ... 52, 72, 74, 88-89, 93, 121, 168-169, 172, 180, 192, 207-208, 229, 233-234, 375, 385-386

U

unity (and strife) .... 74, 150, 208, 256-269, 291-293, chapter 4

V

Varos Meyer Hospital 149, 237
vow (of Jacob and the author) .... 7-14, 22...Divine vow to Abraham...42-44

W

wealth (and wealthy) 27-28, 30, 82-83, 93, 101, 103, 115, 128, 186-187, 195-196, 202-203, 209, 219, 223-225, 227, 246-247, 252-253, 279, 281, 304, 343. (See also *business ventures*)
World War I 74, 243, 289

Y

yarzeit 230
Yeshiva 18, 187, 290
Yishuv (the mitzvah of settling the Land of Israel) .. 133-333, chapter 3, 372-374, 383-384, 387

Z

zealots 122, 127

Name and Place Index

A

Aaron 363-364
Aaron of Karlin 13, 25, 281
Aaron D. Gordon 294
Abaye 19
Abrabanel 40, 114-115
Abraham 5, 14, 41-45, 61, 65, 87, 105, 122, 131, 148, 316, 324-326, 350
Abraham (son of Dov Ber of Mezeritch) 4
Abraham Judah Hakohen 190
Abraham Joshua Heschel of Apt (Opatow) 69-70, 335
Abraham Mordechai of Gur 121, 189
Adret, Shlomo b. Abraham 47, 54
Ahasuerus 23
Alkalai, Yehuda 154
Altshuler, David 63
Amalek 211-213
Asher b. Yehiel (Rosh) 168
Attar, Hayyim b. Moshe 78
Auschwitz 34, 190
Ayash, Judah 145
Azulai, Avraham ben Mordechai 172

B

Babylon 130, 173
Bahya b. Asher 47
Bartenora, Ovadia 42
Bekesosaba 248
Belz 73-75, 242
Berlin, Yehoshuah 213
Berman, Yissakhar Hakohen 183
Blumberg, Yonah Dov 141, 157, 233
Bnei Brak 374
Boaz 181, 283-284
Bohemia and Moravia 69, 255
Bornstein, Abraham 145
Budapest 10, 18, 85, 125, 200, 228, 232, 242, 247, 289, 321, 328, 371, 391, 397

C

Caleb 26, 175, 385-386
Chaldeans 41

Cordovero, Moses 20-21, 48, 222, 380
Cyrus 151

D
Daniel 19, 63
David (King) 14, 22-25, 57-58, 61, 87, 91, 102, 118, 188, 210, 212, 233, 235, 272-273, 293, 305-308, 314-315, 344, 356-357, 364-365, 384
David b. Aryeh Leib of Lida 158
David b. Shmuel Halevi 177
Debrecen 125
Dov Ber of Mezeritch 3-4, 12-13, 341
Dubnow, Simon 3

E
Egypt 6, 32, 44, 65-66, 105, 107, 124, 184, 203, 211-212, 242, 246, 260, 300, 329, 332-333, 356
Eiger, Akiva 33
Elaezar of Worms 28
Elijah, the Gaon of Vilna 160
Elijah of Greiditz 33, 229
Elijah b. Moses de Vidas 20, 53
Elimelekh 136
Elimelekh of Lezajsk (Lizensk) 69, 258
Emden, Yakov Zvi (Yavetz) 30-31, 64-65, 91, 287, 302, 373
Engel, Yosef 50
Ephraim Solomon b. Aaron of Luntshiz 9
Epstein, Baruch Halevi 48, 67
Esau 11
Eybeschutz, Jonathan 21, 30
Ezekiel 24
Ezra 27-28, 30, 286, 386

F
Falk, Joshua 28, 251
Fish, Aaron Yeshayahu 125

G
Gad 22
Galicia 53
Galilee 32

Gedalyah b. Ahikam.. 94, 313
Germany 28, 34, 69, 217, 231, 326
Gerondi, Nisim b. Reuben (RAN) 124
Gerondi, Yonah b. Abraham.. 54
Gikatilla, Joseph.. 65
Ginz, Ya'akov Yosef.. 125
Goebbels, Paul Joseph 275
Gog... 311

H

Hagar... 44
Hager, Israel (Admor of Vizhnitz) 126
Hagiz, Moses.. 172
Hajduboszoreny.. 73, 125
Hajdu 125
Hajduhadhaz 125
Hakohen, Yitzhak b. Shimshon Katz 356
Hakohen, Zadok of Lublin 285
Halberstam, Hayyim of Sanz (Divrei Hayyim).................... 27, 346-347
Halberstam, Yehezkel Shragai (Shiniver Rebbe)............. 121, 139, 322-323, 327
Halberstam, Yeshayah (Tcheniver Rebbe) 327
Halstuk, Meir Yehiel (Ostrowtzer Rebbe) 19
Haman 18
Hamburger, Yitzhak 348
Hannah 34
Hatam Sofer (R. Moses Sofer) 15-16, 27, 51-52, 77, 91-92, 179-180, 213, 381
Hayot, Zvi Hirsch.. 24
Hayyim b. Bazalel 226
Hebron 56
Heilpern, Yehiel 28
Hellman, Hayyim Meir 3
Hertzberg, Arthur 294
Hezekiah... 112
Horowitz, Issac b. Abraham Halevi (Shelah).............. 26, 46, 180-181, 351-352
Horowitz, Pinhas Halevi 180
Horowitz, Ya'akov Yitzhak (HaHozeh Mi-Lublin)................... 12
Hungary 18, 34, 53, 69, 198, 231, 242, 255, 277, 288, 305, 322, 326

I

Ibn Ezra, Abraham 40, 63

Ibn Habib, Moshe b. Shlomo 79
Isaac 4-5, 14, 43, 45, 61, 69, 81, 87, 105, 122, 148, 316, 318, 350
Isaac b. Sheshet 157
Isaac of Komarno 71, 72
Isaac Judah Yehiel of Safrin 71, 148
Isaac Leon ibn Tzur 140
Ishbili, Yom Tov b. Abraham 204
Ishmael 6, 45
Israel b. Samuel of Sklov 145
Isserles, Moshe 347

J
Jacob ... 4-14, 37, 40-41, 43, 61, 63, 69, 81, 87, 104-106, 122, 129, 138-139, 148, 176, 191,
199, 224-226, 236, 244, 256, 261, 265, 279, 304-305, 316-320, 350, 354-356, 377-378,
393
Jacob b. Asher 199
Jeremiah b. Elazar 51
Jericho 18
Jerusalem 6, 14, 25, 28, 30, 50, 56, 67, 85, 94, 96-97, 100, 105, 115, 126, 130-131, 138,
159, 169, 193, 195, 227, 233, 235-236, 268, 298-299, 308, 311, 337, 339-340, 342, 366,
371-372, 374-375, 386
Joshua 26, 45-46, 84, 254-265, 352, 385-386
Joshua b. Hananiah 93
Judah Loew b. Bezalel (Maharal of Prague). 44, 55, 113, 120, 161, 257-258, 265, 384, 391

K
Kallay, Miklos 125, 231, 321, 325
R. Kahana 8-9
Karo, Yosef 13, 29, 42, 175, 274
Katz, Menahem of Prosnitz 381
Katzburg (Publisher) 278
Kimchi, David (RaDaK) 14, 40
Kluger, Shlomo of Brody 62
Kostolany 397

L
Laban 11
Lapronti, Isaac Hezekiah b. Shmuel 54
Levi Yitzhak of Berdichev 3, 25
Lieberman, Eliezer 28

Lithuania 288
Lublin 34, 53, 197, 243
Luria, Isaac (ARI) 32, 52, 72

M
Maimonides (Moshe ben Maimon; Rambam) 37, 39, 45, 62, 75, 140-144, 155-157, 161, 174, 222, 358
Mainz... 217
Majdanek 34
Medzibuz 4
Meir Leib b. Yehiel Michael 127
Meisels, David... 149
Mendel of Przemyslan 263
Menahem Mendel of Rimanov... 70
Meshullam Zusya of Zinkow 335
Mezeritch 4
Miriam 62
Morgenstern, Hayyim Yisrael 227
Moses 4-6, 26, 37-38, 40-41, 45-46, 54, 61, 66, 120-121, 123, 151, 160, 174, 183, 186-187, 240-241, 246, 248, 269, 271-272, 279, 330-331, 359, 361-363, 385-387, 391
Moses Ibn Hayyim Attar 9
Moses b. Yosef Trani 13
Mt. Sinai 38-39, 42, 261, 274
Muscat, Yeshayahu 299

N
Nahman of Bratzlav 13
Nahmanides (Moshe b. Nahman; Ramban) 9, 45-46, 135, 137, 139-140, 155, 158, 214, 218, 222, 240, 283, 304, 309-310, 321, 387
Naftali of Ropshitz 284-285
Napoleon Bonaparte 275
Nathan Zvi Brisk 190
Nebuchadnezzar 313
Nimrod 42
Ninaveh 312
Nitra 35, 288, 314
Nowy Sancz 27

O
Of and Magog 51, 275

Omri 49-50
Oradea 197

P

Pachanovsky, Joseph 226
Papo, Eliezer 154
Perfet, Isaac b. Sheshet.. 303
Persia 130
Piestany (Pishtian).. 313, 397, 399
Pinhas of Koretz 357
Poland... 53, 80, 288
Poprad 34
Przysucha (Pshyshka)... 78

R

Raba 19, 47
Rabbenu Tam 288
Rachel.. 34, 352, 264-265
Radbaz (David ben Shlomo Ibn Zimra) 204
Ran (Nissim Reuben of Gerondi)... 8
Rashi (Shlomo b. Isaac) 5, 14, 17, 20, 24-26, 27-28, 34, 39, 47, 52, 62, 288, 331, 358
Rav 247-248
Reich, Koppel 374
Resh Lakish.. 5
Rhine 300
Ricci, Immanuel Hai ben Abraham 31-33
Rokeach, Aaron of Belz 242-243
Rokeach, Mordechai 244
Roosevelt, Franklin 205
Rosenbaum, Moshe Aryeh Leb Litah Segal 279
Rothschild 66, 93
Ruth... 283-284

S

Saadia Gaon 63
Saba, Abraham 29, 175
Saba, Isaac... 29
Safed... 20-21, 32
Salanta (Nadislanta) 190
Samaria.. 51

Samuel Eliezer b. Judah Halevi 51
Sarah 34, 45
Satoraljaujhely 149
Schiff, Meir b. Ya'akov HaKohen 336
Schindler, Pesach 8, 25
Schlesinger, Akiva Yosef 113, 122-123, 235
Schlesinger, Israel David 200
Scholem, Gershom 6, 8, 50, 52, 101
Schwartz, Naftali Hakohen 190
Shabbetai b. Meir Hakohen 178
Shabbetai Zvi 30, 158
Shamash, Yiftach Yosef 28
Shapiro, Hayyim Elazar (Munkatcher Rebbe) 73, 98, 327-328
Shapiro, Kalonymous Kalman 25
Shapiro, Meir 197
Sharabi, Shalom 266
Shimon b. Menassiah 23
Shimon b. Yohai 10, 61, 180
Shlomo b. Shimon Duran 52
Shneur Zalman of Liadi 3-4
Sihon 51
Simha Bunim of Pzhyshkha 79
Slovakia 34, 81, 150, 397
Sochaczew 145
Sonnenfeld, Yosef Hayyim 232, 371-375
Spain 30, 202, 217
St. Petersburg 3
Sussman, Ephraim Fischel Sofer 232, 371-372, 375

T
Taleki, Count Paul 69
Tashbaz (Shimon b. Zerah) 52
Teichthal, Hayyim Menahem 9, 22, 34, 228
Teichthal, Yissakhar Shlomo 8-9, 327-328
Teitelbaum, Moses b. Zvi 53, 83
Teitelbaum, Moses David 74
Terni, Daniel b. Moshe David 204
Tisadada 192
Tosafists 9
Tranava 35